# CREDIT AND COLLECTION MANAGEMENT

William J. Shultz, LL.B., Ph.D.

Hedwig Reinhardt, Ph.D.

BERNARD M. BARUCH SCHOOL OF BUSINESS
AND PUBLIC ADMINISTRATION, THE CITY
COLLEGE OF THE CITY UNIVERSITY OF NEW YORK

# CREDIT AND COLLECTION MANAGEMENT

## THIRD EDITION

PRENTICE-HALL, INC.

Englewood Cliffs, N. J.

Current printing (last digit):

12  11  10  9  8  7  6  5  4

19183—C

# Preface

Although the major characteristics of mercantile and consumer credit management have changed little during the past eight years, detail modifications have been many. Therefore, both practitioners and students in the two credit fields need an accurate picture of *current* credit tools and practices. Although retaining the basic organization of the second edition, which was widely approved by credit instructors and managers, this third edition of *Credit and Collection Management* has been searchingly revised and updated with this objective in mind.

Course instructors in credit and collection management should especially note the problems appended to most of the chapters in this edition. These are not presented as *cases* from which their students are to derive *new* principles, but as *applications* of the relevant text material to provide an elementary working knowledge of credit and collection practices and to "clinch" prior-studied principles in the students' minds.

Acknowledgment is made to *Credit and Financial Management* for permission to republish as part of this book articles which originally appeared in that magazine.

The authors are greatly indebted to literally hundreds of credit executives and officials of credit agencies and associations with whom they have corresponded or discussed portions of this book, and who have contributed information, illustrations, or ideas embodied in it. A blanket expression of gratitude is hereby extended to these many friends; it is true that without their assistance this book could not have been written.

To the following who read all or portions of the manuscript and helped the authors immeasurably with their suggestions and criticism, we wish to make specific mention of our appreciation: Mr. Mortimer J. Davis, Secretary and Treasurer, New York Credit Men's Adjustment Bureau, Inc.; Professor George F. Helwig, School of Commerce and Finance, University of Detroit; Mr. J. L. McCauley, President, American Credit Indemnity Company of New York, Baltimore, Md.; Mr. John F. Neary,

National Association of Credit Management and Credit Research Foundation, Inc., New York City; Dr. M. R. Neifeld, author of *Neifeld's Manual of Consumer Credit;* Dean Max V. Poffenberger, School of Business, Oklahoma City University; Mr. T. Rodríguez Sánchez, author of *Foreign Credits and Collections;* Mr. Herbert C. Sandner, Vice President and Credit Executive of William Iselin & Co., Inc., New York City; Mr. R. M. Severa, Executive Manager, Credit Bureau of Greater New York, Inc.; Mr. Benjamin Weintraub of Levin & Weintraub, Counselors at Law, New York City; Mr. Leon Ziesel, Dun & Bradstreet, Inc., New York City; and our colleagues, Professor I. Harold Kellar, Department of Business Administration, Professor Charles Martin, Law Department, and Professor John N. Myer and Professor Leo Rosenblum, Accountancy Department, of the Bernard M. Baruch School of Business and Public Administration, The City College of The City University of New York.

All personal and company names in illustrative reports and problems are fictitious.

WILLIAM J. SHULTZ
HEDWIG REINHARDT

# Table of Contents

## PART II · MERCANTILE CREDIT INFORMATION AND JUDGMENT

## PART VI · CONSUMER CREDIT

## PART VII · ECONOMICS OF CREDIT

# Illustrations

**PART I**

# BACKGROUND OF
# MERCANTILE CREDIT MANAGEMENT

# CHAPTER 1

# Introduction

Nearly nine-tenths of manufacturers' and wholesalers' sales in the United States—some 350-400 billion dollars a year—are made "on credit." [1] We can therefore fairly say that "mercantile credit," [2] also called "commercial credit" or "trade credit," is an essential element of the American distributive system. Without its lubricating influence, the channels of market distribution would be constricted, the flow of goods and services through them would be sluggish, and our economic system would have to operate at a lower level of efficiency.

Determination of when mercantile sales shall be made upon credit terms and when they shall not, and the collection of the payments involved when they become due, are now generally recognized as important business functions. Skilled technologies of credit analysis and collection procedure have been developed. The men and women who

---

[1] This estimate represents the 1950-1960 average (*Statistical Abstract of the United States, 1960,* Washington, D.C., 1960, pp. 498, 831).

[2] The terms "mercantile," "commercial," and "trade," as applied to suppliers' credit, are used synonymously. The authors have retained the "mercantile" designation on the ground that it is deeply ingrained in business usage and combines tradition and wide current recognition.

administer these functions, who through training and experience have mastered and apply these technologies, have established themselves as a professional group—"credit managers."

## THE NATURE OF MERCANTILE CREDIT

Mercantile Credit—the sale of goods or services to business concerns upon credit terms—is but one phase of the broad economic institution of Credit in general. To understand the functioning of Mercantile Credit, we must first understand its place in the general structure of the credit system.

### What is "credit"?

Definitions of "credit" and "credit transactions" are almost as numerous as the writers who have discussed the subject. This multiplicity of definitions, with its resulting confusion for students, may be attributed to failure to distinguish among (1) the *credit transaction,* (2) the *credit standing* of the buyer or borrower that is the basis of such a transaction, (3) the *debt obligation* of the buyer or borrower that results from a credit transaction, and (4) the *legal instruments* that embody this obligation. If these four interrelated credit aspects are kept distinct in the student's mind, simple but comprehensive definitions of them which will serve as a firm foundation for further analysis can be framed.

A credit transaction is one in which "a present value is exchanged for the *promise* of future payment." This definition covers the case where the "present value" is a quantity of goods and services sold for a promise of future payment, as in mercantile and retail credit. It covers also the case where the "present value" is currency or the immediately realizable value embodied in a bank checking account given in exchange for the promise of future repayment, as in bank loans, personal loans, and investment credit. Note that both elements of a credit transaction—the "present value" given by the one party and the *promise* of future payment or repayment given by the other—coexist at the moment of exchange.

No promise of future payment or repayment is absolutely certain to be fulfilled. Eventualities are conceivable which would prevent full payment or repayment by the safest and soundest of debtors. In giving present value for the promise of future payment, then, a credit seller or lender accepts not the certainty of future payment or repayment but merely the *probability that the buyer's or borrower's promise* will be fulfilled. Every credit seller or lender necessarily incurs some risk. This chance of loss is balanced against the profit or interest to be derived from the transaction. If the risk of loss outweighs the profit or interest, the transaction is not consummated. If the profit or interest is greater, the sale or loan is made.

Probability that a buyer's or borrower's promise of future payment or repayment will be fulfilled can usually be empirically evaluated in advance of a credit transaction. Whether the evaluation is for investment, bank, mercantile, or retail credit purposes, the elements to be taken into account are: (1) the buyer's or borrower's character, (2) his business capacity (relatively unimportant in the extension of retail credit to wage or salary earners), (3) his financial position and prospects (security of employment and compensation in the case of retail credit extended to wage or salary earners), (4) the collateral security he can give to ensure part or full payment, and (5) extraneous considerations, such as business trends, which may affect his future paying ability. These five elements establish a buyer's or borrower's *credit standing*—that is, the business world's current judgment of the *probability* that he will live up to his promise to pay.

Probability of future payment, for any individual or business concern, is closely keyed to the amount involved. Assuming satisfactory character, a would-be buyer's or borrower's ability, financial position, and collateral security might give a high probability rating to his promise to pay or repay $1,000 at a given future date, whereas if the amount involved were $50,000 the probability rating to be given to his promise might be low. Our final definition of a buyer's or borrower's *credit standing*—or his "credit," as the word is sometimes used—is "the business world's current judgment of the *probability* that the amount he promises to pay will be paid."

Some writers on credit problems have interpreted this *judgment* of the business world as an attribute of the buyer or borrower. They write of "the power of the buyer or borrower to command credit," and of "the buyer giving his credit in exchange for the goods he purchases." Popular language, particularly the phrase "his credit is good," lends support to this interpretation. Such statements imply that a buyer's or borrower's "credit" or credit standing is something absolute, over which sellers or lenders have no control. This implication is at wide variance with actual credit practice. As we have seen, risk of loss on a credit transaction must be balanced against the seller's or lender's profit from the transaction. Since margins of profit differ widely among sellers and lenders, a concern seeking credit may be a satisfactory risk to one seller or lender and not to another. Obviously there is no credit "power" inherent in a concern which "commands" credit in all quarters. Always we must come back to the basic concept of credit transactions as involving: (1) a *promise* of future payment of a given amount, (2) the business world's estimate, based on the circumstances of the would-be buyer or borrower, of the *probability* that this promise will be fulfilled, and (3) the balancing of the risk of loss so ascertained against the profit to be derived by the particular seller or lender from the transaction.

After a credit transaction has been negotiated, the promise of the buyer or borrower to make future payment constitutes a moral and legal obligation. In accounting and financial terminology, such an obligation constitutes a liability of the debtor and an asset of the creditor. Such obligations can be totalled for a single creditor or for a class of creditors or for the country as a whole. Usage has attached the term *credit outstanding* to these totals of debtor-creditor obligations. We may interpret credit outstanding either as having been extended by the lender or seller, or as having been incurred by the borrower or buyer.

### Classification of credit

We may classify credit transactions as follows:

1. Investment credit
2. Mercantile loans of commercial banks
3. Open market credit
4. Agricultural credit
5. Mercantile credit
6. Consumer credit
   a) Retail credit
   b) Personal loan credit
7. Refinancing credit

Each of these credit classes covers a specific field. They have some features in common; but their institutions, procedures, and economic implications differ substantially.

*Investment credit* is extended to governmental units, to business enterprises, and to individuals. It is made available to business enterprises and individuals generally with the understanding that it shall be embodied in fixed assets and working capital. Consequently the terms of such credit are usually long—anywhere from the five years of some equipment notes and the older form of home mortgages to the 999 years of some old railroad bonds. Investment credit is almost without exception evidenced by legal instruments—notes, bonds, and mortgage bonds. Note that shares of corporation stock are not credit instruments, and investment in such shares is not a credit transaction; corporation stock represents equity ownership, not a creditor's right.[3]

*Mercantile loans* are but one phase of the credit activities of commercial banks. All commercial banks purchase readily marketable bonds

---

[3] The student interested in the field of investment credit is referred to R. E. Badger, H. W. Torgerson and H. G. Guthmann, *Investment Principles and Practices,* 5th ed. (Prentice-Hall, Inc., Englewood Cliffs, N.J., 1961).

—government issues and selected corporate issues—for their "investment portfolios" to serve as a "secondary reserve." Many banks also invest in real estate mortgages of various types. Such uses of bank funds may be viewed as an element of the "investment credit" considered in the preceding paragraph. So also may the long-term loans which are being made by some banks to particular business enterprises, since they differ from bond issues only by not being evidenced by formal indentures. Furthermore, many banks now make personal loans to individuals, buy consumer instalment notes from dealers, and give loans to consumer financing institutions—activities that will be discussed in later chapters. Lending to business enterprises, however, is generally viewed as the primary function of the commercial banking system.

In many ways bank loans to business enterprises resemble mercantile credit. They are self-liquidating. They are usually for short terms. They are largely unsecured. They are intended to assist the debtor enterprise in carrying inventory items or receivables, and thus supplement the debtor's own working capital. Bank analysis of the would-be borrower's credit standing is similar to, but somewhat more refined than, the credit analysis that lies behind the extension of mercantile credit.

Nevertheless, the differences in procedure, use, and economic implications between mercantile credit and the mercantile loans of commercial banks warrant their being treated as separate classes of credit. Bank loans create new purchasing power and by temporarily expanding deposit accounts add to the country's monetary supply, whereas mercantile credit has no such effects. Some bank loan instrumentalities, such as the promissory note, with or without collateral, have little place in mercantile credit, while the open book account and the trade acceptance, important instrumentalities in mercantile credit, have no place in bank loan procedure. Furthermore, the allowable risk element in bank loans, because of the thin margin of profit in a bank's interest charge, is generally much smaller than for mercantile credit, so that a credit standing which might be acceptable as a basis for mercantile terms could be unacceptable as a basis for a bank loan.[4]

*Open market commercial paper credit* is not a major method of financing American business. A few large and well-known business and financial enterprises, which cannot obtain sufficient loan accommodation from local banks or which can obtain lower interest rates on the "open market," issue "bearer" promissory notes in convenient denominations. Through a small number of brokers these notes are sold, usually on a discount basis, to banks and other institutions that seek safe. short-term placement of temporarily idle funds.[5]

---

[4] The mercantile loan practices of banks, factors, and finance companies are discussed in Chapter 24 of this volume.

[5] The student interested in the field of open market credit is referred to any standard textbook on business finance.

*Agricultural credit* is extended to farmers. When farmers obtain long-term funds by mortgaging their properties to savings banks, insurance companies, and other mortgagees, or when such mortgages are discounted by federal land banks, we have a species of investment credit. When farmers borrow funds for terms ranging up to three years from commercial banks or through federal farm lending agencies, we have a type of bank credit. The economic effects of these two types of credit extended to farmers differ from those of ordinary business investment credit and bank mercantile loans. Hence it seems advisable to classify them as a separate category of credit.[6]

*Mercantile credit*, the major subject of this volume, differs from investment credit, the mercantile loans of commercial banks, and open market credit in that the "present value" obtained by the debtor in exchange for his promise of future payment is not money but a quantity of goods or services. It is extended by business concerns to business concerns, not as an objective in itself, but as a secondary element in consummating a sales transaction. The sources of information used for mercantile credit differ markedly from those employed for investment and open market credit. As previously indicated, there are many parallels between mercantile credit and the mercantile loans of commercial banks, but differences in their procedures and economic effects are marked.

*Retail credit*, the subject of Chapters 26 to 29 of this volume, is extended by retailers to individual consumers. In some respects it is comparable to mercantile credit. But the crucial point that it is individuals in their personal capacity who receive retail credit has produced administrative developments strikingly dissimilar to those of mercantile credit. Different sources and techniques of obtaining credit information are employed, and different elements enter into the credit decision. The dissimilarities between the two fields of credit, in economic impact as well as in procedures, outweigh the parallels and warrant their separate classification and study.

*Personal loan credit*, the subject of Chapter 30 of this volume, also involves the extension of credit to individuals. But unlike retail credit, the "present value" given for the promise of future payment is cash. Commercial banks, industrial banks, personal loan companies, consumer finance companies, sales finance companies, credit unions, and other institutions that purvey personal loan credit are in an altogether different economic category from the retail specialty stores, department stores, instalment houses, and other dealers that sell on retail credit.

---

[6] The student interested in the field of agricultural credit is referred to W. G. Murray, *Agricultural Finance*, 2nd ed. (Iowa State College Press, Ames, Iowa, 1947); for recent developments, see *Selected Articles from the Bankers Farm Bulletin of the Federal Reserve Bank of Atlanta, 1959-1961*, particularly the study "Merchant Credit in Southeastern Agriculture," September 1961.

There are similarities in the sources of credit information and the credit analysis as between these two fields, but the differences in institutions involved, in terms, in evidential instrumentalities, and in collection procedure establish them as distinct credit fields.

*Refinancing credit* comprehends the factoring (purchasing) or financing (lending on the security of) of mercantile and retail accounts receivable by various financial institutions. This activity has grown into a multi-billion dollar business since World War II. It enhances the liquidity of accounts receivable, and thereby has become a factor in recent continuing credit expansion, particularly that of retail credit. This form of credit is explored in Chapters 23 and 24.

## Contributions of mercantile credit to business

That the existence of mercantile credit has been generally beneficial for business goes without saying. Its advantages are:

1. Business men with ability but with an investment capital too limited to engage effectively in business, or to conduct a business on as large a scale as would otherwise be possible, can operate in part with resources provided by their suppliers. In many cases such business men would not be valid risks for bank loans, but are proper subjects for mercantile credit with its broader risk margin. The extension of mercantile credit to these buyers enables them to operate businesses at profit to themselves and with value to their communities, and enlarges the sales possibilities of their suppliers.

2. Seasonal enterprises that are not valid bank loan risks but measure up to mercantile credit standards can operate with a net worth sufficient for their off-season operations and base their in-season expansion on mercantile credit. If mercantile credit were not available, they would either have to operate with large amounts of "dead" or inactive investment capital during off-season months, or they would find their operations restricted when the time for seasonal expansion arrived. The first alternative would constitute inefficient use of the nation's store of investment capital. The second would limit both the service and profit of seasonal enterprises and their suppliers' sales possibilities.

3. Through the interflow of bank loans and mercantile credit, the beneficial effects of bank credit upon the business system are extended to cases where bank loans could not be directly accorded. A strong seller with a liberal "line" of bank credit may be able to carry with profit a considerable list of customers with lower credit standing who would not themselves be eligible for bank loans. Thus mercantile credit serves as an instrumentality for more extended percolation of bank credit through the business structure.

4. In times of credit restriction by financial institutions, mercantile credit continues to operate and enables business to carry on.

5. If extended and used wisely, mercantile credit may help supplier and customer to avoid at least the extreme impact of business cycle fluctuations, assisting the seller to maintain sales volume, and allowing the buyer to maintain inventory.

Mercantile credit can be abused, and these abuses definitely are harmful to the buyers and sellers involved, and to the business system. Many a buyer, in a position to develop a sound business on a modest scale consonant with his limited capital, has been led astray by his ability to obtain more mercantile credit than was warranted by his financial condition. Such a buyer, overexpanding his business on his creditors' funds, renders himself vulnerable to all the slight breezes and zephyrs of the business atmosphere that hardly affect more stable enterprises. His mushroom concern fails, with ruin for himself and loss to his creditors, when a sounder, less overgenerous credit policy toward him might have produced a lasting business structure. A seller who endeavors to force his sales volume by "selling credit"—*i.e.,* being unwarrantedly liberal in his credit policy—soon finds his working capital frozen in overdue receivables and his profit eaten up by excessive bad debt losses.

## DEVELOPMENT OF MERCANTILE CREDIT

Mercantile credit—the giving of goods in exchange for a promise of future payment—is probably as old as business itself. Any collection of records of business transactions that comes down to us from the older civilizations is certain to contain references to such promissory transactions. Absence of standard moneys in those old times was no bar to the making of credit arrangements; indeed, it seems to have been a stimulus, since an honest merchant's word was often better than the coin immediately available for payment.

When a measure of economic civilization crystallized in western Europe out of the dark Middle Ages, mercantile credit was reborn or revived. The great merchant princes of the Renaissance counted their wealth as much in receivables as in gold and inventories, and the bills of exchange that bore their names were the international currency of European trade. Wide international trade operated to a major extent on credit, and within each country chains of credit linked retailers of all sorts to well-capitalized wholesalers.

### Early American development

In American Colonial times, mercantile credit was the very backbone of trade with England and of internal commerce within the Colonies.

Southern tobacco planters took payment from English commission merchants in the latters' bills of exchange. New England importers bought
from English exporters on open book account. Within the Colonies,
payments between merchants were made usually on the basis of bills
of exchange and promissory notes payable three, five, or ten days after
sight. Where the names on these instruments were well known, they
might circulate extensively as currency by negotiation through endorsement, thus giving their obligors prolonged credit terms. Sales by importing wholesalers to retailers were on terms of twelve months or
longer, since the retailers had to depend upon the annual crops of their
customers for payment. "Credit" prices, in such cases, were considerably
higher than "cash" prices.

The twelve-month term continued to be common practice for half a
century after the Revolution. There was, however, a definite tendency
towards shorter terms, which became more marked as an increasing
proportion of domestic trade was based upon the output of American
manufacturers who lacked the capital to extend long-term credit to
their customers. By the 1850's, mercantile credit terms were commonly
from four to eight months, with 5 to 30 per cent off the "credit" price
as a cash discount; promissory notes and trade acceptances were the
usual instrumentalities of this credit. The volume of credit transactions
and the amount of mercantile credit outstanding increased at tremendous
pace during the period before the War Between the States. One factor
in this increase undoubtedly was the development of commercial banking, whereby bank credit extended to wholesalers, and importers started
chains of mercantile credit reaching down to the retailers.

Wide price fluctuations between 1862 and 1869 made long credit
terms perilous to sellers. Thirty-day terms became customary in many
lines; substantial cash discounts were offered to induce payments within
the ten-day "cash" period. Promissory notes and trade acceptances,
their usefulness diminished under shorter terms, were generally dis-
carded in favor of the open book account.

With a recovery of monetary stability in the fourth quarter of the
nineteenth century, there was some lengthening of terms to two, three,
and four months. But the half-year and year terms of the first half of
the century never returned. Need for them had passed. Sufficient capital
was now available in rural regions to enable retailers there to carry a
large part of their customer credit themselves. Improvements in transportation and communication changed mercantile buying from an annual or semiannual function to a periodic one, with consequent reduction of inventories and long-term credit needs.

Shortening of credit terms had the effect of reducing the amount of
credit outstanding at any one time. Had there been no increase in the
number of buyers and the business transacted per buyer, this reduction

of individual credit outstanding would have resulted in a tremendous contraction of the mercantile credit system. But, allowing for cyclical ups and downs, there was steady secular expansion of American business, carrying with it a corresponding increase of credit transactions. This growth element more than offset the restrictive effect of shortening credit terms, and mercantile credit continued to be an expanding factor in the American economic pattern.

### American development, twentieth century

The volume of American mercantile credit transactions and of mercantile credit outstanding expanded even faster than the rapid growth of American business activity during the first three decades of the twentieth century. Continued improvement in the techniques of credit analysis and collection procedure made possible a steady broadening of the categories of business buyers who could be deemed acceptable credit risks, and thereby continued to widen the credit basis for American business. By the 1930's some 85 per cent of mercantile transactions (dollar value) were on credit terms. Since then, the general proportion has moved nearer to 90 per cent.

This average proportion does not apply to all lines of business, or to all concerns within a line. As shown in Illustration 1-1 there is considerable variation among business categories as to proportions of sales made on credit terms. Exporters in many lines sell exclusively on credit. Manufacturers selling direct-to-retailers generally extend credit more freely than do wholesalers in the same line. Variation in credit liberality is wide, too, as among product lines; tobacco wholesalers in 1954 made only 71 per cent of their sales on credit, whereas the proportion for full-line dry goods wholesalers was 98 per cent. Within particular product lines, variations run the gamut from concerns selling only on cash to those selling entirely for credit. Such variation, however, should not blind us to the emphatic dominance of credit in the mercantile field.

Terms of sale, as we shall see in the next chapter, have crystallized into fairly regular patterns for different lines of business. Thirty- and sixty-day terms, with provision for cash discount, are most common, with occasional examples of custom-established extra terms or seasonal dating. The open book account has established itself as the general mercantile credit instrument, with only a few lines still maintaining the promissory note or the trade acceptance as customary instruments.

Since World War II a rising proportion of industrial and business equipment has been sold on intermediate-term and long-term payment arrangements. These transactions, studied in Chapter 22, involve an interesting merger of mercantile and investment credit.

office—the Central Credit Interchange Bureau in St. Louis, Mo.—provide a nationwide reporting system for ledger experience, a most important source of credit information.

FOREIGN CREDIT INTERCHANGE BUREAU (described more fully in Chapter 24) This Bureau supplies to its subscribers export credit interchange reports on foreign customers. It uses methods similar to those employed in the domestic field. Weekly bulletins and minutes of monthly Round Table Conferences on foreign credits and collections, and semiannual surveys of credit and collection conditions throughout South America are made available to the Bureau's subscribers. The Bureau also provides consultation and export marketing research service, and assists in foreign collections. In recent years, in cooperation with other American and British organizations, it has sponsored a biennial "International Credit Conference."

NATIONAL ADJUSTMENT BUREAU AND COLLECTION SYSTEM (described more fully in Chapters 14 and 18) The NACM provides national collection service through its Commercial Claims Division. In addition, 62 local associations operate adjustment and collection bureaus subject to standards and rules prescribed by the NACM.

FRAUD PREVENTION DEPARTMENT (described more fully in Chapter 17) Since its inception in 1925, this department has been a great help to credit executives. It has been instrumental in investigating more than 3,000 credit frauds, obtaining over 1,800 convictions, and recovering several million dollars from fraudulent debtors. Of great value and importance is the deterrent effect this department has had on those debtors who conceivably might otherwise resort to fraudulent practices.

WASHINGTON SERVICE BUREAU This Bureau, established in 1940, assists members of the NACM to solve problems resulting from sales to federal government agencies. Its services are chiefly of an informative kind but may also expand into additional activities.

PUBLICATIONS The NACM provides its members with several publications: *Monthly Business Letter;* a monthly magazine, *Credit and Financial Management,* with instructive articles by professional experts on current problems and information; the *Credit Manual of Commercial Laws,* edited and republished every year to keep credit executives abreast of federal and state legal and judiciary developments. It prints a number of standardized credit department forms, such as financial statement blanks and bank inquiry forms.

LEGISLATION The NACM sponsors national and state legislation which, in its opinion, will preserve and strengthen the country's credit and financial interests, and will be equitable to both creditors and debtors. It fights legislation which would be inimical to sound credit operations.

CREDIT RESEARCH FOUNDATION The Credit Research Foundation was established by the NACM in 1949 with a variety of functions in education and research. The Foundation took over the operation of the National Institute of Credit which the NACM had set up in 1918. The Foundation provides courses for credit men and women. While it establishes standards and rules for this credit training program, its 65 local chapters administer the courses in cooperation with neighboring universities and colleges; the largest "chapter school" of the NACM is the New York Institute of Credit.

ILLUSTRATION 1-1. Ratios of Wholesalers' and Manufacturers' Credit Sales to Total Sales, by Fields of Business, 1933, 1939, 1948, 1954

| Field of Business | Merchant Wholesalers | | | | Manufacturers' Sales Branches | | |
|---|---|---|---|---|---|---|---|
| | 1933 | 1939 | 1948 | 1954 | 1933 | 1939 | 1948 |
| Amusements, sporting goods | 83.7 | 84.6 | 87.0 | 90.8 | 59.2 | 79.9 | ... |
| Automotive | 64.8 | 35.3 | 61.2 | 75.9 | 85.3 | 62.9 | 78.4 |
| Beer, wines, liquors | ... | 63.7 | 67.6 | 70.9 | ... | 85.8 | 86.9 |
| Chemicals, paints | 87.0 | 90.3 | 88.1 | 92.5 | 96.5 | 97.3 | 96.0 |
| Clothing, furnishings | 94.1 | 95.0 | 95.2 | 96.9 | 99.4 | 99.5 | 99.7 |
| Coal, coke | 87.2 | 96.0 | 97.2 | 96.7 | 76.3 | ... | 98.1 |
| Drugs (full line) | 88.0 | 91.0 | 95.4 | 95.1 | 99.5 | ... | ... |
| Drugs, drug sundries | ... | 87.6 | 87.3 | 90.1 | ... | 99.7 | 99.1 |
| Dry goods (full line) | 95.5 | 94.9 | 96.7 | 97.7 | 99.0 | ... | ... |
| Dry goods (specialties) | ... | 97.6 | 94.1 | 96.3 | ... | 99.7 | 88.5 |
| Electrical goods | 84.8 | 88.1 | 87.6 | 87.7 | 94.3 | 99.5 | 92.1 |
| Farm products (raw materials) | 60.4 | 45.0 | ... | 72.3 | ... | ... | ... |
| Farm products (consumer goods) | 74.1 | 76.7 | 76.5 | 84.0 | 78.2 | 76.8 | 66.6 |
| Farm supplies | ... | 62.0 | 75.4 | 81.6 | ... | 68.1 | 91.5 |
| Furniture, furnishings | 90.4 | 92.6 | 92.4 | 94.1 | 99.4 | 97.2 | 97.7 |
| Groceries (full line) | 80.0 | 81.9 | 82.3 | 84.7 | 83.6 | ... | 92.6 |
| Groceries (specialties) | ... | 78.4 | 81.1 | 85.3 | ... | 91.3 | 84.6 |
| Hardware | 88.3 | 93.1 | 93.3 | 95.3 | 99.0 | 94.0 | 92.5 |
| Jewelry, optical goods | 86.6 | 88.4 | 93.2 | 92.1 | 97.9 | 86.0 | 82.4 |
| Lumber, materials | 88.8 | 94.6 | 93.3 | 96.2 | 98.2 | 97.9 | 95.1 |
| Machinery, equipment, supplies | 85.6 | 90.8 | 86.7 | 91.1 | 93.6 | 97.5 | 95.4 |
| Metals, metal work | 92.6 | 88.1 | 92.2 | 95.0 | 99.5 | 97.9 | 98.6 |
| Paper, paper products | 90.5 | 94.2 | 91.7 | 95.3 | 98.4 | 99.2 | 98.1 |
| Petroleum, products | ... | 86.0 | 90.0 | 93.6 | ... | 72.4 | 94.7 |
| Plumbing, heating | 79.9 | 91.7 | 91.2 | 93.8 | 94.0 | 99.2 | 95.0 |
| Tobacco, tobacco products | 70.0 | 65.7 | 66.5 | 70.8 | 99.6 | 99.8 | 97.0 |
| Waste materials | 81.9 | 76.5 | 93.7 | 94.7 | ... | ... | ... |
| All other products | ... | 81.1 | 89.8 | 88.4 | ... | 97.4 | 64.8 |

Sources: U. S. Bureau of Census, *Census of Business, Wholesale Distribution* series. Credit sales data were not included in the 1958 *Census of Business.*

## DEVELOPMENT OF CREDIT MANAGEMENT

Credit analysis in the modern sense of the term—judgment of a customer's credit standing on the basis of comprehensive information about him and by the application of standardized evaluation techniques—is a relatively recent business development. The beginnings of such analysis are found in the 1840's, but most of the modern science of credit analysis has come into existence since World War I.

Prior to the establishment of "The Mercantile Agency" by Lewis Tappan in 1841, the only credit information available to a seller was what he derived from personal contacts with his buyers and what he might incidentally obtain from reference letters provided by the buyer or written in answer to the seller's inquiries. Something might be learned of a buyer's character and business ability, but only in hit-or-miss fashion. Tappan's Mercantile Agency, which later became R. G. Dun & Co., offered sellers their first opportunity for organized credit inquiry. John M. Bradstreet began selling credit information in 1849, established "Bradstreet's Improved Commercial Agency" in 1855, and printed the first credit rating book in 1857. Various specialized agencies, covering particular business fields, were founded during the last quarter of the century; some failed, others have lasted and enlarged.

Mercantile agencies were only one of the sources of credit information that American business learned to tap as the nineteenth century advanced. Sellers discovered that, in their credit work at least, they had more to gain by interchange of information on mutual customers than by suspicious maintenance of secrecy. Business customers were persuaded that they owed suppliers who sold them on credit terms the obligation of frank information about their financial circumstances. With this wealth of credit information becoming available, credit analysis evolved into an intricate art requiring more expert application than the ordinary business operator could give to it. By the close of the century, credit and collection work had crystallized into a differentiated administrative function in large business enterprises, and credit management was coming to be recognized as one of the business professions. "Credit men" had sufficient recognition and status by 1896 to form their own national professional organization—the National Association of Credit Men.[7]

Significant credit management developments during the first half of the twentieth century have been: (1) improvement in the sources of credit information—more accurate ratings and reports by the mercantile agencies, standardization and widening of interchange of ledger in-

---

[7] In 1958, the name was changed to National Association of Credit Management.

formation, and fuller acceptance by customers provide suppliers with financial statements and (2) refining of the techniques of financial statemen procedures of credit judgment; (3) widening recog agement of the importance of the credit operation, proportion of businesses making provision for skille and substantial credit departments in their operatin (4) a growing professional outlook among the men do the credit work of the nation's business.

Credit management has moved up to the status of an ness profession, with prerogatives, responsibilities, standa This is a far cry from the time when credit analysis and were considered an incidental responsibility of a bookkeep credit manager of today holds a key position in his enter increasing extent he is ranked and treated as an admin policy-making senior executive of the company he serves. quently he is heir apparent to corporate officership—compan or controller.

### Appendix to Chapter I

### The National Association of Credit Management (NA

The NACM is the credit executive's most important professional and organization. It started out in 1896 with a small membership and a tivities that centered on seeking legislation against credit frauds and, on providing credit ledger interchange information. In 1961 the NACM a membership of approximately 35,400 credit managers and had widen scope of activities into all fields connected with mercantile credit. Affil with NACM are 146 local credit associations and 58 "credit women's grou In addition the national association has a few "direct" members in areas wh no local associations function.

Purposes and objectives of the NACM as set forth in its bylaws encomp: the organization of individuals and associations in the mercantile credit fie into a national body; the promotion of honesty and fair dealings; the enac into a national body; the promotion of honesty and fair dealings; the enac ment of appropriate laws, with emphasis on uniformity throughout the nation further development of the exchange of credit information; education, train ing, and research in the field; and efficient facilities to handle insolvencies, to investigate and prosecute fraud, and to perform such other functions as the advancement and protection of mercantile credit may require. Its "Canons of Commercial Ethics" set specific standards for the credit profession.

In accordance with these aims the NACM has established the following organizational elements, and engages in or sponsors the following credit activities:

NATIONAL CREDIT INTERCHANGE SYSTEM (described more fully in Chapter 6) Fifty-eight Credit Interchange Bureaus located in principal trading centers operate under standards and rules established by the NACM but under the control of their local associations. These Bureaus, together with a coordinat-

The Foundation is also in charge of another educational institution set up by the NACM. The Graduate School of Credit and Financial Management, started in 1947, is an advanced school which conducts summer courses for credit and financial executives at Dartmouth College and Stanford University.

Another function of the Foundation consists in conducting statistical studies —for example, on the condition of accounts receivable—and special research studies pertaining to credit in its various forms and phases and in different lines of business. In 1953 the Foundation began holding Credit Workshop Sessions four times a year in different parts of the country, where credit executives from many fields of business discuss their credit problems at a meeting that lasts two or three days.

CREDIT CONGRESS, INDUSTRY CREDIT GROUPS, AND OTHER MEETINGS

Annual national conventions of the NACM, called "Credit Congresses," give members the opportunity to meet for several days, present papers on pertinent subjects, attend discussions, and establish personal and business contacts. The programs of these conventions provide an indication of the multitude and variety of problems facing the credit executive.

In addition to these national conventions, state and district conferences are held throughout the country. Some 1,200 special credit industry groups sponsored by the NACM local affiliates meet every month.

OTHER SERVICES

NACM includes in its functions the sponsoring of voluntary member activities such as promoting credit executives' education in the necessity of proper insurance coverage (National Insurance Advisory Council) and improving credit and financial practices in particular industries (National Committee on Improved Construction Practices). It also provides special advisory and arbitration services.

## SUPPLEMENTARY READINGS

Abramovitz, S., *Inventories and Business Cycles, with Special Reference to Manufacturers' Inventories,* National Bureau of Economic Research, New York, 1950.

Credit Research Foundation, Inc. (NACM), *Analysis and Evaluation of Credit Management Functions,* New York, 1953.

————, *Credit Management Handbook,* New York, 1958.

————, *Training for Credit Management,* New York, 1954.

Federal Reserve Bank of Kansas City, "Trade Credit, a Factor in the Rationing of Capital," *Monthly Review,* June 1957, p. 3.

————, "Forces Behind the Growth in Trade Credit," *Monthly Review,* October 1959, p. 3.

Federal Reserve System, "Credit from Large to Small Business," in *Financing Small Business* (Report to the Committees on Banking and Currency and the Select Committees on Small Business, Washington, 1958), Part II, Vol. 2, p. 482.

Foulke, R. A., *Inventories and Business Health,* Dun & Bradstreet, Inc., New York, 1960.

————, *The Sinews of American Commerce,* Dun & Bradstreet, Inc., New York, 1941.

"Know Your National Association and How it Serves You," *Credit and Financial Management*, series, starting February 1961, p. 18.

Reinhardt, H., "Economics of Mercantile Credit, A Study in Methodology," *The Review of Economics and Statistics*, November 1957, p. 463, reprinted in *Credit Executive*, March 1958, p. 3.

Rodgers, R., "Bank Credit, Mercantile Credit, and Retail Credit," *Credit and Financial Management*, February 1951, p. 14.

## REVIEW

1. Define a "credit transaction." Explain the application of this definition to mercantile credit.
2. What considerations determine a buyer's or borrower's credit standing?
3. Is credit management a profession? Explain.
4. In what respects does bank credit differ from mercantile credit?
5. In what respects does agricultural credit differ from mercantile credit?
6. In what respects do retail credit and personal loan credit differ from mercantile credit?
7. What are the advantages of mercantile credit to the business system?
8. Why were mercantile credit terms shortened after the War Between the States?
9. What proportion of manufacturers' and wholesalers' sales is made on credit terms? Is this proportion fairly uniform for all classes of business, or are there substantial variations?
10. What is the National Association of Credit Management? What services does this organization perform?

# CHAPTER 2

# Mercantile Credit Terms

A contract for a mercantile credit transaction, whether it be embodied in memo form in a salesman's order book, or incorporated in a purchase order and its acknowledgment, or written down in full legal entirety, must state when the buyer is obligated to make payment. Sound business practice dictates that a statement of the payment obligation should be repeated on all invoices covering shipments under the sales contract. If specific statement of the payment terms is not made in the sales contract or other sales documents, the law presumes that any standard terms established by custom for that line of business are intended to apply. We call these formulations of the buyer's payment obligation the "credit terms" or "terms of sale." This payment obligation arises when and as the seller fulfills his obligation to deliver the goods or perform the services that are the subject of the sales contract. The *evidence* of the buyer's obligation to pay takes the form of a "credit instrument," as explained in Chapter 3.

## THEORY OF MERCANTILE CREDIT TERMS

Variety in credit terms is extreme. In some business lines trade custom has crystallized terms that are rigidly adhered to by every seller; in other lines cutthroat competition is reflected as much in the credit terms offered as in the prices asked. Even in lines where custom has gone far to establish standard terms, individual sellers may be found whose particular situation enables them, or forces them, to grant special terms to their customers. And most sellers, though they adhere generally either to the standard terms of their line or to some individual standard of their own, find it necessary to make exceptions to this standard because of special circumstances of particular customers or even whole classes of customers.

Whenever a new line of business develops, there is likely to be wide and erratic variation in terms of sale, although sometimes of necessity they follow those already established in the chain of distribution selected by the seller. Soon, however, through informal exchange of views among the sellers or through the influence of their trade association, a tendency towards uniformity and standardization sets in. Such customary trade terms may be as short as the ten-day period for sales of eggs, butter, and cheese; or as long as the six- to nine-month period for sales of unset diamonds. The most common customary credit terms are 30 or 60 days, with an allowance for cash discount.[1]

### Product factors as credit term determinants

The variations found among "standard" trade terms are not the result of mere chance. To a considerable extent they reflect significant differences in the products handled by various lines. The "product factors" that influence customary credit terms may be classified as follows:

1. The product factor most clearly correlated with credit terms is inventory turnover.[2] The shorter the products turnover period, the shorter are the credit terms. Perishable goods, which must necessarily have a quick turnover, are nearly always sold on 7- to 10-day terms; retail grocers, for example, must pay for their fresh fruits and vegetables within this period, while they have 30-day terms for their canned fruits and vegetables. Standard-brand articles which are well advertised and can be expected to have a quick turnover are generally sold on shorter terms than similar nonstandard items. Some kinds of jewelry which have a slow retail turnover are sold to retailers on terms of six months and longer.

2. Raw materials are usually sold on shorter terms than finished products. This is clearly exemplified in the rayon trade, where yarns and

---

[1] Dun & Bradstreet occasionally publishes a report entitled *Terms of Sale and Average Collection Period for 50 Manufacturing and Wholesaling Lines.*

[2] Federal Reserve System, "Credit from Large to Small Business," in *Financing Small Business* (Report to the Committees on Banking and Currency and the Select Committees on Small Business, Washington, 1958), Part II, vol. 2, p. 485.

fabrics made by the same firms are sold respectively on 30-day and 60-day terms.

3. For a long time industrial business equipment was generally sold on cash terms, on the theory that such purchases should be financed with investment funds which had to be in hand before the purchase could be made. Since the 1930's, however, instalment purchase of industrial and business equipment has become common. Terms on such instalment purchases frequently run to 18 months.

These product factors are major considerations for dissimilarities in terms of sale among the various lines of business. But individual concerns selling several product lines may also offer differing terms for particular lines.

### Buyer circumstances as credit term determinants

Sometimes differences in credit terms as between lines of business, or as offered by a single seller, can be attributed to the character or special circumstances of the buyers. For example:

1. Rural retailers extending credit to customers who pay their bills principally in the crop season often demand and obtain longer terms than urban retailers whose customers are more regular in their payments. This is a waning tendency. Financially sound retailers who sell substantially upon charge account credit may obtain somewhat longer terms than outlets that operate exclusively on a cash basis.

2. Customers located at a distance are frequently given longer terms than customers located close to the seller. A common arrangement, in the case of distant customers, is to date the standard discount and credit periods from the arrival of the goods at their destination instead of from the invoice date. This extra time allowance places them on an equal credit basis with nearby customers.

3. Customers making small unit purchases are sometimes given credit terms shorter than the standard for the trade. A large buyer whose purchases constitute an important fraction of the supplier's total sales may be granted terms longer than the standard.

4. Poor credit risks among buyers may have to accept credit terms shorter than the standard for the trade, or may even be refused any credit terms at all.

5. Customers who are good long-run credit risks, but are temporarily in embarrassed circumstances, may for a while obtain longer terms than the standard from suppliers who are willing to tide them over the stringent period and thereby retain their custom and good will. Sometimes the granting of these extra terms is made conditional upon the evidencing of the extended obligation by promissory notes or trade acceptances or upon paying interest on this extension. Frequently, in

such cases, the standard terms remain unaltered but the collection procedure takes a lenient line.

### Seller circumstances as credit term determinants

Finally we find variations in credit terms resulting from peculiarities in the sellers' situation:

1. Financially weak sellers, without the operating capital to finance credit sales, may have to ask cash terms or exceptionally short credit periods. Thus farmers customarily sell hogs to the meat packing companies on a cash basis.

2. In a line where competition is especially severe, underbidding by competing sellers may take the form of longer credit terms as well as of lower prices. Such practices should be categorically condemned, as they menace the financial soundness of both buyers and sellers. But such "selling of credit" as a premium for the purchase of goods is all too common.

### The business cycle and credit terms

A number of writers have suggested that credit terms also vary with the phases of the business cycle. There is no evidence that this is so. Credit managers' judgments of their customers' credit status, and of the classes of risks they are willing to accept, are unquestionably affected by business cycle developments. But such considerations influence decisions to grant or withhold credit, rather than decisions as to the terms on which credit should be granted. The actual credit period may be extended in a recession, however, by foregoing pressure for payment. This is the more usual way in which credit terms, though nominally unchanged, are in effect, adapted to business conditions.[3]

Monetary policies that influence the business cycle may incidentally affect credit terms. This was found to be the case during various "tight money" periods of the postwar era. Modification of the credit terms of particular concerns during the 1950's can be traced, in part at least, to monetary policy factors.[4] Many other factors, however, were influencing credit terms during this period. Some had the effect of easing terms of sale, others tightened them; no over-all trend in credit terms attributable to monetary factors can be ascertained.[5]

---

[3] H. Reinhardt, *Recent Trends in Credit Practices—Terms of Sale and Collection Practices in 32 Industries* (Credit Research Foundation, New York, 1955). This report was based on an extensive questionnaire about postwar experiences; over 1,200 companies responded.

[4] R. A. Foulke, *Current Trends in Terms of Sale* (Dun & Bradstreet, Inc., New York, 1959), p. 29, lists 257 out of 1,600 concerns consulted whose credit terms were so influenced.

[5] Federal Reserve System, *op. cit.*, p. 494.

## CLASSIFICATION OF CREDIT TERMS

Six classes of credit terms are found in domestic American mercantile dealings. These are (1) prepayment terms, (2) "cash" terms, (3) individual-order terms, (4) lumped-order terms, (5) instalment terms,[6] and (6) consignment terms. "Dating" may be considered either a seventh class of terms or a special variant of individual- and lumped-order terms.

### Prepayment terms

Prepayment terms take three forms: (1) C.B.D. (cash before delivery), (2) C.O.D. (cash on delivery), (3) S.D.-B.L. (sight draft with bill of lading attached). Sellers insist on these prepayment terms —apart from the few instances where they are customary in a line of business—in four cases:

1. When the information on a new account—or the lack of such information—establishes it as an unsatisfactory credit risk, or where information on an old account indicates that it has deteriorated from satisfactory to unsatisfactory standing.

2. When an old account is overdue on past invoices, and the seller wishes to increase pressure for payment or refuses to permit the buyer's obligation to increase beyond its existing level.

3. When an account has become insolvent, or is being operated by a receiver, until satisfactory arrangements have been made for the protection of new debts incurred for continued operation.

4. When a petition for reorganization has been filed, without satisfactory arrangement for protection of suppliers selling during the interim period.

It should be noted that C.O.D. or C.B.D. sales to an overdue account may be a poor method of pressing for collection of a past-due balance. The buyer, if he is really in financial difficulties, has a strong inducement to ignore payment of the past-due balance for so long as he is covering his current needs by the C.O.D. or C.B.D. purchases. In effect, these terms for the new purchases tend to ratify an indefinite extension of the past-due balance. A sounder arrangement is for each C.O.D. or C.B.D. payment to be somewhat larger than the current shipment that it covers, so that the past-due balance is thereby cleared by instalments. Or it might even be better, in the long run, to grant such an account regular terms on new purchases, provided that each new order was accompanied by a payment on the past-due balance; by this means the

---

[6] The topic of industrial instalment terms is not developed in this chapter, but is given full consideration in Chapter 22 of this volume.

account would be brought in time to a current basis without the irritation that is provoked by C.O.D. and C.B.D. terms.

Under S.D.-B.L. terms, the shipment is made to "the order of the seller" with instructions to notify the buyer of its arrival. Thus the seller controls the goods until payment is made or the shipment returned. He prepares a draft or order upon the buyer to pay. After notifying the customer of his action, he sends this draft, with a negotiable bill of lading and other shipping papers, to a bank in the buyer's city (usually through arrangements made by the seller's bank) with instructions to deliver the shipping papers to the buyer only upon receipt of payment. Without these papers the buyer cannot obtain the goods from the carrier. The bank transmits the buyer's payment on the draft, for a moderate charge, to the seller. The one possibility of this arrangement failing is that a scheming merchant will order goods on S.D.-B.L. terms and then, upon their arrival, plead lack of immediate funds and ask for release of the shipping papers, promising to pay the draft within a brief period. The temptation for the seller to accept such an arrangement is strong; otherwise he must stand the costs of both shipment and return of the goods. But if he agrees, he is placed in the position of having extended credit to the worst sort of credit risk. He may protect himself against this contingency by requiring a C.B.D. payment equal to the two-way freight cost or to some fraction, say one quarter, of the invoice amount.

C.O.D. terms give the seller even less protection. Besides the chance that a fraudulent buyer will refuse to accept the goods on plea of lack of funds and ask their release upon a short credit term—a situation parallel to that described above in connection with S.D.-B.L. terms—another danger enters. Unless the carrier is instructed to accept only currency or a certified check in payment, a fraudulent or irresponsible buyer may obtain the goods through a bad check. Therefore every C.O.D. shipment should be preceded by a letter informing the buyer of the date of arrival and notifying him that the payment must be by currency or certified check and the carrier should be directed to accept only such payment.

A seller has complete assurance of payment only if he sells on C.B.D. terms. Credit men exhibit extreme reluctance to ask customers—even the poorest credit risks—to make payment before shipment; they prefer qualified C.O.D. terms that provide for fractional prepayment. C.B.D., however, should be the basis for selling to any buyer whose credit standing does not warrant regular terms, regardless of his feelings. Where the goods involved are a special order, or would not have a regular market after their production, some manufacturers push the C.B.D. principle to the point of requiring a substantial deposit or full payment before the order is put into production.

### "Cash" terms

In trade parlance, "cash" terms mean, not immediate payment upon receipt of goods, but payment in ten days' time from the invoice date. This ten-day period is presumed to allow time for the goods to be shipped from the seller to the buyer, for them to be examined by the buyer, and for the buyer to mail his payment and have it reach the seller. In cases where the goods must move considerable distance by a slow means of transportation, the ten-day allowance may just cover this sequence of actions, so that the buyer is in effect paying immediately for the goods he receives. Where seller and buyer are in close proximity to each other, the ten-day term may actually constitute a significant credit extension. And, of course, there is always a possibility that a hard-pressed, negligent, or fraudulent buyer will fail to put his check into the mail on time, so that the seller finds that this "cash" sale has nonetheless involved him in a collection or bad-debt problem. The credit standing of a customer buying on "cash" terms should be just as thoroughly examined as that of any buyer on regular terms, for practically the same moral risk is involved in both cases.

In one variant "cash" arrangement, payment for each previous shipment is collected on each new delivery. This is known as "bill-to-bill," "drop delivery," "on delivery," or "load-to-load," terms.

### Individual-order terms

Individual-order terms are utilized when a buyer's orders, or shipments on his orders, are made only once or twice a month, and there is no necessity or advantage to lump the payments as of a single date. The credit period—30 days, or 60 days, or whatever it may be—is counted from the invoice date of the particular shipment; so is the cash discount period. In the short-hand of trade custom, such individual order terms without provision for discount are referred to as "net 30," or "net 60," according to the particular term allowed. If a cash discount is permitted, the discount per cent and discount period precede the statement of the net period. Thus "2/10/30" or "2/10 net 30" means "a thirty-day credit period with a two per cent cash discount allowed for payment within ten days of the invoice date."

If a house in New York sells goods throughout the country on 2/10 net 60 terms, it is evident that a buyer in Jersey City would enjoy a distinct advantage over one in San Francisco. The former would receive his goods within 24 hours and have time to check them before making discount payments within the ten-day period, while the house in San Francisco might have to pay before the goods were received in order to take the cash discount. To overcome this disadvantage to distant purchasers, many sellers date invoices to them "R.O.G." (receipt of goods) or "A.O.G." (arrival of goods). This means that the time allowed for taking discount is measured from the date the goods are received by the purchaser. If, however, the purchaser does not avail himself of the discount within the period allowed, the regular terms are usually measured from the invoice date. R.O.G. terms applying to the credit period as well as to the discount period are commonly allowed on water-borne shipments, other slow freight, and sometimes under special circumstances such as transportation strikes.

### Lumped-order terms

Lumped-order terms are found in lines of business where buyers frequently repeat or fill in orders twice a month or more often, or where shipments on orders go out at intervals shorter than two weeks. In such cases all deliveries during a certain period, usually a month, are lumped together and billed as of one date. Credit and discount periods for these shipments begin with this statement date, or at some later date as established in the trade—usually the first of the following month. Such lumping of payment obligations simplifies the supplier's and the buyer's bookkeeping.

There are three bases for lumped-order terms: (1) E.O.M. (end of month), (2) M.O.M. (middle of month), and (3) prox. (proximo—some specified date in the following month).

*E.O.M.*, the most common form of the lumped-order terms, provides that all orders shipped during a month are billed in a single statement as of the end of the month, with the credit and discount periods for all such orders starting at the billing date—or rather, in practice, as of the first of the next month. Sometimes, net E.O.M. terms are used without a cash discount. More often, however, cash discounts are allowed. In such cases, *the credit and discount periods are usually identical,* so that the cash discount is not an inducement for earlier payment, but its denial is a penalty for past-due payment. The common credit and discount period under E.O.M. terms is ten days. Thus, under the 8/10 E.O.M. terms frequently used in the clothing industry, all deliveries to a customer during the month of May would be covered by a statement as of the last business day in May, and payment, with 8 per cent deducted, would be due as of June 10.

E.O.M. terms may appear, at first glance, to be harsh. In reality, they are quite liberal. A buyer who has received goods at the beginning of a month, and is billed for them only at the end of the month, enjoys a credit and discount period up to 40 days. Moreover, for billing purposes, E.O.M. commonly means the 25th or, in some instances, the 20th of the month. All shipments up to that day are lumped on one statement of that date. All later shipments go on the statement for the following month with the credit and discount period starting a full month later. This gives a buyer who orders shipments on or shortly after such a billing date an additional opportunity for a longer credit period. Abuses of this privilege are common and there is little that sellers can do to avoid them.

*M.O.M.* terms are less common than E.O.M. terms, but their use is increasing.[7] Credit and discount periods under such terms—usually identical and usually for ten days—begin at the "middle-of-month" billing date. An M.O.M. arrangement is actually a split E.O.M. term where the buyer pays on two biweekly statements instead of on a single monthly one. Payment on goods shipped to him between the first and 15th of the month must be made by the 25th with the cash discount deducted. Payment for shipments made between the 15th and the end of the month is due on the tenth of the following month.

*Prox.* terms connote payment obligation and a cash discount period in the month following shipment. But so, also, do E.O.M. terms. Actually, in cases where the cash discount and credit periods are identical, there is no distinction between E.O.M. and prox. terms. In one business line, such as textiles, a particular term may be called E.O.M., whereas in the automobile parts trade the same term is called prox. Prox. terms often provide, however, for a discount period shorter than the credit period. Thus "2/10 prox. net 30" would establish a discount date on the tenth of the month following shipments and a due date on the last day of that month. E.O.M. terms rarely add a net due date after the discount period.

### Dating

Under the term "dating" are grouped two unrelated and dissimilar credit term practices—"season" dating and "extra" dating. Such "dated" terms are standard in some industries, but are departures from regular terms in others.

*Season dating* is an extension of the ordinary credit period to induce buyers of seasonal goods to accept delivery well ahead of the time they would normally be sold. Such advanced deliveries enable a manufacturer either to spread out his production schedules or to limit his storage of finished goods. Early availability of the merchandise may or may not expand the customer's sales opportunities. It definitely does burden him with extra storage and extra inventory risk. To require him also to meet earlier payment dates would be unfair even where advanced receipt of the goods might carry some advantages; many customers would refuse advance delivery without "dating." The "dating" may be accomplished

---

[7] Foulke, *op. cit.*, p. 26.

by the addition of an extra month or more to the regular terms—for example, "net 60, 60 ex." The more common arrangement is to give regular terms on an invoice which has been dated ahead to what would be the normal shipment date. Thus a buyer of summer wear might place his order in the preceding fall, obtain delivery in January on 2/10 net 60 terms with the invoice dated May 1. He would then have until May 10 for taking cash discount or until July 1 for net payment.

*Extra dating* is an anomalous but customary way of giving long identical credit and discount periods. A textile converter selling on a 70-day credit and discount period, with the discount at 2 per cent, would not state the terms as 2/70/70 but as 2/10-60 ex. The purchaser is expected to pay the stated price, less 2 per cent "cash" discount, 70 days after the invoice date. He can, if he wishes, pay earlier and deduct additional *anticipation* discount at the rate of one-half of 1 per cent per month—*i.e.*, 6 per cent per annum. Sometimes such anticipation discount is stated in the terms; more often the buyer assumes it—and takes it.

### Consignment terms

Most consignment terms are used in circumstances which are not related to credits, for example when sales of agricultural products are made through commission merchants or when a retailer refuses to be committed to a purchase but is willing to accept the goods and sell them on consignment. But consignment terms may also be employed when a buyer does not qualify as a sound credit risk for regular terms and is unable to buy C.O.D. Title to consigned goods remains in the shipper, the recipient acting purely as the shipper's sales agent. If the recipient fails, the goods constitute no part of his assets available to general creditors but belong exclusively to the shipper. Theoretically, at least, the shipper is protected against failure of the consignee to pay for goods that he has actually sold by the legal consideration that failure to make such payment constitutes embezzlement and is punishable as a criminal offense; in practice, convictions on this count are extremely difficult to obtain.

Unless certain legal requirements are complied with, a consignment contract may be construed as an unrecorded conditional sales contract, and its peculiar benefits may be lost to the consignor. These requirements are: (1) the consigned merchandise must either be segregated from other merchandise in possession of the consignee, or be clearly and distinctly marked as the property of the consignor; and (2) proceeds from the sale of consigned goods must likewise be segregated from the consignee's general funds. Therefore, a consignment agreement should contain directions as to how the consignee is to keep the consigned goods clearly identified. Furthermore, the consignee should be directed to deposit the consignor's share of the proceeds from the sale of consigned goods in a separate bank account, preferably identified as in trust for the consignor. Insurance on consigned goods should be carried in the name of the consignor. The consignee should be required to make periodic reports of his sales and periodic remittances of the proceeds. Because of these legal technicalities, a credit man should not trust his general knowledge of business law to draw up a consignment contract and prepare directions for consignees but should have forms for these purposes prepared by a competent attorney.

## THE CASH DISCOUNT

In most mercantile lines, customers are encouraged to make immediate payment, well in advance of the due date, by the offer of a "cash discount"—a reduction of ½, 1, 2, 3, or even some higher per cent from the invoice price if the buyer's check is received by the seller within ten days, or some other brief specified period, from the invoice date. Such cash discounts can be embodied in individual-order terms or in lumped-order terms. Examples of the former, in trade parlance, would be "1/10/30" terms or "2/10-net 60" terms—in the first case a 1 per cent discount and in the second case a 2 per cent discount for payment within ten days of the invoice date, with the net credit period respectively one month and two months. An example of a lumped-order cash discount would be "2/10 prox. net 60"—a cash discount allowed for payment by the tenth of the following month on all orders shipped during the preceding month, with a net credit period of two months, usually calculated from the first of the following month.

Many so-called "cash discounts" are "cash" in name only. We noted that in E.O.M. terms and sometimes in prox. terms a combined credit and discount period of only ten days is allowed, with the discount amounting to 6, 7, 8 per cent, or even higher. Rarely are these discounts denied in cases of later payment, so that they operate, in effect, as trade discounts. A similar interpretation must be placed on such terms as "2/30/31," common in selling rayon yarns, or on the extra dating terms previously described, when the discounts are not refused on late payment. Should the discounts in any of these cases be disallowed on late payments, they still cannot be considered true "cash" discounts, since the net and discount periods are identical, or practically so. Rather, their disallowance operates as a penalty for delinquencies.

### Anticipation

Closely related to the cash discount is "anticipation"—a deduction, usually at the rate of one-half of 1 per cent per month, allowed for payment before a due date or before the close of a protracted discount period. Anticipation is most common when long dating terms are granted, but may be allowed in connection with E.O.M., prox., and even individual-order terms. In many lines of business, anticipation privileges are specifically stated in the terms of sale. In others they are "silently" understood.

### Legal considerations

Cash discounts and anticipation are permissible under the Robinson-Patman Act, provided they are allowed uniformly to all customers in any business class—that is, all of a company's wholesaler customers, or all its retailer customers. What is not permitted is variation in application of a discount policy. Discounts may not be allowed to some insistent "terms chiselers" who pay after the discount date and be refused to others of a company's customers who pay on their net due dates. Either all customers must be held strictly to discount date payment, or all customers must be allowed the discount regardless of when they pay. Many companies consistently violate the Robinson-Patman Act by giving in to terms chiselers. There is evidence, however, that credit managers are generally becoming more "Robinson-Patman-conscious" in this respect, and are holding terms chiselers more strictly to account.

### Reasons for cash discounts

From a seller's viewpoint there are three definite advantages, translatable into monetary terms, to receiving early payments on his deliveries through the instigation of cash discounts. (1) Cash in hand gives him funds which he may be able to employ with profit. (2) Alternatively, he may be thereby freed from the necessity of bank borrowing and its cost. (3) He may also be enabled to take advantage of cash discounts offered by his suppliers and thereby reduce his purchasing costs.

If we take 4 to 6 per cent bank rates as a measure of saving, a seller who receives payments 50 days earlier from discounting customers under 1/10 net 60 or 2/10 net 60 terms saves, on an annual basis, from .57 to .86 of 1 per cent of the payments involved. Taking all other possible advantages of early payment into account, a generous estimate of what a seller saves when buyers anticipate their due dates by 50 days in order to take advantage of a discount would be approximately 1 per cent. Terms of 1/10 net 60 would pass such a saving on to the discounting customers. Terms of 2/10 net 60, or 1/10 net 30, or 2/10 net 30 obviously give discounting buyers substantial bonuses over and above any saving that accrues to the seller.

Why do sellers in so many lines give such bonuses to discounting customers? The answer is again, as so often in credit matters, ingrained custom. The cash discount established itself in American credit practice during the 1860's and 1870's, when credit terms were long and sellers faced heavy risks from currency depreciation. Trade and economic conditions today are vastly different and offer no justification for substantial cash discounts, but the custom nonetheless persists.

Of course, these bonuses to discounting buyers, if they are taken by a large proportion of the customers of any company or line, must be given weight in pricing. Net prices, therefore, are probably somewhat higher than they would be in fields where large cash discounts are widely taken.

From a buyer's viewpoint, anticipation of payment to take advantage of generous cash discounts is certainly profitable. How much so is indicated by the following tabulation of discount savings to buyers on a per annum basis:

| ½% | 10 | days | net | 30 | days | = | 9% |
|---|---|---|---|---|---|---|---|
| 1% | 10 | " | " | 30 | " | = | 18% |
| 2% | 30 | " | " | 4 | mos. | = | 8% |
| 2% | 10 | " | " | 60 | days | = | 14% |
| 2% | 30 | " | " | 60 | " | = | 24% |
| 2% | 10 | " | " | 30 | " | = | 36% |
| 2% | 40 | " | " | 60 | " | = | 36% |
| 2% | 70 | " | " | 90 | " | = | 36% |
| 3% | 10 | " | " | 4 | mos. | = | 10% |
| 3% | 30 | " | " | 60 | days | = | 36% |
| 3% | 10 | " | " | 30 | " | = | 54% |
| 4% | 10 | " | " | 4 | mos. | = | 13% |
| 4% | 10 | " | " | 60 | days | = | 29% |
| 5% | 10 | " | " | 4 | mos. | = | 16% |
| 5% | 10 | " | " | 60 | days | = | 36% |
| 5% | 10 | " | " | 30 | " | = | 90% |
| 6% | 10 | " | " | 4 | mos. | = | 20% |
| 6% | 10 | " | " | 60 | days | = | 43% |
| 7% | 10 | " | " | 4 | mos. | = | 23% |
| 8% | 10 | " | " | 4 | mos. | = | 26% |

### Abolition of the cash discount?

Credit managers have few arguments in favor of cash discounts, but many against them. Their abolition would mean: (1) simplification of suppliers' cost analysis, pricing, and billing procedures—particularly important in view of the growing mechanization of bookkeeping which makes "informal adjustments" more difficult; (2) saving of time and confusion at both ends; (3) avoidance of much unpleasant correspondence about unearned discounts; and (4) possibilities of price reductions through cost saving.

A few companies have taken the bold step of eliminating the cash discount from their quoted terms of sale in recent years, without any noticeable adverse reactions from their customers. Some of them sugar-coated the pill by lowering price lines, or by holding price lines constant when a general upswing of prices was taking place. Actions of this type, however, have not been too frequent.

Some sales departments still emphasize cash discounts as a selling point, though the prospects most influenced by it are likely to be those whose payments tend to be irregular.[8] Some other sales organizations —particularly those of large companies—require all customers to take the cash discount, and accept orders only from those who do, referring all others to jobbers. They thereby relieve their credit departments of much work.

Generally speaking, the cash discount has lost much of its original attraction. In these days it is rather an anachronism that has been carried over from the period after the War Between the States when monetary instability gave it a justification it does not possess today. Yet its abolition does not appear likely in the near future. Individual sellers may make successful headway against the custom. But it would require collective action sponsored by trade associations to finally do away with it, and this seems hardly feasible in view of the "tradition" in the field and because antitrust laws would presumably block such an undertaking. Like the weather, everyone talks about abolishing cash discounts, but no one does anything about it.

## SUPPLEMENTARY READINGS

"Cash Discount: Friend or Foe of Faster Pay and Good Will?" *Credit and Financial Management,* March 1961, p. 8.

Chapin, A. F., "Once Again Cash Discount," *Credit and Financial Management,* March 1949, p. 4.

―――――, "Reward or Penalty—Which Is the Cash Discount?" *Credit and Financial Management,* April 1951, p. 6.

Credit Research Foundation, *Study on Invoice Datings and Discounts,* New York, 1950.

Foulke, R. A., *Current Trends in Terms of Sale,* Dun & Bradstreet, Inc., New York, 1959.

"Is Cash Discount Operation 75 Years Behind the Times?" *Credit and Financial Management,* September 1953, p. 16.

McKibbin, L. E., "Net Terms versus Cash Discount," *Credit and Financial Management,* March 1960, p. 22.

Reinhardt, H., *Trends in Credit Practices—Terms of Sales and Collection Practices in 32 Industries,* Credit Research Foundation, New York, 1955.

---

[8] Foulke, *op. cit.,* pp. 40, 42.

## REVIEW

1. Are there "standard" or customary terms of sale for particular lines of business? If so, how do they develop?
2. In what ways may the product involved influence the customary terms of sale of a line of business?
3. In what ways may the circumstances of buyers influence the terms of sale granted to them?
4. In what ways may the circumstances of a seller influence the terms of sale he offers?
5. In what ways may business cycle factors influence credit terms?
6. When should prepayment terms of sale be demanded?
7. What considerations should influence a choice between "C.O.D." and "C.B.D." terms?
8. What are "S.D.-B.L." terms? When are they used? How is payment arranged?
9. What is meant by "cash" terms of sale?
10. What does "2/10 net 60" mean?
11. What are "R.O.G." or "A.O.G." terms? When are they used?
12. What are "E.O.M.," "10 prox." and "M.O.M." terms? When are they used?
13. Explain "extra" dating.
14. Explain "season" dating.
15. Explain "consignment" terms. What procedures must the seller adopt to ensure full legal protection of his claims?
16. Distinguish between "cash discount," "anticipation," "trade discount," and "quantity discount."
17. What are the arguments for and against the cash discount?

## PROBLEM

Alpha Mills, a large textile concern with spinning plants and weaving mills in several eastern states, has developed "carlon," a new artificial fiber that can not only be woven into a new "wonder" cloth but also has many industrial uses. Alpha Mills will produce both carlon threads and carlon cloth. Alpha Sales Corp., a subsidiary of Alpha Mills, is established to handle the sale of the thread and cloth. The former will be sold to weaving mills and to industrial users. The latter will be sold to converters, to manufacturers of sheets, pillow cases, and other "white goods," and as "white" piece goods to department and dry goods stores.

1. Should the same credit terms be established for the thread and the cloth? Why?
2. If the decision were made to have different terms for the thread and the cloth, which would be the longer? Why?
3. Should the converters and manufacturers be given the same credit terms as the stores? Why?

4. Where could the credit manager of Alpha Sales Corp. find guidance as to what would be appropriate terms for him to establish?

5. West Coast customers are asking for 10-day longer terms than East Coast customers because it takes more time for their orders to arrive. What should be done about their complaint?

6. An order is received from an industrial company which is the subject of "arrangement" proceedings and is operating under a bankruptcy receiver. Under what terms might the order be accepted?

7. Would Alpha Sales Corp. ever sell on consignment? Explain.

8. Should a cash discount be offered? Why?

# CHAPTER 3

# Mercantile Credit Instruments

The types and characteristics of credit instruments are many, for every field of credit noted in Chapter 1 has developed its own special and peculiar documentary evidences. At one extreme are the federal reserve notes, which are obligations immediately redeemable to the holder and which at present constitute the basic currency of the United States. At the other extreme is the registered bond, an instrument of investment credit, which may have a maturity of scores of years and which is transferable only by a complicated procedure.

The credit man in a business concern engaged in domestic commerce is interested in only three credit instruments—the open or book account, the promissory note, and the trade acceptance. Export trade involves certain other credit instruments—the bill of exchange, and the banker's acceptance on letter of credit—which will be explained in Chapter 24.

## THE OPEN OR BOOK ACCOUNT

Most mercantile credit transactions are evidenced not by a written debt obligation signed by the debtor but by a memorandum notation made by the seller. This memorandum notation, made as an incident to the seller's regular bookkeeping procedure, is the entry in the customer's ledger.

## Types

In earliest rudimentary bookkeeping procedure, sellers kept "day books" in which they entered all financial transactions in the order of occurrence. This "day book" evolved into the "journal," which carried entries in chronological order but with indication of their subsequent classification for posting. At convenient intervals, the entries in the "journal" would be posted to the appropriate ledgers. One of these ledgers would be the "customer sales ledger." Each customer would have his numbered page in this ledger, with his name and business address at the head of the page and, frequently, the credit terms on which he purchased. The amounts of his credit purchases would be posted to this page, and while still unpaid would constitute part of the seller's "accounts receivable." Payments made by the customer would also be posted to this page, so that a running record of his outstanding debt would always be available. Many a small firm still operates with a hand-posted customer ledger of this type.

The customer ledger has not been ignored in the technological revolution of office procedures during the past quarter century. All large companies and many small ones have adopted machine-posted, punch-card, or open-filing customer ledger systems.

In *machine-posted ledgers* there is a separate card for each account (see Illustration 3-1). These are filed alphabetically or in some other sequence. Original entry from invoice copies and payment memos is typed onto each card by a machine which automatically calculates and enters each new balance. These files of ledger cards may be periodically checked for delinquencies, or they may embody visible index or "punched border" systems (described in Chapter 13) which automatically spot past-due accounts.

*Punch-card ledgers* represent a more advanced application of automation to bookkeeping. As with machine-posted ledgers, original entry is made from invoice copies and payment memos. But the data, instead of being typed onto the cards, are coded by punching holes in the cards (see Illustration 3-2). With the information posted in this fashion, each card serves all the purposes of a receivables ledger. In addition, the cards, having been run through accessory machines, can be used for automatic billing and for various managerial analyses. Punch-card machines represent heavy capital investment or rental cost, and would rarely be practicable for exclusive ledger-system use. But a large or medium-sized company that has adapted other operations to punch-card

| | | | | | | |
|---|---|---|---|---|---|---|
| NAME | JOHN DOE CO. | | | RATING | E-2 | |
| ADDRESS | 300 W. ADAMS ST. | | | CREDIT LIMIT | 3,500 | |
| CITY & STATE | CHICAGO ILL. | | | SALESMAN | 2A | |
| | | | | TERMS | REG. | |

| DATE | REFERENCE | CHARGES | √ | CREDITS | | BALANCE |
|---|---|---|---|---|---|---|
| BALANCE FORWARD | | | | | | |
| MAY 12 61 | 2/10 E14 | 1228 00 | A | | | 1228 00 |
| MAY 19 61 | CASH | | | 1203 93 | A | |
| | DISCOUNT | | | 24 07 | A | 00 |
| JUN 19 61 | N/30 F29 | 473 02 | B | | | 473 02 |
| JUL 7  61 | 2/10 G35 | 1728 00 | C | | | 2201 02 |
| JUL 24 61 | NO DISC | | | 1693 44 | C | 507 58 |
| AUG 15 61 | CR MEMO7 | | | 12 01 | B | 495 57 |
| AUG 21 61 | CASH | | | 461 01 | B | 34 56 |
| OCT 9  61 | N/30 | 543 57 | | | | 578 13 |
| OCT 16 61 | CASH | | | 34 56 | C | 543 57 |

A    STANDARD FORM 137 (47)

*ACCOUNTS RECEIVABLE LEDGER*

MAY BE ORDERED IN ANY COMBINATION OF A, B, OR C

syst⊘matic BUSINESS FORMS, INC., NEW YORK, N. Y.

ILLUSTRATION 3-1. Machine-Posted Customer Ledger Card

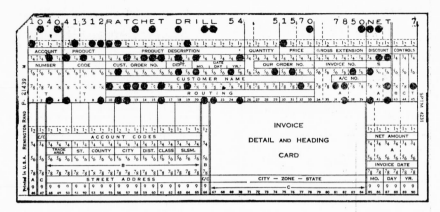

ILLUSTRATION 3-2.    Punch-Card Customer Ledger (Remington Rand)

procedures can profitably use such procedures for its customer ledger system. Some credit managers view punch-card ledgers as an intermediate step to magnetic-tape ledgers electronically processed by cybernetic equipment—a development currently in the experimental stage.

An *open-file ledger* (sometimes called a "ledgerless ledger") is a modification of a machine-posted or punch-card ledger file.[1] For each account there is a pocket or folder into which duplicate invoices, copies of collection correspondence, and other relevant items are inserted. Attached to each folder is an information card on which notations of balance and other account data may be entered. As payment memos come through, the duplicate invoices to which they relate are removed from the pocket. Thus each card-plus-pocket provides current detail as well as summary ledger information on the account. The corner of each pocket is cut away so that a glance can reveal whether it contains invoice copies or is empty, thus automatically distinguishing accounts with balances from paid-up or inactive ones.

### Legal status

An open account, as entered upon a customer ledger, does not of itself establish the debt of the purchaser, as does a promissory note or trade acceptance signed by the purchaser. The existence of the debt can nonetheless be established, upon proper foundation, by the evidence of correspondence, sales memos, purchase orders, duplicate invoices, and shipping papers. A seller can make delivery under a credit sale, without written acknowledgment of the buyer's debt, confident that the

---

[1] The Remington Rand SUIAP (Simplified Unit Invoice Accounting Plan), one type of open-file ledger system, is described in *Credit and Financial Management,* November 1956, p. 14, and August 1957, p. 8.

rules of evidence will enable him to establish his claim upon the buyer should it ever be necessary to do so.

## Advantage

The great advantage of the open account is its flexibility. Cash discounts can be incorporated into the terms of sale, extensions of time can be granted, and other readjustments of the payment obligation can be made, without legalistic procedures yet without the forfeiting by the seller of any of his rights. A memo notation upon the ledger card or page suffices to record the modification of the original agreement. Some of the advantages attributable to such informal procedures may become less plausible with the spread of mechanized, and therefore less flexible, bookkeeping. But it is unlikely that the popularity of the open account will thereby be affected.

One reason for the widespread use of open accounts, though not necessarily an advantage of the system, is the general assumption in many lines of trade that signed acknowledgments of mercantile debt are demanded only of inferior credit risks. This assumption is so general that it can be viewed as an American trade custom. A seller who tried to impose the use of promissory notes or trade acceptances on his customers would risk insulting and losing a large proportion of his best accounts.

## Disadvantages

Since a ledger entry is a one-party notation, never seen by the purchaser, it may not record a true two-party agreement. The buyer may have a different understanding as to price or terms. He may be dissatisfied with the quality of all or part of a shipment, and insist on an allowance for the defect. For so long as there is no complete meeting of the minds of seller and buyer as to all elements of the sale, delivery, and payment, the ledger entry establishes no conclusive debt. All too often such disputes drag a weary course month after month. Where a signed debt instrument is involved, the issue would be brought to a head as soon as the instrument was placed before the purchaser for signature, and solution of the dispute would be expedited.

General use of promissory notes or trade acceptances in mercantile credit would promote prompt collections. Default upon notes or acceptances, with the procedure of protest provided for such cases of default, would make every buyer's delinquency in payment of his obligations a matter of public knowledge. Buyers would be more careful to order only what they could expect to pay for and would make more strenuous efforts to meet payments when these came due. But delinquency on an open account is a private matter between buyer and seller. Through ledger interchange arrangements (discussed in a later chapter) consistent delinquency can be made known to the trade, but the effect of this may be less impelling upon the customer than the public disclosure of default on a signed instrument.

Finally, general use of signed credit instruments would put sellers' receivables into a form in which they would be somewhat more readily financed by banks. Even in the case of sound borrowers, banks may allow a more generous credit line when the borrowing is accomplished in part by discounting customer paper. Where a seller's own credit standing is too poor to enable him to obtain unsecured bank loans, his bank will sometimes discount good customer notes and acceptances for him. Financing open accounts receivable is also feasible. Factors and finance companies engage in this business, and in recent years many banks have also turned to this form of credit extension, at little if any higher charge than for customer paper loans. There are still wide areas of the country, however, where there are inadequate facilities for financing accounts receivable.

## THE TRADE ACCEPTANCE

A trade acceptance is a draft drawn by a seller on a buyer to cover the latter's purchase of goods, directing the buyer to pay a specified amount to the order of the seller on a specified date. When the buyer agrees to these terms by signing his acceptance on the face of the draft, and indicates the bank or other place at which payment will be made at the due date, the paper becomes a full-fledged negotiable instrument.

### Legal and financial status

The form of trade acceptances is determined by two independent considerations—the negotiable instrument laws of the states and Federal Reserve regulations.

In order to be a negotiable instrument under the Uniform Negotiable Instrument Law now in effect in all states, and thus available for discount at a bank, a trade acceptance must conform to the following statutory requirements of negotiability:

1. It must be written, typed, or printed.
2. It must be signed by the drawer (the seller).
3. It must name the drawee (the buyer) or indicate him with reasonable certainty.
4. It must embody an unconditional order for the drawee to pay a certain sum of money.

5. The sum of money must be payable to bearer or to the *order* of the drawer or some third party.
6. The sum of money must be payable at a fixed or determinable date.
7. The order must be unconditionally accepted by the drawee (the buyer), with his signature converting it into an unconditional promise to pay.

Federal Reserve regulations add several further requirements to those established by the state negotiable instrument laws in order to dis-

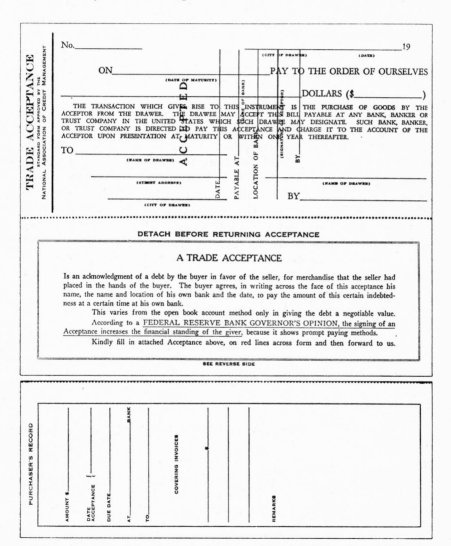

ILLUSTRATION 3-3. A Trade Acceptance Form Obtainable from NACM

tinguish the trade acceptance clearly from other commercial paper:

1. The face of the instrument must bear conspicuously the label "Trade Acceptance."
2. The instrument must bear on its face a statement that it arises out of the purchase and sale of goods.
3. The instrument must be accepted in writing on its face.

With the form of the trade acceptance thus minutely determined, a credit man would be foolhardy to trust to his inspiration or to some vague ideas of commercial law in drafting an acceptance. A slight misjudgment would strip it of many of its advantages as a credit instrument. The wiser policy would be to use or copy exactly the trade acceptance form provided by the National Association of Credit Management. A reproduction of one of these forms is given in Illustration 3-3.

### Collection

If a seller has not discounted a customer's T.A. (trade acceptance) but has retained it in his receivables portfolio until shortly before the due date, he deposits it with his bank for collection. The acceptance written on the face of the instrument names the bank at which collection is to be made. This is usually the bank where the customer maintains his checking account. The seller's bank sends the acceptance through to the named bank as though it were a check, and it is charged to the customer's account like an ordinary check.[2] If the customer should stop payment on the instrument, or if funds in his account should be insufficient to meet it, it need not be protested unless there are endorsers on the instrument, but the procedure of protest is usually followed. A dishonored T.A. is legal foundation for "suit upon the instrument."

If a T.A. has been discounted by the seller, the discounting bank will take the initiative in putting it through for collection. The procedure is the same as indicated above.

### Current use

Many sellers in the fur trade and in the canning industries use the trade acceptance instead of the open account as one of their basic credit instruments. In most lines of business, however, the trade acceptance is used only in one or two special cases. When a customer is generally a sound credit risk, but his working capital position is such that he is bound to be slow in his payments, a supplier will often allow him an

---

[2] There are some states where this procedure cannot be followed. See the National Association of Credit Management's *Credit Manual of Commercial Laws.*

extra 30 or 60 days over the regular credit period but insist on receiving a T.A. for the extended credit term. Thus the supplier acquires a rather firm prospect of prompt payment and, at the same time, the immediate availability of readily discountable paper.

The theory and law of the trade acceptance should preclude its being demanded of inherently weak credit risks or when an extension of credit terms is granted before or after the account becomes past-due. In this latter case, the proper instrument is the promissory note. But in these instances, as in other credit matters, practice does not adhere strictly to theory. Trade acceptances are sometimes used where open account credit is deemed too hazardous and as extension instruments.

### Efforts to promote use

Credit men generally agree that the trade acceptance is much superior to the open account as a credit instrument. Its advantages are:

1. It permits "suit upon the instrument" in case of default. This is much simpler than the "suit upon the contract" which is necessary with the open account.
2. It forces early mutual agreement on amounts due and terms of sale.
3. It places strong pressure on buyers to pay promptly on the due date.
4. It provides sellers with a discountable credit instrument.
5. It may specifically provide for payment of interest on long credit terms.

There is no difficulty about combining the trade acceptance with the cash discount, in spite of some opinion to the contrary, since a practical arrangement can be worked out whereby a buyer either makes his discounted payment within the discount period or returns the signed acceptance for the net amount before the close of the discount period.

Advantages of the T.A. to the supplier are readily evident. The National Association of Credit Management, at its annual meetings, has therefore consistently endorsed the extension of its use. The banking system, however, currently displays little enthusiasm for the idea. In the 1920's the Federal Reserve System tried to promote wide use of T.A.'s. So did the commercial banks and the newly created American Acceptance Council. The idea was to encourage bank mercantile loans on T.A.'s, rather than on borrowers' own notes, thus establishing a distinction between "trade credit" and "finance credit." The campaign did not prove successful. It slowed down and eventually petered out completely. Meanwhile purchasers have maintained a silent, stubborn opposition to general use of trade acceptances. They have nothing to gain from the use of this instrument, and they stand to lose the freedom of late payments that open accounts may allow them. Moreover, a century's custom has earmarked the trade acceptance as an instrument used only for slow payers. Any attempt by an individual seller to require his customers to buy on acceptance terms puts him to the risk of insulting and losing his best customers.

## THE PROMISSORY NOTE

A promissory note, so drawn that it is a negotiable instrument, is an unconditional promise in writing and signed by the maker to pay a certain sum of money on demand or at a determinable future time to order or to bearer. An example is presented in Illustration 3-4.

Although the promissory note is a major instrumentality of bank credit, it holds only a minor place in mercantile credit. It is used widely in the fur and jewelry trades as a basic credit instrument. It is essential in industrial instalment selling, as explained in Chapter 22. Otherwise its only important uses in mercantile credit are:

1. When a customer is not a satisfactory credit risk, but can obtain a co-signer or an acceptable guarantor for his promissory note. A frequent example of this arrangement occurs where an incorporated enterprise is not a valid risk, but one of the officers or shareholders has personal wealth which makes him an acceptable guarantor. The corporation then buys upon its promissory notes endorsed by the officer or stockholder.

$ _____                    _____ 19 __
                    _____ after date _____ promise to pay to
the order of _____
                                            _____ Dollars
at _____
Value received
No. _____ Due _____         _____

ILLUSTRATION 3-4.   Promissory Note

2. When a customer requests an extension of time on a payment and such extension is warranted. In such case, it is customary to ask the customer to sign a note or a series of notes for the additional period of

time granted. A trade acceptance could not be used under these circumstances, since the renewal debt does not arise from a sale of merchandise. The note gives the creditor greater assurance that the debt will be paid on the new due date. It may also, depending on its quality, provide him with a discountable instrument.

Collection of a promissory note given under one of the above circumstances is ordinarily made through the banking system, as in the case of a trade acceptance. No protest is necessary if payment is not made on the terms of the note, but notice of dishonor must be sent to an accommodation endorser to hold him to his obligation, unless he has previously waived such notice. Any extension of a note beyond its original term releases an accommodation endorser, unless he previously agrees to the extension.

## SUPPLEMENTARY READINGS

Credit Research Foundation, *Punched Card Accounting and the Credit Department,* New York, 1957.
———, *Punched Card Systems in the Credit Department and Accounting Operations,* New York, 1957.
Holmes, W. L., "Can We Automate Data for Credit Decisions?" *Credit and Financial Management,* April 1960, p. 14.
Hume, A. C., "Mechanized Accounting Opens New Frontiers," *Credit Executive,* January 1960, p. 8.
Protzel, H. W., "Converting the Accounts Receivable to Punched Cards—a Case History," *Credit and Financial Management,* November 1960, p. 20.

## REVIEW

1. Describe three arrangements for maintaining a customer ledger.
2. Does an open account on a customer's ledger legally establish the purchase debt incurred by the customer?
3. What advantages and disadvantages does the open or book account have as a credit instrument, in comparison with the trade acceptance and the promissory note?
4. What are the advantages and disadvantages of the trade acceptance, as a credit instrument, in comparison with the promissory note? Why is credit use of the trade acceptance so restricted?
5. You are credit manager of the ABC Corp., 40 Broadway, New York City. You approve an order of $150 of your merchandise for John Doe of Fayetteville, N. J., provided Doe will sign a 60-day trade acceptance. Doe banks at the First National Bank of Fayetteville. Invoice for the merchandise is dated April 15, 1960. Prepare the trade acceptance for Doe to sign. Write in, in parentheses, whatever Doe would write in accepting the instrument.
6. As credit manager of the ABC Corp., you approve an order of $200 of your merchandise for Roe Products, Inc., of Steuben, Ohio, provided the

corporation gives you a note with the accommodation endorsement of Richard Roe, president of the corporation. The invoice for the merchandise is dated April 15, 1960. Prepare the note to be sent to Roe Products, Inc.

## PROBLEM

Mr. Howard, office manager and credit manager of Beta Paper Co., a small paper jobber, has just received a letter from a customer asking for a two months' extension on a $218 payment, originally on net 60 terms, which will fall due in a week. The reason given for present inability to pay is a recent cash purchase of a distress stock at very advantageous terms. The customer is an old one. Mr. Howard considers him a good credit risk, and is willing to grant the extension.

1. So that this extension will not seem too casual and set a bad precedent, and to have the added assurance of being definitely paid at the end of the extended term, Mr. Howard is considering sending a 60-day trade acceptance in the amount of $218 for the customer to accept and return. Should he?

2. Mr. Howard wonders whether he should charge 6% per annum interest for the two-month extension. Should he?

PART II

# MERCANTILE CREDIT
# INFORMATION AND JUDGMENT

# CHAPTER 4

# Dun & Bradstreet

To arrive at a sound judgment of a customer as a credit risk, a credit manager needs a wealth of information. He must have data that indicate whether the owners or officers of a business are honest and intend to repay the debt they are incurring. He must have information about the prior history of the concern and its current operations that enable him to judge whether the principals or officers are good business men and whether the enterprise has reasonable hopes of continued operation that will make repayment of the debt possible. He must discover the concern's current financial position—information that not only throws light on the concern's prospects of survival, but also upon the possibility of salvaging some part of the debt should unforeseen contingencies force it out of business in the near future.

A century ago, even half a century ago, obtaining information that would give a rounded picture of a customer as a credit risk was largely a hit-or-miss matter. Credit decisions had to be made "by guess and by gosh." Today the alert credit manager finds out almost as much about his customers as they know about themselves—sometimes more. The sources of his information are the following:

I. From within his own organization:

    A. The customer's ledger card or page showing his past record of purchases and payments.

    B. The credit manager's first-hand judgment of the customer from interviews at either the seller's or the customer's office.

    C. Salesmen's reports.

II. From outside his own organization:
    A. At first hand:
      1. Financial statements and other information supplied by the customers.
      2. Ledger exchange information obtained from other suppliers of the customers.
      3. Information supplied by banks.
    B. At second hand:
      1. Ratings and reports by mercantile agencies.
      2. Consolidated interchange reports of local credit associations and of the National Association of Credit Management.
      3. Information supplied by attorneys and accountants.
      4. Information derived from investor's manuals and other supplementary sources.

Of these many and varied sources of credit information, the one that supplies the most comprehensive coverage of customers as credit risks is the mercantile agency with its ratings and reports. We will therefore direct our first study to mercantile agency reports and ratings, and particularly to those of Dun & Bradstreet, the one general agency that covers all types and classes of commercial and industrial business enterprises.

## HISTORY OF DUN & BRADSTREET [1]

    Lewis Tappan was a partner in Arthur Tappan & Co., a wholesale and retail dealer in dry goods, which failed in 1837 partly as a result of credit extensions and was subsequently reorganized. In 1841 Lewis Tappan established "The Mercantile Agency." This enterprise, based on the credit files that Lewis Tappan had previously accumulated in his dry goods business, which were now enlarged by information obtained from lawyers and other correspondents about the country, offered New York City manufacturers and wholesalers credit information on their customers. The credit reports were written in longhand, and were read off to interested clients. In 1843 a branch was opened in Boston. Subsequently more branches were established in lead-

---

    [1] This account is derived from R. A. Foulke, *The Sinews of American Commerce* (Dun & Bradstreet, Inc., New York, 1941).

ing commercial cities. The organization was changed into Douglas & Co. in 1854, with R. G. Dun as a partner. In 1859, after another reorganization, it became R. G. Dun & Co. This name was continued until 1933.

Meanwhile John M. Bradstreet, a Cincinnati retailer who later practiced law, interested himself in mercantile credit problems. In 1849 he began selling credit information which he had accumulated to New York City wholesalers. Six years later he opened a New York office as Bradstreet's Improved Commercial Agency. In 1857, two years before the publication of the *Reference Book* of the Mercantile Agency, founded by Lewis Tappan, Bradstreet's printed the first rating book—a volume of 110 pages, listing 17,000 businesses located in nine cities.

When credit reporting was inaugurated as a service to business men, the furnishing of information by one person to another in response to a credit inquiry was regarded by the courts as a "privileged communication," and such responses were accorded the protection of that defense in actions for libel. In 1868 the New York Court of Appeals held (*Ormsby v. Douglass*, 37, N. Y. 477) that the defense of "privileged communication" was applicable as well to credit reports furnished by an agency. This decision was important to the development of credit reporting service in this country. R. G. Dun & Co. acquired National Credit Office as a subsidiary in 1931. It was merged with the Bradstreet Agency in 1933, and the corporate name of the consolidated enterprise became Dun & Bradstreet, Inc. It purchased the credit reporting and checking service in the men's and women's clothing fields of Credit Clearing House when that organization ceased operations in 1942. A later acquisition (1958) was the American Foreign Underwriters Corporation, whose export credit reporting services were continued by Dun & Bradstreet's International Division.

## ORGANIZATION OF DUN & BRADSTREET

Dun & Bradstreet is organized into three functional departments—Reporting, Service, and Educational—which gather, prepare, analyze, and disseminate credit and other business information.

The *Reporting Department* prepares the famed D & B reports. The Regular and Analytical reports, studied in detail later in this chapter, are valuable tools for domestic mercantile credit analysis. The International Reports cover foreign accounts of American exporters (see Chapter 24). Beside these "standard" reports, D & B also undertakes special "made-to-order" credit inquiries.

The *Service Department* issues the *General Reference Book*—D & B's 3,000,000-name credit rating volume. It is also responsible for the *Apparel Trades Book*, the *Credit Recommendations* of D & B's Credit

Clearing House Division, and the *International Market Guides.* Among the subunits of this department are the Mercantile Claims Division that operates the D & B collection service, and the Building Trades Division that publishes the monthly *Consolidated Ledger Abstracts* for suppliers in the construction industries.

The *Educational Department* is responsible for Dun & Bradstreet's various publications, including the monthly *Dun's Review and Modern Industry* and the *Dun & Bradstreet Service* (a business news letter). It has issued many booklets and pamphlets, some of which are of key importance to the study of mercantile credit. It has also developed correspondence courses and films on subjects related to credit.

Although Dun & Bradstreet has expanded its activities far beyond the limits of mercantile credit, the compilation of its credit reports and the publication of the *Reference Book* and other credit ratings are considered by far the most important of its operations.

To prepare these, the company has established 42 district offices in the United States and Canada. Some of these cover entire states, as in Colorado and Utah; others confine their operations to particular metropolitan areas, as in New York City. Suboffices and reporting stations bring the total network of offices to 142 in the United States and 18 in Canada. In order to expedite the preparation and distribution of the various types of reports issued, Dun & Bradstreet has divided the country into 12 regions, roughly corresponding to the 12 Federal Reserve Districts. The 42 district offices of Dun & Bradstreet are integrated into this regional structure. In addition to the domestic set-up, Dun & Bradstreet maintains offices in 19 countries, including Australia, the Union of South Africa, Great Britain, France, Germany, Argentina, and Brazil.

Depending on the size of the trading area, from three to more than 200 "reporters" are attached to an office. There were over 1900 throughout the country at the end of 1960. The majority of these are "city" reporters. Periodically, according to a schedule, they visit business concerns to interview their principals and obtain financial statements, data on methods of operation, and other information needed for the credit reports. This includes a list of trade suppliers to whom requests for ledger information are mailed. Following such direct contacts with a concern the reporters interview outside authorities, such as banks, for the purpose of verifying information obtained and in order to get additional facts. Data so accumulated are analyzed, and reports are prepared which carry ratings in symbol form. To the senior, experienced reporters are generally assigned the more technical and comprehensive investigations and reports; they also answer inquiries on specific accounts as "consulting reporters." Newer men usually cover the smaller enterprises. Special "service consultants," in addition, are attached to the offices for closer personal relationship to clients.

Dun & Bradstreet has an additional corps of "traveling reporters" who visit concerns outside the immediate city office area once a year. Furthermore, some 18,000 "local correspondents" in the United States and another 7,500 in Canada—bankers, insurance brokers, lawyers, court clerks, public record clerks, and others—supplement the work of the traveling reporters in areas outside the Dun & Bradstreet office cities.[2] An effort is made to have a local correspondent at every county seat in the country to report on suits, judgments, the recording of deeds and mortgages, and other pertinent record items.

## THE REFERENCE BOOK

Six times a year Dun & Bradstreet issues to its subscribers a volume $11\frac{1}{2}''$ × $16\frac{1}{2}''$ in size, $4\frac{3}{4}''$ thick, containing approximately 4,800 pages and listing over 3,000,000 industrial and commercial enterprises in the United States and Canada.[3] This is the famous D&B *Reference Book* given to subscribers on a loan basis.[4] It lists practically all manufacturers, wholesalers, and retailers who buy regularly on credit and on whom credit reports have been written. The *Reference Book* does not include certain classes of service and professional establishments, such as real estate brokers, barber and beauty shops, and stock brokers, even though credit reports may have been prepared on those businesses. All *Reference Book* listings are compiled from information in the complete credit report. Most of the names are followed by a letter and a number which constitutes the Dun & Bradstreet rating evaluation of an enterprise's financial strength and composite credit appraisal. These ratings are continually reviewed.[5]

The listings of the *Reference Book* are classified by states, and within the states by cities, towns, and villages. In each community, the business establishments are listed alphabetically. A sample section of a page from the *Reference Book* is presented in Illustration 4-1.

---

[2] Abraham Lincoln was for a while a "local correspondent" of R. G. Dun & Co.

[3] Eight sectional editions of the *Reference Book* are published. The subscription cost of one of the sectional editions, suitable for a seller with a local market, is lower than that of the general edition.

[4] The *Reference Book* is not for sale. Subscribers receive their copies as a "loan" from the agency, and must return them if a subscription is discontinued. Old issues have to be returned when new editions are issued. By these means Dun & Bradstreet endeavors to keep its ratings confidential among its subscribers, and maintain their legal status as "privileged communications" to which libel law is not applicable.

[5] In the calendar year 1959, for example, there were over 1,600,000 changes in the Reference Book, or over 6,000 on each business day. This figure included upward and downward rating changes of existing businesses, initial ratings for new concerns, and removals.

**ROPER ▲ Deering 13**

Bk town Flint
Beebe Motor Co ............... Ats 7
Beetle John C NR ...... Plbpsup 4
Biggs E J Baldwin ................
Bourke George ..................
Eaton's Cut Rate ....... DrgSstn 2
Grable Hosiery Mill ..............
Healey Frank A .................
Kennedy Mfg & Sales Co ... Laces
(See Detroit)
Ritter Emil .....................
Thrum Mrs Alice C ......... Cnf 7

**ROTTERDAM ▲ Ellis 197**

Bk town Pryor
Ashworth Henry A S ........ Elcro
Blum Pearl Button Co* ..........

Cleveland William ........ Sawmill
Eldredge Lawrence W ...... Mbcl 7
Farmer Richard ................
Lathrop E F&Co .... Furn Mills Inc
Rotterdam Gardens .............
Scott Geo NR ..................
Seaton Herman .................
Shaver John & Margaret ...... Ggo 2
Smith Jonathan NR ..............
Waters Orland E .................
Zeller W F J ....................

**RUBY (See Hickman)**

**RUSH LAKE 1,214 Forest 2**

Bk town Brushville
Anders Theodore .................
Andrews Clifford ...............
Jones E L ......................
McGuire William W ..............
Nielsen Christopher ............

Noble Herbert W ............... Rct 2
Norris Winfield N ..............
Palmer's Filling Station .. GrSstn

**RYANSBURG 1,022 Wright 13**

Bk town Francis
Alling & Campbell Inc ...... Radios
Bromiley Anthony ...............
Jones Mrs Evelyn M ............
Mitchell Archie ................

**SACKVILLE ▲ Ontario 13**

SACKVILLE BK .................. $85M
Phillips Pr Bryan Townsend Cas
Alberts Thaddeus A ..............
Ballman Ahab J .................
Bluman Frederick ...............
Callahan John ..................
Daume Oscar .....................
Harris & Harris NR .............
Heller F S ......................

**Country Center Motor Co Inc..3**

Crowell Andrew B ......... GCntr 3
Beetle John C NR ...... Plbpsup 4
Danbera Roofing & Sand Co ... Dg
Dawley Kevin ...................
Delmonico Photo Service Inc ...7
Dobbin F G .....................
Dolan Sinclair L ...............
Early & Duggin .................
Edgehill Warren C ..............
Euter Bessie (Mrs A) ...........
Fistoe Ray Motors Inc ..........
Freer Raymond T Co .............
Frost Lumber Co* ...............
Fuirt Marble & Granite Co .. Cntr
George Paul ....................
Gerstein Crushed Stone Co .. Gr 6
(Br of Wooster Ohio)
Gilbert Godfrey ................
Gibson Construction Co.. RoadCntr
Gimsy Geo ......................
Graham Hill Motors .............
Gray Horace G & Sons ..........

Gray Otto P ........ Jc ......
Griffen Homer M ................
Griffon Bros & Son .............
Heather Margaret Smith (Mrs A)

Hight William S ................
Hinckey Horace C Jr NR .........
Milner Raymond .................

Milner William A NR .. Hyml
Nickerson Geo O .. WaterWelldrlg
Peison John & Lucn .. PlbgFiDardot
Rackham Arthur & Co. inc .. DrgLq
Redcliff Ginger Ale Co Inc. Cntr 7
Samson's Service Station NR ...
Tobey Samuel & Son .............
Vurton Elliott A ...............
Voos William O. ................
Winslow Herbert .. HigePlbgcap
Wolfson Benjamin & Rose .. Wnwr

**SANBORN 1,819 Deering 13**

Bk town Weehauken
Boswell George S Jr ......... Dg
Bisbee Arthur A ................
De Laval Henry A ...............
Dodds Layton ...................
Dundee Co-operative Sales Assn
Inc ............................
(Br of St Cloud Minn)
Foster Paynter B ...............
Franklin David .................
Gruber Mrs Emma .. Amher

**RUSH LAKE Fillmore**

DAWSON TR CO ................ $213M
J M Thompson Pr J L Marshall Cas
KNEELAND TR CO .................
(Br of Kneeland)
Allen Electric Co* ........ Cntr
Allen Motor Co* ................
American Electric Supply Co ....2
Andrade Water Co* ..............
Appleton Men's Apparel Shop inc
Arnold Metal Products .. Stamping

Babcock John L Jr ..............
Camabili's Gifts 8 .............
Downs George D .. Drg
Eisner Tire & Linoleum Co .. Frn
Geller Robert R Sons Inc .. Mort
Gentry's Joseph Sons inc .. Sstn 6
Jennings I H .. Sstn 3
Karl Benjamin ..................
Kettle Frank ...................
Lewis Irene .................... Radios
Old Gold Auto Co* ..............
Paddock Frank Electrical Prod
Sanchez Electrical Products Corp
Sanchez H E Paint Store .. W&R
Stelton & Gasiorowski .. Gravel

**SOUTHVILLE (See Leesville)**

**SPELLACY (See Arden Wood)**

**SPERLING ▲ Randolph 81** ..$719M

1st NAT BK ....................
John Tracy Pr Paul Williams Cas

Beln & Winfield .. GrMt
Calzano Frank .................. ChildSh
Callahan's Service Station .....
Crowder Tool & Specialty Co ....
D & M Seafood Co Inc ...........
Decker William C .. StructuralSvc
F & W Products Co Inc .. Canned
(Br of Chicago Ill)
Interstate Decorators .. Wlbcl
Jablow Allen R .................. Sstn
Kazimir Nathan .................
Lomax J J Reynolds ............. Sstn
Lowe Max .......................
Mead Claude L .. FrnHldapl
Metz A Harper .. ElcCntrMshp
Pinus Bros Inc .................. RoadCntr
Wright John N NR ............... SPmll
York Mrs Birdie H .............. Wnwr

**SQUIRES (See Sheppard Falls)**

Meaker William E ............... Mort 6
Merritt Samuel J .. PlyHtchy
Michaels Harry F .. Nursery
Quain Dennis & Sons Inc.. MtlDrg
Seltierriek Bros .. TJStinAtsup
Tobias Mary A (Mrs J F).. Ats 1

**SIEBERT ▲ Kimball 42**

Bk town Sage
Chapin Mary A & Robert .. GrMt
Cortese John B ................. GCntr
Goodrich Lumber Co* ............
Jackson William H .. Atrp
Johnson Virgin .................
Opelthorpe Milling Co .. Flour
Stanley Charles B Sr .. Mason 6
Van Dusen C Emory .. Sstn 6

**SIMMONS 1,911 Ewing 13**

Bk town Swenson
Buchanan Mitchell .. Frm 6
Caffarelli Oil Co .. Petrpt
Drummond W S .. HigPlbgcap
Dugowski Thaddeus .. Elcsup
Excelsior Dry Goods Co inc .....
Fairest Valley Mercantile Co inc

Hawley Everett NR .. Elcsup
Hicks Raymond E & Georgianna ..

Mayo & Green Canning Co Inc...8

Rainer & Weber ..................
Townley Benjamin .. SPmll

**SINGLETON 1,145 Smart 42**

Bk town Ford River
Freemanters Beatrice .. GrMt
Goodrich Lee .. Drg
Strauss Childrens Shop ........
Todd Cut Rate ..................

**SOLEDAD 5,675 Iroquois 49**

EATON TR CO .................... $882M
H D Williams Pr C E Morris Cas
(Also Branches)
LAUREL NAT BK Pr J Lewis Cas .. $320M
J Roscoe Elliott Pr Lewis Cas
Ackerman Louis R ...............
Albright Claude A ..............
Alleyne Hubert B ............... Mont
Bayer Henry & Son.. PlgElcCntr
Belford J R Co* ................. Plbofix
Owens George H ................. Frn
Pin Club ....................... Cntr
Pincus Bros Inc ................
Snitzer Clarence D .............
Stoltz Joseph ..................

Kellinan Kersey G .. Roofg 6
McGerrild Bros.. inc.. PlyElcCntr
Madden J F .....................
Main Street Market .............
Marks Eliot ....................
Marks White & Noonan.. HigEgp
Marvin Nelson James ............

Mascot John B ..................
Megliorn L Nelson ..............
Merritt Fertilizer Co Inc.. RoadCntr
Middleton Irving N .. Radios 9
Millard Wilma (Mrs R R).. PlsuSc

Morehouse Mrs Jessie ........... Jlvrp
Mortimer Stores ................
Mulroy A J & Son ............... GCntr
Nancy Dee Shop .................
National Henry* ................
Olrich Mrs Nettie ..............
Oswald Arthur A ................
Peaton David R ................. Sstn 7
Peters Pr Francis.. ElcPlbgCntr
Puman S H Co ...................
Purdy Harold W NR ..............
Putnam Danzig Inc .. Tractors
Putnam Walter & Sons NR.. Road
Rodell Walter A ................

Roberts J Wiswall ..............
Rogers Lincoln C ...............
Ruskin Everett W .. Atrp
Ruskin Alfred F ................
Snocking Alfred ................
Shore Paul W NR ................ Opblow
Stanley Shortwall .. Grmt
Smith Mary Mary Alice .. Frn
Susley Hillary ..................
Tacconesti Alfred ..............
Townley J G Jr & Co inc.. Mort

Vesey Garage Inc ...............
Vockers Products Corp.. MchTool
Voos Elsie (Mrs W J).. GrMt
Weston Louis M .................
Wilkey Louis R .. PlbgCntr
Williamson Robert H .. Drg
Wilson Orris E ..................

**SHEPPARD CENTER 5,420 York 13**

1st NAT BK Pr J Earl F Martin Cas .. $309M
Curtis Atkins BK Pr J Earl F Martin Cas .. $551M
Oral Whitley Pr James A King Cas
American Millinery ..............

Asbestos Roofing Co .. SmetRoofg
Azerian Carpet Store ...........
Benjam .. Mtl
Binder .. Electric Shop

ILLUSTRATION 4-1. Excerpt from Dun & Bradstreet Reference Book

**54**

As a further aid to credit managers and sales managers, population figures, banking and postal facilities, and county locations are given for all communities. Of particular use to sales managers is the four-digit U.S. Standard Industrial Classification number appearing before the name of each concern. It classifies the business as to function and products. This enables the sales manager of a hardware wholesaler, for example, to pick out rapidly all hardware retailers in a sales area so that his salesman can visit them. Whenever a C precedes the code number, it indicates that the rating of the business has been changed in that particular issue of the *Reference Book*. Whenever an A appears before the code number, it indicates that the name has been added since the previous edition. A numeral immediately preceding the rating represents the last digit of the year the business was started or came under its present ownership within the last ten years. These latter features are of interest to both sales personnel and credit managers. As a further convenience, primarily to salesmen, the *Reference Book* is also published in small single-state pocket-size editions called "State Sales Guides."

## The *Reference Book* ratings

The heart and substance of the *Reference Book*, for a credit manager, are its ratings of listed enterprises. Every subscriber to the Dun & Bradstreet service is given a key to these ratings. Such a key is reproduced in Illustration 4-2.

A Dun & Bradstreet rating represents an overall evaluation of a business concern's credit standing. Two elements are involved: (1) estimated financial strength as expressed in sixteen code letters; and (2) a composite credit appraisal embodied in four categories—"high," "good," "fair," and "limited"—and expressed in figures.

The *estimated financial strength* of a business is an objective factor, commonly measured by its tangible net worth. In some instances, this is not the same as the net worth in a company's financial statement since such intangible assets as good will, patents, and the like may have been eliminated. Estimated financial strength, moreover, is intended to portray the fair, going-concern value rather than the liquidation value of a business. Sixteen net worth classifications are used for this purpose. They are covered by letters, from Aa for enterprises with an estimated financial strength over $1,000,000 to L for concerns with estimated financial strength under $1,000.

The *composite credit appraisal* is a more complicated factor, based on a combination of factual data and judgment. It indicates, in four classifications ("high," "good," "fair," and "limited"), the *degree* with

## KEY TO RATINGS

| ESTIMATED FINANCIAL STRENGTH | | | COMPOSITE CREDIT APPRAISAL | | | |
|---|---|---|---|---|---|---|
| | | | HIGH | GOOD | FAIR | LIMITED |
| Aᴀ | Over | $1,000,000 | A1 | 1 | 1½ | 2 |
| A+ | Over | 750,000 | A1 | 1 | 1½ | 2 |
| A | $500,000 to | 750,000 | A1 | 1 | 1½ | 2 |
| B+ | 300,000 to | 500,000 | 1 | 1½ | 2 | 2½ |
| B | 200,000 to | 300,000 | 1 | 1½ | 2 | 2½ |
| C+ | 125,000 to | 200,000 | 1 | 1½ | 2 | 2½ |
| C | 75,000 to | 125,000 | 1½ | 2 | 2½ | 3 |
| D+ | 50,000 to | 75,000 | 1½ | 2 | 2½ | 3 |
| D | 35,000 to | 50,000 | 1½ | 2 | 2½ | 3 |
| E | 20,000 to | 35,000 | 2 | 2½ | 3 | 3½ |
| F | 10,000 to | 20,000 | 2½ | 3 | 3½ | 4 |
| G | 5,000 to | 10,000 | 3 | 3½ | 4 | 4½ |
| H | 3,000 to | 5,000 | 3 | 3½ | 4 | 4½ |
| J | 2,000 to | 3,000 | 3 | 3½ | 4 | 4½ |
| K | 1,000 to | 2,000 | 3 | 3½ | 4 | 4½ |
| L | Up to | 1,000 | 3½ | 4 | 4½ | 5 |

### CLASSIFICATION AS TO BOTH
### ESTIMATED FINANCIAL STRENGTH AND CREDIT APPRAISAL

| FINANCIAL STRENGTH BRACKET | | EXPLANATION |
|---|---|---|
| 1 | $125,000 to $1,000,000 and Over | When only the numeral (1, 2, 3, or 4) appears, it is an indication that the estimated financial strength, while not definitely classified, is presumed to be within the range of the ($) figures in the corresponding bracket and that a condition is believed to exist which warrants credit in keeping with that assumption. |
| 2 | 20,000 to 125,000 | |
| 3 | 2,000 to 20,000 | |
| 4 | Up to 2,000 | |

### NOT CLASSIFIED OR ABSENCE OF RATING

The absence of a rating, expressed by the dash (—), is not to be construed as unfavorable but signifies circumstances difficult to classify within condensed rating symbols and should suggest to the subscriber the advisability of obtaining additional information.

### INVESTIGATING

"Inv " In place of the rating is an abbreviation of "investigating." It signifies nothing more than that a pending investigation was incomplete when the book in which it appears went to press.

The letters "N. C." on any written report mean not listed in the Reference Book.

*Dun & Bradstreet, Inc.*

ILLUSTRATION 4-2.   Key to Dun & Bradstreet Ratings

which the following eight conditions are met in the appraised business: (1) soundness of its legal structure; (2) sufficient age—at least one year, preferably three or more years; (3) experience of the management; (4) no record of criticized failures or fires; (5) willingness to submit financial statements; (6) sound financial position; (7) favorable financial and business trends; and (8) good payment record. A "high" rating is given to a business, in any of the net worth categories, provided that it fulfills all these eight requirements. In exceptional instances a business that falls short of top standard on one or two factors, but which offsets this deficiency by a particularly favorable position with respect to the others, may still be rated "high." A "good" appraisal is accorded when all conditions necessary for a "high" one are met, but to a somewhat lesser degree. The same standard of relativity is involved in the "fair" evaluations; a business thus appraised might have a top-heavy but still not dangerous financial condition. A "limited" appraisal, not uncommon for small business, rarely applies to companies in the higher financial strength classes. If a large business warrants no better than a "limited" appraisal, it is usually in a position where a "blank" symbol, explained below, is more appropriate.

Whereas there are four classifications of composite credit appraisal, ten different numerals ranging from A1 to 5 are used to indicate into which of these categories a business belongs, depending on its estimated financial strength. The meaning of a "high," "good," "fair," or "limited" credit appraisal is not absolute but relative. It varies with the size of the company's net worth. This is sound principle; risk of failure is always greater for a smaller business than for a larger one. A higher figure (expressing greater risk) within the same appraisal classification is therefore applied to small net worth enterprises than to large-scale businesses. The "high" composite credit appraisal for a $5,000 net worth concern, for example, is expressed by the figure 3 while the same "high" composite credit appraisal for a $500,000 net worth business is indicated by the figure 1. A "fair" composite credit appraisal for each of these concerns would be 4 and 2, respectively.

A number from 1 to 4 without any letter means that the estimated financial strength of the concern is presumed to fall within one of the four ranges indicated in the Key in Illustration 4-2. This information by itself is not much of an indication of the credit risk involved in selling to a concern so listed, but it is better than none, and so is given.

A blank symbol (−) is assigned when Dun & Bradstreet lacks information that would enable it to make any positive rating, or when available information suggests a situation that cannot be reflected in the standard rating symbols. It should not be interpreted as unfavorable, but should indicate to a D & B subscriber the advisability of obtaining additional information on the concern.

## REPORTS

Dun & Bradstreet prepares credit reports on all commercial enterprises listed in the *Reference Book* and on numerous semicommercial service and professional organizations not so listed. These reports are sent to subscribers in response to requests on "inquiry tickets."

D & B domestic mercantile credit reports are presented in two forms —Analytical and Regular. In each case a comprehensive "base report" is prepared on a concern. It is rewritten at least once a year, and is followed up, as occasions warrant, with supplementary reports between the periodic revisions. Such interim reports, as well as copies of any other report written on the account, are supplied to the subscriber automatically within one year following his receipt of the report he had asked for. This follow-up procedure is called "continuous service." If a "base report" on file is over 6 months old when an inquiry arrives, one of the interim reports is prepared; if the base report is over one year old, a new one has to be written. There are, altogether, five occasions for the issuing of an interim report, each one of them indicated by the two letters that preface such reports: AD for additional or later information; IT for items of particular interest to specific subscribers; SN for special notices of newsworthy credit developments; ST for more recent or interim financial statements; TR for later trade payment experience.

### Analytical reports

Analytical style reports are written by highly trained and specialized reporters on approximately 65,000 large or complicated domestic business enterprises. They feature comprehensive descriptions of how the business operates, and detailed comparative financial statements (balance sheets and profit and loss statements). They also include an analysis of the condition and trend of operations and other pertinent credit and financial data.

These reports, regardless of the size or complexity of the business reported on, are written in two sections, as shown in Illustration 4-3. The first, which is revised at least every six months and usually consists of one page, is called the AD-section. The second, termed the CD or "condensation" section, contains the basic information about the company.

The divisions of the AD-section of a D & B Analytical Report are: (1) *Date* on which the report was compiled; (2) *Heading*, giving the Standard Industrial Classification Number (SIC) of the concern, name, address, line of business, starting date, manner of trade payment, net worth, sales volume, number of employees, and the concern's D & B rating; (3) *Summary*, in capital letters, stating in compact form the outstanding financial and operational highlights of the business that are the basis for the rating given; (4) *Trade*, containing a tabulation of the ledger experiences of the concern's suppliers; (5) *Banking*, outlining the concern's bank relationships; (6) *Current*, presenting the trend of the concern's financial condition and operations and significant changes since the date of the latest figures shown in the following section of the report. The divisions of the CD or "condensation" section are: (a) *Financial Statements*, presenting in column form the concern's three most recent balance sheets together with explanatory footnotes referring to the form in which the data were received by D & B, the reserves against receivables and fixed assets, fire insurance carried, and contingent liabilities, if any; (b) *Income Statements and Surplus or Net Worth Reconciliations*, also tabulated for three years; (c) *Analysis*, with a careful interpretation of all data given; (d) *Operation* of the business— a summary statement of its products, distribution, territory, number of accounts, terms of sale, seasons, number of employees, location, and operational facilities; (e) *Subsidiaries* (if any)—the details of any parent-subsidiary corporate relationships; (f) *Management*, stating the names of owners and partners or officers and directors; and (g) *History* of the business and the personal background of the individuals responsible for it.

## Regular Reports

Regular Reports are written on all concerns not handled in Analytical style. These are the smaller and less complicated concerns—the small retailers, wholesalers, manufacturers, and service enterprises which comprise the major part of American business. Apart from being shorter, Regular Reports cover the same ground as Analytical Reports. As shown in Illustration 4-4, they are prepared in a single "section" with the following captioned divisions: (1) *Date;* (2) *Heading;* (3) *Summary;* (4) *Trade and Banking* (if such information is relevant); (5) *Finance*, containing the latest financial statement, sometimes summaries of the financial statements for two or more preceding years, and general financial information supplemented by comments; (6) *Operation*, describing the business, its products, distribution, customers, selling terms, location, and premises; and (7) *History*, presenting the background of the business and its owners.

## Special Notices

A subscriber to the Dun & Bradstreet service is automatically entitled to "continuous service" for one year on every account for which he draws a report. If the report on such a customer is revised during the year he receives a copy of the supplementary report. Between report revisions, pink Special Notices are issued whenever new items of information bearing favorably or unfavorably on the credit status of the customer become available. A sample Special Notice is shown in Illustration 4-5.

*Dun & Bradstreet* **ANALYTICAL** *Report*

| SIC | NAME & ADDRESS | | STARTED | RATING UNCHANGED |

| | | A- AD 10 MAR 15 1961 A | | |
|---|---|---|---|---|
| 56 12 | KING & TODD, INC | MEN'S CLOTHING & FURNISHINGS | 1930 | A A1 |
| | 351 FIFTH AVE | | TRADE | DISC-PPT |
| | NEW YORK 1 N Y | | SALES | $2,240,739 |
| | | | WORTH | $615,289 |
| | | | EMPLOYS | 140 |

**SUMMARY**    SALES OF THIS PROMINENT LOCAL CHAIN WERE OFF 9% IN 1960 AND LOSS OF $18,437 REDUCED WORTH SLIGHTLY. CONDITION IS STILL FINANCIALLY STRONG. SALES CURRENTLY ARE UP 30% OVER LAST YEAR AND EARNINGS TREND IS UPWARD.

**TRADE**

| HC | OWE | P DUE | TERMS | Mar 10 1961 | SOLD |
|---|---|---|---|---|---|
| 25000 | 25000 | | 2-10-EOM | Disc | Over 3 yrs to 3-61 |
| 5000 | 5000 | | 2-10-60 | Disc | Over 3 yrs |
| 4000 | | | 2-10-30 | Disc | Over 3 yrs |
| 3000 | 3000 | | 3-10-EOM | Disc | Over 3 yrs |
| 7500 | 5000 | | | Disc-ppt | |
| 5000 | 5000 | | 2-10-EOM | Disc-ppt | Over 3 yrs to 3-61 |
| 15000 | 10000 | | 30 | Ppt | Over 3 yrs |
| 10000 | 3000 | | 10-EOM | Ppt | Over 3 yrs |
| 1500 | 1500 | | 30 | Ppt | Over 3 yrs to 2-61 |

**BANKING**    High five figure balances maintained at local bank. Loans are on own straight paper to low six figures. Regular clean ups given. Deposit accounts are maintained convenient to store locations.

**CURRENT**    T. B. Johns, Treas., said on Mar 14, 1961 the up trend in sales and operating profits in the last half of 1960 has continued. Jan and Feb 1961 sales are 30% ahead of 1960. With increased mark-up profits are ahead. Merchandise and accounts payable are at low points of $175,000 and $90,000 each and bank debt was paid following the post-holiday annual clearance sales.
3-15-61 (803 75)

PLEASE NOTE WHETHER NAME, BUSINESS AND STREET ADDRESS CORRESPOND WITH YOUR INQUIRY.
The foregoing report is furnished, at your request, under your Subscription Contract, in STRICT CONFIDENCE, by DUN & BRADSTREET, Inc. as your agents and employees, for your exclusive use as an aid in determining the advisability of granting credit or insurance, and for no other purpose.   9R4-1 (30466)

ILLUSTRATION 4-3.   Dun & Bradstreet Analytical Report

## Special Inquiry Reports

In addition to the "standard" Analytical and Regular reports and their supplements, the D & B Reporting Department also prepares Key

```
        KING & TODD, INC                          A CD Page 1
        NEW YORK 1 N Y

Figures prepared from statements signed by T. B. Johns, Treas.  Accountant: Planter, Smith
and Marshall, CPA, New York.

                                          FINANCIAL STATEMENTS

                                 Dec 31 1958        Dec 31 1959        Dec 31 1960

CASH.............................  $    61,106      $    76,219      $    98,420
MARKETABLE SECURITIES............
NOTES RECEIVABLE.................
ACCOUNTS RECEIVABLE..............      227,498           212,431           235,018
INVENTORY.......................      597,620           572,016           502,654
INCOME TAX REFUND................                                            2,100
OTHER CURRENT ASSETS.............
   TOTAL CURRENT ASSETS..........      886,224           860,666           838,192

FIXED ASSETS.....................       92,208            81,418            70,017
INVESTMENTS......................
PREPAID - DEFERRED...............       10,633             9,064            11,463
                       ....
OTHER ASSETS.....................
   TOTAL ASSETS..................      989,065           951,148           919,672

DUE BANKS........................       50,000            50,000            50,000
NOTES PAYABLE....................
ACCOUNTS PAYABLE.................(A)    174,813           158,987           154,977
ACCRUALS.........................       22,756            17,416            19,406
TAXES(Except Federal Income).....
FEDERAL INCOME TAXES.............        5,803             1,019
LONG TERM LIABILITIES (Current)..       10,000            10,000            10,000
                       ....
OTHER CURRENT LIABILITIES........
   TOTAL CURRENT LIABILITIES......     263,362           237,422           234,383

LONG TERM LIABILITIES............       90,000            80,000            70,000
                       ....
RESERVES.........................

PREFERRED STOCK..................
COMMON STOCK.....................      300,000           300,000           300,000
CAPITAL SURPLUS..................
EARNED SURPLUS...................      335,703           333,726           315,289
NET WORTH (Prop or Part).........
   TOTAL LIABILITIES            .      989,065           951,148           919,672

NET WORKING CAPITAL..............      622,862           623,244           603,809
CURRENT RATIO....................        3.37              3.63              3.58
TANGIBLE NET WORTH...............      635,703           633,726           615,289
```

(A)  Includes unredeemed gift certificates.  Inventory valued at cost.  Accounts receivable
are less reserves $16,413.  Fixed assets are less reserves $148,418.  Full fire insurance
carried on inventory and fixed assets under reporting policy.  Federal income tax returns
examined through 1958.  Company is liable for store lease rentals totaling $89,000 in
1961.  No other contingent liabilities reported.
3-15-61

                                                        (CONTINUED)

ILLUSTRATION 4-3   *(Continued)*

Account and Cost Plus reports. These are individualized credit inquiries,
designed to answer specific questions by subscribers about important
customers whose orders are large or whose sales, collection, or inventory
problems are unusual.

```
KING & TODD, INC                           A CD Page 2
NEW YORK 1 N Y
```

INCOME STATEMENTS AND SURPLUS OR NET WORTH RECONCILIATIONS

| FOR THE YEARS ENDED | Dec 31 1958 | Dec 31 1959 | Dec 31 1960 |
|---|---|---|---|
| NET SALES...................... | $ 2,598,708 | $ 2,467,341 | $ 2,240,739 |
| COST OF GOODS SOLD............. | 1,562,494 | 1,480,421 | 1,299,922 |
| GROSS PROFIT (Loss)............. | 1,036,214 | 986,920 | 940,817 |
| EXPENSES....................... | 1,009,356 | 973,343 | 951,584 |
| DEPRECIATION................... | 14,615 | 11,431 | 10,497 |
| NET INCOME (Loss) ON SALES...... | 12,243 | 2,146 | (L) 21,264 |
| OTHER INCOME................... | 9,418 | 6,408 | 3,201 |
| OTHER EXPENSES................. | 6,307 | 6,431 | 2,474 |
| FEDERAL INCOME TAXES........... | 5,803 | 1,100 | (CR) 2,100 |
| OTHER TAXES.................... | | | |
| FINAL NET INCOME (Loss)......... | 9,551 | 1,023 | (L) 18,437 |
| | | | |
| SURPLUS-NET WORTH-START......... | 329,152 | 335,703 | 333,726 |
| ADD: NET INCOME............... | 9,551 | 1,023 | |
| ADJUSTMENTS............... | | | |
| DEDUCT: NET LOSS.............. | | | 18,437 |
| ADJUSTMENTS............... | | | |
| DIVIDENDS................ | 3,000 | 3,000 | |
| SURPLUS-NET WORTH-END........... | 335,703 | 333,726 | 315,289 |

(L) Loss (CR) Credit

ANALYSIS   Decreases 1958 through mid-1960 in sales resulted from reduced consumer demand generally and increased competition from newly opened suburban shopping centers. In the last six months of 1960 sales increased following more aggressive merchandising tactics, expenses were reduced and profits for this interim period partially offset earlier losses.

Despite the downward operating trend, financial position has been consistently strong. Collections average about two months and cash flow is entirely adequate to meet current expenses and take trade discounts.  Current maturities of long term liabilities have about been covered in most years by earned depreciation charges.

Long Term Liabilities:  Debentures to provide funds for expansion issued in 1948 to the Acturia Insurance Company in the amount of $200,000 at 4% interest, maturing $10,000 annually.

OPERATION   Products:  Retails better and high priced men's clothing and furnishings.

Distribution:  To middle and upper income clientele from seven stores.
Territory:  New York City and suburbs.
Accounts:  15,000
Terms:  Cash 35%, monthly charge 40%, 90 day budget 25%.
Seasons:  Fairly steady with holiday peaks.
Employees:  140

Facilities: All locations leased.  Headquarters located in modern skyscraper in midtown New York adjacent to garment district.  Stores located at 351 Fifth Ave., 1 Wall St., and 449 Madison Ave., New York City, Garden City and Scarsdale, N.Y., Greenwich, Conn., and Millburn, N.J.
3-15-61

(CONTINUED)

ILLUSTRATION 4-3   *(Continued)*

## COST OF D & B CREDIT SERVICES

Dun & Bradstreet offers subscribers a wide range of service contracts, with a corresponding range of charges. The cost of

KING & TODD, INC                              A CD Page 3
NEW YORK 1 N Y

MANAGEMENT   Herman L. Todd, Pres.          Harold S. King, Exec V Pres.
             Frank Pine, V Pres.            Ellsworth Price, V Pres.
             Richard Perkins, Sec.          Thomas B. Johns, Treas.
             DIRECTORS:  The officers with Howard Case.

HISTORY      Started: 1930 as a partnership of King and Todd.
             Incorporated: New York August 1, 1940.
Authorized Capital Stock:  30,000 shares Common $10 par value.
Outstanding Capital Stock:  30,000 shares owned 40% each by Todd and King; 5% each
by the other four officers.

Todd, born 1903, married, graduate of Dartmouth 1925.  Employed as a clothing salesman by Banks Bros. Inc., New York, 1925-1930.  He is general manager.

King, born 1902, married, was employed 1919-1930 by Banks Bros., latterly as manager
of furnishings department.  He is general merchandising manager.

Pine, born 1910, married, graduated from Cornell 1933 and entered employ of partnership.  Officer since incorporation.  He is manager of clothing department.

Price, born 1915, married, employed 1935-1941 as salesman by Acme Shirt Manufacturing
Co., 1941-1945 in Armed Forces, 1945 employed here.  Elected to office 1954.  He is
manager of furnishings department.

Perkins, born 1910, married, was employed by Park Bank & Trust Company in personnel
and in branch office supervisory work 1931-1948.  Has general office management.

Johns, born 1918, married, graduate of Wharton School, 1940.  Armed Forces 1940-1945.
Employed by Smith & Smith CPA 1945-1952.  Elected Treasurer here in 1952.

Case is a partner in the law firm Bleeker & Case, New York.
3-15-61 (803 75)

ILLUSTRATION 4-3   *(Concluded)*

a minimum one-year contract that covered 50 reports and two sectional
*Reference Books* would be a few hundred dollars. Provision of several
complete sets of the *Reference Book* and of a large number of reports,

*Dun & Bradstreet Report*

RATING
UNCHANGED

| SIC | NAME & ADDRESS | | STARTED | RATING |
|---|---|---|---|---|

CD 13 AUG 10 1961 N

**59 12**

KENT STORE      DRUGS      1953    E 2

124 KENT ROAD
ST BERNICE MICH
CARLTON COUNTY

TRADE    DISC-PPT
SALES    $89,232
WORTH    $22,901
EMPLOYS   2 P. T.

MILES GROSS, PARTNER
HANNA (MRS MILES) GROSS, PARTNER

**SUMMARY**    SALES ARE INCREASING AND FINANCIAL CONDITION IS SOUND.

**TRADE**

| HC | OWE | P DUE | TERMS | Aug 1 1961 | SOLD |
|---|---|---|---|---|---|
| 2431 | 2000 | | 2-10-30 | Disc | Over 3 yrs |
| 300 | | | 2-10-30 | Disc | Over 2 yrs |
| 250 | | | 2-10-30 | Disc | Over 3 yrs |
| 136 | 136 | | 2-10prox | Disc | Over 3 yrs |
| 75 | | | 2-10-EOM | Disc | Last sale in June |
| 15 | | | 30 | Ppt | Over 2 yrs |

**FINANCE**

Statement June 30 1961

| Cash on hand | $ 304 | Accts Pay | $ 3,724 |
|---|---|---|---|
| Cash in bank | 1,872 | | |
| Mdse | 14,450 | | |
| Total Current | 16,626 | Total Current | 3,724 |
| Fixt & Equip | 9,913 | | |
| Deposits | 86 | NET WORTH | 22,901 |
| Total Assets | 26,625 | | 26,625 |

Net sales year ending June 30 1961 $89,232; gross profit $26,181;
salaries and drawings of partners $6,732; net profit over and above salaries
and drawings of partners $3,457. Monthly rent $150; lease expires 1962.
Fire insurance: Mdse $14,000; Fixt $8,000.
Signed July 20 1961 KENT STORE by Miles Gross, Partner
Received by mail. No accountant indicated.

-----0-----

    Residential construction has stepped up in this section with the re-
sult that both sales and profits of this business have mounted steadily.
Part of earnings have been reinvested in the business every year to finance
its steady growth.
    On August 10 1961 Miles Gross stated that sales are now picking up
slightly as is usual in the Fall. Some thought has been given to opening a
second store, he said, but so far he has not been able to find the right
location.

**OPERATION**    Operates a pharmacy and soda fountain. Drugs and prescriptions account
for 50% of sales, with the remainder equally divided among fountain, sundries
and confectionery. Fixtures and a twenty-foot soda fountain are new. Both
partners are active and there are two employed on a part-time basis. LOCA-
TION: Rents first floor of a two story building in good condition. Store
measures about 20 x 50 feet. It is located in a residential section developed during the past ten years.

**HISTORY**    The style "Kent Store" was registered by the partners on April 30, 1953
This firm was formed March 1953. Starting capital consisted of $10,500
savings, a $3,500 loan from Teachers Credit Union, and a $3,000 loan from the
partners' families, making a total of $17,000. Loans have since been repaid.
    Miles Gross, 41, is native born. He was graduated from Columbia College
of Pharmacy. He then was employed as a registered pharmacist by Wark Pharmacy
and by Ray Drug Co. until this business was started.
    Hannah (Mrs Miles) Gross is 36. She was a school teacher prior to forma-
tion of this firm.
8-10-61 (158 85)

ILLUSTRATION 4-4.    Dun & Bradstreet Regular Report

might involve annual charges of several thousand dollars. Key Account
reports average around $75. The charge for an extensive Cost-Plus
report could range up to $1,000.

```
                    Dun & Bradstreet Report              SPECIAL
                                                         NOTICE

    SIC      NAME & ADDRESS                    STARTED    RATING

             SN 7 APR 5 196- N
 33 91   SLATER MFG CO    IRON & STEEL FORGINGS   1947    E 2½

         200 SOUTH ST
         HAMILTON OHIO
         BUTLER COUNTY

                        BUSINESS PURCHASED

             On April 5, 196-, G. F. Brown, President, stated Slater Mfg. Co., on
         April 4, 196- purchased the inventory and accounts receivable of Union Roto-
         Burr, manufacturers of die castings, 15 Oak St., Mid-City, Ohio. This acqui-
 SPECIAL sition will help to round out Slater's line of products.
 NOTICE      Operations of Union Roto-Burr have been consolidated with those of the
         subject, and Brown says no further capital outlay is expected. Purchase
         price of $2000 was obtained by selling additional capital stock which was
         purchased by the present officers.
         4-5-6- (216 78)


    PLEASE NOTE WHETHER NAME, BUSINESS AND STREET ADDRESS CORRESPOND WITH YOUR INQUIRY.
    The foregoing report is furnished, at your request, under your Subscription Contract, in STRICT CONFIDENCE, by DUN & BRADSTREET, Inc. as your agents and
              employees, for your exclusive use as an aid in determining the advisability of granting credit or insurance, and for no other purpose.   9R5-3 (30435)
```

ILLUSTRATION 4-5.   Dun & Bradstreet Special Notice

## SUPPLEMENTARY READINGS

Foulke, R. A., *The Sinews of American Commerce,* Dun & Bradstreet, Inc., New York, 1941, Chs. VIII-XI.

Rall, L., "Credit Rating Agencies," in H. V. Prochnow (ed.), *American Financial Institutions,* Prentice-Hall, Inc., Englewood Cliffs, N.J., 1951, p. 605.

Sommers, H., "Where Shall We Find the Answers?" *Credit and Financial Management,* August 1950, p. 5.

## REVIEW

1. List ten sources from which a credit manager might derive credit information about a customer.
2. Why are mercantile agencies not subject to suits for libel when they submit unfavorable credit information about a customer?
3. Distinguish between the functions of the following classes of Dun & Bradstreet reporters: (a) city reporters, (b) traveling reporters, (c) correspondents.
4. What services does Dun & Bradstreet supply its customers?

5. What is the theory of the Dun & Bradstreet ratings?

6. Explain the following ratings in the Dun & Bradstreet *Reference Book* or in its reports: (a) A + 2, (b) B 1½, (c) D 1½, (d) H 3½, (e) L 4, (f) 4, and (g)—.

7. Divide a sheet of paper into two columns. In the left-hand column, list the items of information about the Kent Store in the Dun & Bradstreet Regular Report presented on p. 64 that seem to you favorable from a credit viewpoint. In the right-hand column list the unfavorable items of information about this firm.

8. Make the same type of analysis of King & Todd, Inc., covered by the Dun & Bradstreet Analytical Report on pp. 60-63.

9. What are Dun & Bradstreet's Key Account Reports and Cost-Plus Reports?

# CHAPTER 5

# Special-Line Agencies

Besides Dun & Bradstreet, there are approximately 100 mercantile agencies in New York City and an undetermined number in other parts of the country. A number of trade associations maintain credit departments. These other agencies and trade association departments are all specialized in one of three ways: (1) they provide credit information on customers of particular business lines; (2) they provide only special types of credit information; or (3) they operate in limited territories.

Our analysis will cover the special line agencies and departments under three groupings—agencies serving the textile and apparel lines, agencies serving certain other lines, and trade association credit departments. Next we will consider the special service agencies. This chapter will conclude with a general consideration of how to utilize mercantile agencies and their services.

## TEXTILE AND APPAREL AGENCIES

A large number of special line agencies serve sellers in the textile and apparel fields. Among the leading ones are the National

Credit Office, Inc., the Credit Clearing House Division of Dun & Bradstreet, Inc. (which should be classified as a special line agency), and the Credit Exchange, Inc. Two of the many smaller agencies in this

---

$$\text{NCO}$$    CURRENT INFORMATION
AND ANTECEDENTS

| ELECTRONICS MIDWEST, INC. | MFR. DIODES & | CHICAGO 5, ILL. |
|---|---|---|
| WAD:AG-880-A | TRANSISTORS | 5033 Kennedy Place |
| | APRIL 1, 19__ | |

**NEW INFORMATION** - Treasurer Beverly on March 25 reported backlog of $600,000. Stated sales for the first two months were up 8% and earnings were favorable. Company has plans for construction of a plant in Los Angeles at a total cost of $100,000, which they expect to finance without outside borrowings.

**ANTECEDENT COMMENT** - Records clear. Established 1934. Present corporation formed 1957. Management well regarded. E. R. Able, Pres., holds a number of important patents in this field.

| FINANCIAL | 12/31/ | 12/31/ | 12/31/ |
|---|---|---|---|
| Cash | $ 55,900 | $ 213,700 | $ 216,700 |
| Receivables | 177,000 | 199,300 | 251,600 |
| Merchandise | 583,900 | 455,400 | 551,500 |
| Current Assets | 816,800 | 868,400 | 1,019,800 |
| Current Debts | 251,100 | 259,300 | 319,200 |
| Working Capital | 565,700 | 609,100 | 700,600 |
| Term Debt | 45,000 | 15,000 | - |
| Fixed Assets | 383,800 | 379,000 | 406,400 |
| Net Worth | 930,200 | 994,000 | 1,128,000 |
| Sales | 1,892,900 | 1,905,400 | 2,229,100 |
| Profit | 119,300 | 131,000 | 166,000 |
| Dividends | 67,200 | 67,200 | 68,600 |

Accountant: Ernst & Quinn, CPA's, Homestead, Ill.

**TRADE** - EXCELLENT

| HIGH CREDIT | OWING | PAST DUE | TERMS | PAYMENTS |
|---|---|---|---|---|
| $ 9,700 | 3,300 | 0 | 2-10 prox | dis-very ppt |
| 5,000 | 600 | 0 | N 30 | ppt |
| 3,300 | 600 | 0 | 2-10 & 25 | dis |
| 2,600 | 1,600 | 0 | N 30 | ppt |
| 2,500 | 200 | 0 | ½-10 N 30 | dis |
| 2,000 | 500 | 0 | 2-10 prox | dis |
| 2,000 | 0 | 0 | 2-10 N 30 | dis |
| 1,600 | 400 | 0 | 2-10 N 30 | dis |

SUPPLIERS -
Wire Alloys Corp., Milwaukee, Wisc.     Components, Inc., Racine, Wisc.
Germanium Specialties Co., Chicago      Laminations Co., Kent, Ohio

**ANALYSIS** - A well established and successful company in this field which has reported a profit in every year but two since 1940. For the year ended December 31, 19__ sales reached a record high and earnings were at a near record level. Volume increased approximately 17% over 19__, while earnings were up approximately 27%, reflecting continued industry growth and excellent expense control.

Financial condition at year end continued strong with cash and receivables comfortably supporting total debt. Principal liability was provision for taxes on income amounting to $116,900. Deferred debt at year end closing had been completely eliminated. Both receivables and inventory appear well controlled and adequately supported by working capital. Total debt continued modest. Bank comment quite favorable.

**CREDIT SUGGESTION** - (A) - REQUIREMENTS.

ILLUSTRATION 5-1.  A National Credit Office Report

field are Consolidated Credit Investigations and the Women's Apparel
Board of Trade. The services of these smaller agencies are similar, though
performed on a smaller scale, to those of the larger agencies.

NCO *Specialized Service*

ANTECEDENTS
& Method of Operation

ELECTRONICS MIDWEST, INC.          MFR. DIODES &          CHICAGO 5, ILL.
WAD:AG-880                         TRANSISTORS            5033 Kennedy Place
                                   APRIL 1, 19__

E. R. Able, President                        Edwin B. Jones, Exec. Vice Pres.
J. J. Bowdin, Vice Pres.                     R. W. Campbell, Vice Pres.
                     Ralph B. Beverly, Secy.-Treas.

DIRECTORS - The officers and Thomas A. Davis and Paul J. Nixon.

HISTORY - Incorporated Illinois 1957. Succeeded the proprietorship of
E. R. Able established 1934.

In 1957 bought the assets of Radio Essentials for $50,000 and merged
that operation with the subject. In July 1958 sold 10,000 shares of
stock to the public through Davis Securities Co. of Chicago. This
represented a 10% stock interest. In January 1960 completed a 30,000
sq. ft. addition to the plant and administration building.

PERSONNEL - E. R. Able, born 1912. Graduate M.I.T. in electrical engineering. Holds a 75% stock interest. Heads the general management.
Holds title to a number of patents used by the company. Life insured
for $500,000 for the benefit of the business.

Edwin B. Jones, active with the business since 1942. Became Treas. in
1958 and assumed present position in 1960. Holds a 5% stock interest.

J. J. Bowdin, here since 1934. Was plant manager until 1957 when he
became Vice Pres. in charge of manufacturing. Is an electrical
engineer. Graduate of Chicago University. Ralph W. Campbell, born
1917. Active here 1938-1941. Served as a Major in the U. S. Army
during World War II. Returned 1946. In charge of engineering. Ralph
B. Beverly joined the company in 1945 as Comptroller. Elected Treas.
1959. Formerly Vice Pres-Treas. of Hamilton-Brown Electronics, St.
Louis, Mo.

Thomas A. Davis is Pres.-Treas. of Davis Securities Co., Chicago. Paul
J. Nixon is Pres. of Paul J. Nixon Agency, New York City.

METHOD OF OPERATION - LINE - Manufactures germanium, silicon and
crystal diodes and specialty transistors.
DISTRIBUTION - Sells to manufacturers of electronic equipment and U.S.
Government agencies. Utilizes sales agents. Has representation
throughout the world.
EQUIPMENT - Owns the plant occupied which provides 100,000 sq. ft.
Fully modern and air conditioned to provide the necessary close tempera-
ture control. Employs 50.

BANKS - Third Trust & Savings Bank, Chicago, Ill.
        Security Loan National Bank, Chicago, Ill.
        Wall Street Trust Co., New York City

ILLUSTRATION 5-1   *(Concluded)*

# FINANCIAL STATEMENT SUBMITTED TO NATIONAL CREDIT OFFICE, INC.

Name **ELECTRONICS MIDWEST, INC.** Business **Mfr. Diodes & Transistors**

Street and No. **5033 Kennedy Place** City **Chicago** Zone **5** State **Ill.**

⇨ **STATEMENT OF (DATE)  December 31, 19** ⇦

| ASSETS | | | LIABILITIES | | |
|---|---|---|---|---|---|
| CASH IN BANK....$ | | | ACCOUNTS PAYABLE.............. | $ | 83,807 |
| ON HAND.....$ | | 216,703 | DUE CONTRACTORS (without offset) | | |
| U. S. GOVERNMENT SECURITIES............ | | | UNSECURED LOANS PAYABLE | | |
| RECEIVABLES for Mdse. Sold to Customers (Age at Foot of Page) | | | To Banks............... | | |
| ACCOUNTS $ **264,139** | | | To Partners or Officers............ | | |
| Less Res. for Discounts ......$ | | | To Others............... | | |
| Less Res. for Doubtful $ **2,500** | | 251,639 | SECURED LOANS PAYABLE | | |
| | | | Owing to............ | | |
| NOTES & TRADE ACCEPTANCES | | 4,485 | ACCRUED WAGES & EXPENSES...... | | 44,202 |
| (Less $ .......... discounted) | | | TAXES—Accrued and Payable: | | |
| DUE from FACTOR or FINANCE CO. | | | a. Withholding & Payroll........... | | 57,129 |
| | | | b. Federal & State Income...... | | 116,883 |
| | | | c. All Other.............. | | 2,211 |
| PHYSICAL INVENTORY OF MDSE. (Valued at lower of Cost or Market) | | | RESERVE for Income Taxes since last closing | | |
| Raw Materials....$ **293,505** | | | | | |
| In Process...........$ **204,783** | | | MORTGAGE—DEFERRED DEBT— Due within 12 mos. | | 15,000 |
| Finished Mdse ......$ **53,236** | | 551,524 | **CURRENT LIABILITIES** | | 319,234 |
| | | | MORTGAGE—DEFERRED DEBT— | | |
| **CURRENT ASSETS** | | 1,040,821 | Due after 12 mos. | | |
| Due from Partners, Officers, or Employees | | | LOANS Subordinated until............(date) | | |
| Due from Affiliated or Assoc. Companies | | | | | |
| LAND & BUILDINGS $ **313,629** | | | **TOTAL LIABILITIES** | | |
| Less Depreciation..$ **102,574** | | 211,055 | IF CORPORATION Capital Stock Pfd. $ **256,683** | | |
| MCHY., EQUIP., FURN., & FIXT. $ **348,649** | | | Capital Stock Common $ | | |
| Less Depreciation..$ **153,268** | | 195,381 | Capital Surplus......$ | | |
| INVESTMENTS (Describe on opp. page) | | 10,000 | Earned Surplus.....$ **871,339** | | |
| PREPAID & DEFERRED............. | | 6,468 | Deficit (red)........$ | | |
| | | | CORPORATE, PARTNERSHIP, or INDIVIDUAL......NET WORTH | | 1,128,022 |
| **TOTAL ASSETS** | | 1,447,259 | **TOTAL LIABILITIES & CAPITAL** | | 1,447,259 |

| | |
|---|---|
| ACCOUNTANT—Was above statement prepared by an outside accountant? Yes ☒ No ☐ Is he C.P.A.? ☒ Registered? ☐ Licensed? ☐ | RECEIVABLES |
| Accountant's Name.... **Ernst & Quinn** | For goods shipped during months of: |
| Address **2 Main St., Homestead, Ill.** | a. **December** $ 191,231 |
| On what date are your books closed?........ **12/31** | b. **November** $ 456,828 |
| MERCHANDISE—If not valued at Lower of Cost or Market, state | c. **October** $ 25,009 |
| basis used............. | d. Prior Months................ $ 1,071 |
| Is original inventory record retained by you ☐ or outside auditor ☒ | Do these include any consigned goods, uncredited returns, or un-shipped merchandise? Yes ☐ No ☒ |
| Is any merchandise pledged as security for any debt? **No** | Have all bad accounts been charged off or reserved? Yes ☒ No ☐ |
| If so, state amount so pledged. $ | During the past year have you sold, pledged, or assigned any receivables? Yes ☐ No ☒. If so, name financing concern and |
| INSURANCE—Fire: Mdse. $ **500M** , Bldg. & Fixt. $ **350M** | describe transaction:............ |
| Use & Occup. $ **Yes** ; Burglary $ **X** ; Life, Benefit | |
| Business $ on . | |

ILLUSTRATION 5-2.  Photographic Financial Statement and Verification Included in the NCO Report

## PROFIT AND LOSS STATEMENT

**PLEASE LIST OFFICERS, SUPPLIERS, AND BANKS ON REVERSE SIDE**

FOR PERIOD FROM **Jan 1** 19___ TO **Dec 31** 19___

| | |
|---|---|
| GROSS SALES | $___ |
| Less RETURNS | $___ |
| Less DISCOUNTS $ | $___ |
| NET INCOME FROM SALES | $ **2,229,124** |
| Inventory—begin'g | $ **523,069** |
| Purchases—Net | $ **874,208** |
| Labor | $ **290,504** |
| Factory Overhead | $ **57,404** |
| Total | $ **1,745,185** |
| Inventory at end | $ **551,524** |
| Cost of Goods Sold | $ **1,193,661** |
| GROSS PROFIT ON SALES | $ **1,035,463** |
| Selling & Ship. Exp. | $ **395,908** |
| Salaries—Officers or Principals | $ **54,300** |
| Adm. & Gen. Exp. | $ **145,710** |
| Bad Debts | $ **1,232** |
| Depreciation | $ **54,367** $ **651,517** |
| INCOME or (LOSS) ON SALES | $ **383,946** |
| Other Income (exclude discount earned) | $ **2,750** |
| Total | $ **386,696** |
| Deductions from Income **Prof.Sharing** | **41,279** |
| NET PROFIT or (LOSS) before Income Taxes | $ **345,417** |
| Provision for Fed. & State Income Taxes | $ **179,400** |
| NET PROFIT or (LOSS) | $ **166,017** |

## RECONCILIATION OF SURPLUS OR NET WORTH

| | | |
|---|---|---|
| Beginning (date) | | $ **773,901** |
| ADD: Profit for Period | $ **166,017** | |
| Other Credits to Surplus | $___ | $___ |
| Total | | $ **939,918** |
| DEDUCT: Loss for Period | $___ | |
| Div. & Withdr'ls | $ **68,579** | |
| Other Charges to Surplus | $___ | $ **68,579** |
| NET WORTH or SURPLUS at end | | $ **871,339** |

INVESTMENTS—Describe (If subsidiary or affiliated state % owned)

a. **Govt - 5% notes** $ **10,000**

b. ___ $___

LIABILITIES—Merchandise received or charged to you but not included in Assets or Liabilities $ **-**

Amount of Contingent Liabilities $ **-**

Are any liabilities secured in any way? **No** If so, state amount, creditor, and nature of security ___

Annual Rent $___ Lease Expires **1970**

NET WORTH—Has this been decreased since statement date by withdrawal, retirement of capital, payment of dividends, bonuses, or personal Income Taxes? **No**

If so, by what amount? $___

TAXES—Have all Federal, State, and Local tax assessments been paid or shown accrued on statement? **Yes**

Tax Closing date? **12/31** Date of latest return examined by Internal Revenue Service? **12/31/59**

## INDEPENDENT ACCOUNTANT'S OPINION

The accompanying Balance Sheet and Profit and Loss Statement was prepared from an independently verified statement of assets and liabilities except for merchandise inventory. The inventory was certified to us by one of the officers of the corporation as taken at lower of cost or market value and we have test checked its arithmetical accuracy.

**MAR 28**

RECEIVED THROUGH THE MAILS BY NATIONAL CREDIT OFFICE, Inc. | OPENED BY

Accountants Signature *Fritz Ernst* : Address **2 Main St, Homestead**
(Please use your own Letterhead if additional space is necessary)

**TO NATIONAL CREDIT OFFICE, INC.**
Two Park Avenue, New York 16, N. Y.

The undersigned warrants that the foregoing figures and answers are true and accurate in every respect and orders this statement mailed to you with the intention that it shall be relied upon in the extension of credit or insurance by such concerns, including factors or agents, who may subscribe to your service now or hereafter. My (Our) accountants are authorized to supply you with any supplementary information that may be required.

Dated at *Chicago* this **25th** day of **March** 19___

Signed in the presence of:

Name *Georgia Smith*

Address *Chicago, Ill.*

*Electronics Midwest Inc*
(Name of Corporation, Partnership or Proprietorship)

By *E. R. Able*

*President*
(Signature of Officer, Partner or Owner) (Title)

ILLUSTRATION 5-2 *(Concluded)*

## National Credit Office

National Credit Office (NCO), with headquarters in New York City and branches in seven other cities, is the largest of the special mercantile agencies. It was organized in 1900 to report on textile manufacturers and distributors. In 1931 it was absorbed by R. G. Dun & Co. which in 1933 was merged into Dun & Bradstreet. NCO remained an independent subsidiary. The two organizations continue to some extent in competition. NCO is still the major credit reporting agency in the textile field, covering manufacturers and wholesalers (including converters and jobbers) of yarns, cloths, cloth goods, and wearing apparel, as well as department stores, specialty chains, and piece good retailers. In recent years it has expanded widely into credit reporting in other product fields, including metals, electronics, and chemicals. In all, NCO issues reports on some 50,000 companies.

Most NCO credit reports are prepared and issued in three separate parts. Those for small firms are presented in briefer form. The "Antecedent" section gives the history of the concern, short business biographies of its officers, a description of its methods of operation and the names of its principal banks. A "Current Information" section provides condensed financial statements for the three latest years, a trade report with ledger information from suppliers, the names of the principal suppliers, an intensive analysis of current financial trends, and a suggested average credit figure. This last reflects NCO's over-all opinion of the credit soundness of the account, expressed in a letter.[1] The third part of the report consists of a photographic reproduction of the customer's latest financial statement.[2] This photographic method of presentation has the advantage over transcriptions of eliminating error possibilities and speeding the release of information. An example of an NCO report is presented in Illustrations 5-1 and 5-2.

Unlike Dun & Bradstreet, NCO does not publish a general rating book. It does, however, issue surveys of metals and electronics buyers that contain the ratings calculated for the reports on these companies.

Like Dun & Bradstreet, NCO is expanding into reporting and research operations of which some are quite unrelated to mercantile credit.

---

[1] The letters A, B, C, D stand for excellent, satisfactory, fair, and poor. They are applied regardless of the size of the account or credit suggested. If NCO believes that an account is a safe risk for any practicable credit extension, its recommendation is "requirements" instead of a specific figure.

[2] Where this complete, photographed financial statement is lacking, a third report page with the caption "Financial Information" is typed, containing all available figures which reflect the present financial condition of the business.

### Credit Clearing House Division of Dun & Bradstreet

Credit Clearing House was originally an independent organization, with the most extensive rating, reporting, and checking service in the apparel field. Like NCO, it was absorbed by Dun & Bradstreet, but as a divisional operating unit instead of a subsidiary. Besides issuing reports, Credit Clearing House publishes a quarterly *Apparel Trades Book* with over 150,000 names. This volume indicates, through code symbols, the trade styles, branches, and types of merchandise sold by the listed concerns. Their ratings are given by a special code (see Illustration 5-3).[3] Reports, mostly of the D & B Regular type, are issued on the companies listed in the *Apparel Trades Book.*

The heart of the Credit Clearing House Division's operations is its "credit checking," or "credit recommendation service" as D & B calls it. This is designed to assist suppliers in their credit decisions on individual orders as they are received. In the men's and women's wear fields, such a service is vital for two reasons. (1) A large proportion of the retailer customers are small enterprises, financially vulnerable because of limited capital. Consumer demand in this line reacts sharply to such factors as changing styles, weather, and local conditions. These hazards produce an unusually high business mortality among apparel retailers. Hence there is special need for constant watchfulness over customer accounts. (2) A large portion of the suppliers are small concerns that do not have regular credit managers or credit departments.

Although credit checking is of greatest value to small suppliers, many large apparel houses with highly trained credit executives consider the service an important credit tool. They like to compare their own opinions with those of a source which, through pooling inquiries from subscribers all over the country, is able to keep constant track of customer purchases.

Credit Clearing House is the largest of several special-line mercantile agencies that do credit checking for their fields. The technique of credit checking varies according to the agency performing it. There are marked basic similarities, however, in the collection and dissemination of this special kind of credit information. For this reason, the procedures of Credit Clearing House may be presented as an example of this type of agency credit service.

When a subscriber to the Credit Clearing House Division receives an order from a customer, he immediately communicates by telephone or

---

[3] All names listed in the *Apparel Trades Book* are also listed in the D & B *Reference Book.* Their ratings in the two books, while usually embodying identical appraisals, are expressed in different codes.

## APPAREL TRADES BOOK

# KEY TO RATINGS

| | | Estimated Financial Strength | Payments Appraisal | Composite Appraisal |
|---|---|---|---|---|
| ⌶ B · | A | Over $1,000,000 | 1 2 3 4 | A B C D |
| | · · · · | See Note¹ · · · · | 1 2 3 4 | A B C D |
| | C | Over 500,000 | 1 2 3 4 | A B C D |
| ⌶ F · | D | Over 300,000 | 1 2 3 4 | A B C D |
| | E | Over 200,000 | 1 2 3 4 | A B C D |
| | · · · · | See Note¹ · · · · | 1 2 3 4 | A B C D |
| | G | Over 100,000 | 1 2 3 4 | A B C D |
| ⌶ K · | H | Over 50,000 | 1 2 3 4 | A B C D |
| | J | Over 30,000 | 1 2 3 4 | A B C D |
| | · · · · | See Note¹ · · · · | 1 2 3 4 | A B C D |
| | L | Over 20,000 | 1 2 3 4 | A B C D |
| | M | Over 10,000 | 1 2 3 4 | A B C D |
| ⌶ S · | O | Over 5,000 | 1 2 3 4 | A B C D |
| | R | Over 3,000 | 1 2 3 4 | A B C D |
| | · · · · | See Note¹ · · · · | 1 2 3 4 | A B C D |
| | T | Over 2,000 | 1 2 3 4 | A B C D |
| | V | Over 1,000 | 1 2 3 4 | A B C D |
| | W | Up to 1,000 | 1 2 3 4 | A B C D |

X · · · · · · · · Not Classified · · · · · · · · See Note²

§ { The symbol § preceding a rating indicates that an important part of the total worth consists of assets not usually considered working capital.

Note¹ { The letters B, F, K and S in the Estimated Financial Strength column, preceded by the symbol ⌶ indicate in a general way what is considered relative in size. To illustrate: the letter B indicates size comparable to concerns classified in the range A to C inclusive, the letter F, comparable to those from D to G inclusive, the letter K, comparable to those from H to M inclusive, and the letter S, comparable to those from O to V inclusive.

Note² { The letter X is not to be construed as unfavorable but, in the column or columns in which used, signifies circumstances difficult to definitely classify within condensed rating symbols and should suggest to the subscriber the advisability of reading the detailed report.

## CREDIT CLEARING HOUSE

### DUN & BRADSTREET, INC.

SERVING THE APPAREL LINES NATIONALLY

ILLUSTRATION 5-3.   Key to Ratings of the Credit Clearing House *Apparel Trades Book*

mail with the Division, giving name and location of the account, the amount of the order, the selling terms, and his previous ledger experience with the account. If the inquiry is made by telephone, within a minute or two the supplier receives one of three answers:

"The account is favorable";

"It is considered favorable as a slow paying account"; or

"Individual judgment is suggested, and we will send you a copy of the report."

A confirmation slip is mailed to him (see Illustration 5-4).

Credit Clearing House does not advise any subscriber not to sell an account. The third of the above answers is given under two circumstances. (1) A subscriber's judgment on a particular account may be

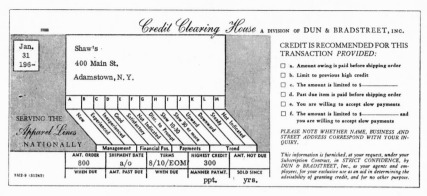

<table>
<tr><td colspan="3">Credit Clearing House A DIVISION OF DUN & BRADSTREET, INC.</td></tr>
</table>

| Jan. 31 196– | Shaw's 400 Main St. Adamstown, N. Y. | CREDIT IS RECOMMENDED FOR THIS TRANSACTION *PROVIDED:* |
| --- | --- | --- |

☐ a. Amount owing is paid before shipping order
☐ b. Limit to previous high credit
☐ c. The amount is limited to $—————
☐ d. Past due item is paid before shipping order
☐ e. You are willing to accept slow payments
☐ f. The amount is limited to $————— and you are willing to accept slow payments

*PLEASE NOTE WHETHER NAME, BUSINESS AND STREET ADDRESS CORRESPOND WITH YOUR INQUIRY.*

SERVING THE *Apparel Lines* NATIONALLY

A B C D E F G H I J K L M
New · Experienced · Inexperienced · Good · Satisfactory · Not Indicated · Disc. to Prompt · Slow 10-30 · Slow 30 or more · Upward · Downward · Steady · Not Indicated

| Management | Financial Pos. | Payments | | Trend |

*This information is furnished, at your request, under your Subscription Contract, in STRICT CONFIDENCE, by DUN & BRADSTREET, Inc., as your agents and employees, for your exclusive use as an aid in determining the advisability of granting credit, and for no other purpose.*

| AMT. ORDER | SHIPMENT DATE | TERMS | HIGHEST CREDIT | AMT. NOT DUE |
| --- | --- | --- | --- | --- |
| 800 | a/o | 8/10/EOM | 300 | |
| WHEN DUE | AMT. PAST DUE | WHEN DUE | MANNER PAYMT. | SOLD SINCE |
| | | | ppt. | yrs. |

3M2-9 (31242)

ILLUSTRATION 5-4.  Credit Clearing House Confirmation Slip

influenced by his own business policy and requirements—his desire and need to move goods, his inventory and receivables situation, his credit and sales policy. Hence a particular borderline account might be an acceptable credit risk for a certain-sized order to one supplier but not to another. When Credit Clearing House give its third answer, it says in effect that in view of the status of the account it cannot make a general recommendation for all and any suppliers, so that each supplier must form his own judgment in the light of his special situation. (2) An account may exhibit some peculiar features that Credit Clearing House feels subscribers should discover from the report and take into consideration in making credit decisions.

Recommendations furnished by the Credit Clearing House Division are based on the judgment of analysts who are specialists in credit problems arising in the apparel industry. These analysts are assigned to specific geographic regions. They arrive at their opinion through the use of: (1) the Dun & Bradstreet *credit reports* on accounts under their jurisdiction, which become a part of the credit folders maintained by the Division, and which are kept up-to-date through the facilities of the Dun & Bradstreet reporting service and by special investigations which the analysts may request in order to review their current opinion; (2) the *master card* (see Illustration 5-5) which is maintained on each account as a record of the purchases, payment experiences, and other pertinent information furnished by subscribers when they place their inquiries. Abnormalities in the pattern of an account's purchases and payments, such as overbuying (evidenced by widespread and overactive inquiry), buying out of season, or slowing payments, catch the analyst's eye as he reviews the master card each time an inquiry on the account is received. A master card would also spotlight the spreading of an account's purchases into new lines or new markets, which might not in

| DATE REC. | SUBSCRIBERS NO. OFFICE | SUBSCRIBER | AMT. OF ORDER (OMIT LAST 2 DIGITS) | DECISION | BY | DATE ANS. | SHPT. DATE | TERMS | HIGHEST CREDIT | OWES NOT DUE | WHEN DUE | OWES PAST DUE | WHEN DUE | PAYMENTS |
|---|---|---|---|---|---|---|---|---|---|---|---|---|---|---|
| 2/5 | | 0 2 8 9 6 | 8 | R | 3 | | | 10/Eom. | | | | | | |
| 3/7 | | 0 2 2 5 | 7 | R | 2 | | | 10/Eom. | 4 | 0 | 3/10 | | | ppt. |
| 3/11 | 7 | 5 6 0 1 | 2 4 | R | AA | | | 30 | 15 | – | | | | ppt. |
| 4/15 | 6 8 | 5 1 5 | 5 | R | 2 | | | 10/Eom. | 4 | 2 | 9/10 | | | ppt. |
| 4/12 | | 3 0 4 | 2 | R | 1 | | | 2/10 Eom. | | | | | | |
| 4/20 | | 4 2 6 0 | 1 3 | R | AA | | | Eom. | 13 | 2 | 4/10 | | | ppt. |
| 5/26 | 2 | 1 3 4 0 | 2 | R | 1 | | | Eom. | 2 | 2 | 4/10 | | | ppt. |
| 5/26 | | 0 3 3 5 0 | 5 | R | 2 | | | 30 | 7 | | | | | ppt. |
| 5/30 | | 0 5 6 5 2 | 1 | R | 2 | | | 14/Eom. | | | | | | 1st order |
| 6/23 | 4 | 0 2 1 0 3 | 3 | R | 1 | | | Eom. | 3 | 1 | 7/10 | | | ppt. |
| 6/24 | | 1 8 6 7 3 | 1 | R | 2 | | | 10/Eom. | 2 | 1 | 7/10 | | | ppt. |
| 4/21 | | 0 5 6 1 0 | 2 | R | 3 | | | Eom. | | | | | | new |
| 7/7 | 4 7 | 7 0 5 | 6 | R | AA | | | 10/Eom. | | | | | | |

ILLUSTRATION 5-5.  Credit Clearing House Master Card

itself be abnormal but would call for investigation and explanation. In addition to performing routine credit checking service, the analysts of the Division frequently act as consultants to subscribers who are faced with complex credit problems not readily solved by the response on a recommendation slip.

## Credit Exchange

Credit Exchange is the second largest credit checking agency. It covers the men's, women's, and children's wear field all over the country. It makes recommendations on individual orders as received by its subscribers. These are usually given by telephone, with subsequent written confirmation in the form of punched cards; these contain not only the decision but many items of credit information on the account such as its credit line, payment record, three-year trend, business composition, starting date, lines of merchandise carried, previous insolvency record if any, and remarks.

Credit Exchange also prepares reports on the accounts it covers. These contain photostatic financial statements. They suggest, furthermore, "lines of credit" for the accounts, or give explanations of why credit should be refused. A "nonrecommending" report is always followed by a "personal opinion letter" with more advice on the account. Subscribers are notified of changes in recommendations on accounts for a year after making inquiry. As a special protective device for subscribers, a

"Weekly Change List" is issued containing the latest information on accounts on which there have been changes in recommendation; the "List" calls subscribers' attention to accounts whose condition has improved, as well as to those which have deteriorated.

## SPECIAL-LINE AGENCIES IN OTHER FIELDS

Other business fields also have their special credit agencies. Usually only one agency in each line is outstanding. Thus the furniture field has Lyon Furniture Mercantile Agency. The Jewelers Board of Trade serves the jewelry field. There is Credit Executives Association, Inc., for hotel and restaurant suppliers. Stationers and Publishers Board of Trade, Inc., covers purchasers of stationery, typewriters, and other office equipment. American Book Publishers Council, Inc., serves book publishers.

Some of these special-line agencies, like Lyon, are operated as reporting organizations to whose services any supplier may subscribe. Others, like The Jewelers Board of Trade, are nonprofit membership associations. These two agencies are described in the following pages.

### Lyon Furniture Mercantile Agency

Lyon Furniture Mercantile Agency, one of the largest special-line agencies, covers the house furnishings field—furniture, carpets, floor coverings, refrigerators, lamps, and other household appliances—and certain business furnishings lines, such as undertakers' equipment. It was established in 1876, and expanded by amalgamation with other agencies operating in this field. Today the Lyon Agency maintains seven offices located in major commercial cities and claims to serve 95 per cent of the manufacturers and distributors in the field. It supplies its subscribers with reports, a rating book, and current supplementary information.

The reports of the Lyon Agency are similar to those of Dun & Bradstreet and the National Credit Office. They give a history of the subject business, brief biographies of the principals, description of the method of operation, financial statement information and analysis, ledger information from suppliers, a summary, and a rating. Sample pages from a Lyon Report are shown in Illustration 5-6. Drawing a Lyon report entitles a subscriber to receive, for a year, "Special Notifications" containing significant news items on the account.

The Lyon rating book contains over 140,000 names. It is issued semiannually and is generally known as the Red Book. It differs from the Dun & Bradstreet Reference Book in a way characteristic of the rating books issued by special-line agencies. There is a key for "estimated financial net worth" as in the Dun & Bradstreet ratings. There is no single key for composite credit appraisal. Instead, there is a number series key for pay ratings, ranging from 1 for discounting customers through 7 for C.O.D. or C.B.D. customers. In addition, key numbers

---

Form 29                                                                          2-60

### LYON RED BOOK REPORT

Lyon Furniture Mercantile Agency, as your agents and employees, furnishes the information herein at your request under the terms of your subscription agreement. The information is for your exclusive use. It is to be held strictly confidential and not to be revealed, made known or shown to those reported. Any disclosure is a violation of the terms of your contract.

```
SMITH HENRY D.                    FC&Apl           BANGOR........ME.
                                                   313 Main Street
Age 40, Md.

REV: (ja-31)  July 1, 1961
```

ANTECEDENTS
        Commenced business at above address as new venture July 1, 1955.

        Henry D. Smith had previously been employed from 1936 to 1948 as buyer and manager by Black & White, Augusta, Me. and from 1948 until early in 1954 was employed as buyer and manager by H. J. Roberts Inc., furniture, Portland, Me.

        Fire and commercial records claimed clear for owner on latest signed statement submitted to Agency.

GENERAL INFORMATION
        Owner is well experienced and well known in this line locally. Operates from rented quarters at above address comprising a two story frame building 40 ft. x 60 ft., centrally located. Premises afford two display windows and subject handles a complete line of furniture, some floor coverings, stoves, etc. Sales are for cash or on short term credit basis. Fair sized stock of merchandise carried.

FINANCIAL INFORMATION

COMPARATIVE SUMMARIZED STATEMENTS

| DATE | ASSETS | LIABILITIES | NET WORTH |
|------|--------|-------------|-----------|
| July 1, 1955 | 19,400.. | 9,500. | 9,900. |
| July 1, 1958 | 20,120. | 9,820. | 10,300. |
| July 1, 1959 | 10,900. | 5,400. | 14,500. |
| Jan. 1, 1960 | 22,320. | 5,570. | 16,750. |
| Nov. 30, 1960 | 24,019. | 10,606. | 13,413. |

        The following statement taken from books as at Nov. 30, 1960 was received by mail:

```
ASSETS:
Cash on hand $636.42; in bank $4000.        4,636.42
Accts. rec., reg.                           2,466.01
Mdse., cost or mkt.-lower                    6,351.47
                 Net Current Assets        13,453.90
Fixt. $550; del. equip. $900.               1,450.00
Real estate & bldg.                         9,000.00
Prepaid ins.                                  115.53
         TOTAL ASSETS. . . . . . . . . . . . . . . . 24,019.43
```

---

ILLUSTRATION 5-6.   A Lyon Furniture Mercantile Agency Report

running up to 120 cover credit status ratings and special situations of interest to the credit manager. The full key to the *Red Book* ratings is given in Illustration 5-7.

One of the most valuable services of Lyon is the *Weekly Supplement,* which reaches subscribers every Monday morning. It records important

---

Form 20                                                                                         2-60

## LYON RED BOOK REPORT

Lyon Furniture Mercantile Agency, as your agents and employees, furnishes the information herein at your request under the terms of your subscription agreement. The information is for your exclusive use. It is to be held strictly confidential and not to be revealed, made known or shown to those reported. Any disclosure is a violation of the terms of your contract.

SMITH HENRY D.                        -2-                        BANGOR........ME.

July 1, 1961

FINANCIAL INFORMATION    (Cont'd)
LIABILITIES:
Accts. pay., not due                          1,361.80
Loan from bank (note)                         6,700.00
Sundries                                         44.25
            Total Current Liabilities         8,106.05
Mtg. on real estate                           2,500.00
            TOTAL LIABILITIES. . . . . . . . . . . . . 10,606.05
            NET WORTH. . . . . . . . . . . . . . . . . 13,413.38

Annual sales $15,000.00

        No mdse. on consignment.  Ins. on mdse. $6000; on fixt. & del.
equip. none.  Business property rented - annual rental $600.

                        (SIGNED)  By:  Henry D. Smith
                            REAL ESTATE

| Location & Description | Title in Name of | Value | Mtg. | Equity |
|---|---|---|---|---|
| Frame house, Portland, Me. | Jane & Henry D. Smith | $9,000. | $2,500. | $6,500. |

ANALYSIS
        Latest statement compared with initial figures reveals a decrease in net worth of about $3,300.

        Comparison of cash and receivables to current liabilities on latest statement reveals liquid position slightly below standard, with current ratio likewise subject to improvement and some margin of protection afforded creditors.  It is noted that bulk of liabilities is represented by loan from bank, with cash item alone well in excess of accounts payable.  Real estate listed is held jointly by subject and wife and is therefore not available for rating purposes.  Turnover rate of less than twice per year is below standard.

        Allowing for depreciations and adjustments, means are estimated at between $3,000. and $5,000.

TRADE INVESTIGATION
        Inquiry June 19, 1961:

(1) DISCOUNT - High recent credit $766.  Owing $766.  Selling since
            Aug. 20, 1955.  Terms 4% Eom, net 60.
(2) DISCOUNT - High recent credit $648.  Selling since Sept. 1955.
            Terms 2% 30 days.
(3) DISCOUNT - High recent credit $344.  Owing $151.  Unfilled orders
            $120.  Selling since Oct. 13, 1958.  Terms 2/10/30.

---

ILLUSTRATION  5-6   *(Continued)*

## LYON RED BOOK REPORT

Lyon Furniture Mercantile Agency, as your agents and employees, furnishes the information herein at your request under the terms of your subscription agreement. The information is for your exclusive use. It is to be held _strictly confidential_ and not to be revealed, made known or shown to those reported. Any disclosure is a violation of the terms of your contract.

SMITH HENRY D.                          -3-              BANGOR........ME.

July 1, 1961

TRADE INVESTIGATION (Cont'd)
(4) DISCOUNT - High recent credit $220.  Selling since Sept. 1955.
              Terms 2/10/30.
(5) DISCOUNT - High recent credit $183.94.  Selling for year.  Terms
              4/70.
(6) DISCOUNT - High recent credit $155.  Selling since July 20, 1957.
              Terms 2/30/60.
(7) DISCOUNT - High recent credit $137.55.  Terms 2/30/60.
(8) DISCOUNT - High recent credit $101.  Selling from Oct. 14, 1959.
              Terms 2/10/30.

SUMMARY
        OWNER EXPERIENCED.  COMMENCED BUSINESS JULY 1, 1955 AS NEW
VENTURE.  RECORD CLEAR.  LATEST STATEMENT SUBMITTED INDICATES LIQUID
AND CURRENT POSITIONS SUBJECT TO IMPROVEMENT.  AMPLE PROTECTION
AFFORDED CREDITORS.  PAYMENTS DISCOUNT.

N:                          Rate 13 - R - 1 - 116

ILLUSTRATION 5-6  *(Concluded)*

credit developments for the field during the previous week, including rating changes, news about new businesses, dissolutions, successions, assignments, receiverships, bankruptcies, and accounts placed for collection. Trade information included in the *Weekly Supplement* is based

# LYON RED BOOK — CREDIT KEY

## CAPITAL RATINGS
### Estimated Financial Worth

| | | | |
|---|---|---|---|
| A | ................. | $1,000,000 | or over |
| B | ................. | 500,000 | to $1,000,000 |
| C | ................. | 300,000 | to 500,000 |
| D | ................. | 200,000 | to 300,000 |
| E | ................. | 100,000 | to 200,000 |
| G | ................. | 75,000 | to 100,000 |
| H | ................. | 50,000 | to 75,000 |
| J | ................. | 40,000 | to 50,000 |
| K | ................. | 30,000 | to 40,000 |
| L | ................. | 20,000 | to 30,000 |
| M | ................. | 15,000 | to 20,000 |
| N | ................. | 10,000 | to 15,000 |
| O | ................. | 7,000 | to 10,000 |
| Q | ................. | 5,000 | to 7,000 |
| R | ................. | 3,000 | to 5,000 |
| S | ................. | 2,000 | to 3,000 |
| T | ................. | 1,000 | to 2,000 |
| U | ................. | 500 | to 1,000 |
| V | ................. | 100 | to 500 |

**Z** No financial basis for credit reported·

### INDEFINITE RATINGS

**F** —Estimated financial responsibility not definitely determined, presumed high.

**P** —Estimated financial responsibility not definitely determined, presumed moderate.

**W**—Estimated financial responsibility not definitely determined, presumed small.

**Y** —Estimated financial responsibility not definitely determined, presumed very limited.

The omission of a rating is not unfavorable but indicates that sufficient information is not at hand on which to base rating.

## PAY RATINGS
### Based on suppliers' reports

1—Discount.
2—Prompt.
3 —Medium.
4—Variable, prompt to slow
5—Slow.
6—Very slow.
7—C. O. D. or C. B. D.

8—Pay rating not established, but information favorable.
9—Claims to buy always for cash.

### SPECIAL CONDITIONS

12—Business recently commenced.
13—Inquire for report.
21—Buys small, usually pays cash.
23—Sells on commission.
24—Name listed for convenience only.
29—Rating undetermined.
31—Financial statement declined, or repeatedly requested and not received.

### SYMBOL INTERPRETATION

● or 12 — Business recently commenced.
✚ or 116 —New statement recently received.
▲—Indicates information of unusual importance.
☉—Sells on installment plan.
(?)—Sells from residence, office or catalogue.

## CREDIT GRANTORS—NOTE

No system of ratings can ALWAYS convey an accurate summarization of existing conditions. Book ratings reflect conditions believed to exist when assigned, and are based upon information obtained from financial statements, from the trade, special reporters, correspondents, financial institutions and other sources deemed reliable, but the correctness thereof is in no way guaranteed.

Conditions are constantly changing, and changes as made are shown in the "LYON Weekly Supplement and Report", and in Lyon Credit Reports.

Should any error, or inaccuracy in rating be noted, it should be reported only to the Agency, in order that correction may be made.

Inquire for Detailed Credit Report on all NEW ACCOUNTS, and make inquiry at least once a year on old accounts or when change in rating is indicated in the "LYON Weekly Supplement and Report".

(OVER)

ILLUSTRATION 5-7.  Key to the Lyon *Red Book* Ratings

# SPECIAL RATINGS

### Key Numbers interpreting Credit Items and Business Conditions; as appear in

## LYON WEEKLY SUPPLEMENT AND REPORT

12 or ●—Business recently commenced.

13—Inquire for report.

21—Buys small, usually pays cash.

23—Sells on commission.

24—Name listed for convenience only.

29—Rating undetermined.

30—Rating in abeyance, pending later information.

31—Financial statement declined, or repeatedly requested and not received.

47—New ownership or change in ownership.

49—Dissolved.

50—Succeeded by —

51—Rating raised to —

52—Rating lowered to —

54—Rating suspended.

55—Given bill of sale, or notice thereof.

56—Reported selling out, or discontinuing.

57—Have sold out.

58—Sold out at auction.

59—Damaged by water.

60—Damaged by flood or storm.

61—Damaged by fire.

62—Burned out.

63—Partially insured.

64—Fully insured.

65—Inventory not insured.

66—No insurance.

67—Will continue.

68—Deceased.

69—Estate continues.

70—Claim placed for collection with Lyon Agency.

75—Suit reported.

76—Execution issued.

77—Judgment reported.

78—Attachment proceedings reported.

79—Closed by Sheriff or Marshal.

80—Sold out by Sheriff or Marshal.

81—Chattel mortgage.

82—Chattel mortgage foreclosed.

83—Deed of trust for benefit of creditors.

85—Real estate mortgage foreclosed.

87—Assignment for benefit of creditors.

88—Petition for Receiver filed.

89—Temporary Receiver appointed.

90—Receiver appointed.

91—In hands of Receiver.

92—Voluntary petition in bankruptcy.

93—Involuntary petition in bankruptcy.

94—Petition for arrangement, reorganization extension or composition.

95—In bankruptcy.

96—Inquire for important new report.

98—Trustee appointed.

99—In liquidation to discontinue business.

100—First dividend paid.

101—Second dividend paid.

102—Final dividend paid.

103—Asking extension.

104—Called meeting of creditors.

105—Offering to compromise.

106—Unable to locate.

107—Discontinued or out of business.

108—Claims should be given immediate attention.

109—Settled and resumed.

110—Settlement paid.

111—Removed to —

113—Capital stock increased to —

114—Name changed to —

115—Cannot report definitely as yet.

116 or ✤—New statement recently received.

117—Received discharge in bankruptcy.

118—Discharge in bankruptcy denied.

119—Not for book listing.

120—Discontinue book listing.

ILLUSTRATION 5-7  (Concluded)

on a *Tracer* sent out weekly to check on customers' paying habits. Suppliers report their current experience with these accounts.

### The Jewelers Board of Trade

The Jewelers Board of Trade is another mercantile agency that covers practically an entire line of business. As a nonprofit membership organization of some 1,500 members, it is sponsored and maintained by jewelry manufacturers and wholesalers and by some other institutions that have dealings with this trade, such as insurance companies and banks. In structure it is comparable to a trade association devoted exclusively to credit information service. It issues a *Rating Book* twice a year, in regular and in pocket sizes, with names and credit standing of some 43,000 jewelry buyers, and prepares credit reports on these accounts. A weekly *Service Bulletin* supplements the *Rating Book* by reporting on current credit developments for this customer group. "Green slips" cover individual customer developments and supplement the reports.

## TRADE ASSOCIATION CREDIT DEPARTMENTS

Approximately 400 national trade associations supply their members with credit information.[4] The credit departments of these trade associations perform one or more of the following functions: (1) promoting and supervising the exchange of ledger information among members as described in Chapter 6 of this volume; (2) supplying current credit information including special reports on members' customers; (3) preparing reports on the industry's financial practices (cash discounts, and so forth); (4) promoting uniformity in terms of trade for lines of business and "trade standards" to assist members in the analysis of financial statements; (5) publishing delinquent lists; and (6) in few instances, acting in collection work. They derive their information usually from the customers or suppliers who are members of the association; they do not use reporters who visit concerns for first-hand information.

The credit reports of The American Fur Merchants' Association, Inc., may be taken as an example for this phase of trade association work. This association, located in New York City, serves the skin dealers and

---

[4] U. S. Department of Commerce, *Directory of National Trade Associations 1956,* Washington, D.C., pp. iv and v.

also banks and others allied to this trade. It prepares reports on practically all skin buyers. These reports are based on: (1) descriptive and historical material supplied by the customer, (2) his financial statements, and (3) daily data on sales to the customer and ledger interchange on him, supplied by the association's members. The reports contain six sections: (1) organization and history of the customer's business; (2) antecedents and personnel records; (3) the latest financial statement and interim trial balance figures; (4) litigation and insolvencies, if any; (5) a general statement on paying habits; and (6) a so-called rating, expressed in letters (such as X, Y, E) to which members have a key. This rating is based primarily on the financial structure of the business with emphasis on its working capital position, and is actually a recommended credit line. Weekly bulletins of the association keep members informed about suits, judgments, insolvencies, and other developments affecting their customers.

### Trade association delinquent lists

Some trade association credit bureaus include, as part of their service to members, the preparation and distribution of "delinquent lists." Members of the association are requested to report any customer when he becomes delinquent—this being interpreted in some instances as being several days behind in payments or, in other cases, as being one or more months in arrears. The names of customers so reported are listed alphabetically, mimeographed, and distributed either weekly or monthly, with an indication of the number of suppliers reporting the delinquency; an example is shown in Illustration 5-8. When a customer reported as delinquent clears his past-due balance, or brings his arrearage within the limit allowed by the association's policy, the supplier notifies the association credit bureau, and if no other members of the association are still reporting the customer, his name is taken off the list.[5]

Of course, a delinquent list does not give a supplier the rounded information that he can obtain from ledger interchange. But on the crucial matter of the slowing of a customer's payments, it provides immediate information. Moreover, existence of such a delinquent list is a powerful collection instrument for all credit men in the line, since they can warn a customer that his slow payments will put him on the list, or induce a customer already reported to clear his past-due balance and thereby remove his name from the list.

A few trade associations require their members to discontinue regular

---

[5] The New York State Liquor Authority publishes a monthly delinquent list for the liquor trade; under its regulations no supplier may make further credit sales to a dealer so listed. Some collection agencies also prepare lists of accounts turned over to them.

credit terms to any customer whose name appears on the delinquent list, thus aiding the collection efforts of their members by imposing a credit boycott on any delinquent customer. The question has been raised whether such action does not constitute illegal restraint of trade. Apparently not. The United States Supreme Court has sanctioned delinquent lists not accompanied by any boycott agreement [6] but has not passed upon the credit boycott issue. Two federal district court decisions,

---

UNPAID ACCOUNTS LIST No. 103

Fur Dressers and Fur Dyers Ass'n, Inc.

We report the following amounts Past Due
as of November 1, 1960,

PRIVATE AND CONFIDENTIAL USE OF MEMBERS ONLY

This list goes into effect on November 15, 1960

Destroy All Previous Lists

| NAME | ADDRESS | NO. OF MEMBERS |
|------|---------|----------------|
| Astor, Martin & Co. | 339 West 27 St. | 1 |
| Baum, Henry Fur Co. | 420 West 29 St. | 2 |
| Cohen & Green Inc. | 329 West 28 St. | 1 |
| Denker, Hertz & Co. | 455 West 29 St. | 1 |
| E. S. & R. Fur Co. | 347 West 27 St. | 2 |
| Grossner Furs | 355 West 29 St. | 1 |
| Holdin & Fried Co. | 397 West 28 St. | 1 |
| Meyer & Kushner Furs, Inc. | 458 West 27 St. | 2 |
| New Style Fur Co. | 486 West 28 St. | 2 |
| Pollack & Cohen, Inc. | 330 West 29 St | 1 |

ILLUSTRATION 5-8.   Excerpt from a Delinquent List

---

however, have upheld boycott practices.[7] They have been widely supported in state court decisions.

## SPECIAL CREDIT SERVICE ORGANIZATIONS

Besides Dun & Bradstreet and the special-line mercantile agencies which provide their subscribers or members with overall

---

[6] *Cement Manufacturers Protective Association v. U.S.*, 268 U.S. 588, 45 S.Ct. 586.
[7] *U.S. v. Fur Dressers & Fur Dyers Association*, 5 Fed. (2d) 869; *U.S. v. Southern California Wholesale Grocers Association*, 7 Fed. (2d) 944.

credit reporting service, there are a number of credit organizations which supply specialized types of credit information. The two most significant of these special credit services are litigation lists and individual credit inquiries.

## Litigation lists

In several metropolitan centers, certain publishers of court records and other legal materials have found a market for daily "litigation lists." These are listings of business men in the city who were served with summons, thereby instituting suit against them, on the preceding day. In New York City, the Credit Bureau of Greater New York, in addition to providing other credit services described in Chapter 27, publishes a *Daily Litigation Bulletin* with over 1,500 subscribers in all lines of business. A sample page is shown in Illustration 5-9.

The information published in litigation lists must be interpreted by credit managers in the light of the size and background of the defendants against whom suits have been entered. If they are substantial concerns with ample capital and a long record of sound performance, the litigation may represent a minor dispute of no consequence credit-wise. On the other hand, notice of suit against concerns of recent origin which have not yet proven their ability for profitable operation, or against small businesses with light capital, may be of vital credit significance. Business enterprises selling to large numbers of small grocery stores, dairy stores, stationery shops, or other small retail outlets (many of them barely clinging to solvency by the margin of an eyelash), must know immediately of any suits against their customers. Frequently a suit marks the beginning of a very quick end—one that generally leaves little salvage for the creditors. A credit manager learning that suit has been instituted against such an account, must inform his salesman to stop credit to the customer immediately and to use every effort to collect all outstanding balances. The credit manager who first learns of litigation initiated against a border-line customer and by forceful action collects the account, saves his company an otherwise inevitable loss, which less vigilant competitors may have to take.

Litigation list publishers are able to offer their subscribers a valuable supplementary service. They also supply reports on suits that have been brought against individual customers over a period of time. A lengthy litigation record may indicate that a financially stable customer is the type that must be treated with utmost severity in collection procedure, since apparently only the ultimate action of suit obtains payment from him.

# DAILY LITIGATION BULLETIN

A Division of The Credit Bureau of Greater New York, Inc.

841 Broadway, New York 3, N. Y.                                    Telephone: SPring 7-7300

A Daily Record of Commercial Suits in all industries in the Metropolitan Area

*Published Daily except Sat., Sun. and Holidays*

INFORMATION APPEARING IN THIS PUBLICATION IS STRICTLY CONFIDENTIAL, FOR SUBSCRIBERS
DIRECT USE ONLY, AND NOT TO BE COPIED OR REPUBLISHED IN ANY FORM FOR RESALE

*In accepting this publication, the subscriber agrees that the information contained herein has been
compiled from sources and by persons deemed reliable, the accuracy of which is in no way guaranteed.*

FOODS and LIQUORS          RESTAURANTS — HOTELS          BUTCHERS — BAKERS — GROCERS

SEPTEMBER 5TH, 1961

| DEFENDANT | SERVED AT | PLAINTIFF | AMOUNT | CD |
|---|---|---|---|---|
| AAA Testing Co. | 900 E 44 St NYC | Community Bank & Trust | 866.20 | NT |
| Abelescu, Steven | 2121 Bedford Ave, Bklyn | Nat'l Corresp.Schools | 215.90 | CT |
| Brigante, Philip | 575 W 86th St, NYC | Rogers Meat Market | 85.56 | GS |
| Bukkelman, Natalie | 444 W 99th St, NYC | Ace Beauty Parlor Sup. | 113.34 | GS |
| Burmeister, Alan | 110 5th Ave, NYC | J-K Clothes Shop | 67.50 | GS |
| Carmington, Peter | 909 Park Ave, NYC | Standard Drug Supply Co | 304.40 | MR |
| Conniston Wire Co. | 1001 1st St, Bklyn | Community Bank & Trust | 1455.80 | NT |
| Creighton, Joseph Z. | 491 Exeter St, NYC | Home Dept. Store | 168.20 | GS |
| Drayton, Peter | 2060 Fox St, Bx | Marcy Paint & Paper | 200.05 | NT |
| Easton Drivers School | 229 W 59th St, NYC | Rent-A-Car Corp. | 666.42 | CT |
| Ellsworth, Phineas | 99 E 106th St, NYC | Nat'l Bank & Trust Co | 316.05 | NT |
| Ensenada Market | 1 W 111th St, NYC | Fruit Exchange | 199.50 | GS |
| Exterior Painting Co | 1211 Broadway, NYC | National Pigment Co | 505.10 | CT |
| Faraway Van Lines | 12 Leight St, Bklyn | Nat'l Tire & Rubber Co | 229.40 | GS |
| Firstenberg, Donald | 8 E 8th St, NYC | Neet Cleaners & Dyers | 46.75 | WL |
| Froeder, Samuel | 2121 -21 St, Astoria | Ace Tiling Co | 416.02 | WL |
| Garabrand, Ignatz | 1205 3rd St, Bklyn | Big G Furniture Co | 322.80 | FL |
| Gerston, Michael | 909 Ave of Americas, NYC | Twin City Transptn Co | 165.02 | WL |
| Gurnee, Aloysius | 405 Home St, Bronx | Wendover Publishing Co | 88.75 | CT |
| Hamart, Gabriel | 741 Anderson Terrace, NYC | Manufacturers Bank | 1262.42 | NT |
| Hernstein, Yetta | 2921 Bathgate Ave, Bx | Day's Work Agency Inc | 41.90 | CT |
| Horder Fumigating Co | 1777 E 99th St, Bklyn | Refined Oils, Inc | 368.62 | GS |
| Humedinger, Ephraim | 498 W 77th St, NYC | Drug Service Co | 181.22 | GS |
| Internat'l Wire Coating Co | 22 Westbridge Ave, Bklyn | Plastics Unlimited | 1338.40 | CT |
| Islam, Frederick | 319 Broome St, NYC | Dianne Caterers Inc | 112.09 | CT |
| Jacobsen, Amanda | 555 E 116th St, NYC | Norma T.V. Service | 31.50 | WL |
| Jones, J. Price | 2 E 1st St, Bklyn | Supermart Grocers | 85.10 | GS |
| Justin, Lawrence | 9 Bedford Ave, Bklyn | Prime Savings & Loan | 315.05 | RE |
| Kalten's Dairy | 1605 -12th Ave, Bklyn | Hale Farm Products Co | 129.40 | GS |
| Kornblatt, Clarence | 401 W 82nd St, NYC | Uptown Pharmacy | 41.50 | GS |
| Kreimer Metallic Containers | 920 E 12th St, NYC | Pride Stamping Corp | 220.60 | WL |
| Lawrence Tailoring Co | 212 5th Ave, NYC | Pyramid Thread Co | 114.22 | GS |
| Lenting, Joseph | 1601 Avedon Ave, Bx | Ward's Serv Station | 40.95 | WL |

ILLUSTRATION 5-9.    Excerpt from a Daily Litigation Bulletin

## Individual inquiry agencies

There exists a considerable number of agencies that make intensive
individual investigations of persons and business organizations for their
clients. Their agents can dig out much more than the general information
to be found in ordinary mercantile agency reports. They interview landlords, business associates, bank officers, and any other individuals who
can throw light on the character and activities of the person or business
under inquiry. The reports of these agencies are necessarily more expensive than ordinary mercantile credit reports. But they are more
thorough and may be more informative.

These individual inquiry agencies are patronized primarily by insurance companies, banks, and employers checking upon key employees.
Their services, however, are used also to a considerable extent by credit

departments that must make decisions upon very large orders from customers about whom the mercantile agency reports leave a wide margin of doubt, particularly where the issue of a moral risk enters.

Among the more widely known individual inquiry agencies are Bishop's Service, Proudfoot's Commercial Agency, Hooper-Holmes Bureau, O'Hanlon Reports—all of New York—and also the Retail Credit Company of Atlanta, Georgia, with numerous branch offices.

## EVALUATION OF MERCANTILE AGENCY CREDIT SERVICES

In many lines a credit manager has a choice between Dun & Bradstreet and one or more special-line agencies that cover his field. Which should he choose? How best can he use the services of the agency of his selection?

### General mercantile agency v. special-line agency

Few of the special-line agencies are in competition with each other, since their specialized fields rarely overlap. All are in sharp competition with Dun & Bradstreet, which reports on all fields of business in the United States and Canada. The selling claims of the competitors indicate a balance of merits between Dun & Bradstreet and special-line agency services.

Dun & Bradstreet states that its system of reporters and correspondents enables it to ferret out information that would not be accessible to suppliers and other business references. Many special-line agencies have to rely on information from customers and suppliers; others have their staffs of reporters. But none of them has built up the blanketing coverage of Dun & Bradstreet.

The special-line agencies claim two advantages over Dun & Bradstreet. *First*, they argue that their report writers are specialists in the line of business and therefore capable of giving a more thorough analysis and interpretation. This claim does not seem substantiated any longer since Dun & Bradstreet has developed, as indicated in the preceding chapter, adequate specialization of its reporters by trades and business lines. *Second*, the special-line agencies claim that their trade and ledger information is fuller than that in the Dun & Bradstreet reports, since they receive fuller ledger interchange cooperation from their subscribers or members. There may have been merit to this argument in the past. In recent years Dun & Bradstreet has claimed as full coverage for its trade reports as any of the special-line agencies.

An unbiased judgment would be that Dun & Bradstreet and many of the special-line agencies are doing superb credit reporting. One or the other may produce a superior report on a particular case, however, so that many credit managers, whose budgets permit, subscribe to both Dun & Bradstreet service and that of the special agency for their line.

## Use of rating books

A mercantile agency rating book provides quick, compact, and usually easily understood credit information on a company's accounts. In many small businesses without trained credit managers, a rating book is used as the exclusive basis for credit judgments. Some concerns, where the person responsible for credit decisions is unable or unwilling to acquire the necessary additional information for sound credit judgment, go even a step further in this oversimplified procedure and sell only to customers given good ratings by the rating book.

Such exclusive dependence on a rating book should be avoided. If a company subscribes to a mercantile agency service, the agency reports ought to be used for all crucial decisions. The rating book should be a supplementary credit tool. All new customers ought to be checked in the rating book. If the risk rating is high and the pecuniary strength rating is appropriate for the order size, the order may be approved on this basis alone. Otherwise the book rating becomes a signal that a report should be drawn. A company's list of customers should be checked in each new edition of a rating book for unfavorable rating changes that may make new reports advisable.

## Use of agency reports

Agency reports are the credit manager's most valuable source of information. He would like to draw reports on all accounts. But few credit departments have such liberal cost budgets, which might easily be extravagant compared to the return they would bring. Commonly, a credit manager considers himself fortunate if he can draw an agency report for each new customer and on each doubtful account. Quite often, however, in lines of business with a rapid turnover of customers, the credit department budget allows the drawing of reports only on a portion of the new accounts.

If at all possible, an agency report should certainly be obtained on a new customer from whom a first order is received. This holds true even for lines of business where other information sources are currently available, for instance in the grocery wholesale line where considerable dependence is placed on salesmen's reports. If the credit department cannot afford otherwise, the credit manager may have to confine himself to getting reports on new accounts only when they are rated "fair" or "limited." Omitting the "high" and "good" ratings may seem justified as they entail less risk. Nevertheless, in many cases a report on such accounts might show weaknesses which are not evident in a condensed rating.

Even with restricted means a credit department has to keep close watch on two developments. First, borderline accounts have to be carefully observed and covered by continuous service reports so that the credit manager receives warning if and when they "go sour." Second, a rating change for a customer, or an unexplained change in his financial position, should prompt a credit manager to seek fuller information.

Agency reports are packed with information, but their value is largely wasted if they are read casually or indifferently. Every fact, every figure usually has definite credit significance, and should be given thought. An example of how an agency report should be analyzed is given in the Appendix to this chapter.

### Use of agency checking service

An individual-order recommendation given by a mercantile agency that provides credit checking service might appear at first glance an unequivocal guide to credit action. It is so taken by many small subscribers that do not have trained credit personnel. Experienced credit managers, however, while finding these recommendations useful as guides to credit judgment, exercise considerable discretion in acting upon them.

Credit checking agencies are known to lean to the side of conservatism in their judgments. An experienced credit manager takes this into account. He may realize that his company is in a position to take risks that others in the line, operating on narrower gross margins, cannot afford; or his own analysis may lead him to the conclusion that a customer's financial weakness, although warranting the agency judgment, is a temporary development which may produce delayed payment but not insolvency. Should his company continue to sell to the customer while some other suppliers withdraw because of the agency recommendation, his company will not only make immediate sales that would otherwise be lost but also will gain valuable good will position with that customer.

APPENDIX TO CHAPTER V

ANALYSIS OF AN AGENCY REPORT

Most agency reports are loaded with significant information. Every line, every word, every figure usually has a bearing on appraisal of the subject concern as a credit risk. A credit report should not be read casually. Each detail in it deserves study and consideration. As an illustration we shall analyze the Dun & Bradstreet report on the Kent Store presented on page 64 of this volume.

The heading indicates that the Kent Store is not incorporated. This is a favorable circumstance, from one viewpoint. Since limited liability is not involved, as would be the case if the business were incorporated, all of the personal wealth of the partners, Mr. and Mrs. Miles Gross, is liable for business debts. On the other hand, any personal financial difficulty is more likely to affect the business assets than would be the case if personal and business finances were segregated.

Miles Gross, one of the partners, is 41 years old, and married. He is in the prime of his life, from a business viewpoint. The fact that he is married raises the presumption of greater responsibility. His wife, Hannah, is his business partner.

Gross had an appropriate education and several years' experience in his line before he became an independent co-owner of a drug store. He graduated from a renowned college where he had studied pharmacy and was then employd for many years as a registered pharmacist. As of the time of the report he has had eight years' experience with his own store, enough to classify him as well experienced in the field. Mrs. Gross, apparently, has not the same vocational background in the drug line as her husband, but she has been working with him since the store's beginning, and her school teaching days have accustomed her to conscientious work.

The store was started with $17,000 in 1953; $10,000 came from savings, $3,500 from a Teachers' Credit Union loan, $3,000 from family loans. All these loans have been repaid. Net worth is now $22,901. In the last years, several thousand dollars have been plowed back into the business. Evidently, a small business is slowly being built up by a couple who know how to run it.

From "Operation" it is apparent that no credit sales are made. This is obvious also from the financial statement that lists no receivables among the assets of the business. The drug store is located in a rented building, in a residential section that has expanded in the past 10 years and evidently is still expanding. The partners are even considering opening another store; it is, however, not quite clear whether they are thinking of a second establishment in the same or in another part of the city. In any case, this is a favorable indication.

The financial statement given for June 30, 1961, presenting exact figures rather than estimates, would indicate that Gross has a bookkeeping system that enables him to submit an accurate balance sheet at the close of his accounting year. No accountant is mentioned. In this respect, however, the information is no better or worse than that submitted by most small drug stores.

The store's current position is not very liquid; 87 per cent of current assets consist of merchandise. Yet, this relatively large inventory has some justification since the store is preparing for the Fall which, according to the report, is its best selling season. The accounts payable of $3,724 are presumably for merchandise and not for the new fixtures and the soda fountain; otherwise notes would be outstanding. Fixtures and equipment apparently are fully paid.

The store also seems to be sufficiently insured against fire; merchandise as well as fixtures are covered. No fires as yet have been reported.

Sales volume, $89,232, is substantial. The monthly rent for the store is not high. Withdrawals of the partners are modest and part of the earnings are continuously reinvested in the business.

The Trade Report is entirely favorable. Nearly all payments are made on a discount basis. Most suppliers have been selling to the store for two to three years; no new suppliers are mentioned.

All in all, this report on Kent Store indicates that, for its line of business and size, it is an eminently satisfactory credit risk. Regular terms of sale, and the normal credit limits that a drug store supplier customarily grants to customers whom it considers good risks, would certainly be justified.

## REVIEW

1. Contrast a Dun & Bradstreet report and a National Credit Office report.
2. Contrast the ratings in the Dun & Bradstreet *Reference Book*, the *Apparel Trades Book*, and the Lyon *Red Book*.
3. What are the advantages and disadvantages of special agency credit reporting compared with Dun & Bradstreet credit reporting?
4. Discuss the use of credit rating books.
5. If a credit department operates on a restricted budget, for what classes of customers should it draw agency reports, and for what classes might it forego reports?
6. Analyze the credit standing of Electronics Midwest Inc., from the report on pages 68-71, in a manner similar to the analysis of Kent Store on page 64.
7. What is agency "credit checking"? Describe the procedure.
8. What credit services might be provided by a trade association?
9. What is a delinquent list? Who prepares it? How is it used?
10. What is a litigation list? What sort of seller would find it profitable to subscribe to it?
11. In what ways does the report of an individual inquiry agency differ from that of a regular mercantile agency?

## PROBLEM 1

1. Analyze the Dun & Bradstreet report on King & Todd, Inc. (pp. 60-63) in a manner comparable to the Chapter 5 Appendix analysis, but set all favorable items and interpretations and all unfavorable ones in separate columns.
2. You are credit manager of Dart Clothes, Inc., manufacturer of high-quality progressive-style men's suits. On June 20, 1961, a salesman sends an initial $12,000 order from King & Todd with the explanation that King & Todd's buyer likes Dart's progressive styling and plans to feature the line; annual orders, the salesman indicates, may run well over $100,000. On the basis of the 3/15/61 Dun & Bradstreet report on King & Todd, would you O.K. the order on the company's regular net 30 terms with the presumption that you would also have to O.K. much larger orders from King & Todd in the near future?

## PROBLEM 2

1. Analyze the Lyon report on Henry Smith's store (pp. 78-80) in a manner comparable to the Chapter 5 Appendix analysis, but set all favorable items and interpretations and all unfavorable ones in separate columns.

2. If you were credit manager for a linoleum floor covering manufacturer, would you on July 18, 1961 O.K. a first order of $1,200 from Smith on 2/30/60 terms, on the basis of the Lyon report?

# CHAPTER 6

# Ledger Information

One of the most useful items of knowledge about an account that a credit executive can have is the account's current credit position and paying habits. The information given in a mercantile agency report may be anywhere from a month to more than a year old, according to the date of its last revision. So too, the information to be derived from the latest available financial statement may be sadly out of date. The credit standing of an account may deteriorate seriously between reports or between financial statements, yet the credit manager who depended exclusively on them would be unaware of it. Information from other suppliers as to their current dealings with an account is immediate and up to the minute.

It may seem incredible, at first thought, that sellers in a competitive line should exchange information about their customers. Surely business men would consider their customer lists, their terms of sale, and data on credit extended and amounts outstanding, as among the most confidential of business information, never to be disclosed to competitors who might seek to steal good customers from them or who might seek to underbid them in credit terms. For a long time, indeed, this was the attitude of a majority of business houses, and the idea of exchanging ledger information for credit purposes was slow to get under way. There are still firms that have not been won over to credit cooperation and stand aloof from any share in the combined credit experience of their trade.

For the most part, however, the lesson has now been well learned that acquiring credit information is a cooperative matter. Only through help given to one another, and to the agencies that collect and disseminate credit information, can credit managers learn many of the facts they need for sound credit judgment. It is a case of their standing together, or standing their losses individually. Even where such interchange of credit information proves damaging to a debtor, it is legally a privileged communication and the credit managers do not have to worry about committing libel. It is furthermore tacitly understood that ledger information given in response to a credit inquiry shall not be used for competitive sales purposes. This standard of professional conduct is generally respected. In the few cases where it is breached, the offending firm soon finds itself blackballed by all other credit managers in the line and cut off from further credit interchange.

## USE OF OWN LEDGER DATA

A business concern's own customer ledger provides its credit manager with a source of information which he uses constantly in making his own credit decisions and in supplying other credit managers with data when he engages in ledger interchange. He may, after long experience, carry the record and current status of every one of his concern's customers printed indelibly in his memory. But this is exceptional, even among the most experienced credit managers. Where the number of accounts runs into several hundreds or into thousands, the credit manager must refer to the ledger book or file. He usually has a clerk look up three items of information for him:

1. A comparison of the new order with previous orders to ascertain whether the new order is of normal size;
2. A check on the record of past payments;
3. A notation of the indebtedness already outstanding, to ascertain whether the indebtedness resulting from the new order will keep the total within reasonable or pre-agreed limits.

When a credit manager receives a request from another credit manager, or from an agency, for ledger information on an account, he takes fuller information from the ledger than when he consults it for his own use. He notes when the account was opened, so that he can report "how long sold." "Highest recent credit" and "amount outstanding" are ascertained from the "balance" column. "Amount past due" may involve a calculation relating invoice entries to terms of sale so as to establish which debit items are past due, but the figure is usually noted in the ledger. "Manner of payment" is found by comparing the sequence of invoice debits with the sequence of payments that cleared them.

For bookkeeping purposes, particular payments by customers need not be related to the specific debit entries they clear. It suffices that the running balance of debits and credits be maintained accurately. For credit purposes, however, payments should be related to their debit items so that the dates of the two entries may show whether the customer paid promptly or, if he was delinquent, how late his payments were. Ledger books and machine ledger cards therefore sometimes carry two narrow columns, one on the debit side and one on the credit, for memorandum entries to identify corresponding debit and payment entries. This is usually done by giving debit entries and their clearing payments the same number or letter so that a glance at correspondingly numbered or lettered items reveals the time taken by the customer for his payments. This procedure is indicated in Illustration 3-1 on page 37 of this volume.

### NATURE OF LEDGER INTERCHANGE INFORMATION

The information that one supplier should give another, for credit purposes, about an account to which they both sell, has become standardized. It comprises six or seven items.[1] The six items that always appear are:

1. *How long sold*. This information is given in the form of "—yrs.," or "—mos.," or "since—." It enables the inquirer to judge how soundly based are any opinions that the respondent may express about the account. But there are further conclusions that may be drawn from this item. By showing a number of new suppliers, it may indicate that the customer is expanding operations, or that old suppliers have tightened their credit extensions to him and he is turning to new sources. In the majority of cases a large number of new suppliers to an established firm may be interpreted as a warning signal.

2. *Highest recent credit*. This is the maximum amount outstanding on the customer's account any time within the past 12 months. It should not be interpreted as the credit limit that the respondent allowed the customer. Perhaps the respondent would have been happy to sell more if the customer had been inclined to buy more. Or, perhaps, after having set a lower limit, the respondent allowed the customer to exceed it temporarily for some special reason. However, although "highest recent credit" is

---

[1] Note that the ledger information that mercantile agencies obtain from suppliers and present as part of their regular "trade reports" usually consists of only five items—Highest Recent Credit, Owing, Past Due, Terms of Sale, and Payments. See the Dun & Bradstreet reports on pp. 61, 62, and 64, the National Credit Office report on pp. 70 and 71, and the Lyon Furniture report on pp. 78 and 79.

no statement of a credit limit, it may help a credit manager to establish one for a new account.

3. *Amount owing.* By itself this figure is of little credit significance. But taken in connection with the figure given for "highest recent credit," it may tell a story. It is to be expected, for customers in seasonal lines of business, that the amount reported "owing" should coincide at the peak of the seasonal buying and for a time thereafter with "highest recent credit." Off-season the amount owing should be considerably lower than "highest recent credit." If several respondents should report that a customer's off-season "owing" was close to his "highest recent credit," it might indicate one of two things—a legitimate expansion of the business into new lines of merchandise, or improper buying either through poor judgment or with fraudulent intent. In any case the credit manager would be cautioned.

4. *Amount past due.* The significance of this item is obvious. Any statement of an amount past due indicates that, with respect to that supplier at least, the customer is failing to conform to the terms of sale. One or two such indications of delinquency do not condemn a customer; they may be due to disputes over particular shipments or to other acceptable reasons. But if several respondents report a customer as past due, the credit manager can draw but one conclusion—that the customer is in a weak financial position. It will not be apparent whether the customer is only temporarily in financial straits or if he is progressing down the road to final disaster. At least, the credit manager has received a warning signal.

5. *Terms of sale.* This information serves two purposes. It enables the credit manager to interpret correctly the significance of an amount reported past due in connection with the date of last sale. Furthermore, if the terms reported are not the customary ones for the line, this may reflect the respondent's judgment of the customer as a credit risk. C.O.D. or C.B.D. terms usually indicate that the respondent considers the customer too poor a risk to be entrusted with any credit terms. If T.A. terms are reported, the account is probably a good long-term risk but for the time being a slow payer.

6. *Method of payment.* The respondent is expected to say whether the customer discounts, pays promptly on the due date, or is slow in his payments. In the latter case, it is customary to report the average number of days' slowness. This information is considered by many credit managers to be the crux of the entire ledger interchange system. It provides a credit manager with the most accurate indication as to the treatment he may expect from a customer.

A seventh item frequently incorporated in ledger interchange, and reported immediately after "how long sold," is *Date of last sale.* This item is valuable for various reasons. If the last sale was made many months ago, the supplier's knowledge about the customer's paying habits cannot be considered up-to-date. The item also dovetails with "how long sold," in indicating a shift to new suppliers. It may help, too, to evaluate some of the other interchange items.

In addition to these six or seven regular items of ledger information, suppliers often give, under the heading of *Comments* or *Remarks*, significant and usually derogatory information. For example, they may report that they had to collect bills through attorneys or collection agencies, or that the customer takes unearned discounts, or that they discontinued selling to him after some bad experiences. Sometimes the additional remarks are favorable, tending to qualify some unfavorable element of information among the preceding items; for example, after reporting a customer as a slow payer, a supplier may add the comments "but satisfactory" or "improving."

## INDIVIDUAL LEDGER INTERCHANGE

With very few exceptions these days, business houses honor requests made to them for ledger information, provided the inquirers establish good faith by submitting corresponding ledger information upon the customers about whom they inquire. Custom has established the information to be exchanged as the six or seven items noted at the opening of this chapter—how long sold, date of last sale (sometimes), highest recent credit, amount outstanding, amount past due, terms of sale, and manner of payment—together with such additional comments as either party may care to make.

### Locating other parties for interchange

When a first order is received from a new customer, it is usual to ask him for three or four business references—other suppliers who will report on his credit standing with them. If a first order is obtained by a salesman, he normally requests such references and transmits them to the credit department, separately or as part of his "salesman's credit report" (Illustration 7-1, page 120). These names are from then on readily available for ledger interchange, but too much weight should not be attached to any information they supply. They may be presumed to be "handpicked" by the customer and always favorable to him. Reports from other suppliers are likely to be more objective. A credit manager may take their names from the report of the salesman who noted the brand names of goods on the retailer's shelves. Or he may receive some through ledger exchange, when other suppliers write to him and inquire about a customer. A credit manager adds the names of such suppliers to the list to whom he subsequently directs his own ledger inquiries.

There is another, usually successful, way of locating other suppliers for ledger interchange. In many lines of business, certain outstanding concerns sell to most, or to a large proportion, of the customers in their field. A small supplier may safely make a blind effort at ledger inter-change with such a major organization. This is quite a common pro-cedure, equally helpful to the inquirer who usually learns what he wants, and to the responding concern which in this way receives much un-solicited information on its customers. This method may also influence the payment habits of some customers. A financially embarrassed buyer often pays his large suppliers promptly and goes slow on others because he knows that the large suppliers are so frequently queried by others in the trade. Therefore the first indications large suppliers often get of credit weakness on the part of a customer are inquiries from smaller sup-pliers who find that payments to them have turned slow.

Still another means of locating other suppliers of a customer for ledger interchange is through the credit group to which a credit manager be-longs. When a customer's name is brought up at a group meeting, each of his suppliers present usually makes note of the others who report selling to him. Individual interchange may be subsequently conducted with these other sellers.

A final source of names for ledger interchange is the credit bureau of certain trade associations. Some associations require all members to register the names of their customers with the association's credit bureau. A file card is then made out for each customer with the names of his sup-pliers. When an association member telephones or writes to his associa-tion for the names of other suppliers of one of his customers, his request can be easily met.

### Procedures of individual interchange

The cardinal rule in exchanging ledger information is that it is a *quid pro quo* transaction—a real interchange between the two parties in-volved. A credit man who expects to receive ledger information should back his request by offering equivalent information. Where he is in-quiring on a new account, he has, of course, no exchange information to offer. But the mere appearance of a first order and a new supplier may be of interest to the concern that has been asked. If an inquirer, ignorant of custom in this matter, makes a request for ledger information without proffering his experience, two courses of action are open to the recipient of the request. He may send the inquirer a courteous note instructing him on the custom of *quid pro quo*, and declare himself ready to give the requested information as soon as the inquirer reciprocates. Or, more graciously, he may supply the information with an accompanying ex-planation of the custom and ask for the inquirer's experience as a return courtesy.

Various forms are used for inquiry about a new account. Some credit managers dictate a brief business letter stating that the customer under inquiry is a new account and that they would appreciate credit informa-tion about him. The reply may also be a dictated letter. Other credit

Credit Department

(THIS SIDE OF CARD IS FOR ADDRESS)

P. O.

TO ———— To ————

Sold from ————
Highest recent credit $ ————
On What Terms ————
Amount owing $ ————
Amount past due $ ————
How long ————
Credit Limit $ ————
Date Last Payment ————
Do you consider this a desirable account ————
Other Information ————
FILE NO. ————

**MANNER OF PAYMENT ANSWER—YES OR NO**

Discounts
Prompt and Satisfactory
Days slow
Slow but collectable
Slow and unsatisfactory
Settles by Dated Checks
Account secured
Notes paid at maturity
Makes unjust claims
Collected by attorney

PLEASE RETURN THIS CARD

BIG FOUR MERCHANDISE CO., INC.

536-38 BROADWAY

NEW YORK, N. Y.

Credit Department

RETAIN THIS CARD FOR YOUR FILE.

New York, N. Y., ————————19————

Please give us in confidence any information you may have concerning

Name ————

City ———— State ———— order for $ ————

From whom we have ————

OUR EXPERIENCE

Sold from ———— to ————
Highest Credit ————
Owes ———— Past Due ————
Terms ————
Date Last Payment ————
How Pays ————

Big Four Mdse. Co., Inc., ∴ 536-38 Broadway, ∴ New York, N. Y.

REPLY CARD

THIS SIDE OF CARD IS FOR ADDRESS

Please note that customer's name does not appear on return card. It bears his file number only, insuring complete privacy. We are always willing to reciprocate.

ILLUSTRATION 6-1.  Ledger Interchange Postcard

managers use a rubber stamp. It imprints a form covering the items of information customary in credit interchange on the very letter received, which is mailed back to the sender.

Where an old account is being checked, many credit offices use a form of printed return postcard sold by business stationers. One of the two attached postcards is addressed to the respondent, and states the name of the account, the code number or letter to identify it, and the inquirer's own experience with the account. The return card is addressed to the inquirer, and bears a form on which the respondent can enter his experience with the account. The two cards are folded and so sealed with a wafer that the name of the account and the inquirer's statement of his experience are concealed on the inside. The return card, when detached and filled in by the respondent, bears only the code identification of the account, so that it is meaningless to anyone but the inquirer. Illustration 6-1 shows one of these inquiry postcards.

Ledger interchange among a group of sellers located within a metropolitan area is frequently conducted by telephone. Credit managers, especially those belonging to the same local association, usually know each other personally. That solves the otherwise difficult question of identifying the inquiring party at the telephone, where practically anybody might pose under the name of a supplier and get information on an account. In cases where the credit managers are not personally acquainted and do not know each other's voices, a respondent can protect himself in only one way. He should hang up the receiver and then call back the company the inquirer says he represents. Telephoning speeds up the interchange of information by several days, and its cost is hardly greater than that of correspondence interchange.

Finally, a credit manager may call personally upon another to discuss a mutual account. This would be a time-consuming and most inefficient procedure if the conversation were limited to the ordinary items of ledger information. It is recommended only for a more searching inquiry—for example, if suspicion of fraud or some other disturbing phenomenon is involved and the inquirer wants to probe into matters that cannot well be committed to paper. For ordinary ledger interchange, mail and the telephone are more economical media.

### Advantages and disadvantages

The great merit of individual interchange of ledger information is its ⁓mediacy. A credit manager faced with an order from a doubtful account, and with only a few days for decision, may find his own files with their several-months-old reports and statements inadequate for judging the present credit status of the customer. Here direct ledger information from other suppliers will be extremely helpful. So also where a credit manager has to make a quick decision on a delinquent account, and his own files do not throw light on the character of the delinquency, which may be temporary or final, with differing courses of collection action indicated for the two possibilities.

Ledger information derived from direct interchange is likely to be fragmentary in three ways. (1) The customer file card may not contain the names of all the customer's suppliers or of even the more important ones. (2) The few suppliers that the credit manager is able to contact may not reflect the customer's current over-all credit relations. (3) The credit manager cannot use individual ledger interchange for all his accounts, as it is time-consuming and, if carried too far, relatively expensive.

## GROUP INTERCHANGE

An unknown number of "credit groups," possibly as many as several hundred, have been organized to enable the credit managers of various lines of business to meet and exchange ledger information within the group. Many of these are sponsored by the 146 local credit management associations which are affiliated with the National Association of Credit Management. The New York Credit and Financial Management Association, for example, has sponsored 32 of the hundred or more such groups in the metropolitan New York area. Others are sponsored by trade associations. Still others have developed without outside sponsorship by mutual action of the credit managers in an area. Some large industries have their own nation-wide groups.[2]

The distinctive feature of a credit group is that all its members sell to the same business class of customers. All the members of a group need not be in identical lines of manufacturing or wholesaling. But they must be in related lines so that their customer lists overlap. Thus a men's wear credit group could include manufacturers of shirts, belts, suspenders, neckties, socks, and underwear, as well as jobbers who handle some of these items.

### Procedure

Group interchange is conducted through written reports and orally. A written report system involves maintenance of an office, or desk space

---

[2] An example is the oil industry with its American Petroleum Credit Association of over thirty years' standing.

in some member's office. Upon a member's request for a group "clearance" on a customer, the group secretary mails out inquiries to the members, compiles their replies, and sends the resulting report to all members who responded. Such clearances take at least several days to complete. Group credit service by correspondence may go beyond ledger interchange. Some groups mail "moral suasion letters" to members' delinquent customers. Others procure financial statements from their members' customers. Others supply members with current information, usually derogatory, on customers in daily or weekly "flashes."

Oral ledger interchange is a common group activity. Weekly or biweekly meetings of the group are arranged, usually at luncheons or dinners. Prior to each meeting, members mail in to the group secretary the names of customers, usually not more than two or three for any member, that they wish discussed at the meeting. A mimeographed list of these names is mailed to all members so as to reach them at least 24 hours before the meeting. Each member who has any of these names on his customers list jots down his ledger information on such accounts and takes it with him to the meeting.

After the luncheon or dinner, the meeting proceeds to the business of interchange. The secretary reads the first name on his list, and the members who have ledger information on the account show their hands. When called on, they report, usually following the formula "how long sold, highest credit, amount outstanding, amount past due, terms, manner of payment, comment." Since all present are familiar with the formula, the speaker frequently does not state his headings but simply gives the facts and figures in rapid sequence. All other members who sell the same account jot down the information for their office files. Sometimes this machine-gun presentation of ledger data is interrupted by the group entering upon a brief discussion of some case that displays interesting or contradictory aspects. A well-directed meeting may cover two to five reports on each of 20 to 25 accounts in the course of an hour.

### Advantages and disadvantages

Group interchange has several important advantages over individual interchange. It eliminates duplication of effort. A single report on a customer by a member at the group meeting conveys its message to all the other interested members who might otherwise have to inquire and be answered individually. Furthermore, group interchange usually gives each credit manager who participates more information from more widely distributed sources than he would be likely to receive through individual interchange.

There is an important disadvantage to group interchange. Its information may be as fragmentary as that obtained by individual ledger interchange, since it is likely to be based on only a fraction of a customer's suppliers, all in the one selling line. The resulting picture of a customer's current credit status may be fairly accurate—or badly distorted.

## AGENCY INTERCHANGE

As we noted earlier, Dun & Bradstreet and some of the special-line agencies include a "trade report," which is a compilation of ledger information, in each of their credit reports. In addition some agencies, such as Lyon Furniture Mercantile Agency, issue special periodic summaries of ledger data on weak accounts. Some trade association credit departments that do not issue reports or rating books make periodic "clearances" or compilations of ledger data on all customers of their members.

The names of suppliers who will provide ledger information are obtained by these organizations in several ways. Agencies preparing reports or ratings ask listed companies, at the time of submitting annual financial statements, to name their suppliers. In response, the companies presumably "hand-pick" the names and omit those suppliers with whom they are not on friendly paying terms. Agencies nevertheless generally get a rather complete picture by inquiring not only from suppliers named by the listed companies but also from suppliers who request reports on these companies. Trade association credit departments, which generally maintain much closer relations with their members than commercial credit agencies do with their subscribers, request these members to keep them constantly supplied with up-to-date lists of their customers. This procedure gives them full interchange lists as far as suppliers in the particular trade are concerned but leaves them without leads to suppliers outside the trade.

Every agency that issues credit reports or ratings on buyers maintains a folder for each buyer which includes a list of his suppliers. When the time comes to make a "clearance"—to collect and compile ledger information on a buyer—blanks similar to those used in direct interchange are sent to all his suppliers. When these blanks are returned, the ledger information on them is tabulated, and becomes the "trade report" included in the general report on the customer (see Illustrations 4-3, 4-4, 5-1) or the "clearance" report distributed to members of a trade association.

### Advantages and disadvantages

Whereas direct and group interchange is likely to give only a few ledger statements, the "trade reports" in agency credit reports may contain up to a score. Dun & Bradstreet "trade reports" generally cover a representative cross section of a customer's suppliers, even though these may belong to widely different lines of business. The special-line agencies and the trade association credit departments may sometimes get fuller coverage of suppliers in their special lines, but they lack comprehensive coverage on suppliers outside their lines. Thus, while the coverage of agency and association "trade reports" is wider and more representative than that of direct interchange, it too is usually far from complete.

Another advantage of the agency and association "trade report" over direct interchange is the reduction in duplication of effort. With interchange centralized in the agency, each supplier is called upon to give his experience on an account only once. The tabulated returns are then available to any and all who receive reports.

But agency "trade reports" lack one great advantage of individual and group interchange—the immediacy of the information derived from such interchange. An agency ordinarily makes a "clearance" of ledger information only when it plans to issue a new report on a customer. This may be once or twice a year; rarely is it more frequent. Thus "trade report" information in an agency report may well be somewhat out of date by the time a credit manager turns to it. Special-line agencies, like the Lyon Furniture Mercantile Agency, may partly compensate for this by making special clearances on doubtful accounts, and embodying these in weekly supplements. Such a procedure is helpful but may not always answer the needs of the individual case when, for example, a credit manager might want immediate ledger information on a particular account. Trade association "clearances" made upon members' requests are not subject to this shortcoming.

## THE NATIONAL CREDIT INTERCHANGE SYSTEM

A national system of ledger information interchange attempting to cover all lines of sellers in the continental United States is sponsored and supervised by the National Association of Credit Management.

This organization and its functions were described in the Appendix to Chapter I of this volume. Here we are concerned with one of its leading functions, the sponsoring of nationwide ledger interchange. Of the 146 local credit associations affiliated with the NACM, 58 own and operate credit interchange bureaus. The NACM provides a coordinating unit, the Central Credit Interchange Bureau located in St. Louis, and a supervising body, the Credit Interchange Board of Governors.

### Operation of the credit interchange system

When a concern takes out membership in a local Credit Interchange

Bureau belonging to the National Credit Interchange System, it is given a code number and is required to submit a list of customers which is supplemented as the member acquires new customers. Later, when the member draws a report on a customer, it is expected to add the names of all creditors of the account known to it. In this way, the Interchange Bureau is able to note the names of many—if not all—suppliers on each customer file card.

If other members have previously reported a customer thus named by a new member, or by an old member completing his customer list to the bureau, the bureau adds the code number of the member now reporting to those already noted on that customer's file card. If the customer has not previously been named, a new file card is made out for him, and the code number of the reporting member is entered.[3]

A "zone of operation" is assigned to every local bureau. It embraces the normal trade territory of its members. Each bureau is reponsible for the preparation of final interchange reports on customers located within its zone. It also has to report to other bureaus the names of all customers which its own members have in these other bureaus' zones and receives, conversely, the same kind of information from other bureaus whose members have customers in its zone. In the latter case, the customer's card carries notation of the other interested bureaus. Thus the customer file of every bureau consists of two groups of names: (1) customers located within its zone whose cards contain the names of suppliers within the zone and the list of other interested bureaus, and (2) customers located in other zones but sold to by suppliers in the bureau's zone whose cards contain the names of the local suppliers and the particular bureau in whose zone the customer is located.

When a member asks for an interchange report he sends an inquiry form to his interchange bureau. If a "clearance" and report has already been made on the customer for some other supplier within the preceding 120 days, the inquirer merely receives a copy of this report. If no report has been compiled within this period or if the member desires a current clearance in spite of such a report being on file, he will receive the latest available report as a temporary measure and the machinery of "clearance" is set in motion.

The first step in making a clearance is to send a "request for information ticket" to every member of the local bureau who is listed on the customer's file card and also to outside references listed by the inquirer

---

[3] Some bureaus do not work on this "customer list, new account" basis but operate instead with "inquiry sheets." Under this method a member does not have to file the names of all his customers. The bureau mails a list of inquiries about customers within the bureau's zone to all members and gets their experience. However, under this system the inquiring member also has to list the names of his customers who are located *outside* the zone.

on the inquiry form. As soon as these "tickets" have been returned, the bureau prepares a preliminary report, covering suppliers within its own zone of operations plus the outside references given by the inquirer. This preliminary report is rushed to the inquirer.

Meanwhile the second step in the "clearance" procedure has already been started. If the customer is located within the bureau's own zone of operation, but his card shows that other bureaus are interested, these other bureaus are notified of the clearance. They, in turn, make clearances for their zones and send the results of their inquiries to the first bureau, which tabulates the results in a final report. This report is now available not only for the original inquiring supplier but also for any other members of the bureau who desire it, and for any members of other bureaus who request it.

If a customer on whom a clearance is requested is located in the zone of operation of some other bureau, the first bureau immediately notifies the other bureau, which is responsible for the final report. The first bureau makes its own local clearance on the customer, and sends it to the other bureau, which embodies it in the general clearance. The report that the inquiring supplier receives is thus prepared by the bureau in whose zone of operation the customer is located.

Illustration 6-2 presents an example of an interchange report prepared by this procedure.

### Contents and interpretation of an NACM credit interchange report

An NACM credit interchange report, as shown in Illustration 6-2, contains a tabulation of all seven items of ledger information that are the basis of credit interchange—how long sold, date of last sale, highest recent credit, amount now owing, amount past due, terms of sale, and payment record—plus a "comments" column. Because of the comprehensiveness of these reports, often covering all the suppliers of a customer and generally all of the more important ones, certain conclusions can be drawn as to a customer's credit status which would be impossible with other methods of ledger interchange.

Much of the value of an interchange report may be wasted if a credit manager merely glances hastily at the statements of amounts past due and of manner of payment. Each column of an NACM report carries a message which may be of significance in arriving at sound credit judgment. Interrelations between the columns, too, have to be carefully observed.

The seven standardized items of ledger interchange have already been interpreted on pages 95-97 of this volume and the reader is referred to that presentation. But some additional information can be derived from an NACM interchange report. The first column in these reports is headed

FORM 6

# NATIONAL ASSOCIATION of CREDIT MANAGEMENT
## Credit Interchange Report

OFFICES IN PRINCIPAL CITIES

---------------- GROCERY CO                ------------, IOWA          AUGUST 18,1960
                                           -------- COUNTY

The accuracy of this Report is not guaranteed. Its contents are gathered in good faith from members and sent to you by this Bureau without liability for negligence in procuring, collecting, communicating or failing to communicate the information so gathered.

| BUSINESS CLASSIFICATION | HOW LONG SOLD | DATE OF LAST SALE | HIGHEST RECENT CREDIT | NOW OWING INCLUDING NOTES | PAST DUE | TERMS OF SALE | DISCOUNTS | PAYS WHEN DUE | DAYS SLOW | COMMENTS |
|---|---|---|---|---|---|---|---|---|---|---|
| DES MOINES 805-409 | | | | | | | | | | |
| Food P | 6-59 | 7-60 | 135 | 35 | | 2-10-30 | x | x | | |
| Gen M | yrs | 7-60 | 150 | | | 2-10-30 | x | | | |
| Food P | yrs | 7-60 | 1347 | 490 | | 2-10-30 | x | | | |
| LOUISVILLE 808-369 | | | | | | | | | | |
| Food P | 6-59 | 7-60 | 24 | | | 2-10-30 | | x | | |
| Mfg | 1959 | 6-60 | 451 | 107 | 57 | 2-10-30 | | x | 30 | Improving |
| MINNESOTA 808-560 | | | | | | | | | | |
| Food P | 1958 | 7-60 | 162 | | | 2-10-30 | x | | | |
| Food P | 1959 | 7-60 | 2270 | 2270 | | 2-10-30 | x | x | 15 | Improving |
| Food P | yrs | 6-60 | 4000 | | | 2-10 | x | | | |
| BOSTON 808-670 | | | | | | | | | | |
| Food P | 1958 | 7-60 | 1260 | | | 2-10-30 | x | x | | |
| Food P | 6-59 | 7-60 | 813 | 517 | | 2-10-30 | | x | 10 | Getting slower |
| CLEVELAND 808-404 | | | | | | | | | | |
| Food P | 7-59 | 7-60 | 327 | | | 2-10-30 | x | | | Takes U/D. |
| OMAHA & NEBRASKA 808-249 | | | | | | | | | | |
| Food P | 2yrs | 7-60 | 650 | 237 | | 1-10-30 | x | x | 10 | No change. |
| Food P | 7-59 | 7-60 | 227 | | | Draft | x | | | |
| CHICAGO 808-301 | | | | | | | | | | |
| Food P | yrs | 7-60 | 945 | 537 | 50 | 2-10-30 | | x | | |
| Food P | yrs | 7-60 | 1705 | 800 | | 2-15-30 | x | x | | |
| | | | | 4993 | 107 | | | | | |
| Bu 36 MJ | | | | | | | | | | |

ILLUSTRATION 6-2.   An NACM Credit Interchange Report

"Business Classification." It indicates the responding suppliers' lines of business and the reporting local credit bureaus. It also gives the date when the reports of these bureaus were tabulated—the first half of the code number under each bureau city stands for month and day. The listing of a customer's suppliers by their lines of business is extremely valuable to a credit manager since it tells him how many concerns besides his own are supplying the customer with the same kind of merchandise. The "highest recent credit" reported by other business enterprises in his line accordingly gives him a rough idea of the proportion of the customer's requirements in this line supplied by his concern. This may be useful information when the credit manager is deciding on a credit limit for the account. Another use of this column is to check whether a customer is buying outside his regular trade channels, geographically and otherwise. If his purchases are not consistent with his line of business, it may be a sign of legitimate or ill-considered expansion, or of speculative buying, or possibly of fraud. Indication that a customer is buying outside his normal buying radius or from too many suppliers in one field might be a warning signal that he can no longer obtain credit from his nearby or customary suppliers and is trying to tap additional sources that may not be aware of his weakness. This interpretation is particularly justified when local suppliers report that he is very slow or that they are selling him on C.O.D. terms, while the new "outside" suppliers report that they have been selling him only a short while.

In Illustration 6-2, the "Business Classification" column gives the following information: ——— Grocery Co. buys food products, confectionery, and general merchandise from suppliers located in seven reporting zones. The report from sellers in the Des Moines area was filled out on August 5, the others on August 8. The indication that ——— Grocery Co. is buying as far away as Boston might arouse suspicion if these Boston houses were new suppliers and if the customer had a bad paying record with suppliers in nearer zones.

Two other columns of the NACM interchange report—"Now Owing" and "Past Due"—have some particular connotations in addition to those analyzed on page 96. The figures of each of these columns are totalled at the bottom of the page. These totals open some interesting perspectives. If the date of an interchange report is close to the end of a customer's financial year, the total "Now Owing" figure should bear some relation to the "Payables" figure in the customer's financial statement. Since all of a customer's suppliers may not be covered by the interchange report, the "Now Owing" total might well be less than the customer's balance sheet "Payables." A "Now Owing" total that exceeded the balance sheet "Payables" figure, however, would raise questions. There may be a negligent or even a fraudulent understatement of "Payables" in the customer's financial statement, and the situation should be investigated. Quite a few financial statement frauds have been exposed in this way.

The "Past Due" total is another crucial item. If this total amounts to a sizable proportion of the customer's outstanding trade debt, he may be marked as a poor risk or, at best, as a slow-paying account. A few delinquencies in number and amounts may not be so important. They may be due to disputes over shipments or even be a matter of policy where the buyer pays local sellers or large suppliers promptly and holds up payments to more distant or smaller ones. But a high proportion of past due obligations should put a credit manager on guard. Although it may reflect an early stage of recovery from a bad situation, it more likely indicates current difficulty or progressive deterioration.

### Trend analysis of NACM reports

If a customer continues for some time in a doubtful category, a credit manager may draw a continuous series of interchange reports on him. From time to time new suppliers will appear in successive reports and old ones may disappear, as the customer changes his sources of supply for one reason or another. But for most businesses a series of these interchange reports will show considerable consistency in responding suppliers. These may constitute only a fraction of the customer's total resources, but they usually represent a large enough sample to provide a basis for definite conclusions about trends in his manner of payment.

For effective trend analysis of interchange information, the data in successive reports should be summarized in some tabular form. Total amounts reported as owing and past due, and the numbers of suppliers reporting different manners of payment, should be entered. Changes in the ratio of amount past due to amount owing, and shifts in the numbers of suppliers reporting prompt or slow payment, provide a rough sketch of the trend in the account's credit status.

### Advantages and disadvantages

NACM interchange reports have several advantages over other systems of ledger interchange information. The most important are their greater coverage of suppliers and, closely connected with this, the cumulative impression they are able to give of a buyer's credit status. These reports do not pretend to complete coverage of suppliers, since the customer cards at the various interchange bureaus do not always contain exhaustive lists of sellers. Also, the local bureaus, though constantly expanding, are still short of 100 per cent supplier membership. Moreover, some suppliers queried in a clearance may not reply. But, even considering these limitations, this service does provide the widest coverage of suppliers at present available from any information source, including trade reports from mercantile agencies. NACM reports also have another advantage over agency reports—the indication they give of suppliers' lines of business, date of last sale, and location, with all the implications such information may have.

NACM reports also compare favorably with other forms of interchange as to *immediacy* of the information received. Whereas the interchange items in agency reports—if they are not currently supplemented

—may be as much as six months to a year old, the maximum age of NACM interchange information is four months. Furthermore, an inquirer may obtain an immediate clearance if he asks for one or if no interchange report is on hand which has been made within the four-month period. In this case, he may get his information with even less delay than if he had made his own direct ledger interchange or waited for an oral interchange at the next meeting of his group.

NACM interchange bureaus also offer an "automatic revision report" service that continues for as long as the member desires. Concerns subscribing to it receive a new interchange report on an account every four or six months.

Costs of NACM interchange reports vary with the number of reports arranged for by members in their one-year contracts. Rates per individual report range from $1.00 to $1.75.

## USE OF LEDGER INTERCHANGE

When an order is received from a new customer, most credit managers whose companies subscribe to mercantile agencies draw a report. If the "trade information" was recently compiled, no other ledger information may be sought. Getting such information from other sources is mandatory if the agency trade report is out of date or if no agency report is obtained. An NACM report may be drawn if the supplier is a member of the local credit association. Or reliance may be placed on group interchange or on personal exchange of ledger information with other credit managers.

A slow-paying account, or one which pays promptly at the moment but is in a weak financial position and might collapse abruptly, should be observed constantly through the exchange of ledger information. Any turn for the worse will thereby be disclosed at an early stage, while other credit information, such as ratings or reports, may lag far behind the course of events. In such cases ledger information from special-line agencies and associations as well as from local credit groups is promptly available and therefore particularly helpful. Any divergence from normal in the buying or paying activity of a customer—an unexplained increase in his buying, a shift from discounting to net-term payment, a change from prompt to slow payment—should also suggest an interchange inquiry to provide a basis for sound interpretation of the indicated developments—favorable or unfavorable.

It is sometimes advisable to look for ledger information as a guide to collection procedure. A credit manager may be faced with the issue whether he can afford to be mild in collection pressure on a delinquent customer, or whether he should immediately use stringent measures to salvage what he can before impending bankruptcy materializes. The probability or unlikelihood of early insolvency is often reflected in ledger interchange information, which thus provides a compass for collection action. Even when a customer with an apparently sound financial position discounts regularly or always pays promptly, it is advisable to check upon his payments at intervals—perhaps once a year, or after some longer period—for assurance that his payment record is good with all his suppliers. An unfavorable turn of general business conditions or a local development that might injure customers in that area should also be the occasion for verifying the payment records of the customers affected.

## SUPPLEMENTARY READINGS

Nuffort, T. H., "Don't Tinker with Ledger Experience," *Credit and Financial Management,* March 1959, p. 12.

## REVIEW

1. Why do competing business concerns allow their credit managers to exchange credit information about their customers?
2. What items of ledger information does a credit manager expect to receive and to give in interchange?
3. If a credit manager wishes to make direct credit inquiries about a customer, how does he locate other suppliers in order to get this information?
4. If a credit manager receives an inquiry about an account but the inquirer does not state his experience with the customer, what should the credit manager do?
5. Explain how the return-postcard arrangement may be used in ledger interchange.
6. What are the advantages and the limitations of telephone ledger interchange?
7. What are the advantages and disadvantages of individual ledger interchange, agency interchange, group interchange, and NACM interchange?
8. What is an NACM interchange "clearance"? Explain the procedure.
9. Explain the implications of the information derived from each of the following items of NACM ledger interchange: (1) Business Classification, (2) How Long Sold, (3) Date of Last Sale, (4) Highest Recent Credit, (5) Now Owing, (6) Past Due, (7) Terms of Sale, (8) Paying Record, and (9) Comments.

## PROBLEM 1

You are credit manager for Cross Pharmaceuticals, a large New York drug wholesaler. Mr. Williams, treasurer of the company, sends you a memo stating that in checking over departmental expense accounts he notes a monthly item of $5 for a Drug Trade Group luncheon in the credit department account. He says he knows you meet other drug house credit managers at these luncheons and probably talk over customer circumstances, but questions whether there is any value in this to Cross Pharmaceuticals since the company subscribes to the Dun & Bradstreet service and is a member of the New York Credit and Financial Management Association, and can obtain all needed customer information through these sources. Write a reply memorandum to Mr. Williams justifying your attending the Drug Trade Group luncheons.

## PROBLEM 2

Interpret the Credit Interchange Bureau report on page 108.

# CHAPTER 7

# Other Sources

Besides mercantile agencies and ledger interchange, a credit manager has a number of other sources of credit information which he may exploit. Chief among these are his own observation of his customers, the customers themselves, and his company's salesmen. Also important in particular instances are banks, accountants, attorneys, and some other more incidental sources.

## THE CUSTOMER

Some credit managers never see, never make personal contact with, their concern's customers. To them a customer is an account number in the ledger file, a signature at the bottom of letters, an impersonal synthetic entity constructed out of words and figures in agency reports, interchange reports, and ledger cards. These men are neglecting one of their most valuable sources of credit information—their own personal impression of the customer's character and ability from man-to-man contact. Most of their credit decisions may still be sound despite this lack of first-hand acquaintance. But for some proportion of their decisions, their judgment will be at fault because this fragment in the mosaic of their credit information is missing. Credit managers thus functioning in ivory towers cannot do a good job. This is fully recognized in the profession. A growing emphasis is being placed on personal contact between credit manager and customer.

## The customer at the credit manager's office [1]

In certain lines of business—the clothing trades, for example—it is common or even customary for the customer to visit the seller's place of business, make his selection of merchandise, and place his order. It is regular practice in these lines for the salesman to invite the customer, as soon as the details of the order have been settled, to drop in and say "Hello" to the credit manager or whoever is responsible for the credit work of the firm. If the time is around noon, the salesman may propose that the customer be his guest at lunch—and that the credit manager join them. In this way a personal impression can be formed and sometimes valuable information gained which would not be obtainable in correspondence or from reports and financial statements.

In lines where buying is not usually done by customers on the sellers' premises, a credit manager should always take advantage of any visit by a customer to the sales department or some other department of his concern. It should be standard practice in all offices that, whatever the basic reason of a customer's visit, he should be persuaded to call upon the credit department, and should be there accorded a courteous and friendly reception. These are golden opportunities for gaining invaluable credit information, as well as for further cementing trade good will.

Still another possibility of personal conversation between credit manager and customer arises when a local account becomes delinquent in payments. The suggestion should be embodied in one of the collection letters sent to such a customer that he drop in and talk over his difficulties with the credit manager. A surprisingly high proportion of delinquent accounts may take advantage of this offer, particularly if the credit manager has shown himself previously to be a sympathetic and experienced counsellor. The major purpose of such a conversation is, of course, to analyze the customer's present troubles and work out some method of payment satisfactory to both parties. However, the wise credit manager looks beyond the immediate situation. He deals with it, but he guides the discussion so that he receives information about a customer's position and future plans.

Credit interviewing, like any other form of interviewing, is a technique

---

[1] In bank credit and retail credit, an interview with the client or customer at the bank or store is usually a prerequisite to the credit extension. The credit interview has accordingly become, for these fields, a much more standardized procedure than it is for mercantile credit. See Chapters 23 and 27 of this volume.

which requires certain innate qualifications. But natural abilities can be improved by self-analysis, study, and training. Good credit interviewers are born, but they are also made. Some have from the outset the necessary qualifications, such as a friendly, understanding attitude, an agreeable voice, and the absence of disturbing mannerisms. Every credit manager, no matter how self-confident he may be that he possesses these attributes, should test himself as an interviewer. An efficient test would be to act an interview scene and have it recorded or a movie taken of it. The credit manager would then know exactly how the customer sees him and reacts. He could then also make the necessary corrections in his "interview manners."

Because not every credit manager has interviewing aptitude, a few large business concerns employ specialized credit interviewers. Such a specialist has the expert's advantages over the general practitioner, but he usually lacks detailed knowledge and the "feel" about a customer which a regular credit manager has acquired.

Credit interviews cannot be standardized or "patterned." Each must be tailored to the particular customer and his special circumstances. But advance planning of each interview is imperative. The specific information sought, the manner of dealing with the customer, the questions to be asked, even the phrasing of particularly delicate questions, should be predetermined.

There is some difference of opinion about how to start and conduct a credit interview in the credit manager's office. Some credit managers prefer the indirect approach. They argue that a customer resents direct questions and that if they are forced on him he will give evasive answers. He will feel less restraint and talk more freely about himself, his business, and his plans if the interview is started on some side issue. This may be true to some extent. In recent years, however, a different line of thought has developed. Credit managers are more than ever expected to advise their customers, and their counsel is greatly appreciated. A customer discussing his finances with a supplier's credit manager feels that, just as in a doctor's or a lawyer's office, he must give all necessary pertinent information and face direct questions in order to receive correct diagnosis of his case and sound advice. This, of course, is largely a matter of personalities and mutual trust. But with the credit profession growing in stature, more emphasis is placed today on this kind of open-minded confidential relationship than ever before. A really good credit manager should be able to get all the information he wants by directly asking for it.[2]

---

[2] New York Credit and Financial Management Association, *How Credit Interviews Are Conducted* (New York, 1955), contains a tabulation of questions (derived from a survey in which 3750 members participated) which credit executives might ask their companies' customers, their banks, or their accountants.

A customer interview in a credit manager's office should usually be a two-way communication. The customer gives information. The credit manager may give advice. An experienced credit manager is often in a position to provide helpful counsel to his company's customers. How to proffer such counsel so that it will be appreciated and not resented— that is a problem not peculiar to the credit manager-customer relationship. The credit profession is aware of the growing importance of the credit manager's client advisory role, and increasing attention is being paid to it.[3]

### The credit manager at the customer's place of business

Ordinarily a credit manager does not have the time for intensive investigation of each account at first hand. But cases may arise where such procedure is advisable. For example, a mill or factory may buy all or nearly all of its raw material from a single supplier. Such a supplier's credit manager would be warranted in visiting the account and making a thorough first-hand inquiry. He might even find it helpful to take one of the company's engineers along to judge the technical aspects of the customer's operations and make suggestions to improve them.

On such visits the credit manager should go directly to the subject matter. The customer, fully aware that the supplier has a big stake in his orders, should recognize the supplier's right to complete knowledge about his business.

Many successful credit executives make it a regular practice to take an annual "swing around the circle"—a two- or three-week field trip during which they visit as many of their accounts as possible. A searching advance study is made of these accounts, but an informal approach is usually adopted. The talk may start with a word of praise on the customer's plant or store, and then go on to his plans and prospects. If circumstances warrant it, the credit manager may also raise the question of the slowness of the account, suggest a specific payment plan and arrange it with the customer on the spot. But the major profit to the credit manager from such a visit is a first-hand impression of the customer and the picture of his premises and business methods. A supplementary benefit is the promotion of customer good will.

In recent years some companies have experimented with a "traveling credit man"—usually a junior credit assistant who accompanies the salesman on his route and thereby establishes a personal liaison between the credit department and the customer.

---

[3] This topic was given major consideration at the Credit Research Foundation's 1959 "Credit Management Workshop" at Carmel (Cal.), where all participants reported that many of their customers had discussed frankly and helpfully such problems as products, prices, and costs.

### SALESMEN

A company's salesmen have daily first-hand acquaintance with its customers. A natural query is, why should not these salesmen be a primary source of information for the concern's credit department? Why go to the expense of agency reports when a salesman can ask a customer all the pertinent questions that could be put by an agency reporter?

#### Limitations on salesmen as sources of credit information

Salesmen are generally opposed to gathering credit information for the credit departments of their companies. Often they are supported in this attitude by their sales managers.

Salesmen paid upon a commission basis feel that time spent collecting credit information would be more profitably used in visiting more customers, making more sales, and earning larger commissions. Moreover, they are often convinced that asking the customer questions which will reveal his credit status may spoil the hypnotizing build-up of their sales talk and endanger the sale. Even after the customer has put his name on the dotted line, the delicate balance of his assent could easily be shattered by a request for a financial statement, or a query as to how his payments are being made; in a fit of pique he might revoke the order on the spot.

Salesmen seem also generally not well fitted by experience, temperament, and interest to be reliable credit reporters. Good credit judgment requires a comprehensive understanding of business practices and finance that the ordinary salesman does not have opportunity to acquire. Most good salesmen, furthermore, are congenital optimists, who view the world, and especially their customers, through rose-colored glasses. This optimism and exuberant appreciation is one of the factors that enables them to override their customers' hesitations and persuade reluctant orders, but it tends to blind them to defects in the customers which may render the latter poor credit risks. Besides, could any salesman be expected to discourage the shipping of a hard-won order because the customer was a poor credit risk? He would rather exaggerate every favorable consideration and minimize every factor to the customer's discredit.

#### Possibilities of obtaining credit information through salesmen

These limitations, nevertheless, do not disqualify salesmen completely as sources of credit information. But only certain types of credit information should be sought from them—information which cannot be obtained from other sources. Furthermore, the salesmen should be carefully conditioned, trained, and controlled in the exercise of this function.

A salesman can request two specific items of credit information from new customers without endangering his sales. These are the name of the customer's bank, and the names and addresses of three or four references. Such inquiry is expected by most buyers when they give a first order, and the query arouses no resentment. Beyond this a salesman should not ask a customer for specific information. But he should keep his eyes and ears open. Before entering a prospect's store or plant, he can judge the advantages and disadvantages of its location, he can note whether competing stores are close at hand, and he can judge whether a storefront makes an effective display. Once upon the premises, in the course of the sales talk, he can evaluate the layout and display of the store, the efficiency or indifference of the business methods in evidence, the business personality of the customer himself, and competing lines carried in stock. Finally, from other salesmen in the same or related fields, and sometimes from local sources, he can pick up stray comments and judgments that may throw revealing light upon a new account.

### Salesmen's credit report forms

To ask salesmen to report generally upon new customers would result in vague generalities of but little value to a credit manager. He must prepare a credit report blank providing for specific answers. Where the salesman's judgment is demanded, it should be expressed in some standard comparative form. Some salesmen's credit reports provide for three judgment categories—"excellent," "satisfactory," and "poor." Others provide for five judgments categories—"excellent," "very good," "good," "poor," and "bad." A salesman's credit report form prepared upon these principles is shown in Illustration 7-1.

Salesmen generally need some education in credit matters before they can or will cooperate effectively with the credit department in procuring credit information on new accounts. Credit managers can promote the credit education of their companies' salesmen by preparing a "Salesmen's Credit Manual" along the lines of the model *What Your Salesmen Should Know About Credit and Collections,* issued in 1953 by the New York Credit and Financial Management Association.

A credit manager seeking to develop his company's sales force as a source of credit information should always obtain the cooperation of the sales manager. The latter should be consulted upon the preparation of the credit report form and the salesmen's credit manual. Any pet idea of his as to content or appearance of such a form or manual, if at all feasible, should be deferred to. The sales manager should then instruct his salesmen accordingly, and be held subsequently responsible for the

# SALESMAN'S CREDIT REPORT

Date ................

Name of firm ...........................................

Address ...............................................

.......................................................

Type of store or business ...............................

Names of principals ....................................

Bank ..................................................

References: 1. ........................................

           2. ........................................

           3. ........................................

           4. ........................................

Brands carried: .......................................

.......................................................

.......................................................

Check:

| | |
|---|---|
| Location: | Excellent__ Satisfactory__ Poor__ |
| Competition: | Slight __ Normal __ Bad __ |
| Appearance of building: | Excellent__ Satisfactory__ Poor__ |
| Window display: | Excellent__ Satisfactory__ Poor__ |
| Layout: | Excellent__ Satisfactory__ Poor__ |
| Counter display: | Excellent__ Satisfactory__ Poor__ |
| General interior appearance: | Excellent__ Satisfactory__ Poor__ |
| Choice of merchandise: | Excellent__ Satisfactory__ Poor__ |
| Manager's sales personality: | Excellent__ Satisfactory__ Poor__ |
| Character of employees: | Excellent__ Satisfactory__ Poor__ |

Remarks: ..............................................

.......................................................

.......................................................

.......................................................

.......................................................

Signed .........................

ILLUSTRATION 7-1.   Salesman's Credit Report Form

quality of their reports. Grading and competitive rewarding of salesmen according to the credit quality of their accounts, discussed in Chapter 21 of this volume, is often an inducement to careful preparation of such credit reports by the sales force.

Special care must be exercised in using the information in a salesman's credit report. The strictly factual data, such as a customer's bank, references, and other suppliers, can be accepted without qualification. But the salesmen's judgments must sometimes be taken with a grain of salt. Personal acquaintance with his company's salesmen may enable the credit manager to judge which reports may be accepted at their face value and which have to be discounted for salesmen's ingrained optimism. But where such personal contact does not exist the credit manager must look at the salesman's report with a touch of skepticism. If agency reports confirm them—fine! But if an agency report presents a less rosy picture than a salesman's report, the former should be given more weight.

Obviously, a salesman's report can never substitute for an agency report. But many credit managers with a limited budget for drawing agency reports on new accounts have been forced to compromise. They often establish arbitrary order and credit limits for new accounts. Providing a customer's orders stay within these limits, they judge him on his reference book rating and on the salesman's report. If orders exceed these limits they draw an agency report and make a more thorough analysis.

### Primary dependence upon salesmen's credit reports

In certain lines of business—wholesale groceries may be taken as an example—a large proportion of the customers are small retail outlets from which neither the agencies nor the sellers can obtain adequate financial information. Credit managers in such lines must depend heavily upon credit information garnered by their sales force.

However, the salesmen serving these small retail outlets are generally able to transmit exceptionally valuable credit information. The full story of the success or failure of such stores is written upon the very face of these establishments for experienced eyes to read. Salesmen's visits are frequent—sometimes weekly, more frequently biweekly, or at the very least monthly. They commonly act also as collectors so that they are instantly aware of any tendency on the part of a customer to fall behind in his payments. And they often have an incentive to conservative credit judgment that salesmen in other lines lack; they may have to absorb a percentage of the bad debt losses on their accounts. Salesmen's credit report forms under such circumstances are at least as full as the one shown in Illustration 7-1. They may include lines for the salesman's estimate of the value of the customer's stock, for whether the customer's premises are rented or owned, and for other financial information which the salesman can obtain by direct inquiry. Such reports are submitted by salesmen not only on the occasion of first orders but also whenever the customer requests a higher credit limit or when any delay in his payments occurs.

In these lines the functions of sales manager and credit manager are often combined in one individual. Knowing his salesmen intimately, he can evaluate shrewdly the soundness of their credit reports. Experience has taught him that in many, if not most, instances, these salesmen's reports are his most dependable form of credit information.

## BANKS

Banks are a recognized source for certain elements of credit information, particularly where first orders from new accounts are concerned.[4]

### Direct inquiry

A new account is always asked for its banking connections. The credit manager should immediately write to the bank, stating that a first order of a given amount has been received, and requesting the bank's experience with the account. Less frequently, credit managers write to a customer's bank when he falls behind in his payments. In such cases it is customary to send to the bank, with the request for the bank's information, a regular interchange report of the supplier's own experience with the customer. Occasionally a credit manager requests a customer's bank to verify the cash item in his financial statement.

These credit requests involve labor and cost to the banks. Some banks reimburse themselves by charging a small fee for submitting a credit report. Most, however, perform this service gratis. They, too, frequently send out requests for interchange information on their clients, and they feel themselves obligated to give their reports when requested.

The replies that banks give to credit inquiries vary widely, ranging from a bare acknowledgment that the customer maintains an account with them to an extended appraisal of the customer as a credit risk. Most bank replies, however, are cast in a standardized mold. They contain the following information, and no more:

1. How long the customer has maintained an account with the bank.
2. Average size of the account, stated in general terms—"a moderate

---

[4] National Association of Credit Management and the Robert Morris Associates, *Statement of Principles in the Exchange of Credit Information between Banks and Mercantile Concerns* (New York, 1959).

three-figure balance," "a low four-figure balance," "a high four-figure balance," and so forth.

3. If the customer borrows from the bank, the line of credit—stated in general terms as above—which the bank allows, the current debt balance, and whether such borrowing is upon open line or upon notes, discounted commercial paper, or other collateral (including guaranties and endorsements).

4. If the customer borrows from the bank, a statement as to whether he repays promptly, or if there has been any delinquency in his repayments.

5. If the customer has defaulted on any trade acceptances or notes collected through the bank, or has had checks returned because of insufficient funds, a statement to that effect.

6. Sometimes a statement of the community opinion of the customer as to his character and business ability.

7. Sometimes a statement, in broad terms, that the bank considers the customer good for a "moderate," or "reasonable," or "liberal" line of credit, or more favorable still, that the customer is "good for his requirements."

It is generally a wise precaution, in addressing a credit inquiry to a bank, to request specific information under the seven headings listed above. This indicates to the bank exactly what the credit manager is looking for, and it facilitates a detailed reply.

Some banks use a large stamp, similar to that used by some credit departments for giving ledger interchange information (see page 101), which imprints the standardized headings for a bank credit report on the inquirer's letter. The standard information is then inserted, and the original letter mailed back to the inquirer. In other cases a bank officer will dictate the reply in letter form. It is common practice to stamp or type in red, at the bottom of a bank credit reply, the following sentence or one similar to it: "Confidential information which is furnished at your request and without any responsibility on the part of the bank or its officers." This sentence is intended to establish the credit reply as a "privileged communication" under the law of libel and to disclaim such responsibility for the statements contained which might be basis for a claim for damages should the information, through no deliberate intent or wilful negligence on the part of the bank officer, prove to be false or misleading.[5]

Such information from a bank obviously pictures only a fragment of a customer's credit position. But it is a valuable fragment. More extended

---

[5] See *Park & Tilford Importing Corporation v. Passaic National Bank and Trust Co.*, 129 N.J.L. 436, 30 Atl. (2nd) 24.

knowledge can sometimes be obtained by personally interviewing an officer of the customer's bank.

### Indirect inquiry

For a large and valued client, a bank will do many favors that it refuses to smaller clients. The credit manager of a large corporation can occasionally request his company's bank to ask a customer's bank about the customer. There are many things about a client that one bank will tell another bank but will not disclose to a business concern. For example, it may have obtained a financial statement or interim financial information from the customer as a basis for its own lending decision, or its loan officer may have obtained revealing information from conversations with him, or special inquiries may have been made about him. The bank's general opinion of the customer based on such information might be expressed in a report given to an inquiring supplier, but none of the background detail would be included. Upon inquiry from another bank, however, even though the letter stated that the inquiry was being made on behalf of a client, the customer's bank might send copies of the statement, conversation memo, and report—such are the courtesies which banks render to each other. The recipient bank, in turn, would transmit this information to its client.

## ACCOUNTANTS

Next in line as a source of credit information, and becoming increasingly important in this capacity, is the accountant. Credit managers in all lines of business, as will be shown in the following chapter, correspond with their customers' accountants about details in the customer's financial statement that they have prepared. In the textile and apparel field particularly, but also in other trades, accountants are proving to be a valuable source of supplementary credit information on their clients. They do not confine themselves to the elucidation of the financial statements. Quite frequently, they supply the inquiring seller with trial balances and confidential information about the customer's business. Usually, customers authorize their accountants to provide suppliers with such information. In many cases, however, the accountants obviously respond to a credit manager's inquiries without specific authorization— raising thereby a delicate point of accountancy ethics. The American Institute of Certified Public Accountants takes a clear stand on this matter. According to No. 16 of the Rules of Professional Conduct for the members of the Institute, no violation of the confidential relationship between accountant and client is permitted. The Institute interprets this to mean that, in the absence of prior authorization from a client, no member may give third parties information additional to that contained in reports and statements prepared by the member.

## ATTORNEYS

During the nineteenth century, attorneys were a major source of information about customers who lived in out-of-town, small communities. Mercantile agency reports on such customers were generally inadequate, banks were not yet educated to credit cooperation with suppliers, and general ledger interchange among suppliers was practically nonexistent. Local attorneys, who combined a general knowledge of business procedure derived from their legal activities, a knowledge of how to check upon the mortgages and judgments outstanding against a local business man, and a first-hand knowledge of the business men of their communities and their standing, were a logical source of credit information. The fees charged for credit reports were a welcome item of income to many a struggling small-town attorney. He was doubly anxious to make these reports, since such a contact with a supplier often led to later arrangements for undertaking collections and suits on behalf of the supplier in his community.

Since then the mercantile agencies have improved their services to such an extent that their routine reports on small-town business men are likely to be superior to the best reports a competent attorney could prepare. Use of attorneys as a source of general credit information has, therefore, declined substantially.

### Current role of attorneys' reports

Some business concerns still place great reliance on attorneys' reports and require them for all out-of-town customers located in small communities. They find an attorney's report a valuable supplement to their credit information from other sources under certain special circumstances. When the basis for extending credit to an out-of-town customer is not so much the current financial status of his business, but rather his personal ownership of property which can be reached by creditors in case the business fails, a local attorney is better able to check the property records and report upon the market value of the property and any mortgages or other liens standing against it. When the credit status of an account may be clouded by claims and suits, a local attorney can readily discover the facts by checking legal records. The same holds true when there is suspicion that a customer has assigned or pledged his receivables.

In such cases, timely notice derived from an attorney's report has saved many a supplier from subsequent losses.

Attorneys' credit reports are often expected to include an estimate of a credit limit for the customer and to state the probability of collection in case of nonpayment. The credit manager may get answers to these questions but they are not likely to be worth much. The attorney, without credit experience, without the customer's financial statement, and without ledger interchange information, is much less equipped than the credit manager himself for making an estimate of a sound credit risk. Except for hearsay knowledge, he has little basis for any conclusion as to whether the customer may be "judgment proof," or whether some recovery could be made in case of default. Furthermore, his opinions on such matters may be colored in favor of the customer who is a fellow townsman and possibly even a local client. Finally, since attorneys receive only trifling fees for making credit reports, or in some cases no fee at all—the hope of receiving future collection work from the inquiring creditor being deemed sufficient compensation—they frequently make only casual, inadequate investigations.

### How to obtain an attorney's report

To locate a local attorney from whom a credit report on an out-of-town customer may be obtained, a credit manager usually has to consult a "law list." Several publishing companies issue such lists [6] periodically, registering thousands of lawyers in small towns and county seats who have submitted their names and paid a fee for such listing. No attempt is made by the publisher to rate the credit-reporting capacity of the lawyers thus named since this is generally the least important of their professional activities. "Law lists" are used primarily by city attorneys seeking local correspondents to conduct local suits, and by collection agencies that have to make local collections or prosecute local suits. Their use for credit information purposes is incidental and today relatively rare. Generally these "law lists" are distributed gratis by the publishers upon request to lawyers and collection agencies.

Once the listed local attorney is ascertained from the list, the supplier's attorney or credit manager may enter into direct correspondence with him and request credit information. Some local lawyers make a small charge for a credit report. Others prepare such reports gratis on the tacit understanding that the inquiring concern will give them any local collection and suit cases that may arise.

---

[6] Among them *American Lawyers' Quarterly* (Cleveland), *B.A. Law List* (Milwaukee), *Clearing House Quarterly* (Minneapolis), *Commercial Bar* (New York), *Columbia List* (New York), *Forwarder's List of Attorneys* (Chicago), and *Martindale·Hubbell Law Directory* (Summit, N.J.).

## MISCELLANEOUS

An alert credit manager overlooks no possible source of information on his company's customers. He may consult insurance agents, landlords, legal records (such as county clerks' files and court reports), and all sorts of publications. Trade magazines and papers are as useful to him as to the sales manager. Frequently a news item in one of the journals tells a story that warrants the raising of credit limits to some customer in improving circumstances or the increasing of collection pressure upon another whose position is deteriorating.

Some credit managers claim that they find corporation stockholder reports and investment manuals occasionally useful as sources of credit information. This may be so under special circumstances. But usually the information so available is not the kind the credit manager is looking for. Sometimes a credit manager may become doubtful about a customer's business ethics and would like to have his suspicions confirmed or dispelled. In such a case, he should write to the Board of Trade, Chamber of Commerce, or Better Business Bureau of the community in which the customer is located and inquire about his past record.

The credit manager, as well as the other executives of his company in the sales and production fields, must anticipate general business conditions in the trade that will affect the ability of his customers to pay as well as their willingness to buy. There are many professional forecasters who are willing to read the future for him; if his business concern subscribes to their services he will have the benefit of their educated "guesstimates." But he will still have to form his own judgment. For this purpose, statistical data, analyses of business trends, regional descriptions, and trade reports are helpful. They are found in the U.S. Department of Commerce publications, such as *Survey of Current Business;* in publications of the Department of Agriculture, such as the *Agricultural Finance Review;* in the *Federal Reserve Bulletin;* in the monthly *Reviews* and *Business Letters* of the twelve Federal Reserve Banks and of commercial banks, such as the First National City Bank of New York and the Cleveland Trust Company; in *Dun's Review* and other Dun & Bradstreet publications; in *Credit and Financial Management* published by the National Association of Credit Management; in current studies of the Credit Research Foundation, such as its *Accounts Receivable Survey;* in Chamber of Commerce reports; in trade magazines and journals; and in current studies of such business research groups as the National Industrial Conference Board, the National Bureau of Economic Research, and the Committee on Economic Development.

## SUPPLEMENTARY READINGS

Dunn, W. R., "The Credit Side of Customer Relations," *Credit and Financial Management,* January 1950, p. 7.

Manning, I., "From a Banker to a Credit Man," *Credit and Financial Management,* September 1950, p. 12.

Marks, Jr., L., *Credit Orientation and Training for Salesmen,* Credit Research Foundation, New York, 1958.

National Association of Credit Management, "Counseling Customers Pays in Added Sales," *Credit and Financial Management,* July 1960, p. 8.

New York Credit and Financial Management Association, *How Credit Interviews Are Conducted,* New York, 1955.

## REVIEW

1. How should a credit manager conduct a conversation with a customer who visits the credit department?
2. What information can a credit manager obtain on a field trip that he cannot derive from sources of information available to him at his office?
3. Why do salesmen generally make poor credit reporters?
4. What valuable information about new customers should salesmen be asked to report to the credit department?
5. In what lines of business must primary dependence be placed on salesmen's credit reports? Why?
6. What credit information on a customer will his bank ordinarily supply?
7. When may a credit executive approach his own company's bank to ask a customer's bank for credit information on the customer? What sort of credit information might he obtain in this way?
8. Under what circumstances would an attorney's report be a particularly valuable source of credit information?
9. What kind of credit information about a customer would a credit manager expect to obtain from the customer's accountant?
10. How could a credit manager get the name and address of an attorney who would make a report on an out-of-town customer?
11. What credit information can be derived from corporation manuals?
12. Where could a credit manager obtain information that would help him to anticipate improvement or deterioration of general business conditions in his customers' lines of business?

# CHAPTER 8

# Credit Use of Financial Statements

Two major considerations in any credit decision are the customer's business ability and his general financial position. The sources of mercantile credit information already studied throw light on both of these factors, particularly on the former. For all large- and medium-sized enterprises, and for some small ones, however, the most valuable source of information on a customer's financial position, and a valuable supplementary source of information on his business ability, is his latest financial statement.

As will be developed more fully in subsequent pages of this chapter, a financial statement usually consists of two parts—a balance sheet which summarizes the capital position of a business at the close of an accounting period and a profit-and-loss statement which summarizes the results of its operations during the accounting period. A third part—a "reconciliation of surplus" or a "reconciliation of net worth"—is sometimes prepared to reconcile apparent discrepancies between the profit-and-loss statement and the stated net worths of the preceding and current year. These documents, on their face, do not measure the managerial ability applied to a business or the soundness or weakness of its financial position. In the first place, the figures in a financial statement may have to be qualified and subjected to adjustments before they are of any use in credit analysis; these qualifications and adjustments are studied in this chapter. Second, certain analytical procedures, which go by the name of "financial statement analysis," must be applied to these figures before they can reveal the ability and financial position of the company issuing the statement; the techniques of financial statement analysis are studied in Chapters 9 and 10.

Besides balance sheets, profit-and-loss statements, and reconciliation statements, a credit manager can sometimes obtain supplementary financial information from the customer's accountant and from the customer himself. The first category—accountants' reports—are studied in a later part of this chapter. The second category—insurance statements, trial balances, and budgets—will be analyzed in the closing pages of Chapter 10.

## HISTORY OF CREDIT
## USE OF FINANCIAL STATEMENTS

The history of the financial statement as an instrument of accounting practice is a long and interesting one but does not concern us here. Submission of financial statements by buyers to sellers was a late development. Effective analytical use of such statements for mercantile credit purposes has been made only in the second quarter of this century.

### Submission of financial statements by borrowers and buyers

As early as the 1870's, mercantile credit agencies were able to obtain some neatly arranged financial statements from large mercantile houses in the East. Largely through the pressure of these agencies, the practice of issuing financial statements as a basis for credit extensions was developed through the 1870's and 1880's.[1]

The next source of pressure for financial statements was the commercial banks. To an increasing extent during the 1880's and 1890's, they insisted on obtaining financial statements from their borrowers. In 1895 the Executive Council of the New York State Bankers' Association adopted a resolution recommending that loan applicants be requested to submit financial statements.[2] A year later the Pennsylvania bankers adopted some of the statement forms developed by the New York association. Bankers' associations in other states followed the lead of the New York and Pennsylvania associations, and during the first decade of the 1900's the giving of financial statements to banks became quite common. In 1914 the Federal Reserve Board added impetus to the use of

---

[1] R. A. Foulke, *The Sinews of American Commerce* (Dun & Bradstreet, Inc., New York, 1941), p. 337.

[2] R. A. Foulke, *Practical Financial Statement Analysis*, 4th ed. (McGraw-Hill Book Co., New York, 1960), p. 15.

financial statements as a basis for commercial bank lending by providing that, for borrowers' notes to be eligible for federal reserve rediscount, the makers of the notes must have given financial statements to the lending bank. Standardization of financial statement practices was promoted during the 1930's by the reporting requirements established by the Securities and Exchange Commission.

It is impossible to determine exactly when individual sellers first started asking customers for financial statements and obtaining them, but probably it was as early as the 1880's. The National Association of Credit Men, from its very inception, interested itself in this matter, and by 1898 had prepared standard "property statement" blanks—balance sheet forms—for the use of its members. The practice of requesting financial statements from customers was slow in developing, and was not widespread during the first decade of this century. By the 1920's, however, a substantial proportion of credit managers had become aware that their customers' financial statements were useful sources of credit information, and a substantial proportion of buying concerns had come to recognize that their suppliers were entitled to ask for and receive their financial statements as a basis for giving credit terms.

Some concerns are still reluctant to submit copies of their financial statements to their suppliers upon request for three reasons: (1) trade custom in some lines of business; (2) the self-confident assumption of some large companies that their suppliers should be only too happy to sell them on credit terms without any detailed financial information; (3) the preference of some business concerns to forego the credit advantages of issuing financial statements rather than expose their financial operations to competitors, tax authorities, or other interested parties. Apart from these exceptions, requesting financial statements and receiving them in due course is generally accepted policy in mercantile credit. Refusing a financial statement is usually taken as an indication that the buyer is concealing an unsatisfactory financial picture.

### Development of financial statement analysis

The development of effective techniques of financial statement analysis is fairly recent and still in process. Investment analysts, not bank or mercantile credit men, were the first to see the possibilities of these techniques and to exploit them. The first suggestions for ratio analysis appeared in a book on railroad security investment analysis, published in 1900.[3] Bank and mercantile credit men made little effort, for two decades, to follow in the footsteps of the investment analysts but confined themselves to use of the current ratio. In the *Federal Reserve Bul-*

---

[3] J. N. Myer, *Financial Statement Analysis,* 3rd ed. (Prentice-Hall, Inc., Englewood Cliffs, N.J., 1961), p. 7.

*letin* of March 1919 Alexander Wall published an article, "Study of Credit Barometrics," which explored the possibilities of ratio analysis of financial statements for bank and credit work. Bank and mercantile credit managers were profoundly influenced by this article, and after having been unwarrantedly ignored, the possibilities of financial statement analysis for a while were grossly exaggerated. Because early proponents of the new technique claimed too much for it, in some cases presenting it as an infallible formula for credit judgments, there was soon an unfavorable reaction and many credit managers, after initially experimenting with the technique, dismissed it as an empty academic exercise.

While mercantile credit managers generally turned their backs on financial statement analysis after their first uncritical enthusiasm for it, bank loan officers continued to use it. They soon learned that valuable, though qualified, judgments could be derived from its proper use. Impressed with the bankers' experience, many mercantile credit managers have turned their attention again to financial statement analysis and have found that, while it can be no absolute determinant of their credit judgments, it does provide them with elements of knowledge about their customers that can be helpfully combined with the information they derive from other sources.[4]

## THE FINANCIAL STATEMENT DATE

Customarily the date of a financial statement is the closing day of the concern's accounting year or other accounting period. The balance sheet summarizes the company's assets and liabilities as of that date. The income statement summarizes the results of its operations for the preceding accounting period—usually a year, but sometimes less in the case of a new business or one that is changing its accounting year.

A majority of the country's business enterprises use the calendar year as their accounting year. The remainder employ "natural" fiscal years better suited to the seasonal character of their operations. There is a trend toward "natural" accounting years.[5] This movement was stimulated

---

[4] There is growing cooperation between the accounting and credit professions. For more than a decade, for example, the "Credit Executives Committee on Cooperation with Certified Public Accountants" of the New York Credit and Financial Management Association and the "Committee on Cooperation with Commercial Credit Grantors" of the New York State Society of C.P.A.s have met annually and discussed mutual problems.

[5] According to tabulations of the Internal Revenue Service derived from corporate income tax returns, the number of corporate taxpayers filing returns that use a "natural" accounting year expanded from 14 percent of all corporate returns in 1933 to 49 percent in 1958. These "natural" accounting years are used primarily by newly formed and smaller companies, while larger and older business establishments are inclined to stand by their original calendar year choices. (H. F. Reiss, "Trend Continues to Natural Business Year," *Journal of Accountancy,* August 1960, p. 25.)

by the creation, in 1935, of the Natural Business Year Council through cooperation of the National Association of Credit Men, the Robert Morris Associates, the National Association of Accountants, and the American Institute of Certified Public Accountants. The Natural Business Year Council studied the seasonal variations of the different lines of business and recommended certain low activity points as suitable determinants of their accounting years. Some of the "natural" closing dates recommended for various lines of business are shown in Illustration 8-1.

ILLUSTRATION 8-1.  Some Recommended Natural Business Year Closing Dates

| Business Lines | Recommended Natural Business Year Closing Date (end of the month) |
| --- | --- |
| Advertising agencies | December |
| Automotive accessories manufacturers | July or August |
| Automobile dealers | October |
| Automobile manufacturers | September |
| Book publishers | June |
| Breweries | October |
| Broom and brush manufacturers | June |
| Candy wholesalers | July |
| Canners of fruits and vegetables | January or February |
| Clothing (men's work) manufacturers | November |
| Coat and suit (women's) manufacturers | November |
| Crockery and glassware manufacturers | January |
| Dairies and produce companies | February or March |
| Department stores | January |
| Drug retailers | January |
| Drug wholesalers | June |
| Dry goods wholesalers | November or December |
| Flour millers | March to June |
| Furniture manufacturers | November or December |
| Grocery wholesalers | June |
| Hardware retailers | January |
| Hat manufacturers | October |
| Heating and plumbing contractors | December |
| Hotels (residential) | June or July |
| Ice cream manufacturers | December |
| Jewelry and silverware retailers | January |
| Laundries | June |
| Mail order houses | January |
| Meat packers | October |
| Millinery retailers | June |
| Photographers | April |
| Radio and television wholesalers | January |
| Ready-to-wear (ladies') retailers | January |
| Refrigerator manufacturers | July |

Source: R. A. Foulke, *Practical Financial Statement Analysis,* 4th ed. (McGraw-Hill Book Co., Inc., New York, 1960), pp. 212-214.

As a result of the expanding use of "natural" accounting years, the financial statements received by a credit manager from some concerns may have a calendar year date, whereas statements from others in the same line may have one or more "natural" year closing dates. This aggravates the difficulties of analysis, both for income statements and for the balance sheets of seasonal businesses. Rations based on items such as income, cost, receivables, inventory, and current liabilities vary according to the date for which these figures are reported. In comparative financial statement analysis, it is essential that the comparison be made for concerns with the same closing date or that adjustments be made for differences.

## CONTENTS OF A BALANCE SHEET

A balance sheet is a summary of the capital position of a business at a particular moment, customarily the close of the last business day of a concern's accounting year, which may be either the calendar year or a "natural business year."

The financial position of a business, as pictured in its balance sheet, consists of a summary tabulation of its assets—what it owns—offset by its liabilities—what it owes. The net balance represents owners' equity—"net worth" in the case of unincorporated enterprises, "capital and surplus" in the case of corporations. Accounting practice has established the following standardized classifications of business assets and liabilities:

| *Assets* | *Liabilities* |
|---|---|
| Current | Current |
|   Cash | Fixed (long-term, funded) |
|   Receivables | Capital (owners' equity) |
|   Merchandise (or "inventory") | |
|   Other current | |
| | |
| Fixed (noncurrent) | |
| Intangible | |
| Miscellaneous | |
| Total Assets | Total Liabilities |

Since the item "capital" is the difference between total assets and the current and fixed liabilities, the figures for "total assets" and "total liabilities" are always identical.

Accounting practice has not only standardized the major classifications of the balance sheet but has also been successful to a substantial extent in determining how to attribute the various ledger items to the balance sheet headings. However, there are still many borderline situations where this remains undecided. Moreover, differing methods are used to give dollar values to certain book items, so that the same dollar figure for a particular balance sheet item in two different statements may have widely disparate significance—for example, the last-in first-out method of valuing inventories undervalues inventories in periods of rising prices, overvalues them in periods of falling prices. Hence the balance sheet of a business must not be read with a casual eye. A credit analyst should probe beneath the given figures to ascertain how they were determined, what they really represent, and whether they serve his purpose which is different from that of the management of the company, its accountant, or an investor examining the same data.

### Current assets—cash

The asset item of "cash" includes money on the company's premises —in the cash drawer, cash register, or safe—and bank deposits. Ordinarily no uncertainty attaches to the reporting of this item. Sometimes, however, through ignorance of proper accounting procedure, small business men may improperly include post-dated checks in their "cash on hand." There have been cases, moreover, where two related concerns have, as an incident to fraud, exchanged checks in order to raise their bank balances. Each has deposited the other's check and included the amount in its "cash in bank," without reporting the corresponding liability of the check it has given.

### Current assets—receivables

"Receivables" consist of two items—"(trade) notes and acceptances receivable" and "accounts receivable." The former are customers' promises to pay the reporting company for goods sold or services performed, evidenced by promissory notes or trade acceptances. The accounts receivable are also customers' promises to pay for goods or services, but evidenced only by the entries in the reporting concern's customer ledger.

Notes given by officers or employees of the reporting concern for loans received, or notes given by affiliates or other business units for loans to them, are not current assets. They should not be included in this category, since they do not possess the liquidity of trade paper, but should be separately reported.

In the jewelry, fur, and some other lines, customer notes or acceptances are the normal type of receivables. They are normal, too, for retailers and others who sell on instalment terms. Otherwise they may be an indication of credit outstanding to customers who cannot be sold on regular terms or who were delinquent on open accounts. Where this is the case, their liquidity, and even their soundness, may be open to question.

A past-due note or acceptance on which a customer has defaulted is not, of course, as sound an asset as one which has not yet matured and on which payment at the due date may still be expected. Consequently, some balance sheet forms provide for separate statement of the amount of notes and acceptances in default.

If customers' notes or acceptances have been discounted with a bank, the bank is a preferred creditor with respect to them, and they do not constitute a real asset for the suppliers. The asset value of accounts receivable is also reduced to the extent that any of them are pledged, assigned, or factored, as explained in Chapter 23. Therefore balance sheet forms commonly provide either for separate statement of any amount of notes, acceptances, or book receivables discounted (see Illustration 23-4), or for exclusion of discounted receivables from the tabulation of current assets (see Illustration 8-2).

Seasonal variations affecting receivables also have to be kept in mind. The experienced credit manager knows his customers' normal receivables pattern and notes any deviation.

### Current assets—merchandise

The item of "merchandise" consists of the value of the inventories of raw materials, work in process, and finished goods which a business has on hand at the close of its accounting year. In the case of manufacturers it is helpful to a credit manager to know the distribution of the total merchandise item among its three component parts. For one thing, a manufacturer's stock of raw materials is more readily salable than his stocks of finished goods and work in process, and so has higher salvage value in case of liquidation. Furthermore, the figure for raw materials, stated separately, may provide an indication of whether the manufacturer indulges in speculative buying, while a separate figure for work in process may throw light on the efficiency of his production planning and control. Consequently the balance sheet forms sent to manufacturers by banks and some mercantile credit departments provide for separate statement of the component merchandise items (see Illustration 23-4). Many mercantile credit managers, however, do not insist on having manufacturers' merchandise figures broken down and ask only for the over-all total (see Illustration 8-2). On the other hand, they do require that goods held on consignment should not be included in inventory, but separately reported, as title and ownership are vested in the consignor and not in the consignee. Also, where inventory has been pledged as loan collateral under a factor's lien or through a warehouse receipt, such circumstance should be clearly stated. In addition to these points, credit managers are apt to observe the *seasonal* aspects of merchandise inventory in a customer's balance sheet even more carefully than in the case of his receivables, for the inventory figures will be the first to indicate if a customer is not adhering strictly to his seasonal line.

Another important consideration in evaluating a reported merchandise figure is when and how it was determined by the customer. The physical volume of the customer's inventories should have been ascertained by actual count—the "physical inventory" taken at an appropriate and convenient date. Many small retailers with casual accounting practices, however, merely "guesstimate" their stocks of goods. If a retailer's merchandise figure is an important consideration in a credit judgment, the basis of its determination should be checked.

Furthermore, there may be question as to the values placed by the customer on the merchandise in his inventories. The most common acceptable valuation basis is the cost or market price of the goods, whichever is lower. There are other acceptable procedures, however, which may, under certain price situations, produce quite different results. There are also various methods of determining the cost of inventory items. The most common is the first-in first-out (FIFO) method, but far from uncommon are the base stock, average cost, retail, standard cost, and last-in first-out (LIFO) methods. Finally, a credit manager must bear in mind the possibility that an irresponsible customer may have utilized some unauthorized valuation method that inflates his reported merchandise figure. Most balance sheet forms sent out by credit men require a statement as to merchandise valuation method used (see Illustrations 8-2 and 23-4); these statements do not ordinarily cover, however, the method of cost determination applied.

**Other current assets**

Besides cash, receivables, and merchandise, a customer may have some other asset which can be readily converted to cash. Such an asset is properly rated as current. The most common case of "other" current assets is readily marketable securities owned by the customer; the cash surrender value of a life insurance policy held by a customer may also be included. Deferred charges, or prepaid expenses which might normally be part of current assets, are usually not so regarded by credit managers.

**Fixed assets**

The fixed assets of a business consist of owned land and buildings, machinery, and other equipment, including furniture and fixtures used in the business. Credit managers, who are concerned primarily with the *current* aspects of a customer's business, take only a secondary interest in the balance sheet figure of fixed assets. Through sale or use as loan collateral, however, fixed assets may sometimes be converted into additional working capital. Moreover, if a customer's current circumstances establish him as a borderline credit risk, the investment in fixed assets may determine whether or not the salvage aspect of the business makes the risk acceptable. Under certain circumstances excessive investment in fixed assets may be taken as an indication of poor business ability.

Good accounting practice requires that the initial cost or value of each fixed-asset item should be reduced every year by some acceptable depreciation procedure. A credit manager using a balance sheet fixed-assets figure for any purpose wants to be sure that it has been properly depreciated. Hence balance sheet forms for credit purposes always ask either for the net depreciated value of these items or for their gross undepreciated value balanced by a figure for depreciation reserves (see Illustrations 8-2 and 23-4).

If the land and buildings of a customer are mortgaged, or if there are chattel mortgages upon any of his machinery or equipment, the security value of these assets to trade creditors is reduced accordingly. Therefore, such encumbrances have to be brought to the attention of the credit manager. Balance sheet forms used for credit purposes either contain a direct query as to real-estate and chattel mortgages, or provide for reporting the specific amounts involved in the liability column of the balance sheet (see Illustrations 8-2 and 23-4).

### Other assets

The credit manager is interested in various asset items other than those termed "current" and "fixed." These should be enumerated under a separate asset heading. Among them are: investments not includable in current assets; loans to subsidiaries, stockholders, officers, or employees; advances to suppliers; deferred charges or prepaid expenses; and copyrights, patents, good will, and similar "intangibles." A credit manager gives little or no weight to such items in determining the acceptability of a credit risk. If they constitute substantial amounts in the balance sheet, his suspicion may be aroused that the customer's business practices are not sound.

### Current liabilities—accounts, notes, and acceptances payable to the trade

Liability figures are factual and present no question of valuation, as do certain of the asset figures. Hence, unless a customer fraudulently or by mistake has omitted or understated his trade liabilities, a credit manager can take the figures given for accounts, notes, and acceptances payable to the trade as indisputable. He does, however, want the overall figure for trade liabilities separated into accounts payable and notes and acceptances payable (see Illustrations 8-2 and 23-4). Except for certain lines of business, such as the jewelry and fur trades, a report of notes or acceptances payable indicates that a customer is having payment difficulties with some of his other suppliers. Notes payable are generally a sign that he has fallen past due and has had to give promissory notes for obtaining an extension of payment time. If acceptances payable are reported, some of his suppliers are obviously refusing him ordinary open account terms. A credit manager also wants to know whether a customer is past-due on any of his accounts or notes and acceptances payable. Hence balance-sheet forms sent to customers usually provide for some report on this point (see Illustrations 8-2 and 23-4).

As indicated in an earlier chapter, it is a wise precaution to check the "payables" figure in the balance sheet with the total reported as "owed" by the concern in an NACM interchange report—provided that such a report is available as of the same, or nearly the same, date.

### Current liabilities—notes payable to banks and finance companies

An unsecured bank loan, apart from adding to the total of a customer's current liabilities, is generally a favorable consideration from a credit manager's point of view. Bank credit standards for unsecured loans are very high. Consequently, if such a liability item appears on a customer's balance sheet, it is commonly taken as the mark of a high credit rating.

The discounting of customers' notes and acceptances with a bank has always been a recognized financial practice. The assignment of accounts receivable to banks or finance companies as security for loans carried formerly a certain credit stigma, but is now generally accepted as no more a sign of credit weakness than the discounting of customer paper. Either practice, however, makes the lending bank or finance company a preferred creditor as to the pledged notes and acceptances or accounts receivable and so reduces the assets available as security to the general creditors. As already indicated in discussing the asset side of the procedure, this should be made known to the credit manager. Consequently, financial statement forms provide space for this information (see Illustrations 8-2 and 23-4).

### Other current liabilities

Any other obligation of a business that must, or may, be paid within a year's time should be included in current liabilities. Among such items are accrued taxes, interest, payrolls, and other accrued expenses, short-term loans from officers of a corporation (sometimes even from subsidiaries if they settle their accounts regularly with the parent company) or from sources other than banks and finance companies, instalment payments under conditional sales contracts or chattel mortgages, and forthcoming amortization payments on real estate mortgages. Also a lump-sum mortgage payment due within the year should properly be included with current liabilities unless its renewal is absolutely certain.

### Fixed liabilities

Fixed or noncurrent liabilities are those which do not become due during the accounting year following the balance-sheet date. The most common ones are real estate mortgages, sometimes the later instalments of chattel mortgages, bonded debt, and medium- and long-term loans from banks, government agencies, and other financial institutions.

Deferred liabilities are frequently secured by some fixed assets of a business: a real estate mortgage by land and buildings, a chattel mortgage by the equipment it financed, and bonded debt by particular categories of a corporation's assets in accordance with the indenture. To the extent that these assets are pledged to the mortgagees and bondholders they constitute, of course, no security for its general trade creditors.

### Reserves

In the liability columns of some balance sheets are items called "reserves." These are "book" adjustments, set up to take account of certain factors which directly or contingently may reduce the net worth of the business. A credit manager takes account of reserves according to their nature.

A *bad debt reserve* may be established as a partial offset to expected losses on notes and accounts receivable. Usually such a reserve is shown in the Assets column of a balance sheet as a deduction from gross receivables. Occasionally it figures independently in the Liabilities column. A *depreciation reserve* may be set up as a Liabilities item to cover annual depreciation of buildings, machinery, and equipment. This reserve item may instead appear in the Assets column as a deduction from the gross value of the depreciable assets. In recent years several companies have established *valuation reserves* to cover the risk of price losses on inventory. Such valuation reserves may also figure either as Liabilities items or as deductions from the inventory figure in the Assets column. When reserves of these kinds are set up as Liabilities items, credit managers who analyze customer financial statements usually subtract them from both Total Liabilities and the particular Assets items to which they relate. Such an adjustment makes a customer's balance sheet a more candid reflection of his true credit position.

Sometimes reserves are set up to cover operating expenses known to have accrued but whose amount is not certain or which have not matured as of the balance sheet date. Such a reserve is treated by a credit manager as though it were a current liability like accrued expenses.

*Contingency* reserves, such as many corporations established during World War II in anticipation of postwar reconversion costs, may be viewed as part of the customer's surplus.

## Capital

The difference between the total assets of a business and the sum of its current, deferred, and reserve liabilities constitutes its net worth. This term is actually used in the case of unincorporated enterprises. For corporations this balance is called "capital stock and surplus." Either term connotes the "ownership value" of the business.

## Contingent liabilities

Contingent liabilities—specific liabilities that may develop in the near future for a business because of some definite act or occurrence—may be crucial financial factors in credit judgments. A business man who has given his accommodation endorsement on a promissory note for some other party, for example, will become liable for the amount of such note if the maker fails to pay it, and such liability might be a determining consideration in his solvency. An unfavorable verdict in a pending lawsuit, a commitment under a contract to a losing venture, or a heavy tax deficiency judgment, might convert an account abruptly from a good credit risk to an insolvency case.

The range of possible contingent liabilities is so wide and often so vague that it would be futile to ask customers to indicate all of them. One type of contingent liability, however—the amount for which a business or business man is contingently liable as endorser, surety, or guarantor for third parties—can be definitely determined, and is a valuable item of information to credit managers. Accordingly, most balance sheet forms prepared for credit purposes make specific inquiry on this matter (see Illustrations 8-2 and 24-3).

## CONTENTS OF INCOME AND RECONCILIATION STATEMENTS

An income (or profit-and-loss) statement is a classified tabulation of the operating results of a business enterprise for an accounting year or other period, with the resulting balance of net profit or loss. In contrast to the balance sheet which portrays a static situation as of a given date, the income statement is more dynamic in character, reflecting the development of the subject concern over an accounting period. It is this aspect of the income statement which makes it of particular importance for credit purposes.

A reconciliation of surplus or of net worth takes the difference in the surplus or net worth of a business shown by two successive balance sheets and explains such difference on the basis of the income statement for the intervening accounting year and of financial transactions not included in the income statement.

Accounting practice recognizes a number of ways of presenting income statements. The traditional ones agree in providing for a determination of "gross profit from sales" separate from other items of income. "Gross profit from sales" is determined as follows:

Gross receipts from sale of goods or services
    Less: Returns, allowances and sometimes discounts
Net receipts from sale of goods or services
    Less: Cost of goods or services sold
Gross profit from sales

The item "cost of goods or services sold" in the above calculation is determined as follows:

Inventory of goods or materials (if any) at beginning of year
Cost of materials or merchandise bought for manufacture or resale
Wages and salaries directly associated with manufacture or service
Other costs directly associated with manufacture or service
    Total of above items
        Less: Inventory of goods or materials (if any) at close of year
    Cost of goods or services sold

From "gross profit from sales" are subtracted selling expenses and general administrative expenses. The resulting "net operating profit" is then adjusted by (a) adding "other income" (e.g., interest, proceeds from sale of land, purchase discount), and (b) deducting "other income expenses" (e.g., interest payments, loss on sale of fixed assets); the result is either "net profit" or "net loss."

Banks have always required their borrowers to submit, in addition to their balance sheets, detailed profit-and-loss statements and reconciliation statements (see Illustration 23-4). Mercantile agencies ask for profit-and-loss statements, as well as balance sheets, from all but small enterprises. Mercantile credit managers, however, have only in recent years become aware of the analytical value of customers' income statements, especially with regard to sales and expense figures. Financial statement forms now sent to buyers provide not merely for bare sales figures but for a complete income and expense breakdown. Customers' response to this request has so far not been too cooperative.

## LIMITATIONS ON CREDIT USE OF
## FINANCIAL STATEMENT INFORMATION

One reason for the laggard development of financial statement analysis as a credit inquiry procedure is the unreliability of so many of the financial statements submitted to mercantile agencies and suppliers. Many statements obtained from small businesses are utterly inadequate for purposes of credit analysis. Or the requested information may be submitted in full detail, but with nonstandard classifications, so that comparison of the financial position of the concern in question with others in the same line of business, or even with its own financial position in earlier years, is difficult if not impossible. In a small minority of cases deliberate fraudulent misrepresentation may be involved.

## Inadequacy

The adequacy of a customer's financial statement depends initially on the efficacy of his accounting system. Many small businesses are conducted by owners who themselves have not the slightest idea of sound accounting procedures and who are innocent of any guidance or advice from accountants. Not merely do many of them lack knowledge of the elementary mysteries of double-entry bookkeeping, but not infrequently they do not even keep records which would enable them to calculate the totals of their sales or purchases for a year. The financial estimates they give to a supplier or agency can, therefore, be no better than a series of guesses, some of them quite blind. To apply analysis procedures to such statements would be a waste of time.

Suppliers who sell to small retailers realize that no dependable financial information can be obtained on many of their accounts and usually do not even bother to ask for formal statements. Even for such customers, however, certain items of financial information may be available—the figure for the past year's sales, the total of receivables at the close of the year, the value of merchandise at that date if an inventory was made, the amount owed to creditors, and the value of a house and any other property owned by the proprietor including the amount of any mortgages against such property. Even though such items of information do not constitute a formal financial statement, nor even an estimated one, they throw some light on a customer's financial circumstances and provide some guide to credit action.

Even more provoking are the cases of customers who fill out some details of the financial statement forms submitted to them but leave important queries unanswered. They may fail to state the amount of accounts receivable that are past due, or how their merchandise is valued, or whether any of their accounts payable are past due, or if any assets are assigned or pledged to secure liabilities, or whether there are contingent liabilities. In some instances a customer may actually lack such information; for example, he or his accountant may not have segregated overdue accounts receivable at the close of the accounting year. More often, however, a customer is well aware of the information but purposely fails to enter it on the supplier's financial statement form because of its unfavorable implications. If a credit manager overlooks such omissions, his analysis and conclusions will be equally defective. The customer, moreover, is encouraged to continue his deceitful habits.

The practice is growing, among credit managers, of sending to customers who have submitted deficient financial statements a "supplementary financial information form" (see Illustration 8-3) which requests the missing items of information. The customer may respond; in any case, he is impressed with the supplier's alertness and with the importance placed on the financial statement.

Fortunately for credit analysis work, the character of financial statements submitted by small business enterprises is steadily improving. Some of this advance is attributable to the school systems of the various states which have made the fundamentals of elementary business education a part of their required curricula. Social security and withholding tax reporting requirements have compelled many small businesses to adopt some sort of bookkeeping routine. In part the advance may also be credited to the increase in number of trained accountants whose services are now available, on reasonable terms, to small businesses. In part it must be attributed to thousands of credit managers who have sympathetically cooperated with their customers and encouraged them to establish bookkeeping systems that will not only produce the necessary credit information but also will place the customers' businesses upon sounder financial foundations.

### Lack of standardization

Financial statement analysis is largely based on comparison—comparison of an account's current financial statement with his prior ones and with those of other similarly circumstanced concerns in the same line of business. If the financial statements received by a credit manager are not constructed on identical patterns he cannot draw valid conclusions from such comparisons. Unfortunately, such standardized patterns are only partly developed. The general organization of balance sheet information is fairly well established. However, there is still considerable variation in the classification of particular items that are important in credit analysis. For example, instalment payments under a conditional sales contract or a chattel mortgage that will have to be made during the coming year are often included under fixed liabilities instead of under current liabilities. Investments of a nonliquid character may be listed as a current asset instead of under the heading "other assets."

If customers and their accountants always adhered to sound accounting practice, this difficulty of nonstandard and hence misleading statements would not exist. The long-term attack on the problem, therefore, is further improvement in the accounting education of business men and of some accountants. The immediate solution is the preparation of financial statement forms that will leave no room for ambiguity in the classification of balance sheet items. Forms prepared by individual suppliers for their customers are often defective in this respect. The standard forms prepared by the National Association of Credit Management are much better. If the customer answers them correctly, there is little room for uncertainty in the information the supplier's credit department receives.

## Accounting conventions

The great progress already made in accounting standardization has been accomplished in part through the development of certain accounting conventions relating to the valuation of assets and the classification of purchases between capital outlays and expenses. Standard procedures of inventory valuation, the various methods of determining inventory costs, and the formulas for calculating depreciation, are examples of these conventions.

These conventional techniques usually portray fairly a concern's financial position. But in individual cases and under certain circumstances they may produce a distorted and misleading picture. Cost-or-market valuation of inventories, for example, understates the realistic asset value of this item in a period of rapidly rising prices, whereas cost valuation overstates it when prices decline sharply. A straight-line method of depreciating machinery may not disclose the imminent obsolescence of some items.

A credit manager's knowledge of business conditions in his customers' lines may enable him to correct some but not all of these distortions. Whatever conclusions he derives from a financial statement analysis must accordingly be subject to qualification.

## Falsity

Submission of a false financial statement for credit purposes is punishable under both state and federal criminal law, as described later in this volume (Chapter 18). Prosecution of the makers of false financial statements is vigorous. Consequently this type of fraud is rare, and many credit managers never have to deal with it throughout their careers. But the possibility that a gang of credit racketeers may seek to victimize a supplier, or that one of his customers on the verge of bankruptcy may take the desperate step of falsifying his financial statement, is always present. It is often difficult to detect the fraud from the statement itself. In many cases, it is only discovered in a later bankruptcy. A credit manager should never assume that he will always be one of the lucky ones who will never be faced with this unpleasant issue.

### Auditor's certification

It is current practice for the banks to require an "auditor's certification" on the borrower's financial statement. Mercantile agencies do the same, wherever possible, with regard to the accounts on which they report; they usually state when they reproduce a balance sheet in their report whether or not it was audited. Credit managers who receive financial statements directly from their buyers attach considerable importance to this certification, which they regard as a confirmation that the statement figures may be relied upon, and as an avenue to further information.

The actual significance of the certification statement depends on the nature of the audit and the corresponding responsibility accepted by the accountant—both expressed in the wording of the certification. The following certification statement, for example, establishes a financial statement as the result of skilled and responsible work:

We have examined the balance sheet of the X Company as of _____ 19 __, and the related statements of income and surplus for the year then ended. Our examination was made in accordance with generally accepted auditing standards, and accordingly included such tests of the accounting records, and such other auditing procedures as we considered necessary in the circumstances.

In our opinion the accompanying balance sheet and statements of income and surplus present fairly the financial position of the X Company at _____ 19 __, and the results of its operations for the year then ended, in conformity with general accounting principles applied on a basis consistent with that of the preceding year.

Setting up standards for the wording and meaning of auditors' certifications has been a primary task of the American Institute of Certified Public Accountants. In its "Statement on Auditing Procedure No. 23" it formulates three requirements. (1) Whenever a C.P.A.'s name is associated with a financial statement, he must either give his opinion on the fairness of the statement, or indicate that he is unable to express an opinion and why. (2) His report shall follow one of four well-recognized forms, depending on circumstances. (3) He may give:

(a) an *unqualified opinion* where he has no reservations;

(b) a *qualified opinion* when he regards the statement as generally fair but disagrees with certain stated points;

(c) *no opinion*—if he has not devoted sufficient time and effort on the statement or if he takes exception to a substantial part of its contents; or

(d) a statement that he has *not made an audit,* if circumstances warrant it.[6]

---

[6] The American Institute of Certified Public Accountants checked on the effectiveness of Statement 23 for the period 1952-1954. Four-fifths of the financial statements in the sample conformed.

The credit profession watches with keen interest the progress that is being made in standardizing and safeguarding certification procedures. The reliability of financial statements on which credit managers base their judgments depends to a large extent on the success of such accounting endeavors.[7]

## OBTAINING FINANCIAL STATEMENTS

The financial statements which a mercantile agency obtains from a business are embodied in the agency report on this company. It may be *summarized* (see the Dun & Bradstreet Regular Report, Illustration 4-4), or *copied* (see the Dun & Bradstreet Analytical Report, Illustration 4-3), or reproduced by *photography* (see the National Credit Office Report, Illustration 5-1).

Even when their departments subscribe to a mercantile agency service most credit managers request financial statements directly from their customers for three reasons:

1. They may not draw reports regularly on all accounts.

2. A statement received directly from a customer may reach the credit manager much sooner than an agency report containing the same statement.

3. Asking a customer directly for his statement impresses him with the alertness of the supplier's credit department and gains his respect. It also opens the way to direct questions and answers on some statement items. This may be of particular importance in the case of a new account or a doubtful one.

Most buyers are accustomed to provide their suppliers with financial statements and do not resent the request for it.

### The financial statement form

Every customer of whom a financial statement is requested should be provided with a form on which the information may be entered. Otherwise many customers would not take the trouble to obtain forms on their own account or to write out the statement headings as well as the figures. Moreover, such statements would vary so widely as to classifications adopted and detail given that they would be useless for analytical purposes.

---

[7] In a resolution adopted at the 56th Credit Congress (1952) the National Association of Credit Management recognized the efforts made and stated: "The American Institute of Certified Public Accountants and various state societies have subscribed to certain procedures wherein the certification assumes responsibility for the method of evaluating assets and liabilities. This is welcomed as a step towards uniform, informative and reliable balance sheets, operating statements and accounting practices."

Many large suppliers, whose customers belong to a particular line of business, prepare and have printed financial statement forms adapted to the special financial circumstances of their customers. If such special forms have been carefully thought out so that they conform with the customers' accounting systems and elicit all needed details of financial information, there is everything to be said in favor of the practice. Many of these private financial statement forms, however, are inadequately planned. They may fail to check on whether customers' inventories contain goods on consignment. They may neglect to check upon the assignment of accounts receivable or the discount of notes and acceptances. Their format may also confuse customers more familiar with standard forms. It is, therefore, likely to help both supplier and customers if the former sends out one of the widely used financial statement forms printed and sold by the National Association of Credit Management (see Illustration 8-2).

No one standard financial statement form is appropriate for all classes of credit buyers. The detail needed to reflect the complicated financial structure of a large customer would be meaningless and confusing to a small one. A manufacturer's inventory should be subdivided into raw materials, work in process, and finished goods; no such subdivision is needed for the inventory of a wholesaler or retailer. Hence suppliers who sell to different classes of customers should use a selection of financial statement forms suited to the differing needs of these customers. The National Association of Credit Management offers several different forms in its series.

### Requesting a financial statement

Some suppliers provide their salesmen with financial statement forms, to be given to new customers on the occasion of taking a first order. The customer is told to fill out the form at his early convenience and mail it to the supplier's credit department. Many sales managers object, however, to such introduction of credit matters into sales interviews with new customers. Consequently the more common practice is for the request for a financial statement to be made by letter.

The financial statement letter to a new customer should combine a promotional effort with the request for the statement. It should open by welcoming the customer and thanking him for his order or inquiry. The request for financial statement information should be explained as customary. Complimentary phrases should be introduced wherever possible. This is also a good opportunity to ask for the previous financial statement in order to be able to compare figures; the customer may be flattered by this request if he is told that it is made to observe his progress. The following is an example of a type of letter for new customers that should promote good will while soliciting a financial statement:

Dear Mr. _____:

Thank you for your order of _____. It calls for a well-selected assortment of our merchandise. You will be pleasantly surprised when you discover what wonderful sales leaders these items are.

As you know, it is customary for our customers to provide us with their latest financial statements so that we can provide them with proper

---

Form 5W

Date_____19____

**FINANCIAL STATEMENT OF**_____

Kind of Business_____ Address _____

At Close of Business on_____19__ City_____ State_____

**ISSUED TO**_____ ←{ Name of firm asking for statement

[THIS FORM APPROVED AND PUBLISHED BY NATIONAL ASSOCIATION OF CREDIT MANAGEMENT]

For the purpose of obtaining merchandise from you on credit, or for the extension of credit, we make the following statement in writing, intending that you should rely thereon respecting our exact financial condition.

[PLEASE ANSWER ALL QUESTIONS. WHEN NO FIGURES ARE INSERTED, WRITE WORD "NONE"]

| ASSETS | Dollars | Cents | LIABILITIES | Dollars | Cents |
|---|---|---|---|---|---|
| **Cash In Bank** | | | Accounts Payable (for Merchandise) | | |
| On Hand | | | Notes & Acceptances Payable for Merchandise | | |
| **Accounts Receivable** | | | Owe to_____ Bank | | |
| (Amt. 60 Days Past Due $_____) | | | (When Due_____Secured) (Unsecured) | | |
| (Amt. Sold or Pledged $_____) | | | Income Taxes. Accrued | | |
| **Notes and Trade Acceptances Receivable** | | | Other Taxes. Including Sales Taxes. Accrued | | |
| (Amt. Sold or Pledged $_____) | | | Interest. Accrued | | |
| **Merchandise Inventory,** Not on Consignment or | | | Rental, Payrolls. etc.. Accrued | | |
| Conditional Sale, at Cost or Market whichever is lower. | | | Payables to Partners, Relatives. | | |
| (Amount Pledged $_____) | | | Other Current Liabilities (Describe) | | |
| **Other Current Assets** (Describe) | | | | | |
| | | | **TOTAL CURRENT LIABILITIES** | | |
| **TOTAL CURRENT ASSETS** | | | Mortgage on Land and Buildings | | |
| **Land and Buildings** (Depreciated Value) | | | Chattel Mortgage on Mdse. or Equipment | | |
| **Machinery, Fixtures and Equipment** (Depreciated Value) | | | Liens on Mdse. or Equipment | | |
| **Due from Officers or Non-Customers** | | | Other Liabilities. No Current (Describe) | | |
| **Other Assets** (Describe) | | | | | |
| | | | **TOTAL LIABILITIES** | | |
| | | | Net Worth or {Capital $ / Surplus $ } | | |
| **TOTAL ASSETS** | | | TOTAL NET WORTH AND LIABILITIES | | |

**BE SURE TO ANSWER ALL THESE QUESTIONS**

| | | INSURANCE CARRIED |
|---|---|---|
| Amount you are liable for as endorser, guarantor, surety $ | What books of Account do you keep? | Fire |
| Amount of delinquent taxes: Sales tax $_____Income tax $_____ Property tax $_____Other taxes $_____ | Date of latest inventory | Merchandise $_____ Furn. & Fixt. $_____ |
| Amount of merchandise held on consignment $ | Date of latest audit | Building $_____ Extended Coverage $_____ |
| Amount of machinery or equipment held under lease $ | Title to business premises is in name of | U & O $_____ |
| Amount of machinery or equipment under conditional sale $ | If premises leased state annual rental | Liability General $_____ Auto & Truck $_____ |
| Amount you pay per month on lease or conditional sale contract $ | Name of your bank(s) | Burglary $_____ Life for Benefit of Business $_____ |

**BUY FROM THE FOLLOWING FIRMS**

| NAMES | ADDRESSES | AMOUNT OWING |
|---|---|---|
| | | |
| | | |
| | | |
| | | |

The statement above and on the back of this form has been carefully read by the undersigned (both the printed and written matter), and is, to my knowledge, in all respects complete, accurate and truthful. It discloses to you the true state of my (our) financial condition on the_____day of_____19___ Since that time there has been no material unfavorable change in my (our) financial condition, and if any such change takes place I (we) will give you notice. Until such notice is given, you are to regard this as a continuing statement. **The figures submitted are not estimated. They have been taken from my (our) books and physical inventory taken as on date shown.**

Name of Individual or Firm_____
If Partnership. Name Partners } If Corporation. Name Officers }_____
How long established_____ Previous business experience_____ Where_____

Date of Signing Statement_____Street_____City_____State_____

Witness_____ Signed by_____
Residence Address of Witness_____ . Title_____
25M-1-60

NO ENVELOPE IS REQUIRED
JUST FOLD, STAMP, AND MAIL

ILLUSTRATION 8-2. Financial Statement Blank Prepared by the NACM

credit accommodation. Accordingly I am enclosing a financial statement form for you to fill out and mail back to me. It is a self-sealing type that needs no envelope, and our address and a stamp are already on it; just fill it out, drop it in the mailbox, and the postman will take care of the rest.

We are confident that this is the beginning of a long business relationship that will be pleasant and profitable for both of our companies.

Incidentally, could you also send us copies of one or two of your previous statements so that we may take full note of your recent progress?

Sincerely yours,

A different sort of letter should be devised to obtain financial statements from old customers—unless this is a regular annual routine and needs no particular explanation. Such requests may vary somewhat according to the customers' individual credit circumstances, but they should be alike in being promotionally complimentary. The following illustrates a financial statement letter of this type:

Dear Mr. _____:

On reviewing your ledger card recently, I was impressed by the growing volume of your purchases from us and your excellent record of payments. I take this opportunity to express our appreciation on both scores.

As you know, we like to follow our customers' progress through their financial statements as soon as these are available so that we may always be ready to advance them proper credit accommodation. Accordingly, I am enclosing a copy of our regular financial statement form for your accountant to fill out when the figures are ready.

Our best wishes for your continued success.

Very truly yours,

### Requests for supplementary financial statement information

When a credit manager receives a financial statement that omits needed items of information, he should write immediately to the customer, or to the accountant who prepared the statement, and ask for the necessary implementation. Otherwise the statement may be of little use for credit analysis. A follow-up request for missing figures, if properly formulated, should not cause resentment but should contribute to the respect which customers have for suppliers with alert credit departments.

A request to a customer for supplementary financial information should be made as impersonal as possible in order to avoid any implication that doubts exist about this particular buyer's financial position. A personal letter, accordingly, is not advisable. The better method is to use a mimeographed or printed request form that shows, on the face of it, that it has been prepared to cover questions arising from any incomplete financial statement and is not geared to this individual case. Illustration 8-3 is an example of such a form.

A request for supplementary information from a customer's accountant,

THE ABC CO.
17 W. 42ND STREET
NEW YORK CITY

. . . . . . . . . . . . . . . . . . . . . .

To . . . . . . . . . . . . . . . . . . . . . .
. . . . . . . . . . . . . . . . . . . . . . .
. . . . . . . . . . . . . . . . . . . . . . .
. . . . . . . . . . . . . . . . . . . . . . .

Gentlemen:

The ABC Co. takes seriously its obligation to provide its customers with the credit they need for profitable operation. So that we may fulfill this obligation effectively, we ask our customers' cooperation in providing us with certain details of financial statement information. Will you help us meet our credit obligation to you by supplying us, in addition to the financial statement you recently sent us, with the items of information checked below.

Where possible, please note your reply on this sheet and return it to us in the enclosed, self-addressed envelope.

Thank you.

THE ABC CO.

. . . . . . . . . . . . . . . . . . . . . . . . . . . . . . . . . . . . . . . . . . . . . . . . . . . . . . . . . .

___ 1. Date of financial statement
. . . . . . . . . . . . . . . . . . . . . .

___ 2. If an aging of your past-due accounts receivable is available, please send us a copy.

___ 3. Amount, if any, of raw material included in merchandise inventory $. . . . . . . . . .

___ 4. Amount, if any, of merchandise held on consignment $. . . . . . . .

___ 5. Specific nature of investments listed under "Current Assets"
. . . . . . . . . . . . . . . . . . . . . . . . .
. . . . . . . . . . . . . . . . . . . . . . . . .

___ 6. Specific items included under "Other Current Assets" . . . . . .
. . . . . . . . . . . . . . . . . . . . . . . . .

___ 7. Amount, if any, of past-due notes and acceptances payable $. . . . . . . . . .

___ 8. Amount, if any, of past-due accounts payable $. . . . . . . . .

___ 9. Amount, if any, of notes and accounts payable to officers, directors or stockholders $. . . . . . . . .

___10. Amount, if any, of installment payments due this year under conditional sales or chattel mortgages $. . . . . . . . .

___11. Amount, if any, of fixed liability maturing this year $. . . . . . . . .

___12. Provision for federal taxes $. . . . . . . . .

___13. Specific nature of "other liabilities" . . . . . . . . . . . . . . . . . . . . .
. . . . . . . . . . . . . . . . . . . . . . . . .

___14. Amount, if any, of notes and acceptances discounted or pledged for loans $. . . . . . . . .

___15. Amount, if any, of accounts, receivable discounted, assigned or pledged $. . . . . . . . .

___16. Amount of sales $. . . . . . . . .

___17. Proportion of sales made on credit or installment terms . . . . . . . . . .%

___18. Amount of purchases of materials or merchandise $. . . . . . .

___19. Contingent liabilities, if any
    Nature           Amount
. . . . . . . . . . . . . . . $. . . . . . . . . .
. . . . . . . . . . . . . . . $. . . . . . . . . .
. . . . . . . . . . . . . . . $. . . . . . . . . .

ILLUSTRATION 8-3.   Form for Obtaining Supplementary Financial Statement Information from a Customer

151

# PEPPERELL
### FOUNDED IN 1844
*Manufacturing Company*
INCORPORATED

*Executive Offices* 160 State Street, BOSTON

*Sales Offices* NEW YORK  BOSTON  CHICAGO  DALLAS  LOS ANGELES  ATLANTA

*Plants* BIDDEFORD, MAINE    LINDALE, GEORGIA    PEPPERELL, ALABAMA    LEWISTON, MAINE    FALL RIVER, MASS.

40 Worth Street, NEW YORK CITY 13

**CREDIT DEPARTMENT**

Gentlemen:

     Re:

The above concern has furnished us with a financial statement as of
, showing a Net Worth of

Will you be kind enough to answer the following questions in order
that we may be able to complete our credit files.

1. Are you a C. P. A.?
2. Did you prepare a certified statement?
3. How often do you audit this company's books?
4. Are all Accounts Receivable for merchandise sold and delivered
   to customers?
5. Did you verify Accounts Receivable by direct communication?
6. Did you age Accounts Receivable? ____ What portion, if any, is
   over four months old?
7. Have all bad Accounts Receivable been written off?
8. Did you supervise the taking of the inventory?
9. Have you verified all known liabilities by direct communication?
10. Have any Accounts Receivable, Merchandise or any other assets
    been assigned or pledged as collateral for advances or loans
    during the past year?*
11. Is the above net worth subject to reduction as a result of Federal,
    State, local taxes, renegotiation or any other contingencies?*

   * If affirmative, please give details on reverse side.

We would be grateful if you would let us have this information as soon
as possible.  An addressed envelope is enclosed for your convenience.

                        Very truly yours,

. . . . . . . . . . . . . .         Credit Department
Accountant's signature

ILLUSTRATION 8-4.   Form for Obtaining Supplementary Financial Statement Information from an Accountant

on the other hand, does not have to take into consideration the customer's
feelings in the same way as when he is being directly asked. Before an
accountant can accede to such a request, he must be duly authorized by
the customer. A credit manager may endeavor to obtain the desired information through a telephone call. Written communication is usually
preferred. Some credit departments have printed forms for supplemen-

tary inquiries addressed to accountants; an example is shown in Illustration 8-4. The accountant's verification form that is part of the financial statement included in National Credit Office reports is, in effect, a supplementary accountant's statement (see Illustration 5-2).

## SUPPLEMENTARY READINGS

See page 198 of this volume.

## REVIEW

1. What organizations first endeavored to obtain financial statements from buyers or borrowers? What was the next class of organizations to promote the giving of financial statements for credit purposes? What part did the National Association of Credit Management have in developing this practice?
2. Is it usual or unusual for a credit manager today to request a customer's financial statement? Are such requests customarily honored or refused?
3. How dependable is financial statement analysis as a technique for developing credit judgments?
4. In what ways is the closing date of a financial statement significant in interpreting the data it contains?
5. What is the balance sheet of a business? What is the profit-and-loss statement? Explain their importance in credit analysis.
6. What are the major balance sheet classifications of assets and liabilities? What is reported under each heading?
7. Why should notes payable to trade creditors, notes payable to banks and finance companies, and notes payable to officers and others be stated separately in a balance sheet?
8. What are "reserves," and what are "contingent liabilities"? How should the credit manager interpret such items?
9. What is the "net operating profit" of a business, and how is it detemined?
10. What profit and loss statement items are of primary interest to the credit manager?
11. What allowances and qualifications must a credit manager make with respect to the data of the financial statements he receives from customers?
12. What is the meaning of "auditor's certification" on the financial statement obtained from a customer?
13. Why does the National Association of Credit Management offer a choice of several financial statement forms?
14. Write form letters to be used by the credit manager of the ABC Plastic Materials Co. in asking for financial statements from new customers and from old ones.
15. What supplementary information may the credit manager receive from the accountant who has prepared the customer's financial statement?

# CHAPTER 9

## Comparative Financial Statement Analysis

If an adequate financial statement has been received from a customer, two types of analysis are possible:

1. Comparative analysis, whereby the customer's financial position is compared with that of other similarly circumstanced concerns in the same line of business.

2. Trend analysis, whereby the customer's financial position shown by his latest statement is compared with that shown in earlier statements.[1]

### USE OF COMPARATIVE
### FINANCIAL STATEMENT FORMS

If financial statement information on a customer is to be compared with that of other companies, or with its own financial pic-

---

[1] The nomenclature of financial statement analysis is still confused, and each writer on the subject must specify the meaning he gives to particular terms. In this and the two following chapters the term "comparative" analysis is used for the comparison of the financial statement ratios of a particular customer with ratios derived from similarly circumstanced firms in the same field of business. This is called by some writers "external" or "vertical" analysis. Comparison of the financial position of a customer as shown by his latest financial statement with his financial position according to earlier statements is here termed "trend" analysis. This is sometimes called "internal" or "horizontal" analysis.

ture for earlier years, the organization of the two financial statements must be identical. But identical financial statement forms may not be filled out identically by different customers; because of variant accounting practices, the figures reported under particular headings may not always have the same meaning. Some adjustment of the reported figures may be necessary before valid comparison can be made.

Many bank and mercantile credit managers who undertake analysis of their customers' statements use "comparative financial statement forms" to which the information in the customers' statements is transferred after adjustment has been made. Since these forms cover three or more years, trend analysis as well as comparative analysis is facilitated. Such a form may be a printed sheet or card which is kept in the customer's general credit department file. In some cases it is printed on the credit file folder. An example is shown in Illustration 9-1.

### Adjustments

If a customer's financial statement has been prepared in accordance with standard accounting practice, and a credit manager is satisfied that all balance sheet items appear under the proper headings, the financial statement figures may be transferred without modification to the comparative statement form. Often, however, two types of adjustments—reclassifying items and "shaving" specific figures—may have to be made.

Common reclassifications are eliminating such items as illiquid investments or loans to officers from "current assets" and including them in "other assets," and transferring items of instalment debt from "fixed liabilities" to "current liabilities." Such transfers, although they affect the calculation of the customer's net working capital and current ratios, do not change the totals of his assets and liabilities or his net worth.

Many credit managers find it necessary to shave or reduce asset items that they deem inflated in view of the true values behind them. They eliminate "good will," patents, and copyrights if these are given substantial asset value, except in cases where special circumstances warrant their retention. Investments in subsidiaries may be substantially written down if there is reason to believe that the book value given them exceeds a reasonable market price. If merchandise is valued at cost instead of the lower of cost or market values, a conservative-minded credit manager may lower the merchandise figure by some moderate proportion in a period of falling prices. If a substantial volume of past-due receivables is reported or suspected, particularly if the customer's receivables-turnover ratio is lower than normal, the figure for receivables may be shaved. Similarly, should a low inventory-turnover ratio indicate that the customer's merchandise may be overvalued or include "dead stock," the reported merchandise inventory figure may be lowered.

Name.................................... Acct. No. ..........
Address.........................................
.............................................
Business............................ Balance Sheet Date............

| | 19— | 19— | 19— | |
|---|---|---|---|---|
| *Assets* | | | | |
| Cash | | | | |
|   Bills and notes receivable | | | | |
|   Accounts receivable | | | | |
| Total receivables | | | | |
|   Raw materials | | | | |
|   Work in process | | | | |
|   Finished goods | | | | |
| Total merchandise | | | | |
| Other current assets | | | | |
|    TOTAL CURRENT ASSETS | | | | |
| Land | | | | |
| Buildings | | | | |
| Machinery, equipment, fixtures | | | | |
| Intangible assets | | | | |
| Other assets | | | | |
|    TOTAL ASSETS | | | | |
| *Liabilities* | | | | |
| Accounts payable | | | | |
| Bills and notes payable to trade | | | | |
| Notes payable to banks | | | | |
| Other current liabilities | | | | |
|   TOTAL CURRENT LIABILITIES | | | | |
| Fixed liabilities | | | | |
| Reserves | | | | |
| Other liabilities | | | | |
| NET WORTH | | | | |
|    TOTAL LIABILITIES | | | | |
| Sales | | | | |
| Credit sales | | | | |
| Net operating profit | | | | |
| *Ratios* | | | | |
| Current | | | | |
| Sales to merchandise | | | | |
| Credit sales to receivables | | | | |
| Sales to net worth | | | | |
| Net worth to current liabilities | | | | |

ILLUSTRATION 9-1.   Example of a Comparative Financial Statement Form

Shaving assets in these ways reduces not only particular assets and total assets, but also net worth, since the latter figure is the difference between the customer's assets and liabilities. This is the primary intent of such shaving, since if any asset items are inflated above their true values the figure for net worth is correspondingly exaggerated. As a result, the customer's net worth ratios, as well as his current ratio and the ratios involving the particular shaved assets, all become less favorable.

If a customer's assets figures are shaved as a preliminary to judging his financial position, it is advisable for a credit manager to make record of both the original financial statement figures and the adjusted ones. For this purpose two columns of his comparative financial statement sheet are used for each year's record instead of one. The first column contains the actual figures from the customer's statement, with at least the merchandise and receivables ratios calculated on the original figures. The adjusted figures and the ratios based on them are entered in the second column.

## COMPARATIVE ANALYSIS

The essence of comparative financial statement analysis is the calculation of certain ratios from a customer's financial statement, and their comparison with the corresponding "typical" ratios for similarly situated concerns in the same line of business. Such a comparison does not give any forecast of the customer's probable financial development. It does place his financial position, as of his last statement date, in the perspective of what is considered normal in his field.[2]

We shall first study the ratios used in comparative financial statement analysis. Then we shall proceed to the important subject of how the "typical" ratios used as a basis for the comparison are established. Comparative financial statement analysis for credit purposes commonly employs eight major ratios. They are: (1) sales divided by inventory ("inventory turnover"), (2) credit sales divided by receivables ("receivables turnover"), (3) sales divided by net worth ("net worth turnover"), (4) sales divided by expenses ("expense ratio"), (5) net profit divided by sales ("profit-on-sales ratio"), (6) net profit divided by net worth ("profit-on-invested-capital ratio"), (7) current liabilities divided by net worth ("current debt ratio"), and (8) current assets divided by current liabilities ("current ratio"). In addition, there are several other ratios which are useful in certain lines of credit work and under special customer circumstances.

---

[2] Comparative financial statement analysis is used in investment analysis and in various types of managerial analysis, but with differing ratio interpretations.

## Sales divided by inventory

The first ratio calculation a credit manager usually makes is that of net sales divided by inventory—commonly called "inventory turnover" or "merchandise turnover." It is presumed to indicate the number of times a customer "sells through" his inventory in the course of the year.

Actually, the figure resulting from dividing sales by the dollar amount of inventory is far from being a true statement of merchandise turnover. In the first place, the balance-sheet merchandise figure is reported at its cost price—or possibly even lower in the case of cost-or-market valuation —while the sales figure is determined by selling price. As a result, in the case of wholesalers and retailers, the true turnover ratio is overstated by a proportion which represents the mark-up of the goods; in the case of manufacturers, value added to the raw material and to work in process by manufacture is ignored. In the second place, the merchandise inventory which a firm has on its balance sheet date may be far from the average held through the year; in many cases, the balance sheet date which closes the accounting year is purposely set at a time in the year when inventory will be at its lowest. This circumstance causes the ratio of inventory to sales to exaggerate still further the true merchandise turnover for many concerns; in a few cases the ratio may understate the true turnover.[3]

However, while sales divided by merchandise may not give a true merchandise turnover ratio either for a particular customer or for the line of business to which he belongs, nonetheless it provides a ratio that is considered useful for comparative credit analysis. Merchandise mark-up is fairly uniform for any particular line of business. Therefore the circumstance that sales-price value is placed on sales and purchase-price value on inventories for both the particular customer and his line of business does not invalidate a comparison of their ratios. We may not be comparing their actual merchandise turnover ratios, but the two ratios compared are modified by the same unknown mark-up, and so the relationship remains the same.

Differences in inventory levels at varying times of the year are a factor which, if not allowed for, would invalidate comparison of the sales/ merchandise ratio between a particular customer and his line. "Typical" ratios used for comparison should be based on concerns in the line that have the same accounting years, and hence balance sheet dates, as the

---

[3] Note that retailers, in calculating their own "stock turns," avoid both of the above distortions by (1) either valuing inventory at the retail sales price or using "cost of goods sold" instead of "sales," and (2) using monthly average inventory figures. A store with a suitable accounting and inventory system can make these calculations from its own records. Customer financial statements submitted to suppliers or mercantile agencies usually do not provide the information necessary for such calculations.

particular customer under consideration. If typical ratios cannot be calculated on this basis, the credit manager should make an adjustment of the particular customer's merchandise figure, and of certain other balance sheet items, on the basis of his knowledge of the customer's line of business, so that the ratios derived from these figures are comparable with the available standard ratios.

The absolute sales/merchandise ratio of any customer is of no significance, because of the wide variation in merchandise turnover according to lines of business. A sales/merchandise ratio of seven would be high for a manufacturer of stoves; one of thirty would be low for a meat wholesaler.[4] The sales/merchandise ratio of any particular customer is significant only in relation to the normal or typical ratio for similarly-circumstanced concerns in his line of business. A customer ratio higher than the typical ratio may be a sign of a superior sales policy, or of superior purchasing and stock control—in either case an indication of good management. There is a presumption, moreover, that little of the inventory value reported is either obsolescent or overvalued. A customer sales/merchandise ratio substantially below the typical is generally taken as an indication of weak selling or purchasing policies, with the probability that the reported merchandise figure is overvalued or contains obsolescent stock, and should be shaved.

A low sales/merchandise ratio that cannot be reconciled with other features of a financial statement analysis may raise a suspicion of fraud in the preparation of the statement, through false overvaluing of the merchandise inventory.

### Credit sales divided by receivables

The next ratio which most credit managers analyze is that of credit sales divided by receivables—commonly termed the "receivables turnover" ratio.[5] It requires careful study because its components, like those of the merchandise turnover ratio, may have to be adjusted before they are usable in the ratio calculation.

A sales figure from a customer's financial statement can generally be used without modification to calculate "receivables turnover" if a manu-

---

[4] This and subsequent statements of normal or typical ratios are derived from Dun & Bradstreet's annual publication, "14 Important Ratios in 72 Lines of Business." See Illustration 9-2.

[5] Instead of a "receivables turnover" ratio, the Dun & Bradstreet typical ratios include an "average collection period." This is calculated by dividing credit sales by 365, then dividing the resulting figure of "average credit sales per day" into total receivables. Calculating the ratio this way has the advantage of making it directly comparable with a customer's credit terms. It has the disadvantage of involving an extra calculation—dividing by 365—in determining each customer's ratio. Any receivables turnover can be translated into an "average collection period" by dividing it into 365.

facturer or wholesaler sells only on credit terms—as the great majority do. Where sales are made both for cash and on credit, as is usual with retailers, the analyst should include nothing but *credit* sales in his computation. He can usually learn the approximate proportion of a customer's credit sales to his total sales from a mercantile agency report.

Receivables, the other component of this ratio, is a factual figure of what is owed to the customer. No valuation is involved. The volume of receivables at the balance sheet date, however, is not necessarily an average for the year. For seasonal businesses which close their accounting years at a date of low inventory following their heavy selling season, the balance sheet figure for receivables is likely to be considerably above the annual average, since the heavy volume of receivables accumulated during the selling period which reduced the inventory does not get paid off until a month or two later. Consequently a customer's ratio of credit sales divided by receivables rarely reflects his true receivables turnover for the year. However, as in the case of the sales/merchandise ratio, this does not impair the usefulness of the receivables turnover ratio for credit analysis. If the credit sales/receivables ratios of concerns in the same line of business and using the same accounting year are compared, the differences in their credit and collection policies will be validly reflected.

A higher-than-typical credit-sales/receivables ratio for a customer indicates that his credit or collection policy is abnormal for his line of business in one or more of the following three ways: (1) he grants shorter credit terms; (2) he has a larger proportion of discounting customers, possibly because he allows more generous cash discounts; (3) he applies a stricter or more effective collection policy. A lower-than-normal ratio would mean that he allows longer credit terms than is usual, or has fewer discounting customers, or has a poorer collection policy, or some combination of these possibilities. In any case, a low credit-sales/receivables ratio should be made the occasion for obtaining, if possible, an aging-of-accounts statement from the customer, in order to see how much ought properly to be shaved from his reported receivables before calculating his net worth and current ratios.

### Sales divided by net worth

A credit manager is always vitally interested in a customer's tangible net worth, after certain intangibles have been eliminated. It is the customer's own investment in his business, and constitutes the margin of protection to his creditors against shrinkage in the value of the business assets if the business incurs losses in the near future or if it has to be liquidated. The crucial question concerning a customer's net worth is whether this is adequate in relation to the magnitude of operations conducted. A valuable guide on this matter is the ratio of the customer's sales divided by its net worth, sometimes called the "net worth turnover." Incidentally, this ratio may also throw light on whether a net worth adequate to the size of the business is being effectively employed.

There is no absolute standard of a sound proportion of sales to net worth for all types of business. If an enterprise requires a heavy investment in fixed capital, it should be made in substantial part with the owner's money. Therefore such an enterprise should have a lower sales/net worth ratio than one operating without large fixed capital. A relatively low sales/net worth ratio would also be characteristic of a business with slow-moving inventory and hence substantial inventory investment in relation to sales. A business selling entirely on credit terms and accumulating large receivables would also need relatively more equity capital, and hence have a lower net worth turnover, than a cash-terms enterprise. Thus we find a sales/net worth ratio around 1.2 typical for petroleum producers and refiners, who have tremendous investments in land and equipment. A ratio around 1.9 is typical for furniture retailers selling largely on instalments, who must carry large inventories of merchandise and of instalment receivables. In contrast, net worth turnovers for lumber wholesalers range around 5.1; those for fruit and fresh produce wholesalers are around 10.1.

Small enterprises in any line of business customarily operate with smaller net worths, relative to their sales, than do their larger competitors. This is one of the reasons for the general consideration given to relative business size as a credit risk factor. It also reflects the circumstances that small businesses generally have relatively smaller investments in fixed assets than do larger ones, and that they have greater flexibility in their financial management.

The mere fact that the sales/net worth ratio of a customer is somewhat in excess of the normal for his type of company and line of business should not in itself be taken as a sign that he is doing too large a business on too little net worth and operating excessively on his creditors' funds. A moderately high net worth turnover may well be a sign of superior efficiency—the result of a highly geared sales policy, or efficient purchasing and collection management. But when the sales/net worth ratio of any business is double the normal, or higher, the credit manager has a warning sign.

Whether a high net worth turnover is attributable to "shoestring" operation or to superior efficiency may be checked to some extent by other ratios derived by financial statement analysis. If it is accompanied by high merchandise and receivables turnovers, and high profits on sales, the explanation is probably efficiency. If it is accompanied by a low ratio of net worth to current liabilities, as described below, the conclusion that the customer has insufficient net worth is confirmed. Such a "shoestring" business is vulnerable to every adverse business fluctuation and to extraneous circumstances that would not bother a more conservatively financed enterprise.

A low sales/net worth ratio, accompanied as it often is by a high net worth/debt ratio, may be comforting to the credit manager from one viewpoint. The business is obviously operating with an ample margin of net worth, and should it fail in the near future the creditors would not lose much, if anything, on their claims. But a net worth turnover ratio that is substantially below normal, particularly if it is accompanied by low merchandise and receivables turnover ratios, is a clear indication of poor management. Such a customer, if not already on the down grade, must before long lose ground before his better managed competitors. Losses will eat into his net worth, so that the present protection for his creditors will dwindle. He is still an acceptable credit risk, but must be carefully watched.

### Expense divided by sales

The so-called "expense ratio" has become a most important item in judging a credit situation, provided the supplier's credit manager is able to procure the expense figures from the customer. Without an income statement he is usually at a loss; but this financial document is being made available to him more and more frequently. Once he is in possession of a customer's expense figures, the question arises as to the "right" or "wrong" proportion they indicate relative to sales. Except for some re-tailing lines [6] there are no "typical" expense ratios that are generally acceptable. A credit manager therefore must make up his own "typical" ratios for the field, from the financial statements received from all of his customers in a given line.

A high expense ratio may be attributable to excessive expenses—high rents for stores, operating inefficiency, excessive compensation to owner-executives. It may also be due to lagging sales resulting from poor store location, sharp competition, unsound pricing, poor promotion or selling. In any case, an abnormally high ratio is likely to be a finger-post to serious long-range business weakness, and a warning to a credit manager to watch the account carefully.

### The profit ratios

High profit on sales and/or on net worth is not necessarily an indication of managerial effectiveness, nor are low profit ratios a sure sign of

---

[6] Dun & Bradstreet has published several "typical" operating ratios—total expenses, wages, owner's compensation, occupancy cost, bad debts, advertising expenses—for 41 lines of retail trade (see Illustration 9-3). Several trade associations have occupied themselves with this problem in their respective fields and so have some university bureaus of business research.

managerial failure. Extraneous circumstances may for a long or short period exercise stronger influence on the profit ratios than internal management. Or long-range policy may dictate short-term holding of profits at higher or lower levels than is normal for the line. Still, in most cases, these profit ratios provide a valuable pointer to the efficiency with which a customer's business is operated, although they may require interpretation.

Of the two profit ratios, profit/sales is considered the more valuable for credit analysis. Profit/net worth too often reflects net worth rather than profit factors—a "shoestring" enterprise, for example, might show a striking profit/net worth ratio without being particularly well run. Usually a high or low profit/sales ratio is confirmed by a similar profit/ net worth ratio. When they diverge an explanation should be sought; the explanation may be a valuable item of credit analysis information. Low profit/sales and a normal or high profit/net worth, for example, might point to a retailer conducting a good business on cut-price policies, or to a company not particularly effective in its basic business operation but deriving supplementary income from other sources, or to a not-too-efficient "shoestring" operator. Normal or high profit/sales combined with low profit/net worth might indicate a good operating enterprise with ultraconservative financing—a credit manager's happiest find.

### Current liabilities divided by net worth

A credit executive is interested in the fixed liabilities of a customer if there is substantial risk of insolvency in the near future. The fixed assets of the business should liquidate for something in excess of the fixed liabilities they probably secure, so that there may be some balance left over to divide among the current trade creditors.

In the case of a solvent customer, however, a credit manager is more interested in the current liabilities of the business. One point he wants to know, and will find in the "current liability" ratio—the relationship between current liability and net worth—is how the customer is financing his current operations. Is he relying on creditors' funds, or does he carry a reasonable share of his financing through equity capital?

Some credit managers calculate this "current liability" ratio by dividing net worth by current liabilities, others by dividing current liabilities by net worth. On the basis of the first procedure, the higher the ratio the better the customer's financial position; on the basis of the second procedure, soundness is indicated by a low ratio. We shall employ the second procedure—dividing current liabilities by net worth—since the Dun & Bradstreet "typical" ratios, which are frequently used for comparison, are so calculated.

There is considerable variation among lines of business as to the customary sharing of current financing between owner and creditors. For example, towards the end of the 1950's the current liabilities/net worth ratio for petroleum operators was typically 16 to 27 per cent, while for wine and liquor wholesalers it exceeded 100 per cent. A ratio of 30 to 40 per cent was common for a good many lines of business. Like all the other ratios, the "current liabilities" ratio for any customer becomes significant only when compared with what is typical for the line of business.

If the current liabilities/net worth ratio for a customer is substantially higher than the typical ratio for his line, he is being overfinanced by his creditors, and is a "shoestring operator" or is "trading on creditors' equity" as this situation is commonly described. If he is an energetic, capable operator, he may still be an acceptable credit risk and may develop into a sound large-volume purchaser. Should his financial statement *also* reveal poor merchandise or receivables turnover ratios, and particularly if the balance sheet or an interchange report shows that he is past due on any substantial part of his accounts payable, the credit manager has warning of a customer with an unhealthy financial condition.

### The "current" and "acid test" ratios

Comparative financial statement analysis for a long time gave major weight to the ratio of current assets divided by current liabilities, or even confined itself to this "current ratio." This was not unwarranted, since this ratio does reflect a number of factors that are crucial in determining a credit risk. To view this ratio comparison as the be-all and end-all of financial statement analysis was shortsighted, however; the pendulum is now swinging the other way, and many credit analysts treat the current ratio as a supplementary rather than a basic tool.

The more a customer operates his business with his own funds—*i.e.,* the greater his net worth in relation to his capital needs—the less will be his need of bank loans or of trade credit, the smaller will be his current liabilities in relation to his assets, current and other, and the higher will be his current ratio. A high current ratio may also be produced by aggressive selling that moves merchandise from the shelves soon after it has been received, by sound purchasing and stock control policies that prevent the accumulation of "dead" inventory and facilitate rapid clearing of liabilities, and by an effective credit and collection policy that prevents the "freezing" of substantial parts of the receivables asset. Any favorable element of financial or business management that reduces current assets less than current liabilities, or increases current assets more than current liabilities, tends to raise the current ratio.

Contrariwise, bad business or financial management lowers the current ratio. Poor sales, purchasing, or credit policies result in accumulated, slow-moving merchandise or receivables and necessitate a corresponding enlargement in the volume of current liabilities. So does excessive investment in fixed assets that absorb net worth which otherwise could finance current operations.

For a long time 2:1—two dollars of current assets to every dollar of current liabilities—was taken as an arbitrary standard for current ratio soundness. It is now recognized that normal or typical current ratios differ by lines of business, for differently circumstanced concerns in each line of business, and even from year to year according to business cycle developments. Whereas the typical current ratio towards the end of the 1950's averaged nearly 6 for dry goods retailers, for wine and liquor wholesalers it was 2. The giants in any business field commonly have current ratios many times higher than the small units in the line.

The so-called "acid test" or "quick" ratio is commonly applied as an adjunct to the current ratio. It divides cash plus receivables by current liabilities. The exclusion of merchandise inventory, it is claimed, provides a clearer picture of a customer's current operational liquidity. This may be of significance where substantial amounts of "dead" inventory distort the current ratio. Otherwise the "acid test" ratio has about the same importance—or lack of it—as the current ratio itself.

### Other ratios

Many other ratios, besides the eight studied above, can be calculated from financial statement figures. Some would be of no use at all for credit purposes. Others may provide useful additional information on particular types of customers.

*Receivables divided by inventory.* The more efficient a company's selling or purchasing policies, the larger will be the ratio of its receivables to its inventory. Receivables are the more liquid type of current asset. Hence if this ratio is high it is a favorable credit point. Similar information is derived, however, from the merchandise turnover ratio.

*Net working capital divided by inventory.* Net working capital is the excess of current assets over current liabilities. This ratio is favorably influenced, therefore, by either a low level of current liabilities which increases the working capital figure, or by a low level of merchandise inventory relative to other current assets. The current ratio including the "acid test" and the merchandise turnover ratio, taken separately, may indicate more clearly what favorable or unfavorable factors are involved. But many credit analysts prefer the net working capital/merchandise ratio.

*Sales divided by net working capital,* or the "net working capital turnover" ratio. Where investment in fixed assets is too large, the resultant freezing of a substantial part of net worth may compel heavy dependence on current liabilities, and so produce a low net working capital. This situation will be reflected by a disproportionately high sales/working capital ratio where the sales/net worth ratio might otherwise indicate normalcy. This ratio is sometimes useful as an alternative to the fixed-assets ratios surveyed below.

*Sales divided by fixed assets.* A low ratio of sales to fixed assets would indicate excessive investment in, or inefficient use of, land, machinery, and other equipment. This ratio may be a useful check upon enterprises that normally must operate with substantial fixed assets.

*Fixed assets divided by net worth.* A high ratio of fixed assets to net worth may indicate either excessive investment in fixed assets or inadequate net worth for an otherwise balanced enterprise. This ratio became a significant supplementary tool in credit analysis after World War II. Investment in fixed assets was to some extent favored by war and postwar inflationary developments; some large establishments may have been prompted to buy more real estate and equipment under these circumstances. Very frequent, however, were the cases where small retailers, particularly the ones that had started business only a short time before, began putting attractive fixtures into their stores and using up more funds than they could afford. It is not surprising, therefore, to find that in many recent bankruptcy cases, large proportions of the tangible net worth were tied up in fixed assets. A high fixed-assets ratio is certainly a warning signal,[7] and it is understandable that many credit managers have made this ratio an important element of their credit analysis.

*Total debt divided by net worth.* Fixed assets, if not excessive, do not influence the working capital positions of solvent going concerns. Hence, for them the total debt/net worth ratio has little credit significance. But if other ratios point to financial weakness and if a large deferred liability is present, a total debt ratio excessively high for the line or type of business underlines the indicated weak condition.

*Funded (long-term) debt divided by net working capital.* In some ways this supplementary ratio is deemed to be more helpful to credit analysis than the preceding one based on total debt. Long-term obligations may safely exceed the net working capital in many lines of business. In connection with other factors reflecting a doubtful financial position, however, a high funded debt/net working-capital ratio may become significant.

---

[7] In some lines, where heavy investment in expensive equipment is normal, a *low* fixed asset ratio might be an adverse indication. It might reflect a situation requiring expensive rental of equipment or profit-consuming subcontracting.

## "TYPICAL" RATIOS

Throughout the preceding discussion of ratio analysis, it was emphasized that the absolute ratios derived from a particular financial statement are meaningless. Only by comparison with "typical" or "normal" ratios of some sort do they throw light upon the relative financial position of the customer and his status as a credit risk.

Where can a credit manager find typical ratios for a customer's line of business? He has two sources. If he is fortunate he may find that "standard" ratios [8] have been published for his customer's business line. More often he will find himself compelled to calculate appropriate "typical" ratios from his own files, provided he has enough comparable customers to make such calculation possible.

### Currently available standard ratios

A credit executive can obtain standard ratios from various sources. Dun & Bradstreet has published annually since 1931 tables containing 14 comparative ratios for 72 lines of business (see Illustration 9-2). These are based upon the financial statements of several thousand enterprises with net worths above $75,000. Dun & Bradstreet has also published, at irregular intervals, tables containing ten standard "operating" ratios for 41 retail lines (see Illustration 9-3). The Robert Morris Associates calculate a series of ten comparative ratios widely used by bank loan officers. The Federal Trade Commission and the Securities and Exchange Commission publish quarterly summary operating ratios for manufacturing, wholesaling, and retailing corporations. A number of trade associations have upon occasion published studies of standard ratios for the lines of business served by their members.

Most of the standard ratios are the median figures of the ratio ranges for the business fields covered; in the Dun & Bradstreet comparative ratios, the first and third interquartile figures are also given. These median ratios are acceptable as roughly "typical" or "normal" for their *lines of business*. The difficulty is that this is too broad a base on which to calculate a trade "typical" ratio that will be a safe guide in comparative financial statement analysis. Within each business line, ratio ranges may differ substantially for subgroups determined by such factors as size of the business unit, location, type or grade of product manufactured or sold, whether the concern operates in owned or rented premises, and, in the case of retail stores, whether sales are primarily for cash, on charge account, or on instalment terms. "Typical" ratios for such subgroups,

---

[8] The term "standard" is applied to a *published* calculated "typical" financial statement analysis ratio for a line of business.

Upper Quartile
MEDIAN
Lower Quartile

| Line of Business (and number of concerns reporting) | Current assets to current debt (Times) | Net profits on net sales (Per cent) | Net profits on tangible net worth (Per cent) | Net profits on net working capital (Per cent) | Net sales to tangible net worth (Times) | Net sales to net working capital (Times) | Collection period (Days) | Net sales to inventory (Times) | Fixed assets to tangible net worth (Per cent) | Current debt to tangible net worth (Per cent) | Total debt to tangible net worth (Per cent) | Inventory to net working capital (Per cent) | Current debt to inventory (Per cent) | Funded debts to net working capital (Per cent) |
|---|---|---|---|---|---|---|---|---|---|---|---|---|---|---|
| Airplane Parts and Accessories (42) | 3.49 / 2.14 / 1.47 | 4.59 / 2.65 / 1.09 | 12.24 / 7.60 / 4.25 | 24.28 / 12.73 / 6.30 | 4.30 / 3.23 / 2.11 | 7.72 / 4.98 / 3.57 | 34 / 56 / 61 | 7.4 / 4.9 / 3.3 | 30.3 / 40.6 / 55.7 | 22.6 / 59.7 / 118.9 | 47.2 / 68.0 / 138.0 | 55.3 / 84.8 / 157.5 | 68.2 / 88.3 / 137.0 | 12.7 / 23.2 / 47.4 |
| Automobile Parts and Accessories (74) | 3.62 / 2.69 / 1.88 | 5.88 / 3.23 / 1.63 | 15.21 / 8.50 / 4.54 | 25.89 / 14.14 / 7.52 | 3.66 / 2.59 / 2.22 | 7.40 / 4.65 / 3.35 | 33 / 42 / 49 | 7.8 / 6.4 / 4.1 | 24.6 / 36.8 / 56.4 | 22.8 / 32.8 / 69.2 | 31.7 / 56.3 / 105.6 | 55.1 / 82.7 / 127.8 | 58.2 / 94.7 / 127.2 | 8.6 / 35.0 / 59.7 |
| Bedsprings and Mattresses (62) | 6.32 / 3.50 / 2.01 | 3.24 / 1.74 / 0.17 | 8.87 / 5.39 / 1.25 | 13.36 / 8.37 / 2.44 | 5.53 / 2.76 / 2.36 | 7.75 / 6.29 / 4.73 | 26 / 35 / 48 | 10.0 / 8.1 / 6.0 | 15.1 / 22.8 / 40.9 | 14.6 / 23.3 / 54.4 | 33.3 / 62.2 / 89.5 | 46.2 / 68.4 / 90.9 | 45.4 / 63.0 / 108.3 | 8.8 / 23.9 / 39.1 |
| Bolts, Screws, Nuts and Nails (56) | 4.04 / 2.96 / 1.82 | 6.19 / 3.48 / 1.78 | 16.69 / 10.91 / 3.46 | 27.13 / 18.22 / 11.22 | 4.42 / 2.52 / 1.77 | 8.86 / 4.62 / 3.28 | 25 / 31 / 37 | 9.7 / 6.3 / 5.0 | 37.5 / 56.4 / 73.1 | 19.7 / 29.2 / 51.8 | 33.2 / 52.2 / 85.5 | 61.8 / 83.4 / 110.2 | 48.0 / 76.8 / 130.2 | 13.6 / 35.7 / 64.0 |
| Brewers (34) | 3.22 / 2.34 / 1.54 | 4.89 / 3.63 / 0.08† | 14.52 / 7.78 / 0.05† | 42.93 / 28.00 / 0.78 | 3.00 / 2.35 / 1.92 | 9.77 / 8.62 / 6.49 | 12 / 18 / 24 | 21.7 / 16.7 / 11.4 | 61.1 / 77.0 / 104.7 | 13.6 / 23.3 / 38.5 | 35.5 / 48.1 / 92.6 | 38.6 / 53.2 / 80.6 | 97.8 / 128.6 / 207.2 | 34.5 / 65.6 / 190.8 |
| Chemicals, Industrial (67) | 3.79 / 2.66 / 1.86 | 6.91 / 4.54 / 3.04 | 15.96 / 11.07 / 5.91 | 40.04 / 22.10 / 10.94 | 3.25 / 2.29 / 1.58 | 7.36 / 4.26 / 2.72 | 32 / 40 / 46 | 9.7 / 7.1 / 4.9 | 32.2 / 58.0 / 76.3 | 19.6 / 29.3 / 54.2 | 49.8 / 65.2 / 109.7 | 44.2 / 61.5 / 93.3 | 72.0 / 91.9 / 135.9 | 31.9 / 54.4 / 98.2 |
| Coats and Suits, Men's and Boys' (190) | 3.49 / 2.15 / 1.67 | 1.91 / 1.05 / 0.58 | 9.20 / 5.06 / 2.84 | 11.15 / 6.07 / 3.02 | 6.80 / 4.86 / 2.71 | 7.53 / 5.13 / 3.04 | 27 / 48 / 77 | 6.5 / 5.2 / 4.3 | 2.5 / 6.6 / 15.8 | 35.2 / 71.9 / 73.1 | 68.2 / 134.4 / 206.1 | 55.9 / 84.2 / 128.1 | 65.1 / 93.0 / 133.4 | 6.3 / 16.3 / 48.0 |
| Coats and Suits, Women's (85) | 2.79 / 1.83 / 1.47 | 1.87 / 0.69 / 0.22 | 14.40 / 6.65 / 3.00 | 15.98 / 8.20 / 3.68 | 12.30 / 6.50 / 5.04 | 13.53 / 9.23 / 6.22 | 31 / 45 / 52 | 16.4 / 9.5 / 5.0 | 3.6 / 7.4 / 15.3 | 49.8 / 93.7 / 158.0 | 84.1 / 141.2 / 196.7 | 57.9 / 88.3 / 123.1 | 91.2 / 132.3 / 220.5 | 10.8 / 29.9 / 56.9 |
| Confectionery (41) | 3.83 / 2.97 / 2.25 | 3.60 / 1.93 / 0.75 | 10.81 / 6.54 / 2.53 | 22.60 / 11.45 / 3.72 | 4.61 / 2.83 / 2.19 | 10.61 / 6.45 / 4.71 | 12 / 19 / 38 | 18.1 / 8.5 / 6.5 | 28.8 / 43.2 / 56.2 | 19.7 / 30.2 / 37.6 | 36.2 / 42.8 / 61.6 | 48.6 / 77.0 / 98.9 | 52.6 / 74.8 / 124.1 | 13.5 / 35.7 / 58.3 |
| Contractors, Building Construction (159) | 2.77 / 1.81 / 1.35 | 3.24 / 1.33 / 0.33 | 13.42 / 7.66 / 3.27 | 21.35 / 12.45 / 4.18 | 8.64 / 5.85 / 2.70 | 14.40 / 8.49 / 6.03 | * / * / * | * / * / * | 8.8 / 20.4 / 35.1 | 34.8 / 75.7 / 165.4 | 53.0 / 120.0 / 220.2 | * / * / * | * / * / * | 9.9 / 21.8 / 49.5 |

†Loss. *Building construction contractors, and electrical contractors have no inventories in the credit sense of the term. Building construction contractors only carry materials such as lumber, bricks, tile, cement, structural steel, and building equipment to complete particular jobs on which they are working. Electrical contractors carry electrical equipment and supplies to complete particular jobs on which they are working. Concerns operating in these lines generally have no customary selling terms, each contract being a special job for which individual terms are arranged.

ILLUSTRATION 9-2. Excerpt from Dun & Bradstreet, "14 Important Ratios in 72 Lines of Business"

rather than for general business lines, are needed for truly effective comparative ratio analysis.

Standard ratios have a second weakness which is difficult, if not impossible, to remedy. They are in many cases based on the financial reports of concerns with different balance sheet dates. As we noted above, the volumes of accounts receivable, merchandise, and current liabilities for seasonal businesses may vary widely from month to month. Ratios involving these items will vary accordingly, for a line of business as well as for an individual concern, according to the balance sheet dates involved. Standard ratios for a seasonal line of business calculated from financial statements with different balance sheet dates cannot be representative, except by chance, for the particular balance sheet date of any individual concern.

A third weakness is the derivation of standard ratios from financial statements based on differing accounting procedures. Some statements may base inventories on LIFO, some on FIFO. The first method—"last-in-first-out"—inflates the dollar value of inventories in inflationary periods and deflates them in deflationary periods. FIFO—"first-in-first-out"—produces the opposite distortion. Differing depreciation and reserve practices produce differing asset and liability results. Standard ratios derived from statements based on divergent accounting procedures may or may not be fairly representative for a business line.

Finally, it should be noted that financial statement relationships for nearly all lines of business and subgroups vary substantially with year-to-year changes in general business conditions and the special year-to-year changes in the circumstances of particular lines of business. For example, from 1955 through 1959 the trend in typical current ratios for manufacturers of industrial machinery was upward; it was slightly downward for furniture stores and grocery wholesalers during this period. Most currently published series of standard ratios are not available to credit managers until a year or more after the financial statements on which they are based were issued. In periods of rapid economic change, credit managers must accordingly allow for possible obsolescence of their standard ratios. This is even more relevant when such ratios are calculated at longer than annual intervals.

### Calculated "typical" ratios

Available standard ratios are sadly deficient in many ways, but they have their usefulness within a limited scope of applicability. The credit manager, therefore, should not discard them but should try to remedy their imperfections. By long experience in his field of business he

ILLUSTRATION 9-3.  Operating Ratios

SELECTED
OPERATING
EXPENSE

| LINE OF RETAIL TRADE | Year | Cost of Goods Sold | Gross Margin | Total Expense | Net Operating Profit | Owners' Compensation | Employees' Wages | Occupancy Cost |
|---|---|---|---|---|---|---|---|---|
| | | PER CENT | PER CENT | PER CENT | PER CENT | PER CENT | PER CENT | PER CENT |
| Appliance-Radio-Television Dealers........ | 1958 | 64.5 | 35.5 | 34.4 | 1.1 | 3.1 | 15.6 | 2.5 |
| Auto Accessory and Parts Stores.......... | 1955 | 65.6 | 34.4 | 31.7 | 2.7 | 10.5 | 9.8 | 4.7 |
| Auto Dealers............................ | 1958 | 85.1 | 14.9 | 14.7 | 0.2 | — 7.5V — | | 1.2 |
| Bakeries................................ | 1955 | 58.1 | 41.9 | 38.3 | 3.6 | 10.6 | 11.3* | 6.1 |
| Bars and Taverns........................ | 1953 | 54.2 | 45.8 | 43.4 | 2.4 | 10.9 | 15.5 | 6.8 |
| Book Stores............................. | 1954 | 61.9 | 38.1 | 35.1 | 3.0 | 9.2 | 6.9 | 6.7 |
| Camera and Photographic Supply Stores..... | 1954 | 69.1 | 30.9 | 28.5 | 2.4 | 9.8 | 6.7 | 4.8 |
| Candy, Nut and Confectionery Stores....... | 1955 | 64.2 | 35.8 | 35.4 | 0.4 | 13.9 | 6.3* | 8.5 |
| Children's and Infants' Wear Stores........ | 1957 | 67.5 | 32.5 | 30.8 | 1.7 | 9.4 | 7.2 | 6.9 |
| Department Stores§....................... | 1958 | 68.1 | 31.9 | 31.3 | 0.6 | — 18.3 — | | 2.9 |
| Drug Stores............................. | 1958 | 65.3 | 34.7 | 29.5 | 5.2 | 8.0 | 11.2 | 2.2R |
| Dry Goods and General Merchandise Stores. | 1957 | 70.5 | 29.5 | 27.6 | 1.9 | 8.6 | 8.6 | 4.5 |
| Family Clothing Stores.................... | 1956 | 69.4 | 30.6 | 27.9 | 2.7 | 9.4 | 7.7 | 4.2 |
| Farm Equipment Dealers.................. | 1958 | 82.5 | 17.5 | 14.2 | 3.3 | 2.2† | 4.3* | ** |
| Farm Supply Stores...................... | 1956 | 84.1 | 15.9 | 14.4 | 1.5 | 4.2 | 4.8 | 1.6 |
| Floor Coverings Stores.................... | 1954 | 64.3 | 35.7 | 34.0 | 1.7 | 9.0 | 12.4 | 4.5 |
| Florists................................. | 1953 | 52.6 | 47.4 | 44.1 | 3.3 | 12.6 | 11.7 | 7.0 |
| Furniture Stores§........................ | 1958 | 61.6 | 38.4 | 37.9 | 0.5 | — 21.0 — | | 6.2 |
| Gasoline Service Stations................. | 1956 | 76.8 | 23.2 | 22.1 | 1.1 | 6.3 | 8.1 | 4.0 |
| Gift, Novelty and Souvenir Stores......... | 1957 | 60.0 | 40.0 | 38.1 | 1.9 | 13.8 | 7.0 | 8.7 |
| Grocery Stores.......................... | 1952 | 84.1 | 15.9 | 14.4 | 1.5 | 6.0 | 3.9 | 2.7 |
| Grocery and Meat Stores................. | 1950 | 83.7 | 16.3 | 14.3 | 2.0 | 3.7 | 5.4 | 1.9 |
| Hardware Stores........................ | 1958 | 69.5 | 30.5 | 29.5 | 1.0 | 8.1† | 10.6 | 3.7 |
| Jewelry Stores (Cash and Open Credit)...... | 1953 | 55.6 | 44.4 | 40.7 | 3.7 | 15.3 | 8.9 | 7.4 |
| Jewelry Stores (Installment Credit)......... | 1953 | 52.5 | 47.5 | 41.7 | 5.8 | 10.1 | 12.3 | 6.9 |
| Juvenile Furniture Stores................. | 1954 | 66.6 | 33.4 | 30.2 | 3.2 | 10.0 | 6.1 | 6.8 |
| Liquor Stores (Package).................. | 1955 | 80.3 | 19.7 | 17.1 | 2.6 | 7.6 | 2.9 | 2.9 |
| Lumber Dealers......................... | 1955 | 75.5 | 24.5 | 21.1 | 3.4 | 5.5 | 8.7 | 1.8 |
| Meat Markets........................... | 1954 | 79.3 | 20.7 | 19.3 | 1.4 | 6.8 | 6.4 | 2.3 |
| Men's Furnishings Stores................. | 1952 | 67.2 | 32.8 | 29.3 | 3.5 | 9.8 | 6.5 | 6.4 |
| Men's Wear Stores...................... | 1958 | 65.5 | 34.5X | 32.1X | 2.3X | 7.0 | 11.0 | 2.9R |
| Music Stores............................ | 1956 | 64.2 | 35.8 | 33.3 | 2.5 | 9.6 | 9.2 | 5.2 |
| Office Supply and Equipment Dealers....... | 1958 | 64.7 | 35.3 | 32.8 | 2.5 | 4.3† | 18.5 | 3.0 |
| Paint and Wallpaper Stores............... | 1956 | 66.9 | 33.1 | 30.1 | 3.0 | 11.4 | 6.9 | 4.9 |
| Restaurants............................. | 1950 | 52.7 | 47.3 | 44.0 | 3.3 | 7.9 | 21.8 | 6.7 |
| Shoe Stores (Family)..................... | 1958 | 63.1 | 36.9 | 33.1 | 3.8 | 10.1† | 8.6 | 4.0R |
| Sporting Goods Stores.................... | 1953 | 71.4 | 28.6 | 26.6 | 2.0 | 9.3 | 5.4 | 5.1 |
| Toy Dealers............................. | 1958 | 64.2 | 35.8 | 24.4S | 11.4S | 0.0S | 8.2 | 7.8 |
| Women's Accessory and Specialty Stores.... | 1954 | 66.3 | 33.7 | 31.5 | 2.2 | 11.2 | 5.8 | 7.5 |
| Women's Ready-to-Wear Stores............ | 1953 | 67.7 | 32.3 | 29.4 | 2.9 | 8.2 | 8.8 | 5.4 |
| Women's Wear Stores§................... | 1958 | 64.5 | 35.5 | 34.5 | 1.0 | — 18.4 — | | 3.8 |

The bracketed ratios are based on net sales

* Does not include manufacturing labor.   ** Not available.   R—Rent only.   † Salaries of owners and managers
S—Before owners' salaries were drawn.   § Ratios shown are for stores in the following volume groups: department stores with

| Adver-tising | Bad Debts | Inventory Turnover Per Year | | | SOURCE OF SURVEY |
|---|---|---|---|---|---|
| PER CENT | PER CENT | TIMES | | | |

The ratios compiled by DUN & BRADSTREET, INC., may be reproduced or used publicly with credit to DUN & BRADSTREET, INC. The ratios compiled by others are provided through the courtesy of the compilers and cannot be included in published material or used publicly without permission of the compilers.

| Adver-tising | Bad Debts | Inventory Turnover | | | SOURCE OF SURVEY |
|---|---|---|---|---|---|
| 2.8 | 0.7 | 4.6 | . | . | National Appliance and Radio-Tv Dealers Association, 1141 Merchandise Mart, Chicago 54, Ill. |
| 1.2 | 0.1 | 3.9 | . | . | Dun & Bradstreet, Inc., New York, N. Y. |
| 0.8 | ** | ** | . | . | National Automobile Dealers Association, 2000 K Street N.W., Washington 6, D. C. |
| 0.6 | ** | 18.7 | . | . | Dun & Bradstreet, Inc., New York, N. Y. |
| 0.7 | ** | 13.5 | . | . | Dun & Bradstreet, Inc., New York, N. Y. |
| 1.7 | ** | 3.3 | . | . | American Booksellers Association, Inc., 175 Fifth Ave., New York 18, N. Y. |
| 1.9 | 0.0 | 3.2 | . | . | Dun & Bradstreet, Inc., New York, N. Y. |
| 0.3 | ** | 11.8 | . | . | Dun & Bradstreet, Inc., New York, N. Y. |
| 1.3 | 0.0 | 2.6 | . | . | Dun & Bradstreet, Inc., New York, N. Y. |
| 1.7 | 0.2 | 2.5 | . | . | Bureau of Business Research Bulletin No. 155, Harvard University, Graduate School of Business Administration, Soldiers Field 63, Boston, Mass. |
| ** | ** | 3.8 | . | . | Eli Lilly and Company, Indianapolis 6, Ind. |
| 1.3 | 0.0 | 2.4 | . | . | Dun & Bradstreet, Inc., New York, N. Y. |
| 1.5 | 0.0 | 2.3 | . | . | Dun & Bradstreet, Inc., New York, N. Y. |
| 0.6 | 0.2 | 2.8 | . | . | National Retail Farm Equipment Association, 2340 Hampton, St. Louis 10, Mo. |
| 0.3 | 0.1 | 14.2 | . | . | Dun & Bradstreet, Inc., New York, N. Y. |
| 1.8 | 0.0 | 3.7 | . | . | Dun & Bradstreet, Inc., New York, N. Y. |
| 1.8 | 0.1 | 11.8 | . | . | Dun & Bradstreet, Inc., New York, N. Y. |
| 5.2 | 1.0 | 2.6 | . | . | National Retail Furniture Association, 666 Lake Shore Dr., Chicago 11, Ill. |
| 0.5 | 0.0 | 21.3 | . | . | Dun & Bradstreet, Inc., New York, N. Y. |
| 1.2 | ** | 2.4 | . | . | Dun & Bradstreet, Inc., New York, N. Y. |
| 0.1 | 0.0 | 13.6 | . | . | Dun & Bradstreet, Inc., New York, N. Y. |
| 0.4 | ** | 17.2 | . | . | Dun & Bradstreet, Inc., New York, N. Y. |
| 1.6 | 0.2 | 2.0 | . | . | National Retail Hardware Association, 964 North Pennsylvania St., Indianapolis 4, Ind. |
| 2.2 | 0.0 | 1.2 | . | . | Dun & Bradstreet, Inc., New York, N. Y. |
| 3.4 | 1.7 | 1.4 | . | . | Dun & Bradstreet, Inc., New York, N. Y. |
| 2.6 | 0.0 | 3.4 | . | . | Dun & Bradstreet, Inc., New York, N. Y. |
| 0.3 | ** | 5.9 | . | . | Dun & Bradstreet, Inc., New York, N. Y. |
| 0.7 | 0.3 | 4.3 | . | . | Dun & Bradstreet, Inc., New York, N. Y. |
| 0.2 | 0.0 | 53.3 | . | . | Dun & Bradstreet, Inc., New York, N. Y. |
| 1.3 | 0.0 | 2.1 | . | . | Dun & Bradstreet, Inc., New York, N. Y. |
| 2.8 | 0.3 | 2.4 | . | . | New York University on Grant from MEN'S WEAR MAGAZINE, 7 E. 12th St., New York, N. Y., July 24, 1959. |
| 2.1 | 0.0 | 3.0 | . | . | Dun & Bradstreet, Inc., New York, N. Y. |
| 1.2 | 0.2 | 3.0 | . | . | National Stationery and Office Equipment Association, 740 Investment Bldg., Washington 5, D. C. |
| 1.4 | 0.2 | 3.2 | . | . | Dun & Bradstreet, Inc., New York, N. Y. |
| 0.5 | ** | 35.5 | . | . | Dun & Bradstreet, Inc., New York, N. Y. |
| 2.9 | ** | 2.0 | . | . | Washington University, St. Louis on Grant from MEN'S WEAR MAGAZINE, 7 E. 12th St. New York, N. Y., July 24, 1959. |
| 1.7 | 0.0 | 2.5 | . | . | Dun & Bradstreet, Inc., New York, N. Y. |
| 2.7 | ** | 3.1 | . | . | PLAYTHINGS Magazine, 71 W. 23rd St., New York 10, N. Y. |
| 1.0 | 0.0 | 2.6 | . | . | Dun & Bradstreet, Inc., New York, N. Y. |
| 1.3 | 0.0 | 4.1 | . | . | Dun & Bradstreet, Inc., New York, N. Y. |
| 2.6 | 0.3 | 4.5 | . | . | Bureau of Business Research Bulletin No. 155, Harvard University, Graduate School of Business Administration, Soldiers Field 63, Boston, Mass. |

X—Total expense plus net profit does not equal gross margin.   V—Does not include mechanics' wages.

annual sales volume under $250,000; furniture stores between $250,000 and $500,000; women's wear stores under $250,000.

usually knows what is "typical" for individual concerns in the line, and he can accordingly modify the published ratios. To a certain extent he will be able to arrange them to suit his needs. He may also attempt to bring them up to date in periods of strongly fluctuating business conditions when they are apt to be out of focus already by the time they are issued. In this way he is cooperating with the institutions that prepare such ratios and are as eager to improve them as the credit managers who want to be able to use them.

Concerns that have a considerable number of customers in a particular business line can do better than merely modify or update published standard ratios on the basis of their empirical knowledge of the customer line. For any group of fifteen or more comparable customers (reasonably related in type of operation and size, and with the same accounting periods) for which he has financial statements, either from mercantile agency reports or received directly, a credit manager can calculate his own "typical" ratios. Even so small a number as fifteen, if truly comparable, may provide comparative ratios that may be more reliable, for a company selling to a particular class of customers, than any published set of standard ratios that does not relate specifically to that class. If the number runs to scores or hundreds, the probability of superior reliability is greatly enhanced.

A credit manager calculating his own "typical" comparative ratios should not let himself fall into the trap of using arithmetic averages, particularly if there is significant variation among his customers as to size or character of operations. The same considerations that dictate calculation of median and interquartile figures by the organizations that publish standard ratios apply to a credit manager who "rolls his own."

APPENDIX TO CHAPTER 9

EXAMPLES OF COMPARATIVE FINANCIAL STATEMENT ANALYSIS

The three following case studies of comparative financial statement analyses show respectively a normal good risk, a questionable risk revealed by "shaving" the balance sheet, and a questionable risk revealed by ratio analysis.

CASE 1

The following financial statement is submitted by a paint and varnish wholesaler:

| Assets | | | Liabilities | | |
|---|---|---|---|---|---|
| Cash on hand | $ | 416.16 | Notes to bank | $ | 205,000.00 |
| Cash in bank | | 57,961.73 | Accounts payable | | 221,520.76 |
| Notes receivable | | 46,493.56 | Accruals | | 16,549.19 |
| Accounts receivable | | 709,515.15 | Total current | $ | 443,069.95 |
| Inventory | | 804,691.04 | | | |
| Total current | | $1,619,077.64 | Fixed liabilities | | 166,000.00 |
| Fixed assets | | 365,421.79 | Capital and surplus | | 1,715,106.18 |
| Loans to officers | | 8,000.00 | | | |
| Investments | | 331,676.70 | | | |
| Total assets | | $2,324,176.13 | Total liabilities | | $2,324,176.13 |
| Sales | | $3,598,463.72 | | | |
| Net profit before income tax | $ | 17,992.32 | | | |

The standard median ratios for this type and size of business, and the ratios derived from the financial statement, are as follows:

| | Standard Ratios | Company Ratios |
|---|---|---|
| Current ratio | 3.5 | 3.6 |
| Sales/merchandise | 5.1 | 4.5 |
| Sales/receivables | 10.4 | 4.8 |
| Sales/net worth | 3.3 | 2.1 |
| Current liabilities/net worth | 32.0% | 25.8% |
| Net profit/sales | 1.5% | 0.5% |

Two of the customer's ratios—current and current liabilities/net worth,—are better than standard. The other four—merchandise turnover, net worth turnover, receivables turnover, and net profit/sales—fall somewhat short of the standard; receivables turnover is substantially below standard. It should be remembered, however, that the customer may be selling to retailers, who normally get 60-day terms. The higher-than-standard receivables turnover ratio is probably strongly influenced by industrial distributors in this line, who sell largely on 30-day terms. In general, the comparative analysis indicates a well-capitalized business, conservative in its financial management, but rather unprogressive in its merchandising and credit policies.

## Case 2

The following financial statement is submitted by a manufacturer of electrical goods:

| Assets | | Liabilities | |
|---|---:|---|---:|
| Cash | $    60,915.41 | Notes payable for mer- | |
| Notes receivable | 27,720.15 | chandise | $    44,192.16 |
| Accounts receivable | 122,535.18 | Accounts payable | 133,016.11 |
| Inventory | 528,464.43 | Accruals | 23,200.08 |
| Total current | $  739,635.17 | Total current | $  200,408.35 |
| Fixed assets | 773,815.93 | Notes payable, deferred | 674,481.92 |
| Investments | 127.00 | Subtotal | $  874,890.27 |
| Miscellaneous receiv- | | Preferred stock | 985,400.00 |
| ables | 4,164.17 | Common stock | 165,000.00 |
| Prepaid expense | 20,071.62 | Earned surplus | (D)339,071.31 |
| Developmental expense | 148,404.07 | | |
| Patents | 1.00 | | |
| Total assets | $1,686,218.96 | Total liabilities | $1,686,218.96 |
| Sales | $1,406,799.04 | | |
| Net loss | $  290,014.47 | | |

The standard median ratios for this type and size of business, and the ratios derived directly from the financial statement, are as follows:

| | Standard Ratios | Company Ratios |
|---|---|---|
| Current ratio | 2.8 | 3.7 |
| Sales/merchandise | 4.8 | 2.7 |
| Sales/receivables | 8.0 | 9.4 |
| Sales/net worth | 2.9 | 1.7 |
| Current liabilities/net worth | 38.2% | 24.7% |
| Total debt/net worth | 68.3% | 107.8% |

At first glance this business may seem a reasonable risk. The current, current debt/net worth, and receivables turnover ratios are better than the standard, indicating a liquid position. Other ratios—merchandise turnover, net worth turnover, and total debt/net worth—however, are far below the standard, reflecting a less efficient sales management than the "liquidity picture" might lead one to suspect. The high total debt/net worth ratio in itself is not necessarily a danger sign, but in connection with the other unfavorable ratios and such unexplained items as the net loss and the deficit in earned surplus, the deferred debt item becomes a cause for concern. Finally, the substantial asset items designated "Prepaid expense" and "Developmental expense" represent no tangible security for creditors.

Once his doubts are aroused, the credit manager should "shave" the assets of this customer. He eliminates "Prepaid expense" and "Development expense," and in view of the low merchandise turnover, "Inventory" is given only three-quarters of its balance sheet value. The revised balance sheet and the ratios based on it now appear as follows:

| Assets | | Liabilities | |
|---|---|---|---|
| Cash | $ 60,900 | Total current | $ 200,400 |
| Receivables | 150,200 | Deferred | 674,500 |
| Inventory | 396,400 | | |
| Total current | $ 607,500 | Subtotal | $ 874,900 |
| Fixed assets | 777,800 | Net worth | 514,700 |
| Other assets | 4,300 | | |
| Total assets | $1,389,600 | Total liabilities | $1,389,600 |

The ratios calculated on the basis of this revised balance sheet are:

| | |
|---|---|
| Current ratio | 3.0 |
| Sales/net worth | 2.7 |
| Current liabilities/net worth | 38.9% |
| Total debt/net worth | 170.0% |

These revised ratios, and particularly the current liabilities/net worth ratio, together with the current net loss and the deficit on earned surplus, definitely place the concern in the questionable category. (For a trend analysis on this case, see page 195 of this volume.)

## Case 3

The following financial statement is submitted by a department store:

| Assets | | Liabilities | |
|---|---|---|---|
| Cash | $ 43,052.81 | Due to banks | $ 20,400.00 |
| Accounts receivable | 157,017.93 | Accounts payable | 197,871.75 |
| Inventory | 205,618.71 | Accruals | 26,516.92 |
| Total current | $ 405,689.45 | Total current | $ 244,788.67 |
| Fixed assets | 607,561.93 | Mortgage | 250,000.00 |
| | | Net worth | 518,462.71 |
| Total assets | $1,013,251.38 | Total liabilities | $1,013,251.38 |
| Sales | $1,953,016.62 | | |
| Net profit before income tax | $ 61,043.81 | | |

The standard ratios for this type and size of business, and the ratios calculated from the financial statement, are as follows:

| | Standard Ratios | Company Ratios |
|---|---|---|
| Current ratio | 3.5 | 1.7 |
| Sales/merchandise | 5.8 | 9.5 |
| Sales/net worth | 3.0 | 3.8 |
| Current liabilities/net worth | 27.2% | 47.2% |
| Net profit/sales | 2.0% | 3.1% |

The high merchandise turnover ratio reflects aggressive sales policy, and the impression of efficiency is to some extent confirmed by the high profit ratio. The low current ratio and the high proportion of current liabilities to net worth indicate that the store is operating with inadequate working capital. This situation might be remedied by an increase in net worth, or by an expansion of fixed liability, to clear the excess of current liability.

The picture is one of mixed strength and weakness. If net worth should be built up, this customer may become a promising account from both sales and credit viewpoints. As matters stand, it is highly vulnerable to any financial mischance. (For the trend analysis on this case, see page 197 cf this volume.)

## SUPPLEMENTARY READINGS

See page 198 of this volume.

## REVIEW

1. What is a "comparative financial statement form"? How is it used?
2. What sort of adjustments or "shaving" may be applied to a customer's financial statement before it is used for credit analysis purposes?
3. What is the significance, in comparative financial statement analysis, of the following ratios: (a) sales/merchandise, (b) credit sales/receivables, (c) sales/net worth, (d) current liabilities/net worth, (e) the current ratio, (f) receivables/merchandise, (g) net working capital/merchandise, (h) sales/net working capital, (i) sales/fixed assets, (j) fixed assets/net worth, (k) total debt/net worth, (1) the "acid test" ratio, (m) net profits/sales, (n) net profits/net worth?
4. What are some of the sources of published standard financial statement ratios?
5. What are the defects of present published standard financial statement ratios?
6. What combination of ratios would indicate a customer to be (a) a successful "shoestring" operator, (b) a rather inactive business man but, at least at present, a good credit risk, (c) a dangerous speculator?

## PROBLEM 1

Make a comparative financial statement analysis of the 12/31/60 statement of King & Todd on pp. 61-62. Ratios for men's clothing retailers from Dun & Bradstreet's "14 Important Ratios in 72 Lines of Business" are:

| | | | |
|---|---|---|---|
| Current | 2.61 | Net Prof/Sales | 1.96% |
| Net Sales/NW | 2.50 | Net Prof/NW | 4.38% |
| Net Sales/Inventory | 3.7 | Current Debt/NW | 48.8 % |

## PROBLEM 2

Make a comparative financial statement analysis of the 11/30/60 statement of Henry D. Smith on pp. 78-79. Ratios for furniture stores with 50% or more instalment sales from Dun & Bradstreet's "14 Important Ratios in 72 Lines of Business" are:

| | | | |
|---|---|---|---|
| Current | 3.71 | Net Prof/Sales | 1.54% |
| Net Sales/NW | 1.80 | Net Prof/NW | 3.03% |
| Net Sales/Inventory | 4.4 | Current Debt/NW | 38.2 % |

# CHAPTER 10

# Financial Statement Trend Analysis

       When a credit manager has not only the latest financial statement of a customer, but also the preceding one, and perhaps statements of earlier years, he is able to make a "trend" analysis—he can study the development of the customer's financial position over a period of time and determine whether he is improving or deteriorating.

Trend analysis is not an alternative to comparative ratio analysis. The two complement each other. A relatively weak financial position revealed by the ratios in a financial statement has altogether different significance according to whether trend analysis on the basis of the preceding years shows the customer to be recovering from still greater weakness or retrogressing from an earlier strong condition. In the first case, despite the weak present position, the customer may be deemed an acceptable credit risk if general business conditions warrant the continuance of the recovery already under way. In the second case, and particularly if the customer's downward trend is attributable to factors that are not likely to change during the current year, he may be marked down as an unacceptable credit risk.

Credit managers are attaching increasing importance to trend analysis for two reasons. *First*, they can apply it in circumstances where no valid standard ratios are available to which a customer's ratios can be compared. Earlier financial statement figures at least give historical perspective for present computations. *Second,* and more important, trend analysis, particularly in its form of ratio trend analysis, is finding growing use as a basis for *forecasting.* We saw how difficult it is to interpret the figures of a financial statement with regard to future developments. Trend analysis offers guidance in this connection. Its reliability, especially for forecasting, depends on the factors establishing the trend. If external factors are responsible, there is little presumption for *continuity* of the trend—unless there is inherent continuity in the external factors. For a trend largely due to internal factors, there is considerable presumption for continuity.

Trend analysis suffers from a weakness not applicable to comparative analysis. Over a period of a year or longer, inflationary or deflationary price developments may operate with varying intensities upon different elements of the financial statement. Dollar sales, for example, may be affected by price upswings and downswings quite differently than inventories, accounts receivables, payables, and fixed assets. Hence, trend changes in financial statement relationships may reflect dollar value fluctuations as well as internal business developments.

## SOURCES OF PAST
## FINANCIAL STATEMENT INFORMATION

A credit manager who insists on regularly obtaining financial statements from all his customers accumulates, in time, files that go back several years on the older accounts. As each statement is received, its figures, as they appear or after adjustment, are transferred to a comparative statement sheet or card. In due course this provides all the figures necessary for trend analysis on the customer. As indicated in Illustration 9-1, comparative statement sheets or cards generally have space for calculation and entry of the significant ratios so that immediate comparisons can be made of the ratios as well as of the items themselves.

New accounts are generally asked to submit their most recent financial statement. It is not as customary to request past-year statements, but such demands are becoming more frequent and, if properly worded, generally meet with favorable response. Mercantile agency reports, moreover, usually contain financial statements for two or three years. In the case of small concerns the earlier financial statements may be presented in summary form only (see Illustration 4-4); with large companies, however, the earlier statements are given in full detail and in a form comparable with the latest one (see Illustration 4-3).

## RATIO TREND ANALYSIS

We saw in Chapter 9 that the relative financial strength or weakness of a business may be revealed through various relationships of the financial statement figures which were conveniently calculated in ratios. Noting year-to-year changes in these ratios is one of the most common and most instructive techniques to determine a customer's financial development and prospects.

Study of the trend of financial statement ratios for a single concern is not beset by all the difficulties and qualifications that plague comparative analysis. A business generally adheres to its accounting conventions and practices once they are adopted. The accounting year, though it may be an unusual one for the line of business, generally remains unchanged for long periods of time; so do classifications given to various assets and liabilities, and valuation methods for fixed assets, inventories, and intangibles. Any deviation from prior practice would become immediately obvious. And finally, the credit manager does not have to bother about the availability or validity of standard ratios.

### Significant ratio trends

The same ratios that are deemed significant in comparative analysis and were studied in Chapter 9 are the basis of trend analysis.

*Sales/merchandise.* A rising merchandise turnover ratio reflects either an improvement in sales policy, or an improvement in purchasing and stock control policies. Which factor is responsible for the improvement can be determined from the trend in other ratios, or by comparison of the actual sales and inventory figures for the successive years. Improvement in either factor is a favorable consideration.

*Credit sales/receivables.* A rising receivables turnover ratio usually reflects improvement either in the customer's credit policy or his collection techniques, or in both. There may be cases, however, where an earlier credit or collection policy was too strict, so that a decline in the receivables turnover ratio indicates a shift to a more liberal and sounder policy; comparative and trend analysis would clear up this point. Also, in a year of business recession it must be expected that a concern will have more difficulties in its collections, so that a decline of the receivables turnover ratio in a bad year is not necessarily an indication of poorer credit management; it may even be a sign of wise policy.

*Sales/net worth.* The significance of a change in this ratio depends on which of the two factors—net worth or sales—was responsible for the ratio change. A reduction in the ratio attributable to an increase in net worth because profits were ploughed back into the business or new capital was invested, would be a favorable development. An increase of the ratio due to a reduction in net worth resulting from operating losses, or the charging of a capital loss to surplus, or withdrawals by partners, or the payment of dividends in excess of earnings out of surplus, would be an unfavorable development.

A rising ratio due to an increase of sales might be a favorable or unfavorable sign, depending on the customer's previous net worth situation. If he was previously a "shoestring" operator, carrying on or expanding his business to a disproportionate extent upon creditors' funds, a further rise in his sales/net worth ratio would unquestionably be a bad sign. If, however, the concern had previously been overcapitalized for the magnitude of its operations, and perhaps ultraconservative in its management policies, a rise in the sales/net worth ratio might reflect a healthy expansion of its operations and a more progressive and aggressive business policy. A decline in the sales/net worth ratio attributable to a decrease in sales might also have either a favorable or unfavorable connotation depending on the precedent circumstances.

It should be evident that a change in either direction of the sales/net worth ratio may be very significant, but its meaning cannot be ascertained exclusively from the trend itself. Upon noting a change in this ratio, a credit analyst should study changes in other ratios and possibly make a horizontal trend inquiry as described later in this chapter.

*Expense/sales.* A rising trend in this ratio—particularly if it is getting out of line with the usual proportion in the customer's field of business—should always be viewed as an unfavorable sign, regardless of whether it is caused by rising costs, falling sales, or both. Rising expenses may sometimes be unavoidable under the impact of inflationary conditions, but sales should also rise, even if not fully proportionately, under the influence of such conditions and thereby hold down the ratio. Where internal factors are responsible for a rise in this ratio, a credit analyst is put upon warning to inquire into the cause.

*Profit ratios.* At first glance, a rising trend in a customer's profit ratios is generally welcomed by a credit manager. On second thought, he should be careful not to exaggerate their importance. Special reasons, usually not openly advertised, may be behind a rising or declining profit trend. One company may adjust P & L items to show an apparently low profit for tax and other purposes. Another company may endeavor to report a magnified profit in order to attract new investors or for other reasons. Generally, however, an upward trend in profit ratios may be interpreted as a good sign, and a downward trend as a poor showing for the business.

*Current liabilities/net worth.* A decline in this ratio is, of course, categorically favorable, from a credit manager's viewpoint, whereas a rise is unfavorable. A rise indicates that the share of current financing of the business carried by its creditors is increasing relative to the owner's equity, so that the creditors' margin of protection is shrinking. The true significance of a change in this ratio, however, is not its immediate favorable or unfavorable connotation but the light it throws upon changes in the sales/net worth and current ratios. A rise in the current liabilities/ net worth ratio magnifies the unfavorable impact of a rise in the sales/net worth ratio or a decline in the current ratio.

*The current ratio.* This ratio—with or without the "acid test"—occupies a slightly more important place in trend studies than in comparative analysis. By itself it may not explain the causes of growing liquidity or illiquidity of a concern. In combination with other ratio trends the "current" development helps to throw light on a complicated situation.

## Common-size analysis

Some writers on financial statement analysis suggest what they call "common-size" or "100 percent" analysis as a method of studying trends in a customer's financial position. Under this system, all asset items in a balance sheet are calculated as percentages of total assets, and all liability items, including net worth, as percentages of total liabilities. The percentage distributions of successive years are then compared, as shown in Illustration 10-1.

ILLUSTRATION 10-1. Example of Common-Size Balance Sheet Analysis

| | BALANCE SHEETS | | COMMON-SIZE ANALYSIS | |
|---|---|---|---|---|
| ITEM | 1960 | 1961 | 1960 | 1961 |
| *Assets* | | | | |
| Cash .............. | $ 5,943 | $ 10,416 | 2.5% | 3.7% |
| Receivables ......... | 47,621 | 61,011 | 20.1 | 21.4 |
| Merchandise ........ | 70,908 | 90,401 | 30.2 | 31.7 |
| Other current ....... | 22,000 | ...... | 9.5 | ... |
| Total current ...... | $146,472 | $161,828 | 62.3% | 56.8% |
| Land .............. | 24,470 | 29,062 | 10.4 | 10.2 |
| Other fixed ......... | 61,081 | 90,911 | 26.0 | 32.0 |
| Other .............. | 3,017 | 2,741 | 1.3 | 1.0 |
| Total assets ........ | $235,040 | $284,542 | 100.0% | 100.0% |
| *Liabilities* | | | | |
| Notes payable ....... | $ 2,646 | $ 1,461 | 1.1% | 0.5% |
| Accounts payable ..... | 67,544 | 63,550 | 28.8 | 22.3 |
| Total current ....... | $ 70,190 | $ 65,011 | 29.9% | 22.8% |
| Reserves ........... | 8,944 | 16,041 | 3.8 | 5.6 |
| Capital stock ........ | 150,000 | 175,000 | 63.8 | 61.4 |
| Surplus ............ | 5,906 | 28,490 | 2.5 | 10.2 |
| Total liabilities ..... | $235,040 | $284,542 | 100.0% | 100.0% |

Common-size analysis is a form of ratio trend analysis, but an utterly useless one. A set of ratios based on comparison of single asset and liability items to total assets and total liabilities is of no significance in credit judgment. Trends in most of these common-size ratios are also quite meaningless. Comparing *relative* changes in certain sets of common-size percentages could yield information, but this would only be ordinary ratio trend analysis done under unnnecessarily difficult circumstances.

## HORIZONTAL TREND ANALYSIS

The second approach to financial trend analysis applied to a customer's financial statements is the "horizontal" one. In the horizontal analysis the year-to-year comparison is that of the actual figures of a series of statements, instead of ratios between sets of figures.

Horizontal analysis may be used independently or in conjunction with ratio trend analysis. Credit managers who do not make comparative ratio studies often confine themselves to horizontal trend calculations, since the burden of mathematical computation is thereby held to a minimum. Exclusive use of horizontal analysis is sufficient in many cases to provide the credit manager with a clear picture of the customer's development. But it does not establish causative factors; doing this is the great advantage of ratio trend analysis. Horizontal trend analysis therefore develops its outstanding value when it is combined with ratio trend analysis. The following example shows the application of the combined methods and the resulting significant conclusion.

Assume that A, a drug wholesaler, had a net worth of $100,000 in two successive years, and that its sales were $500,000 in the first year and $300,000 in the second year. Assume further that B, also a drug wholesaler, had sales of $500,000 in two successive years, but that its net worth was $100,000 in the first year and $167,000 in the second. In both cases there would be a change in the sales/net worth ratio from 5 to 3. The significance of the change would be quite different in the two cases—unfavorable for A in view of the decline in sales, favorable for B because of the increase in net worth.

The key financial statement figures to be followed "horizontally" from year to year are current assets, merchandise inventory, current liabilities, net worth, sales and, if available, expenses. The data on a customer are systematically transferred to his comparative statement sheet or card, as was recommended earlier in this volume. Each asset and liability item, or income and expense item, stands thus in alignment over a number of years, and relative trends can be recognized without effort.

## Base-year treatment of horizontal trends

Instead of tabulating the amounts of the various asset and liability items year after year, or in addition to doing this, many credit managers calculate the *percentage changes* these items undergo. There are two techniques for this procedure: (1) simple base-year horizontal trend analysis, and (2) progressive base-year horizontal trend analysis.

*Simple base-year computation* relates the various balance sheet items year after year to one arbitrary base year—usually the earliest year for which a customer statement was available—which represents 100 per cent. The variations in percentages of the later-year items from the 100 per cent of the indicated base-year show the relative changes that have occurred since then. The obvious shortcoming of this method is that these relative changes are clearly evident only for the first year following the base year. Thus, in the comparison of the 1959 and 1960 financial statements of the X Department Store shown in Illustration 10-2, the 1960 percentages for merchandise and sales, based on 1959, are respectively 171 and 162, indicating that both increased, but that there was a slight slowing of merchandise turnover. Similarly, it is evident that both net worth and current liabilities increased between the two years, but the latter to a larger extent. The same information could have been obtained from ratio trend analysis, with the added advantage that it would have been possible to see how each factor involved in a ratio contributed to the ratio change.

When a third year, and a fourth year, and still later years are brought into a series, and the figures of each successive year are related to the original base year, a "simple" base-year trend computation loses much of its usefulness. A credit manager is interested primarily in the developments of the latest year. But the increase or decrease percentages of the latest balance sheet items, computed on the basis of the original base year, may throw little light on developments during the latest accounting year. Thus the percentages in the 1961 column of Illustration 10-2 indicate that in the two years beginning with 1959 the merchandise inventories of the X Department Store doubled while sales increased by less than 60 per cent, but unless a credit analyst compared the 1960 and 1961 percentages he would not realize that the greater part of this unfavorable development occurred in the 1961 accounting year and involved an increase of inventories at a time when sales were decreasing. Comparison of the relative percentages of two items in both the 1960 and 1961 columns requires a double mental calculation which should be avoided if possible.

This weakness of simple base-year trend analysis is avoided in *progressive base-year* trend analysis, where the financial statement figures of each successive year are related, not to any single base year, but to the year immediately preceding. The year-by-year changes in the component figures of a customer's financial statements are immediately reflected in each year's percentages. Thus in the progressive computation given in Illustration 10-2, the 1961 percentages make it immediately evident that X Department Store's sales during its 1961 accounting year

ILLUSTRATION 10-2. Example of Base-Year Horizontal Trend Analysis

| ITEM | 1959 | 1960 | 1961 |
|---|---|---|---|
| *Balance Sheet Figures for X Department Store* | | | |
| Cash ................. | $ 19,060 | $ 21,452 | $ 8,415 |
| Receivables ........... | 46,441 | 57,966 | 89,556 |
| Merchandise .......... | 204,608 | 351,447 | 424,309 |
| Total current assets ... | $ 270,109 | $ 430,865 | $ 522,280 |
| Fixed ............... | 171,051 | 165,951 | 157,693 |
| Other ............... | 13,501 | 11,611 | 12,401 |
| Total assets ......... | $ 454,661 | $ 608,427 | $ 692,374 |
| Notes ............... | 20,000 | $ 45,000 | $ 30,000 |
| Accounts payable ...... | 73,760 | 93,771 | 185,451 |
| Total current liabilities | $ 93,760 | $ 138,711 | $ 215,451 |
| Fixed liabilities ....... | 25,000 | 25,000 | 25,000 |
| Net worth ........... | 335,901 | 444,656 | 451,923 |
| Total liabilities ...... | $ 454,661 | $ 608,427 | $ 693,374 |
| Sales ............... | $1,046,460 | $1,701,433 | $1,651,603 |
| *Simple Base-Year Trend Computation* | | | |
| Receivables .......... | 100% | 125% | 193% |
| Merchandise .......... | 100 | 171 | 202 |
| Current assets ........ | 100 | 159 | 193 |
| Current liabilities ...... | 100 | 147 | 232 |
| Net worth ........... | 100 | 132 | 135 |
| Total assets and liabilities | 100 | 134 | 152 |
| Sales ................ | 100 | 162 | 159 |
| *Progressive Base-Year Trend Computation* | | | |
| Receivables .......... | . . . | 125% | 153% |
| Merchandise .......... | . . . | 171 | 120 |
| Current assets ........ | . . . | 159 | 121 |
| Current liabilities ...... | . . . | 147 | 155 |
| Net worth ........... | . . . | 132 | 102 |
| Total assets and liabilities | . . . | 134 | 114 |
| Sales ................ | . . . | 162 | 98 |

were lower than for the preceding year, while its merchandise inventories increased. Also the relative changes in net worth and current liabilities of the store between 1960 and 1961 become more manifest than in the simple base-year analysis.

Progressive base-year trend computation is no more difficult than financial statement ratio calculation. It has the advantage of showing, at a glance, not only changes in the relationship between two financial statement factors, but also in what way each factor contributed to a change in relationship. There is no need, as in ratio trend analysis, for a credit manager to study the absolute figures of successive financial statements in order to determine factor responsibility for relationship changes.

Progressive base-year trend analysis has one important shortcoming. It cannot be associated conveniently with comparative financial statement analysis, as can ratio trend analysis. If progressive base-year trend percentages are calculated for trend analysis, a separate calculation must be made of ratios for comparative analysis, thus doubling the computation labors of a credit department.

In practice we find that credit managers who doubt the validity of comparative financial statement analysis commonly base their trend analysis on the progressive base-year method. But where both comparative and trend analyses are made, the ratio technique is employed for the trend as well as the comparative analysis.

## Graphic presentation

The actual figures of significant financial statement factors for a series of years can be plotted on arithmetic charts, and the lines connecting corresponding figure points from year to year will indicate visually the increases and decreases of these various factors, as shown in Illustration 10-3. Such graphic presentation, however, is of little use to a credit manager. He wants to see relative variations in the financial statement factors. An arithmetic chart shows absolute variations; because of the different magnitudes involved, relative variations are distorted out of recognition. Thus, in Illustration 10-3 the increase of X Department Store's sales from 1960 to 1961 appears much greater than the increase in its merchandise inventory, yet the percentage increase of the latter was 171 as against 162 for the former.

Relative variations can be shown graphically on a semi-logarithmic chart, whereon differences between all magnitudes are reduced to the same scale. Illustration 10-4 presents a semi-logarithmic charting of the financial statement figures for X Department Store used in Illustrations 10-2 and 10-3. Note that the slant of any line corresponds to the percentage increase between two years, no matter whether the amounts involved are in the low hundred thousands or over a million. If two

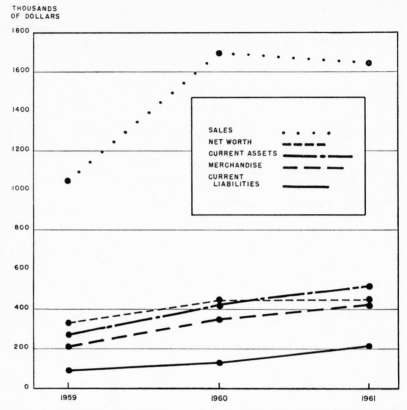

THOUSANDS
OF DOLLARS

SALES
NET WORTH
CURRENT ASSETS
MERCHANDISE
CURRENT
LIABILITIES

ILLUSTRATION 10-3.   Graphic Presentation of Horizontal Analysis, Absolute Scale

lines slant at about the same angle, the percentage increases of the
factors they represent are approximately the same. If one line slants at
a sharper angle than another, the factor represented by the first line
increased by a greater percentage than did the factor represented by
the second line.

Any increase or decrease shown by a progressive base-year trend
computation can be represented visually on a semi-logarithmic chart in
a manner as readily comprehensible as by the computation. Developments over a series of years can be recognized more readily from the
lines of a semi-logarithmic chart than from the series of percentages in
a progressive base-year trend table. Moreover, no computations are necessary in making the chart; the figures can be entered directly on the
chart from the comparative financial statement card or sheet. A semi-
logarithmic chart is a more efficient and time-saving substitute, then, for
a progressive base-year trend computation. Like that computation, however, it cannot be tied in with comparative financial statement analysis,
since it does not provide the actual ratios needed for such analysis.

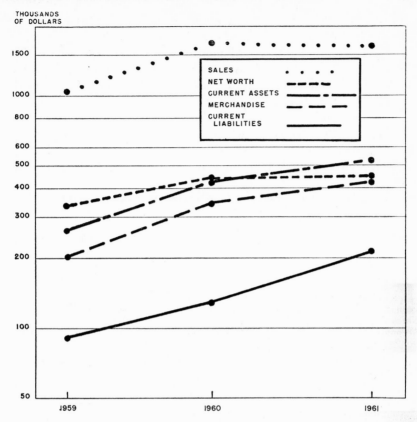

ILLUSTRATION 10-4.    Graphic Presentation of Horizontal Analysis, Semi-Logarithmic
Scale

### Where-got where-gone analysis

A where-got where-gone analysis is a simplified version of what accountants call a "statement of sources and application of funds."

Every change in a business concern's balance sheet affects its net
worth—the arithmetic difference between its total assets and total
liabilities. An increase in assets or decrease in liabilities results in a
rising net worth; a decrease in assets or increase in liabilities causes it to
decline. This rise and fall of net worth is the basis of where-got where-
gone computations. All changes in asset or liability items producing
*increases in net worth,* such as additions to assets or deductions from
liabilities, are tabulated in the "where-gone" column. All changes in
asset or liability items producing *decreases in net worth,* such as deductions from assets or additions to liabilities, are tabulated in the "where-
got" column. The total at the end of each column must, obviously, be

identical for both, as the successive financial statements from which the items of change were taken had to be in complete balance.

The origin of this rather odd nomenclature is not quite clear. The idea, apparently, was that if assets increase or liabilities decrease funds are being used for these purposes and "go" into these items. On the other hand, when assets decrease or liabilities increase, funds are not absorbed or "gone"; they are received or "got."

Illustration 10-5 shows a "where-got where-gone" calculation. First the increase or decrease of each asset and liability item of the X Manufacturing Corporation was computed. Then all asset decreases and

ILLUSTRATION 10-5.     Example of "Where-Got Where-Gone" Computation

| ITEM | BALANCE SHEETS | | INCREASE OR DECREASE | WHERE GOT | WHERE GONE |
|---|---|---|---|---|---|
| | 1960 | 1961 | | | |
| *Assets* | | | | | |
| Cash ............... | $ 58,938 | $ 57,841 | —$   1,097 | $   1,097 | |
| Notes receivable ...... | 502 | 1,322 | +    820 | | $    820 |
| Accounts receivable ... | 22,204 | 36,333 | +  14,129 | | 14,129 |
| Inventory ........... | 72,853 | 100,906 | +  28,053 | | 28,053 |
| Total current ....... | $154,497 | $196,402 | +$ 41,905 | | |
| Fixed assets, net ...... | 71,481 | 157,051 | +  85,570 | | 85,570 |
| Leasehold improvements | 15,727 | 27,966 | +  12,239 | | 12,239 |
| Due from officers ..... | 2,567 | 1,122 | —   1,445 | 1,445 | |
| Prepaid items ........ | 2,252 | 2,189 | —     63 | 63 | |
| Miscellaneous receivables | 7,000 | 9,655 | +   2,655 | | 2,655 |
| Development expense .. | 33,010 | 94,335 | +  61,325 | | 61,325 |
| Patents ............. | 1 | 1 | ...... | | |
| Total assets ........ | $286,535 | $488,721 | +$202,186 | | |
| *Liabilities* | | | | | |
| Due to banks ........ | $ ...... | $ 30,000 | +$ 30,000 | 30,000 | |
| Accounts payable ..... | 9,117 | 31,935 | +  22,818 | 22,818 | |
| Accruals ............ | 12,544 | 35,526 | +  22,982 | 22,982 | |
| Advances from customers | 43,178 | 71,738 | +  28,560 | 28,560 | |
| Due to officers ........ | ...... | 1,661 | +   1,661 | 1,661 | |
| Total current ....... | $ 64,839 | $170,860 | +$106,021 | | |
| Serial notes payable ... | 45,000 | 112,375 | +  67,375 | 67,375 | |
| Deferred royalty income | 19,000 | 7,000 | —  12,000 | | 12,000 |
| Common stock and capital surplus ....... | 149,372 | 149,372 | ...... | | |
| Earned surplus ........ | 8,324 | 49,114 | +  40,790 | 40,790 | |
| Total liabilities  .... | $286,535 | $488,721 | +$202,186 | | |
| Net sales ........... | $208,794 | $269,116 | | | |
| Net profit . .      . | 10,319 | 40,790 | | | |
| Where-got where-gone totals ......................... | | | | $216,791 | $216,791 |

liability increases were copied into the "where-got" column and all asset increases and liability decreases into the "where-gone" column. Totaling the two columns was merely an arithmetical check.

Where-got where-gone analysis does not provide any information that cannot be obtained from straight visual inspection of two successive financial statements. Its virtue is that it classifies this information in a form whereby certain relationships may become more evident.

In the case presented in Illustration 10-5, a credit manager comparing 1960 and 1961 statements would note immediately that there has been an exceptionally sharp rise in current liabilities. Current assets and net worth both increased too, but not in proportion to current liabilities. Ratio trend analysis, progressive base-year trend analysis, and graphic presentation would all show that the financial position of the company was weaker in 1961 than it had been in 1960 but would not indicate the reasons. By careful comparison of individual items in the two balance sheets, the credit manager could spot the significant factors. He would probably arrive at this result more quickly if he had the two statements set up in where-got where-gone form.

Current liabilities increased by over $100,000, and the company's serial note debt was augmented by over $67,000. Inventories and receivables both grew, but the increase was trifling beside that of liabilities. The two items that stand out in the "where-gone" column are the $85,570 increase in fixed assets and the $61,325 rise in capitalized development expense. The increase in fixed assets may prove in the long run an investment in productive capacity, but an item such as capitalized development expense is always highly questionable in credit analysis. This case is no exception to the rule. If these costs had been noted as actual expenses instead of being capitalized into an asset item, the company's 1961 profit would have been converted into a loss. As it stands, the credit manager sees readily that three-fifths of the increase in current liabilities can be accounted for by this single "where-gone" item. One of the few favorable indications is the substantial increase in sales in 1961. The rise of "earned surplus" however, is merely fictional, as a balancing figure. "Where-got where-gone" computations established these points more obviously and readily than progressive base-year analysis would have done, but that was its only advantage.

Where-got where-gone analysis can also be based on a company's latest financial statement and its current budget forecast. Such a "cash- or funds-flow summary," as it is called by some writers,[1] provides a picture of the company's *anticipated* funds flow—obviously helpful to a credit analyst.

---

[1] W. J. McDonald, "Modern Concept and Uses of Funds Flow Statements as Signposts to Both the Creditor and the Debtor," *Credit and Financial Management*, April 1960, p. 12.

## SUPPLEMENTARY FINANCIAL INFORMATION

Banks, factors, finance companies, and upon occasion mercantile credit executives may request their clients or customers to provide them with trial balances, budgets, cash- or funds-flow summaries, or insurance statements. With the aid of such supplementary financial reports, a credit manager can often sharpen his analysis, particularly as to a customer's *current* financial condition.

### Trial balance

A trial balance is a schedule of the assets and liabilities of a concern as of a given date, and of income and expenses from the preceding balance sheet date to the trial balance date. Surplus or net worth figures are not current but are carried over from the preceding balance sheet. The same applies to merchandise, unless the company has a "perpetual inventory" system that permits the taking of inventory at any time and not only at the close of books. All other balance sheet items can be drawn from a company's ledger and currently listed in a trial balance; asset and expense items are usually tabulated together in a Debit column, liabilities and income items in a Credit column. Unless errors have occurred in posting or computation, the totals of credits and debits should balance.

Concerns with complete sets of books usually draw trial balances at the end of each month. In this way they check periodically the accuracy of their books and obtain information helpful in managerial control.

Credit managers have discovered that customers' trial balances are frequently a useful source of supplementary credit information. A customer's latest financial statement may be as much as 13 months old. His circumstances may have altered radically during the interval. With an *interim balance sheet* constructed from his latest monthly trial balance, his financial picture can be brought up to the month, if not to the minute. If a customer's financial statement does not contain a full income statement but only figures for sales, at least the relationship of various classes of his expenses to his sales income can be studied from the trial balance. Furthermore, a trial balance pictures a customer's finances at a date when they have no chance of being window-dressed by low inventories and other circumstances peculiar to the closing of an accounting year.

Accordingly, some credit managers make it a practice to request new customers to submit their latest trial balance as well as their latest financial statement, particularly if the agency rating indicates that the customer may be a questionable credit risk. Slow-paying customers who are given extra terms on a trade acceptance basis may be subjected to this requirement; so also may customers who have been granted extensions after failure to pay their accounts at their due dates. In certain lines of business, such as the clothing industry and fur trades, where a large proportion of the operators are marginal credit risks and where there are ever-present dangers of obsolescence of inventories through style changes, monthly trial balances are asked for almost as freely as financial statements. Some mercantile agencies serving sellers in these fields ask accounts they cover for monthly trial balances on which to base their own credit judgment; these balances are reported to subscribers unless an account requests the agency to keep such figures confidential.

Illustration 10-6 indicates the form in which a February 1961 trial

ILLUSTRATION 10-6.  Example of Trial Balance

TRIAL BALANCE
*The Ewing Shirt Co.*

February 28, 1961

|  | DEBIT | CREDIT |
|---|---|---|
| Cash in bank | $ 1,942.31 | |
| Cash on hand | 73.94 | |
| Accounts receivable | 42,739.17 | |
| Reserve for bad and doubtful accounts | | $ 2,177.62 |
| Inventory (12/31/60) | 33,414.62 | |
| Machinery and fixtures | 7,714.00 | |
| Reserve for depreciation | | 2,123.33 |
| Deposit with supplier | 400.00 | |
| Accounts payable | | 23,101.91 |
| Notes payable—bank | | 8,000.00 |
| A. Ewing—capital (12/31/60) | | 42,183.64 |
| Sales | | 37,943.52 |
| Returns and allowances | 1,498.32 | |
| Sales discounts | 118.93 | |
| Freight out | 159.17 | |
| Purchases—materials | 13,915.41 | |
| —supplies | 2,140.40 | |
| Freight in | 116.92 | |
| Purchase discounts | | 301.18 |
| Wages | 7,016.63 | |
| Office salaries | 728.50 | |
| Withdrawals—A. Ewing | 450.00 | |
| Miscellaneous selling expense | 631.33 | |
| Rent | 280.00 | |
| Insurance | 715.45 | |
| Legal and auditing | 140.00 | |
| Telephone and telegraph | 118.90 | |
| Stationery and printing | 13.34 | |
| Light and power | 27.18 | |
| Factory expense | 18.73 | |
| Miscellaneous general expense | 1,214.04 | |
| Postage and carfare | 131.36 | |
| Interest | 112.55 | |
| Totals | $115,831.20 | $115,831.20 |

ILLUSTRATION 10-7.    Example of Balance Sheet Construction from Trial Balance

PART 1

TENTATIVE BALANCE SHEET

| *Assets* | | *Liabilities* | |
|---|---|---|---|
| Cash | $ 2,016.25 | Notes to bank | $ 8,000.00 |
| Accounts receivable | 42,739.17 | Accounts payable | 23,101.91 |
| Inventory | | Total current | $31,101.91 |
| Total current | $ | Reserves | 4,300.95 |
| Machinery and fixtures | 7,714.00 | Net worth | |
| Other | 400.00 | | |
| Total assets | | Total liabilities | |

PART 2

COMPUTATION OF 2/28/61 INVENTORY

| | | |
|---|---|---|
| Inventory (12/31/60) | | $33,414.62 |
| Plus: Purchases—materials | | 13,915.41 |
| —supplies | | 2,140.40 |
| —freight in | | 116.92 |
| Wages | | 7,016.63 |
| Total | | $56,603.98 |
| Less: Gross sales | $37,943.52 | |
| Deduct returns and allowances | 1,498.32 | |
| Net sales | $36,445.20 | |
| Deduct estimated 20% gross profit | 7,289.04 | |
| Estimated cost of sales | | $29,156.16 |
| Estimated inventory, 2/28/61 | | $27,447.82 |

PART 3

COMPLETION OF ESTIMATED BALANCE SHEET

| *Assets* | | *Liabilities* | |
|---|---|---|---|
| Cash | $ 2,016.25 | Notes to bank | $ 8,000.00 |
| Accounts receivable | 42,739.17 | Accounts payable | 23,101.91 |
| Inventory | (27,447.82) | Total current | $31,101.91 |
| Total current | ($72,203.24) | Reserves | 4,300.95 |
| Machinery and fixtures | 7,714.00 | Net worth | ( 44,914.38) |
| Other | 400.00 | | |
| Total assets | ($80,317.24) | Total liabilities | ($80,317.24) |

balance might be submitted to a credit manager, though fragmentary trial balances containing only a few essential items are more frequently used. To construct an *interim balance sheet* as of the trial balance date, the credit manager would set up the reported asset and liability items, other than the December 31, 1960 figures for inventory and net worth, in regular balance sheet form as shown in Part 1 of Illustration 10-7. He would then take the December 31 inventory figure and add to it purchases of materials, supplies, and wages. From this total he would subtract gross sales less returns, allowances, and the estimated gross profit on sales, as shown in the second part of Illustration 10-7. The gross profit percentage for the latter figure is derived from either the previous income statement or the credit manager's knowledge of the particular customer or the customer's line of business. The result would be an estimate for the inventory as of February 28, 1961, which would then be inserted into the incomplete interim balance sheet. Thus, total assets would be determined. The same figure would now be set up as "total liabilities," and the other liabilities would be subtracted to produce the residual figure for net worth as shown in the third part of Illustration 10-7.

The interim balance sheet thus constructed from a trial balance may be analyzed as to its component parts to see if any evidences of structural weakness are immediately evident. It can also be compared with the preceding balance sheet by ratio-trend and where-got where-gone analysis for indications of improvement or deterioration of the concern's financial position.

## Budget

A business budget, or "operating forecast," may be described as a preplanning of a concern's expenses for a forthcoming period in the light of its anticipated sales during such period.

Budgeting is a well-established technique with most large business enterprises, and medium- and small-sized concerns are adopting it in increasing numbers. Its primary purpose is improved managerial control. Its use as a basis for credit judgments is incidental but of growing importance and strongly recommended. Bank loan officers have generally educated their clients to the viewpoint that a borrower who prepares a budget for his own guidance should submit it to the bank when he applies for a loan. In mercantile credit the same idea is gaining ground for the customer-supplier relationship.

The first step in preparing a budget is undertaken by the sales department of a concern, which forecasts its sales for the coming budgetary period. In the case of seasonal businesses, this budgetary period is usually a year; for nonseasonal enterprises it may be a half year or a quarter. Upon the basis of this anticipation of sales and of other items of income, each department, including the sales department, prepares an estimate of its expenses for the coming year. Discrepancies between estimated income and estimated expenses are ironed out at a conference of the department heads, and a schedule of expenses for each department during the coming budgetary period is approved. For control purposes, these schedules are broken down into monthly allotments which take account of seasonal variation in the concern's operations.

The department schedules of income and expenses can be, and usually are, consolidated into an over-all anticipated profit-and-loss statement for the coming budgetary period. The monthly schedules can likewise be combined into a series of anticipated monthly profit-and-loss statements. These are the financial documents submitted to a bank or a credit department as the budget of the borrowing or buying concern. By relating these anticipated profit-and-loss figures to the concern's last preceding balance sheet, anticipatory balance sheets can be prepared for the projected period. Such anticipatory balance sheets may be included in the budgets submitted for credit purposes by borrowers and buyers.

It should be recognized that a business budget is only a guess—but a very educated one. Its value depends largely on sales forecasts and the reliability of the statistical techniques on which these forecasts are based. Since business expenses in their relation to sales can be fairly well controlled, the expense schedules of a budget are generally valid to the same extent as the sales forecast.

In a budget the management of a business sets up the operating and financial goals it intends to achieve. Realization of this plan may be modified or prevented by unforeseen circumstances. In spite of this uncertainty, customer budgets are particularly helpful to a credit manager in two cases. The first is that of a customer who is increasing his purchases to such an extent that they exceed the limit the supplier has set for the account. The credit manager may go along with such a customer if he has submitted a clear budget statement, and it shows that he has planned and is undertaking a well-conceived program of expansion. The second case is that of a customer who is a poor credit risk because he is operating with insufficient net worth. If a budget from such a customer shows that he plans either to restrict operations to a level more consonant with his net worth, or to obtain additional capital for his enterprise, this may be the crucial consideration in the credit manager's decision to sell him on regular terms.

### Insurance statement

No business can be conducted without risk. Against some risks, however, a business may take out insurance. Because of the premium expense, most concerns insure against only a few of their insurable risks.

The extent of a customer's insurance coverage is important to his suppliers for two reasons. First, the fuller the coverage, the less the chance of insolvency produced by an extraneous loss, with resulting bad debt loss to the creditors. Second, wide insurance coverage is an indication of business caution. Credit managers prefer cautious customers to venturous ones who might involve their suppliers in their gambles.

Mercantile agency reports generally give information only on a customer's fire insurance coverage. Some standard financial statement forms, such as those supplied by NACM, contain questions about liability insurance, life insurance for the benefit of the business, and about the apportionment of fire insurance coverage among a company's assets. Otherwise, if a credit manager wishes to discover what business insurance a customer carries, he must write and ask the customer about it.


APPENDIX TO CHAPTER 10


EXAMPLES OF FINANCIAL STATEMENT TREND ANALYSIS


In the two following case studies, financial statement trend analysis is applied to the two companies studied in Cases 2 and 3 of the Appendix to Chapter 9. Comparative analysis showed that the customers were questionable risks. Before making his final decision, the credit manager would want to know whether their present condition was an improvement from a still worse position, or a deterioration from a better one. Under the first circumstance, the poor showing of the comparative analysis would be ameliorated. Under the second circumstance, it would be further confirmed.


CASE 1

The last three financial statements for the electrical goods manufacturer studied in Case 2 of the Appendix to Chapter 9 were:

| Assets | Earliest Year | Next Year | Current Year |
|---|---|---|---|
| Cash | $ 29,641.18 | $ 55,715.91 | $ 60,915.41 |
| Notes receivable | 24,315.91 | 18,815.46 | 27,720.15 |
| Accounts receivable | 92,515.12 | 77,110.22 | 122,535.18 |
| Inventory | 672,014.79 | 733,905.16 | 528,464.43 |
| Total current | $ 818,487.00 | $ 885,546.75 | $ 739,635.17 |
| Fixed assets | 811,015.19 | 804,131.26 | 773,815.93 |
| Investments | 127.00 | 127.00 | 127.00 |
| Miscellaneous receivables | 919.43 | 2,814.61 | 4,164.17 |
| Prepaid expense | 61,042.71 | 19,316.44 | 20,071.62 |
| Developmental expense | 44,217.71 | 130,615.82 | 148,404.07 |
| Patents | 1.00 | 1.00 | 1.00 |
| Treasury stock | 114,600.00 | . . . . . . . | . . . . . . . |
| Total assets | $1,850,410.04 | $1,842,552.88 | $1,686,218.96 |

*Liabilities*

| | | | |
|---|---|---|---|
| Notes payable for merchandise | $ 354,716.01 | $ 58,416.27 | $ 44,192.16 |
| Accounts payable ........... | 141,021.42 | 238,406.62 | 133,016.11 |
| Accruals ................. | 16,307.15 | 31,115.81 | 23,200.08 |
| Total current ............. | $ 512,044.58 | $ 327,938.70 | $ 200,408.35 |
| Notes payable, deferred ...... | ......... | 442,300.00 | 674,481.92 |
| Subtotal ................. | $ 512,044.58 | $ 770,238.70 | $ 874,890.27 |
| Preferred stock ............. | 1,100,000.00 | 985,400.00 | 985,400.00 |
| Common stock ............. | 165,000.00 | 165,000.00 | 165,000.00 |
| Earned surplus ............. | 73,365.46 | (D)78,085.82 | (D)339,071.31 |
| Total liabilities ........... | $1,850,410.04 | $1,842,552.88 | $1,686,218.96 |
| Sales ..................... | $1,188,567.62 | $1,167,514.21 | $1,406,799.04 |
| Net loss .................. | $ 116,629.19 | $ 114,715.05 | $ 209,014.47 |

The ratios calculated directly on these financial statements were:

| | Earliest Year | Next Year | Current Year |
|---|---|---|---|
| Current ratio ............ | 1.6 | 2.7 | 3.7 |
| Sales/merchandise ....... | 1.8 | 1.6 | 2.7 |
| Sales/receivables ........ | 10.2 | 12.2 | 9.4 |
| Sales/net worth .......... | 1.0 | 1.1 | 1.7 |
| Current liabilities/net worth | 38.3% | 30.6% | 24.7% |
| Total debt/net worth .... | 38.3% | 71.8% | 107.8% |

It will be remembered that, for comparative analysis purpose, the current year assets were "shaved" because of the low merchandise turnover and because of the intangible natures of the "Prepaid expense" and "Developmental expense" items. These considerations dictated "shaving" the assets of the two earlier years, as well as of the current year. The balance sheets so revised appeared as follows:

| *Assets* | Earliest Year | Next Year | Current Year |
|---|---|---|---|
| Cash ...................... | $ 29,700 | $ 55,700 | $ 60,900 |
| Receivables ............... | 116,800 | 95,900 | 150,200 |
| Inventory ................. | 336,000 | 326,100 | 396,400 |
| Total current ............. | $ 482,500 | $ 477,700 | $ 607,500 |
| Fixed assets ............... | 811,000 | 804,100 | 777,800 |
| Other assets ............. | 1,000 | 2,900 | 4,300 |
| Total assets ............. | $1,294,500 | $1,284,700 | $1,389,600 |
| *Liabilities* | | | |
| Total current ............. | $ 512,000 | $ 327,900 | $ 200,400 |
| Deferred ................. | ........ | 442,300 | 674,500 |
| Subtotal ................. | $ 512,000 | $ 770,200 | $ 874,900 |
| Net worth ................ | 782,500 | 514,500 | 514,700 |
| Total liabilities ........... | $1,294,500 | $1,284,700 | $1,389,600 |

The ratios calculated on the basis of these revised balance sheet figures were:

| | Earliest Year | Next Year | Current Year |
|---|---|---|---|
| Current ratio ............ | .9 | 1.5 | 3.0 |
| Sales/net worth .......... | 1.5 | 2.3 | 2.7 |
| Current liabilities/net worth | 65.4% | 63.7% | 38.8% |
| Total debt/net worth .... | 65.4% | 149.7% | 170.0% |

Using the original merchandise turnover ratio, and the revised figures on the other ratios, the following conclusions were reached:

1. Merchandise turnover, though still subnormal, had been improved during the past year by a reduction of inventory associated with an increase in sales.

2. Because of the conversion of substantial amounts of current liability into deferred liability in each of the two later years, both the current ratio and the current liabilities/net worth ratio showed marked improvement despite a substantial decline in net worth between the earliest year and the two later ones.

3. Because of the substantial increase in deferred liability and the decrease in net worth, the total debt/net worth ratio had deteriorated disastrously.

4. Net worth had declined substantially between the earliest and the second year, and experienced only a trifling increase in the next year.

5. The record of consistent and apparently increasing loss was a most unfavorable trend development.

The only real favorable trend development for this company was the rise in merchandise turnover. The apparent improvement in the current and current liabilities/net worth ratios was fictional; it was produced by a conversion of current liability to fixed liability. All the other trend developments were unfavorable. The combination of unfavorable comparative and trend analyses for this concern marked it as an unacceptable credit risk.

CASE 2

The last three financial statements for the department store studied in Case 3 of the Appendix to Chapter 9 were:

| Assets | Earliest Year | Next Year | Current Year |
|---|---|---|---|
| Cash | $ 25,518.26 | $ 23,042.17 | $ 43,052.81 |
| Accounts receivable | 45,371.40 | 95,421.72 | 157,017.93 |
| Inventory | 128,846.73 | 153,791.18 | 205,618.71 |
| Total current | $ 199,736.39 | $ 272,255.07 | $ 405,689.45 |
| Fixed Assets | 501,765.93 | 553,819.27 | 607,561.93 |
| Investments | 25,436.23 | ........ | ........ |
| Total assets | $ 726,938.55 | $ 826,074.34 | $1,013,251.38 |
| *Liabilities* | | | |
| Due to banks | $ 6,000.00 | $ 25,000.00 | $ 20,400.00 |
| Accounts payable | 28,041.12 | 77,287.75 | 197,871.75 |
| Accruals | 7,203.35 | 17,415.16 | 26,516.92 |
| Total current | $ 41,244.47 | $ 119,702.91 | $ 244,788.67 |
| Mortgage | 250,000.00 | 250,000.00 | 250,000.00 |
| Capital stock | 400,000.00 | 415,000.00 | 430,000.00 |
| Earned surplus | 35,694.08 | 41,371.43 | 88,462.71 |
| Total liabilities | $ 726,938.55 | $ 826,074.34 | $1,013,251.38 |
| Sales | $ 657,231.41 | $1,075,419.96 | $1,953,016.62 |
| Net profit | $ 7,448.19 | $ 24,616.71 | $ 61,043.81 |

The ratios calculated on these financial statements were:

| | Earliest Year | Next Year | Current Year |
|---|---|---|---|
| Current ratio | 4.8 | 2.3 | 1.7 |
| Sales/merchandise | 5.1 | 7 | 9.5 |
| Sales/net worth | 1.5 | 2.4 | 3.8 |
| Current liabilities/net worth | 9.5% | 26.2% | 47.2% |
| Net profit/sales | 1.1% | 2.3% | 3.1% |

The threefold increase in sales, accompanied by the doubling of merchandise turnover and the tripling of the profit ratio, were strikingly favorable developments. The explanation was found in the mercantile agency report, which told of the hiring of a new manager early in the second of these three years. He had the store refurnished and redecorated, vitalized selling techniques, promoted charge account selling, and instituted more aggressive advertising. In the following year an uptown branch of the store was opened; this was immediately successful.

Against these favorable trends stood the unfavorable developments in the current ratio and the sales/net worth and current liabilities/net worth ratios. Net worth had been increased by liberal ploughing back of profit and through the purchase of additional stock by the shareholders, but this increase in net worth was insufficient in view of the great expansion of the store's business. There was nothing wrong about the financial position of this store that would not be cured by a $100,000 addition to its net worth. But until such addition was made, the store would be financially vulnerable, and would have to be watched closely by its creditors.

## SUPPLEMENTARY READINGS

Chiuminatto, P. M., "Working Capital—Key to Credit," *Credit and Financial Management*, August 1956, p. 12, and September 1956, p. 20.

Credit Research Foundation, *Methods of Calculating Reserves for Doubtful Accounts*, New York, 1958.

Dun & Bradstreet, Inc., *How to Build Profits by Controlling Costs—a Small Business Handbook*, New York, 1959.

Flint, F. P., "Making and Using the Financial Forecasts is Essential to Sound Business Operations," *Credit and Financial Management*, September 1957, p. 14.

Foulke, R. A., *Genesis of the Fourteen Important Ratios*, Dun & Bradstreet, Inc., New York, 1955.

————, *Inventory and Business Health*, Dun & Bradstreet, Inc., New York, 1960.

————, *Practical Financial Statement Analysis*, 4th ed., McGraw-Hill Book Co., Inc., New York, 1959.

Gee, E. F., *The Evaluation of Receivables and Inventories as an Integral Phase of Credit Analysis*, Bankers Publishing Co., Cambridge, Mass., 1953.

Gum, W. L., *Fiscal Year Reporting for Corporate Income Tax*, National Bureau for Economic Research, New York, 1956.

Hopiak, G. A., "Credit Analysis versus Investment Analysis—Tools and General Purpose Identical but not Approach," *Credit and Financial Management*, March 1961, p. 18.

"Insurance as Added Security for Credit," *Credit and Financial Management*, October 1959, p. 8.

McDonald, W. J., "Modern Concept and Use of Funds Flow Statements as Signposts to Both the Creditor and the Debtor," *Credit and Financial Management*, April 1960, p. 10.

Myer, J. N., *Financial Statement Analysis*, 3rd ed., Prentice-Hall, Inc., Engle-wood Cliffs, N.J., 1961.

National Association of Credit Management, *Danger Signals Shown in Financial Statements—Important Check-Points in Credit Analysis*, 3rd ed., New York, 1961.

————, *What to Look for in Financial Statements*, New York, n. d.

Penny, L. H., "What to Look for in Report of Accountant," *Credit and Financial Management*, December 1958, p. 9.

Preville, M. S., "Credit Men Should Watch for Hidden Tax Claims," *Credit and Financial Management*, January 1950, p. 30.

Sanzo, R., *Ratio Analysis for Small Business*, Small Business Administration, Washington, D.C., 1957.

Sommers, H. M., series of articles on "Financial Statement Analysis," *Credit and Financial Management*, April 1950 through June 1951.

"Why Close Your Books at December 31?" *Credit and Financial Management*, January 1950, p. 28.

## REVIEW

1. From what sources might a credit manager obtain earlier-year financial statements of a new customer, so that he can make a trend analysis?

2. Why may a ratio trend analysis on a customer be accepted with fewer qualifications than a comparative analysis?

3. What conclusions could be drawn from either a rising trend, or a falling trend, in any of the following ratios for a particular customer: (a) sales/merchandise, (b) credit sales/receivables, (c) sales/net worth, (d) current liabilities/net worth, (e) current ratio? What would the following combination of ratio trends indicate: rising sales/merchandise, declining sales/receivables, rising current liabilities/net worth?

4. What is "common-size" analysis? What is its value?

5. What is "horizontal" trend analysis? What does it show that is not apparent in ratio trend analysis?

6. Distinguish "simple" and "progressive" horizontal trend analysis.

7. What are the advantages and disadvantages of progressive horizontal analysis compared with ratio trend analysis?

8. Compare semi-logarithmic horizontal trend charting with progressive horizontal trend analysis.

9. Explain "where-got where-gone" analysis. What are its advantages?

10. What is a trial balance? How can it be used to construct an interim balance sheet? What other information of value to a credit manager can be derived from it?

11. How is a business budget prepared? What can a credit manager learn from a customer's budget?

12. Of what value is a customer's insurance statement to a credit manager?

13. What is a cash- or funds-flow summary and how does it help a credit manager's judgment about a customer?

## PROBLEM 1

Do a ratio trend analysis and a horizontal trend analysis of King & Todd from their 1958, 1959, and 1960 financial statements on pp. 61, 62.

## PROBLEM 2

Do a 1959-1960 where-got where-gone analysis of King & Todd from their financial statements on pp. 61-62.

# CHAPTER 11

# Analyzing the Credit Risk

Before the credit manager of a large manufacturing corporation lies a duplicate sales slip, sent to him under regular office routine by the sales department. It is a substantial first order which, if duly paid, will produce a good profit. Future orders from this customer, if duly paid, will mean still more profit.

When this sales slip arrived several days earlier, the credit manager immediately drew a Dun & Bradstreet report and an NACM interchange report, sent inquiries to the customer's bank and his references which were noted on an accompanying memo sent by the sales department, and wrote a courteous letter to the customer requesting a financial statement. The reports, the replies, and the statement have all been received. The conclusions of a ratio analysis of the financial statement have been entered on a form which is attached to the statement itself. The credit manager has studied all these items carefully. He finds the picture of the customer a mixed one. Some items indicate him to be a good credit risk. Some items are unfavorable.

Shall the credit manager's decision be "yes" or "no"? Or is there some compromise solution? How is he to make his decision?

## BASIC CONSIDERATIONS

The credit manager's function has sometimes been described as that of saying "no" to the sales department.

This generalization is utterly misleading. "No" may sometimes save a loss, but it never earns a profit.

The credit department is, or should be, a profit-producing department that says "yes" to the sales department wherever possible. Its ability to do so depends upon its competent performance of the following five functions:

1. Determination of the marginal class of risks to which the concern should sell on regular terms. This lowest class of acceptable risks is that group of customers whose bad debt losses, over a reasonable period of time, may be expected to fall somewhat short of the profit (gross sales minus costs of production and delivery) derived from the purchases of those in the group who eventually make full payment, so that some net profit results from selling to the group. Special circumstances, discussed later, may temporarily warrant setting an "order-checking level" above or below this marginal risk class.

2. Determination of the degree of risk attaching to each account, as accurately as is possible upon the basis of available information, so that it may be classified for approval or rejection.

3. Persuasion of submarginal customers to buy upon special terms or under special arrangements which will eliminate or reduce the excessive risk that makes them otherwise unacceptable.

4. Development and application of collection procedures that will reduce the risk of nonpayment involved in all sales, even those to highest-risk customers.

5. Counseling marginal and submarginal accounts in appropriate ways so that their credit status may eventually rise to unqualified acceptability.

### The principle of risk categories

A credit manager should view his concern's customers to some extent as an insurance actuary views his company's policy holders.

In the case of life insurance, the actuaries have established, on the basis of mortality tables, that a certain percentage of men of a given age will die in the current year. The chance that any particular individual within the age group will die cannot be thus determined. But conclusions as to the group rest on the firm foundation of probability mathematics. The insurance company can establish a premium rate for the group that will yield a predictable net profit on insurance taken out by the group, despite unpredictability as to its individual members. Similar principles are applied in accident, fire, marine, and other insurance fields.

Similarly, credit analysis of a seller's individual customers cannot determine which of them, over any period of time, will certainly involve the seller in bad debt losses and which will pay, promptly or laggardly, all their obligations in full. Like insurance policy holders, credit customers fall into risk groups. The over-all loss for each group may be predetermined with some degree of accuracy, though by no means with the mathematical precision possible to insurance actuaries. For each individual customer in a risk category, however, there is only a relative *probability* of loss, a degree or percentage of risk determined by the over-all loss that may be anticipated from his group.

An insurance actuary must establish definite risk categories for *all* policy holders covered by his company, since varying premium rates must be calculated for all categories. A credit manager in some ways has an easier problem. He has only one decision to make—whether or not to check orders from particular customers. He does not have to classify all his accounts and all new orders into their particular risk categories. Only one category of accounts has to be clearly defined in his mind—the "marginal" or "break-even" one, whose bad debts loss for the class as a whole will just barely leave some net profit on the total sales to the class. The credit manager will approve, within certain credit limits established for the individual accounts (as discussed in Chapter 12 of this volume), all orders from customers in this marginal class. He will lump all better risk categories into a "certainly acceptable" risk class and, with allowance for credit limits, he will approve all orders from customers in these categories. Below the marginal group he will lump all inferior risk categories into a "submarginal" class to whom he will refuse regular credit terms but with whom he may endeavor to make special terms-of-sale arrangements.

How will a credit manager define this marginal risk category that is certain to produce some bad debt losses but whose orders will yield a gross profit sufficient to cover, with some margin to spare, these bad debt losses? The credit rating classes established by Dun & Bradstreet and by the special line agencies that make ratings provide a crude but workable classification of customers into risk categories. They do not, however, indicate the degree of risk, in per cent terms, attached to each category. This information the credit manager should have. He can determine it individually for his own company by keeping sales records of his accounts classified by rating categories. Sales and bad debt losses would be totalled annually for each category and the loss ratio calculated. Such tabulation and computation would be a relatively simple task for even a small credit office, and the results would be a valuable though not an exact guide. A large concern, that used punch-card tabulating machines for its sales and other records, could easily have the customer cards punched for their credit ratings and have all the calculations made automatically by machine.

A single year's experience, so tabulated, would be of some value in indicating quantitatively the risk of loss involved in each category of customers. Cumulative experience over several years would enlarge the sample. A still better result would be achieved if a number of credit managers associated in a credit managers' group were to tabulate their loss experience in similar fashion and pool their finding.[1]

### Risk categories and the seller's profit margin

It is important that the classification of accounts into risk categories should be in terms of the percentage of expected bad debts to gross sales for each group. As stated above, most companies under ordinary circumstances should sell to customers in the lowest risk category for which profit on the sales to the class exceeds the bad debt losses for the class. Unless the percentage of expected bad debt loss for each class— or at least for those classes around the margin—is known, there is no way of determining whether the credit department's policy is too lenient or too strict.

Illustration 11-1 is a graphic demonstration of the principle of deriving maximum profit by selling to the lowest risk category for which profit on sales to the class exceeds the bad debt losses for the class. Assume that a firm receives $1,000,000 in orders on which its gross profit over direct operating and delivery costs, if all payments were made, would be 20 per cent. Its customers fall into ten risk categories. For the first category from which $100,000 orders are received, the probability of bad debt loss is practically nil, and $20,000 gross profit may be expected. For the second category, from which another $100,000 of orders are received, $2,500 of nonpayments must be expected—a bad debt loss anticipation of $2\frac{1}{2}$ per cent; not only will the $500 of gross profit expected on these "bad" orders be lost, but also the $2,000 operating and delivery costs on these "bad" orders are a loss which must be offset against the $19,500 profit on the "good" orders in this category, so that the net profit on $100,000

---

[1] This determination of acceptable and nonacceptable credit risk categories by correlating bad debt loss experience and mercantile agency rating categories provides a mechanical credit checking procedure but does not eliminate the need for intensive credit analysis. Any good credit manager would want to assure himself, particularly in the case of accounts in or near the marginal category, that the agency's rating agreed with his own judgment. He would also want to follow such accounts more closely than would be possible by merely noting changes in agency rating classification.

Procedures for determining credit risk categories are usable only for the limited purpose specified—ascertaining the *class* of risk to which credit sales may profitably be made by the particular seller.

## PROFIT AND LOSS ON RELATIVE CREDIT RISKS

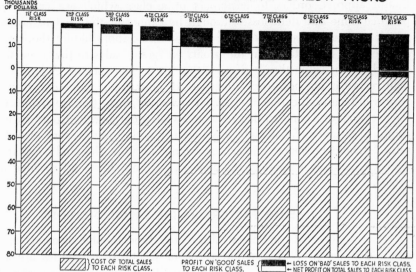

ILLUSTRATION 11-1.  Demonstration of Relationship of Acceptable Risk Categories to Seller's Gross Profit Margin

sales to this category will be only $17,500. The third category has a $5,000 bad debt loss expectation, and net profit on the $100,000 sales to this category will be only $15,000. For each successive category, the expectation of nonpayment for the class is $2,500 higher, and the net profit on the $100,000 of sales to the class is $2,500 lower.

As indicated in Illustration 11-1, some profit is to be derived from selling to the eighth category, for which the anticipated bad debt loss is $17,500, or 17½ per cent. If sales were made to the ninth class, the company would just break even on its direct operating and delivery expenses, though indirectly some profits might result from sales to this class since overhead costs would be spread over a greater volume of production and sales. But sales to the tenth category of customers, for which 22½ per cent of nonpayment is anticipated, would result in a $2,500 direct operating loss.

Obviously, the credit manager of this hypothetical concern should approve orders for all categories of accounts down through the eighth category, possibly even through the ninth. If he checked orders through the eighth category, $70,000 of bad debt losses would have to be expected on the $800,000 of sales, but the maximum net profit of $90,000 would be achieved. If the credit manager were overconservative, and refused to check orders to the eighth category of customers, the company's bad debt loss would be reduced to $52,500 on $700,000 sales, but total net profit would be only $87,500.

The conclusion to be drawn from this analysis is that a credit manager should approve orders to customers of a class which are certain to produce some bad debt losses, though he cannot at the time determine which particular customers in the class will be responsible for the losses. But he must be certain that the profits on "good" sales to that class will exceed the losses on the "bad" sales that are to be expected. A high bad debt record is not necessarily the mark of poor credit judgment. It may very well be an indication of excellent credit judgment that is maximizing the net profit of a concern that sells on a wide profit margin. Contrariwise, complete absence of bad debt loss together with a high record of order refusals could be sound ground for prompt firing of the credit manager who was actually strangling the concern's selling effort and slashing its profits.

### SELLER FACTORS IN THE CREDIT DECISION

As indicated above, the fundamental elements of a credit decision are: (1) determination of what risk categories are acceptable to the seller, and (2) determination of whether the customer is within one of the acceptable categories. What risk categories are acceptable to the seller, depends upon circumstances of the selling concern—the profit margin on which it operates, the market for its goods in relation to its production capacity, its competitive position, possibilities of moving dead stock, any need for special promotional outlets for its goods, its working capital position, its collection techniques, and similar considerations.

#### The seller's profit margin

As a rule, the wider a concern's profit margin on its sales, the poorer the class of credit risks it can afford to supply. Taking the hypothetical case presented in Illustration 11-1, it is the seller's 20% margin of gross profits over direct operating and distribution costs that makes it profitable to sell to eighth-class risks. If its profit margin were only 10%, it would be limited to selling to fourth-class risks, or at the most to fifth-class risks. If it sold to any group of poorer risks, it would lose more on the nonpayments resulting from such sales than it would gain as profit on the acounts on which it collected. A seller whose profit margin was 30% could sell profitably to even lower classes of risks than are shown in Illustration 11-1.

#### Market and production capacity

The relation between the market for a seller's goods and its production capacity may influence determination of the acceptable credit risk level in two ways.

A seller with a market demand for its goods greater than its production capacity can exercise selectivity among its customers. A factor which may influence its choice is their credit standing. It may choose to sell its limited output of goods only to the highest categories of credit risks, even though it would make a net profit on sales to lower categories. Thus, if the hypothetical firm in Illustration 11-1 had a capacity of only $600,000 worth of goods, it would be ridiculous to exclude some customers in the first six risk categories, in order to sell to customers in the seventh and eighth classes and incur greater debt losses. Under these circumstances, the credit manager would approve orders only through the sixth-risk category of customers.

Such credit restriction based on limited output occurs in practice under two circumstances. The first is the case of sellers of quality products that have deliberately chosen to limit their production to a given capacity, because they do not want to risk the quality reputation of their products by seeking mass markets or incur the risks incumbent upon expansion. Some of these quality-product sellers feel that to maintain their product reputation they should market only through quality outlets, with high credit standing. A number of well-known concerns in the men's wear line follow such credit practice. The second circumstance is where extraneous factors limit the output of particular sellers or large classes of sellers. The shortages that developed in so many civilian production lines during World War II forced thousands of manufacturers and wholesalers to restrict their sales to levels far below demand. One way of accomplishing this restriction was to lift the line or margin of credit acceptability which they had previously applied in their credit decisions.

In certain cases production capacity may influence a seller's level of credit acceptability in just the opposite way—it may cause the margin of acceptable credit standing to be lowered. This somewhat anomalous situation is found in manufacturing lines that have very high overhead costs. Such concerns must maintain production at capacity, or at a certain high percentage of capacity, if they are to show profit. When business conditions or a competitive situation cause their sales to fall below the figure necessary to maintain their production at capacity or near-capacity, one method whereby they can bring their sales up to the required figure is to lower their credit standards—to deliberately sell to classes of customers below the credit risk standard established by their profit margin on direct operating costs. Of course they will incur a net loss, calculated against direct operating and distributing costs, on these sales. But their unit overhead will be reduced because total overhead will be spread over the greater production and sale, and this saving on overhead may offset, at least to some extent, the credit loss. The net result may be increased final net profit, or decreased final net loss.

## Competition

Sellers operating in a bitterly competitive market will commonly sell to poor credit risks that they would never consider if they had an exclusive market. Some writers on credit have decried this tendency, holding that a company's standard of acceptable credit risk should be divorced from competitive considerations. There is some justice to this claim, for in these competitive fields we sometimes see efficient sellers forced into insolvency by the failure of customers who were obviously bad credit risks—so bad that, on the basis of the profit margin principle discussed above, sales to them should never have been approved.

There are, however, sound occasions for such practice. If a company has high overhead costs and excess capacity, it may be well advised to sell to poorer-risk categories. Although an apparent net loss will have to be taken on these sales, more widely distributed overhead may make the rest of the sales more profitable. There is also the chance that the expected bad debt loss on the submarginal customers may be held down by shrewd and effective collection procedures so that some net profit may be wrung even from these sales.

## Disposal of "dead" stock

A selling concern sometimes finds itself burdened with "dead" stock —an excess of seasonal goods as a result of misjudging a seasonal demand, a model that did not take the fancy of the market, or stock beyond the needs of its ordinary market purchased at bargain prices through a bankruptcy sale. Such dead inventory ties up working capital and storage space. If it remains unsold too long, it will have only scrap value. The sales force is instructed to make every effort to sell—possibly extra commissions are given to salesmen who get the orders. Suppose several of these orders come from customers who, when investigated, are found to belong to submarginal risk categories. Should they be refused? Probably not. The possible nonpayment loss on such orders may be high—higher than could ordinarily be taken on a risk category in view of the seller's general profit margin. But the certain loss that would ensue from failure to sell the "dead" stock would be still higher. Common sense should dictate approving at least these special orders to the submarginal customers. The credit manager is always free to refuse to check subsequent orders from them which do not involve any of the concern's "dead" stock.

## Maintenance of special promotional outlets

Certain manufacturers of quality men's clothing feel that a lasting market for their product is developed by promotional efforts directed at college men. The young man who becomes used to the style and quality of a particular brand-line of suits, shirts, or other articles of wearing apparel during his impressionable college years may remain a customer of that brand for life. Therefore these manufacturers make every effort to find and keep outlets for their product in as many college towns as possible. Sometimes the only clothing store in a college town that can carry their line is submarginal by their credit risk standard. In such case, the credit consideration is outweighed by the promotional consideration; orders to such an outlet will be approved—though with a self-notation by the credit manager to keep a particularly sharp eye on payments by the account. Nonpayment losses on such sales of course run very high—high enough, possibly, to wipe out all profit on this class of sales. Such net loss, however, is viewed as part of the company's promotional expense.

In other lines of business similar considerations often determine continued selling to substandard outlets which have special promotional value. Greater nonpayment loss can be taken on these accounts than would be warranted by strict consideration of the ordinary profit principle.

### The seller's working capital position

One intermediate risk category generally recognized by credit managers is the group of customers who may eventually be expected to pay their accounts in full but who, because of weak working capital positions, are practically certain to be "slow pays" for some time to come. Persistent collection pressure will obtain their checks for all purchases—but 30 to 60 days late, or with even longer delays. A seller with a good working capital position can afford to carry such accounts, and the eventual net profit on sales to them is only slightly less than that on sales to prompt-paying customers. But a seller with a weak working capital position may not be able to take on such buyers. The certain delay in receiving payments from such customers may leave its bank balance so depleted that it will be unable to meet its bank and trade debts as they fall due, thereby injuring its own credit standing and making more difficult the obtaining of the future credit accommodations it will undoubtedly need. Regretfully the credit manager of a seller pinched for working capital must say "no" to orders from such customers, even though they otherwise constitute an acceptable risk category, and even though competitors are not merely willing, but glad, to sell to them.

### Collection techniques

The more efficient a credit department is in its collection procedures, the poorer are the credit risks to which it may safely sell. In effect, a vigorous collection technique reduces the nonpayment loss that may be expected from each risk category. Such reduction of loss probability by collection efficiency may make a poor-risk category of customers acceptable.

A particular application of this principle may be observed in the case of a concern that obtains its orders primarily through traveling salesmen who visit their accounts at short intervals—semi-monthly, monthly, or bi-monthly. There are limitations to the use of salesmen as collectors, as we shall see in a later chapter. Where such collection technique is possible, however, the probability of nonpayment by poor-risk customers is reduced. If terms are net 30, and a salesman visits a customer every 60 days, he is able to act personally on any item before it becomes more than 30 days overdue. Dealing face-to-face with the customer, he may succeed in making collections which might not be obtained if the credit department depended exclusively on correspondence. Consequently, a credit department can approve sales to a poorer-risk category of customers if such personal collection procedures are applied.

### Limitation of credit department work

One reason why many manufacturers prefer to sell through jobbers rather than directly to retailers or industrial consumers is that the former practice saves them credit difficulties as well as merchandising difficulties. Instead of having to check thousands of retailer and manufacturer accounts, many of them of marginal character, the credit department need concern itself with the accounts of only a few wholesalers, who as a class generally are of a higher credit standing than the mass of retailers and small manufacturers. Some large manufacturers of quality and well-known brand products, however, have developed a compromise procedure which enables them to sell directly to a limited number of retail and manufacturing accounts without unduly increasing their credit function. They make direct sales at a substantial cash discount—smaller, however, than the trade discount which they give to jobbers, so that the manufacturer and the discounting customer in effect split the jobber's "spread" between them—to retailers and manufacturers of only the highest credit standing; in many cases, indeed, their direct sales are limited to discounting customers. All other buyers must purchase through jobbers who offer less generous cash discounts and may charge higher net prices.

The credit department of a manufacturing company operating on such a credit policy obviously foregoes the profits that might be derived from customers in lower credit categories but recovers at least a part of such lost profits by the sales to jobbers. It is a common practice in many lines of business—for example, in the rayon industry.

## CUSTOMER FACTORS IN THE CREDIT DECISION

Determination by a credit manager of what categories of credit risks his company, in view of its particular circumstances, may accept is only the preliminary step in the making of his credit decisions. It provides a background to his major task—determination of which would-be customers fall into the category of acceptable credit risks, and which must be handled as submarginal cases.

It is commonly said, by practicing credit managers as well as by teachers of mercantile credit, that an account is rated, for credit purposes, on the "three C's"—the customer's Character, Capacity, and Capital.[2] The alliteration of the "three C's" is a convenient aid to memory, if their meaning is clearly understood. "Capital," for example, is not confined to the customer's net worth as it appears in a balance sheet. It represents the *general financial position* of a customer, of which balance sheet net worth is only one element.

### Character

In a credit sale, the seller exchanges his goods for the customer's *promise* to pay at a future date. That promise is worth little if a customer does not intend to keep it, or if he is a moral weakling who will fail a promise that has become irksome to perform, or if he has vices that may bar him from fulfilling his promise.

Admittedly, evidence of highest character in the past is not a guaranty of continued business probity. Many business frauds have been perpetrated by individuals whose prior record was untarnished. Nevertheless, all credit managers consider previous character an important factor in grading a customer as a credit risk. Many credit managers rate character the most important of all the factors.

How can a credit manager learn of a customer's character, of his distinctive inner nature which motivates his actions and his relations with other men?

There is no objective yardstick for so subjective a factor as personal character. All that a credit manager seeks are scattered outward signs that may reflect or correlate with that inner complex of compulsions and inhibitions of the customer that we call character. He does not hope

---

[2] Some writers add a fourth C for Conditions. This is not a customer factor, however, and does not properly belong with the three other C's. In our analysis, study of "conditions," or extraneous factors which influence the credit decision, follows the present analysis of customer factors.

to build up rounded character pictures of his customers from available objective information. But enough may be learned to give him a basis for determining the *probability* that a customer's promise of future payment is honestly given and that its fulfillment will be resolutely attempted.

The most important customer character sign for which a credit manager looks is a record of actual frauds or of actions that may possibly have been fraudulent. Any such record noted in a mercantile agency report would establish a would-be customer as a zero moral risk. A record of bankruptcies or of fires covered by insurance, particularly if contested, would raise the suspicion—unwarranted in a particular case, perhaps, but nonetheless raised—that the man had previously cheated his creditors or might have committed arson, and hence might do it again. The discovery, through ledger interchange, that a would-be customer persistently takes unearned discounts, or that his trade debts are frequently turned over to collection agencies or brought to suit (indicating that he wilfully avoids payment until the last crucial pressure is applied), would likewise condemn him as a moral risk.

If a customer is reported as intemperate in his addiction to liquor, a race track habitué, or indulging in speculation, these vices are viewed as reducing the probability that he will fulfill his promises of future payment. They indicate an element of irresponsibility which may carry over to his business relations. They may also, at times, absorb resources needed for the payment of his business obligations and so prevent such payment.

A family man is deemed a better moral risk than a bachelor or a divorced individual, even though the head of a family usually has greater personal liabilities than an unmarried man. The responsibilities of a family are supposed to make him more careful, more conservative in his business ventures. While conservatism may check a man from reaching the pinnacles of success to be achieved by taking risks, it makes him a preferable risk from the credit viewpoint. A very large family—five or more children—may lower the "character" rating of a customer operating a small business, since it may weaken its financial security.

Church and civic affiliations are viewed as indications of good character. But a business man who also holds a responsible public office may be deemed an inferior credit risk, for in such cases the customer's attention to public affairs may interfere with efficient conduct of his business.

Finally, a credit manager must take into account a customer's reputation—what other business men think of him. The mercantile agency report may state, "Enjoys good reputation." The letter from the customer's bank may say, "Well thought of in the community." Replies from other suppliers with whom the credit manager has exchanged ledger information may contain comments either favorable or unfavorable. Other items of reputation may be gleaned from the "Remarks" column of the NACM interchange report. These comments reflect character judgments by other credit managers, some of whom may have had more intimate associations or longer experience with the customer than the credit manager faced with making his credit decision. Some of these comments may have to be taken with reservation—those of the bank, for example, and those from the customer's references. But the others deserve, and are usually given, great weight.

## Capacity

More business failures may be traced to the incapacity of their proprietors than to any other cause. "To have a business of my own" is the dream of hundreds of thousands of men who chafe at taking orders from an employer and who feel that they could earn more in a business than they look forward to receiving as wages or salaries. They do not realize that success in business, even in a small retail store, requires a combination of abilities not possessed by all individuals. Every year several thousand men stake their hopes and their little accumulations of capital on some "business of their own"; the greater part of them fail within a few years.

Assessment of capacity must be made not only in the case of founders of new enterprises but also time and again during the life of the business. A supplier receives an order which indicates that a customer is adding new lines, or is enlarging his enterprise. While the business was conducted on a smaller scale, the abilities of the owner were commensurate to the problems he faced. But will his abilities measure up to the intricacies of the enlarged business? Many a man who was successful in a small enterprise has failed conspicuously to master the different and more difficult techniques of a large-scale undertaking. Or the case may be that of a one-man enterprise built around the capacity of an individual now in his 60's. Are his energy, his mental alertness, beginning to decline? How long before the disabilities of age will cause his business to deteriorate? What are the possibilities that his death may leave the business with nothing but a salvage value or complicated estate entanglements? In a further example, a corporation replaces a key executive. Does the new man have the capacity of his predecessor? Will the business improve or decline under his guidance?

Granting that a customer is a good moral risk, his long-run credit standing is determined primarily by his ability. The third judgment factor—the customer's general financial position—is, as we shall see, primarily a short-run determinant.

A special aspect of "capacity"—legal capacity of the owner of an unincorporated business to incur debts—will be considered before turning to the subject of general business ability. In most states a person under 21 is deemed an "infant" who can at any time prior to his majority disaffirm a contract; in some states majority is reached at the age of 18, in some others if the person marries before 21. When a contract is disaffirmed by an "infant," the seller may recover the goods unless they have been sold or otherwise disposed of. There are variations, too, among the states as to the extent to which a married woman can be held responsible for debts which she contracts without the consent of her husband, and as to whether she can act as surety for her husband. A mercantile agency report would, of course, indicate whether a customer were an infant. An agency rating for an infant's business would be "poor" and so would discourage the granting of credit. Still, an order from an infant may be received before his business has been reported by the agencies. Therefore orders from a new customer not covered by the agency rating book should provoke inquiry, among other matters, as to the age of the purchaser. And where a customer is a married woman, a credit manager should check in the NACM *Credit Manual of Commercial Laws* as to her rights. He will find those rights curtailed in a number of states.

Much of the information on a customer's capacity is indirect and inferential. First and foremost, in the case of established concerns, there is the past record of the business. Has it been in existence under the present management for any considerable length of time? That in itself is a favorable point, for mere survival in the competitive business struggle demands ability of a fairly high order. Is the business on the up-grade or the down-grade? Are its production techniques efficient? Is its marketing policy sound? Are its labor relations mutually satisfactory? If the business is a new one, what was the previous business record of the owner or manager? Did he have experience in the line he is now entering, or is it a completely new venture for him? What was his educational background? Answers to all these questions can usually be found in an agency report on the customer.

Trend and comparative analysis of the customer's financial statements usually throws considerable light on his business ability. In the first place, if the statements disclose the absence of an adequate accounting system, the customer stands condemned as lacking even the rudiments of present-day business knowledge. Trend analysis of the statements should indicate, more accurately than any generalized comment in an agency report, whether the business is an improving or a deteriorating one. Comparative analysis shows up such faults, indicative of bad business judgment, as excessive overhead, excessive inventory, poor control of receivables, a bad working capital position, or inadequate net worth.

A salesman's report on the appearance of a customer's store, and his judgment on the man's business methods, may provide good pointers to the man's ability. Best of all, when it can be obtained, is the credit manager's own judgment of the customer from an interview with him.

## General financial position

Few credit executives would subscribe without qualification to Juvenal's comment that "a man's credit is proportional to the money he keeps in his storeroom." [3] However, a customer's general financial position is unquestionably the all-important consideration in determining a credit manager's immediate decision on particular orders. Does the available information on the customer indicate the probability of his early failure? And if such failure is likely, will the salvage value of his assets cover his trade and other debts? Is the customer fundamentally financially sound but temporarily suffering from a weak working capital position so that, although a good long-run credit risk, he is certain for a while to be "slow pay"?

Indications of imminent failure are generally good reason for refusing further credit to a customer and for pressing him to pay any owed balances. The difficulties of a business on the down-grade are cumulative, and once the foreshadows of business failure appear, the question generally is not "Is recovery possible?" but "How short a time remains before bankruptcy?" Ordinarily the salvageable value of a failed business is only a fraction of its liabilities, and the creditors receive as bankruptcy dividends only small percentages of their claims. Hence it behooves any seller to discontinue further credit sales and clear an account as far as possible once a customer's financial position becomes precarious; continued support of a failing customer, in the desperate hope that such support may enable him to recover, often results in throwing good money after bad.

Occasionally, however, an unincorporated enterprise that is on the verge of failure may be an acceptable credit risk if the owner or partners possess judgment-liable property not associated with the business, sufficient to satisfy the liabilities of the enterprise, which may be reached by creditors of the business. This situation could not arise with a corporation, of course, because of the limited liability of the shareholders, unless independently well-to-do officers or stockholders of the corporation guarantee its liabilities. Some credit managers disapprove the authorizing of further credit sales solely on the basis of a customer's personal assets. They feel that such action would only swell the ultimate liabilities of the business without preventing its downfall. Many credit managers, how-

---

[3] "Quantum quisque sua nummorum servat in arca tantum habet et fidei"—Juvenal, *Satires*, III, 143-144.

ever, salve their conscience in this matter with the argument that the business should be given one last chance to redeem itself.

Sometimes analysis of a customer's current financial position shows that his sales are moving satisfactorily, that he has a substantial net worth, and that in other ways he is a sound credit risk in the long run. Possibly, however, as an incident to expansion with limited funds, a disproportionate part of his capital, for the time being, may be tied up in equipment or other fixtures; or part of his capital may be "frozen" in excessive inventory; or he may have slow-paying receivables; or a substantial mortgage payment or term loan repayment may have recently been made or may soon mature. With his operating capital position thus impaired, the customer cannot possibly pay all his trade accounts as they come due. He must become delinquent upon some of them. In time, by clearing his excess inventory, or liquidating some of his "frozen" receivables, or plowing back his profits, the customer will again achieve a liquid position and be able to pay promptly. Still, at present he has no choice but to be "slow pay."

Such a customer clearly is not a top-class credit risk. Neither should he be considered submarginal, except for sellers that must be paid promptly or that have their own operating capital positions impaired. He falls into an intermediate category, earmarked for special treatment. Perhaps he may be allowed the regular terms but be subjected to more diligent collection follow-up. Perhaps his special situation may be frankly recognized and longer terms than the regular ones be granted with the understanding that he will pay these promptly. Perhaps such longer terms are placed upon a trade acceptance basis. In any case, his peculiar financial condition gives rise to special credit treatment.

A "financial position" consideration of great importance is, as already previously indicated, whether the account carries adequate insurance. Without it, a small business that was otherwise an excellent credit risk might be wiped out in an hour by fire and its creditors would probably take almost complete losses on what it owed them. If it carried adequate insurance, it would receive a cash reimbursement that could clear all its obligations. Similarly a customer without automobile liability insurance might be forced abruptly into bankruptcy, with consequent loss for all its trade creditors, if a heavy award against it were made for death or injuries inflicted by one of its delivery trucks. By slow and painful education, credit managers are becoming aware of the importance of insurance as an element in a customer's financial position, and are learning to inquire about the insurance carried by their customers and to advise them about it.

Information on a customer's current financial position is derived from two sources—his financial statement (plus any supplementary financial information that he or his accountant submits) and ledger interchange among his suppliers. The financial statements may be obtained from agency reports or directly from the customer. They are interpreted in accordance with the techniques of financial statement analysis discussed in the three preceding chapters. Ledger interchange gives more immediate information about a customer's trade liabilities and how he is meeting them. One detail that should be checked in the case of a doubtful noncorporate customer is the exemption law of his state, as summarized in the *Credit Manual of Commercial Laws.* As will be shown in Chapter 19, the element of legal exemption can seriously affect the salvage possibility of an insolvent, noncorporate account.

## Relative weights of customer credit factors

It is difficult to assess the relative weight of the credit factors on the customer side. The importance of each of the C's varies with the individual case and the surrounding circumstances. No arbitrary assignment of certain percentage values to each "C" should be made.

Sometimes character is the only factor on which a credit manager can base his decision. He will have to do that, for example, in the cases of small retail or service enterprises that start with a low capital which they gradually increase as they plow back profits over the years, and where at the beginning the business capacity of the owner is an unknown factor. Such situations faced credit managers with regard to a whole trade in the early 1930's when the sale of liquor was relegalized. Dispensers and retail stores were established for the most part by individuals with little capital, and often with no experience in the field they were entering. The beer and liquor manufacturers and the wholesalers either had to sell to a large proportion of accounts that on financial and capacity grounds were the lowest type of credit risks, or not sell at all. Hence, for some time the main factor in the credit decisions in this line was the character of the proprietor. Inquiry through mercantile agency reports and salesmen's information was directed primarily to this point.

Most credit managers take the position that they will not give credit terms to a customer who has a record of fraud, or whose record raises a strong suspicion of fraud. In such instances character becomes not merely the most important of the three customer credit factors, but the decisive one. Apart from this situation, character and ability are viewed as essentially long-term factors. Where a customer's character and ability are rated favorably, and an initial study of his financial statement shows him to be in a satisfactory position, a credit manager will commonly give a liberal credit limit. The account thereafter receives a minimum of attention. Its rating is checked as a matter of course with each new issue of the rating book to make sure that there has been no change. Each year the customer's financial statement is examined to see if the satisfactory financial position has been maintained. But the drawing of an agency report may be omitted for a year or two if the credit manager has to economize; NACM interchange reports may not be drawn at all under such conditions as long as the financial statements remain favorable. Orders from the account are for the most part checked through automatically on the basis of its credit limit.

If the character or ability ratings of the customer are low the credit manager will tab the account for constant watching, even though the initial financial position may be satisfactory. A low credit limit is set, so that the general credit position of the account is reviewed frequently whenever new orders bring the balance to the limit. Ledger interchange information is followed closely, either through repeated NACM reports or by raising the name at credit men's group meetings. Any weakening of the financial position or payment record of such an account is a danger signal.

Where a customer has a poor general financial position, the account must also be observed continuously and carefully, no matter how high its character and ability ratings. It is vulnerable, and further deterioration is dangerous. For such an account a credit manager not only seeks all available ledger interchange material, but also subscribes to agency continuous service. An Argus-eyed vigilance must be exercised.

Few customers remain forever gilt-edge risks. For most of them the credit picture changes from year to year, sometimes from month to month. A man believed completely trustworthy does something that throws doubt upon his character. With experience a man's ability rating may rise; with age it may fall; or a corporation changes managers, with resulting improvement or lessening of its ability rating. Bad financial positions may gradually improve; good ones may deteriorate slowly or overnight. As these transformations occur, the credit manager must not only readjust the ratings of his customers as to character, capacity, and financial position; he must further readjust the relative importance of these factors for each particular case and reshape his treatment of the accounts.

## EXTRANEOUS FACTORS IN THE CREDIT DECISION

A credit executive must never ignore business trends and other extraneous conditions, either in establishing acceptable and nonacceptable credit risk categories for his concern, or in ranking his accounts in those categories. His own standards of acceptability should vary as business conditions change, and the credit positions of his customers may alter violently with shifts in the business picture.

## Business conditions and the seller's standards
## of credit risk acceptability

Should rising costs, falling prices, or a decline in the volume of production and sale, narrow the profit margin that a seller has been accustomed to earn on its sales, with the prospect that this reduced gross profit will have to be accepted for some time to come, the credit manager ought to review his credit standards and tighten them, since some customers that were acceptable risks under the old profit margin may no longer be acceptable under the new one. Contrariwise, if for any reason increased profit margins develop, with a prospect of their being maintained, the credit manager should liberalize his credit standards.

The credit manager of a business that must maintain near-capacity production to earn its profit should always be scanning the business horizon to anticipate the demand for his company's products. It is not enough for him to liberalize his credit policy after sales have actually fallen off, in order to restore the sales volume. He should anticipate the ebb and flow of market demand and readjust his credit standards in advance of the actual shifts of demand, so that when a slackening does occur, it will already have been compensated by a liberalized credit policy, and sales will be maintained at the capacity level. Anticipation of a seller's market is not so important, since a credit manager can always instantaneously cut off approval of orders to poorer-risk customers when his concern's output is being largely absorbed by high-rated buyers.

## Business conditions and customers' credit risk status

It is even more important for a credit executive to foresee business conditions in his customers' fields. Here he must not only forecast general trends on a national scale but also local developments that influence his customers' ability to pay even more crucially. The credit manager of a clothing manufacturer who correctly anticipated a general boom in clothing purchases would make costly mistakes in credit authorization if his forecast failed to take into account a buying slump in a particular community where employment depended primarily on an industry that was in severe straits. Favorable local conditions, on the other hand, together with a general boom situation may make a customer with no business ability whatsoever, and with inadequate financial means, a good credit risk for so long as the boom continues. A general depression on a national scale, or bad local conditions due to poor regional crops, or a protracted strike in the dominant industry of a town, or a flood, will wipe out not only the businesses of men with little ability or low capital but also many inherently well-managed enterprises as well.

Some lines of business are more sensitive to business cycle and price variations than others. A slight recession hardly felt in retail lines, for example, might cause the business of machine tool companies to decline to a minor fraction of its preceding level. Lines that must carry heavy inventories of goods are particularly vulnerable to price recessions. Textile converters, for example, tend to buy with an eye to speculative price changes as well as from regular supply considerations. A converter having purchased merchandise would have considerable difficulty in making payments if gray goods prices subsequently dropped. Similarly, a fall in the price of finished fabrics might leave converters with goods which they could sell only at prices insufficient to meet their trade debts on that merchandise. Such considerations are specially pertinent because small textile converters frequently operate on shoestring net worth. Hence, a credit manager must not only endeavor to forecast business conditions and price trends in his customers' lines, but he must also judge the relative severity of the impact of these business and price fluctuations upon his various classes of customers and even on individual accounts. Delicate problems may also arise for the credit manager whose company sells to two or more customers who compete with each other and whose competitive position he is therefore influencing.

### Government policy and customers' credit risk status

Government policy may, in some cases, be a key consideration in the credit standing of a class of customers or particular buyers. For example, the tax situation can be important. A business suffering a current-year loss may be eligible for a substantial "carry-back" refund of previously paid income taxes. A credit manager considering a buyer with a poor current financial position, but whose financial statements show substantial income tax payments for preceding years, should realize that this situation may make all the difference between the customer being an acceptable or unacceptable credit risk. Another example of the credit importance of government policy is provided by the system of awarding government contracts, and particularly the possibility that the recipient of a defense contract may get it financed by a government-guaranteed loan. A customer qualifying for such a loan might be an excellent risk; without it he might be unacceptable.

Government policy, on the other hand, may also adversely affect a customer's credit standing. Wartime price ceilings during the 1940's, unfavorable allotments of scarce raw materials, and renegotiation of government military supply contracts to reduce profits, are examples of such possibilities; taxes may also work in this direction. In some periods a credit manager may have to review continuously the situation of some of his customers, particularly those with doubtful financial positions, with regard to positive or negative implications of governmental policies.

## SPECIAL CREDIT ARRANGEMENTS WITH SUBMARGINAL CUSTOMERS

When a new customer is found to be submarginal with respect to regular credit terms, or the financial position of an old customer deteriorates to that level, he may still be converted to an acceptable risk if special arrangements can be made to protect the supplier.

### Cash, prepayment, and consignment terms

The most common special arrangement with submarginal customers is "cash" or no-credit terms of sale.

As indicated in Chapter 2, "cash" terms generally mean payment within ten days of the invoice date, so that risk of nonpayment still remains. But this risk is reduced in two ways; the customer's orders tend to be smaller, and there is little likelihood of cumulation of unpaid deliveries.

C.O.D. and S.D.-B.L. terms, if firmly enforced, eliminate all risk of nonpayment of trade debt, but they involve the supplier in risk of a different kind. If a customer is unable to pay on arrival of a shipment or had ordered with fraudulent intent, and the supplier's credit manager refuses to allow the carrier to release the shipment without payment, his company not only loses a sale but has to pay two-way freight costs.

C.B.D. terms give 100 per cent security to the seller. They are particularly to be recommended where a customer's low credit rating is attributable to the moral risk involved, and when selling to a business operated by a bankruptcy receiver or trustee. Where the low credit rating is due to the customer's weak financial position, there is little probability that C.B.D. terms will be accepted, unless the order is absolutely essential to continuation of his business; if he honestly cannot find funds to meet his overdue trade obligations, he is not likely to be able to pay in advance of receipt of goods. But no harm is done by a diplomatic offer of C.B.D. terms, and occasionally a sale that would otherwise be missed can be effected thereby.

A not uncommon practice for customers that are borderline cases because of financial weakness is to offer to sell them on "split-shipment" terms—part C.B.D., part regular. One-quarter or one-half of the total invoice amount may be requested before delivery, the remainder to be paid on the regular net 30 or net 60 basis. Such an arrangement does not completely impugn the customer's credit standing, and his good will is thus maintained; yet the credit manager has substantially reduced any loss that his firm might have to sustain should the customer eventually default.

Consignment terms, explained in Chapter 2, involve so much supervision of the buyer by the seller that they are not commonly employed for ordinary merchandise. In those instances where automobiles, durable household equipment, and similar items of substantial size and value are involved, or where a large delivery of raw material can be earmarked to a particular production order on which the manufacturer is engaged, consignment may be the only practicable means of selling to a sub-marginal customer and still protecting the seller.

When a customer orders on regular terms, and a credit manager decides that the sale should be made only on one of the special terms noted above, he is not free to direct shipment on one of these special terms and then notify the customer. No legal contract has been made that would bind the customer. The customer's purchase order presuming regular terms, or the salesman's slip that embodied the customer's purchase order, was a legal offer to buy. But when the credit manager refused to authorize the sale on regular terms, this offer was not accepted. The credit manager must make a new offer of the sale on the special terms to the customer, and the customer must accept it before a valid contract comes into existence.

A letter offering the customer special terms affords the credit manager an opportunity to exercise his finest talents as a correspondent. The situation is a delicate one. He must somehow tell the customer that the latter is not a satisfactory credit risk, yet maintain his good will to the extent of obtaining an order on terms that will probably aggravate the customer. The letter should, in one way or another, assist the customer to maintain his self-esteem. In a line where "repeat" orders are not an important element, special terms may be proposed as a means of speeding delivery while more favorable credit information is sought. While referring to the factor that temporarily makes the customer a poor credit risk, his self-importance can be built up by also mentioning favorable factors.

Confidence may be expressed in the customer's ability and certainly in his integrity. His feelings may be salved by not singling him out as an individual case, but merging him in a group, by use of expressions such as "anyone" or "any business man." His difficulties may be attributed to causes outside his control by reference to some "unexpected circumstance" or local situation. The opportunity should be seized to show him that the special terms offered will benefit him by assuring him of a cash discount. It should also be implied that the arrangement can be revised, by phrases such as "for the time being," or "until conditions improve." The credit manager should emphasize that his company is genuinely interested in the customer's success and values him as a customer. The following is an example of a letter embodying these principles: [4]

---

[4] H. M. Sommers, "The Psychology of Credit Letters," *Credit and Financial Management,* December 1942, p. 10.

Gentlemen:

Thank you for your order and for the opportunity to demonstrate our service and the quality of our merchandise.

The usual credit investigation preliminary to opening a new account has brought us a Dun & Bradstreet report giving us the interesting history of your business, and details of your present financial situation.

You are securing a very good volume, but when we compare it with your receivables, it is apparent that your customers are not cooperating with you properly in paying their bills. The money you have tied up in amounts overdue from your customers could be used to reduce your own indebtedness, which we feel is rather heavy, and to eliminate the reports of slowness up to 90 and 120 days which are coming from your creditors.

It is not in the spirit of criticism that we mention this, for no doubt you are already taking steps to bring this situation under control. Our policy, however, does not provide for credit accommodations where payments are slow to this extent, and we therefore regret that we cannot ship your order on open account. We should, however, like to review your situation again in six months, and take up the matter of credit with you then.

In the meantime, may we suggest that you permit us to ship your requirements on a cash basis. You can earn a discount of . . . per cent, which certainly gives you a much more substantial return than current interest rates.

If you will let us have your reply promptly, we can still get the goods to you in time for Saturday's business.

Your customers will certainly like the sheer beauty of this style, and you can depend upon its giving good service.

Yours very truly,

## Collateral security

A substantial proportion of bank loans are made on the basis of collateral security, rather than exclusively on the client's credit standing. Collateral security is also a factor in personal loans, and in mercantile instalment credit. It does not commonly enter ordinary mercantile credit. The usual mercantile credit office is not equipped to deal with collateral security in the form of stocks, bonds, mortgages, assigned commercial paper, or other instruments. In several instances, however, collateral security is recognized and made a basis of ordinary mercantile credit extensions; such usage is increasing.[5]

The one class of collateral security that can be introduced without excessive complication into mercantile credit procedure is the *third-party surety or guarantor*. A submarginal customer may become a good credit risk if another party with good credit standing will accept liability for the customer's debt should the customer himself fail to make payment. The guaranty, of course, is as good or bad as the guarantor. This third party may be a relative, wife, or friend owning property,[6] or it may

---

[5] See H. Reinhardt, *Recent Trends in Credit Practices—Terms of Sale and Collection Practices in 32 Industries* (Credit Research Foundation, New York, 1955), p. 10.

[6] A credit manager should check carefully in the NACM *Credit Manual of Commercial Law* whether a married woman can be a guarantor of another person's debt in the particular state.

be the sound parent of a weak subsidiary corporation, or the sound subsidiary of a weak parent corporation, or even a salesman with special faith in an account. The major supplier of an important promotional outlet may guarantee its accounts with other suppliers. An officer or major stockholder of a weak corporation may accept responsibility for its debts.

These third party undertakings may assume either of two forms. More commonly, a weak customer may be required to give promissory notes, with the third party's accommodation endorsement or, more rarely, co-signature. If the customer fails to pay an endorsed note at maturity, the seller may protest the nonpayment and proceed against the third party. The other form of third party undertaking is the separate contract of guaranty, under which the third party guarantees payment of the customer's account up to a stated maximum balance. Should the customer default, action lies against the guarantor on his contract. In each form of third party undertaking, the consideration for acceptance of the customer's liability by the third party is the sale by the supplier to the customer upon the specified credit terms.

An examination should always be made into the capacity or authority of a third-party guarantee. Is such action within the scope of a partnership agreement? Would a third-party guarantee by a corporation be *ultra vires?* Does a particular corporate officer have the authority to bind his company in this matter?

A second and not uncommon form of mercantile credit collateral is assignment of payments under a contract. A manufacturer who has obtained a substantial order but whose weak credit standing precludes him from buying materials and supplies for the operation on regular terms, may sometimes obtain the needed credit extensions by assigning to his suppliers part of the payments that will be made to him under the contract.[7]

Still another form of collateral security is the statutory lien upon land and structures thereon given by law in most states to suppliers of building materials used in building construction. It is called a *mechanic's* or *materialman's lien.* In states that follow the so-called "Pennsylvania" system, materialmen who supply a building contractor with his materials may obtain a lien upon any building into the construction of which their materials specifically enter, and upon the land on which such building is erected. This lien is superior to the principal contractor's lien upon the property. Should the owner of the property fail to pay the principal con-

---

[7] Note that assignment of payables to suppliers is generally not feasible as far as government contracts are concerned. Here payments may be assigned only to financial institutions; exceptions to this regulation, such as assignments to suppliers, need the special permission of the contracting government unit in order to be effective and are rare.

tractor so that he in turn cannot pay his materialmen, or should the principal contractor be paid but fail to make his due payments to the materialmen, these latter can establish liens upon the property for the amounts owed to them. Under the so-called "New York" system, materialmen do not obtain a direct lien upon the property, which may be had only by the principal contractor. They may give written notice to the owner of unpaid claims, and require him thereupon to retain such funds due the contractor as remain in his hands, and apply such funds to payment of the materialmen; upon his failure to do so, they have right of action against him or may secure a lien upon the property.

These legal rights may be of significant importance to the credit manager of a concern that supplies materials to building contractors. Some of these contractors may be submarginal credit risks, yet they can safely be sold on credit terms if a materialman's lien can be established. For this purpose materials must be sold to the contractor for exclusive use on a particular property. Without this provision, the lien could not apply. The credit manager of the supplier company would also have to ascertain that the contract between the builder and the owner of the property did not preclude liens in the four or five jurisdictions where such clauses can block the materialman's lien. He would have to study carefully, in any case, the details of the mechanic's or materialman's lien laws in the *Credit Manual of Commercial Law* published by the National Association of Credit Management.

The building supply line enjoys still other forms of collateral security. Many contractors, particularly those working on public structures, are compelled by their principals to take out *performance bonds* and *labor and material payment bonds* for the protection of subcontractors, material suppliers, and workers on the construction. Such bonding of the contract gives a materials supplier greater security than a materialman's lien since, if the contractor fails to pay the supplier, the latter has immediate recourse to the bonding company. So-called *retainages* are amounts up to 20 per cent withheld from construction payments until completion of the job in conformity with contract specifications. Unpaid materialmen can claim payment from these retainages.

### Subordination of claims

Sometimes balance sheet study of an unacceptable credit risk shows that a substantial element of its liabilities is owed to officers or other principals of the company. If the seller's claims could have priority over these others, the account would be acceptable creditwise, at least for the time being. Such priority can be obtained by having these "internal" claims subordinated, through specific agreement involving the creditors' consent,[8] to those of the seller. On rare occasions, a key supplier may also be able to obtain subordination of the claims of other *trade* creditors as a condition of continuing to sell on credit terms to a weak customer.

### Placing "slow pay" customers on a T.A. basis

Suppose that trade reports indicate that a customer, new or old, is substantially late in payments to a goodly proportion of his suppliers, and analysis of his financial statements shows that, while he is fundamentally sound, his operating capital position is weak and he simply cannot avoid lateness in many of his payments. Given such circumstances, it would generally be optimistic self-delusion for a credit manager to expect that his concern will be paid promptly. His realistic objective should be to obtain some airtight assurance that he will be paid in an extended period not longer than, or possibly slightly shorter than, that for other suppliers. This can often be achieved by arranging trade acceptance terms with the customer.

Despite the advantages of the trade acceptance as an instrument of mercantile credit, indicated in an earlier chapter of this book, it must be recognized that most customers view trade acceptance terms as a reflection on their credit standing and resent any proposal to place them upon such terms, no matter how well warranted such proposal may be. The letter embodying the proposal must be a little masterpiece of diplomacy if the good will of a customer who is, after all, a good long-run risk is not to be sacrificed. Like letters proposing "cash," C.O.D., or C.B.D. terms, previously discussed, it should flatter the self-esteem of the customer while pointing out the plain circumstance of his general delinquency in payments. A good opportunity exists, however, for picturing the T.A. proposal as a minor return favor which the customer will grant in exchange for a major favor—extension of the terms of sale—which the seller proposes to grant. Thus, if the customer is averaging 120 days in his payments, and the seller's regular terms are net 30, the letter might read, after the introductory discussion of the customer's slow payment record:

> Our regular terms, as you know, are net 30. We recognize, however, that prompt payment in accordance with these regular terms might temporarily work hardship upon you. For the next few months, while you are restoring a more favorable working capital position, we wish to cooperate with you by allowing you a special 90-day term.

Then, and not without some such introduction, would follow the proposal that the customer give trade acceptances on his invoices. This proposal

---

[8] Such an agreement has exacting legal requirements and it should be prepared by an attorney familiar with this field of law, or be based on the sample subordination agreement form presented in the *Credit Manual of Commercial Laws, 1961,* p. 712.

should not appear to be a special requirement demanded of this particular customer, but as a general procedure followed by the supplier with regard to a group of customers; the disarming preamble to the T.A. proposal might be a sentence such as the following:

> Whenever we arrange extended terms for a customer, such as yourself, in whose success we have faith, it is our policy to ask the return favor of a trade acceptance.

In such manner the request for trade acceptances can be made to appear a concomitant to special terms offered to sound credit risks instead of a degrading penalty imposed upon "slow pays."

In securing a trade acceptance from a slow-paying account, a credit manager reduces only slightly the long-run risk of nonpayment. He does improve his chances of collecting promptly at the agreed time, however, for most businessmen will arrange to meet a signed obligation when due whereas they might permit an open account to lag. This is a distinct collection gain. Finally, instead of endangering the customer's good will by an exigent series of collection letters, the credit manager has placed his concern in the favorable light of sympathetically cooperating with the customer in his temporary difficulty.

## SUPPLEMENTARY READINGS

Ballard, G. F., "Retainage Changes 5 Billion Dollars from Working Capital to Waiting Capital," *Credit and Financial Management,* August 1959, p. 12.

"Can Federal Contracts Be Assigned?" *Credit Executive,* October 1951, p. 5.

Carey, H. D., "Use, Nature, and Functions of Three Basic Legal Instruments," *Credit and Financial Management,* February 1958, p. 9.

*Credit and Financial Management,* annual insurance number.

Cushman, R. I., "Credit Problems in Construction," *Credit and Financial Management,* November 1951, p. 10.

National Association of Credit Management, *Appraising and Accepting a First Order,* New York, n.d.

————, *Bonds on Public Works,* New York, 1960.

————, *Converting Marginal Accounts into Profit Customers,* New York, n.d.

————, *Increased Profits from Marginal Accounts,* New York, n.d.

Surety Association of America, *Bonds of Suretyship,* New York, 1959.

————, *Public Bond Issues for New Projects—Surety Safeguards,* New York, 1958.

Weintraub, B., and H. Levin, *What the Business Executive Should Know about Guaranties of Debts and Subordination of Claims,* New York Credit and Financial Management Association, 1957.

## REVIEW

1. What four functions must be successfully performed by a credit department so that it can properly approve a maximum number of orders received?
2. What is the lowest risk category of customers that should be given credit terms by any seller? How might a credit manager determine this risk category for his company?
3. Under what circumstances might a very low bad debt loss ratio be a sign of poor credit policy?
4. Under what circumstances might a concern's policy cause it to refuse credit terms to categories of possible customers who would be acceptable credit risks on the basis of the seller's margin of profits on sales?
5. Under what circumstances might a supplier extend credit terms to customers who are not acceptable credit risks on the basis of the seller's margin of profits on sales?
6. Is there ever justification for a seller deliberately to accept only superior credit risks in order to reduce the work in the credit department?
7. In what ways is the standard of credit acceptability influenced by a company's collection policy?
8. How may a seller's working capital position affect its standards of credit risk acceptability?
9. Indicate favorable and unfavorable types of character information on a customer, and the sources where such information may be obtained.
10. Give examples of the sort of information that sheds light on a customer's business capacity and indicate the sources for such information.
11. Should the personal wealth of an owner, partner, officer, or stockholder of a business have any bearing upon a credit manager's judgment of the credit status of the business?
12. If the financial statement of a customer indicates that his current situation will not permit him to pay all his trade liabilities promptly, does he have to be established as an unacceptable risk or is he still acceptable? On what terms might he be acceptable?
13. Are credit terms ever refused or granted entirely on the basis of a customer's character?
14. How would credit treatment of a customer differ if the credit factors on his side—the "three C's"—showed the following combination: (a) favorable character and financial position with unfavorable history of capacity; (b) favorable capacity and unfavorable reports on character and financial position; (c) favorable character and capacity but unfavorable financial position?
15. How may changing business conditions of a general or regional character affect a credit manager's standards of acceptable credit risks with regard to his own concern and with regard to the credit status of particular customers?
16. In what ways might governmental policy be an important factor in determining a customer's credit risk status?
17. Why is it not always advisable to offer cash, C.O.D., or S.D.-B.L. terms to a substandard customer?

18. How may a third party be made security for a financially weak customer's liabilities?

19. When may contract assignment be used as a means of securing payment from a buyer?

20. What is a "materialman's lien"? What is a "performance payment bond"? What are "retainages"? Compare the importance of these forms of collateral to a supplier.

21. When should a credit manager insist on receiving T.A.'s?

## PROBLEM 1

You are credit manager for Gamma Chemical Corp. One of the company's products is Akform, a plastic with exceptional stress- and heat-resistant qualities. A company salesman sends in a $78,000 order for Akform from Sigma Plastics Co., with the explanation that the company has just obtained a large government order for missile components for which Akform is the most suitable material.

An NCO report indicates that Sigma Plastics is a manufacturer of plastic novelties. It is wholly owned by a Mr. Sigma. He established the business twelve years ago. It had a rapid, profitable growth for eight years, but has sustained losses in three of the past four years. Last year's sales were $438,000, with a $2,814 net loss. The end-of-year balance sheet shows current assets of $216,000 against current liabilities of $93,000, but $161,000 of the current assets is inventory, which seems excessive in view of the sales volume, and half of the current liabilities are trade notes payable. The trade report indicates that the company is past due on a number of its accounts, and that at least two suppliers are shipping it on a CBD or COD basis. Four years ago there was a fire with a $75,000 insurance settlement. NCO reports that Mr. Sigma is "not well regarded" in the trade and the report conclusion is "A line of credit is not suggested."

NCO bulletins issued since the report indicate that Sigma Plastics has had another fire which destroyed much of its stockroom inventory, that it is suing one of the insurance companies with which it had coverage, and that it has received a $215,000 subcontractor order for missile component parts.

What is your decision on the Sigma Plastics order? Why?

## PROBLEM 2

Mr. Brown operates the only men's clothing store in Dartherst, a New England college town. Mr. Brown is a poor businessman and for years the store has barely clung to solvency. Trade reports indicate that he is late on payments to nearly all his suppliers.

Two companies have just received first orders from Mr. Brown. One is Noble Co., manufacturer of the Noble brand of men's suits, a high-price, high-quality, "prestige" line sold through over a thousand stores throughout the country. Noble Co. sets its prices so as to obtain a 20 per cent gross margin—fairly substantial for this line. Its credit manager, Mr. Hull, is considered an expert in his field.

The other company is Welford Inc., a haberdashery wholesaler in the area including Dartherst. Mr. Welford's superb business management has resulted in operating economies which have enabled him to shave prices somewhat, thereby reducing his gross margin percentage, compared with competing wholesalers in the area. This, and a good sales organization, have resulted in a phenomenal expansion of Welford's business that is currently straining its financial resources. Mr. Welford is his own credit manager.

1. If either of these companies accepted the orders on regular terms from Mr. Brown, which would have the greater justification? Why?

2. Are CBD, COD, consignment, or T.A. terms to Mr. Brown a possibility for either or both of these companies? Explain.

# CHAPTER 12

# Credit Limits [1]

No subject is more shrouded in confusion, in the minds of writers upon the subject as well as in the minds of credit managers themselves, than that of "credit limits." There is widespread bewilderment as to what they really are, how they should be determined, and how they should be used. Yet every large credit office must, in one way or another, establish and use credit limits for its customers unless it is to lose itself in a maze of repetitive reviewing of customers' credit positions as individual orders come in.

The penalties for misjudgment in setting credit limits are substantial. If they are set too low, either credit office work is wastefully multiplied or good orders are lost by unwarranted rejections. If they are set too high, the bad debt loss mounts.

Inept use of limits also carries penalties. If limits are viewed as rigid, semipermanent limitations on the balances that customers are allowed to

---

[1] In commercial banking these "credit limits" are called "credit lines." The term "credit line" has recently been making appearance in mercantile credit literature. "Limit" has a negative connotation, "line" a positive one, so the newer term has a semantic advantage. "Credit limit" is, however, still more widely used; we therefore have continued to employ it in this book.

incur, they will sometimes cost the seller perfectly good orders, on other occasions open wide the door to bad debt losses.

Probably no other detail of a credit manager's work better reflects his ability, and contributes more to his success or failure, than the way he handles credit limits.

## PURPOSES OF CREDIT LIMITS

A credit limit may serve one of three purposes. It may be set as the maximum amount of credit on regular terms which a customer will be allowed to have outstanding. It may be set as the maximum amount which a customer's ledger balance will be allowed to reach without review of his general credit position. It may be set for a customer who is being supplied on "must-discount" terms—i.e., he is expected to discount but does not always comply; in such cases it acts as a penalty for his failure to discount or as an inducement to better paying habits.

### The credit limit as a maximum for the customer's regular-term credit

Many credit managers view their credit limits—wrongly, as we shall see—as the maximum amounts they will allow their customers to buy on regular terms. By one or another of the methods considered later in this chapter, they calculate the ledger balance which they feel each customer may be safely allowed to accumulate on regular-term buying. When that limit is reached by a customer who is past due on any part of his balance, further orders are held up until the delinquency is cleared. If there is no past-due balance, the customer's financial position is re-examined. Thereupon his limit may be raised, or he may be asked to anticipate some part of the balance not yet due, so that the additional obligation on the new order will keep his outstanding balance within the limit previously established.

There is one situation where rigid use of credit limits may be warranted. The credit manager may have on his books a number of small marginal accounts that ought to be kept under constant surveillance. But his departmental budget does not permit him to subscribe to agency "continuous service" on all of them, or perhaps the pressure of work on the limited personnel of his department does not permit constant observation of these accounts. A practical compromise is to risk some limited amount—$50, $100, or $200—on each. If such a customer wishes to buy above this limit, he must pay on cash terms, C.O.D. or even C.B.D. If he refuses to buy on these terms, and turns to a competitor, the credit and sales departments do not grieve too deeply—they are content to let some other supplier take a risk which they refuse.

Except in this special case, a credit limit which is truly a limit on a customer's regular-term buying is an unwarranted strait-jacket on the selling efforts of the business. It is an indication either that the credit manager is not aware of the proper use of credit limits, or is unwilling to devote the time and incur the trouble that proper use of credit limits involves.

## The credit limit as a "STOP, LOOK, LISTEN" sign

In general, a credit limit should be a maximum amount which a customer's ledger balance will be allowed to reach *without review of his over-all credit position*.

As we shall see, the figure set for a customer's credit limit should be based both on his expected buying needs and on the probability of his consistent prompt payment. A credit limit so determined reflects the credit manager's judgment of the amount of debt to his company which, in the light of the customer's present circumstances, the latter can safely incur and repay. Thus, whenever a customer exceeds his credit limit, it is a sign either that he has increased his purchases over what seemed a reasonable amount when his credit position was last analyzed, or that he has fallen behind in his rate of payment so that new order debt is cumulating on top of past-due payables. Either of these developments should be a warning to the credit manager that the facts on which he based his last credit judgment have altered. The change need not necessarily be for the worse; a successful customer may be soundly expanding his business, and for that reason be buying more. But a change of one sort or another has occurred, and every change in a customer's business should be the occasion for a review of his credit position. The credit limit is a "STOP, LOOK, LISTEN" sign for the credit manager.

What action should a credit manager take when he discovers that a customer's latest order brings his ledger balance over the previously established credit limit? Refusal to ship the order on regular terms may be the correct procedure if the exceeding of the credit limit was due to bad buying judgment on the part of the customer or a deterioration of his financial position. But it would obviously be disastrously wrong if the reason for the enlarged ledger balance was sound expansion or a shift of the customer's sources of supply in favor of the credit manager's concern. When a customer exceeds his credit limit, it is a signal not to take action on the customer, but to make inquiry.

Let us assume that an order from A, a customer of some two years' standing, brings his balance over the limit previously established. A glance at the ledger card indicates that the customer is taking the net terms and paying promptly. The passing of the limit has been caused by an increase in the size of his recent orders, not by slow pay. The last agency report discloses a growing business operated by a capable proprietor. The three financial statements on file confirm this impression. Without further ado, the credit manager O.K.'s the order. He might also immediately set a higher credit limit. But, properly cautious, he calls for an NACM ledger interchange "clearance," the last interchange report in his file being six months old. The new report shows that A has added some new sources of supply, that his "highest recent credit" with several of his old suppliers has somewhat increased and that he is maintaining a good paying record— a number of "discounts," most of the rest "prompt," and a few cases of "10 to 15 days slow." The credit manager's last doubts are cleared, and now, with an easy mind, he raises A's credit limit to a figure more consonant with his expanded business.

Now take the case of B, whose latest order likewise would bring his ledger balance over his credit limit. The ledger card shows his purchases running normal. But whereas he previously averaged 15 to 20 days slow on his payments, he has become 30 to 40 days slow, and this cumulation of unpaid amounts accounts for the increase of his ledger balance. The "slow-pay" tendency is confirmed by a recent interchange report. A check on the data in B's credit folder indicates that he is a generally sound account, though with a somewhat poor working capital position caused, primarily, by slow turnover of his excessive inventory. The credit manager now phones the sales manager and learns that the salesman who handles B's account will be in the office two days later. The order is marked "Hold" and put temporarily in suspense. From the salesman the credit manager hears that business in B's neighborhood has been unusually slow for the season; for a number of reasons money is "tight," and people are not buying in their normal volume. The credit manager now has the picture he needs to appraise B's situation. He writes B a friendly letter, analyzing his inventory situation in the light of the slack business of his neighborhood and suggesting some special sales to "unfreeze" part of this merchandise and obtain funds to clear some of the overdue trade debts. Would he not also reconsider the new order? Whatever he definitely needs, the customer will receive immediately on regular terms. So much for the letter. The credit limit remains unchanged, and the credit manager is satisfied that he has caught a potentially dangerous situation at the right moment, thus protecting his company against future loss, aiding a good customer, and retaining his good will.

In another case the credit limit may flag a customer in the early stages of disintegration. In still another it may enable the credit manager to discover overbuying with intent to perpetrate a fraud. It may disclose that a customer is accumulating inventory for speculative reasons, because he believes that a price increase or a shortage is imminent. Or it may point to a customer who has increased his capital through taking in a partner, so that the sales department should devote special attention to him. All these situations can be found only by making inquiries, and not by simply refusing orders and standing pat. Except for the special cases noted, credit limits, therefore, should primarily be signals to investigate—that is, "STOP, LOOK, LISTEN" signs.

There is one class of customers to whom no automatic credit limit should be allowed. This is the customer whose financial position makes him a marginal risk, and whom the credit manager watches carefully through agency "continuous service" reports or constant ledger interchange information. Every order from such a customer should involve the fullest possible review of his current situation.

In a large credit office which must operate with a staff of only partly trained or relatively inexperienced assistants, the credit limit performs a useful organizational function. The assistants are authorized to approve all orders that maintain customers' ledger balances within their limits. This takes care of most of the daily flow of orders, and the credit manager's time is freed for matters that require his experience and judgment. Only those cases are referred to him where an order could bring a customer's ledger balance over the limit. Similar definition of delegated authority may be made by the central credit office of a large company to the district offices. Such division of credit department responsibilities obviously promotes efficiency.

## DETERMINING CREDIT LIMITS

To determine a credit limit that will be an effective "STOP, LOOK, LISTEN" signal on an old customer is a fairly simple procedure. It is more difficult in the case of a new customer, but far from being as complex as many credit managers seem to fear. In most cases, indeed, not merely a year-round limit should be calculated, but separate in-season and off-season limits can and should be determined.

### "Experience" limits

If a customer has been sold to regularly for a year or more, determination of a credit limit for him is a simple matter.

His ledger card shows his past-year orders and their monthly distribution. These figures are taken as a starting point and adjusted for any probable variants, such as growth or decline of the customer's business, or an anticipated boom or recession in his line.

Next a monthly average for the customer's high in-season buying may be calculated, and another for his low off-season buying. This differentiation is very important for seasonal businesses. A credit limit suitable for the off-season purchases of such a customer would be too restrictive for his in-season needs, and a fair in-season limit would not serve the credit manager as a "STOP, LOOK, LISTEN" sign in off-season periods. Of course, where a customer's purchases are spread fairly evenly through the year, only one average of anticipated monthly purchases need be calculated.

If the customer pays promptly within the net term, his average monthly purchases—separated if necessary into in-season and off-season—are multiplied by the number of months allowed under the seller's terms of sale. Thus, with net 30 terms the multiplier would be 1; with net 60 terms it would be 2. Some upward adjustment may then be made to give a certain leeway and cover the possibility that a payment check may arrive a few days late, with a further order meanwhile coming up for consideration. Such carefully calculated and observed in-season and off-season limits will flag any unanticipated increase of the customer's buying or any delinquency in his payments, and warn the credit manager that an inquiry is in order. They also lend themselves easily to mechanized, automatic procedures.[2]

In the case of a slow-paying customer, the multiplier applied to average monthly purchases cannot be determined by the seller's regular terms of sale, since the delinquency in payment would constantly cause the customer's ledger balance to exceed the credit limit. The multiplier for such a customer should be the number of months payment period to which the credit department actually holds him. For example, if the regular terms are net 60, but a fairly sound customer with working capital difficulties is generally 30 days late and, according to trade reports, can be expected to continue being late, the multiplier should be 3 instead of 2. In-season and off-season credit limits so calculated would give a credit manager prompt warning if such a customer deviated in his buying and paying procedures from the anticipated pattern. The following two examples illustrate the calculation of credit limits for two customers that are similarly sized and circumstanced but have differing paying records.

EXAMPLE 1

Customer A, owner of a hardware store, according to his ledger card buys from $15,000 to $17,000 annually from the seller; last year his purchases totaled $15,699.25. Seventy per cent, more or less, of the total of his annual orders are shipped to him, on semimonthly deliveries, in September, October and November. The 30 per cent balance, consisting of fill-in orders, is shipped during January, February, and March. Terms are net 60. A generally pays promptly.

Business reports indicate that consumer purchases for the coming season in A's region will run about 5% lower than they did in the preceding year.

---

[2] I.B.M.'s "RAMAC 305" (Random Access Method of Accounting and Control), for example, used for a variety of controls, is also employed in this connection. Credit limits are fed into the computer, purchases are added, and payments are deducted. If a new order is inserted which brings the balance over the established limit, the order is automatically rejected by the machine and taken to the credit manager for decision. (See *Credit and Financial Management,* February 1960, p. 10.)

The seller's credit manager judges accordingly that A's purchases should not run over $15,000 for the coming year. Deliveries of $10,500 will presumably be made, at the rate of $3,500 a month, during September, October, and November. Fill-in orders of $4,500 will be shipped at the rate of $1,500 a month during January, February, and March. Strict adherence to the terms-of-sale rule would produce an in-season limit of $7,000 and an off-season limit of $3,000. The credit manager decides to allow, however, for the possibility that A may send a check a few days late, so he adds $1,750 (the amount of one anticipated semimonthly in-season shipment) to the in-season limit, making it $8,750, and $500 (a purely arbitrary figure, since off-season shipments to A are generally irregular rush orders of small amounts) to the off-season limit, making it $3,500.

EXAMPLE 2

The picture as to Customer B is identical, except that, although he is a good credit risk, for one reason or another he often pays up to 30 days late.

The seller's credit manager calculates that in-season deliveries will probably be around $3,500 a month and off-season deliveries around $1,500 a month. Instead of multiplying these figures by 2 to get his credit limits, as he did initially with Customer A, he multiplies them by 3, since as a realist he accepts the fact that some of B's checks will come in at the end of three months, instead of within two months, as they should. He makes no further adjustment, however, as he did in the case of A, since he wants warning if B's lateness at any time should exceed 30 days with further shipments still to be made to him. Thus B's credit limits are set at $10,500 in-season and $4,500 off-season.

At first glance it may seem contrary to all credit logic to allow a larger credit limit to a slow-paying and therefore poorer risk customer than to a prompt-paying, substantially better-risk one. Second thought should indicate, however, that such allowance is sound; without it, the account would be constantly flagged to no purpose. A customer's ledger balance reflects not merely one factor—his buying rate—but two factors—his buying rate and his paying rate. The decision of a credit manager that a customer is an acceptable risk presumably has taken full account of both factors, and the credit limit for the account should be established accordingly.

## Formula calculation for new accounts

The credit limits for a new customer, or for one who has not bought for some time,[3] may be determined also by applying the sellers' terms of sale, or the customer's anticipated payment period in the case of a slow-paying customer, to the monthly averages of in-season and off-season purchases. But a credit manager cannot turn to a ledger card for a new

---

[3] E. I. Du Pont de Nemours & Co., for example, handles orders from customers who have not purchased for one year or more as "first orders" and applies "first order" limits to them—Credit Research Foundation, *Punched Card Accounting and the Credit Department* (New York, 1957), p. 2.

customer to determine what his anticipated purchases will be. Possibly the sales department can give him a good estimate; if not he can make his own calculation of the customer's probable purchases from his credit inquiry information by a four-step formula:

1. Calculate "cost of goods sold" from the customer's latest financial statement by taking "cost of goods purchased" from the income statement and adjusting it for the difference between beginning- and end-of-year inventories. For retailer customers a simpler calculation is possible—subtract an estimated normal markup for that type of store from the "sales" figure.

2. Adjust "cost of goods sold" (a) upward to take account of anticipated increased sales or replenishment of insufficient inventory, or (b) downward to take account of anticipated reduced sales or reduction of excessive inventory. This adjustment must obviously be arbitrary, based on the credit manager's judgment of business trends in the customer's field and territory and on his interpretation of the customer's inventory situation. This figure may be called "cost of anticipated current-year purchases."

3. Estimate the share of "cost of anticipated current-year purchases" attributable to goods of the type sold by the credit manager's company. The "Business Classification" column of an NACM interchange report, read in connection with the "Highest Recent Credit" and "Amount Owing" columns, will often picture the distribution of a customer's purchases by types of goods and volume of buying. The sales force can sometimes assist a credit manager in this estimate. The resulting figure may be called "customer's current-year needs in the seller's line."

4. Estimate the share of the above amount that the credit manager's own concern can hope to supply. The basis for this estimate is the credit manager's knowledge of his company's competitive position. If it can expect to supply the new customer with an exclusive line, its share of the "customer's current-year needs in the seller's line" is 100 per cent. Generally, however, a credit manager must assume that his concern will supply only a fraction of the customer's needs in the line. NACM interchange reports indicating the number of suppliers for certain lines of goods, and salesmen's reports, may be helpful in deciding on the proper fraction.

Once a new customer's probable purchases from his company are thus determined, the credit manager calculates a credit limit by the same procedure as for old customers. The usual differentiation would be made in establishing limits for in-season and off-season, and for prompt and slow customers. A new customer's probable period of payment can generally be anticipated fairly closely by analysis of his working capital position as revealed in his last financial statement and a check on his current paying record as it appears in trade reports.

EXAMPLE

The latest financial statement of a new customer, a retailer, gives his purchases as $52,468, sales as $62,693, end-of-year inventory as $12,511. The preceding financial statement showed a $9,973 inventory. The credit manager believes that current consumer buying in the customer's area will be about 5 per cent higher than in the preceding year. Approximately one-third of the items sold by this customer are produced by this seller, but on the basis of trade practices and the salesman's report, the credit manager judges that the best his company can hope for is to supply one-half the customer's needs in these lines. His calculation of the customer's probable purchases from his company would be made as follows:

1. Using round numbers for the calculation, $10,000 beginning-of-year inventory plus $52,500 purchases minus $12,500 end-of-year inventory, gives $50,000 cost of goods sold. (Had the figure for purchases not been given, assuming that the retailers' usual mark-up in the customer's line was 25 per cent, the credit manager could have calculated cost of goods sold by the formula: four-fifths of $63,000 sales equals $50,400 cost of goods sold. The calculation then would have proceeded with this slightly higher figure.)

2. Adjustment for the 5 per cent increase expected in the customer's sales gives $52,500 for his probable current-year purchases (starting with the $50,000 prior-year cost-of-goods-sold figure).

3. One-third of this amount, or $17,500, is the amount that the credit manager's concern could sell to this customer if it could exclude all competition.

4. One-half of $17,500, or $8,750, is the probable amount of this customer's purchases from the credit manager's concern in view of the competitive situation.

From this $8,750 probable purchases figure the credit manager would calculate the customer's credit limits or limit, taking into account the probable seasonal distribution of his purchases, the selling concern's terms of sale, and the probabilities of prompt or slow payment by the customer.

## Arbitrary lump-sum credit and order limits for new accounts

Many credit managers have solved the problem of establishing credit limits for accepted new customers where the purchase amounts are relatively small by allowing an arbitrary credit limit—$100, or $200, or $500, or some other round amount, according to the line of business and the general nature of the customers. This arbitrary limit is maintained for a testing period, say of six months. During this period it is reviewed every time an order brings the customer's ledger balance over the limit. Such study may indicate that the order should be approved. Or it may lead the credit manager to decide to hold the limit for the time being and ask the customer to take cash terms or anticipate some of his outstanding debt so as to keep his balance within the limit.

At the end of the testing period, the limit is raised for a customer with a satisfactory payment record whose purchases obviously warrant a higher allowance. This second limit is again an arbitrary one, and such arbitrary limit for a large-buying customer may be subject to frequent rechecking.

Possibly a third, or even a fourth, arbitrary limit may be used during the first year or year-and-a-half that a new customer is on the seller's books. Sooner or later, however, the accumulation of ledger experience is sufficient to enable the credit manager to discard these arbitrary limits for an "experience limit" of the type discussed earlier in this chapter.

### "Net worth" limits and "net working capital" limits for new accounts

Many credit managers arbitrarily give every new account a credit limit measured by a certain percentage—5, 10, or 15 per cent—of its net worth. A variant of this is to divide the customer's net worth by the probable number of his principal suppliers, as indicated by an NACM ledger interchange report or as assumed by the credit manager from his knowledge of the buying customs of the trade. Since a customer's net worth range is indicated in most mercantile agency ratings, these credit limit procedures do not require customer financial statements or agency reports.

Some credit managers who use these credit limit procedures try to defend themselves by the argument that a customer's net worth is his suppliers' protection in case he fails. This argument overlooks the fundamental consideration that the basis for most mercantile credit extension is not the salvage value of a customer but the probability that his operations as a going concern will provide incoming funds to meet his trade obligations as they fall due. Net worth becomes a protective or buffer factor only when the customer fails.

A second defense is that there is some correlation between a customer's net worth and his purchasing power. This is true, but the correlation is too slight to be of value for credit purposes.

Furthermore, even if there were some merit in taking net worth as the measure of a customer's total mercantile credit need, the next step of arbitrarily taking 5, 10, or 15 per cent of the net worth figure would rob the result of any pretense of realism. Equally unrealistic is the procedure of dividing net worth by some presumed number of principal suppliers. Even where their number can be ascertained, the credit manager has no assurance that his company may expect a pro rata share of the customer's purchases.

The best that can be said for the net worth credit limit procedures is that they are no worse than the arbitrary lump-sum credit limit allowances previously discussed, and for small buyers they provide a time-saving and a not unreasonable device. If more exact limits can be calculated by formula, this should be done. Otherwise a net worth limit may be set initially, and adjusted upward or downward as subsequent circumstances dictate. Eventually it can be replaced by an "experience" limit.

A few credit managers calculate credit limits by taking an arbitrary percentage of net working capital or by dividing net working capital among principal suppliers. They argue that customer ability to pay trade obligations is more closely related to net working capital than to net worth. In theory this is true. In practice, because of the arbitrary character of the proportion of net working capital that is used as a credit limit, the result is little, if any, superior to the net worth procedure. Moreover, net working capital cannot be taken from an agency rating, but requires a financial statement or an agency report for its calculation.

### "Follow-the-leader" limits

Many credit managers of small concerns base the credit limit they set for a new customer on the "highest recent credit" reported by some other supplier known to have an efficient credit department. Several dangers attach to this practice. In the first place, we know that a stated "highest recent credit" may bear little relation to the credit limit set by the reporting supplier. The customer may be buying less from that supplier than his credit limit would permit. Or he may be exceeding that limit due to expanded purchases or retarded payment. More important than these considerations, the customer may be purchasing much more from this reporting supplier than he will from the inquiring supplier, so that the former's credit limit would be much too high to serve as a "STOP, LOOK, LISTEN" sign to the latter.

Nonetheless, a credit manager setting a credit limit for a new account does himself no harm to glance at the "highest recent credit" reports of other suppliers. They have had some experience with that customer, and their reports may give him a worth-while check on the figure he has reached by his own formula calculation or by some arbitrary system. But unless he has reason to believe that his concern will sell approximately the same amount to the customer as some other supplier whose credit limit is based on experience, he should be chary of "following" closely any other supplier's "highest recent credit."

### Revision of credit limits

Nothing can be more dangerous to a credit department than a set of credit limits which are revised only upward to accommodate the expanded purchasing of good customers. It is just as important, possibly even more important from the viewpoint of preventing bad debt losses, that credit limits have a downward flexibility. When, for any reason, a customer reduces his purchases and there is evidence that such condition may last for some time, his limit should be reduced. When a customer's credit position deteriorates to a point where he becomes a marginal risk and must be kept under constant surveillance, the credit limit previously accorded to him should be suspended, and his orders individually checked.

A customer's credit limit ought to be reviewed, with the possibility that it may be revised upward or downward at regular intervals, on the following occasions:

1. Whenever an order would cause a customer's ledger balance to exceed his credit limit by any substantial margin. The review may indicate that the limit should be raised, or that it should be maintained with the present order approved, or that special credit terms should be arranged for the customer or some other special action taken.

2. Upon receipt of a new financial statement. This may indicate a probability that his purchase requirements for the coming year will be greater or less, or that his payment period will be shorter or longer, or that his financial position has disintegrated to a point where no credit limit should be allowed.

### Credit lines established by agencies

Several special-line agencies in their reports or ratings recommend credit "lines" for their clients' customers. In some instances, such credit lines are for all practical purposes the same as credit limits. In others, they are not supposed to be viewed in this light. The National Credit Office, for example, regards the "line of credit" it recommends in a report on a customer (see Illustration 5-1) only as a guide for the inquiring subscriber, and a flexible one at that. It does not intend it to be interpreted as a credit limit.

Various methods are being used by the different agencies for determining such credit lines, from rigid formulas applicable to all accounts to selective calculations adapted to the individual case. Some standardize their calculation system. They determine, first, the total trade debt a customer may reasonably be expected to have outstanding during his period of peak purchases, based on his prior-year record of buying and paying, and modified as to probable increases and decreases in his business during the coming year. This total is then divided by the number of his suppliers, excluding incidental suppliers of small amounts. Other agencies use more flexible computation methods that are more closely geared to the individual case. National Credit Office, for instance, bases its recommendations not only on the seasonal purchase requirements of the business and the number of suppliers but also on several additional factors pertaining to the structure and even on the "atmosphere" of the enterprise.

Such agency-recommended credit lines are very valuable to the supplier. The agency generally has more information on the customer and his business operations than the single seller would be able to obtain.

Its judgment, therefore, should be at least as reliable as his own, if not more so. However, an agency line should be used with proper qualifications and adjustments. Depending on how the agency computes its recommendation figure and the degree of conservatism in its general attitude, its line may be too high or too low for unqualified use by the supplier. For example, a mere division of customer purchase requirements by the number of leading suppliers results in a very arbitrary credit line if applied by each supplier to this account. The customer's purchases from one supplier may be several times greater than from another. He should logically receive a larger limit from the first than from the second. Agencies, also, are usually rather conservative in their judgment, and suppliers on this basis alone often decide on a higher credit line than the one recommended. In general, the credit manager learns from experience with the agency and with his concern's customers how to apply the necessary adjustments to the *average* line which the agency provides.

A particular situation with regard to credit lines exists for the credit *checking* agencies. As explained in Chapter 5, they advise the inquiring subscriber whether he should ship a given order on regular credit terms. They do not report or recommend a line of credit for the inquired account, but they must have some such calculation on their books for each customer they cover, in order to be able to recommend to a supplier the acceptance or nonacceptance of an order he has received. Such an indication of the possible volume of acceptable orders appears frequently in some form or other at the top of a customer's "Master Card" that contains the account's purchase and paying record (see Illustration 5-5). This figure may be calculated in many different ways; the larger agencies usually take a variety of factors into consideration. The smaller ones frequently apply such simplified procedures as the "arbitrary" methods previously described—lump-sum, percentage of net worth, percentage of net working capital. They all review such credit lines established for their own orientation at frequent intervals and regard them generally as flexible even for current use.

## INFORMING CUSTOMERS AND
## SALESMEN OF CREDIT LIMITS

Opinion among credit managers is divided as to whether customers should be informed of the credit limits set for them. Those opposed argue that if a customer is informed of an initial low limit that may subsequently be revised upward, he may feel that it is a reflection on his credit standing, and so his good will may be lost. On the other hand, though he would be a good risk for a higher credit limit, he may confine his purchases to the established one. The credit department is never called upon to review and raise it, and good orders are meanwhile missed. Credit managers who favor the practice argue that if it should be desirable at some future time to hold a customer's regular-term credit to the established limit, the customer's prior knowledge of that limit enables the credit manager to invoke the restriction without its appearing to be an arbitrary action.

In this matter, as in so many others in credit practice, circumstances determine cases and there can be no one always-valid rule. Where a new customer's financial position makes him a marginal risk whose regular-term credit must be confined to a prescribed maximum, it is unquestionably good practice to let him know this limit. Any subsequent letter reminding him of it can use the phrase "the line of credit upon which we both agreed last——," even though there was no "agreement" between the two parties, but a one-sided determination by the seller's credit manager. In this way, the limit does not appear to the customer as a surprise factor sprung upon him without warning but as a contractual arrangement to which he has been subject all along. Another occasion when it is useful to notify the customer of a credit limit is when a first order is received from a sound customer from whom the seller hopes to get much larger orders in the future, and whose credit limit is set with those larger orders in mind. In his letter acknowledging the order and welcoming the new customer, the credit manager has the opportunity of saying, "We have opened a $..... line of credit to your account." This is a sales promotional phrase, flattering the customer and inviting him to expand his orders.

A credit limit that is truly intended as a "STOP, LOOK, LISTEN" sign to the credit department should never be communicated to the customer. He will not necessarily be held to that credit balance, and it would be bad promotional tactics to make him think that a brake was being applied to his buying. If ever the time comes to apply restrictive policies to him, they will have to be based on some consideration other than a credit limit which is intended exclusively for the internal management of the credit office.

Salesmen should always be informed when a weak account is restricted as to its buying on regular terms, and they may as well be told when such restriction is established by a fixed credit or order limit. They should also know if a high credit limit has been set for a customer. In such cases the established figure is more like a sales quota and a challenge to the salesman to use his promotional skills to achieve it. There is little purpose to informing salesmen of "STOP, LOOK, LISTEN" credit limits. They would be meaningless to the salesmen without constant up-to-date information on the customer's ledger balance, and might have the adverse effect of hampering sales effort.

## SUPPLEMENTARY READINGS

Anderson, M. H., "Setting Up and Controlling the Lines of Credit," *Credit and Financial Management,* August 1959, p. 18.

"Setting Up Lines of Credit—Not by Formula but by Getting the Facts," *Credit and Financial Management,* February 1956, p. 8.

Smith, G. H., "Third Letter Writing Contest—Informing Customer about a Credit Limit," *Credit and Financial Management,* March 1951, p. 18.

## REVIEW

1. When is a credit limit properly used as an arbitrary maximum to the amount of credit extended to a particular customer?
2. Explain what is meant by the statement that a credit limit should be treated as a "Stop, Look, Listen" sign.
3. What administrative use may be made of credit limits within a large concern's credit department?
4. Why should two credit limits, one for in-season buying and one for off-season buying, be calculated for some customers?
5. Explain how "experience" credit limits may be calculated.
6. Why should slow-paying customers be given higher credit limits than comparably circumstanced prompt-paying customers?
7. How may a credit manager estimate a new customer's probable annual purchases from his concern, in order to calculate his credit need?
8. How might a credit manager reasonably set a credit limit for a new customer whose purchases would be relatively small?
9. What are the arguments for and against determining a credit limit based on the customer's net worth or net working capital?
10. To what extent is the "highest recent credit" figure obtained from some other supplier of a customer useful in determining a credit limit for him?
11. When should a customer's credit limit be reviewed and possibly revised?
12. What qualifications must be set on suggested credit lines calculated by mercantile agencies?
13. When might it be advisable to notify a customer of the credit limit assigned him?
14. Under what circumstances should salesmen be informed about a customer's credit limit?

## PROBLEM

You are credit manager for Dart Clothes, Inc., manufacturer of high-quality, progressive-styled men's suits. The company sells on net 30 terms. On June 21, 1961, a salesman sends an initial $12,000 order from King & Todd, a men's clothing chain with stores in New York City and the suburban area, with the explanation that their buyer likes Dart's progressive styling and plans to feature the line; annual orders, the salesman indicates, may well run over $100,000. You drew the Dun & Bradstreet report on King & Todd (shown on pp. 60-63) and decide to approve the order.

From experience you estimate that suits constitute one-half to three-fifths of the sales in clothing stores such as those operated by King & Todd. If they feature the line, as the salesman indicates, sales of Dart suits could be up to one-fifth of their total sales of suits. This annual sale of Dart suits would be divided about 60 per cent for the fall-winter line and 40 per cent for the spring-summer line. If their ordering follows the pattern of most clothing stores, they will order about 65-75 per cent of their fall-winter requirements for delivery August through October, with the balance on a fill-in basis during the following months. Likewise, 65-75 per cent of their spring-summer line purchases will be for delivery February through April, followed by fill-in orders.

What credit limit would you establish for King & Todd? How would you calculate it?

# PART III

## MERCANTILE COLLECTIONS

# CHAPTER 13

# Collection Principles and Procedures: 1

Some customers regularly discount or mail their checks on or before the net due date. They present no collection problem.

But rare indeed is the credit office that deals only with such customers. Even where a seller's special circumstances permit it to select customers of only the highest risk categories, some of them will occasionally lapse on their payments for longer or shorter periods. Any supplier seeking a mass market, who sells to intermediate- and poor-risk categories of customers, must expect that a substantial proportion of his accounts will fall behind in their payments.

A credit manager should make every effort, not merely to collect what is owed to his concern, but also to collect it promptly.[1] He has six reasons for so doing. (1) If lax collection policy results in an accumulation of "overdues," a proportion of his company's assets will be "frozen" in these receivables, to the detriment of its own working capital position. (2) The longer an account is allowed to become delinquent, the greater

---

[1] It is astonishing how much consistent slow-pay is tolerated in most lines of business. The justifications advanced are trade custom, competition, pressure from sales departments, and special circumstances of the customer. See H. Reinhardt, *Trends in Credit Practices—Terms of Sales and Collection Practices in 32 Industries* (Credit Research Foundation, New York, 1955), p. 9.

is the probability that it will eventually result in a bad debt loss.[2] (3) Slow collections result in lost sales, since an honest overdue customer is reluctant to add to his indebtedness by buying more, while the seller's credit department tends to restrict the credit extended to such an account. (4) A firm but courteous collection policy maintains customer respect. (5) The reputation of a concern for alert and efficient collection policy is in itself an important factor in obtaining prompt payments. (6) When a credit department acquiesces in cases where delinquency results from overbuying, it is cooperating with the customer in jeopardizing himself.

If sound credit judgment be deemed the primary function of a credit department, effective collection must be viewed as a second function ranking only slightly behind the primary one. The two are closely interrelated. Lax credit policy should not be compensated by strict collection procedure or vice versa. Both should be well-balanced. But where balance cannot be achieved, liberal credit policy and firm collection is the best combination.

## BASIC CONSIDERATIONS

The three basic principles of collection procedure that every credit manager should always bear in mind are:

1. GET YOUR MONEY.
2. GET IT PROMPTLY.
3. RETAIN YOUR CUSTOMER'S GOOD WILL WHILE COLLECTING FROM HIM.

Another consideration, only slightly less important than these three, is:

4. SEEK EVERY OPPORTUNITY TO MAKE YOUR COLLECTION PROCEDURE CON-TRIBUTE TO YOUR CONCERN'S SALES POLICY.

It may seem contradictory to say that a collection procedure should both be efficient in obtaining customers' payments and yet maintain their good will. It may seem even more impossible that an effective collection system should contribute to sales policy. Yet as all credit managers learn sooner or later, these two objectives of collection policy are categorical *musts;* good collections should never be accomplished through long-run sacrifice of sales.

### Differentiation among delinquent customers

There is no one single collection procedure that should be applied to all delinquent customers. Slow-pay has many causes, and each calls for different treatment. A credit manager should be prepared with a

---

[2] A good aphorism to remember in this connection is: "Flowing water and credit do not freeze easily. Stagnant water and credit do."

range of collection procedures suited to the different categories of delinquency. Among the reasons why customers fail to pay promptly, and the procedures appropriate to them, are the following:

1. A new customer may have honestly misunderstood the terms of sale. This may be the fault of the sales department, and possibly also of the credit department, which should have expressly mentioned the terms of sale in its initial confirmatory letter. If a "reminder" letter or card to the customer produces this explanation, the credit manager owes him an apology. Of course, the explanation may not be true, but the credit manager should always treat it as though it were. It can be offered only once by any customer, and on that one occasion he is allowed the benefit of doubt.

2. The seller's billing department may have failed to mail an invoice or statement, or may have failed to do this on time. If a customer makes this charge, it must be accepted, at least on the first one or two occasions, and evoke an apology from the credit department.

3. A sound customer, or one of his clerks, may have been careless for once in keeping track of his payables, or the customer may be generally inefficient in his business methods so that such oversight occurs frequently. A "reminder" letter or card will generally clear up this type of delinquency whenever it occurs.

4. A sound customer may have ignored a small payable, intending to include it subsequently when he pays for a larger accumulation of orders. This practice is quite common in retail credit, rare in mercantile credit, but occasionally businessmen will follow it. A "reminder" letter or card should obtain results in this case. If the customer repeats the procedure, a friendly letter indicating the trouble that his practice causes the seller's bookkeeping and credit departments may win his response. But often the situation just has to be accepted.

5. Unknown to the credit department, there may be a dispute between the customer and the sales department over details of a delivery, and the customer is holding back payment as pressure to obtain early and favorable settlement. If this is revealed as the cause of delayed payment, the credit manager should try to persuade the customer that payment of the due amount and the dispute are unrelated matters, and that the latter should not influence the former. Should this persuasion fail, the credit manager has little choice but to await the settlement of the dispute, meanwhile putting diplomatic pressure of his own on the sales department to achieve an early settlement.

6. A sound customer, who could pay promptly, may be repeatedly slow by habit and by nature. Such a customer must be pressed constantly by collection correspondence. Delicate discrimination should be used in the type of collection letters written to him, so that he is prodded

into fairly early payment without being so aggravated that he turns to a competitor. "Stunt" letters, which are generally inadvisable as collection devices, may sometimes be effective with this type of customer.

7. In times of general business slowdown, some small firms and occasional large ones are inclined to use "me-too" tactics. They know that other companies are not paying on time, and they feel that they should be permitted to do the same. Courteous firmness is the collection answer to this situation.

8. A customer who could pay on time, if he were not drawing so much from the business for his personal expenses, may find it inconvenient to pay promptly. He is not a good moral risk, of course. There is an element of irresponsibility in his character that may eventually wreck his business, although it is sound at the moment. Therefore it is doubly important that he should not be allowed to fall too far behind on his obligations, particularly if the business outlook for his line or region is cloudy. The tone of the collection letters addressed to him should be stronger, from the outset, than those addressed to the preceding classes of slow-pays, and they should be mailed to him in more rapid sequence. More chances may be taken that a strong collection procedure may alienate his good will, since his character weakness makes him a marginal and less desirable account—except perhaps in a boom period when even such customers do not constitute much of a risk.

9. A relatively sound customer, because of factors outside of his control, or because of poor business management, may have inadequate operating capital and find it impossible to pay all his suppliers promptly. Under certain circumstances it may be wise either to tolerate the late payment or to allow him a special long term, possibly secured by trade acceptances. If the difficulty arises suddenly, because of unforeseen exigencies, he may be permitted an extended term on his past-due debt, secured by a promissory note. Whatever the regular or special terms, he should be the subject of a diligent collection follow-up, to obtain the earliest possible payment. Most of these "operating capital" cases succeed in paying some suppliers fairly promptly, at the expense of others whose accounts are longer delayed. The credit manager of any particular supplier should make every effort to have his company be one of those paid promptly. By so doing, he reduces his risk of loss (in case adjustment or liquidation procedures subsequently become necessary) and keeps the customer's account and respect. This case calls for the fullest exercise of the credit manager's virtuosity as a correspondent. He must express his confidence in the customer, be properly sympathetic with obvious difficulties, and perhaps occasionally give advice, yet all the time press delicately for payment by appealing to the customer's good will and sense of fair play, by subtly threatening him with the loss of a valued credit standing, and by emphasizing all the advantages that ac-

crue from prompt payment. Here, above all, is a situation calling for the seemingly contradictory approaches of applying firm collection pressure and yet maintaining the customer's good will.

10. A customer may fall far behind in his payments because he is failing and rapidly approaching insolvency. Once this is realized, the credit manager should bring all the heaviest weapons of his collection arsenal into play. If bankruptcy does not appear too imminent, he may make an attempt to collect by correspondence. The sequence of such letters should be brief—in all probability already a number of them have been sent while the account was being treated as an "operating capital" case—and the strongest possible appeals should be used. An attempt may be made to collect by draft. If this fails, there is no alternative but to place the account in the hands of a collection agency or attorney.

11. One of the most disagreeable collection problems is that of the customer who could pay promptly but holds back his payments until they are squeezed out of him. This is not a case merely of payment habitually late, but one of latent dishonesty; the customer hopes to wear out the seller's collection efforts and eventually to avoid payment completely by default, while he turns to some other source of supply. Some credit managers, once they discover that a customer belongs to this class, simply refuse orders to him on regular terms. Others continue to sell to him, willing to match their collection persistency against his passive resistance. The collection techniques to be employed in these cases, whether or not further orders are approved, are the strongest possible collection letters, attempts at collection by draft, warnings that the customer will be reported to credit organizations, and the institution of suits. Not infrequently, such a customer may be converted into a prompt or reasonably prompt payer to a supplier who applied "mailed fist" tactics, while he continues to be delinquent to less resolute creditors.

12. Finally, if a credit manager has reason to believe that a customer is perpetrating a fraud—either a deliberate mercantile swindle or the desperate venture of a man grasping at any straw in the hope of heading off bankruptcy—the account should immediately be placed in the hands of a collection agency, which may by its strong-arm methods be able to get eleventh-hour-payment. Further action, however, is incumbent upon any credit manager who suspects a customer of fraud. He should communicate his suspicions and any confirmatory evidence to a fraud prosecution agency (discussed in Chapter 17). Aiding in every way possible in the detection and prosecution of credit fraud is one of the professional duties of a credit manager.

### Ascertaining that an account is delinquent

One of the essentials of effective collection procedure is prompt dispatch of the first "reminder" notification. If these reminders are not received by delinquent customers until weeks after their accounts became due, they feel that they have open invitation to take their time about paying such a casual and indifferent creditor.

The source for learning when a customer becomes delinquent is usually his ledger sheet or card. There will be found the dates of invoices to a customer and his payments. By noting the entry dates for invoices as yet unpaid and adding thereto the credit period allowed the customer, the credit manager, or a clerk checking for him, can see whether the customer is past due on any of his obligations. In many concerns that sell on lumped-order monthly terms, it is regular routine for some clerk in the bookkeeping or credit department to check through the customer ledger a few days after the monthly payment date to note unpaid accounts and report them to the credit manager. Where the concern sells on individual-order terms, the ledger should be checked over twice a month, or even weekly, if too great delinquency is to be avoided.

This procedure of repetitive inspection of the customer ledger book or file is practicable where only a few accounts are involved. It cannot be applied where the number of active accounts is large. In such case, for reasons of bookkeeping as well as for credit efficiency, a seller should use some sort of "visible index" or "keysort" ledger card system.

A "visible index" ledger card system is a dynamic refinement of the familiar machine-bookkeeping ledger card file. Each ledger card is attached to a slotted holding-card, the top or bottom edge of which shows the number and name of the account and is marked with monthly or weekly divisions. A colored marker can be slid along this edge (see Illustration 13-1). When the first invoice amount is entered on a ledger card for a new customer (or after a period of account inactivity for an old customer), the marker is set at the month or week when payment is due. No further adjustment of the marker is made for new invoice entries on the ledger card until payment is made on the first entry. On receipt of payment on the first invoice entry, the marker is moved ahead to the month or week of the next due date as it appears from the ledger card. Thereafter the marker is moved on the occasion of each payment.[3] Supplementary tabs or markers with different colors may also be attached to the "visible index" edge to indicate such matters as the steps in collection procedure that have been applied to a delinquent account, or which accounts have been placed on C.O.D. terms, or which accounts require special watching.

Twenty-five or more of these slotted holding-cards, each with its attached ledger card, are hinged to a panel in such manner that the top

---

[3] An alternative procedure is to set the marker at the month or week from which the credit period starts. An account is visibly current under this system when the marker is not further back than the present date minus the credit period. This system is practicable only if all accounts have identical credit terms.

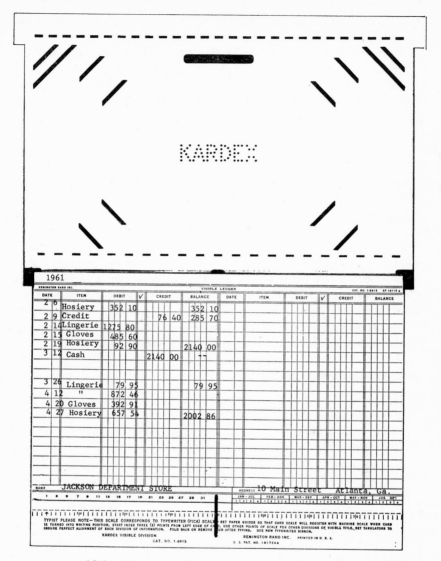

ILLUSTRATION 13-1.  Customer Ledger Card in Remington Rand Kardex Visible File

or bottom edge of each, with the name of the account and the marker, is visible. The panels, in turn, may be arranged so that they slide out of a cabinet, or tilt backwards and forwards in a tub. Since all the cards are in a fixed position on the panel, their visible edges with names of the accounts and the markers are in uniform file. A glance along a panel picks out instantly any markers which have not been advanced to a due date beyond the current month or current week. A few minutes' work on the part of the posting clerk once a month or once a week produces a full list of delinquent accounts upon which collection procedures should be started.[4]

"Keysort" ledger cards, made by the Royal McBee Corporation, do not have to be attached to hinged holding-cards. They have holes punched around their edges (see Illustration 13-3). These holes can represent months or weeks according to the credit terms granted by the seller. Other data can be code-punched around the edges. When the cards are standing in the file, all these holes are in line.

Two ledger files are ordinarily maintained when these "keysort" cards are used, one for currently active accounts which have obligations outstanding, and a second for accounts which have no liabilities for the time being. When a payment is received from an active account, a slot is punched above the hole for the month or week of the payment's due date, and also above the holes for the following months or weeks up to, but not including, the due date of the next payment. Delinquent accounts can be located at any time by running a skewer through the line of holes of the file cards which represents the month or week just past (see Illustration 13-3). The cards for accounts which are paid-up have slots above this hole and slip down from the skewer. Cards for delinquent accounts have not had slots punched above the hole in question; they remain on the skewer and can be lifted from the file.

### Collection procedure timing

After collection procedure on a delinquent account has been initiated by a "reminder" notice, it should be consistently followed up until payment is received or the account is written off. A systematic follow-up, properly timed, has much more chance of success than a haphazard one. Part of the effect of a collection letter series depends upon their cumulative repetition; this is lost if letters are sent out at irregular intervals, whenever the matter arises casually in the credit manager's memory. But while this timing in collection procedure should be systematic, it should not be uniform for all customers. For some, as already indicated, the sequence of letters and possible subsequent direct collection steps should be rapid. For others it may be drawn out.

---

[4] The "visible index" principle is also used in Remington-Rand's "Kolect-A-Matic" ledger system (see Illustration 13-2). Instead of machine-bookkeeping ledger cards attached to hinged slotted holding-cards, the "Kolect-A-Matic" ledger consists of a file of pockets hinged on a panel. Each pocket has a "visible-index" edge, with the name of the customer and a marker. Instead of posting invoice and payment amounts to a ledger card, the duplicate invoices themselves are filed in the pockets, to be removed therefrom when paid. The markers are used in the same way as in the "visible index" card system. The "Kolect-A-Matic" system definitely saves bookkeeping time, and is just as efficient in pointing up delinquent accounts as is the ledger card system. It gives no indication of a customer's past record of purchases and payments, however. Consequently, while it is widely used, not all credit managers are enthusiastic about it.

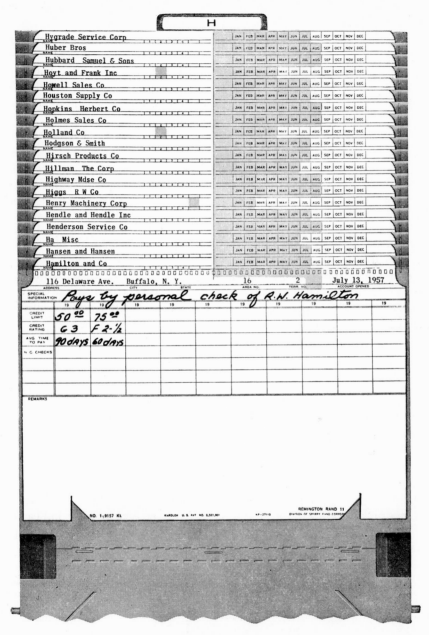

ILLUSTRATION 13-2. Remington Rand Kolect-A-Matic Visible Record System for Accounts Receivable

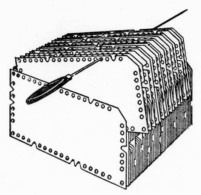

ILLUSTRATION 13-3.  "Keysort" Cards and Sorting Procedure

Collection timing is accomplished by either a tickler system or a desk diary. A tickler system, as used for this purpose, is a card file of which the tab cards are the days of the month for a one- or two-month period. An example is shown in Illustration 13-4. Each time a credit department receives from the accounting department notice of a past-due account, a "collection follow-up card" is made out for it.[5] On this will be noted each collection action as it is taken.

ILLUSTRATION 13-4.  Tickler File for Collection Follow-Up (Remington Rand)

The card is then filed ahead at the date for the next action. Every morning the credit manager or his assistant checks the cards filed for that date. If payment has been made, the card is withdrawn from the file. Otherwise the appropriate collection action is taken and noted on the card, which is again filed ahead. A tickler file is thus a mechanical means of tickling the credit manager's memory.

A desk diary may be used instead of a tickler file where not more than half a dozen delinquent accounts are expected to come up for follow-up treatment in any one day. Instead of filing a card ahead in the file, the credit manager writes the name and address of the account, together with the next collection step in the diary for the day on which the stated action is to be taken. A diary has the disadvantage, compared with the tickler file, that it does not contain the full record of previous collection efforts on the account, together with possible comments that the credit manager may have made for his future guidance.

No general rule can be laid down for the timing of collection letters and collection steps. In some cases, after the sending of an initial "reminder," it might be advisable to postpone further action for a month, to give the customer opportunity to include the past-due amount in his next month's remittance. An even longer follow-up delay is, of course, indicated where the credit manager had agreed to a 60-day extension of time on a payment. In contrast, subsequent steps have to be speeded up to one or two days in cases where immediate telegraphic reply has been demanded to a telegram threatening that the account will be placed with a collection agency or that suit will be brought. Where the customer is in a highly seasonal business, it may be advisable to press a very rapid collection procedure during the seasonal period when his receipts are coming in. If, however, collection has not been made during these months, the follow-up during the off-season time may be widely spaced to serve merely as a reminder of the debt, for which collection will be pushed in the next season.

## DEALING WITH "TERMS CHISELERS"

Few credit managers have been so fortunate as to escape experience with "terms chiselers"—customers who pay after the cash discount period has expired but nonetheless take the discount deduction. A show of sternness on the part of the seller's credit manager can bring some of these "terms chiselers" quickly to heel and make them abide by the terms of sale. Others succeed in continuing their cheating

---

[5] In some offices the credit department receives duplicate invoices. These are immediately placed in the tickler file according to their due dates. If not paid then, they serve as "collection follow-up cards" thereafter.

by threatening to carry their business to competitors if they are not allowed to take discounts whenever they pay.

### Preventive measures

The first step in curing "terms chiseling" is to prevent or discourage it. Too often salesmen tend to slide over the matter of discount terms in making a sales presentation, fearing that an explicit statement may irritate a customer and lose a sale. Experience has shown that such procedure is penny wise and pound foolish; in the vagueness of the salesman's exposition of terms the "terms chiseler" finds an excuse for his practices. Here is a field for cooperation between sales departments and credit departments. Sales managers must direct their salesmen to be specific in their statements on terms of sale.

Another preventive measure can be taken when the credit manager writes his letter of welcome to the new customer. Unobtrusively but specifically the terms of sale should be confirmed. They should be printed in red ink on invoices and statements; a rubber stamp with adjustable amount and date figures can be used for the purpose. Less satisfactory, but used to a considerable extent, are stickers with a discount motto which can be attached to invoices and statements.

### Curative measures

Preventive methods eliminate some taking of unearned discounts, but they do not discourage the hardened "chiselers." When a check from such a customer arrives late but with cash discount deducted, the credit manager is faced with a hard decision. Shall he be fair to his concern and all his other prompt-paying customers, and insist on full payment, thereby risking loss of this customer's trade? Shall he acquiesce in the cheat, but compensate by silently "adjusting" prices or lowering quantity discounts on future orders to this customer? Or shall he knuckle under, and accept the cheat without compensatory subterfuge? The last is certainly the path of least resistance, but it constitutes surrender that may be unnecessary. The second line of action could have adverse repercussions. Firmness, or at least an initial show of it, is the recommended attitude in dealing with "terms chiselers." No credit manager has ever lost a "terms chiseling" customer by sending him, on the first occasion when discount is improperly taken, a firm courteous letter—see page 306—refusing to condone the practice. The letter can make reference to the well-known Curtis Candy Co. case [6] which established the taking of unearned discounts as a violation of the Robinson-Patman Act. For moral effect, the customer's check with discount improperly deducted

---

[6] Federal Trade Commission, Complaint 4556.

may be returned.[7] It is less impressive, though possibly productive of the same result, to accept the check and bill the customer for the improper deduction. Against a hardened, chronic chiseler stronger letters and methods—such as draft—may be appropriate.[8]

"Terms chiseling" may be attempted in other ways than by late mailing of a check with deduction of unearned discount. The check may arrive on time, but have a discrepancy between the amount as written and as stated in figures, or it may be without signature. Or there may be a letter stating that the check is enclosed, without any accompanying check. The "terms chiseler" expects that the seller's credit manager will send back the check for correction, or reply to the letter. This means delay at both ends of the correspondence. Eventually, the customer sends through a valid check, with discount deducted, anywhere from ten days to a month late. But a knowing credit manager can circumvent these tricks. The check with a discrepancy can be corrected to the right amount. An unsigned check, though usually returned, may be handed by the credit manager to his bank for clearing. When the customer's bank receives the check it will ask the customer to authorize payment. In the case of the letter without enclosed check, the credit manager draws a draft on the customer, deposits it with his bank for collection, and notifies the customer that this action was taken as the most convenient way of rectifying the mistake.

Most "terms chiseling" customers react favorably to firm but courteous treatment. They gain an added respect for a supplier who, without giving offense, maintains his rights, and this respect is a valuable element of good will for all future dealings. But some hardened "chiselers" stand pat in the face of letters or action such as suggested above, and confront the supplier with the choice of either accepting the cheat or losing them as customers. The choice that the credit manager then makes must be determined by his company's position. If it is favorably situated and can pick and choose as to its outlets, the credit manager can maintain his firm attitude and force the "chiseler" either to abide by the terms of

---

[7] Some business men think that if they deposit a customer's check with discount improperly deducted, they thereby ratify the deduction and preclude themselves from asking for the discount amount. This view is in error. Unless the maker of the check has written "in full satisfaction," or some phrase of similar intent, upon the check, its acceptance by the creditor does not estop him from claiming the full amount of the invoice or statement. The only purpose of returning a customer's check is the moral effect of the action.

[8] A survey of over 1200 credit managers on their handling of "terms chiseling" indicated that 74 per cent do not permit it, 11 per cent permit it sometimes, 12 per cent permit it generally (3 per cent did not answer the question). Of the 85 per cent who do not permit it or permit it only occasionally, three-quarters accept the customer's check, deposit it, and either bill the customer for the "chiseled" difference or just ask him not to repeat. The others return the customer's check and request a new one for the full amount. See H. Reinhardt, *op. cit.*, p. 5.

sale or seek another supplier. If the supplier cannot afford to lose a customer, even one of the "chiseling" type, the credit manager must surrender with as much dignity as he can.

Much is being done, and more can be done, by credit and trade associations, to check "terms chiseling." Members of some of these organizations report "chiselers" among their customers to the associations, which list them. Whole lines of business thus obtain advance warning. Many of these associations encourage their members to present united fronts to "chiseling" customers.

## THE PRE-DUE NOTIFICATION OR STATEMENT

Where goods are sold on lumped-order terms, so that payments become regularly due on the 10th, or the 15th, or at the end of a month, most sellers send the customer a monthly statement, timed to arrive a few days before the due date. It serves the customer both as a reminder and as a check upon his payables record. Before mechanized bookkeeping became prevalent, such statements were the bane of the bookkeeping department. They demanded substantial amounts of time at periods when the department was carrying peak loads in other duties. Accordingly, credit managers for a while gave serious thought to whether this custom of sending out monthly statements should not be discontinued,[9] at least for the large number of customers who apparently pay from invoices rather than from statements. Mechanized bookkeeping procedures can handle pre-due notices without difficulty. The argument for eliminating them has thereby been weakened.[10]

Where goods are sold on individual-order terms, pre-due notification can be accomplished by sending the customers duplicate invoices. These are timed by a tickler file maintained by a bookkeeping clerk and mailed to arrive a few days before due dates. Undoubtedly the system has value in preventing honest oversight on the part of some customers.

## THE FIRST REMINDER

Two or three days' grace should be allowed every account before it is sent a reminder that a due date has passed without receipt of a check. Such a grace period used to be the normal result of

---

[9] In some instances such statements are required by law. In New York, for example, the Alcoholic Beverage Law compels manufacturers and wholesalers to send out pre-due notices and retain copies as evidence of their compliance with the law.

[10] A 1954 survey indicated that 90 per cent of the companies covered sent out pre-due statements; a minority of these sent them only at customers' requests. See Reinhardt, *op. cit.,* p. 8; see also "They Prefer to Send Monthly Statements," *Credit and Financial Management,* August 1958, p. 8.

ordinary office routine. Hand entry of payments upon the customers' ledgers, copying off a list of delinquent accounts, and transmitting the list to the credit manager usually took a day or two. By the time the credit manager received the list, corrected for last-minute payments, the ordinary grace period had generally expired and the "reminder" notices could be sent out immediately. With the increasing speed-up of mechanized accounting and office procedures, a delinquent list may reach a credit manager the day after the due date. Under these circumstances a grace period, if it is to be allowed, should be a matter of deliberate collection policy.

A first "reminder" notice should be truly a reminder, and nothing more. A customer who has accidentally or deliberately failed to send in his check by the due date cannot be offended by a brief impersonal reminder of his obligation, but he might resent sharply a letter which apparently singled out his default.

One of the simplest and most effective of first "reminders" is a duplicate statement or invoice. A seller with a large proportion of customers that miss their due dates may find it time-saving to have an extra carbon copy made of all statements or invoices for such later use. If only a small proportion of customers are ordinarily delinquent, duplicated copies of the invoices will best fulfill this purpose. Nothing could be more impersonal, and hence less likely to give offense.

Some offices have a special form for their "reminder" duplicate statement or invoice which has "PLEASE REMIT" or "PAST DUE" printed in red at the top or across the face of it. Or this emphasis may be achieved by rubber stamping the duplicate statement or invoice in red with "PLEASE REMIT," or "PAST DUE," or "HAVE YOU FORGOTTEN US?", or, even more effectively, with the single word "PLEASE." Or a short notation—such as "Did you realize you overlooked us last month?"—may be written or typed in red across the bottom of the statement. Unquestionably such procedures emphasize that the account is past due and payment is desired. The question remains, however, where appropriate "reminding" ends and overemphasis, which could produce some resentment, begins. A credit manager must decide this issue individually for each case.

"Collection stickers" may be attached to duplicate statements or invoices. They bear some brief statement suggesting remittance of the past-due account and have several advantages over printed or stamped notices. They attract attention because of the strongly colored gloss paper on which they are usually printed. Their messages can be courteous, explanatory, or humorous, as the occasion demands. Since they come in series, a different message can be used on successive occasions. Examples of these "reminder" stickers are shown in Illustration 13-5. They can be purchased from most commercial printers.[11]

---

[11] There are even machines on the market, such as the "Pick-a-Phrase and Collect Automat," which print according to selection one of twelve available reminders.

ILLUSTRATION 13-5. "Reminder" Collection Stickers

A few business houses send out their "reminders" in the form of printed cards with some such message as the following:

> "A friendly reminder that your present payment of $.... on our ........statement was due on............"
>
> The A.B.C. Corporation

The name and address of the customer, as well as the amount past due, the month of the statement, and the due date, are usually written in by hand. In some cases these cards are sent without the name and address of the customer appearing on the card. The impersonal formality of this type of reminder is counted on to remove any implication of specific or personal criticism.

### SUPPLEMENTARY READINGS

See page 283 of this volume.

### REVIEW

1. State the four basic principles of collection procedure.
2. State 12 reasons for customer delinquency and the collection treatment to be applied in each case.
3. How may a credit manager be made aware of his customers' delinquencies shortly after each due date?
4. How may a tickler file or desk diary be used to control collection follow-up? Which is the more efficient?
5. What is the best time interval between collection steps?
6. What is "terms chiseling" and how should "terms chiselers" be treated?
7. Should statements and duplicate invoices be sent to customers in advance of due dates?
8. How may duplicate statements and duplicate invoices be used as "first reminder" notices?
9. What considerations should guide a credit manager in planning the method or form of his concern's "first reminder" notices?
10. Give four or five statements which might be found on reminder "stickers."

# CHAPTER 14

# Collection Principles and Procedures: 2

## FOLLOW-UP CORRESPONDENCE

If the "reminder" notice does not produce a check from the customer, a follow-up procedure, which may be quite protracted in some cases, must be started. It is based, in most credit offices, primarily upon a series of letters. The first of the series may be little more than a mild reminder. The intensity of the following letters rises, on a carefully graduated scale, through friendly pleas for payment, to warnings of the inconveniences of the collection actions that will ensue if payment is not made, and finally to threats that drastic collection procedures will be resorted to if payment is not immediately forthcoming.

Collection letter writing has to observe certain principles as to content and form. It is an art that requires intensive study. Chapters 15 and 16 of this volume are devoted to it.

## FOLLOW-UP BY TELEPHONE

The answer to a collection letter is often—much too often—SILENCE. Breaking that silence, getting an explanation—any explanation, true or false—of why the customer has become delinquent is an important step in obtaining payment. Therefore, even where primary collection emphasis is placed on correspondence, it is a desirable and common practice at some advanced stage of the collection effort to endeavor to reach the customer directly by telephone in order to establish a personal contact.

Telephone conversation with a delinquent customer has many advantages. If the customer himself, or some responsible member of his organization, can be brought to the other end of the wire, the deadening silence that has weighed down the preceding collection correspondence is broken. The credit manager may obtain a specific promise of payment at some date in the near future. The promise may not be kept, but at least it gives the credit manager a new and powerful point of argument in any subsequent credit correspondence. In the course of the telephone conversation, the customer may be persuaded to explain the financial situation that is holding up his payment. This explanation may be used later by the credit manager in his letters as a springboard for suggestions and advice to the customer which may really help him to improve his circumstances. The credit manager can propose extended terms or other special arrangements appropriate to the situation. Difficulties that could be cleared up only by days, or even weeks, of correspondence may be smoothed out in a few minutes by telephone. A credit manager with a friendly voice can often say things that would appear cold or harsh in the black and white of a letter, but that lose their sting when imparted by the spoken word. Finally, the fact that the credit manager has taken the initiative of putting through a telephone call, particularly a long-distance one, may impress the customer with the importance attached to him and his delinquency. In any case, it is harder to be indifferent to a telephone call than to a collection letter which can be dropped into the waste-paper basket without being read.

There are also drawbacks to telephone follow-up. It is easier for some customers to give, unblushingly, evasive or even untrue answers over the telephone that they would never put in writing. Also, a delinquent customer may instruct his secretary to answer any phone call from the supplier's credit manager with the information that the customer is out of his office at the moment. Nevertheless, the balance of opinion is in favor of the telephone as a collection tool.

Many credit offices make inadequate collection use of the telephone because of the costs involved. They look only at the difference between a four-cent stamp and the cost of a toll call—especially if it is a long-distance one. On this basis, they deem the telephone too expensive, even for local collections. Such a view overlooks all the indirect costs associated with the dictating and writing of a letter. Dictated letters cost from $.70 to $2.45 apiece, form letters from $.08 to $.20.[1] Total expense of a local telephone call, including attributed cost of overhead and the credit manager's time, would be far less than that of a dictated collection letter, and not much over that of a form letter. Even toll calls to out-of-town customers would frequently be more economical than long, dictated letters.

## COLLECTION TELEGRAMS

If a customer has ignored a series of collection letters, or has repeatedly promised by letter or by telephone to pay at specific dates and has broken those promises, a telegram may sometimes jolt him into making the payment.

It has been found by test that past-due customers respond to the persuasive powers of the telegram for a number of reasons. A telegram goes directly to the man to whom it is addressed. It attracts individual attention. It gets to the point quickly. It means business—and it is businesslike. It impresses upon the customer the urgency of the message. It compels action. Yet because of its very impersonality, it does not forfeit customer good will. Used at the right stage of the collection procedure, the telegram has been found to be distinctly helpful. The general experience of those who employ it for collecting delinquent accounts is that it may stir the debtor into action whereas letters go unheeded and unanswered. The Western Union Telegraph Co. has case histories on file showing results from collection telegrams of up to 95 per cent effectiveness.

Collection telegrams are legal everywhere. The sending of a telegram for the purpose of collecting a past-due account involves no more legal risk than mailing a letter for the same purpose. There is no statute or rule of law that prohibits the sending of a telegram demanding payment of a just debt—so long as the communication does not contain libelous matter or extortion. A threat to sue would not come under either of these limitations. But a threat to institute bankruptcy proceedings, a criminal prosecution, or to render an unfavorable credit report to the members of a credit association, intended to coerce payment of the account, may make the sender liable in some states. Such liability for coercion or libelous collection language is not confined to collection by telegraph. It applies to any collection communication—by letter, by telephone, or otherwise.[2]

For the assistance of credit executives, Western Union Telegraph Co.

---

[1] *Credit and Financial Management,* September 1958, p. 20.
[2] See National Association of Credit Management, *Credit Manual of Commercial Laws,* 1961, p. 260.

ILLUSTRATION 14-1.    Western Union Form Telegram

offers a list of suggested collection message texts which may be adopted to suit individual needs. These are shown in Illustration 14-1.

## THE SALESMAN AS COLLECTOR

There has long been a major controversy among credit and sales executives as to whether salesmen should be used as collectors on customers that do not respond to ordinary collection procedures by correspondence or telephone. Credit managers are inclined to take the position that the salesman is available for visits to delinquent accounts and that his previously established personal relationship with the customer should be capitalized for collection purposes. Sales managers, on the other hand, usually resent such efforts by the credit department. They insist that collection tasks do violence to a salesman's nature and vocation. Sales force morale, they argue, would be threatened by any effort to turn the salesman into a collector, particularly when he is not compensated for such activity. On balance, much can be said for and against each side of the dispute.[3] In practice, collection by salesmen is confined to special lines of business and particular circumstances.

Where the salesmen of a concern doing business primarily with small retailers visit the customers regularly at short intervals, they commonly perform the collection function to the virtual exclusion of all other methods. Indeed, so established is this custom in some retail lines that the customers refuse to pay in any other way. If, because of a salesman's illness or for any other reason, he cannot make his regular trips on the route, the sales department may be able to get orders from the customer by mail but few payments. Most customers simply wait until they can pay the salesman upon his next visit. This is trade custom, and there is little a credit manager can do about it without losing customer good will. In such lines of business, not only is great weight accorded to the salesmen's judgment in determining which would-be customers are acceptable credit risks but the salesmen are also given major responsibility on collection decisions. If a customer announces that he does not have the funds on hand to pay for the last order, the salesman must decide on the spot whether to take a post-dated check, or to take a part payment as basis for authorizing a new order, or to authorize a new order without any payment on the preceding one, or to refuse any further sale on regular terms until the preceding order has been fully paid.

Even where primary collection responsibility is not placed on the salesmen, they should be brought into the collection procedure whenever a customer's nonpayment has caused the credit department to refuse authorization of any further orders to him on regular terms. A salesman has a personal interest in collecting from such an account, since until collection is made he must forego further sales and commissions on it. The friendly personal relations between him and the customer may enable him to succeed where the correspondence of the credit manager had previously failed. At least, he may possibly obtain an explanation of the delinquency from the customer that will enable the credit manager to work out some practicable basis for subsequent limited authorization of orders, or for special terms of sale.

Without using salesmen directly as collectors of overdue accounts, they can be tied into collection procedure. They may be given duplicate statements of their customers' overdue accounts, and instructed to discuss the payment situation with them. Even if their conversations do not result in immediate receipt of checks, they will frequently elicit information of

---

[3] *Credit and Financial Management* in its March to June numbers, 1952, ran a poll "Should Salesmen Collect Accounts?" to be answered by both sales and credit executives. The published answers indicated a slight majority of affirmative replies, but they were always qualified with regard to circumstances. Comments on this question have appeared intermittently in later issues of this publication, and the debate continues.

great value to the credit manager for his follow-up campaign and also for his future credit judgment on the accounts.

## THE CREDIT MANAGER AS COLLECTOR

Normally the credit manager cannot travel to visit his slow-pays and talk man-to-man with them about the situation. His ordinary place of business is his office, where he makes credit decisions and handles collections through correspondence or telephone, or puts other collection machinery to work.

But the annual "swing around" for the purpose of obtaining first-hand acquaintance with key or difficult accounts, that every credit manager should make, can also include a certain amount of collection work. Whenever a substantial bad debt loss threatens, a credit manager should make an effort at personal collection before abandoning the account to a collection agency or instituting suit. He is in a better position than anyone else to combine pressure for payment with diplomatic maintaining of good will. In direct conversation with a customer, he may be able to work out a sound program of deferred or instalment payment. Far from being insulted by such a personal visit of the credit manager, a delinquent customer is likely to experience some feeling of flattery that his case was considered so important to the supplier that the credit manager himself called.

Some credit managers whose concerns are compelled by competitive circumstance to deal with local poor-risk customers make collection a regular part of their routine activity. They earmark one, or two, or three afternoons a week for calling on their delinquent customers. Only by this intense personal treatment of their collection problem can they hope to hold down the losses from such marginal accounts sufficiently to clear some net profit on sales to them.

## SPECIAL COLLECTION EMPLOYEES

Only a large supplier, with territorial concentration of fairly substantial accounts, would find it worth while to have an employee who specialized exclusively on collection visits. But a supplier that finds it practicable to employ a man specialized in credit interviewing, particularly a traveling credit man, can use him effectively for collection purposes.

Unfortunately, such an employee will presumably set obtaining payment above the maintenance of the customer good will. He has hardly any choice in this, since his success or failure is generally measured by the collections he makes. In his eagerness to establish a good collection record, he may adopt an attitude that is not in line with his company's policy. He may use threats that will prove boomerangs. He may make promises that the collection department is reluctant to keep. Customers may resent his high-pressure methods, and the collections actually obtained may not compensate for the resulting sacrifice of customer good will.

## COLLECTION BY DRAFT

After every other collection procedure has failed, there is one penultimate step that may be taken before turning the account over to a collection agency or instituting suit. This is threatening to draw a draft on the customer, and actually doing so if the threat does not produce results. A draft may also be used to collect from a hardened "terms chiseler" who persists in taking unearned discounts. It would cover the amount of his illegitimate deduction.

### Nature of a draft

A draft is an order drawn by a creditor on a debtor, directing the latter to pay, on sight or after a certain demand period, a certain sum of money. It differs from a trade acceptance in that it does not bear on its face a statement that it arises from a purchase and sale of merchandise, and there is no acknowledgment or acceptance by the debtor. As used in mercantile collections, it is drawn by a supplier upon a delinquent customer and is sent either to the customer's own bank or, if he does not maintain banking connections, to some other bank in his community, for presentation to the customer.[4] It is commonly accompanied by a request [5] that, if the customer fails to pay on the draft, the local

---

[4] Many credit managers prefer to deposit the draft with their own bank for collection. This bank forwards the draft to the customer's bank, or to some other bank in his community, for presentation. If the payment is made, it is transferred by the local bank to the supplier's bank. If the draft is dishonored, it is sent back, by the same way. The advantage of this arrangement is that the local bank may be more expeditious in acting for the supplier's bank, for reasons of inter-bank courtesy, than it would be for the supplier directly. But note that, under this arrangement, the draft, if dishonored, cannot immediately be transmitted by the local bank to a local attorney, unless specific instructions to this effect have been given.

[5] This covering letter must not impute dishonesty, insolvency, or fraud to the customer, as such imputation would be libelous. The following letter to a bank, accompanying a draft to be presented, was held libelous: "Present (this draft) again and if not paid please turn over to some Justice of Peace with instructions to sue on the knowledge of the fact that Mr. Ferdon is about to leave the state for the purpose of defrauding his creditors. The account is long past due and if Mr. Ferdon's intentions were honest and sincere he would have remitted a long time ago since he has sold out his business and ought to have the means received from the sale."—*Ferdon v. Dickens,* 101 Ala. 181, 49 So. 888.

bank report the reasons for nonpayment given by the customer. Occasionally the draft may be accompanied by a request that, if it is dishonored, it be transmitted to a local attorney for collection. If payment is made upon presentation of the draft, the bank transmits the funds to the supplier. If the draft is dishonored, it is returned to the supplier. The bank involved usually charges a small fee for the service, whether or not the collection is made.

A draft sent to a customer's bank as a penultimate effort at collection —to be followed by agency action or suit—is generally a severe blow to a customer's credit standing. The bank is thereby informed that the supplier has exhausted the ordinary procedures of collection. If the customer has been obtaining credit from the bank, such knowledge may result in its discontinuance, at least for some time to come. In any case, the bank will be bound to state, in reply to any subsequent credit inquiries, that collection has been made upon the customer by draft; such information will hardly be a credit recommendation. Subsequent interchange reports on the customer will also carry the remark "Collected by draft."

Any customer upon whom collection is made by draft is certain to resent the procedure, whether or not it was justified by the circumstances. He will probably never again buy from that supplier. Therefore a credit manager should never employ draft collection unless he is certain that his concern wants to rid itself of that customer, either because he has proved to be an unsatisfactory moral risk, or because the evidence as to his ability and financial position indicate that he will shortly fail. So long as any hope remains that the customer may be salvaged for future selling, other less stringent collection procedures should be continued, at least for some time.

Some credit managers misuse the collection draft. They employ it to try to force early payment from essentially sound customers with working capital trouble who must delay on some or all their obligations. Or they employ it in a dispute with a customer over an invoice amount or an issue of damaged goods, to bludgeon him into compliance. It is sometimes applied under sellers' market conditions as a collection short cut. Such misuses have weakened the effect of the draft, which can and should be a tremendously powerful next-to-the-last collection weapon. Credit men's groups and other agencies, therefore, are currently endeavoring to educate credit managers to proper use of the draft.

### Notice of draft

Because collection by draft can work serious injury to a delinquent customer's credit standing, a customer who has resisted all preceding collection pleas and procedures may often be induced to pay by the mere threat of this collection weapon. Warning should therefore always be given to the customer before dispatching a draft to his bank. The customer is entitled to such warning, so that he may have a last chance, if at all possible, to arrange payment and thereby avoid the sharp blow to his credit position. The credit manager has everything to gain and nothing to lose by giving the warning, since it may produce the payment and obviate sending the draft.

Notice to a delinquent customer that a draft will be presented for collection may take the form of a brief letter explaining that the supplier has received no reply, or an unsatisfactory answer, to previous collection letters and that, unless payment is received by a specified date, a draft for the amount of his obligation will be drawn upon the customer and presented through his (or some other specified) bank. Or the credit manager may prefer to use a printed notice of draft, perhaps a form supplied by the same printer or collection agency that provides his draft forms, on the ground that the formal nature of such a printed notice is more impressive than an ordinary typewritten letter.

## COLLECTION BY AGENCY OR ATTORNEY

The final effort at collection in many cases—when a credit manager knows that a delinquent customer is "judgment-proof" and that a successful suit will yield only an uncollectible judgment—is to turn the delinquent account over to an agency or attorney for collection. This ultimate step may also be taken when a credit manager is fed up with unsuccessful collection attempts and all his efforts to maintain an acceptable sales relationship with a customer have failed.

### Collection agencies and their operations

There are two classes of collection agencies—those privately operated, and those operated by credit agencies and associations. Among the latter are the Mercantile Claims Division of Dun & Bradstreet, the Commercial Claims Division of the National Association of Credit Management, the collection divisions of several special-line agencies, the 62 collection bureaus operated by credit associations affiliated with the NACM, and the collection divisions of the credit bureaus of various trade associations. These collection bureaus are supervised by their parent credit organizations to ensure the safety of the clients' funds that they handle. The accounts of the collection bureaus affiliated with the NACM, for example, are audited annually by the central office of the NACM, and these bureaus cannot receive the approval of the central office unless their agents are bonded and they maintain properly secured trust funds for collections made on behalf of their clients.

Most private collection agencies, particularly those which have been long established, are reliable. Some are not. There have been cases where collection agencies embezzled funds they had collected for clients. There have been cases where private agencies, operating irresponsibly in ignorance of the law, have involved their clients in serious libel suits or extortion prosecutions, for in this matter the agency is the agent of the client, and the latter is responsible for the acts of the agent. A private collection agency, therefore, should not be selected casually from a classified telephone directory or on the basis of a direct-mail advertising letter. Careful investigation of the agency should precede submission of any accounts to it for collection; in particular, there should be assurance that its employees are bonded, and that it maintains proper trustee arrangements for safeguarding collections made on behalf of its clients.[6]

A collection agency has no means of collection not available to an ordinary credit office. All the agency can do is mail one or more collection letters, and possibly send a representative to call upon the delinquent customer. Yet the agencies succeed in obtaining payment in a large proportion of cases where the credit office has failed. There are two reasons for this. First, the collection agency has no interest in preserving the good will of the customer while endeavoring to obtain payment from him. Consequently, it can press its demands in uncompromising language. Some customers who can resist the more politely phrased requests of the credit office succumb to direct, vigorous demands of the agency. Second, if the agency is one of those associated with Dun & Bradstreet, a special-line mercantile agency, the NACM and its affiliates, or a trade association credit bureau, the customer knows that his failure to respond to the agency's demands will immediately affect his rating and be communicated in credit reports.

The first step in agency collection is often delegated by the agency to the supplier's credit office. The credit manager receives from the agency a stock of stickers or inserts, to be attached to a letter warning delinquent customers that their accounts will be turned over to a collection agency. In some cases a collection agency supplies its clients with printed or multigraphed "free demand" notices, or with a "final demand" and warning of reference to the agency to be sent to the customer on the seller's own letterhead. These notices have spaces for filling in the customer's name and address, the amount due, and other pertinent data. They state either that the account will be turned over to the agency

---

[6] A beginning was made in state legislation to require licensing and bonding of collection agencies in 1949 when Wisconsin enacted such a law. Few other states followed. The debates on this issue have shifted to a different plane—the question whether collection agency activities constitute improper practice of law, as the bar associations in some states maintain. To require licensing of these agencies might be interpreted as legislative recognition of their status and would thus weaken the argument of the opposing bar associations.

immediately if payment is not made forthwith, or that the account has already been submitted to the agency and payment should be made to the agency. A memo of the sending of the notice is transmitted to the agency, which posts it in a tickler file for further use. In other cases the agency sends out the "free demand" letter. Sometimes a so-called "double demand" service is used; supplier and agency mail letters to the delinquent account on the same day. In any case, if payment is made on a "free demand" notice, the agency makes no collection charge, and the matter ends. When, however, a reasonable time has elapsed without payment, the agency starts its procedure.

A collection agency's first direct action is to write a letter, either announcing that the case is in its hands, or following up a "free demand" letter already sent out. The customer is warned that if payment is not made forthwith, or some settlement arranged with the supplier, "immediate drastic action" will be taken.[7] If this letter produces no results, it may be followed by another, or the agency may send a representative in an attempt to accomplish personal collection, according to the type of service contracted for by the supplier. The agency may also attempt to collect by draft. Should these steps fail, the agency's function ends.

Collection agency charges vary according to agencies and according to the type of collection service to be given. For sending a series of "agency" collection letters, the charge may be 5 per cent of any amount collected by reason of the letters, or even less. Where personal visits of agency representatives to the clients are involved, or where the agency endeavors to collect by draft, or where it undertakes other collection procedures, the charge may range up to 18 per cent of any amounts collected. No charge is made if no collection is accomplished.

### "House agencies"

A large supplier, selling to a class of customers of such character that a substantial number each year become proper subjects for agency collection, may find it advisable to establish its own "house collection agency." Some factors that finance their clients' receivables without recourse,[8] and have substantial uncollected customer accounts on their hands, have also established "house" agencies. Such an agency is not a separate collection organization, but merely a name and address that the supplier's or factor's credit department uses for its final collection letters to make them appear as though they were being sent by a bona fide collection agency. The name chosen for a "house agency" may be

---

[7] Note that a credit manager may state in a collection letter that the account will be turned over to an attorney for suit if payment is not made, but a collection agency may not make such statement in any of its letters as this would constitute extortion in some states. Its threat must be nonspecific, as in the phrase "immediate drastic action."

[8] See Chapter 23.

anything, provided it has the words "collection agency" in it and bears no resemblance to the supplier's regular name. The address may be a post-office box number, permitting the "agency" to operate from the supplier's regular office.

The advantage of a "house agency" is that, on the "agency's" letter-heads, the supplier or factor can press collections with all the vigor that would be used by a regular agency, and thus obtain whatever success could be achieved by such an organization, without having to pay its substantial charges. The customer does not know that his account is not in the hands of a regular agency. Moreover, the supplier's credit department is at all times in full control of the "agency" collection procedure, so that in appropriate cases it can modify the usual exigent language of the "agency" letters in an endeavor to preserve some shreds of the customer's good will. Should a customer survive the financial difficulties responsible for the strenuous collection action directed against him, and subsequently become a desirable credit risk, the supplier can disclaim responsibility for the harsh correspondence of the "agency" and endeavor once again to sell to such customer.

## Collection by attorney

Instead of giving a delinquent account to an agency for collection, it may be submitted to a lawyer in the customer's community. One advantage of such action is that, if the attorney fails to make collection by correspondence or visit, he may immediately initiate suit. Even if the supplier has decided that bringing suit will not be worth while, and so notifies the attorney, the customer does not know this and the attorney can still press for payment with the expressed or implied threat that he will immediately bring suit if payment is not forthcoming. The entrance of an attorney upon the scene appears to many small business men as the actual beginning of legal action, whereas they view agency collection as one last step before legal action. Another advantage of collection by attorney is that, as a local man, he may be better able to win the confidence of a delinquent customer and, in cases where full payment is impossible, work out a compromise that enables the supplier to salvage something from the account.

An attorney experienced in collection work usually opens his dealings with a delinquent customer with a letter stating that the account has been placed in his hands for collection and, if need be, legal action. He continues that his client wishes to avoid bringing suit, if possible, and asks the customer for immediate payment of the due balance or, if that is not possible, that the customer propose some practicable arrangement by which the account may be settled. If that letter fails to produce a response, the attorney may make a personal visit to the customer, or he may choose to make a final attempt at collection by a stronger letter such as the following:

Dear Sir:

On March 15 I wrote you regarding your long overdue account with the XYZ Corporation.

To date I have received no reply from you.

Under the circumstances I have no choice but to issue a summons against you for court action on this matter. The judgment will require you to pay not only the full amount of your overdue account, but also court costs involved in the suit. You can avoid these additional costs by settling the XYZ Corporation's claim before papers are served upon you. For such settlement I must have your check within four days of the date of this letter.

Very truly yours,

If the visit or such final letter produces no results, the attorney either institutes suit or drops the matter, according to the instructions given by the supplier.

The name and address of a local attorney may be obtained from one of the "Law Lists" described earlier in this volume.[9] Or a collection agency, having failed in its efforts, will, upon the supplier's approval, transmit the claim to a local attorney of its selection. Or the supplier may submit the claim to its own law firm, which will forward it to a local attorney. Some mercantile agencies and trade associations have designated attorneys in different parts of the country, who, under special arrangements, undertake collection action for the agency's subscribers or the association's members.

The usual commission for collection of a mercantile debt by an attorney, as established by the Commercial Law League, is

20 per cent on the first $750 collected;
15 per cent on the next $750;
13 per cent on the excess over $1,500;
$20 minimum.

In some cities the bar associations have established higher rates for their members.

### PART PAYMENT AND DELAYED PAYMENT

Sometimes a delinquent customer, in response to a collection letter, explains that it is impossible to pay his past-due bal-

---

[9] See p. 126. Some of the publishers of these directories stand responsible for any claims collected by a listed attorney, provided the creditor notifies the publisher, on a form supplied by the latter, at the time the claim is placed. Upon receipt of such notice, the publisher will bond the attorney selected by the party for the indicated collection claim.

ance now, but offers to pay part of it at present and the balance in instalments, or explains that he will be able to pay the full amount in the near future and requests an extension of time on his account. It may also happen that a credit manager discovers a delinquent customer to be suffering a temporary financial reverse and wonders whether he should take the initiative in proposing part payment or the postponement of payment to some specific future date. In either case, agreement to part payment or delayed payment is a surrender of part of the supplier's rights, and the credit manager should endeavor to obtain some counterbalancing consideration from the customer in exchange for it.

### Part payment

Where a customer who has been analyzed as essentially sound but suffering from working capital difficulties sends on the due date a check for a part of his obligation and explains the situation, he should be regarded as worthy of considerate treatment. He cannot pay all of his accounts promptly, and he has taken the honest step of rationing his payments among his suppliers instead of favoring some to the detriment of others. A credit manager receiving a part payment under such circumstances should acknowledge it, express appreciation of the customer's effort to meet his obligations; and suggest a date or dates for payment of the balance. Additional security in the form of notes should not be requested of such a customer. The statement of specific dates for payment of the balance, however, is a wise procedure. The appreciation expressed for the part payment should win the customer's good will and the dates set for subsequent payment help to hold him to the fulfillment of his obligation. Without such specific dates, even the well-intentioned customer may use his funds as received for the payment of other, more pressing suppliers.

The case is quite different where, after persistent follow-up letters, a delinquent account decides, possibly at the suggestion of the supplier, to send in or to propose part payment. For one thing, the customer has not displayed himself as a high moral risk. There is less assurance that the balance of payments will come through when promised. Furthermore, a particular part payment arrangement must not be allowed to appear as a precedent to which the customer can revert in the future at any time when full payment seems inconvenient to him. Yet, on the principle of "a bird in the hand is worth two in the bush," a credit manager will rarely forego part payment where it can be obtained. But he should also be careful to ascertain that such part payment cannot later be construed by an unreliable customer as having been accepted in full payment of the account.[10]

A precaution that many credit managers take when accepting or assenting to, or proposing part payment, is to explain that it is contrary to the supplier's general credit policy, but that an exception is being made in the present case. This is done to emphasize the obligation of prompt full payment, and to indicate that the particular part payment arrangement is not to be taken as a precedent. Another advisable precaution is to prepare a series of promissory notes for the subsequent payments and mail them to the customer for his signature. Notes will bind the customer to payment of the balance on the specific dates agreed upon. If he does not meet the notes when they are sent through to his bank for collection, it is a more serious blow to his general credit standing than if he merely failed to pay an open-account item. If suit must eventually be brought against the customer, action on notes is in many ways preferable to suit on the general claim. That the supplier incidentally acquires discountable negotiable instruments, upon which he can borrow, is a less important consideration. These are not the kind of notes that banks would readily discount.

It is common practice to notify a customer two or three days before a note is put through for collection. This may save him the embarrassment of having overlooked the imminence of its presentation, and he should be accordingly grateful. By allowing him several days to ensure that the funds to meet the note are available, the probability that the note will be honored upon presentation is increased.

### Delayed payment

Every credit manager has the experience, sooner or later, of the customer who in reply to some letter in a collection series explains that he cannot pay immediately and asks for a month or two-month extension of time. Such letters usually state an honest case, and the credit manager has no choice but to assent. He should always, in such circumstances, set a specific date for the payment. Generally it is also good practice to cover the extension by a promissory note sent to the customer for his signature.

Sometimes a customer's request for extension of time on his account is only a delaying action. He has no greater expectation of being able to pay at the later date than currently, but the extension will give him a reprieve from dunning letters for a month or two. If, from past expe-

---

10 As a rule, a check for less than the due amount, although marked "in full of the account," will not release the debtor of his obligation. This would happen only where there is a *dispute* as to the amount of the claim. In such a case, the creditor must not accept the check marked "in full payment" but should return it and demand the full amount he claims. (See *Credit Manual of Commercial Laws,* 1961, p. 325.)

rience with the customer, or from study of ledger interchange reports, the credit manager believes that the request for an extension of time is merely a ruse of this sort, there is no point to his granting it. At the conclusion of the extension period the customer will ask for a further one, or the collection procedure will have to start all over again. The only reasonable course open to the credit manager is to refuse the request, and press more forcibly than ever for full, immediate payment of the account.

### Post-dated checks

It is very common practice, where extension of time is granted, to ask for and receive a check dated as of the day when payment will be due under the extension. Salesmen who regularly collect on the customer's past order when taking a new one must often accept checks post-dated by two days, or three days, or a week, in order to make their collections.

If there are insufficient funds in the customer's account when the check is presented, it will return to the payee like any other bad check. In most states a post-dated check is deemed not to be an implied representation by the drawer that, at the time of drawing the check, he had funds on deposit in that bank sufficient to meet it upon presentation.[11] Hence the customer cannot be criminally prosecuted under the bad check laws. In these states, a post-dated check has the same legal character as a promissory note. It is a negotiable instrument containing a promise to discharge a present obligation at a future date. But in Ohio, Illinois, Missouri, and possibly other jurisdictions, a dishonored post-dated check has been held to come under the state's bad check law and the maker may be subjected to prosecution. This interpretation, prevailing only in few states, would make a post-dated check an even stronger enforcement instrument for postponed payments than a promissory note.

Many customers who would resent the request for a promissory note as a condition for an extension of payment time will give a post-dated check without cavil. They feel that a post-dated check, which carries on its face no indication of their inability to meet an earlier due date, does not reflect on their credit standing as a promissory note may do. Yet dishonor of a post-dated check casts exactly the same shadow upon a customer's position as dishonor of a note and, as indicated above, there may be criminal penalties attached to nonpayment of the check that do not exist for nonpayment of a note. Whenever a credit manager discovers that a customer would rather bind himself on a postponed payment by

---

[11] The cases that have established this view in most of the states are cited in National Association of Credit Management, *Credit Manual of Commercial Laws*, 1961, p. 336.

post-dated check than by note, there is no reason why the customer's preference should not be indulged.

One use of post-dated checks should be definitely discouraged—the remittance with cash discount deducted. A check that cannot be deposited until a week, or ten days, or two weeks after it has been received is not a cash payment, and the attempt to treat it as such is a form of "terms chiseling."

## CHARGING INTEREST ON PAST-DUE ACCOUNTS

The suggestion that customers should pay interest on their past-due balances is certainly a reasonable one. Nevertheless, for a long time it faced such violent customer opposition that only a few uniquely situated suppliers dared to apply such a policy. Apparently there is less opposition today, and the practice is moderately used. One problem that arises is whether the rates are stiff enough to compel a delinquent customer to make strong effort to pay. Six per cent per annum, the usual rate, is not very much, but higher charges would not be legal in most jurisdictions. Another factor that may work against its smooth application is the differential that exists in all states between the legal rates allowed for this purpose and the higher maximum for contract rates.[12] Particularly in times of tight money a customer would have to pay more for a bank loan to clear his mercantile delinquency than to pay interest on the delinquency.

## WRITING OFF BAD DEBTS

Finally, a credit manager sometimes must decide when to give up collection procedures and resign himself to a bad debt loss. Many credit managers are reluctant to take this step. They would rather drag along the dead weight of uncollectible accounts receivable than acknowledge their demise. Such an attitude is understandable but wrong. A high ratio of bad debt loss may reflect on a credit executive's judgment; a "normal" proportion, however, is to be expected and should be squarely faced. Each case must be judged on its own merits within the framework of the credit department's special policies and procedures. If a company maintains bad debt reserves, as do most firms with doubtful accounts,[13] a credit manager has more motivation to write off accounts that are truly hopeless. Without such precautions the decision to write off bad debts may be more painful but just as unavoidable.

---

12 See *Credit Manual of Commercial Laws,* 1961, p. 328.

13 A survey made by the Credit Research Foundation in 1958 confirms this opinion —*Methods of Calculating Reserves for Doubtful Accounts* (New York, 1958), p. 2.

## SUPPLEMENTARY READINGS

"Charging Interest on Past-Due Accounts—4 to 1 against it," *Credit and Financial Management,* August 1960, p. 8.

"Collection Techniques—Emphasizing Sales Factor and Tabulating Equipment," *Credit and Financial Management,* February 1960, p. 8.

"Credit Executives Give Ten Reasons Why Using Toll Lines Pays Dividends," *Credit and Financial Management,* January 1961, p. 26.

*How to Control Accounts Receivable for Greater Profits—The Function, Control and Effective Collection of Receivables* (A Small Business Handbook, Dun & Bradstreet, Inc., New York, 1959).

National Association of Credit Management, *Better Collecting from Interview to Legal Safeguards,* New York, n.d.

Phelps, C. W., *Improving Collections from Credit Sales,* Small Business Administration, Small Business Aid No. 49, Washington, 1959.

Reid, C. A., "Berserk Unearned Cash Discounts," *Credit and Financial Management,* March 1952, p. 13.

"Should Salesmen Collect Accounts?" *Credit and Financial Management,* March to June 1952.

*Ten Keys to Basic Credits and Collections,* Dun & Bradstreet, Inc., New York, 1956.

"The Telephone's Role in Jet Age Credit Service," *Credit and Financial Management,* September 1960, p. 8.

## REVIEW

1. What are the advantages and disadvantages of using the telephone for collection purposes?
2. What are the advantages and limitations of using telegrams for collection purposes?
3. Should salesmen be used in collection procedure? Explain the issues.
4. What are the possibilities of personal collection visits by the credit manager?
5. What are the possibilities of using collection men in mercantile credit work?
6. Explain collection by draft.
7. Under what conditions should an account be turned over to a collection agency?
8. How does a collection agency operate?
9. What are the advantages of submitting a delinquent account to a local attorney for collection?
10. When should a credit manager accept, or even propose, part payment on a delinquent account?
11. When is it advisable to agree to an extension of time on a delinquent account?

12. Under what circumstances are post-dated checks acceptable in payment of an account?

13. Should interest be charged on past-due accounts? Why?

14. When should a credit manager write off an account?

## PROBLEM

You are credit manager for Omega Hardware Co., a wholesaler selling on EOM net 30 terms. One of your accounts is the Theta Hardware Store of Milltown, which has been buying from Omega Hardware at an average of $1,200 a month. Mr. Theta generally pays promptly but occasionally is 10 to 15 days late because of working capital difficulties. In January, the salesman who calls on the Theta store about the 20th of each month received a much smaller order than usual, and was told by Mr. Theta that the Grand-O factory, the major employer in Milltown, had laid off half its employees, that there was talk of its closing down completely, and that his store's sales had fallen as a result. As of February 5, you have received no payment on Theta's $1,161 December balance due January 31.

1. Plan your collection procedure for the next 30 days. Explain your reasons.

2. Assuming that your collection efforts on the December balance have produced no results by March 5, and that no check has been received by then for the January balance, plan your collection procedure from here on. Explain your reasons.

# CHAPTER 15

# Collection
# Correspondence: 1

Most collections of past-due items are made through
correspondence.

The collection letters that a credit manager sends to his customers
have a double importance. Their primary purpose is, of course, to obtain
payment of a past-due item. But they have also important sales significance. If they are harsh or insulting in tone, a good customer may be
irrevocably lost. If courteous, respectful but firm collection letters are
sent to a customer who appreciates that tone in his business correspondence, or if informal, good-natured but firm letters are sent to the different
type of customer who likes to receive such communications, his respect
will be gained and his good will maintained, to the advantage of the supplier's selling effort. Furthermore, collection letters to a good but slow-
paying customer can actually combine direct sales promotion with collection appeals.

## BASIC PRINCIPLES OF
## COLLECTION LETTER WRITING

A collection letter should, of course, conform to all the
principles of good business letter writing. Its language should be simple

clear English. It should avoid the parroted clichés of thoughtless dictation which irritate many readers. It should be neatly typed, with a good letterhead format. It may include a stamped, self-addressed envelope as a further stimulus to reply.

But collection letters, like sales letters, must do more than merely request or give information. They must perform the difficult task of persuading the recipient to part with money, and they must do so in a manner that will retain his good will and even accomplish a bit of sales promotion on the side. Frequently, therefore, credit executives consult their sales department or their public relations or advertising department about form, style, and procedure in their collection correspondence. Collection letter writing is an advanced and refined branch of the general art of business letter writing.[1]

### Adaptation of letter style to recipient

James Whistler, the famed American painter and wit, once sent a flippant reply to the secretary of a London club who had notified him that his account at the club was past due. The secretary answered:

Dear Mr. Whistler:

    It is not a Nocturne in Purple or a Symphony in Blue and Gray that we are after, but an Arrangement in Gold and Silver.

Not only was the account paid immediately, but Whistler was soon telling London, as his own bon mot, that an artist enjoyed certain financial advantages over other men in that he could pay his bills in Arrangements in Gold and Silver.

Such a collection letter would have been meaningless to most men, insulting to most artists. But James Whistler being James Whistler, it was the perfect collection letter to address to him. That club secretary applied brilliantly a fundamental principle of collection letter writing—the letter should be adapted to the personality of the customer.

For purposes of collection letter style, customers may be divided into two broad categories—those who like a joke and the "good fellow" approach, and those who view business, and particularly such matters as payment on overdue accounts, as a sober, serious matter.

Collection letters to customers of the first type may be jovial, ebullient, lightened by a well-told anecdote, well spiced with humor, slangy language, and even "stunts." In the pages that follow, a number of such "good fellow" letters will be presented as illustrations of various types of collection letter appeals.

A gay, good-natured letter that has outstanding success with "good fellow" customers might produce a distinctly adverse reaction upon a

---

[1] See particularly R. H. Morris, *Credit and Collection Letters—New Techniques that Make Them Work* (Channel Press, Inc., Great Neck, N.Y., 1961).

more reserved type of customer who does not take his delinquency lightly. He expects a dignified courtesy in letters addressed to him and will resent breeziness or playful use of slang.

The best way for a credit manager to learn into which of these categories a customer should be placed is by personal interview. Where this is not possible, the customer's personality may be discovered after a while from his own correspondence. If the supplier's salesmen are expected to make credit reports on new customers, they may be asked to report also on this detail. One large company asks its salesmen on their credit reports to check whether the customer is a "good fellow" or a "sour puss," and the credit department of this company has found that this salesmen's classification is an excellent guide to the tone of its collection correspondence. Another has its salesmen submit personality sketches of chronic slow-pays so that the collection letters to them can be "custom tailored."

Collection letters should be further adapted to the individual case by the introduction of complimentary or otherwise pleasant individual comment, or by helpful discussion of the customer's affairs. If a financial statement showing an improved condition is received from a slow-paying customer, the next collection letter to him should take occasion to congratulate him upon this improvement and express the expectation that he will soon take his place with the supplier's long list of prompt-paying customers. Possibly a "special occasion" letter embodying these congratulations may be sent immediately after receipt and analysis of the statement. If a salesman reports that a "good fellow" customer has recently become a father, the credit manager's next letter to him should carry a congratulatory postscript. Where financial statement analysis or ledger interchange reports indicate a weakness in the customer's conduct of his business, and the credit manager really can give some helpful advice, he should do so in his next collection letter—provided he knows that the customer is a type that will appreciate such advice rather than resent it.

### General considerations on collection letter style

As a rule, short collection letters are better than long ones. A long letter may distract the customer's attention from the main point at issue— his delinquency. Or, recognizing from the opening sentences that he has a collection letter before him, a customer may not have the patience to read through a long missive. It is tossed aside practically unread, its purpose defeated by its excessive length. Of course, length cannot be avoided if a collection letter embodies detailed discussion of the customer's business and some advice upon it,[2] but length for length's sake should be avoided.

---

[2] F. Hardesty, "Who Says All Collection Letters Must Be Brief?—It All Depends on the Message," *Credit and Financial Management*, April 1959, p. 14.

The sentences in a collection letter should be short. Complex and compound sentences should be avoided. Each idea should be embodied in a separate sentence. These, in turn, should be combined into short paragraphs. One-sentence paragraphs often produce an effective collection-letter style. Key words like "PROMPT," "60 DAYS PAST DUE," or "YOUR HIGH CREDIT STANDING" may be typed in capital letters for emphasis.

Here is an example of an effective short collection letter—a perfect specimen of its kind:

Gentlemen:

It isn't going to take much to balance your account—you owe so little. That's why I'm so sure this reminder will bring us your check by return mail.

Am I right?

Very truly yours,[3]

As we shall note subsequently, there are several different appeals that can be directed to a delinquent customer to induce him to make payment. Ordinarily, two or more should not be combined in a single letter. This would divide the customer's attention. Only one appeal at a time can be fully effective. In each letter of a series, the customer can be reminded of other appeals previously used, but each letter should be built around one single appeal.

A credit manager should not apologize for writing a dunning letter. If the customer is fair minded, he will recognize its necessity and propriety. Hypersensitive or explosive customers, on the other hand, are more likely to be goaded to abuse by a cringing attitude on the part of a creditor than by quiet courteous presumption by the credit manager of the justice of his position.

The customer's pride should be flattered both by positive phrases of approval and by exclusion of negative words of criticism. Although a particular letter may center on some other appeal, the customer's pride should always be built up by such expressions as "a good customer like yourself," or "a person of your caliber," or "your excellent record," or "the progress shown in your business." If possible, the writer should avoid negative phrases and words of weak reproof, such as "your failure to pay," or "your unfortunate delay in payment," or "your neglect." Quite apart from the danger of libel involved, no use should be made of such innuendoes as "doubt the honesty of your intentions," or "you are taking a dangerous step on the road to business failure." By preserving a customer's self-respect in collection correspondence, a credit manager not only keeps him favorably disposed towards discharging his obligations but also preserves his good will for possible future orders.

---

[3] L. E. Frailey, *Effective Credit and Collection Letters* (Prentice-Hall, Inc., Englewood Cliffs, N.J., 1941), p. 59.

No matter what else a collection letter says, one message must unmistakably be conveyed to the customer—a request for payment. Some credit managers, fearful of offending their customers' sensibilities, beat about the bush, hint that a check would be acceptable but hesitate to say directly "Send us your check." This is a mistake. Everything else in a credit letter is secondary to that courteous but categorical request for the customer's check, or for an explanation of why no check is forthcoming.

### Combining collection and sales promotion

When a collection letter is written to a customer who is slow in his payments but nonetheless an acceptable credit risk for further orders, a sales promotion postscript may be added to the letter. Perhaps the customer can be gently reproved for not having sent in a customary order. Or his attention may be called to some new line that the supplier has recently put on the market. Or he may be advised to take early advantage of some price reduction, or to place an order before a projected price increase goes into effect.

Sales promotion in a collection letter serves a double purpose. It may obtain an order that otherwise would not have come through. It also performs the valuable credit function of indicating to the customer, by implication, that despite his delinquency the supplier considers him a good credit risk and values his purchases. His pride is built up, and some of the inevitable unpleasant flavor of the preceding dunning missive is removed.

To be able to include such promotional notes in his collection letters, a credit manager must of course maintain close liaison with the sales department. He must check on its general sales program and also recent experience with the particular customer before making any promotional postscript.

### Collection letters and the law

Any statement which is defamatory of a second party, holds him up to contempt or ridicule, or injures him in the practice of his profession or business, and which is communicated to any third party, is actionable libel. When sent by letter, it may also be an infringement of the postal laws. If a collection letter embodies threats, it may constitute the crime of extortion under the law of some states. Deceptive statements may be adjudged unfair trade practices.

A dunning letter hand-written by a credit manager, sealed by him in its envelope, and sent to a customer operating a one-man enterprise who was known to open his own mail, could accuse that customer of the worst sort of fraud, impugn his business ability, or charge him with being insolvent, without being libelous, since its contents were not communicated or "published" to any third party. But if a credit manager dictates a letter to a stenographer, it is deemed "published" to her; [4] or if the letter is transmitted open to a mailing clerk for folding and mailing, it is deemed "published" to such clerk; or if the credit manager had reason to believe that the letter might be opened and read by a secretary or clerk of the customer before it reached him, the letter would be deemed "published" to such secretary or clerk.[5] Under such circumstances, any defamatory matter in a collection letter would be "published" and would constitute a libel.

To communicate by writing to a third party an unquestionable fact, even though it be injurious to a man in his business or profession, is not libelous. Thus, if a customer is delinquent, a collection letter could contain the phrase that he does not pay his debts and not be libelous [6] (though such a statement would be contrary to the principles of good collection writing as stated above). But if a dunning letter should go beyond the bare fact of nonpayment of a debt, and charge the customer with insolvency or bankruptcy,[7] or charge him with fraud or dishonesty,[8] or even that he is unwilling or refuses to pay his just debts,[9] it is libelous.

Another legal aspect of communicating even bare facts of private indebtedness is that it may be actionable as an "invasion of the right of privacy" in some jurisdictions.[10]

### THE REMINDER LETTER

As indicated in an earlier chapter, many credit managers feel that the initial reminder to a customer that he has failed to make a due payment should be accomplished by sending him a duplicate statement or invoice, or a printed card. They feel that the impersonality of such procedure frees the reminder from any imputation that the writer exaggerates the importance of a few days' lateness in payment, or that he considers it a reflection on the customer's credit standing, or that it requires summary collection action. These implications should also be avoided by the credit manager who prefers to send reminder letters in-

---

[4] *Gambril v. Schooly*, 93 Md. 48; *Ostroe v. Lee*, 256 N.Y. 36.

[5] *Rumney v. Worthley*, 186 Mass. 184.

[6] But note that even this statement would be libelous if there was dispute between the supplier and the customer as to the amount of an invoice or some defect in the quality of the goods, so that no specific debt was established, and it would not be an unquestioned fact that the customer was delinquent.

[7] *Hays v. Mather*, 15 Ill. App. 30; *Holmes v. Jones*, 121 N.Y. 461.

[8] *Fogg v. Boston Railway Corp.*, 148 Mass. 513.

[9] *Nichols v. Daily Report Co.*, 30 Utah 74.

[10] *Trammel v. Citizens' News Co.*, 285 Ky. 529.

stead of duplicate statements, invoices, or cards. Brevity and a friendly informality will accomplish this. The example below is brief and informal and includes an "approval" touch:

Dear Mr. _____:

Just a friendly reminder.
Your check on our _____ invoice has not arrived with customary promptness.

Sincerely yours,

Such a reminder letter or card can be used effectively only at the beginning of a collection letter series. The reminder principle may be adapted, however, to later stages of collection correspondence. The following "aged-statement" type of reminder is sometimes effective with a customer who is past due not merely on one payment, but upon several:

---

### A. B. C. SELLING COMPANY

*Terms*

Name _____ Accounts payable in
Address _____ full in thirty
_____ days

Your attention is again called to the past-due portion of your account. Prompt payment will be appreciated.

| Over 4 Months Past Due | 120 Days Past Due | 90 Days Past Due | 60 Days Past Due | 30 Days Past Due | Current | Total |
|---|---|---|---|---|---|---|
|  |  |  |  |  |  |  |

---

## Appeals in follow-up letters

If a "reminder" does not bring payment, a credit manager must resign himself to a program of dunning letters. The first or second may succeed in persuading the customer to send his check. Sometimes four, five, or six may be needed to extract payment or to induce the customer to make a satisfactory arrangement for meeting his debt. In a few cases, the series of letters may fail to achieve their purpose, and the credit manager will have to decide whether to turn the account over to a collection agency, initiate suit, or write off the claim.

The essential message of every collection letter is "You owe us money. Pay us now." Such a bald demand would not be in accord with the customs of business diplomacy. A delinquent customer is fully aware that this is the meaning of a collection letter, and that the credit manager realizes that he knows this. But the customer's face must be saved. So the iron fist of the creditor's legal right is clothed in the velvet glove of courtesy and amenity. Moreover, a credit manager can buttress his legal claim to be paid by appealing to the customer's sense of fairness or business pride, by indicating business advantages that will result to him from payment, or by pointing to business injuries that he will suffer if he fails to pay.

These supplementary reasons for payment are the so-called "appeals" upon which collection correspondence is constructed. There are five basic "appeals" which, with variants, are found in good collection letters— "oversight," "explanation," "pride," "fair play," and "self-interest." They are analyzed and illustrated below, together with another weak appeal of "we need the money."

### "Oversight" appeal

A credit manager knows perfectly well that a customer who has failed to pay on the due date, and has made no reply to a "reminder," has not accidentally "overlooked" his obligation. The reason for nonpayment is that the customer did not have sufficient balance in his bank account to meet that particular obligation together with others that also had to be paid. The low bank balance may have been due to a poor working capital position, or to an unanticipated slump in sales, or to withdrawals for personal expenses, or any combination of these and other possible causes. Although the customer could not pay the account on the due date or upon receipt of the "reminder," another gentle prod a week or ten days later may bring a check from him. If the check does come, the credit manager will be quite content, and will still view the customer as a good credit risk to whom his firm will want to make future sales. Therefore, he does not want his gentle prod to imply that he doubts the customer's ability to pay, or in any other way to cast any reflection on the customer as a credit risk.

The solution of this problem is the time-worn, face-saving fiction that nonpayment of the account has been an "oversight" on the customer's part. Both parties recognize the fictitious character of this appeal. It is, actually, a "second reminder" which should not diminish the customer's good will and may even increase it if worded in a considerate manner. The example below, suitable for an old customer, cleverly draws upon the customer's pride in a previous good record, besides proffering the excuse of oversight.

Dear Sir:

We have been wondering what happened to prevent your check from reaching us this month. It usually arrives promptly on the 10th, or a few days later. As it may have been overlooked, we enclose a copy of the statement.

Very truly yours,

Many credit managers feel that the "oversight" appeal has been used so often and so long that most customers recognize it as a meaningless subterfuge, and lose respect for a supplier who employs it. The majority opinion, however, is that it is still useful as a face-saving first or second "reminder."

### "Explanation" appeal

If a delinquent customer can be persuaded to give an excuse or reason for his delinquency, a major element of his resistance to payment has been broken down. In reply to the customer's letter of explanation, the credit manager can present a strong counterargument, or he may propose a specific extension of time for payment and enclose a note for the customer's signature, or he may propose a specific part payment within the customer's capacity and set a definite date or dates for payment of the balance. Such proposals can be so phrased that they appear as generous favors, and a customer would have to acknowledge himself as churlish, fraudulent, or insolvent to refuse them. Therefore, in one or more of the follow-up letters after the initial reminders, a credit manager should suggest to a delinquent customer that, if he cannot immediately clear his account, he owes an explanation of why payment is not forthcoming. If this request is accompanied by a phrase in which the credit manager intimates that, on the basis of an explanation, he may be able to work out a payment arrangement convenient to the customer, he increases the probability of obtaining payment on the account, and also places his company in the favorable position of being reasonable and understanding about the customer's difficulties.

A request for an explanation is sometimes made as a supplementary appeal combined with others. More often it is used for one letter in a series with varying appeals. Two such letters are shown below. The first would be used for a "good fellow" customer, the second for a more reserved type.

Gentlemen:

No BEATING AROUND THE BUSH.

It's not our job to concoct excuses for you, giving this or that suggestion as perhaps the reason for your not having paid our bill. We're not playing a guessing game. You know the answers; we don't.

If you feel our account is wrong, we know you will tell us why you think it is; if it is right, you'll send your check.

Very truly yours,

Your account consists of: _____ [11]

---

[11] *Credit and Financial Management,* September 1938, p. 32.

Dear Mr. _____:

You must have a good reason for not having paid anything on your account since October—we're sure of that. But you don't tell us what the reason is.

If we only knew what the situation is, no doubt some arrangement could be made that would relieve your mind of the worry of an overdue debt, and satisfy us, too.

If you can, send in a part payment with your answer. But whether you can do that or not, at least tell us just what's wrong. Give us a chance to help. What do you say?

Yours sincerely,[12]

---

[12] L. E. Frailey, *Handbook of Business Letters* (Prentice-Hall, Inc., Englewood Cliffs, N.J., 1948), p. 1189.

## "Pride" appeal

*Noblesse oblige* is a strong motivation with many businessmen. Sometimes, too, though it may not be initially present, it can be awakened and built up by the praise, deserved or undeserved, of outsiders. The appeal to a customer's pride may often be helpful to a credit manager seeking to make collection. As indicated earlier in this chapter, such an appeal should be made, subtly and indirectly, wherever the circumstances of credit correspondence permit. If the customer is a long-established concern with a distinguished record in its field, or if it is a leader in its line or its community, a letter may be framed exclusively upon the "pride" appeal. Experience shows that such a letter, written to an appropriate concern, can be strikingly effective.

EXAMPLE

Gentlemen:

When our salesman brought us your first order two years ago, we felt proud. You are the leading hardware retailer of _____, and we feel that it reflects honor upon us to serve you.

Therefore we were doubly disappointed when your March check did not arrive on the 10th, in accordance with your usual custom, and when you did not reply to our letter of March 20th.

May we expect that we will receive payment on the March account together with that on the April account this month, or that you will communicate with us on the matter?

Very truly yours,

## "Fair play" appeal

Most businessmen are responsive to an appeal for "fair play." This appeal may be made in several ways. The most direct is to develop the theme, "You have received our goods; it is only fair that we should receive payment for them." Another approach may be built around the idea of "Put yourselves in our shoes." Certain types of customers may be influenced by a little homily on American business dealings being based not so much on legal obligations and their enforcement as on the cooperation and mutual good will of buyers and sellers. A "fair play" letter to a "good fellow" customer may be given a hearty tone; for a more reserved customer the appeal should be expressed in dignified language. Examples of several ways of using the "fair play" appeal are presented below; the second example is a highly effective combination of the "put yourself in our shoes" approach with suggestions of appeals to pride and self-interest.

EXAMPLE 1

Dear Sir:

Before you read this letter, glance at the attached statement. It is more than ninety days old.

You cannot have realized how long you have allowed this account to run. We have written to you twice and sent statements four times.

Put yourself in our shoes. Haven't we done more than our share? Haven't you done less than your share?

Meet us half way and make it a 50-50 proposition by sending your check or an explanation.

Please do not disappoint us this time.

Very truly yours,[13]

EXAMPLE 2

Sirs:

You no doubt have customers owing you who have allowed their accounts to become in arrears. You dislike to ask them to pay up because you know they are absolutely good. At the same time, you feel that you have given them the same good service and quality merchandise that you have given your other customers who pay promptly.

You, therefore, know just how we feel about your account with us. We want to continue giving you the best possible service and high quality products as well as the benefit of our regular terms. To that end we seek your cooperation in the matter of settlements.

It occurs to us that you may be waiting to pay your account in full. Please don't do that, because the older it gets the worse it looks on our books. We want to make favorable reports when called upon, and hope you can place us in a position to do so by making at least a part payment by return mail.

We suggest that you send us a check for, say, $ _____, the amount of your _____ and _____ bills. That will put your account in much better shape and enable us to give you additional time on the remaining bills. Will you do this?

Yours very truly,[14]

_____

[13] D. Tomlin, *How to Make Collections,* McGraw-Hill Book Company, Inc., New York, 1940, p. 56.

[14] *Credit and Financial Management,* August 1938, p. 32.

EXAMPLE 3

Gentlemen:

Re: Our Invoice No. _____, Date _____, Amount $_____.

When you ordered the merchandise represented by the above amount and your order was accepted, we both assumed an obligation. Ours was to ship promptly the goods as ordered and in this instance to extend credit under our regular terms. Your obligation was to pay the account in accordance with these terms or, being unable to do this, write us explaining the situation and making definite arrangements for settlement.

We have done our part. Will you do yours?

Sincerely yours,[15]

## "Self-interest" appeal

The sequence of appeals in a collection letter series should be: (1) reminder and "oversight," (2) the idealistic appeals of "pride" and "fair play," and (3) appeals to the customer's self-interest. It is advisable to reserve the self-interest appeals for the later letters in the series for three reasons. First, if a customer does make payment in response to one of the earlier appeals, his "face" is saved—he did the "right" thing, like the honorable businessman that he considers himself to be. He tends to feel grateful for the chance accorded him to make his delayed payment in a gracious manner. Second, the "self-interest" appeals carry a concealed threat, are more coercive, and hence more powerful. Third, many credit managers consider them their strongest appeals. If they are expended in the early letters in a collection series, the later letters must fall back on weaker arguments, and are in the nature of an anticlimax. Thereby the series of letters loses one of its objectives—a steadily rising scale of tension and pressure.

Self-interest appeals can be made on both positive and negative bases. The positive appeals hold forth the prospect of advantage to the customer in making immediate payment. The negative appeals are directed to his fears. He faces the loss of his business reputation if he fails to fulfill his obligations.

There are four specific "self-interest" appeals—two positive and two negative—that can be addressed to a delinquent customer. The first is the claim that the supplier's price schedule and the services it renders to its customers are based on the assumption of prompt payment, and could not be continued if any considerable proportion of customers continued late in their payments. This is not a very strong "self-interest" appeal since the customer may properly doubt whether his own delinquency, or even that of a substantial group of customers, would have such an effect. Some credit managers, however, value this appeal. They hold that it is a polite fiction, like the "oversight" appeal, which they can use occasionally

---

[15] *Printers' Ink,* June 22, 1939, p. 62.

without repeating themselves on a customer who is frequently delinquent.

The second positive "self-interest" appeal is the obvious argument that immediate payment will save the customer the annoyance of receiving further dunning letters.

The third "self-interest" appeal—a negative one—is the warning that, if payment is not received, the supplier will have to suspend selling to the customer on regular terms. The fourth, and strongest of all, is the warning that the seller will be compelled to report, in giving ledger interchange information, that the customer is delinquent, which will injure the customer's credit standing in the trade. This last type of letter may have actionable implications, as previously indicated in this chapter, and should be carefully formulated.

Naturally, the last two "self-interest" warnings do not tend to increase the customer's good will toward the supplier. Therefore the bitter pill should be sugar-coated. One way to do this is to write of the benefits the customer will derive from payment—that he will avoid the annoyance of receiving dunning letters, that he can continue to buy on regular terms, that he will preserve his credit standing. The other way is to explain that the supplier will take the particular action to the customer's disadvantage only with extreme regret and reluctance. If the credit manager can say that he is compelled to take such action by extraneous pressure, so much the better. Note how this sugar-coating, as well as various subtle appeals to the customer's pride, are embodied in the following examples of "self-interest" letters.

Example 1

Dear Sir:

We won't ask you whether you want us to continue selling you standard qualities for the lowest prices in the _____ line. We know your answer in advance.

Perhaps you do not realize that we are able to offer you these low prices only because all of our customers cooperate with us by paying promptly on our thirty-day terms.

We will continue to give you the best buys in the _____ line—but only if your checks keep coming in promptly, as they always have in the past.

Make out a check for $ _____ —the amount past due on our invoices of _____ and _____. Make it out right now, while this letter is before you. You don't have to bother about an envelope or stamp, because there is a return-postage envelope enclosed for you.

Your account will then be current, and you will be doing your share toward keeping the ABC brand the best buy in the _____ market.

Very truly yours,

Example 2

Dear Mr. _____:

I have just approved your order for $ _____ of our _____, although you have made no payments on our _____ and _____ state-

ments. I did this because I consider you one of the best business men in
_____ and feel certain that, whatever the temporary cause of your
present delay in paying us, your check will come through in the very near
future.

You and I both want me to be able to check through your next order
for immediate delivery on regular terms. The long-established custom of our
company will not permit me to do this, however, unless you have established
yourself on a more current basis.

May I expect your check on the _____ and _____ statements,
or at least on the _____ statement, within a week's time?

Very truly yours,

EXAMPLE 3

Dear Mr. _____:

"Do they pay promptly?"

It is nothing unusual for us to be called upon by mail or phone, to
tell of our credit experiences with a jobber to whom we sell.

In fact these requests come in every day, and we are HONOR BOUND
to give an honest and truthful reply. What should we say when a request
comes in asking about you? There's a balance of $ _____ due us ever
since last _____.

Won't you clear it up, Please! We never can tell—you know—a call
about you may come in tomorrow.

Very truly yours,[16]

## "We need the money" appeal

Sometimes a credit manager who has made various unsuccessful appeals to a delinquent customer, tries an appeal to his sympathy by plead-
ing that the supplier badly needs the customer's payment to meet its own
obligations.

It is generally a mistake to use this appeal, no matter how true it may
be. Sympathy, as a motivation of business actions, ranks lower than self-
interest, lower even than principles of "fair play." Where appeals to fair
play and self-interest have failed, a sob story has no chance at all. What
is worse, a "we need the money" appeal may appear to be a confession
of financial weakness on the part of the supplier, and is likely to cost him
the respect of the customer. This reduces still further the supplier's
chances of obtaining payment. In the case of a customer with whom the
supplier hopes to have further dealings, the loss of respect injures future
sales prospects.

That it is not impossible to construct an effective collection letter based
on the "we need the money" appeal, however, is shown by the example
below. It is dignified. The "help us" appeal is placed on the basis that
the supplier needs the payment in order to carry out obligations to others
—to employees, to investors, and to customers.

---

[16] *Printers' Ink*, May 25, 1939, p. 36.

EXAMPLE

Gentlemen:

Four letters have been addressed to you requesting settlement of your account, but for some reason you have not responded. And you have replied to none of these letters, informing us neither as to the reason why you have not paid nor as to when we may expect payment, a courtesy to which we are entitled.

There is a much deeper motive underlying our requests for settlement than the mere desire to collect the amount due us.

We owe an obligation to our employees, who have contributed to the success of this business, to keep them as steadily employed as possible and at good wages. We owe an obligation to our stockholders to provide them with a reasonable return on their investment which made this business possible. We owe an obligation to the trade to furnish them with the highest quality material at the lowest possible price.

In order to discharge these obligations, it is necessary for us to operate this business as economically as possible, which requires that we collect our outstandings as they mature.

It takes a lot of money to operate this business, and when we fail to collect our receivables rapidly enough to furnish the necessary operating capital, it becomes necessary to borrow that capital, thereby increasing the cost of our operations, which handicaps us in attaining our objectives.

Our ability to discharge the obligations mentioned depends on the prompt discharge of the obligations due us from the trade we serve.

May we depend on you to do your part by mailing your check for $ _____ today?

Cordially yours,[17]

## SUPPLEMENTARY READINGS

See page 216 of this volume.

## REVIEW

1. In what ways should collection correspondence be differentiated according to the personalities of customers to whom it is directed? How can the credit department learn about its customers' personalities?
2. Why should most collection letters be short, with short sentences and short paragraphs? What are the arguments for longer letters?
3. Is it better to build a collection letter around a single payment appeal, or around several appeals? Why?
4. Why should a credit manager always endeavor to flatter customer pride in collection correspondence? How may it be done?
5. Discuss the possibilities of making collection letters promotional.
6. When would an abusive statement in a collection letter be libelous?
7. What should be the purpose and contents of a first reminder letter?

---

[17] D. Tomlin, *op. cit.,* p. 109.

8. Why should a collection letter be sent that implies that nonpayment was a mere oversight on the part of a customer, when the credit manager is practically certain this was not so? Write an "oversight" letter that might be sent by the credit department of a cardboard carton manufacturer to customers who miss their due dates.

9. Write a letter asking for explanation of nonpayment of a past-due account that might be sent by a manufacturer of dresses to a small department store.

10. Write a "fair play" letter that might be sent by a drug manufacturer to delinquent drug wholesalers.

11. Indicate four "self-interest" payment appeals that could be made to delinquent customers. Why shouldn't they be sent immediately after a first reminder letter has failed to achieve results?

12. Is the "we need your money" appeal helpful in collections? Explain.

# CHAPTER 16

# Collection Correspondence: 2

## WARNING LETTERS

When all appeals have failed, the next step is warning —warning that more forceful collection procedures, such as sending a draft, turning the account over to a collection agency, or instituting suit, will be applied if payment is not forthcoming. The warning may be given in an indirect, softened semifinal form by the so-called "president's letter," to be followed by the unequivocal direct final warning. Quite frequently this semifinal step is omitted, and the final warning letter follows immediately upon a series of unsuccessful appeal letters.

### The "president's letter"

A delinquent customer expects to receive collection letters from a supplier's credit manager and takes them for granted. One after another the appeals come in but the customer discounts them. He has made up his mind to pay his account in his own good time. A letter from the president of the supplier, however, is something he does not expect. It has a subtly flattering touch, in spite of its dunning objective. The customer is given a sense of importance when it appears that his case is receiving the personal attention of the president. Because of the unexpectedness and flattery of a "president's letter," because it abruptly transforms collection from a routine procedure into an apparently spotlighted individual action, such a letter may capture the customer's attention and prod him into payment where all preceding appeals have failed.

A "president's letter" is not usually dictated by the president of a concern. It is customarily prepared by the credit manager on the president's letterhead and is signed by the president without his ever reading it, possibly without his even noting the name of the delinquent account. The customer does not know this, and so the letter makes its effect.

A "president's letter" should never be phrased in boisterous "good fellow" language. Its tone must be dignified, in consonance with the prestige of the president's position. It usually conveys the warning of impending relentless collection action by stating that the account was referred to the president's attention by the credit department for his approval of such drastic action. It lays claim to the customer's good will by stating that the president has restrained the credit department from taking such harsh measures in order to make a personal appeal to the customer to save himself from the unfortunate results of continued delinquency. It closes with the warning that a draft will be presented through the customer's bank, or the account will be given to an agency for collection, or suit will be instituted, as the case may be.

In large corporations, where the president could not be expected to concern himself with such matters, this letter may appear on the letterhead of the treasurer and be signed by him. Where previous collection correspondence has been handled by a junior credit man, the same effect of "higher-up" interest may be obtained by a letter of this type signed by the credit manager.

EXAMPLE OF A "PRESIDENT'S LETTER"
Dear Sir:

Our Collection Department has referred your account to me for attention.

Because of your failure to remit, they request my authority for handing the matter to our legal representative for such steps as he may deem necessary.

While I agree that you have been accorded every opportunity to adjust the account or make known your intentions, I am reluctant to feel that the action suggested is necessary. Therefore this personal communication asking the courtesy of a prompt reply—your check preferably, or an idea of what we may definitely count upon.

Failing to hear from you, no other consistent course presents itself than turning the account over for legal attention.

Very truly yours,[1]

---

[1] *Printers' Ink*, April 13, 1939, p. 37.

### Warning of collection by draft

As indicated in an earlier chapter, a customer faced with forthcoming collection by draft will usually pay upon notice that the supplier intends to take this action. Therefore a credit manager should always give warning of his intention since this may obviate actual sending of the draft. In any case, even the most obdurate customer, one that the credit manager no longer considers a desirable credit risk for his company, is entitled to the courtesy of such warning.

If the supplier subscribes to a collection service that includes the furnishing of draft forms and printed notices of draft, he can use such printed notice. They are generally couched in impersonal unequivocal language. But not every credit manager has such printed notices of draft available. Or he may wish to soften the impact of the warning so as to preserve some element of the customer's good will against the day when the latter may again be an acceptable buyer. Under such circumstances he will prefer to write with a more personal touch, appealing once again for payment or explanation, but closing with the clear notice that a draft will be drawn if payment is not received by a specified date.

EXAMPLE

Dear Sir:

I have tried every friendly means to have you tell us what is holding up payment of the balance of $ _____ on your account, but without response.

You must agree that we are entitled either to your check or to an explanation why we do not receive it.

If I have received no reply from you by _____, under the rules of our house I shall be compelled on that date to draw a draft upon you and present it for payment to the _____ Bank.

Please do not compel me to take this step, which would be a matter of regret for both of us.

Very truly yours,

### Warning that account will be submitted to agency

As in the case of collection by draft, a warning that an account will be submitted to a collection agency will often bring payment and save bringing in the agency. Some collection agencies provide "free demand" letter forms for this purpose. The credit manager may devise a more personal, more friendly warning that may preserve some customer good will. The example of a draft warning given above could be used for a warning of collection agency action by modifying the third paragraph.

### Warning of legal action

A credit manager may decide against instituting legal action against a customer who has resisted all other collection devices, because he knows that a judgment from a successful suit would probably be worthless. Even so, nothing is lost and something may be gained by warning the customer that the claim against him has been placed in an attorney's hands for suit. Possibly a customer on the verge of insolvency may have such unreasoning fear of legal proceedings, or may so wish to stave off a collection suit that would precipitate all his other creditors upon him, that he will pay the creditor who warns of suit while remaining delinquent on his other obligations. A warning that produces no result need not be followed by actual suit if the credit manager believes that such action would be fruitless. In cases where suit is definitely intended, the giving of notice or warning, to allow the customer to take last-minute action to avoid it, is an established business courtesy to which a credit manager should conform.

A warning of suit is most effective when it is specific. To write indefinitely of "legal proceedings," or of "placing the claim in the hands of our attorneys," does not impress the customer so sharply as when the name of a specific attorney or law firm is mentioned and a specific date given. Apart from these considerations, the credit manager has the choice of phrasing his warning letter in friendly or stern language, according to the type of customer with whom he is dealing.[2] An example of each type of warning letter is given below.

EXAMPLE 1

Gentlemen:

I hate to do it. . . .

I hate to take the certain final step that will ultimately force payment of the balance of your account.

I hate to jeopardize your good standing in the field and your credit rating with other manufacturers.

And what's more, I hate to lose my confidence in you, because you have always paid your bills promptly, and I sincerely believe that you will continue to meet all of your obligations in the future.

But the fact remains that you owe us $ _____ since last _____. You have made no attempt to pay nor to explain why.

Unless I hear from you by Monday night, much as I hate it, I will be forced to turn your account over to _____, our attorneys, with instruction to begin immediate suit.

Please—don't let me lose my confidence in you.

Very truly yours,

EXAMPLE 2

Dear Sir:

You have paid no attention to our repeated requests for payment on your balance of $ _____ due since last _____. Although we offered

[2] A printed warning notice that *simulated* a summons or other legal document, while it might be effective in terrifying some delinquent customers into making payments, would expose a creditor to criminal action in most states. See *Credit Manual of Commercial Laws*, 1961, p. 261.

you every cooperation up until last week, you have entirely ignored us.

Today we placed your account in the hands of our attorneys, _____ _____. The only way you can now stop the sure, swift, and costly proceedings of a suit is to wire us—immediately.

ONLY A WIRE WILL STOP IT NOW.

Yours truly,

## COLLECTION LETTER SERIES

In a truly difficult collection case—where the customer is in financial difficulties affecting all of his payments, or where he is obstinately holding back payment because of some fancied grievance against the supplier, or simply because he is the sort of businessman who delays on all his payments unless he is dealt with firmly—the effectiveness of collection letters depends not alone on the appeal of each individual letter but as much or even more upon the cumulative effect of a series of letters sent in regular sequence and successively more intense in the pressure they impose.

The number of letters to be included in any series and their timing depend upon the type of customer involved and his case. If he is in a very weak financial position, two or three letters might be all that should be sent before drawing a draft upon him or turning his account over to an attorney or agency for collection. The timing in this case should be very short—two or three days' interval between each letter—particularly if the customer is known to take advantage of leniency. A series of seven or eight letters might be mailed to a customer who was deemed a good long-term risk, though a poor working capital position or some temporary difficulty was delaying his current payments. Such a customer might be allowed two or three weeks, or even a month, before a follow-up letter was sent. Appropriate timing in this as in any collection letter series may be controlled by a tickler file or desk diary as explained in Chapter 20.

The sequence of appeals in a series of collection letters should always be from mild to strong—from "reminder" through "explanation" to "fair play" and "self-interest." If two "reminder" letters are sent, or several variants of the "fair play" or "self-interest" appeals are used, each successive variant should be stronger than the preceding one. A mild appeal after a strong one weakens the cumulative effect of an entire series of letters.

Each letter in a collection series should refer to the preceding letters which the customer has not answered. Thus the customer is reminded, in a fashion that grows more emphatic with each letter, of his own discourtesy in not replying and of the credit manager's persistency in following up the delinquency. If a customer answers one of the letters in such a series and gives reasons or excuses for the delay, the credit manager's next letter should take account of the reply.

An example of a series of collection letters, with the adaptations made necessary by the customer's replies, is presented in the Appendix to this chapter.

## SPECIAL CIRCUMSTANCE LETTERS

Besides the regular collection letters addressed to delinquent customers, a credit department must sometimes send letters concerned with special collection situations. It may also include in its correspondence various classes of good will letters intended to supplement the activities of the sales department.

### "Terms chiseler" letters

The problems presented to a credit manager by a "terms chiseler"—a customer who pays after the discount date but none the less takes the cash discount—were indicated in an earlier chapter. Composition of the letter to such a customer, with or without the return of his check, deserves exceptional care. It should differ in content, form, and tone, according to whether the recipient is a first or casual offender or a hardened chiseler.

A letter refusing an unearned discount should always be short and clear and, if possible, casual. Lengthy discussion would only irritate the customer without achieving its goal of making him retract. He may, perhaps, already have a slightly guilty conscience that renders him oversensitive to the implications of a letter refusing him the discount, but that does not excuse clumsy tactics that aggravate his irritability. Unskillful treatment may obtain a check for the discount amount—accompanied by a sarcastic letter promising that the customer will not trouble the supplier with any future business.

If he is a casual offender, a customer's pride should be saved by placing his motives above suspicion. He should be assured that the credit manager realizes that the discount was taken in good faith. Perhaps he may be complimented on being a discounting customer, one whose business acumen and financial position make him a valued account. BUT— the letter continues—the privilege of discount is based upon a time factor. The customer reaps a gain from discounting out of all proportion to any advantage to the supplier of receiving early payment. Therefore in fairness to its own interests, as well as to other discounting customers, the supplier should hold the customer strictly to the terms of discount. If, for moral effect, the customer's check is returned, the letter should close with a request for a new check covering the full amount, without any reduction, to be sent by return mail. If the check received is deposited, the letter should close with a request for a check to cover the balance.

With a hardened terms chiseler, a credit manager will have to take a tough line in his correspondence—unless company policy forces him to submit to the imposition. Generally, however, with such a customer, no saving of face or feelings is necessary. He should be told that he is deliberately violating the terms of the sales agreement and should be ordered to remit the due balance without delay. He may even be warned that his failure to remit will result in collection of the due amount by draft.

### "Bad check" letters

A customer may deliberately send an uncovered check, as a means of staving off further dunning letters for a short while. Or, the lack of funds in the account may be accidental. A bookkeeping error may have misled the customer as to the state of his balance, or he may have anticipated the depositing of an expected check that did not arrive in time.

When a credit manager notifies a customer that a check has been returned for insufficient funds, regardless of his suspicions, his language should embody the assumption that the deficiency was accidental. Thereby he saves the customer's face and preserves his good will.

The ordinary procedure with a bad check is to return it to the customer and request that another check be sent which will "go through" when deposited. Often there will be no response to this letter, and a new series of collection letters must be sent to get another check. Some credit managers meet this situation by notifying the customer that, "for the convenience of both parties," the bad check is not being returned but will be held for a certain number of days—enough to enable the customer to receive the letter and reply by return mail if necessary. After that, it will be redeposited with the supplier's bank with instructions to forward it once again for collection. An alternative and even more effective technique is to inform the customer's bank that the check will be sent back again for collection. A copy of this notification is sent to the customer. Such a letter is shown in the example below. These procedures of redeposit, preceded by notice of such action, preclude any delay in the sending of a new check, and eliminate the excuse of accident. If the redeposited check is returned a second time for insufficient funds, the credit manager is in a position to take a stern tone, even to the extent of warning the customer that he has made himself subject to prosecution under the bad debt law of the state.

EXAMPLE

Gentlemen:

The _____ bank has just returned to us a check dated _____ _____, in the amount of _____, drawn on your bank by Mr. _____. This check was marked "insufficient funds."

We feel that through some oversight funds were not on hand to cover this item when originally presented. Accordingly, three days from the above date, we shall re-enter this check with our bank for collection. We shall appreciate your courtesy in advising Mr. _____ when this check is presented.

A copy of this letter is being forwarded today to Mr. _____ in order that he may have information on this re-entry of his check.

Yours very truly,

## Letters based on special customer circumstances

If a credit manager learns of some extraneous event that may affect a customer's ability to pay his account, such as a flood, a fire, or a widespread strike in the customer's community, it is good policy to anticipate that the customer's payments may be delayed thereby, and to propose special terms if they are needed. Upon receipt of such a letter, the customer is assured of the supplier's sympathetic interest in his affairs and reasonable understanding of his payment difficulties. A customer will probably make efforts to meet the payments to such a sympathetic supplier ahead of his obligations to others who indifferently seek collections on the basis of their original terms of sale. The two letters presented below, sent at two weeks interval, evoked highly favorable response from the recipients.

EXAMPLE

Gentlemen:

During the past few weeks the papers have been filled with reports of floods that caused injury or loss to many business men in your neighborhood.

Therefore, even though our February account amounting to $ _____ is due according to terms, we hesitate asking for the money lest you may be one of those who sustained direct loss and need temporary assistance.

Will you inform us promptly if you were affected, and we will be pleased to arrange new payment terms that will take your present circumstances into account and protect your payment record as it appears on our books. If you are one of the fortunate ones not touched by the recent natural disasters, please send us your check immediately since we are mobilizing our current resources to aid those of our customers who have been less fortunate.

Very truly yours,

Gentlemen:

We assume that your failure to answer our letter of _____ is an indication that you did not suffer damage from any of the numerous major catastrophes experienced through your area during the past Winter and Spring, for which we are glad.

We therefore ask again that you favor us with your check for the February account. Please send us at the same time your Spring order for items needed to round out or expand your stock, so that you can more adequately serve your growing register of satisfied customers.

Very truly yours,[3]

---

[3] *Credit and Financial Management*, March 1937, p. 30.

## Seasonal collection letters

Certain holidays and certain seasons provide the credit manager with the opportunity to work in topical collection appeals, or even write special collection letters based on the holiday or season. One credit manager reports good results with a Christmas collection letter beginning "Is there a Santa Claus?" and ending with Christmas greetings. Another has had success with a New York letter telling how, in China, all debts had to be cleared with the closing of the old year and any man who did not so clear his debt had to go around on New Year's Day carrying a lighted candle. The opening of a buying season provides an opportunity for a letter that combines dunning for past-due balances with sales pro-motion for the new seasonal line. Approach of the close of the supplier's fiscal year may afford a basis for a special "help us" collection appeal, as shown in the example below:

Dear Sir:

As a good business man, you can appreciate that, when the close of our fiscal year arrives three weeks from now, we want to have our books in the best possible condition for our auditors. We are particularly anxious to bring your account, and those of a few other customers, to a current basis so that we can make a perfect showing on our receivables.

Will you cooperate with us?

A check for $ _____, covering your _____ and _____ accounts, now past due, will enable us to write "CURRENT" on your ledger card.

Very truly yours,

## STUNT LETTERS

In a laudable effort to avoid monotony and clichés, credit managers sometimes turn to "stunt" collection letters. The intent of a "stunt" letter is good—to capture the customer's attention by some unusual opening, or by an unexpected enclosure, or by an unusual letter format. Such a letter is not likely to be ignored or swiftly forgotten.

But inability to pay a past-due account is not a humorous matter to a customer in financial difficulties. When he opens a dunning letter and discovers an exhibition of mental acrobatics or some sophomoric humor, his response is likely to be a resentful "Hm, the young man evidently thinks he's clever," or "What does he think I am—a baby to be amused?" No doubt there are some "good fellow" customers who respond favorably to "gags" and infantile rhymes in collection correspondence. But many even of the "good fellows" find it difficult to see the joke in being past due, and reserved customers are more likely to be offended than cajoled by a "stunt" letter. Credit managers are therefore less and less inclined to use them. The two "stunt" letters below, which were actually mailed to customers, are presented as examples of collection letters that debase the dignity of a credit manager and are likely to offend more customers than they amuse.

EXAMPLE 1
Gentlemen:

If you'll kick in with a check for $12.50, representing your past-due balance, you'll surprise our bookkeeper to death. That will please us, because we want to get rid of her anyway.

> Yours truly,

EXAMPLE 2
Dear Mr. _____:

In re: THE ALMIGHTY $.

There i$ a little matter that ONE of our cu$tomer$ ha$ $eemingly forgotten entirely. $ome make u$ promi$e$ but do not keep them. To u$ it i$ an imporant matter—it'$ nece$$ary in our bu$ine$$. We don't like to $peak about $uch remi$$ne$$. NUF $ED.

> Very truly your$,

Good "stunt" letters—good either for a certain type of customer, or even good for any class of customer—can be written and many have been written. If based on humor, the humor must be subtle rather than slapstick, often with a wry little twist appropriate to the circumstance of unpaid debts. A really good anecdote, a clever rhyme, or an adroit metaphor can be the foundation for a letter that will capture the customer's attention without provoking his resentment. An enclosure of some sort may be tied in effectively with a clever or friendly letter. The unexpected—which is the foundation of all "stunt" collection letters—may be introduced by means of an unanticipated request, or by unusual format, or by apparently being written by some person other than the supplier's credit manager.

EXAMPLE (APPARENTLY WRITTEN BY THE CREDIT MANAGER'S SECRETARY, BUT ACTUALLY PREPARED BY HIM.)

Dear sir:

Our Credit Manager, Mr. Pitts, left Saturday for Richmond, Virginia, to attend the National Wholesale Credit Men's Convention and won't return until about the 16th. I happen to be his stenographer, who has typed all his letters to you for the past year, so I feel free to call on you to work with me on a little surprise I'm trying to spring on Mr. Pitts when he returns to his desk.

Without his knowing about it, and in his absence, I'm taking the liberty of writing all of our customers who are a little behind with their payments and requesting that they send in checks before he gets back. Don't you think that will be a pleasant surprise for him? I do. And I may as well confess that I am hoping that that pleasant surprise will prove to Mr. Pitts that I am worthy of being promoted from the position of stenographer to that of a credit woman in his department.

I hope you will understand and forgive the impudence, and possibly the imprudence, of an ambitious young woman. And please send your check for $ _____ so that it will be on Mr. Pitts' desk by next Tuesday.

Sincerely yours,

(signed)  Edith Bailey [4]

## FORM LETTERS

There is never-ending controversy among credit managers as to whether collection letters should all be written individually or whether form letters should be prepared to be used for similar cases.

The argument against form letters is that they do not have specific application to each individual case, so that they lack the pertinent effectiveness of the individually dictated letter. Moreover, if a customer receives identical collection letters several times in the course of successive delinquencies, he can hardly be much impressed.

The major argument in favor of form letters is their great saving of time and cost. A well-constructed form letter can be used in dozens of cases, and save the dictation of a corresponding number of individual letters. One estimate sets the cost range for dictated letters at $.70 to $2.45, and that for form letters at $.08 to $.20.[5] A second consideration is that not all credit managers are consistently effective letter writers. With a substantial amount of collection dictation to do, they are likely to take refuge in trite clichés. Awkwardness in style may creep into some of these messages, unfortunate twists of meaning into others. A form letter, written and polished at leisure, avoids such pitfalls.

The advantages of form collection letters would seem to outweigh the disadvantages, particularly since they may be made adaptable to individual circumstances by provision for insertion of personal touches. Many credit managers have prepared their own sets of form letters. Others use sets prepared by credit associations,[6] trade associations, and individual authors.[7]

---

[4] Adapted from *Credit and Financial Management*, September, 1936, p. 24. Such a letter, while highly successful on the occasion it was used, could be a boomerang, since customers who responded to it might develop an interest in the career of the enterprising stenographer, and disclosure of the "stunt" might provoke their resentment.

[5] *Credit and Financial Management*, September 1958, p. 20.

[6] The New York Credit and Financial Management Association, for example, has published such a collection under the title, *How to Step Up Your Collections by Mail*, New York, rev. ed., 1961.

[7] See specifically L. E. Frailey, *Handbook of Business Letters*, section on "Credit and Collection Letters," (Prentice-Hall, Inc., Englewood Cliffs, 1948); and R. H. Morris, *Credit and Collection Letters—New Techniques That Make Them Work* (Channel Press, Great Neck, N.Y., 1961).

For effective use of form collection letters, the following rules should be observed:

1. "Letter books" or "letter manuals," with samples of collection letter series, should be prepared. Every series should be key-lettered and every letter in the series key-numbered, so that the credit manager as the occasion arises has only to direct that "Letter B-5" be sent to Mr. Doe or "Letter K-6" to Mr. Jones.

2. These letters should never be used in printed, mimeographed, or multigraphed form except possibly for an initial brief reminder note. They should always be copied from the "letter book" sample by a typist and have the appearance of individually dictated letters.

3. Half a dozen or more form letters should be worked out for each situation that may have to be covered. A customer who is repeatedly delinquent should not receive an identical sequence of letters upon each successive delinquency. Such repetition, if recognized by the customer, would rob the letters of much of their effectiveness. This can easily be avoided. Each time a customer is delinquent, a notation would be made on his "collection card" of the particular sequence of letters mailed to him, so that a different series would be used on the next occasion.

4. Several different complete sequences should also be prepared to meet the needs of customers with different characters and personalities. There could be, for instance, a series for the "good fellow" type and another for the more reserved type, and still another for the "tough" type who is a hardened "terms chiseler" or holds back payments until firmly pressed.

5. Special form letters, such as those answering a customer's request for additional time or an arrangement for spreading part payments over a period, should provide sufficient blank space for an initially dictated paragraph while the balance of the letter continues along form lines.

Form letters, including form collection letters, were one of the earliest applications of office automation. The original printed, multigraphed, or mimeographed form collection letters bypassed secretary or typist (except for typing name or address); they betrayed their "form" character to the eye, however, thereby largely defeating their purposes. The automatic typewriter enabled standardized form letters to look like individually-typed, if not individually-dictated, communications. Now credit managers may use "push-button selector" automatic typewriters which permit incorporation in a basic collection letter of a wide selection of special-purpose paragraphs or sentences; "individualized" mechanically-produced form collection letters are now possible.

EXAMPLE OF COLLECTION CORRESPONDENCE

The following correspondence, between a credit manager and a delinquent customer, obtained from the files of a large paint company,[8] illustrates both the sequence of a collection letter series, and the treatment of replies that may result from such letters. It also emphasizes the point, too often overlooked in discussions of collection procedure and correspondence, that even a good collection letter series cannot be counted upon always to draw payment from a past-due account.

May 16, 1961

Sunnyside Auto Paint Co.,
217 Main St.,
Sunnyside, Cal.

Gentlemen:

Please refer to our statement of May 1st, on which you will note there is a past due balance of $387.15.

In calling the matter to your attention at this time, we feel sure that you will favor us with your check to cover.

Very truly yours,
A. ATKINS, Credit Department

———

May 26, 1961

Sunnyside Auto Paint Co.,
217 Main Street,
Sunnyside, Cal.

Gentlemen:

Following our letter of May 16th, to which we have had no reply, we are again calling your attention to the past due balance of $387.15, which is still open on your account with us.

Can it be that our previous letter and statements have miscarried? We must insist on immediate settlement of this item.

Very truly yours,
A. ATKINS, Credit Department

———

May 29, 1961

Mr. A. Atkins, Credit Department,
I Lead Paint Co.,
2nd & Howard Streets,
San Francisco, Cal.

Dear sir,

I aint got $387.15 and that is why I aint sent it to you to pay my bill.
I got lots of money owed me, but I can't collect it now.

---

[8] Adapted from *Credit and Financial Management,* January 1940, pp. 21-22.

If you will just be patient with me, I will get mine and will send you yours as soon as I get it.

JOE BONO

---

June 1, 1961

Mr. Joe Bono,
Sunnyside Auto Paint Co.,
217 Main Street,
Sunnyside, Cal.

Dear Mr. Bono:

Thank you for your favor of May 29, wherein you advise of your collection troubles and request a slight extension of time on the $387.15 now past due on your account with us.

We have set our file ahead to June 15, and trust you will be able to clean this item up prior to that date.

Assuring you of our willingness to co-operate at all times, we are,
Very truly yours,<br>A. ATKINS, Credit Department

---

June 19, 1961

Mr. Joe Bono,
Sunnyside Auto Paint Co.,
217 Main Street,
Sunnyside, Cal.

Dear Mr. Bono:

What success have you had in collecting your accounts?

We have not been favored with your remittance to cover the $387.15 which is past due on your account with us.

An extension of time was granted, at your request, to enable you to make collection of your accounts and forward payment to us.

Having had no word or remittance from you, we must now demand settlement at once, by return mail.
Very truly yours,<br>A. ATKINS, Credit Department

---

June 22, 1961

Mr. A. Atkins, Credit Department,
I Lead Paint Co.,
2nd & Howard Streets,
San Francisco, Cal.

Dear sir,

You give me time ½ month. That aint enough. Look. I tell you how it is. Mr. Zamperini owe me $72.00. His grape no dam good this year because it rain all the time. So he got no money. He and his wife and 7 kids they go on relief and I got to wait till next year.

All the other fellers what owe me money, their grapes no good from rain and they got relief and I got to wait till next year.

You and me, we hope they all get good grape next year and get good price, maybe $50.00 ton, and we get paid.

You help get good price by drink lots of wine.

So you wait till next year and we both get our money.

JOE BONO

June 23, 1961

Mr. Joe Bono,
Sunnyside Auto Paint Co.,
217 Main Street,
Sunnyside, Cal.

Dear Mr. Bono:

We have your favor of June 22nd, and regret to advise that it is not possible for us to wait until next year for settlement of your account with us.

If you can not make payment of the entire amount at this time, no doubt you could send us a part—say $25.00—each week until it is paid in full.

Please let us have your reaction to this suggestion.

Very truly yours,
A. ATKINS, Credit Department

July 6, 1961

Mr. Joe Bono,
Sunnyside Auto Paint Co.,
217 Main Street,
Sunnyside, Cal.

Dear Mr. Bono:

Please let us hear from you, without further delay, regarding your paying at least $25.00 per week on your old balance with us.

If we do not hear from you within ten days from date of this letter, we shall assume that you do not wish to make any settlement of this account and will place same in hands of our Attorneys for immediate suit.

Very truly yours,
A. ATKINS, Credit Department

July 11, 1961

Mr. A. Atkins, Credit Department,
I Lead Paint Co.,
2nd & Howard Streets,
San Francisco, Cal.

Dear sir,

I did not rite you befor on account of I got married and have been pretty busy at that.

I cant make any money with my shop, so I sell him and get married.

Now I cant pay you no $25.00 a week, or even 25¢ a week because

I got no job. Maybe you will give me a job and pay me $45.00 a week, and you could keep $5.00 a week and soon you get $387.15 that way, and I would have a job too, and we would both be O.K. What you say?

JOE BONO

---

July 14, 1961

Mr. Joe Bono,
225-9th Street,
Sunnyside, Cal.

Dear Mr. Bono:

We are sorry to inform you that we can not give you a job at this time, as you suggest. However, you might see our Mr. Baker, at our South San Francisco plant, but we understand that they are not taking applications at this time.

You must make some arrangements to pay this account, and at once, if you do not wish us to hand the matter to our Attorneys who, no doubt, could find some method of forcing payment.

Very truly yours,
A. ATKINS, Credit Department

---

July 20, 1961

Mr. A. Atkins, Credit Department,
I Lead Paint Co.
2nd & Howard Streets,
San Francisco, Cal.

Dear sir,

We have got on relief. Aint it lucky I got married? If I warnt married I would only get $66.50 per month, but now, on account I am married, I get $110.30 per month. So aint it lucky I got married.

I cant pay you because I am on relief and the relief lady says that I cant spend the relief money to pay bills with. So you are out of luck.

I am sorry for you.

JOE BONO

## SUPPLEMENTARY READINGS

Buckley, E. A., *How to Write Better Business Letters*, McGraw-Hill Book Co., New York, 4th ed., 1957.

Dartnell Corp., *Tested Credit and Collection Letters*, Chicago, published annually.

Frailey, L. E., *Handbook of Business Letters*, section on "Credit and Collection Letters," Prentice-Hall, Englewood Cliffs, N.J., 1948.

Little, J. D., *Complete Credit and Collection Letter Book*, Prentice-Hall, Englewood Cliffs, N.J., 1953.

Moran, E. B., and Roper, R. L., *The Selling Side of Credit Correspondence— 101 Credit and Collection Letters Especially Selected for Sales Value*, National Association of Credit Management, New York, 1956.

Morris, R. H., *Credit and Collection Letters—New Techniques that Make Them Work,* Channel Press, Great Neck, N.Y., 1961.

Prout, J. B., *Adjustment Letters Handbook,* Prentice-Hall, Englewood Cliffs, N.J., 1954.

Shurter, R. L., *Effective Letters in Business,* McGraw-Hill Book Co., New York, 2nd ed., 1954.

Smart, W. K., McKelvy, L. W., and Gerfen, R. C., *Business Letters,* Harper & Bros., New York, 4th ed., 1957.

## REVIEW

1. Discuss the possibilities of a "president's" collection letter.
2. Write three letters giving warning respectively of: (a) collection by draft, (b) submission of a delinquent account to a collection agency, (c) submission of a delinquent account to an attorney for purpose of bringing suit.
3. Discuss the timing of a collection letter series.
4. Discuss the sequence of appeals in a collection letter series.
5. Write letters to (a) a customer who repeatedly sends his check, with discount deducted, ten days after the discount date, and (b) a customer who takes the discount when paying a past-due bill.
6. What procedure and type of letter are suggested when a customer's check is returned because of insufficient funds?
7. Write a letter that the credit manager of a clothing manufacturer might send to a prompt-paying clothing retailer in the marketing town of a rural area whose main crop has just been ruined by severe hail storms.
8. Write a Thanksgiving season collection letter that might be sent by a hardware wholesaler to his delinquent customers.
9. If form collection letters are to be used, how should they be prepared?
10. Why do most credit managers deem "stunt" letters to be inadvisable?

## PROBLEM

You are treasurer and credit manager for Lamda Co., a jobber of special papers. One of your accounts is Kappa Lamp Co., which buys substantial amounts of parchment and other lampshade papers. They place two to four orders, ranging from $25 to $350, a month, on net 60 terms. Their sales have been declining for several years because of the competitive situation in the lamp field. They have been reported 30 to 60 days slow in payments to other suppliers but heretofore have paid Lamda's account promptly.

1. Invoice KL367, for $215.89, due April 17, is unpaid as of April 27. Write an appropriate letter concerning it.
2. You receive a check for invoice KL367 on April 29. On May 3 invoice KL368 for $39.47 falls due, and on May 11 invoice KL369 for $163.32. Write an appropriate letter.
3. By May 21 no answer has been received to the preceding letter. Meanwhile invoice KL370 for $308.19 is due. Write an appropriate letter.
4. On May 29 you receive a letter from Mr. Arthur Kappa, president of Kappa

Lamp Co. enclosing a check for $200 in part payment of the past-due balance and giving as the reason for payment delay that Kappa Lamp Co. has been having difficulties in collecting from some of its accounts. The letter promises payment of the remainder of the past-due balance and other maturing invoices by June 1. It also requests that Kappa Lamp Co.'s existing obligations and future purchases be on net 90 terms. Write your reply to this letter.

5. There is no check from Kappa Lamp Co. by June 5. Write an appropriate letter.

6. There is no answer to your June 5 letter by June 15. What do you do?

7. A letter is received from Mr. Kappa on July 3. It states that a very successful lamp salesman has invested in Kappa Lamp Co. and will become its sales manager. The sum invested will be applied to part payment of overdue suppliers' accounts, including that of Lamda Co. if Lamda Co. is willing to continue supplying Kappa Lamp Co. For six months Kappa Lamp Co. would want to buy on net 90 terms. By then, all back balances should be paid off and Kappa Lamp Co. would be able to return to net 60 terms. Write your reply.

# CHAPTER 17

## The Protection of Creditors' Rights

The protection of creditors' rights is—with the exception of bankruptcy procedures and prosecution under the postal law of senders of false financial statements—a matter of state law. On a few matters, such as negotiable instruments, sales, and conditional sales, uniform laws are in force in most states. But by and large, the commercial law of the states varies from state to state in minor and important details.[1]

---

[1] A "Uniform Commercial Code," covering a large number of commercial subjects, including various aspects of creditors' rights, was prepared during the 1940's under the sponsorship of the American Law Institute and the National Conference of Commissioners on Uniform State Laws. Its text was published in 1951 and amended in 1957. From the start indications were that widespread adoption, if it came about, would be a slow process. Pennsylvania enacted the Code in 1953 in its original form and amended it in 1959. Massachusetts and Kentucky, in 1957 and 1958 respectively, adopted the amended version of 1957. Connecticut and New Hampshire adopted it in 1959, Rhode Island in 1960. The following years brought an upsurge of adoptions; by the end of 1963 there were 28 "code states."

Sellers' rights have been substantially trimmed under the Uniform Commercial Code. Out-of-state suppliers are often not aware of this when they sell in Code states. They are advised to insert a clause—permissible under the Code—selecting either the law of the Code state involved in the transaction or the law of their own non-Code state (C. B. Everberg, "Clause Inserted in Contract Permits Shipper to Select Law of Code or Non-Code State," *Credit and Financial Management*, March 1959, p. 16). If both parties are in Code states, no such selection need or can be made since the same Code provisions apply in both states.

The laws of the 50 states and the District of Columbia provide suppliers who have sold merchandise on credit and who have not been paid by the due date, or who learn before the due date that the purchaser has become insolvent, with the following procedures for recovering the debt or the goods:

1. Goods not yet delivered to purchaser—
    a. Retention of the unshipped goods under an unpaid seller's lien;
    b. Stoppage in transit of goods already shipped but not yet delivered to the buyer, resumption of possession, and application of an unpaid seller's lien.

2. Goods already delivered to purchaser—
    a. Suit for collection;
    b. If goods were obtained fraudulently, an action, founded upon deceit by the buyer, for recovery of the delivered goods or their value.

In addition, all the states have bulk sales laws which provide suppliers with preventive protection against certain types of debtor fraud.

Finally, there are various criminal actions against fraudulent buyers which may be brought by the public authorities upon the instigation of the defrauded seller.

Legal action on behalf of mercantile creditors should be conducted by attorneys whose training and experience give them competence in such matters. Every credit manager, however, should be well versed in the fundamentals of the law of creditors' rights. He ought to know when his company has a claim that can be enforced against a delinquent customer, so that he may place the case before an attorney with the necessary instructions to act. He should also be able to collect and prepare the evidence for the attorney so that the latter is in a position to sustain the company's case. For all these purposes, there is no substitute for comprehensive study in commercial law, supplemented, for the practicing credit manager, by constant reference to the *Credit Manual of Commercial Laws* (published annually by the National Association of Credit Management).

## RETENTION OF GOODS UNDER "UNPAID SELLER'S LIEN"

A contract of sale binds a seller to deliver goods to the buyer, as it does the buyer to receive the goods (if they conform to the contract specifications) and to pay for them in accordance with the credit terms of the contract. If a seller learns of a buyer's insolvency before goods purchased by the latter through a credit sale have actually been delivered to him, however, the seller does not have to complete delivery.

Under such circumstances the Uniform Sales Act, and other sales legislation of the various states and territories, give sellers an "unpaid seller's lien"—*i.e.*, right to refuse delivery under the sales contract and to retain the goods until paid for—which they can enforce for their protection.

A seller who seeks to enforce an "unpaid seller's lien" should have convincing evidence of the buyer's insolvency. Knowledge of the filing of a petition of bankruptcy by or against the buyer, or of an assignment for benefit of creditors is, of course, a clear warrant for such action by a seller. The law will also accept such indications of insolvency—in the equity sense of the buyer being unable to meet current obligations as they become due—as discovery, through interchange information, that a buyer is becoming widely delinquent in his payments or is allowing notes or drafts to go to protest. Should a seller refuse to make deliveries under a contract, or stop delivery of shipments already in the hands of a carrier, without such convincing grounds for doubting the solvency of the buyer, he has committed a breach of the sales contract, for which the buyer has several remedies. He may bring an action for replevin to recover the goods and/or he may sue for damages resulting from the original nondelivery.

A seller who still possesses goods covered by a sales contract may enforce his "unpaid seller's lien" by certain actions prescribed by the Uniform or other sales law. He may resell the goods immediately if they are perishable. Otherwise he must request the buyer to agree to cancellation of the sales contract in view of his insolvency, or notify him that the goods will be shipped only after his check has been received, deposited, and cleared. Should the buyer neither agree to cancellation of the contract nor make advance payment, the seller must allow the buyer some additional payment time after the due date under the original contract,[2] whereupon he may resell the goods to the account of the buyer and hold him for any resulting deficiency, or he may rescind the contract and dispose of the goods according to his will.

### Stoppage in transit

A seller who learns of a buyer's insolvency after the purchased goods have been delivered to a carrier for shipment to the buyer, but before actual delivery has been made by the carrier to the buyer, may regain the goods and apply his unpaid seller's lien by exercising his right of stoppage in transit.[3] To exercise this right a seller should have received the

---

[2] Section XXXII (4) of the Uniform Sales Act authorizes rescission of the contract if "the buyer has been in default in the payment of the purchase price for an unreasonable time."

[3] If the goods have been shipped under a negotiable bill of lading, and if the buyer has endorsed the bill of lading to a third party before the seller seeks to exercise his right of stoppage, the right no longer applies.

same evidence of the buyer's insolvency that would have warranted application of an unpaid seller's lien. In order to stop delivery of the goods, the seller need only notify the carrier not to make delivery and to return the goods to the seller at his expense or otherwise dispose of them according to the seller's instructions. The carrier then has a "reasonable" time in which to transmit instructions for the stoppage to such of its agents as are in immediate control of the goods. Should the carrier wilfully deliver the goods to the buyer, or fail to exercise due diligence in notifying its agents not to make delivery, it would be subject to action by the seller for conversion of the goods—that is, an action for damages measured by the value of the goods—or to suit for breach of contract.

Once the seller has repossessed the goods through stoppage, he may proceed with application of his unpaid seller's lien as though the goods had remained continuously in his possession.

## SUIT FOR COLLECTION

When every other means of collection from a past-due account has been exhausted, a seller may turn the account over to an attorney with instructions to bring suit. Responsibility for conduct of such suit rests with the attorney, but the seller's credit manager must cooperate closely with him. Hence all credit managers should know the basic principles of suit for collection. A brief résumé of the procedures involved is accordingly presented in the following pages.

### Jurisdiction for bringing suit

Suit for collection must be brought in a state or federal court with the appropriate jurisdiction. In the first place, the state and judicial district where the suit may be instituted is determined by the location of the debtor's residence or his principal place of business. In the second place, the states have widely differing hierarchies of general courts and special courts, with differing jurisdictions as to area, kinds of suits entertained, and maximum amounts recoverable. Only an attorney of the state where suit is to be brought can know which is the correct court in which to bring suit.

Where out-of-state suit is involved, the seller's attorney establishes contact with a local attorney in the jurisdiction where suit must be brought. The latter may be located through a Law List (described in Chapter 7). Some of the publishers of these directories stand responsible for any claims collected by a listed attorney, provided the publisher is notified at the time the claim is placed.

## Suit procedure

When a past-due account, or a dishonored promissory note or trade acceptance, is given to an attorney with instructions to bring suit, he should be furnished with all the documentary evidence needed for purposes of the action. In the case of suit upon an instrument, these will be the unpaid promissory note or trade acceptance itself, the bank's memorandum of nonpayment, and copies of any notices of dishonor sent to the buyer and any accommodation endorsers. In the case of a suit upon an open account, the documents which should be furnished the attorney are: (1) copies of the original written orders for the merchandise (if any); (2) copies of the invoices showing dates of delivery, terms of sale, nature of the merchandise, and the amounts in suit; and (3) copies of the bills of lading showing delivery to the carrier for transportation to the buyer or the signed drivers' books or receiving reports showing direct delivery to the buyer. Various affidavits by the seller are required, but the nature and contents of these will be indicated by the attorney.

With the necessary documents and affidavits in his hands and usually, also, some advance payment or security for costs, the attorney can commence suit by service upon the debtor of a summons (see Illustration 17-1) or such other process as is required by the laws of the state where the action is brought, together with a statement of the claim in the form of a complaint or other required paper. The debtor is then allowed a specified period of time in which to answer the allegations in the seller's complaint. If the debtor files no "answer" to the complaint within the prescribed time, the seller's attorney may then obtain a judgment "on the complaint" for the amount involved. But the debtor may file an "answer" making a general denial of the seller's allegations, or setting up defenses against the seller's claim, such as the statute of frauds or the statute of limitations, or setting up counterclaims based on charges of nonperformance by the seller of all elements on his side of the sales contract. If the debtor's answer sets up "new matter"—anything other than a general denial—the seller's attorney has a specified period of time in which to serve a "reply." After that, the issue is deemed joined, and the action is set upon the calendar of the court for trial. Under the laws of most states the parties are entitled to a trial by jury as a matter of right, but jury trial may be waived in most states by consent of the two parties, so that the action may be tried by a judge without a jury, thus saving costs.

## Attachment

One of the most valuable auxiliary proceedings in a collection suit is "attachment." Under this proceeding, any real or personal property or

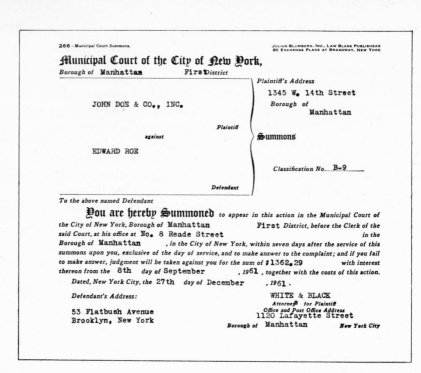

266—Municipal Court Summons.

JULIUS BLUMBERG, INC., LAW BLANK PUBLISHERS
80 EXCHANGE PLACE AT BROADWAY, NEW YORK

# Municipal Court of the City of New York,

Borough of **Manhattan**       First District

Plaintiff's Address

1345 W. 14th Street

Borough of

Manhattan

JOHN DOE & CO., INC.

*Plaintiff*

**Summons**

*against*

EDWARD ROE

Classification No. **B-9**

*Defendant*

To the above named Defendant

**You are hereby Summoned** to appear in this action in the Municipal Court of the City of New York, Borough of **Manhattan**       **First** District, before the Clerk of the said Court, at his office at **No. 8 Reade Street**                                    in the Borough of **Manhattan**       , in the City of New York, within seven days after the service of this summons upon you, exclusive of the day of service, and to make answer to the complaint; and if you fail to make answer, judgment will be taken against you for the sum of **$1362.29**        with interest thereon from the **8th** day of **September**             , 1961 , together with the costs of this action.

Dated, New York City, the **27th** day of **December**    , 1961 .

Defendant's Address:

WHITE & BLACK

*Attorneys for Plaintiff*

53 Flatbush Avenue
Brooklyn, New York

*Office and Post Office Address*
1120 Lafayette Street

Borough of **Manhattan**          *New York City*

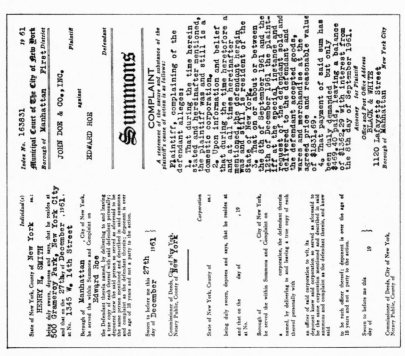

ILLUSTRATION 17-1.    Summons in Mercantile Litigation

interest therein of the debtor that would be subject to a writ of execution is seized in advance of the trial and placed in the custody of the law, to secure such property so that it will be available to satisfy a writ of execution under judgment.

In the New England states and some others, practically all actions are started by attachment. An attorney bringing suit for collection usually prepares at once a writ of attachment naming all the banks in the town where the debtor is located, together with any other persons who may have property of the debtor in their possession, and delivers this writ to the sheriff. This officer then serves the writ upon the debtor and the other named parties. Thereafter the debtor cannot dispose of any of the attached property, or draw any of the attached funds from his bank accounts, unless he files a bond to release the writ.

In most states, however, a writ of attachment is not issued as a matter of right in any action, but may be obtained through a special proceeding under specified circumstances. The most usual grounds for obtaining attachments in these states are:

1. The debtor is a nonresident or a foreign corporation.
2. The debtor has absconded from the jurisdiction or is in concealment.
3. The debtor has removed or is about to remove, conceal, assign or otherwise dispose of his property to the detriment of his creditors.

The attaching creditor may have to post a bond to cover payment of any damages his attachment might produce if it should prove to be unwarranted. If this is done the debtor can usually release the attachment by filing a counterbond in the amount of the attached property.

A seller who has a clear case against a delinquent customer should instruct his attorney to institute attachment proceedings as an incident of the collection suit, if grounds for such procedure can be established. Thereby collection on the judgment through execution is assured, provided the debtor has sufficient funds or property to satisfy the judgment at the time the action is started. Moreover, the abrupt tieing-up of the debtor's funds and property through the attachment may jolt him out of an attitude of indifference to the debt and the suit upon it, and result in immediate settlement without the necessity of court action. This has been the experience of many sellers who have directed their attorneys to employ this procedure when possible.

Arbitrary use of attachment process as a "blackmailing" procedure in a groundless suit, or where the legal basis for attachment averred does not in fact exist, is likely to be a costly error on the part of a plaintiff. In such cases, the defendant is entitled to recover damages for all injury suffered through the attachment. Under certain circumstances these may be substantial. They are not limited to the bond posted by the plaintiff, which is only an assurance that some part of any damage award to an injured defendant shall be collectible.

## Judgment and execution

If the seller is successful in his suit against a customer who has not paid, the court will issue a decree called a "judgment" (see Illustration 17-2), which determines the amount due from the debtor. This judgment constitutes a judicially established claim of the seller upon the debtor. In itself a judgment does not necessarily result in payment, since the debtor may refuse to pay the judgment, or claim that he is unable to do so, as he did on the original debt. It constitutes a lien upon the real property of the judgment debtor for a period of from 5 to 20 years, depending on the law of the jurisdiction, and no third party may acquire such property from the judgment debtor without assuming the liability for the judgment lien.

If a judgment remains unpaid, and if the seller believes that the debtor has funds or property which would satisfy the judgment, he may direct his attorney to apply for an "execution." This is an order of the court, based on the judgment, directing the sheriff or other officer of the jurisdiction to seize the debtor's property to satisfy the judgment. The proceeds of such seizure are then paid to the seller. Within the state of the judgment, an execution can be applied for, and will be recognized, in any jurisdiction where the debtor has property. If the debtor's property is located in another state, suit "on the judgment" must be brought in that state in order to obtain a judgment effective against such property.

## Garnishment

A judgment debtor may have no funds or other property upon which execution may be ordered to satisfy the judgment, but may have claims for money or other property against third parties. The laws of most states give a judgment creditor, under such circumstances, the right to bring "garnishment," "trustee process," or "judgment execution" proceedings against such third parties. The purpose of this action is to discover the amount of the debtor's claims against the third parties, and to compel them to satisfy the creditor's judgment out of such claims instead of paying them to the debtor.

## CIVIL DECEIT ACTIONS

If goods were shipped to a customer on the basis of a false financial statement or other fraudulent misrepresentation on his part, the seller might, as will be seen, instigate criminal proceedings against the customer by the proper public authorities. But the fraudulent action of the buyer also makes available to the seller certain civil remedies in

323B—Judgment on Inquest or After Trial. Municipal Court. (1956)          b          JULIUS BLUMBERG, INC., LAW BLANK PUBLISHERS
80 EXCHANGE PLACE, AT BROADWAY, NEW YORK

## MUNICIPAL COURT OF THE CITY OF NEW YORK,
Borough of **Manhattan**     **First** District

Index No. 163831 19 61

| JOHN DOE & CO., INC. | |
|---|---|
| | *Plaintiff* |
| *against* | |
| EDWARD ROE | |
| | *Defendant* |

Judgment Rendered in Favor of
**JOHN DOE & CO., INC.**     *Plaintiff*

Residing at

**1345 W. 14th Street
New York City**

| | | |
|---|---|---|
| Amount awarded after *Inquest* / *Trial* - - - - - - - - - - - - - - - | $ | 1362.29 |
| Interest - - - - - - - - - - - - - - - - - | | 34.05 |
| Total | 1396.34 | $ |
| Costs by Statute - - - - - - - - - - - - - - - - | $ | 37.50 |
| Service of summons and complaint - - - - - - - - | | 2.90 |
| Filing of summons and complaint - - - - - - - - | | 4.00 |
| Prospective Marshal's Fee - - - - - - - - - - | | 1.00 |
| Filing of Notice of Trial - - - - - - - - - - - | | 1.00 |
| | | 1433.84 |
| Total | 1441.84 | $ |

**State of New York, County of New York**          **ss.:**

being duly sworn, deposes and says that   he is
the attorney   for the plaintiff   in the above entitled action. That the disbursements above specified
have been or will necessarily be made or incurred therein and are reasonable in amount; that a decision
has been rendered after                                    in favor of the plaintiff  .

being duly sworn, deposes and says that   he is   **HENRY H. SMITH**
the attorney   for the plaintiff   in the above entitled action. That the disbursements above specified
have been or will necessarily be made or incurred therein and are reasonable in amount; that the defendant.   answered but has not appeared on the   **9th**   day of **February**     **1962** , the time
set for the trial thereof and judgment is requested by default for the plaintiff  .

Sworn to before me this
**13th** day of **February**     19 **62**

*Henry H. Smith*
................................
**Henry H. Smith**

**Notary Public**

**Judgment** entered the **13th**   day of **February**     **1962**
The summons and complaint in this action having been personally served on

**EDWARD ROE**

the defendant   herein on the **27th**   day of **December**     **1961**   and the judgment rendered
in favor of plaintiff   against said defendant   after
on the   **9th**   day of **February**     **1962**

**Now, on motion of**
attorney   for the plaintiff   it is,
**Adjudged** that     **JOHN DOE & CO., INC.**                         plaintiff ,
residing at **1345 W. 14th Street, New York City**
do   recover of     **EDWARD ROE**                         defendant ,
residing at     **53 Flatbush Avenue, Brooklyn, N. Y.**
the sum of $ **1362.29**     with interest of $   **34.05**     making a total of $ **1396.34**
together with $   **45.50**     costs and disbursements, amounting in all to the sum of $ **1441.84**
and that the plaintiff   have execution therefor.

*Charles Miller*
..........................................Clerk
**Charles Miller**

ILLUSTRATION 17-2.   Judgment upon Litigation for Nonpayment of Merchandise
Sold and Delivered

addition to the suit for collection analyzed above. These are actions for
(1) deceit, (2) replevin, and (3) under fraudulent conveyance laws.

The basis of all these actions is nonpayment on a credit sale made as
the consequence of deceit of the seller by the buyer. There are various
possibilities of such deceit. The buyer may have fraudulently ordered
goods with no intention of paying for them. Or he may have submitted
a false financial statement on the basis of which the seller sold him the
goods. In this second case the deceit may be fraudulent—that is, involving
wilful deception on the part of the buyer—or the falsity of the financial
information may be the result of innocent error by the buyer or of a
deception practiced upon him. Under either circumstance the seller has
a civil action for recovery of the value or the goods involved. A third
type of deceit involves the fraudulent conveyance by the buyer of his
assets so that he thereby becomes unable to meet his obligations.

It is very difficult to prove that a buyer placed an order with no intention of paying. Even the fact of the buyer's insolvency at the time the
order was placed is generally not taken as proof that he did not intend to
pay, since he may have bought in good faith with the hope or expectation that disposal of the purchased goods would provide him with the
funds to pay for them. In a few jurisdictions the courts have allowed
replevin on a doctrine of "constructive fraud" where a purchase was
made in good faith but the buyer's actual financial condition was such
that his chances of actually being able to pay were extremely remote,
but this liberal attitude toward creditors is exceptional. Responsibility for
determining whether a buyer is solvent at the time he places an order is
deemed to rest with the seller. If he makes delivery to a customer without inquiry into that customer's financial position, the courts will generally not aid him by imputing deceit to the transaction. Where falsity
of a financial statement can be established, however, orders solicited and
accepted on the basis of that statement are categorically presumed to
be tainted by deceit.

### Action for deceit

An action for deceit seeks damages for the loss—the unpaid account—
suffered by the seller through the deceit of the buyer. Ordinarily there is
little point to bringing such an action. If the buyer is solvent, recovery
can be had through an ordinary collection suit. If the buyer is insolvent,
the chances of collecting the judgment on the deceit action will be
slight.[4] But where a third party is involved in the deceit, such third party

---

[4] In some jurisdictions, a "body execution" may be obtained upon a judgment in a
deceit action. Under this "body execution," the defrauding debtor may be arrested
and jailed if the judgment for damages is not satisfied. This gives added strength to
the deceit action in these jurisdictions.

can be joined with the buyer in the action, and recovery may be had from the third party if not from the buyer. Thus, if a false financial statement for a corporation has been signed by an officer of the corporation, and he has property in his own right, a judgment under a deceit action may be collected from him though the corporation itself is insolvent.

## Replevin

An action for replevin may be instituted to recover property obtained by deceitful action of a buyer and still in his possession, or in the possession of any other party who is not an innocent purchaser for value. The title of such goods has usually passed to the buyer.[5] By virtue of the deceit involved, however, his title is voidable. Under a replevin action the seller establishes rescission of the sales contract, gives a bond of indemnity, and recovers the actual goods.

If a customer is insolvent, a judgment in a collection suit is worth little. In bankruptcy proceedings the seller usually recovers at best only a fraction of the value of the goods sold. The advantage of a replevin action, when grounds for it can be established, is that the seller recovers the goods actually delivered to the buyer.

The important requirement of the replevin action is that the seller's goods be identifiable in the buyer's possession, or in the possession of any other noninnocent third party who has received them from the buyer. If the seller's goods have been intermingled with other goods of the same character, so that there is no way of distinguishing and separating one from the other, a writ of replevin cannot operate. However, if they have been turned into any other assets—including money which is identifiable as proceeds of the seller's property—this other asset can still be recovered by replevin.

Replevin procedures differ widely among the states. Most commercial actions involving replevin are started by petition to the court of proper jurisdiction for a writ of replevin, upon affidavit stating the basis for the application. The applicant must post a bond to cover any damages that would result to the holder of the property if the seizure under the writ should prove to be wrongful. The sheriff or other officer of the court then serves the writ upon the buyer or other party holding the property, and takes possession of it. The buyer or other party may regain possession of the property by also posting a bond for its value and any other damages claimed by the seller. Upon trial of the action, the rightful ownership of the property is determined.

---

[5] Replevin is also frequently used in conditional sales or chattel mortgage contracts. In the former instance, title has not passed; in the latter, it usually has passed as of the time of the transaction, but is voidable. In both cases, replevin action facilitates repossession of the goods.

### Actions under fraudulent conveyance laws

Under common law, a conveyance made, or obligation incurred, by a person who is or will thereby be rendered insolvent is fraudulent as to his creditors, without regard to his actual intent, *if the conveyance is made or the obligation incurred without a fair consideration.*[6] Twenty states have adopted a Uniform Fraudulent Conveyances Act. It standardizes the details of this feature of common law.

Under such law, a seller who discovers that a customer whose account is past due has made a fraudulent conveyance or has incurred such a fraudulent obligation, may bring action to have the conveyance set aside or obligation annulled to the extent necessary to satisfy his claim. Or—a less common procedure—the seller may disregard the conveyance and attach or levy execution upon the property conveyed. If the customer's payment is not yet due, the seller may petition in a court of competent jurisdiction to have a receiver appointed to take charge of the property, or to restrain the defendant from disposing of the property, or to have the conveyance set aside or the obligation annulled, or to obtain such other relief as may be required by the circumstances of his case.

## ACTIONS UNDER BULK SALES LAWS

All the states have statutes to protect creditors of a merchant against the possibility that he may sell his fixtures and entire stock of merchandise in bulk outside the regular channels of his business and dispose of the proceeds of such sale without paying his business debts. It is the intention of the *bulk sales laws* to prevent this type of fraudulent conveyance and to provide remedies where such transfers have been made in defiance of the law. These statutes are not intended to interfere with legitimate sales of business establishments or liquidations of stock of merchandise in the regular course of business. They require, primarily, that advance notice of such transactions be given to creditors of the merchant who is "selling out," in order to enable them to protect their interests. They state, furthermore, the consequences of not complying with such requirements. If, for instance, advance notice is not given in accordance with the statute, the creditors may hold the purchaser as a receiver of the goods or disregard the sale and levy on the transferred merchandise. Conformity with these laws, nevertheless, does not preclude action by the creditors under a fraudulent conveyance act if elements of fraud appear in the case.

---

[6] Note that not every conveyance contributing to a debtor's insolvency is deemed fraudulent. Payment of an antecedent debt in good faith, or property appropriately conveyed to secure existing obligations, would not be fraudulent conveyances.

Several states require only that the proposed "bulk" sale be *recorded* at the proper public office at least 14 days in advance. Most provide that notice to the creditors of a "bulk" seller must be given *personally* or by *registered mail* at least five or ten days before the sale.

Most bulk sales laws also require that:

1. prior to the sale a "bulk" seller must make a detailed inventory showing the quantity and cost price of each article to be included in the sale; and
2. a "bulk" seller must give the buyer a sworn list of names and addresses of all of the former's creditors and the amount owed to each.

The former Pennsylvania statute provided further "bulk sale" protection for creditors. It made a "bulk" purchaser responsible for the proper application of the sales proceeds to the claims of the creditors. This feature has been taken over as an *optional* clause by the Uniform Commercial Code. Some of the Code states (Pennsylvania and Kentucky) adopted it; others (Massachusetts, Connecticut, New Hampshire, and Rhode Island) did not.[7]

In all cases and under all statutes, failure of a "bulk" seller to comply with the law gives his creditors the right to treat the sale as void and have it set aside.

The proceedings that may be instituted vary in different jurisdictions. In some states creditors may attach the property, obtain judgment against the seller who has made the noncompliance sale, and levy immediate execution against the merchandise. Some states permit garnishment proceedings against the purchaser for the property itself or, if it is no longer in his possession, for the purchase price. If the bulk purchaser no longer holds the goods he may also become personally liable in equity, in this case not for the purchase price but for the agreed inventory value of the property, which may be considerably lower. Replevin action has generally been held inapplicable since there was no fraud in the original sale by the creditors to the bulk seller, and hence no reversion of title to these creditors. Generally no action can be taken, under bulk sales laws, against subsequent purchasers in good faith from the original bulk purchaser.

Bulk sales laws give trade creditors substantial protection. If the bulk seller is insolvent, or bordering on insolvency, the purchaser must protect himself by literal compliance with the letter of the law, and the seller's creditors benefit accordingly. In many bulk sales, where the assets of the sold business well exceed its liabilities and the purchaser has ample financial responsibility, seller and purchaser avoid the trouble of detailed

---

[7] This problem of control over sales proceeds has gained added significance since, in recent years, bulk sales procedures are being used to increasing extent instead of bankruptcy proceedings for liquidating insolvent businesses (see Chapter 19).

compliance with the law by providing that (1) the purchaser shall assume all trade liabilities of the sold business, with the price adjusted accordingly, or (2) the purchaser shall withhold for a time a part of the purchase price, or pay it to a third party in trust, sufficient to cover outstanding trade liabilities of the business. Such procedures may involve the purchaser theoretically in added risk but they give the creditors as much protection as they would obtain from compliance with the law.

### CRIMINAL PROSECUTION OF FRAUDULENT BUYERS

A fraudulent buyer may be sued by the defrauded seller through one of the civil actions previously discussed. In addition, he may be criminally prosecuted by the public authorities under state false financial statement laws, or bad check laws, or under the federal criminal code.

Credit crimes are mostly perpetrated by men engaged in legitimate business who, for reasons beyond their control or because of their own ineptitude, find themselves insolvent and turn to fraud as a last desperate gamble to avert bankruptcy. However, several hundred thousand dollars a year are also lost to sellers through another form of credit fraud that has assumed the proportions of a racket. It is operated by criminal groups who may number as few as three or four or as many as a score.

Such gangs operate in various ways. They may establish a new business with an impressive name—"American," "International," "Amalgamated," and so on—and issue a false financial statement showing an excellent condition. Under fictitious supplier names, members of the gang furnish sellers with references praising the paying habits of the business. Initial orders are then placed on a cash basis or small "trial" purchases are made on credit terms and paid promptly, to be followed by larger credit orders. As the goods arrive, they are reshipped to "fences" who dispose of them at cut prices. This activity continues for as many weeks or months as the gang feels safe. As soon as they discover the investigators of the NACM Fraud Prevention Department or of the postal system on their trail, they decamp.

Instead of operating as a completely new enterprise, the gang may obtain an address on the same street and close to some well-known concern with a good credit rating. They will then adopt a name for the business that resembles very closely that of the established business. Thus, in one case that cost shippers $250,000 or more in less than two months, the name chosen for the racketeers' business was "Oceanic Merchandise Company (not Inc.)" in imitation of the well-rated "Oceanic Merchandise Co., Inc." A careless assistant to a credit manager, seeing the name of the established concern in a rating book, may fail to note the slight discrepancy of name and address and check through substantial orders.

Under a third variant of the fraud, one even more difficult to detect during its operative period, the racketeers buy out some established concern with a good credit rating. They then exploit this rating by enlarging their purchases from the concern's previous suppliers, and by adding new sources of supply. Even alert credit managers may be caught by this form of fraud, since the change of ownership may be concealed from the reporting agencies and the NACM interchange bureaus for several months.

### False financial statement laws

All states have "false pretense" statutes which punish issuance of false financial statements with view of thereby obtaining funds or merchandise. In most of the states special false financial statement laws have been enacted, based on a model approved by and developed largely through the efforts of the National Association of Credit Management.

The New York statute may be taken as typical of these false financial statement laws. It provides that a person shall be guilty of a misdemeanor and shall be punishable by not more than one year in jail, or a fine of $1,000, or both, if the prosecutor can prove "beyond a reasonable doubt":

1. That the defendant made the statement or representation in writing, or caused it to be sent to a supplier.
2. That the statement or representation was materially false—that is, the false items were so misrepresented that, if the true facts had been shown, an ordinarily cautious businessman would not have extended credit upon the strength of the statement whereas, on the basis of the falsification, extension of credit would have been warranted.
3. That the statement or representation was made or used for the purpose of procuring credit or the extension of credit.
4. That the statement or representation was made or used with intent that it should be relied upon, which may be proven by the circumstances under which it was delivered, such as delivery to a credit agency for distribution to its members, or delivery to a particular seller who requested it as a basis for extending credit terms.
5. That the statement or representation was made in the county in which the prosecution is sought.

There is no need to establish, under the false financial statement laws of New York or of the other states, that the statement on which the prosecution is based was sent through the mails.

The federal Criminal Code (U.S.C.A., Title 18, §1341) provides:

Whoever, having devised or intending to devise any scheme or artifice to defraud, or for obtaining money or property by means of false or fraudulent pretenses, representations, or promises . . . , for the purpose of executing such scheme or artifice or attempting so to do, places in any post office or authorized depository for mail matter any matter or thing whatever to be sent or delivered by the Post Office Department, . . . or takes or receives therefrom any such matter or thing, or knowingly causes to be delivered by mail according to the direction thereon, or at the place at which it is directed to be delivered by the person to whom it is addressed, any such matter or thing, . . . shall be fined not more than $1,000, or imprisoned not more than five years, or both.

This section has been construed to apply to the sending of false financial statements by mail, and is frequently invoked, because it provides a longer jail penalty than the state laws, because federal prosecuting officials have shown themselves more energetic in prosecuting this type of fraud than have the officials in a number of the states, and because the prosecution can be instituted in the district where the false statement was received instead of that in which it was made. To establish the crime, the prosecutor must prove "beyond a reasonable doubt" the same first four points as under the state false financial statement laws noted above together with a fifth point—that the false financial statement or representation was sent by mail. Unless this last point is established, the federal courts have no jurisdiction over the case.

The most effective way to prove that a false financial statement was sent through the mails is by introducing as evidence the false statement itself attached to the postmarked envelope in which it was mailed. This may be done only if a principal or employee of the company which received the statement can testify that it is regular routine in that company's office to pin or staple all financial statements to the envelopes in which they were mailed. The evidence is still stronger if the routine includes dating and initialling the statement and envelope by the person opening the letter. A presumption is thus established before the jury that the envelope attached to the false statement is actually the one in which it was enclosed and passed through the mails. The presumption is not conclusive, however. The defendant's attorney invariably endeavors to shake the testimony of the witnesses as to the infallibility of the routine of attaching statements and envelopes in the seller's office, and to raise doubt as to the authenticity of the attached envelope offered in evidence. Sometimes he succeeds in persuading the jury that the testimony does not establish the sending of the particular statement through the mails in the particular envelope "beyond a reasonable doubt." This weakness in the prosecution's case under federal law is eliminated if a credit manager sends all his customers self-mailing statement forms, either specially printed or obtained from the National Association of Credit Management, of the type shown in Illustration 8-2.

### Bad check laws

Every state has a bad check law of one sort or another. These statutes differ widely in their details but agree in their basic principle—that a person who issues a bad check with intent to defraud, knowing that there are insufficient funds in his account to cover it, is guilty of a crime. A period of grace, from three to 30 days, is generally provided, during which the bad check may be made good and the offense thus be purged. Statutory penalty maximums range from $100 to $5,000 fine in addition or alternative to a jail sentence ranging from six months to 14 years.

In most states the crime of issuing a bad check is committed only when the check is given for something of *present value*. Therefore giving a bad check in payment for a pre-existing debt, including payment by a bad check of a trade liability on its due date or at any other time after the goods have been received, is not an offense under most bad debt laws, since the creditor still retains the same right to receive payment that he had before and has not given up anything of value for the bad check. The statutes of New York and of a few other states are exceptions in extending the crime to checks given in payment of past-due indebtedness.

When a customer's check is returned stamped "NSF"—insufficient funds—the best procedure for a credit manager to follow is to return the check with a request that it be made good by return mail. If new payment does not arrive within this period plus 48 hours, he may try a touch of "legal blackmail." A second letter may be sent stating that "the bad check law of (the customer's state) allows (the specified statutory period) for making a bad check good. We anticipate that a new check for $. . . . . . . . . . , including protest fees on the returned check, will be in the mails by (date)." Most small businessmen are not aware that the bad check laws (with a few exceptions, as noted above) do not apply to checks for payment of such accounts, and the implied threat may induce payment that otherwise would have lagged still further. But such a letter must not contain any suggestion or threat of prosecution, for that would constitute punishable extortion or blackmail.

Post-dated checks do not come under most of the bad check laws. If they "bounce," they are merely in the same category as defaulted drafts.

### Instigation of prosecution

A criminal prosecution for fraud is not, like a civil suit for collection, instituted by the injured party. If the prosecution is under state law, it must be instituted by the county or district attorney of the area where the crime was committed—usually the area where the fraudulent customer's business is located. If the prosecution is under the federal Criminal Code, it must be instituted by the federal attorney of the proper jurisdiction.

A credit manager's role in a criminal fraud prosecution is twofold. First, he must bring the fraud to the attention of the proper prosecuting official.

Second, he must be prepared to cooperate with that official—to supply him with the documentary evidence needed to sustain the prosecution, and probably to testify at the trial of the fraudulent customer.

This cooperation necessarily makes demands on a credit executive's time and may expose him to vexations. The fining or imprisonment of a fraudulent customer, moreover, does not recover any bad debts for his company. Consequently some credit managers avoid involving themselves in fraud prosecutions. They may use the threat of a fraud prosecution to enforce payment from a customer whom they have detected in fraud, but they bring no cases before the prosecuting officials and they offer no cooperation in prosecutions instigated by other creditors.

Such a "hands-off" policy must be categorically condemned. Quite apart from the moral responsibility that rests upon every credit manager to advance the public interest by aiding the exposure and punishment of this field of crime, he has a dollars-and-cents interest in the widest possible prosecution and punishment of credit frauds. The writing of a bad check is a crime that can never go undetected. The making of a false financial statement to avoid business failure is discovered in most cases, since the respite gained is rarely more than temporary. If prosecution and punishment invariably followed detection of these crimes, few customers would incur the risk of almost certain punishment, and the resulting losses to sellers would be avoided.

Credit departments that subscribe to the fraud prevention service of the National Association of Credit Management have a powerful ally in their struggle against credit frauds. The Fraud Prevention Department of this organization is described in the Appendix to Chapter I of this volume. It may be recalled here that since its inception in 1925, it has been instrumental in obtaining convictions in over 1,800 credit fraud cases and in recovering millions of dollars for defrauded sellers. Its mere existence, moreover, has a deterring effect on credit crime. Subscribers to this service, upon the slightest suspicion that they are being made the victims of a credit fraud, notify the Department, which has representatives in all principal cities and makes immediate inquiry into the case. If a fraud is being perpetrated, the Department notifies the proper state or federal officials, meanwhile pursuing its own investigation and collecting evidence that will help convict the criminals. As part of the service, the subscribers also receive bulletins analyzing the current types of credit frauds being perpetrated and warning the subscribers of the earmarks of such frauds.

APPENDIX TO CHAPTER 17

ILLUSTRATIVE FRAUD PROSECUTION CASE [8]

The "gang" in this case numbered seventeen. Several of its members posed as operators of chain stores. Four stores were actually established in as many cities in eastern Pennsylvania—the Weiss Department Store of Allentown, the Wagner Variety Store of Chester, the E. J. Bauman Installment House of Pottstown, and Serhan's Furniture & Merchandise Co. of Wilkes-Barre.

These four stores were essentially "fronts" to impress salesmen. Little selling was done from them. Quite often the apparently well-stocked shelves and storerooms were filled with little more than empty boxes. Whenever it was found necessary, merchandise was moved from one establishment to another in order to bolster the inventory at a store when it was needed. Also, from time to time the deposits in the local banks were inflated and the bankbooks exhibited to show a healthy growing condition, but at no time were these deposits permitted to remain for any period beyond that for which they served their purpose; they "revolved" among the four cities even more than did the merchandise of the stores.

From these four stores false financial statements were issued and mailed. On the basis of these statements, and the reports of salesmen who called at and were impressed by the stores, the gang secured large quantities of merchandise. All identification marks and tags were removed from such merchandise, making it practically impossible to identify. It was then immediately sold to "fences" at prices far below its market value.

After several months of operation, the four stores were apparently insolvent, and petitions of bankruptcy were filed. The assets, of course, proved to be negligible. One of the creditors of the Weiss Department Store, a subscriber to the NACM Fraud Prevention Service, became suspicious and notified the Fraud Prevention Department. It instituted an investigation. As soon as use of the mails for transmitting fraudulent financial statements was indicated, the postal authorities were informed, and their investigators joined the inquiry. Statements were obtained from former employees of the stores which revealed the methods of the gang and the fraudulent character of the statements that had been mailed. Several of the creditors had kept the envelopes in which the statements had been mailed and the statements themselves attached, so that prosecution under the federal criminal law could be made.

As a result of the investigation, some twenty individuals were indicted by the Federal Grand Jury, and all but three were taken into custody shortly thereafter. Seventeen were placed on trial. Five of them immediately pleaded guilty. The other 12 preferred to stake their chance on the trial. They lost. The following sentences were imposed: three years' imprisonment for four of the defendants, two years' imprisonment for another five, 16 months' imprisonment for one, and nine months' imprisonment for the remaining seven with the sentence suspended for two of them.

---

[8] Supplied by the Fraud Prevention Department of the National Association of Credit Management.

## SUPPLEMENTARY READINGS

"Check Frauds—the Fastest Growing Crime," *Credit and Financial Management,* July 1958, p. 20.

Eager, S. W., *The Law of Chattel Mortgages, Conditional Sales, and Trust Receipts,* Dennis & Co., Buffalo, 1941, and current supplements.

Everberg, C. B., "Bulk Sales Could be a Substitute for Bankruptcy," *Credit and Financial Management,* March 1951, p. 21.

Glenn, G., *Fraudulent Conveyances and Preferences,* 2 vols., Baker, Voorhis & Co., New York, 1940, and current supplements.

Ledbetter, W. J., and A. Gallen, "Changing Credit Practices Under the Uniform Commercial Code," *Credit and Financial Management,* February 1961, p. 8.

Mattuck, M. S., "False Financial Statements—Detection and Prosecution," in National Association of Credit Management, *Danger Signals Show in Financial Statements—Important Check Points in Credit Analysis,* 3rd ed., New York, 1961.

National Association of Credit Management, *Credit Manual of Commercial Laws,* annual.

National Conference of Commissioners on Uniform State Laws, *Why Your State Should Enact the Revised Uniform Commercial Code,* Chicago, 1958.

New York Credit and Financial Management Association, *Commercial Crime Prevention,* New York, 1961.

"The Rights of Creditors—Some Practical Aspects," *Credit and Financial Management,* February 1958, p. 8.

Wasserman, A. T., *Credit Executives' Outline of Uniform Commercial Code,* New England Association of Credit Executives, Boston, 1959.

Weintraub, B., and H. Levin, "Bulk Sales Law and Adequate Protection of Creditors," *Harvard Law Review,* January 19, 1952, p. 418.

## REVIEW

1. Explain the principle and legal circumstances of "stoppage in transit." When would a credit manager exercise this right?
2. Explain the steps that must be taken to bring a suit for collection to trial.
3. What are the grounds for obtaining an attachment in most states? What is the advantage of obtaining an attachment of the debtor's property in connection with a collection suit?
4. What is a "judgment" in a collection suit?
5. What is an "execution upon judgment"?
6. What is a "garnishment proceeding"?
7. What is an "action for deceit"? When would such an action be instituted against a delinquent customer instead of an ordinary collection suit?
8. Explain "replevin." When is such an action advisable?
9. What is the nature and purpose of an action under a fraudulent conveyances law?

10. What are the rights of a supplier under the bulk sales laws?
11. How may a customer who gives a false financial statement or any other false representation for credit purposes be prosecuted?
12. Does a customer who gives a bad check in payment of an account commit a crime? Explain.
13. What are the obligations of a credit manager when he discovers or suspects the perpetration of a credit fraud?

## PROBLEM

What action should you as credit manager of Epsilon Textile Co., a large New York converter, take on each of the following situations?

1. The Beta Dry Goods Store in Hartford, Conn., four months past-due on $700 of piece goods purchases, has not replied to your collection letters and telegrams, and you have decided to sue.
2. Epsilon Textile Co. has obtained judgment in the suit against the Beta Dry Goods Store, but the store claims it is unable to pay the judgment.
3. An hour after your shipping department has delivered to the railroad a large order destined for Rota Dress Co., the salesman who handles the Rota account phones in that he has just learned that a petition of bankruptcy has been filed against the company.
4. A second shipment under the Rota purchase order is due to be sent in five days' time.
5. A week ago you approved a $500 shipment of piece goods to the Gamma Store, an unincorporated business operated by Arthur Gamma in Lancaster, Pa., on the basis of a favorable financial statement sent to you by Mr. Gamma. Now you learn that the financial statement was false, and that two days ago Mr. Gamma transferred the store lease and sold all the fixtures and stock of the store to his brother-in-law.

# CHAPTER 18

# Adjustments

If a customer is hopelessly insolvent in the bankruptcy sense—that is, his assets are grossly insufficient to meet his liabilities—his creditors have no recourse but to liquidate his business in accordance with one of the procedures described in Chapter 19 and salvage from it whatever they can. A liquidated customer, however, means not only losses on the unpaid balance, but also foregoing all possibility of profit on future sales to him. Therefore, when circumstances warrant, credit executives generally endeavor to work out an "adjustment" whereby a customer in difficulties may be preserved in business, so that he can pay off his debts, in whole or in part, at a not-too-distant future date, and so that profit can be made on further sales to him.

There are two groups of procedures for arranging adjustments with embarrassed customers: (1) out-of-court extensions and compositions, and (2) arrangements and reorganizations under the Bankruptcy Law.[1]

## EXTENSIONS AND COMPOSITIONS

A customer may have assets well in excess of liabilities yet not be able to pay these liabilities as they become due—*i.e.*, he may

---

[1] Equity receivership adjustment procedures used to some extent before the 1938 Chandler Act amendment of the federal Bankruptcy Law have since then been generally abandoned.

be "insolvent" in the *equity* sense of the term. The fault may be his—misjudgment in purchasing policy, poor inventory control, unwise credit extensions. Or the insolvency may be due to forces beyond his control. In either case, his basic business structure and prospects may be sound, and there may be good prospects of his recovering financial equilibrium within six months, or a year, or 18 months, if only he is allowed some "breathing spell." This would be a proper occasion for an *extension*—an agreement among creditors to give some specified extra time on past-due obligations so that he can undertake his rehabilitation free of the pressure of dunning letters and the threat of collection actions.

Where a customer's condition is more desperate, where he is truly insolvent in the *bankruptcy* sense, with liabilities in excess of assets, a mere extension is not likely to help much toward recovery. If there is any possibility of saving him, his creditors must usually do more than simply allow him extra time. They must join in reducing their claims upon him, thereby lowering his unsecured liabilities and restoring him to technical solvency. By sacrificing a fraction of their claims, they enhance their chance of having the balance eventually repaid and maintaining a possible source of future profit. Such a debt-cutting agreement is called a compromise settlement or *composition*.

Creditors' agreements to allow a debtor extra time or to reduce their claims upon him may be achieved through the machinery of the federal Bankruptcy Law or by mutual agreement out of court. The terms "extension" and "composition" are usually reserved for the out-of-court agreements. Such adjustments outnumber those accomplished through Bankruptcy Law procedure.

### Conditions precedent

Not every customer who finds himself in difficulties and unable to meet his obligations is necessarily a proper subject for an extension or a composition. Nor, given a customer who is a proper subject, can an individual credit manager arrange an extension or composition. These types of adjustment require the combination of a proper subject and voluntary group action by his creditors.

There are four customer prerequisites for an extension or composition to have a reasonable chance of success:

1. The customer must be a good moral risk. No group of responsible credit executives would ever consider extending the helping hand of extension or composition to a businessman unless his moral record was unimpeachable.

2. The customer must have sufficient ability to rehabilitate the business after the arrangement has gone into effect. Otherwise, the sacrifices of the creditors would be futile. If they continued selling to the customer,

as is generally expected in an out-of-court adjustment, they would be throwing good money after bad.

3. The customer's financial situation after the proposed adjustment must have good prospects of recovery. If a customer would still be "frozen" at the conclusion of a six-months' moratorium, the extension would have failed of its purpose. So, too, would a debt cancellation of any proportion if it left the debtor still insolvent and without hope of financial restoration. If the terms of the adjustment itself do not establish the customer in a good working capital position, he must have reasonable prospects of raising new equity capital or borrowing for this purpose.

4. General business and local competitive conditions must be such that a merchant aided by an extension or composition can thereafter recover. It would be folly for sellers to prop up a foredoomed customer. Moreover, where excessive local competition is an important factor in a merchant's distress and his creditors sell also to his competitors, these competitors might be strengthened and made better credit risks by liquidating the distressed merchant.

There are five creditor prerequisites for successful extensions and compositions:

1. *All* the creditors must agree in order to make an out-of-court extension or composition effective. Dissenting creditors would be able to wreck any majority agreement by attaching the customer's property or, under certain circumstances, starting bankruptcy proceedings against him. It may, therefore, be necessary to pay off small dissenting creditors in part or in full. This may be done from liquid assets of the business. In some cases small payments to the dissenters are made pro rata by the other creditors who want to arrive at an agreement. Should the amounts demanded by dissenting creditors be substantial, however, plans for an out-of-court adjustment may have to be abandoned, and the coercive machinery of the federal Bankruptcy Law utilized.

2. The creditors must be prepared to make concessions sufficient to give the customer a good chance of recovery. If a 12-month extension is obviously needed, a 6-month moratorium is futile. If a 40 per cent debt slash is necessary to restore a customer to technical solvency, a 20 per cent composition is little if any better than none.

3. The general body of creditors usually appoints a committee of three to five members to supervise and advise the debtor during the adjustment period. Service on this committee is voluntary and without compensation. The responsibility is usually undertaken by the representatives of the major unsecured creditors, who will gain most from success of the adjust-

ment.[2] If an adjustment bureau is associated with the proceeding, as described below, its representative will also be a member of the creditors' committee and will usually serve as its secretary.

4. Major creditors are generally expected to continue supplying the customer with the merchandise he needs on regular terms. If they stopped such selling to him, the business probably would not be able to continue. Certainly its recovery would be hampered. Extension and composition agreements ordinarily do not make specific commitments on this point. The major creditors, however, usually recognize and abide by this condition.

5. In the case of compositions, the creditors must be willing to give the debtor, upon satisfactory fulfillment of his obligations under the agreement, written releases for the excused amounts of his debts to them.

## Procedures

Some extensions and compositions are negotiated directly between debtor and creditors. A growing number of such adjustments, however, is arranged through adjustment bureaus such as those affiliated with the National Association of Credit Management and operated by their local associations. There are 62 such bureaus performing adjustment and liquidation services.

The process of negotiating an extension or composition with the help of a recognized adjustment bureau may be summarized in six steps:

1. The embarrassed debtor, or a group of his creditors, submits to the bureau a general statement of the case. If the debtor has taken the initiative in applying to the adjustment bureau, he is asked to add a full list of his obligations and creditors to the general statement. If a creditors' group has submitted the case, the bureau approaches the debtor, offers its friendly cooperation and requests a list of his debts and his creditors.

2. On the basis of the list of creditors and their claims, the adjustment bureau calls an initial, informal meeting of the principal creditors, usually at the bureau's office. The debtor is generally asked to attend in order to give information and show pertinent records. At this meeting, frequently, a decision is made either to liquidate the business or to attempt an arrangement to keep it alive.

3. If the case seems capable of adjustment, the creditors attending the meeting usually engage the services of the bureau to assist in carrying through the adjustment procedure. The bureau may make an exhaustive study of the debtor's business. If it does, its report, together with a current financial statement of the debtor's business, is sent to all creditors and

---

[2] If a major creditor has special guarantees, or other security or preferences, he may have interests that conflict with those of the general body of unsecured creditors. and should not be a member of the creditors' committee.

## NEW YORK CREDIT MEN'S ADJUSTMENT BUREAU, INC.

### AFFILIATED WITH NATIONAL ASSOCIATION OF CREDIT MANAGEMENT

**71 West 23rd Street, New York 10, N. Y.**

WAtkins 4-0100

Please Address Reply Attention of

October 3, 1960          M. J. Davis

TO THE CREDITORS OF:

ARTHUR ARNOLD SONS
120 Fifth Avenue
New York City

Gentlemen:

We have been requested to call a meeting of the creditors of the above concern. This meeting will be held on –

DATE:     Tuesday, October 11, 1960

TIME:     2 p.m.

PLACE:    NEW YORK CREDIT MEN'S
          ADJUSTMENT BUREAU, INC.
          71 W. 23 St.,   11th floor
          New York, N.Y.

It will benefit all creditors if each will refrain from individual action on their claims until a further report and recommendation can be made by a Creditors' Committee to be appointed at the meeting.

Yours very truly,

NEW YORK CREDIT MEN'S
ADJUSTMENT BUREAU, INC.

BY *[signature]*
          Secretary and Treasurer

MJD:EG

ILLUSTRATION 18-1.   Adjustment Bureau Letter Calling a Creditors' Adjustment Meeting

they are requested to attend a formal creditors' meeting at the bureau's office. They are also asked to take no individual action against the debtor in the meantime (see Illustration 18-1).

4. At the formal meeting there may be further discussion of the case or there may be only the election of the creditors' committee.

5. The creditors' committee, its counsel, and its secretary, after investigation, formulate an appropriate extension or composition proposal.

6. These proposals are submitted by the creditors' committee to the creditors and the debtor. As soon as they have *all* agreed in writing the arrangement becomes a valid contract binding upon all parties. If there are few small creditors who refuse otherwise to sign, they may have to be paid in part or in full, or the idea of a friendly arrangement must be dropped.

### Provisions

While the indicated *process of negotiating* extensions and compositions usually follows a similar pattern for both kinds of adjustments, the *arrangements themselves*—extension agreements and composition settlements—differ considerably in form and contents.

An *extension agreement* does not require a specific form. It is adapted to and worded according to the individual case. The core of this arrangement is always: (1) statement of the waiting period for the creditors, which may cover several months or years; and (2) provision for the creditors' committee remaining in existence for the duration of the agreement and in control over the business. The usual contents of an extension agreement are built around these two points in the following way:

1. Each creditor signing extends the time of payment of his unsecured claim against the debtor for the stated period. The debtor undertakes the obligation to pay these claims or parts of them at a stated time or at stated intervals and may give notes for such instalments.

2. The debtor usually agrees to some form of control and may deposit documents with the creditors' committee for this purpose. If the debtor is a corporation, 51 per cent of its outstanding voting stock may be given in escrow; so may tentative written resignations of the officers and directors. If the debtor is a single proprietorship or partnership, chattel mortgages on assets may be filed with the committee or an assignment for the benefit of creditors may be escrowed with the committee—these are filed subsequently only in case of default. The creditors' committee may be given other documents of control, such as statements authorizing the countersigning of checks and the approving of purchases, sales, payments, and salary increases of officers.

3. The debtor is authorized to carry on the business during the extension period under the supervision of the creditors' committee or the board of directors selected by the committee.

4. The creditors' committee, with the representative of the adjustment bureau frequently its acting secretary, is authorized to exercise its control functions, such as countersigning checks and approving purchases, sales, and payments. It may also be authorized to pay claims of small creditors up to a certain amount, to substitute accountants of its own choice for those of the debtor, to prolong the extension beyond the stated period if

necessary, in its discretion to waive any breach or default of the agreement or, conversely, to declare the debtor in default if he fails to meet an instalment payment or incurs an operating loss that would endanger future business profitability, and to suspend operations of the business or liquidate it at any time it sees fit.

5. It is commonly provided that, should it subsequently become necessary to file a petition for an "arrangement" under Chapter XI of the Bankruptcy Act, as explained later in this chapter, the extension agreement shall constitute the plan for the "arrangement," and acceptance of the agreement shall constitute the acceptance needed to make this "arrangement" plan effective.

6. There may be a provision that, in any subsequent insolvency proceeding, priority shall be granted to all creditors who extend further credit after the extension agreement is declared to be in effect.

7. Upon successful consummation and termination of the agreement— no default in payments and no breach of any other clauses of the agreement—the documents of control are to be returned to the debtor and he is to be restored to full control and operation of the business.

A *composition settlement* does not have to comply with a specific form. It is more standardized, however, than the general run of extension agreements. Its chief provisions are: (1) the reduction of creditors' claims by a uniform percentage; (2) the debtor's obligation to pay the adjusted claims at a stated date or dates; and (3) provisions for the supervision of the settlement by the creditors' committee.

Small creditors have learned that they enjoy a valuable "nuisance advantage" in composition settlements provided the total of their claims does not constitute any substantial proportion of the customer's over-all indebtedness. They can refuse to accede to any scaling down of the amounts owed to them. Rather than resort to the more expensive coercive provisions of Bankruptcy Law procedures, the larger creditors are often willing to agree that debts up to $50, or even up to $100, shall be paid in full.

A composition settlement usually simply scales down a customer's debts, with no extension on the past-due balance. Upon the customer's making immediate cash payment of such balance, the settlement is consummated, and the creditors' committee dissolves. Other types of settlement provide an extension on part or all of the balance, with the extension covered by notes to the individual creditors. In most instances the settlement is deemed consummated upon the delivery of the cash and/or notes in question to the creditors. The work of the creditors' committee is completed upon such delivery, and it then dissolves. Many composition settlements, however, like extension agreements, provide for supervision of the debtor by the creditors' committee until full payment on all the notes has been made. Whatever control instruments were originally deposited with the creditors' committee are returned to the debtor upon the dissolution of the committee.

## ARRANGEMENTS AND REORGANIZATIONS UNDER THE BANKRUPTCY ACT

The federal Bankruptcy Act of 1938, known as the Chandler Act, with subsequent amendments, provides not only for liquidation of hopelessly insolvent business, but also offers two adjustment procedures, covering composition as well as extension, for financially embarrassed enterprises. Bankruptcy Act adjustments have two advantages over out-of-court extensions and compositions: (1) Dissenting minority creditors are compelled to accept adjustments approved by the majority group, thus preventing "hold-up" tactics by a handful of small creditors, or the blocking of reasonable adjustments by the obstinacy or ill will of a few individuals; (2) fuller protection against possible fraud is ensured. Against these favorable aspects of the Bankruptcy Act adjustments are their slower procedure and greater cost.

Chapter XI of the federal Bankruptcy Act supplies a procedure whereby an individual, partnership, or corporation may effect a settlement of its *unsecured* debts by an "arrangement" which involves extension or composition. If a complete corporate financial reorganization, involving publicly held shares and bonds or secured debts, is to take place, the procedure must be one of "reorganization" under Chapter X of the Bankruptcy Law.[3] Significantly, both of these chapters refer to the concern or corporation involved as "the debtor," in contrast to use of the term "bankrupt" in other chapters of the Bankruptcy Act, to avoid the stigma attached to the latter term.

### Arrangements under Chapter XI

Chapter XI arrangements apply usually to closely held corporations, partnerships, or proprietorships, regardless of size. Most of them, however, involve only relatively small or medium-sized business units.

A petition for an arrangement may be filed only by the debtor, not by the creditors.[4] A form for such a voluntary petition is shown in Illustra-

---

[3] The Chandler Act also provides two adjustments procedures which rarely apply in mercantile credit management—Chapter XII deals with debts of individuals secured by real property, Chapter XIII with wage earners' arrangements. In addition, the act regulates agricultural compositions and railroad reorganizations (Chapter VIII), municipal adjustments (Chapter IX), and procedures for other classes of institutions in financial trouble.

[4] Proceedings initiated under Chapter X can be transferred by the court to Chapter XI and vice versa. For example, a business assumed to require a reorganization of its entire financial structure and therefore petitioned under Chapter X may prove to be

In the District Court of the United States for the

District of

**New York**

In the matter of

In Proceedings for an Arrangement

**WILLIAM JONES, INC.**

Debtor.

No.......**1183**...

### PETITION IN PROCEEDINGS UNDER CHAPTER XI

To the Honorable
    Judge of the District Court of the United States for the
**Southern**District of **New York**

THE PETITION of **WILLIAM JONES, INC.**
a corporation engaged in the business of **selling eye glasses and kindred commodities**

which corporation has not been known by any other name or trade name for the past six years.

RESPECTFULLY REPRESENTS:

    1. Your petitioner is a **business** *corporation organized and existing under the laws
of the State of **New York** and has had its principal office and its principal place of business
at **1100 East First Street, New York, N.Y.**
within the above judicial district, for a longer portion of the six months immediately preceding the filing of
this petition than in any other judicial district.

    2. †No bankruptcy proceeding, initiated by a petition by or against your petitioner, is now pending.

    3. Your petitioner is insolvent [or unable to pay its debts as they mature], and proposes the following
arrangement with its unsecured creditors:

        **a) To pay administration claims in cash upon confirmation**

        **b) To pay its unsecured creditors 100%,**

           **payable 25% upon confirmation of the plan and 25% every**

           **3 months thereafter.**

        **c) To pay priority claims in such instalments as shall be agreed**

           **upon between the Debtor and the said priority claimants.**

*Moneyed, Business or Commercial.
†If Bankruptcy proceeding is pending and this petition is brought under Chapter XI, Section 321, strike out this allegation and recite proceedings heretofore had.

ILLUSTRATION 18-2.   Form for Petition for Arrangement under Chapter XI of the
Bankruptcy Act

4.  The schedule hereto annexed, marked Schedule A, and verified by the oath of the undersigned officer of your petitioner, contains a full and true statement of all its debts, and, so far as it is possible to ascertain, the names and places of residence of its creditors, and such further statements concerning said debts as are required by the provisions of the Act of Congress relating to bankruptcy.

5.  The schedule hereto annexed, marked Schedule B, and verified by the oath of the undersigned officer of your petitioner, contains an accurate inventory of all its property, real and personal, and such further statements concerning said property as are required by the provisions of said Act.

6.  The statement hereto annexed, marked Exhibit 1, and verified by the oath of the undersigned officer of your petitioner, contains a full and true statement of all its executory contracts, as required by the provisions of said Act.

7.  The statement hereto annexed, marked Exhibit 2, and verified by the oath of the undersigned officer of your petitioner, contains a full and true statement of its affairs, as required by the provisions of said Act.

WHEREFORE your petitioner prays that proceedings may be had upon this petition in accordance with the provisions of chapter XI of the Act of Congress relating to bankruptcy.

*William Jones, Inc.*

Petitioner

**WILLIAM JONES, INC.**

By *William Jones*

**William Jones**

(SEAL)

**President** of said corporation

**Richard Roe, No. 1 Main Street,**

Attorney **New York 2, N. Y.**

STATE OF **New York**

COUNTY OF **New York**      } ss.:

**William Jones**                                              being duly sworn deposes and says that he is the

**President** of **William Jones, Inc.**

the petitioner named in the foregoing petition, and does hereby make solemn oath that the statements contained therein are true, according to the best of his knowledge, information and belief; that the reason why this verification is made by deponent and not by the petitioner herein, is that said petitioner is a corporation; and that deponent is the officer of said corporation duly authorized by its Board of Directors to execute and verify said petition on its behalf.

Subscribed and sworn to before me this
**3rd** day of **April**                        1961      *William Jones*

                                                **William Jones**

**JOAN SMITH, 111 River Av., New York 1, N. Y.**

*Joan Smith*

(*Official Character*)

N. B.—Oaths to the above petition, and the schedules thereto annexed, may be administered by officers authorized to administer oaths in proceedings before Courts of the United States, or under the laws of the State where the same are to be taken; and diplomatic or consular officers of the United States in any foreign country.
Petitioner's attorney cannot act as notary.

ILLUSTRATION 18-2   (*Concluded*)

tion 18-2. The filing usually takes place in the district where the business is located. The proceedings may be transferred to any other jurisdiction for the convenience of the court [5] or the creditors. The contents of the petition are: (1) the debtor's statement that he is unable to meet his obligations as they mature, or is insolvent in the bankruptcy sense, with liabilities equaling or exceeding assets; (2) the plan of an arrangement he proposes; [6] (3) a list of contracts, liens, and so forth; and (4) a schedule of the debtor's assets and liabilities and an income statement. The fulfillment of this fourth requirement may be postponed to a later date. In place of this schedule a summary of assets and liabilities together with the names and addresses of creditors may be submitted with the petition, if sufficient cause can be shown for the delay.

Upon acceptance of the petition, the court usually refers the case to a *referee* in bankruptcy who thereafter has full charge of the procedure. The debtor is usually left in possession and operation of the business, though he may be required to post an indemnity bond against loss in operations. Sometimes, however, upon application of the creditors, a *trustee* or a *receiver* may be appointed by the court to take charge of the business.[7]

At this stage of the procedure, after the petition has been filed and before the first official creditors' meeting has been called by the referee, an adjustment bureau frequently enters the case on behalf of the unsecured creditors. It calls an informal meeting to arrange the formation of a creditors' committee which will confer with the debtor and formulate an arrangement plan or, possibly, revise the plan previously filed. Thereafter the adjustment bureau may also inform the court of the creditors' wishes, arrange with the court the investigation of the business, its books, inventory, and other particulars, and send reports to the creditors. It actually becomes an unofficial focal point in the proceedings.[8]

---

adjustable by arranging not more than its unsecured debts and leaving the other parts of the financial set-up untouched. It can be transferred to Chapter XI proceedings. Or a concern that originally sought an arrangement of its unsecured debts under Chapter XI is found to need adjustment beyond this scope. It can be transferred to Chapter X proceedings.

[5] The term "court" in descriptions of judicial procedure refers to the presiding judge.

[6] A petition without a plan will be accepted by the court only if a complete list of creditors, with names, addresses, and amounts owed, is attached. The court will then give the debtor a reasonable time to file his plans.

[7] The appointment of this trustee is tentative in character; he takes office only if the arrangement procedure fails and the debtor goes into bankruptcy. The receiver, on the other hand, assumes his responsibilities immediately if the debtor is not left in possession of his business.

[8] The adjustment bureau, though, is rarely if ever appointed by the court as a receiver or trustee in adjustment proceedings under Chapter XI or Chapter X because the law calls for complete independence of such appointees. However, if the Chapter XI (or Chapter X) proceedings should fail and the business be placed in liquidation in bankruptcy court, an adjustment bureau may be elected trustee in bankruptcy by the creditors.

The referee, eventually, after thorough examination of the case, calls the first official meeting of creditors upon ten days notice by mail. Accompanying this notice is a copy of the arrangement proposed by the debtor and a summary of his assets and liabilities. The creditors, in turn, file their claims. They are entitled to do that any time up to the date of confirmation of the arrangement by the court.

The referee presides at the first official meeting. Proof of claims may be filed by creditors, and allowed or disallowed. A creditors' committee may be formed, but this is not required; if an informal committee already exists, it usually now becomes the official one. The debtor is examined by the referee and the creditors. Other witnesses may be called and examined. The arrangement proposed by the debtor may be accepted as it stands, or upon consultation among creditors or their committee it may be altered. The debtor's assent must be obtained for any such modification.

If the proposed arrangement is accepted at this meeting by the required majority of creditors, their written acceptances are now examined. A majority in number and amount of proven and allowed claims of each class of creditors is necessary to make the arrangement effective. The referee then fixes the time when the debtor shall make his payments and directs the receiver or trustee, if such has been appointed, or some other person to receive and disburse these payments. If the plan is not accepted at this meeting, it may be adjourned for a certain period at the discretion of the referee. After that, the arrangement may be accepted by the necessary majority of creditors at that later date or, if no agreement can be reached, it will have to be dropped. In this case the debtor will go into liquidation through bankruptcy.[9]

An arrangement accepted by the majority of the creditors still needs the *confirmation* of the court. This confirmation will be given, provided that (1) the arrangement is feasible and in the best interest of creditors; (2) the debtor has not been guilty of fraudulent or other improper acts, or failed to perform his duties, so as to bar his later discharge as a bankrupt; or (3) the proposal itself and its acceptance have been made in good faith and have not been made or procured by means forbidden in the Act. The confirmation makes the arrangement binding on all parties, including minority creditors who did not agree to it and creditors who did not file claims. Upon confirmation and consummation of the plan, all controls on the business (except those needed to secure deferred payments) are removed, and the debtor is *discharged* by the court as to

---

[9] The debtor may already be in bankruptcy—adjudged a bankrupt—at the time he files the petition under Chapter XI. The filing of the petition or its acceptance by the court would not automatically stay the bankruptcy proceedings, but the judge may grant a stay upon the debtor's request for the duration of the Chapter XI procedure. If this succeeds, the suspended bankruptcy proceedings would be terminated. If the Chapter XI arrangement fails, the bankruptcy proceedings would be resumed.

all debts covered by the arrangement. He may not, however, file another petition under Chapter XI within the next six years, unless the present adjustment was an unqualified extension with no scaling down of claims. Confirmation and discharge of the debtor may be set aside by the court within six months upon petition of any creditor if he should discover that fraud was practiced in procuring the arrangement. In such a case, hearings may follow, leading to a new arrangement, or the court may adjudge the debtor a bankrupt.

### Reorganizations under Chapter X

If a corporation seeks a reorganization of its entire financial structure, including secured debts, and also shares and bonds in the hands of the public, it must avail itself of Chapter X proceedings where certain safeguards are provided for protection of the public interest. Obviously, Chapter X reorganizations are intended for large corporations, not for small units. They are also more complicated. The procedure under Chapter X resembles that under Chapter XI in the basic concept of preserving embarrassed or insolvent concerns that can be saved, and in specific points such as requiring no 100 per cent agreement of creditors for a binding settlement and giving the debtor a discharge as to his liabilities; but there are many differences as to detail.

### Procedure

A voluntary petition under Chapter X may be filed by a debtor, or an involuntary one by three or more creditors with claims aggregating at least $5,000, or by an indenture trustee. A Chapter X petition has to contain: (1) the statement of insolvency (this is the only clause in content which is the same under Chapter XI); (2) specific facts showing the need for relief under Chapter X and why adequate relief cannot be obtained under Chapter XI; and (3) in case of an involuntary petition, the allegation of an act of bankruptcy, such as adjudication as a bankrupt, appointment of receiver, or preferential transfer of assets. No schedule of the debtor's assets and liabilities, or income statement, or list of liens and contracts has to be filed at this stage. Also no plan of reorganization need be submitted, although the desire to effect such a reorganization has to be expressed.

An *answer* to an involuntary petition under Chapter X may then be filed by the debtor corporation within ten days or within a longer period if allowed by the court. Answers may also be filed by the other creditors, or the indenture trustee, or by any stockholder if the company is not insolvent in the bankruptcy sense. If no answer is filed or if the judge finds that the substance of the petition stands despite the answer, he approves the petition.[10]

The judge is authorized to transfer the proceedings under Chapter X to a referee in bankruptcy. But usually, in contrast to what is done under Chapter XI, he personally keeps charge of the procedure, issues all necessary orders, and refers only special problems to the referee. He may leave the debtor corporation in possession and operation of the business or appoint one or more disinterested trustees [11] in his discretion. But he *must* appoint one or more trustees if the liabilities of the debtor exceed $250,000. If the debtor retains the management of the business, the judge may appoint an examiner who will have to perform some of the functions otherwise attributed to a trustee. In practice, appointments of such examiners are rare.

Upon approval of the petition and after the decisions as to the management of the business have been made, the schedules of assets and liabilities including liens, executory contracts, and similar obligations—and furthermore the names and addresses of creditors and stockholders of each class—have to be filed by the debtor or by the trustee management of the business. The court may also direct any investigation into the business and examine its officers and directors.

An adjustment bureau is frequently engaged in the Chapter X proceedings on behalf of the unsecured creditors as it is in Chapter XI proceedings. It usually starts its activities before the first official creditors' meeting has been called by the court. The role of an adjustment bureau is more limited in Chapter X cases than in Chapter XI ones, for the simple reason that unsecured debts which are the core of Chapter XI arrangements are normally not as important an element in Chapter X proceedings. However, as soon as a committee of unsecured creditors has been formed, the bureau may immediately cooperate with other committees representing stockholders, bondholders, leaseholders, and others, for the purpose of arriving at a plan that will be satisfactory to all classes of creditors.

Within 30 to 60 days after approval of the petition, a first hearing must be held upon notice to all interested parties including the Securities and Exchange Commission. At this meeting, objections may be raised to continuance of the debtor in possession of the business or to the trustee or trustees who have been appointed. At this stage or later, a plan of reorganization may be filed. Where the debtor corporation has been con-

---

[10] Approval of a petition under Chapter X acts as a stay to a prior bankruptcy proceeding; under Chapter XI such a stay has to be specifically granted (see footnote 9).

[11] Note that a trustee in adjustments under Chapters X and XI of the Bankruptcy Act is *appointed by the court,* whereas a trustee in liquidations under Chapter XIX (studied in our next chapter) is usually *elected by the creditors.* Their functions are also quite different.

tinued in the management of the business, such a plan may be filed by the debtor corporation, or by any creditor, or by the indenture trustee, or by any stockholder (provided the company is not insolvent in the bankruptcy sense), or by an examiner if appointed and so directed by the court. Not one plan but several plans may be presented.

At the second meeting called by the court at which the federal Treasury Department may be represented, the plan or plans of reorganization are considered. Before approval, a plan may be referred for examination and advice to the Securities and Exchange Commission. It *must* be referred to this agency if the indebtedness exceeds 3 million dollars. After receiving the S.E.C. report [12]—which is purely advisory and does not compel the court to act or withhold any action—or upon a notice that no S.E.C. report will be submitted, the court sets a time period within which the plan must be accepted by the creditors and stockholders.

Acceptance of a reorganization plan under Chapter X requires approval of the creditors in each class holding two-thirds of the claims in amounts filed and allowed; numbers of creditors do not count. If the corporation is solvent (*i.e.*, not insolvent in the bankruptcy sense), the plan must also be accepted by a majority of the stockholdings in each class; again, the number of stockholders is irrelevant. Should any one class of creditors or stockholders entitled to vote reject a plan which is acceptable to the other classes, the plan may nonetheless be put into effect despite their rejection but with protection of their interests.

Upon approval of the plan, a third meeting of all interested parties is called by the court for the *confirmation* of the plan. This confirmation will be given if the court is satisfied that the plan is equitable, fair, and feasible and that the proposal of the plan and its acceptance are in good faith and have not been procured by means or promises forbidden by this Act. The confirmation makes the plan binding on all interested parties—upon the debtor and every other corporation issuing securities or acquiring property under the plan, and upon all creditors and stockholders regardless of how they are affected by the plan. After the confirmation, the property dealt with in the plan is free and clear of all claims and interests of the debtor, creditors, and stockholders, except as provided in the plan or in the order confirming the plan.

A plan, however, may be altered by the court upon proposal by interested parties, even after confirmation, if in the opinion of the judge the change does not adversely affect the interests of creditors and stockholders.

Finally, upon consummation of the plan—when all payments, transfers,

---

[12] Although this S.E.C. report is purely advisory, the value of S.E.C. intervention in reorganizations involving a public interest is so great that such cases are sometimes transferred from Chapter XI proceedings (where the S.E.C. does not enter) to Chapter X proceedings (where it does) expressly to bring the S.E.C. into the picture.

and actions provided by it have been accomplished—a decree is entered by the court *discharging* the debtor corporation from all debts covered by the plan, discharging the trustee or trustees if any were appointed, and terminating the rights and interests of stockholders, except as provided in the plan or in the order confirming the plan. Here as under Chapter XI, confirmation and discharge can be set aside within within six months if fraud was involved.

## Plan of reorganization

The law establishes certain provisions that a plan of reorganization under Chapter X *must* contain and others that it *may* contain.

The mandatory provisions are:

1. Modification or alteration of the rights of creditors generally, or of any class of them, secured or unsecured, through the issuance of new securities of any character or otherwise.

2. Payment of all costs and expenses of administration and other allowances which may be approved or made by the court.

3. Specification of what claims, if any, are to be paid in cash in full.

4. Specifications of the creditors or stockholders, or any class of them, not to be affected by the plan, and the provision, if any, with respect to them.

5. Adequate protection for any class of creditors which is affected but does not accept the plan by the two-third majority in amounts required by the statute. Several ways of protection are named.

6. If the debtor corporation is solvent (in the bankruptcy sense), provision for any class of stockholders which is affected but does not accept the plan by the majority required by the statute. Several methods of protecting their interests are indicated.

7. Provision for adequate means for the execution of the plan which may include a number of specified items, such as retention or sale of property, mergers, consolidations, and other arrangements.

8. Provisions with regard to the manner of selecting directors, officers or voting trustees upon consummation of the plan, and their respective successors.

9. Provision for inclusion in the debtor corporation's charter or that of any corporation organized or to be organized for the purpose of carrying out the plan, of specific provisions, such as forbidding the issuance of nonvoting stock, assuring the fair and equitable distribution of voting power among several classes of securities, determining the terms, rights, privileges of several classes of securities, and other items.

Permissive elements are:

1. Provisions dealing with all or any part of the debtor corporation's property.

2. Provision for the rejection of executory contracts except contracts with public authority.

3. Where any indebtedness is created or extended under the plan for a period of more than five years, special provision for the retirement of such indebtedness.

4. Provision for settlement or adjustment of claims belonging to the debtor corporation, and as to such claims not settled or adjusted in the plan.

5. Any other appropriate provision not inconsistent with the Bankruptcy Act.

### Effectiveness of Chandler Act adjustment procedures

Chapters X and XI of the federal Bankruptcy Law constitute a great improvement over business adjustment procedures available prior to 1938. Previously, while extensions and compositions could be arranged under federal bankruptcy law, the debtor had first to be adjudicated bankrupt. This stigma was a heavy price to pay for adjustment. Hence, adjustments for insolvent businesses were accomplished almost exclusively through common-law procedures or equity receiverships, which usually could not encompass corporate reorganizations. The Chandler Act made the wide flexibility of federal law, and its protection for creditors, available for adjustment cases without the prerequisite of bankruptcy adjudication. It made possible adjustment of the most complicated financial structures and situations. As a by-product, it promoted out-of-court adjustments by inducing reluctant creditors frequently to accept such settlements under the threat that the debtor would petition under Chapter XI and obtain an arrangement, possibly less favorable to them, which they would be compelled to accept.

APPENDIX TO CHAPTER 18

ILLUSTRATIVE ADJUSTMENT CASE [13]

In February a debtor, operating a small family shoe store in a secondary business section of a New Jersey city, was threatened with suit by a creditor with a sizable claim. He sought advice of an attorney, who immediately communicated with the secretary of the New Jersey Association of Credit Men and asked that he call a meeting of creditors. At the meeting it was disclosed that no proper books of account had been maintained other than a payables ledger and a sales book which showed a continuous falling off

---

[13] This case study is derived from the files of the National Association of Credit Management.

in sales. The debtor could give no helpful explanation as to how he had arrived at his present condition other than to attribute it to general conditions, poor sales, and falling prices. There was no doubt as to his honesty and he was insistent that he wanted to pay 100 per cent, that all he sought was additional time.

His financial condition was: Accounts receivable, $745.50; Merchandise, $11,147.91; *Total assets*, $11,893.41: Accounts payable, $9,858.45; Bank loan, $1,455.00; Personal loan, $450.00; Rent due, $795.00; *Total Liabilities*, $12,558.45. Annual sales were about $33,000.

The extension was agreed to and a creditors' committee was selected which included two merchandise creditors and a representative of the association's adjustment bureau.

First a tentative budget was set up based on such information as was available, and proper records were installed. Next a sale was decided on to stimulate business, move winter stocks, and provide cash with which to make necessary spring purchases.

For the sale the advice of a sales manager was had, and it was determined to promote a sale, starting March 4th. The debtor had never conducted a sale and was opposed to it, but the committee was insistent.

The sale was a complete success and was continued for three weeks. From there on, the debtor, relieved of all worry regarding his creditors, was able to devote his entire attention to the other phases of his business. Over the period of the extension he was able to show a modest though steady increase in sales at a time when comparable stores were experiencing a decline.

Monthly operating figures were compiled and progress checked by the committee and the adjustment bureau. A physical inventory was taken every four months, and an Income Statement and Balance Sheet prepared, copies of which were mailed to all creditors. A small net profit was shown from the beginning. Most of the creditors extended new credit, thus eliminating any fear of depleting the inventory which at the beginning was rather low. Had this new credit not been available, and had the original schedule of payments been even approximated, the case would have collapsed in six months or less.

An eighteen months' extension was contemplated in the beginning, but it took just two years to work out the plan. The debtor's condition at the close of the two-year recovery period was: Cash, $248.73; Accounts receivable, $497.55; Merchandise, $11,849.19; *Total assets*, $12,595.47: Accounts payable, $5,636.13. Bank loan, $240.00; Rent due, $210.00; *Total liabilities*, $6,086.13. The second-year sales were $39,000.00. The fees and expenses charged by the adjustment bureau for its services were $855.00, or 8.7 per cent of the total funds disbursed.

While it is true that at the end of this two-year period the debtor did not yet show a perfect condition, the creditors had received 100 per cent, and there was a surplus of current assets over liabilities of $6,509.34, as compared with a deficit of $665.04 when the debtor first called on the credit men's association. There were eighteen creditors in the case who during the extension received approximately $54,000 of business, and had an appreciative account still on their books.

## SUPPLEMENTARY READINGS

"Are Compromise Settlements Ever Justified?" *Credit and Financial Management*, August 1952, p. 8.

Levin, H., "Debtor and Creditor Insolvency Adjustments Out-of-Court and in Chapter XI Proceedings," *New York Law Journal*, December 13/15, 1954, vol. 132, no. 112/114.

National Association of Credit Management, *Credit Manual of Commercial Laws*, New York, 1961, Chs. 25 to 27, including text of the Chandler Act.

New York Credit Men's Adjustment Bureau, Inc., *Guide for Suggested Procedures by Creditors Committees, Certified Public Accountants, and Attorneys in Handling Cases of Financially Embarrassed Debtors*, New York, 1961.

Weintraub, B., and H. Levin, "Availability of Bankruptcy Rehabilitation to the Middle-Sized Corporation: The Third Circuit's Interpretation," *Rutgers Law Review*, Spring 1960, p. 564.

————, "Chapter XI Approaches Its 'Teens," *Cornell Law Quarterly*, Summer 1950, p. 725.

————, "Chapter XI Proceedings—Recent Amendments to the Bankruptcy Act," *New York Law Journal*, August 19/20, 1952, vol. 28, nos. 35 and 36.

————, "Some Practical Aspects of Debtor and Creditor Adjustments for the General Practioner," *New York Law Journal*, October 2/3, 1951, vol. 126, no. 65 and 66.

————, *What the Business Executive Should Know about Chapter XI of the National Bankruptcy Act*, New York Credit and Financial Management Association, New York, rev. ed. 1960.

Weintraub, B., H. Levin, and L. G. Novack, "Chapter X or Chapter XI: Co-Existence for the Middle-Sized Corporation," *Fordham Law Review*, Winter 1955/56, p. 616.

## REVIEW

1. What must be a debtor's circumstances to warrant his creditors granting him an adjustment?

2. What actions and agreements by the creditors are necessary for a successful adjustment?

3. Describe the procedure leading up to an adjustment agreement on a mercantile debtor.

4. Under what circumstances may a business seek an "arrangement" under Chapter XI of the Bankruptcy Act? Who is permitted to petition for such an arrangement? Describe the procedure.

5. Under what circumstances may a business not seek an "arrangement" under Chapter XI of the Bankruptcy Act but may be reorganized under Chapter X? Who is permitted to petition for such a reorganization? Describe the procedure. What provisions must appear in a reorganization plan? What provisions may appear?

# CHAPTER 19

# Liquidation of Insolvent Customers

For customers who are hopelessly insolvent in the bankruptcy sense—with liabilities exceeding assets and no prospect of recuperation—there is usually no solution but liquidation. To protect their companies' interests, credit executives must upon occasion participate directly in liquidation proceedings. Hence some knowledge of insolvency law and liquidation procedure is one of the prerequisites for effective credit management.

Three classes of liquidation procedures are available to the creditors of an insolvent business: (1) three *out-of-court* procedures—liquidation by common consent of debtor and creditors, common-law assignment, and corporate dissolution; (2) two *state judicial* procedures—statutory assignment and state court receivership; and (3) *federal bankruptcy* proceedings.

These procedures vary widely in the safeguards they afford the debtor and creditors and the speed and cost with which they can be effected. Which procedure should be selected in a particular case depends on a number of factors—the trust the creditors have in the debtor, the confidence the creditors have in each other, the legal simplicity or complexity of the claims involved, and the unanimity of opinion among the creditors.

Before analyzing these six liquidation procedures, we shall survey briefly the volume and causes of business failures and two legal factors— exemptions and release or discharge of debtors—involved in most non-corporate liquidations.

## BUSINESS FAILURES

The annual number of business failures and the liabilities involved vary from year to year with the cyclical fluctuations of business. The peak year for failures during the past half century was 1933,

ILLUSTRATION 19-1.   Business Failures in the United States, 1945-1960

| Year | Number in Business (Thousands) | Number of Failures (Thousands) | Aggregate Gross Liabilities (Millions) | Per Cent of Total Failing | Average Gross Liability (Thousands) |
|------|------|------|------|------|------|
| 1945..... | 1,909 | 0.8 | $ 30.2 | a | $37.5 |
| 1946..... | 2,142 | 1.1 | 67.3 | 0.1 | 59.7 |
| 1947..... | 2,405 | 3.5 | 204.6 | 0.1 | 58.9 |
| 1948..... | 2,550 | 5.3 | 234.6 | 0.2 | 44.7 |
| 1949..... | 2,679 | 9.2 | 308.1 | 0.3 | 33.3 |
| 1950..... | 2,687 | 9.1 | 248.3 | 0.3 | 27.1 |
| 1951..... | 2,608 | 8.1 | 259.5 | 0.3 | 32.2 |
| 1952..... | 2,637 | 7.6 | 283.3 | 0.3 | 37.2 |
| 1953..... | 2,667 | 8.9 | 394.2 | 0.3 | 44.5 |
| 1954..... | 2,632 | 11.1 | 462.6 | 0.4 | 41.7 |
| 1955..... | 2,633 | 11.0 | 449.4 | 0.4 | 41.0 |
| 1956..... | 2,647 | 12.7 | 562.7 | 0.4 | 44.4 |
| 1957..... | 2,652 | 13.7 | 615.3 | 0.5 | 44.8 |
| 1958..... | 2,675 | 15.0 | 728.3 | 0.5 | 48.7 |
| 1959..... | 2,708 | 14.1 | 692.8 | 0.5 | 49.3 |
| 1960..... | 2,708 | 15.4 | 938.6 | 0.6 | 60.8 |

a Less than 0.05%
Source: Dun & Bradstreet, Inc.

when they numbered 31,822, with gross liabilities of $928 million. The record low year for failures was 1945, when only 800 enterprises failed, with gross liabilities of $30 million.

As shown in Illustration 19-1, since 1945 the proportion of business failures in any year has been only a fraction of a per cent of the total of business concerns as listed by Dun & Bradstreet. A disturbing consideration is that throughout this period this proportion has slowly but persistently increased—from less than 0.05 per cent in 1945 to 0.6 per cent in 1960. The average liability of business failures, after touching a low of $27,000 in 1950, has also exhibited a rising trend; in 1960 the figure was $61,000. One third to one half of failing businesses have no distributable assets upon liquidation. The proportion of assets to liabilities for the others varies widely in different years.

The actual salvage that unsecured mercantile creditors usually obtain from their failure accounts is invariably much less than the assets remaining to the bankrupt enterprise upon adjudication. Secured creditors must be given the assets to which they can establish their special claims. Certain priority creditors must be satisfied in full. Substantial administrative expenses and fees have to be paid. Only then, if any assets remain, may the ordinary mercantile creditors recover some small fraction of their claims—frequently not more than a few cents on the dollar.

### Causes

Various attempts have been made to determine the basic causes of business failures. While no generally valid conclusions have been reached which would cover every single case, such studies have resulted in narrowing down the approach to business failures to the most frequent cause of disaster: *inefficient management* due largely to inexperience.[1] Other factors may be contributory forces. The general business situation in the different phases of the business cycle, for example, cannot be ignored. There will always be a larger number of failures in periods of recession than in a boom. Some business enterprises, moreover, may be more strongly affected by such fluctuations than others. But the cyclical impact will rarely be the whole story, though many failing buyers may blame their misfortune entirely on it.

Inefficient management leading to failure may take many forms—poor product planning, poor buying, bad financial management, weak production management, unsound personnel policy, bad marketing policy, inadequate promotion, or any combination of these. The business owner may have misjudged the requirements of the business and his own capability to cope with them. Too many people, for example, think that retailing success depends only on the purchase of merchandise offered to them by a salesman who may be using high-pressure methods, and then being personally available to sell the goods to the public. They do not realize that even small-scale retail business has become a technical art, involving skilled buying, effective stock control, promotional selling, careful financing, and sound accounting control. Inefficient operators may hold out in flush times, even in the face of competition. They are bound to collapse in slack periods when their deficits rise and absorb their capital. It is not surprising that the greatest incidence of business failures occurs in the small retail and service fields where inefficient management is most common.

---

[1] Dun & Bradstreet, Inc., *Survival Qualities of American Business,* New York, 1951, pp. 8 and 9; *The Failure Record Through 1959—A Comprehensive Failure Study by Location, Industry, Age, Size and Cause,* New York, 1960, p. 12.

Inadequate capital is another frequent cause of business failures. Too many enterprises start on a "shoestring." Some succeed in accumulating the necessary capital over the years by retaining profits. Others remain in their initial precarious financial position, highly vulnerable to minor set-backs. New enterprises are not the only ones that may lack the necessary "buffer" that a comfortable capital basis provides. A growing business may make the mistake of financing its expansion by increasing its indebtedness. It may intend to correct this faulty financial balance at a later date by plowing back earnings, but it may never have the opportunity to do so. A misjudgment in a single major transaction, or external circumstances, may ruin it while it is still waiting to strengthen its capital position.

Dishonesty and fraud account for some insolvencies. The number of cases where they are listed as the main or sole cause of failure is small. The true proportion is unquestionably higher, but cannot be known, since only the frauds discovered and convicted are recorded, and many undoubtedly go undetected.

## EXEMPTIONS

Not only the remaining business assets of an insolvent unincorporated business but also the personal estates of its owner or partnership owners are subject to the claims of the business creditors. Not all the owners' personal assets, however, must be included in the business liquidation. Every state has prescribed, by constitutional or statutory provision, certain items or monetary amounts that an insolvent person may retain as against his creditors. These are "exemptions." Though established by state law, they are recognized by the federal Bankruptcy Act, and the property covered is beyond the reach of bankruptcy creditors.

All but four states and the District of Columbia grant a "homestead" exemption—freedom from seizure by creditors of the value of a dwelling place, and in some cases a farm, owned and occupied by the debtor. The exempt homestead value differs widely from state to state, ranging from $500 in Georgia to $10,000 in Nevada. Where the homestead exemption applies to farms, the allowance is usually 160 acres.

Besides the homestead, wearing apparel and household goods of debtors and their families are usually exempt up to specified amounts. Tools and equipment used in a trade or profession are also commonly covered by exemption laws. Particular articles of many kinds—from church pews and burial lots to books, musical instruments, and domestic animals—are specifically mentioned in some exemption statutes. In some states the personal property exemption is stated as a certain value—$400, $500, $750,

$1,000, or more—of cash or personal articles selected by the debtor. Wages are substantially exempted in most states.[2]

## DISCHARGE OR RELEASE OF DEBTORS

Liquidation proceedings against an incorporated business commonly involve dissolution or abandonment of the corporation, and the creditors have no further interest in it, regardless of how little or how much they have salvaged from the liquidation. Individual or partnership owners of insolvent, noncorporate businesses live on after such businesses have been liquidated and may subsequently acquire assets. Unless their owners were discharged by law or released by agreement of the creditors from debt balances remaining unpaid after liquidation of their insolvent businesses, their after-acquired assets would be subject to claim by the creditors of the liquidated businesses. Owners of insolvent, unincorporated businesses are obviously sharply interested in freeing themselves from continuing liability for debt balances remaining unpaid after liquidation. Creditors of such businesses would prefer such liability to be preserved, on the chance that subsequent recovery might be realized upon it.

Only through a federal bankruptcy proceeding can the owner of an insolvent, unincorporated business obtain a *discharge* that frees him from liability for debt balances remaining unpaid after liquidation.[3] As an incident of an out-of-court or state-court liquidation, however, the creditors of an insolvent, noncorporate debtor may agree to *release* him from unpaid debt balances.

Where the liquidation of an unincorporated business will be fairly simple, and where the creditors have full faith and trust in the debtor and each other, they are likely to prefer out-of-court or state-court liquidation to federal bankruptcy procedure, because of the greater freedom of liquidation procedure and the lower costs, which mean larger proportionate recoveries for them. A debtor not satisfied with his creditors' proposed treatment of him can always force a federal bankruptcy procedure by filing a voluntary petition. He is thus in a position to compel his creditors to agree to release him from continuing liability on unpaid balances, as a condition to *his* agreeing to forego federal bankruptcy procedure. Indeed, if he is a shrewd bargainer, he can often, in addition, obtain their consent to his retaining some part of his personal estate, which otherwise would have to go in its entirety, except for the exemp-

---

[2] There has been a pronounced trend in recent years toward increasing the amounts of property and wages exempted from execution. In 1959 alone, nine states liberalized their exemptions (*Credit Manual of Commercial Laws, 1960*, p. xlii).

[3] Corporations, though, may apply for a "discharge" under the Bankruptcy Act. The procedure for noncorporate and corporate discharge is described in a later part of this chapter.

tion allowance, to satisfy the business creditors. The "trading advantage" in this bargaining is not entirely on the debtor's side, since the creditors can advance the argument that an out-of-court liquidation will generally be construed as less of a blot on his credit record, if he subsequently establishes another business, than would a federal bankruptcy proceeding.

## OUT-OF-COURT LIQUIDATION

Three out-of-court liquidation procedures are available when the legal aspects of the debtor's obligations are not complicated, and when the creditors trust the debtor and each other. These are liquidation by the debtor under auspices of the creditors, common law assignment, and corporate dissolution.

The two great advantages of these out-of-court liquidations are their low cost, and the liberal choice of methods for disposing of the debtor's assets. As a consequence, the creditors are usually able to make higher proportionate recoveries than are possible under either state-court or federal bankruptcy procedures. Their weaknesses are that the creditors are vulnerable to fraud by the debtor or the person liquidating his business, and that there must be unanimous agreement among the creditors. Dissenters could commonly block an out-of-court liquidation by attaching the debtor's assets in the hands of the assignee or obtaining liens against them, or by forcing state-court receivership or bankruptcy procedures.

### Liquidation by debtor under auspices of the creditors

If all creditors consent, an insolvent debtor may undertake liquidation of his business on their behalf, paying them pro rata from the proceeds of the liquidation. He may do this in any ways approved by the creditors, including bulk sale of his business assets subject to the provisions of the bulk sales law of the state.

Such a liquidation procedure costs the creditors nothing in outlay or time. Obviously, however, it is applicable only if all the creditors have complete trust in the debtor's good faith, since they have practically no protection against fraud on his part, except in states which have bulk sales laws patterned on the original Pennsylvania statute which held a bulk buyer responsible for distributing bulk sale proceeds to his creditors. A creditors' committee, including an adjustment bureau representative, may be formed in connection with such a liquidation. Although its functions are usually limited it can render valuable services to the creditors by listing inventory, checking creditors' claims, advising on procedure of disposal, and arranging for a meeting to be held for final creditor approval. By arrangement between debtor, purchaser, and interested creditors a participating adjustment bureau may act as escrow agent—depository and distribution agent for funds to be shared among creditors.

## Common-law assignment

Under a common-law assignment for benefit of creditors, title to the assets of an insolvent business is transferred to an assignee or trustee, who undertakes their liquidation and the distribution of the proceeds among the creditors.

Appointment of an assignee, and determination of his powers, is made by the debtor. The latter may, or may not, consult with his creditors before taking this step. He may, or may not, provide for bonding of the assignee. The assignee may operate completely on his own responsibility under the debtor's appointment, or he may accept and be guided by the advice of a creditors' committee.

Transfer of the debtor's assets to the assignee may be accomplished in some states by a deed of trust, in others by the execution of chattel mortgages or power of attorney. Customarily the assignment is accompanied by a schedule of assets, and by a schedule of creditors and the liabilities owed to them. The duties and responsibilities of the assignee may be detailed, or he may be left to his own discretion subject only to his obligations as a trustee under equity law. Provision may be made in the assignment instrument for the assignee's compensation, or this may subsequently be settled by agreement between the assignee and the creditors, or the statutory compensation for assignees may be tacitly assumed by all parties. No filing of this assignment instrument is necessary.

If all the creditors agree to the assignment arrangement, the assignee takes over the debtor's property. Under the terms of the assignment instrument, or by agreement with the creditors, he may operate it as a going concern for a while to sell off remaining stock through regular trade channels. Otherwise he seeks to dispose of the stock by bulk sale, and the equipment and fixtures by whatever means seem most expedient. In any case, he presses collection of all debts owed to the debtor, and he notifies the creditors to file their claims.

The assignee may make partial distributions on a pro rata basis to the creditors as the liquidation proceeds, or he may hold all receipts from the liquidation until it is completed and then make a single distribution. When the liquidation is completed and all distributions are made, the assignee presents a final accounting of his office to the debtor and the creditors. If the creditors accept this accounting, the assignee is ordinarily thereby discharged of his office.

Creditors are generally fairly well protected under common-law assignments. The assignee, though appointed by the debtor, is a trustee operating for the creditors, and they have equity remedies against him for improper actions. Indeed, the most vulnerable party under a common-law assignment is the assignee, since he is generally personally liable to the creditors for the propriety of all his actions in connection with the assignment. Still, although the creditors have remedies against fraud on the part of the debtor or the assignee if it is *discovered*, one or more creditors in any group are likely to wonder whether some *hidden* fraud may not be perpetrated on them. Or they may question the competence of an assignee in whose appointment they have had no say. For one reason or another, many common-law assignments are upset, and the liquidation procedures brought under state or federal judicial supervision. Consequently, this liquidation procedure finds favor in only a few states.

### Corporate dissolution

This third procedure is obviously available only for insolvent corporations.

Some of the state corporation laws provide for some form of verification of the distribution of a dissolving corporation's assets among its creditors. In such states, if the management of an insolvent corporation and its creditors are in agreement, these corporation dissolution procedures may be used as an instrument of liquidation. Where there is complete trust, the creditors may leave the entire liquidation procedure up to the management of the debtor corporation; or the members of a creditors' committee or the officials of an adjustment bureau may be appointed directors of the corporation for the period of its dissolution. The corporation addresses the appropriate dissolution petition to the secretary of state, and the liquidation and dissolution are carried through in accordance with the statutory provision. In some states, as indicated below, corporate dissolutions are effected through state court receiverships.

For this procedure also, unanimity among the creditors is essential, since dissenters could force bankruptcy or state court receivership.

## STATE INSOLVENCY PROCEDURES

The states all have insolvency laws that antedate the federal bankruptcy law. Like the federal act, these include liquidation procedures that bind creditor minorities by the will of the majority and discharge debtors from balances remaining unpaid after completion of liquidation. By constitutional provision, the federal law superseded all these state laws with respect to provisions for discharge of debtors. State insolvency procedures remain available, however, for cases of corporate insolvency where the corporate entity is to be abandoned and for noncorporate insolvencies where all the creditors agree to release the debtor from liabilities remaining unpaid after liquidation. Two such state insolvency procedures, stemming either from specific statutory provision or from general judicial law, are available—statutory assignment and state court receivership.

These state insolvency procedures may be more costly than out-of-court procedures, but they afford the creditors more protection against fraud or misdoing on the part of the debtor or assignee. Compared with federal bankruptcy procedure, they may be considerably less costly, but have five shortcomings. (1) Unanimity of the creditors is essential, since dissenting minorities can upset the procedure by forcing federal bankruptcy action. (2) A statutory assignee may experience some difficulty in obtaining control of the debtor's property in other states. (3) The debtor cannot be examined against his will in some jurisdictions. (4) Other protections against fraud are lacking or less effective. (5) Judicial discharge of a debtor from any remaining unpaid balance of his debt is not possible. Still, there are many "friendly" liquidations where these shortcomings of the state procedures have no bearing, and considerable recourse is had to them, particularly the statutory assignment, despite the alternative availability of federal bankruptcy procedure.

### Statutory assignment

In some of the states which cover assignments for benefit of creditors by statutory provision, the statutory procedure is exclusive and replaces the common-law assignments previously described. In the other states both assignment procedures are available. Statutory assignments are identical with common-law assignments, except for the following details:

1. The provisions of the assignment instrument are prescribed, and it must be filed in an appropriate public office.
2. The assignee or trustee usually must be bonded.
3. Creditors may have the appropriate equity court replace the original assignee. In order to avoid tensions between creditors and assignee, it is a growing practice to make a creditors' representative—an individual or a qualified adjustment bureau—the original or replacement assignee.
4. The assignee's final accounting must be made to the appropriate equity court.

### State court receivership

Appropriate courts of equity in many states are authorized, upon petition of the creditors of an insolvent business, to appoint a receiver for such business. In some states a judicial receivership is part of the statutory machinery for effecting liquidations of insolvent companies through corporate dissolution.

A state court receiver operates in liquidations in all respects like a statutory assignee. He is, however, an officer of the court, and neither the debtor nor the creditors have any say in his appointment.

## LIQUIDATION OF INSOLVENT BUSINESSES UNDER FEDERAL BANKRUPTCY LAW

Article I, Section 8, of the federal Constitution provides that "Congress shall have power . . . to establish . . . uniform laws on the subject of bankruptcy throughout the United States."

Four times bankruptcy laws were enacted by Congress under this Constitutional authorization—in 1800, in 1841, in 1867, and in 1898. The first three were all short-lived. The Bankruptcy Act of 1898, frequently amended, is still in force, and from all indications will continue indefinitely to be part of our federal system of law. Important revisions of the federal bankruptcy procedure were made by the Chandler Act of 1938. In its present form, the Bankruptcy Act serves four purposes with regard to liquidating insolvent businesses:

1. It aids creditors by providing a procedure whereby insolvent debtors can be liquidated with proper safeguards against fraud by the debtor during or prior to the liquidation, and with equitable distribution of the debtor's available assets among his creditors.

2. It benefits insolvent debtors who cannot effect recovery through an adjustment, by discharging them from the remainder of their liabilities after their assets have been distributed. They are thus enabled to start new business or employee careers, unhampered by the burden of antecedent debt.

3. It helps both creditors and debtor by establishing judicial jurisdiction over creditors and over the debtor's assets throughout the country.

4. It serves the general public by aiding the business community as indicated above.

### Prerequisites

When a business is insolvent in the bankruptcy sense, *i.e.*, with liabilities exceeding assets, there are two ways under the Bankruptcy Act for accomplishing its liquidation: (1) by voluntary petition filed by the debtor, and (2) by involuntary petition filed by the creditors. Such petitions are filed in the federal district court for the district of the bankrupt's residence or principal place of business.

A voluntary petition may be filed by any businessman, partnership, or corporation, except municipal, railroad, insurance, or banking corporations, or building and loan associations. This petition must allege, among other matters, that the debtor "owes debts which he is unable to pay in

1060—Corporation Debtor's Petition in Bankruptcy.
Bankruptcy Act of 1938.

JULIUS BLUMBERG, INC., LAW BLANK PUBLISHERS
80 EXCHANGE PLACE AT BROADWAY, NEW YORK

In the District Court of the United States for the   SOUTHERN         District of   NEW YORK

In the matter of

OVAL CORPORATION

Bankrupt.

In Bankruptcy

No. 41824

## PETITION

To the Honorable

Judge of the District Court of the United States for the

**Southern** District of **New York**         :

THE PETITION of **OVAL CORPORATION,**

a corporation engaged in the business of **conducting a luncheonette,**

which corporation has not been known by any other name or trade name for the past six years.

RESPECTFULLY REPRESENTS:

1. Your petitioner is a **domestic**          *corporation organized and existing under the laws of the State of **New York**          and has had its principal office and its principal place of business at **10 Oval Avenue, New York City,** within the above judicial district, for a longer portion of the six months immediately preceding the filing of this petition than in any other judicial district.

2. Your petitioner owes debts and is willing to surrender all its property for the benefit of its creditors, except such as is exempt by law, and desires to obtain the benefit of the Act of Congress relating to Bankruptcy; and that its Board of Directors has duly authorized such acts on its part and the statements herein made in its behalf.

3. The schedule hereto annexed, marked Schedule A, and verified by the oath of the undersigned officer of your petitioner, contains a full and true statement of all its debts, and so far as it is possible to ascertain, the names and places of residence of its creditors, and such further statements concerning said debts as are required by the provisions of said Act.

4. The schedule hereto annexed, marked Schedule B, and verified by the oath of the undersigned officer of your petitioner, contains an accurate inventory of all its property, real and personal, and such further statements concerning said property as are required by the provisions of said Act.

WHEREFORE, your petitioner prays that it may be adjudged by the court to be a bankrupt within the purview of said Act.

OVAL CORPORATION
*Petitioner*

By *Richard Rutherstone*
Richard Rutherstone
**President** of said corporation

(SEAL)

H. Burton Stanley
*Attorney*
1673 Broadway
New York City

STATE OF   NEW YORK
COUNTY OF   NEW YORK   } ss.:

RICHARD RUTHERSTONE
being duly sworn deposes and says that he is the
**President** of OVAL CORPORATION
the petitioner named in the foregoing petition, and does hereby make solemn oath that the statements contained therein are true, according to the best of his knowledge, information and belief; that the reason why this verification is made by deponent and not by the petitioner herein, is that said petitioner is a corporation; and that deponent is the officer of said corporation duly authorized by its Board of Directors to execute and verify said petition on its behalf.

Subscribed and sworn to before me this
**19th** day of **February**          1962     *Richard Rutherstone*

**Mary Roe**                              RICHARD RUTHERSTONE

**500 Elk Avenue, New York 1, N.Y.**
*(Official Character)*

N. B.—Oaths to the above petition, and the schedules thereto annexed, may be administered by officers authorized to administer oaths in proceedings before Courts of the United States, or under the laws of the State where the same are to be taken; and diplomatic or consular officers of the United States in any foreign country.
Petitioner's attorney cannot act as notary.
*Moneyed, Business or Commercial.

ILLUSTRATION 19-2. Form for Voluntary Bankruptcy Petition

full and that he is willing to surrender all his property for the benefit of his creditors except such as is exempt by law." The debtor, in this petition, also "prays that he may be adjudged by the court to be a bankrupt within the purview of said (bankruptcy) act" (see Illustration 19-2). He adds to his petition two schedules, one listing all his liabilities and the creditors to whom they are owed, the other containing an inventory of all his assets.

An involuntary petition of bankruptcy may be filed against any business that could file a voluntary petition, given the following circumstances:

1. The debtor must owe debts totalling $1,000 or more.

2. If there are fewer than 12 creditors, any one creditor with a claim of at least $500 may file the petition; if there are 12 or more creditors, the petition must be signed by three or more with provable claims totalling $500 or over.

3. Within four months preceding the filing of the petition, the debtor must have committed one or more of the six acts of bankruptcy indicated below, and the petition must allege such commission.

The six acts of bankruptcy, of which one or more must have been committed by the debtor before an involuntary petition of bankruptcy may be filed against him, are:

1. Fraudulent conveyance, transfer, concealment, or removal of assets by the debtor, *while insolvent*, with intent to hinder, delay, or defraud his creditors. (As defense to this allegation the debtor may prove that he was solvent at the time.)

2. Transfer by the debtor, *while insolvent*, of any portion of his property to one or more of his creditors, thereby giving such creditors a preference or an advantage over the others. This would constitute a preference. (Payments made within four months of the bankruptcy, even though in the regular course of business, may be deemed such a preference if the effect is to give the creditor a greater percentage of his claim than other creditors of the same class receive. No intent to prefer has to be established. The mere act of transfer or payment constitutes the preference.)

3. Suffering or permitting, *while insolvent*, any creditor to obtain a *lien* upon any of his property through legal proceedings, and failing to vacate or discharge the lien within thirty days from the date thereof or at least five days before the date set for any sale or other disposition of property. (A businessman permitting the establishment of liens by certain creditors on his property is in effect passively allowing them preferences as against other creditors. Note that this third act of bankruptcy provides a means whereby creditors may force an obdurate insolvent debtor into bankruptcy. Any one of the creditors can bring suit against the debtor and obtain a judgment lien against his property upon which execution could be enforced. Upon his being unable to vacate this judgment lien

within 30 days' time, the other creditors can file an involuntary bankruptcy petition alleging the third bankruptcy act.)

4. Making a general *assignment* by the debtor *for the benefit of creditors*, whether or not he is insolvent at the time. (This provision enables a creditor, or a group of them, mistrustful or dissatisfied with a debtor's attempt at liquidation through assignment, to transfer the whole liquidation proceeding to the bankruptcy court where their interests will be more adequately safeguarded.)

5. Procuring, permitting, or suffering by the debtor, voluntarily or involuntarily, *while insolvent* in either the bankruptcy or equity sense, appointment of a *receiver* or *trustee* to take charge of his property. (This provision, like the fourth, enables dissatisfied creditors to remove receivership liquidation or adjustment proceedings from the debtor's control, or from the control of some other group of creditors, to the bankruptcy court.)

6. *Admission in writing* of the debtor's inability to pay his debts and his *willingness* to be adjudged a bankrupt, without regard to whether he is insolvent or solvent at the time.

### Adjudication

Upon the filing of a petition of involuntary bankruptcy, a subpoena (equivalent of a summons) and a copy of the petition are served upon the debtor. He has ten days, unless the court [4] sets a longer period, to make an answer and state any defenses, such as denial of the court's jurisdiction, or denial of having committed the alleged acts of bankruptcy, or allegation that he was not insolvent when the acts were committed. If the debtor files such an answer he is then entitled to a trial by jury on the issues of law and fact thus raised. Ordinarily, however, debtors do not contest involuntary petitions of bankruptcy, and are adjudicated bankrupts by default in answering, without the necessity of a trial.

### The referee in bankruptcy

Upon adjudication, the case is transferred by the court to a *referee* in bankruptcy who thereafter acts as the court in all present and future matters affecting the case. We encountered this referee earlier in the adjustment procedure under Chapter XI of the federal Bankruptcy Act (see page 350 of this volume); but here he acts in liquidations. The court appoints him and may re-appoint him, for a six-year term, at an annual salary up to $15,000 for full-time and $7,500 for part-time work as a referee.[5] He must be a competent, disinterested person, not connected

---

[4] The term "court" in descriptions of judicial procedure refers to the presiding judge.
[5] Referees' Salary Act of 1946 as amended in 1952 and 1956.

with any of the parties involved. His principal duties as an officer of the court, as enumerated by the Act, are to:

1. notify all parties interested in the proceeding of all steps taken in connection with it;
2. direct the bankrupt to file schedules of his assets, liabilities and creditors, or to prepare such schedules and statements himself if the bankrupt should fail to do so;
3. examine and, if necessary, direct the amendment of all schedules and statements required to be filed in connection with the proceeding;
4. declare the dividends to be distributed to the creditors and prepare the requisite dividend sheets;
5. keep all records pertinent to the proceeding, and furnish such information as is requested by the parties to the proceeding.

### The trustee and receiver

The person next in importance to the referee in a bankruptcy proceeding is the *trustee* [6] who takes custody of the debtor's assets after he has been adjudged a bankrupt and disposes of them for the benefit of the creditors. He is usually elected by the recognized creditors at their first official meeting. A majority vote in number and amount of allowed claims is necessary. He must be approved by the court. He may be appointed by the court if the creditors cannot reach the necessary majority for his election at that meeting. The trustee acquires title, as of date of the filing of the bankruptcy petition, to all the bankrupt's property including (a) any powers or rights of action which the bankrupt might have exercised to his own benefit, (b) any property transferred in fraud of creditors, (c) any property held by an assignee for benefit of creditors appointed under an assignment preceding the bankruptcy action, and (d) all property which vests in the bankrupt within six months after his bankruptcy by bequest, devise, inheritance, or succession.

The following are the main responsibilities of the trustee:

1. examining the bankrupt at the first creditors' meeting, if he has not theretofore been fully examined, in order to determine whether he has other assets than are indicated in the schedules he has filed, and discovering whether there have been fraudulent or preferential transfers or liens;
2. taking possession of the bankrupt's property, reacquiring possession of any fraudulently or preferentially transferred property, and setting aside any preferential liens;

---

[6] Note that the trustee and the receiver are usually individuals; but they may also be adjustment bureaus or corporations authorized by their charter or by law to act in such capacity.

3. collecting all debts owed to the bankrupt, bringing suit to do so where necessary;
4. converting all other assets of the debtor into cash on the most favorable terms and depositing such funds in authorized depositories;
5. examining all proofs of claims submitted by creditors and making appropriate objections;
6. paying out dividends to the creditors within ten days of their declaration by the referee;
7. opposing the discharge of the bankrupt if it appears advisable to do so and examining the bankrupt at any hearing upon objections to discharge;
8. filing a report within one month of appointment, and every two months thereafter, and submitting a detailed statement of his administration at the final creditors' meeting.

A third person may be engaged in the bankruptcy procedure—the *receiver*. He may be appointed by the judge upon application of any creditor [7] to safeguard the creditors' interest during the considerable time which sometimes elapses between the filing of the petition in bankruptcy and the election of a trustee by the creditors at their first meeting. The receiver's chief duty is to preserve the debtor's assets. He therefore usually takes possession of the debtor's business, in some cases also operates it. He prosecutes or defends any action relating to the business and institutes actions on behalf of the business. Should the petition of bankruptcy be dismissed, the receiver turns back the business to the debtor. If the adjudication in bankruptcy is made and a trustee is elected, the receiver subsequently surrenders his functions to the trustee.

Compensation of trustees and receivers in bankruptcy is not based on a fixed salary schedule as is the payment of the referee. Trustees' and receivers' compensation is determined according to detailed provisions of the law, by the amount of their receipts. They are allowed extra remuneration if their function includes operation of the debtor's business, or if they serve otherwise than as mere custodians of the debtor's assets.

### The first creditors' meeting

Not sooner than ten days and not later than 30 days after a bankruptcy adjudication and the appointment of a referee, the latter calls, upon at least ten days' notice, the first meeting of the creditors. Their names are obtained from Schedule A filed by the debtor in case of a voluntary petition, or from a list furnished by the petitioning creditors to the referee in

---

[7] Note that the creditor filing an application for such a receiver in involuntary cases has to post a bond; so has the receiver, in order to qualify for the appointment by the judge.

case of an involuntary petition. Notification of the creditors is made both by mail and by publication.

A preliminary, unofficial meeting of creditors may have preceded the official one. It may have been called by a recognized adjustment bureau for whose advice and services a creditors' group is apt to ask. At such a meeting at the bureau's office, the circumstances of the case are surveyed, and the creditors are able to discuss further tactics. They may predetermine the composition of a creditors' committee and other steps to be taken.

Creditors may submit proof of their claims to the referee prior to the first official creditors' meeting, or at the opening of it (see Illustration 19-3). After that, they may file proofs of claim within six months, to be passed upon by the trustee. At the first official creditors' meeting the referee examines the proofs of claim hitherto submitted in the presence of all the creditors attending the meeting. Objections to any particular claim may be raised by the other creditors. The acceptance of these proofs of claim establishes the right of the creditors who submitted them to vote at the meeting. Creditors who have not filed their proofs of claim at that time, have no voting right.

The next business of this meeting is usually the election of the trustee who then becomes the center of the proceedings. Very frequently, the creditors elect as trustee a representative of the adjustment bureau that advised them during the preliminary stages of the bankruptcy procedure. A creditors' committee may also be chosen at this time, but this is not compulsory. Such a committee, if elected, has no control over the administration of the debtor's assets. It does have the right to advise the trustee and to be heard by the court on any question affecting the proceeding.

Another item on the program of the first official creditors' meeting is the examination of the debtor, to disclose any concealed assets or fraudulent transfers or liens. This examination may be conducted either by the referee prior to the election of the trustee, or by the trustee after he has been elected. The creditors present have the right to join in the examination. The bankrupt has the duty, under the law, to afford all cooperation to the referee or trustee and the creditors in this examination. Should he prove recalcitrant and refuse to divulge pertinent information requested of him, he may be denied discharge or be referred to the judge for commitment for contempt of court. He is also subject to arrest if he fails to appear for examination as ordered by the court, provided that the court finds his failure to appear contemptuous. The same applies to any other person being examined on the acts, conduct, or property of the bankrupt.

### Subsequent procedure

From this time on until the final creditors' meeting at which the bank-

## IN THE DISTRICT COURT OF THE UNITED STATES
## FOR THE   SOUTHERN   DISTRICT OF NEW YORK

*IN THE MATTER*
*OF*
**OVAL CORPORATION**

*Bankrupt*

*IN BANKRUPTCY*

No. 41824

STATE OF NEW YORK
COUNTY OF NEW YORK } ss.:

**WILLIAM BENJAMIN**    *of No.* 63 Crosley Street
*in* New York City   *County of* New York   *State of* New York
*being duly sworn, deposes and says:*

1. (a) *INDIVIDUAL*

       *That   he hereinafter designates himself as claimant (or as appears below)*

   (b) *CO-PARTNERSHIP*

       *That   he is a member of*
*a co-partnership, hereinafter designated as claimant, composed of deponent and*
          *of*

*and carrying on business at No.*
*County of*       *State of*       *(or as appears below)*

   (c) *CORPORATION*

       *That   he is the       of*
*a corporation organized and existing under the laws of the State of       and carrying on business*
*at No.       in*
*County of       State of       and is duly authorized to make this*
*proof of claim on its behalf. Said corporation is hereinafter designated as the claimant.*

2.    *That the above named Bankrupt was at and before the filing by (or against) said Bankrupt of the petition for adjudication of Bankruptcy, and still is, justly and truly indebted (or liable) to claimant in the sum of $* 479.28

3.    *That the consideration of said debt (or liability) is as follows: goods, wares and merchandise sold and delivered to the said Bankrupt at the special instance and request of said Bankrupt at the agreed price ̶a̶n̶d̶ ̶r̶e̶a̶s̶o̶n̶a̶b̶l̶e̶ ̶v̶a̶l̶u̶e̶ set forth in the annexed statement which is made a part hereof.*

4.    *That no part of said debt (or liability) has been paid. That there are no set-offs or counterclaims to said debt (or liability). That claimant does not hold, and has not, nor has any person by his order, or to deponent's knowledge or belief for his use had or received any security or securities for said debt (or liability). That the instrument upon which said debt is founded is attached hereto. That no note or other negotiable instrument has been received for such account or any part thereof (or that the said debt is evidenced by a note (or other negotiable instrument), which is attached hereto); that no judgment has been rendered thereon, except*

### *POWER OF ATTORNEY*

*To* MARK H. CRAIG, Attorney at Law, 270 Broadway, New York City *or representative:*
*The undersigned,* William Benjamin
*of* 63 Crosley Street, New York   *County of* New York   *State of* New York
*does hereby authorize you, or any one of you, with full power of substitution, to attend all meetings of creditors of the bankrupt aforesaid, and all adjournments thereof, at the places and times appointed by the court, and for the undersigned, and in the name of the undersigned to vote for or against any proposal or resolution that may be then submitted under the Act of Congress relating to bankruptcy, to vote for a trustee or trustees of the estate of the said bankrupt and for a committee of creditors, to accept any arrangement or wage-earner's plan proposed by said bankrupt in satisfaction of his debts, and to receive payment of dividends, and payment or delivery of money or of other consideration due the undersigned under such arrangement or wage-earner's plan, and for any other purpose in the undersigned's interests whatsoever; and with like powers to attend and vote at any other meeting or meetings of creditors, or sitting or sittings of the court, which may be held therein for any of the purposes aforesaid.*

*IN WITNESS WHEREOF, the undersigned has hereunto signed his name and affixed his seal, or caused these presents to be executed by a duly authorized officer, and its seal to be hereunto affixed, the* 1st *day of* March   19 62.

Sworn to before me this 1st   day
of March   , 1962 , *said subscriber
being known to me to be the person described in and who
signed and swore to the above instruments and duly acknowledged that he executed them and was authorized to
execute them.*
**Mary Roe**
500 Elk Avenue, New York 1, N.Y.
*Notary Public or Commissioner of Deeds*

*William Benjamin* (L. S.)
*Sign name of individual, partner or officer here*
**WILLIAM BENJAMIN**
_____ (L. S.)
*Sign name of firm here*

*Annex duplicate of your invoice
Corporation affix seal here*

ILLUSTRATION 19-3.   Form for Bankruptcy Proof of Claim

rupt is discharged, the procedure is primarily in the hands of the trustee, advised by the creditors' committee if such has been elected. Further meetings may be called at the discretion of the referee, or upon written request made by one-fourth of the proven creditors and signed by a majority in number and amount of such creditors. But these special meetings are exceptional. They are called only if some serious unforeseen contingency arises or if the creditors believe that the trustee is not fulfilling his duties.

As the trustee gains possession of the bankrupt's property, he proceeds to convert it into cash if the receiver has not already done so. He collects receivables, not with persuasion like a credit manager who wants to keep a customer's good will, but applying all permissible pressure, such as warning of instant suit if immediate payment is not forthcoming. He institutes suit if the warning is not heeded. If examination of the debtor or another person connected with the debtor has disclosed transfers of property or liens voidable because of fraud or preference, the trustee brings suit to recover the property or to void the lien. With regard to the sale of merchandise and fixtures, the trustee has some discretion as to the methods to be employed. One or more appraisers are appointed by the court to set a fair value upon such property. Upon authorization of the referee and with the advice of the creditors' committee if such exists, the trustee may arrange bulk sales of the merchandise and fixtures, or he may sell them through auction or other approved methods. In no case, however, may the property be liquidated without consent of the court at less than 75 per cent of its appraised value. The funds collected by the trustee are deposited in an approved bank.

The trustee does not have to wait until all the bankrupt's property has been liquidated before asking the court for permission to make a partial distribution to the creditors. He does usually wait until the six-month period is over in which creditors may still file proofs of claim to be approved or rejected by him. In practice, no disbursements are made before this period has lapsed, although the law permits a distribution of funds by the trustee upon authorization of the referee within 30 days after the first official creditors' meeting if the funds in the hands of the trustee exceed 5 per cent of the allowed claims in excess of priority debts, and thereafter whenever the funds available to the trustee exceed 10 per cent of allowed claims. A final distribution is made on the closing of the proceeding.

Ordinary business creditors of a bankrupt do not have first claim upon the funds that accrue to a trustee in bankruptcy. The following classes of claims have priority over all others:

1. All costs associated with the bankruptcy proceeding.
2. Wages and salaries, up to $600 per claimant, earned by employees of the bankrupt within the three months preceding filing of the petition.

3. Creditors' costs incurred in (a) successfully preventing the bankrupt's discharge, or (b) producing evidence resulting in conviction of a person for a criminal offense under the Bankruptcy Act.
4. Federal, state, and local taxes owed by the bankrupt.
5. Any debts given priority under federal law, and rent owed by the bankrupt for the three months prior to filing of the petition provided such rent claim is given priority by state law.

Only after these priority claims have been satisfied out of funds in possession of the trustee can he make distributions to the general creditors of the bankrupt.

A final meeting of the creditors is called, upon 30 days' notice, when the trustee has completed his liquidation and distributions and the entire proceeding is ready to be closed. At this meeting the trustee's final account comes before the scrutiny of both the creditors and the referee.

### Discharge of the bankrupt

Adjudication of any person (other than a corporation) as a bankrupt automatically constitutes an application for his discharge. A corporation must file a petition for discharge within six months of its adjudication.

Discharge releases a bankrupt from all debts except the following:

1. Taxes owing to state or local governments.
2. Liabilities for obtaining money or property by false pretenses and for wilful and malicious injuries to person or property.
3. Unscheduled claims.
4. Claims against the bankrupt for breach of a fiduciary duty.
5. Wages earned within three months of the filing of the petition.
6. Moneys deposited by employees as security for the faithful performance of their duties.

By agreeing to the bankrupt's discharge, his business creditors sacrifice all of their claims upon him except for such dividends as they receive from the liquidation of his property, which in most cases prove to be only a small fraction of the original claims. They therefore have the right to object to and prevent his discharge if there has been any element of fraud associated with the bankruptcy, or if the bankrupt has failed to give his full cooperation during the bankruptcy proceeding. Objection to the discharge of the bankrupt may be raised by any creditor, by the trustee acting on behalf of the creditors, or by the U.S. attorney, on any of the following grounds:

1. The bankrupt has committed an offense, punishable by imprisonment, under the Bankruptcy Act.
2. The bankrupt has destroyed, mutilated, falsified, or failed to keep books of account, unless the court finds such failure justified.

3. The bankrupt obtained property on a materially false statement in writing.
4. The bankrupt made a fraudulent transfer within twelve months before the petition, with intent to defeat the provisions of the Act.
5. The bankrupt had been granted a prior discharge in bankruptcy, or had a composition, or a wage-earner's arrangement plan by way of a composition, confirmed within six years.
6. The bankrupt has refused to obey orders of the court or answer material questions.
7. The bankrupt has failed to explain the deficiency of assets to the satisfaction of the court.

After examination of the bankrupt at the first meeting of the creditors, or at a special meeting called for that purpose, the referee enters an order fixing a time for filing objections to the discharge of the bankrupt. If no objections are raised by the parties competent to raise them during this time, the court enters the discharge of the bankrupt. If objections have been raised, a hearing is held at which the bankrupt may make his defenses. As a result of the hearing either the objections are dismissed and the bankrupt is granted his discharge, or the objections are held valid and the bankrupt receives no discharge of his liabilities.

### Evaluation of bankruptcy procedure

The 1938 Chandler Amendment of the federal Bankruptcy Act, and subsequent minor revisions of the law, have remedied the worst of the major abuses which formerly marred bankruptcy procedure. Gone are the days when fraudulent bankruptcies were relatively safe and profitable, when "rings" operated insolvent business concerns as a bankruptcy "racket," when referees, trustees, and receivers combined with creditors' attorneys to "milk" bankruptcy assets for their own gain. Rampant dishonesty in bankruptcy operations has been replaced by a generally prevailing honesty, to the great advantage of all creditors. The remuneration of referees, trustees, and receivers in bankruptcy is now closely controlled by law and regulations. Integrity and competence are established as criteria for their appointment.

Agreement is general, however, that further improvement in the law and its administration is still possible and desirable. Fees and expenses of bankruptcy procedures, for one thing, still run too high. In recent years they have been absorbing around one quarter of "available" bankruptcy assets. This is well under the one-third to one-half proportion that prevailed in some years before 1938, and this progress in aiding creditors is not to be belittled. Still, many impartial authorities on bankruptcy feel that lower fee and cost allowances would be possible without discouraging individuals with high administrative ability and business understanding from the practice of bankruptcy work.

Bankruptcy abuses still remaining should not be blamed exclusively, or even to a major degree, on the bankruptcy law and its official administration. Creditor indifference and negligence during bankruptcy procedure opens doors to fraud, mismanagement, and exaggerated costs that the best law and official administration cannot keep closed. The creditors of a bankrupt business, particularly the credit managers of the major creditors, owe it to themselves and to one another to assume a share of bankruptcy administration.

When a credit manager learns that one of his company's customers has filed a bankruptcy petition, or that an involuntary petition has been filed against a customer, a responsibility rests upon him to become an active participant in the subsequent proceedings. He should contact the credit executives of other suppliers of the customer about whom he has learned or with whom he has become acquainted through ledger interchange, discuss the case with them, and endeavor to reach an understanding as to choice of a suitable trustee and the membership of a creditors' committee. A possible result of these conversations may be a decision to bring an adjustment bureau into the proceeding. The credit manager should attend the first creditors' meeting in person and be prepared to take an active part in the election of the trustee and committee and the examination of the bankrupt. He should be prepared to accept the responsibility, if it is voted upon him, of serving on the creditors' committee. If, during the course of the liquidation, he suspects maladministration, or fraud and collusion on the part of the trustee, he should take the steps necessary to verify his suspicions. Here the Fraud Prevention Department of the NACM, which concerns itself largely with bankruptcy frauds, may give him a helping hand. If his suspicions are verified, he must further act to inform the other creditors of his discoveries so that a special creditors' meeting can be called to deal with the situation.

In any bankruptcy proceeding there are nearly always a number of creditors who operate small businesses without the services of trained credit managers. Such creditors are generally unaware of the pitfalls of bankruptcy procedure and contribute little to safeguarding their own interests, let alone those of their fellow creditors. The experienced credit managers present at a creditors' meeting must therefore assume a double burden of protecting these "little" creditors as well as their own companies' interests. Often they are compelled to do battle against these "little" creditors for their common interest, for it is these "little" men who become the dupes and often the unwitting accomplices of any fraudulent interest in a bankruptcy proceeding.

## SUPPLEMENTARY READINGS

Abrams, H. J., "Using Assignments as a Less Expensive and Faster Procedure," *Credit and Financial Management,* February 1958, p. 8.

*Bankruptcy Act* (pamphlet edition), Matthew Bender, New York, 1959.

Dun & Bradstreet, Inc., *The Failure Record Through 1959—A Comprehensive Failure Study by Location, Industry, Age, Size and Cause,* New York, 1960.

National Association of Credit Management, *Credit Manual of Commercial Laws, 1961,* Chapters 25 to 27.

United States Courts, Administrative Offices, *Tables of Bankruptcy Statistics,* current.

Weintraub, B., and H. Levin, "Assignments for the Benefit of Creditors and Competing Systems for Liquidation of Insolvent Estates," *Cornell Law Quarterly,* Fall 1953, p. 3.

————, "General Assignments for the Benefit of Creditors," *New York Law Journal,* May 19 and 20, 1950, vol. 123, no. 97, 98.

## REVIEW

1. Discuss the principal causes of business failure.
2. What is the significance of "exemptions" in liquidation proceedings? What is a "homestead exemption"?
3. What are the two kinds of "assignment for benefit of creditors"? Describe their differences.
4. Describe the procedure of a corporate dissolution applied to an insolvent business.
5. Name and explain briefly two procedures for liquidation of insolvent business in state court.
6. What are the benefits of federal bankruptcy legislation?
7. Who may file a voluntary bankruptcy petition? Explain the schedules that must accompany it.
8. Against what types of business enterprises may an involuntary bankruptcy petition be filed? What precedent circumstances are necessary?
9. Explain the six "acts of bankruptcy."
10. What is meant by the adjudication of a debtor as a bankrupt?
11. Explain the functions, in a bankruptcy proceeding, of (a) the referee, (b) the receiver, (c) the trustee, (d) the creditors' committee.
12. Describe the procedure of a first creditors' meeting in a bankruptcy proceeding.
13. What types of claims have priority over those of ordinary mercantile creditors in distribution of the proceeds of a bankrupt's estate?
14. Does discharge from bankruptcy release a bankrupt from all liabilities? On what grounds may a bankrupt be refused discharge?
15. Discuss the responsibilities of a credit manager whose company is a substantial creditor in a bankruptcy procedure.

## PROBLEM

As credit manager for a major trade creditor, what liquidation procedure for an insolvent customer would you prefer under each of the following circumstances? Why?

1. Two of the customer's trade creditors brought suit for unpaid balances and obtained judgments six weeks ago. Upon liquidation, the customer's assets will amount to about $8,000—70 per cent of his liabilities. The two judgment creditors insist on being paid in full.

2. Mr. Jones, owner of the Jones Hardware store in Harrisburg, Pa., has become insolvent. He has communicated with you and with his seven other business and four personal creditors explaining his situation and offered to turn over all his business assets, his savings bank account, and the paid-up balance of his life insurance policy to the creditors if they will all release him from any balance of liabilities. He believes that the liquidated value of his assets will be from 70 to 80 per cent of his total liabilities. You have always considered Mr. Jones completely honest.

**PART IV**

MERCANTILE CREDIT
OFFICE MANAGEMENT

# CHAPTER 20

# The Credit Department: Personnel and Equipment

Efficient credit department operation requires sound office management practices. The proper personnel must be hired and trained, and must operate under effective functional organization. Filing systems suitable to the needs of the department must be set up. Thought must be applied to its layout and to the preparation of suitable forms for conducting work routines.

## PERSONNEL

In a small concern, credit work may be handled as an incidental detail by the proprietor or one of the partners, or perhaps by the bookkeeper. The credit analysis and collection techniques considered in the preceding chapters may be applied in rudimentary form and with only indifferent success. Or, as happens not infrequently, the individual responsible for the credits and collections of the enterprise may make a conscientious study of the credit function and perform it ably. While the personality and ability of the individual who performs the credit function in a small concern may handicap the business or contribute to its success, such a business cannot be said to have a credit department personnel problem. The individual charged with the credit work of a small firm, whether he does such work well or ill, is predetermined by other considerations.

Personnel considerations make their first appearance in credit management when a business attains a size that warrants the employment of an individual to devote all or a major part of his time to credit and collection work. A properly qualified credit manager, man or woman, should be selected for this position. A secretary and file clerk, or a secretary-clerk, must also be assigned for full- or part-time to the work of even a small credit office.

Some large business organizations have credit departments with several hundred employees. Many companies have a dozen or more men and women in their credit offices. Efficiency requires organization of the work of such credit units into specialized categories and the hiring and training of employees with a view to particular responsibilities.

### The credit manager—responsibilities

A credit manager may bear one or more of four distinct classes of business responsibility: (1) he may be the one to formulate his company's credit and collection policy; (2) he may share in the formulation of general company policy; (3) he may operate as a departmental executive; and (4) he may carry out the routine of the actual credit and collection work of his company.

Sound credit and collection practice requires the preformulation of appropriate policy on such matters as determination of regular and special credit terms, acceptable risk categories, credit limits, nature of collection pressures and procedures, giving extensions, charging interest on past-due accounts, closing weak accounts, writing off bad debts, insuring receivables, and participating in adjustments and bankruptcy proceedings. In some companies a top management executive to whom the credit manager is subordinate may reserve to himself ultimate decision on some or all of these elements of credit and collection policy formulation. However, to an increasing extent top management is leaning toward the view that when a capable and experienced credit manager is employed, he is the one person in the company organization who is most qualified to establish credit and collection policies that will best promote the company's over-all interest. The credit *manager* has become a credit *executive*.

In large companies that develop their general marketing policies through a Marketing Committee composed of the departmental executives and consultants whose work has a bearing on marketing problems, the credit manager is likely to be a member of such committee. He is often in a peculiarly favorable position to contribute information and ideas on channels of distribution and upon current business and financial trends. To fulfill his responsibilities as a member of his company's Marketing Committee, a credit manager must obviously acquire a much broader background of knowledge of the company's operations, and think along broader lines, than would be required if he were solely a credit executive. There is a growing trend, also, to include credit managers on company Finance Committees. In numerous instances credit managers are also the comptrollers or treasurers of their companies, with all the responsibility for financial policy attached to such positions.

The head of a large credit department necessarily is preoccupied with executive duties. If his company has no personnel department, he must contact and interview applicants for positions in his department. If there is a separate personnel department, the credit manager must still prepare the job analyses and specifications on the basis of which the personnel department will make its initial selection among applicants and must make his choice from among the selectees sent to him by the personnel department. Some of his time has to be devoted to training new members of his department, or at least to supervising their training. There is the never-ending task of supervising the work of the department—assigning new accounts as they are opened to the junior men, keeping track of the work of all members of the department, settling intradepartmental disputes and complaints, and generally maintaining a productive and happy atmosphere. Furthermore, as a departmental head, the credit manager must also frequently give time to conferences with other executives of the company. He has to see the general manager on matters concerning the general office administration—the personnel and budget requirements of his department, promotions and salary increases for deserving subordinates, matters of office layout or interdepartmental organization of work, issues concerning his department and the sales or accounting departments, discussion of the credit and collection policies he has established and their results. If interdepartmental cooperation is to be effective, the credit manager must be closeted quite often with the sales manager, with the head of the accounting department, and sometimes with the heads of the shipping, law, and public relations departments. Probably he must prepare annual reports on the department's work. There are usually bi-weekly meetings of his credit group, and also the annual convention meetings of the National Association of Credit Management which he wants to attend.

A credit executive with only one or two assistants usually devotes most of his time to the daily routine of credit decisions and collection correspondence. The burden of administrative duties and policy activities resting on the manager of a large credit department is often so great that he has little time for actual credit analysis or collection work on his company's accounts. At most he may reserve a few of the largest and most crucial accounts for himself, or the determination of credit limits over a certain figure, or require that accounts be submitted to him for review when they exceed their credit limits, or that accounts be brought to his attention after a certain degree of delinquency. By these means, while maintaining himself relatively free from the routine of the department's activity, he nonetheless keeps acutely aware of all the important issues that face it and makes his superior knowledge and experience available to the department where it is most needed.

### The credit manager—qualifications

The manager of a large credit department, with dozens or scores of assistants and juniors under him, may be so commanded by his other responsibilities that he has no opportunity to check individual orders or dictate letters to delinquent accounts. Still, he must previously have been a top-flight credit analyst and collection man—either as a junior and assistant in his present company or as the credit manager of some other smaller company—to have reached his present exalted position. Most credit managers, while they have policy and executive responsibilities, must at the same time be good credit and collection practitioners.

Successful credit and collection practice requires not only a thorough knowledge of the techniques that have been analyzed in the preceding chapters of this book but also certain psychological and personality traits. In his emotional reaction to the world about him, a credit manager should strike the happy realistic balance between optimism and pessimism. A constitutionally optimistic credit manager would be shading his judgment in favor of doubtful credit risks because of his faith that things would always turn out well. Such an attitude in a sales manager is an asset, but it would be a liability in a credit manager since it might lead him to approve too many accounts that would produce losses. A credit manager who was a confirmed pessimist would probably avoid most bad debt losses for his company, but by shading his judgment against all doubtful cases he would turn away an entire marginal group of customers from whom the profit would outweigh the bad debt losses.

A credit manager must constantly render dispassionate judgment, within the stated general policy of his company, on whether an account should be accepted for credit terms, on the collection policy that should be applied to a delinquent customer, on whether an adjustment should be made with a distressed customer, on the general credit policy to be followed in the light of anticipated business conditions. Having done so, he should have the strength of character to stand by his judgment in the face of opposition. He should be able to resist the threats or entreaties of a customer who, because of his deteriorating position, has been placed upon a C.O.D. or C.B.D. basis. The sales manager of his concern may raise questions when a new account is turned down or credit is shut off from an old one which has become delinquent; the credit manager should maintain his decision and endeavor to persuade the sales manager of its correctness. The treasurer of the company may disapprove of a bad debt record that the credit manager deems reasonable in the light of the credit policy adopted and followed; again the credit manager should stand by his conclusions and endeavor to convince the treasurer of their reasonableness. Intelligent pertinacity is a prime requisite for a credit manager.

Quite as important as pertinacity is the capacity to make friends and influence people. In spite of the occasional differences of opinion upon the checking of particular accounts that inevitably arise between sales and credit departments, the credit manager must have the respect and liking of his sales colleague. The sales manager should feel that the credit manager is his active collaborator in promoting sales, an ally and not an antagonist. The credit manager must also hold the friendship of the head of the accounting department while persuading him to maintain a receivables ledger system that conforms to the credit department's needs. He should win the close cooperation of the billing division that mails the statements to customers upon his request and of the shipping division that sends out the merchandise. He should be on friendly terms with the advertising and public relations departments that may be helpful to him. To the subordinates in his department the credit manager ought to be an inexorable taskmaster who obtains a maximum of work from them, an expert practitioner in the credit art whose superiority they respect, and a friend who understands and encourages them and who fights loyally for their promotional and other personal rights in the company.

The credit manager's educational and experience background is of considerable importance. College courses in business administration, particularly in subjects related to his future profession—credit, finance, accounting, commercial law—are helpful. Substantial experience in the credit field, preferably in the same or a similar line of business, is also prerequisite. A combination of academic studies, practical training and experience is best.

## The assistant credit manager

Where the size of the department warrants it, there may be an assistant credit manager. He takes over some of the administrative responsibilities of the head of the department and shares with him some of the supervision of the department's work. An assistant credit manager acts largely as office manager for the department. He relieves the credit executive of the routine tasks of hiring and training its personnel and supervising their work.

### Division of work among junior credit personnel

Division of work among the junior men of large credit departments varies considerably according to the managerial philosophies of the department head. Probably the most common arrangement is simply to divide the accounts among the junior credit men on an alphabetical or a territorial basis, so that everyone has an approximately equal work load. Each man has full responsibility for all phases of credit analysis and collection on each of his accounts—determination as to whether a new account is an acceptable credit risk (with borderline cases referred to the credit manager or the assistant credit manager), setting of a credit limit and its subsequent revisions (again with reference of uncertain cases to the credit manager or assistant credit manager), checking of orders from the account, and the handling of collection correspondence routine. Such division of credit department work permits each junior member of the credit department to become thoroughly acquainted with all aspects of each of his accounts and to be guided by this knowledge in collection procedures, if and when they have to be applied.

"Functional" organization of the work of large credit departments is also fairly common. Some of the junior credit men have the responsibility of analyzing the credit risks of the customers and checking the orders as they are received, while others undertake the collection of delinquent accounts. In hiring members of the first group, emphasis is placed on their analytical abilities and experience with the various sources of credit information. Similarly, men who are to concentrate on collections are hired for their ability as correspondents and their knowledge of commercial law. One of the disadvantages of this "functional" arrangement is that neither the analyst nor the collector becomes as intimately acquainted with an account as does a man who handles both phases of the work. Furthermore, a certain duplication of effort is unavoidable since the collector must repeat some of the analyst's work in order to acquire the necessary background knowledge of the case.

Occasionally, where a large company sells several distinct types of products, the customer accounts may be divided among the junior credit men according to the type of product ordered. This arrangement, used in many industrial companies, has the advantage of enabling each junior credit man to become a specialist in the line of business that orders a particular class of the company's products. It has the disadvantage that a customer who buys two or more of the company's types of products will be handled by several of the company's credit men, with division and possible confusion of credit responsibility.

A large credit department may also have one or more investigators who visit customers at their offices, and otherwise make first-hand inquiries, in cases where the ordinary sources of credit information fail to give an adequate picture of the credit risk. Such investigators become experts in the application of their special technique. The advantage is diminished by some duplication of effort, since the investigator must learn all that the regular analyst knows of the account, as a starting point for his special inquiry.

### Character and training qualifications of junior credit personnel

In a functionally specialized credit department—one in which the tasks of credit analysis, collection, and investigation are assigned to different individuals—different abilities should be sought in the various groups of junior credit personnel.

Junior credit analysts should be selected on the basis of having cool, critical intellects that can brush aside irrelevancies and recognize the pertinent details in the heterogeneous mass of information that is accumulated on credit accounts. They should not be prone to snap judgments, but be willing to probe all sources of information before reaching a conclusion. They should have confidence in their own judgments, for a credit analyst who unmade his mind immediately after reaching a conclusion, or who forever worried over each of his judgments, would soon become a psychiatric case. A college education adds little to a high school diploma by way of specific vocational preparation for credit work, unless the curriculum includes courses in business administration, mercantile credit, and accounting. It may, however, provide a wider perspective and broader knowledge of associated fields, apart from generally sharpening a student's way of thinking. The main background requirement for the position—the ability to evaluate credit data on an account and a certain "feel" for situations that may be implicit though not explicit in credit information—comes only from experience, either derived in time from the job itself or gained previously from work in some other credit office. The secondary background requirement, a penetrating knowledge of the lines of business in which the company's customers are engaged, must also be acquired on the job, to some extent by study of files and cases but mainly by day-to-day dealings with reports and other information on customers.

The personnel of the collection division should have some analytical ability, though not as much as an analyst, in order to judge, from information available, the true causes for a customer's delinquency. They must be good correspondents since, as was indicated in Chapter 16, even in a department where form collection letters are used, personal sentences and paragraphs applying to individual customers have to be worked into form letters to make them effective. Collection men must also be good telephone conversationalists, as this instrument is one of their most effective collection tools.

If investigators are employed, they should possess that rare type of personality that can win friends while asking embarrassing questions. The customers visited by a credit office investigator are usually uncertain borderline cases. Many of them may prove in the long run to be profitable accounts and their good will should be preserved. Their financial weakness, however, renders them sensitive and prone to take offense. An investigator's manner should be particularly ingratiating under these difficult circumstances so that he obtains the information needed yet leaves the customer with friendly feelings towards him and his company. The same appreciative attitude should result when such an investigator inquires about a customer from third parties.

A junior credit man who is responsible for both analysis and collection work should combine the qualifications indicated above for the analyst, the collector, and the investigator.

### Women in credit work

The qualities that make a good credit junior or a good credit manager are as likely to be found in women as in men. The business world has generally recognized this. Masculine prejudice against placing qualified women in positions of responsibility may still bar them from top credit positions in some concerns. But the credit manager of many a medium-sized or larger company today turns out to be a very competent woman.

### Compensation and career possibilities in the credit profession

Few pertinent generalizations can be made about compensation in the mercantile credit field. Here, like in any other business field, juniors begin at whatever is the starting office salary level for the times. Advancement depends upon ability demonstrated and the opportunities that chance to develop in the particular employing company.

Salaries for credit managers start at about $7,500 and may go up to $50,000, with an average somewhere between $15,000 and $20,000. Size of the employing company, and the relative importance of the credit function in its operations, are the major factors in determining its credit manager's compensation. But even with respect to these factors there are, according to studies made by the Credit Research Foundation, wide disparities among similar-sized concerns in the same business line.

To an increasing extent, among medium- and large-sized corporations, the position of credit manager is a stepping stone to that of the company's top financial official—controller or treasurer, as the case may be.

## CREDIT OFFICE TRAINING MANUALS

A good training manual is often a key personnel instrument in medium- and large-sized credit offices. To explain personally to new credit trainees all the routine details of the credit department would take quite a few hours of a manager's or assistant manager's time. He would find, moreover, that many of the explanations would have to be repeated at intervals before they were fully understood or became a matter of automatic habit for the new employee. At each change of personnel in the office, this time-consuming educational process would have to be repeated. Managers of large credit offices have found that they can reduce this labor by preparing a manual of their office principles and procedures. It is given to new employees, or to anyone else who may need guidance. At the same time, it provides the office with standards of practice and thus gives uniformity to the work of its various members.

Few generalizations can be made about these credit office manuals, since each one is prepared to meet the special needs of a particular company and its credit office. Of course, its core is a detailed and exact statement of the company's credit procedures—what sources of information are to be used on accounts, how this information is maintained in the files, just what constitutes an acceptable credit risk for the particular company, how credit limits should be determined, what deviations are permissible from the regular terms of sale and when, what leeway of late payment is allowed, how collection procedure is timed, how collection correspondence is handled with an explanation of the use of the form letter manual, what to do when it is necessary to bring suit, or enter adjustment arrangements, or participate in bankruptcy proceedings. Since credit trainees understand *what* to do better when told *why* it should be done, an office credit manual should give at least summary explanations for the procedures that it prescribes.

Credit office routines cannot remain static. They must be altered with developments in the organization of the office, with changes in the markets and sales policy of the company, with changes in external business conditions. Therefore a credit office manual can never be written as a final, unalterable opus. It should be revised whenever conditions change. For this reason it is best prepared in some sort of loose-leaf binder, so that individual pages can be rewritten and replaced easily whenever necessary.

## RECORDS AND FILES

The working tools of a credit department are its records—the customer ledger which provides a record of each account's purchases and payments, various classes of credit information on the accounts, and the records of collection procedure on delinquent accounts. The most important item of equipment for a credit office, therefore, is its filing cases and file boxes. Add to these the requisite number of desks and typewriters, a few shelves for the departmental library, possibly one or two calculating machines to be used in financial statement ratio analysis, possibly some dictaphone machines for the manager and the collection correspondents, and a credit department is basically equipped.

Automatic equipment for data processing and control has recently been developed; some of it has mercantile credit applications. Automation is also contributing to modernization of accounts receivable systems.[1] In large companies this equipment is generally operated by a central "tabulating department" which services the operating departments, including the credit department. Credit departments of small concerns that would not find it economically practicable to purchase or rent such equipment may nonetheless establish automated procedures by utilizing the services of "data processing centers" established in major metropolitan centers by National Cash Register Co. and other producers of such equipment.

### The customer ledger file

As stated earlier, the customer ledger serves a dual purpose. It is an essential bookkeeping control and also an important source of credit information. It should be readily accessible to both the accounting and credit departments, including its collection division.

To maintain duplicate customer ledger files for the two departments, with both files kept constantly up to date for all postings, would involve a duplication of cost and effort not warranted by the advantage of separate files. Some large companies, however, have found it practicable to duplicate the accounting department's customer ledger for credit department use by Recordak photography upon continuous strips of film, as shown in Illustration 20-1. These miniature reproductions of the ledger cards are studied through an enlarger. The entire ledger file is rephotographed weekly, bi-weekly, or monthly, so that the credit department's miniature duplicates are always relatively current.

Where only a single customer ledger file is maintained by the accounting department, the credit manager should arrange to have it kept so as to meet his department's needs as well as satisfy bookkeeping procedures. Hand- or machine-posted cards should be of the visible index or keysort type described in Chapter 13, so that past-due accounts can be promptly and readily detected. It should be made a regular part of the posting clerk's routine to prepare periodically a list of past-due accounts for transmission to the credit department, and also to notify the credit de-

---

[1] See page 36 of this volume.

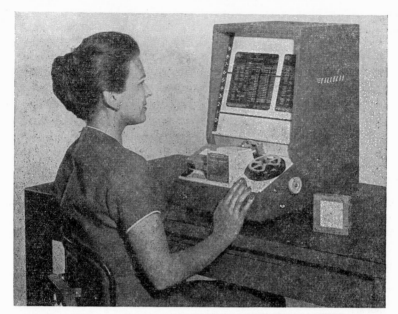

ILLUSTRATION 20-1. Customer Ledger Cards Photographed on Microfilm Are Viewed on Screen of Recordak Film Reader

partment when payments are made by accounts previously listed as past due. Also, the posting clerk should be instructed to key-number or key-letter all debit and credit entries so that payments are related to the charges to which they apply; thereby members of the credit department can readily determine whether an account has a record of prompt payment or what his average of lateness is. Punch-card ledger systems can be coded to produce this information automatically.

### The account folder file

For convenience of reference, all items of credit information on a customer except his ledger card—the agency reports on him, salesmen's reports, any attorney report, all ledger interchange reports, his financial statements, his statement comparison sheet—should be assembled in a folder. Correspondence about credit terms or collections may be included, or a separate file for such correspondence may be maintained. The credit folders are filed alphabetically, geographically, numerically, or by any other system that promotes convenience of reference.

The simplest and cheapest type of folder is the kind made of stiff manila paper with a set of creases at the bottom that permit it to be expanded as its contents increase. More expensive types have provision whereby the contents of the folder may be stapled by their tops or edges to the back of the folder, or fastened by their edges to its bottom.

### The summary file

The complete credit folder on a customer is not called for and its contents studied upon the occasion of every order received from the customer. The decision having once been made that the customer is a good risk for orders within a certain limit, all that the credit manager need do thereafter, upon the receipt of each new order, is remind himself that the customer has been judged a sound risk within the specified limit, and check with the customer ledger to assure himself that the new order will not exceed it. For this purpose a credit manager keeps a "summary" file on his accounts. The full credit folder for a good customer is referred to only when the pre-established credit limit is overstepped, or when a new financial statement is received, or when a new report or new ledger interchange information comes to hand. The summary file is the immediate reference and in many credit offices the only one, for all orders as they come in.

| NAME | | | | $ _____ LIMIT |
|------|--|--|--|----------------|
| ADDRESS | | | | |

REFERENCES

| DATE | D & B | INTERCHANGE | LEDGER | REMARKS |
|------|-------|-------------|--------|---------|
| | | | | |
| | | | | |
| | | | | |

ILLUSTRATION 20-2.   A Credit Summary File Card

The information contained in a summary file should be held to the barest minimum necessary to indicate which orders may be approved on credit terms without further inquiry, which must definitely be sent on C.O.D. or C.B.D. terms, and which necessitate reference to the customer's credit folder for a review of the account. Some credit offices have found satisfaction in summary files which consist merely of colored cards containing the names and addresses of the accounts and their credit limits.

One color is used for accounts that can be checked through within the credit limit indicated. A second color is used for the accounts which are to be sold only on C.O.D. or C.B.D. terms. A third color is used for accounts for which, because of their borderline financial condition, or because of developing delinquency in their payments, or for some other reason, the full credit folder should be studied on the occasion of each new order. The most common type of summary file, however, consists of 3" x 5" cards which, besides the name and address (and possibly number) of the account, contain the following information: credit limit, credit terms, agency rating, general interchange picture, references, ledger status, and remarks (see Illustration 20-2). These cards may be colored to indicate the treatment of the accounts, as previously described, or such treatment may be indicated by a tab system.

Some credit offices have the summary file form printed on the front of the general credit file folders. This, of course, saves the necessity of a separate card file. But it sacrifices the convenience of quick reference to a card file kept on or in the credit manager's desk.

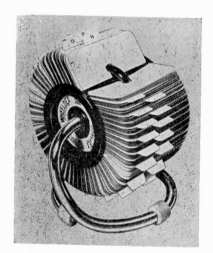

ILLUSTRATION 20-3. A "Wheeldex" Credit Summary File

Where the number of accounts that a credit manager is responsible for runs over a thousand, a "Wheeldex" summary file may prove more convenient than the usual card file box or drawer. Here, the summary cards, 3" x 5" size or smaller, are hinged to the rim of a wire wheel which can be revolved by a touch of the hand. Gravity causes the cards to open up at the top of the wheel, so that one card is always fully exposed (see Illustration 20-3). The particular card wanted is found more rapidly by revolving the wheel than by searching through a file box or drawer, and when found is fully visible without being drawn forth.

With a punch-card ledger system, most or all of the summary information on an account may be punch-coded into its card. Processing the card makes the information available to the credit manager.

### Tickler files and desk diaries

Successful operation of a credit department depends to a considerable extent on timing—promptness in determining the credit risk of a new account and clearing its first order, promptness in spotting delinquencies, a consistent follow-up of collection letter series. A credit manager's unaided memory cannot be depended upon to remind him of every one of the constantly changing series of significant dates for each of his accounts. As indicated in Chapter 13, he should provide himself with the mechanical memory of a desk diary or a tickler file.

While a single tickler file could be used for all reminder needs in a credit office, it is more common practice to use two or three tickler files. One may be used for new accounts to ensure consistent quick action upon them. A second might be set up to hold duplicate invoices of individual-term orders. These invoices would be filed at some grace period— two or three days, or possibly as much as a week—after their due dates. The receivables clerk would have the duty of sending the credit department a daily list of payments. Each day's group of duplicate invoices, as they turned up in the tickler file, would be checked against these payment lists. If an invoice had been paid, it would be destroyed. If unpaid, it could be transferred to the collections tickler file to serve as a record sheet in that file, or a card might be made out for the collection file.

The third and most common tickler file in a credit department is the collection file. The technique of thus controlling the timing of collection procedure has already been described. When payment is finally received, the card for that account is removed from the file. It may be placed in a "dead" file from which it can be recovered when a new delinquency occurs, or it may be placed in the account's general credit folder as a record of the delinquency and the steps that had to be taken.

Some credit offices maintain a fourth tickler file—the "revision" file. The account cards in this file carry the date when the customer issues his annual statement. Each card is first placed in the file in accordance with this date. When the card comes up it reminds the credit manager to request a new financial statement and, if the case seems to warrant it, to draw a new agency report and an interchange report. The card is then filed a couple of weeks ahead to remind the credit manager to check if these items have been received and, if they are in the customer's folder, to review his credit status. Special cards may be inserted in this file as a reminder to review a doubtful account in a month's time, or in three months' time, or at some other interval. The "revision" tickler file should obviously cover at least a year.

### Form letter files

If form collection letters are used, as discussed in Chapter 16, a credit office should have a number of copies of these letter forms on file. Every member of the department who ever has occasion to send out collection letters, and every secretary or typist who may be called upon to type them, should have a copy of the file.

## Credit library

Even the smallest credit office ought to make provision for a minimum credit library. A single bookshelf may be sufficient to accommodate this "library," but it should include a number of important items. The latest edition of the *Credit Manual of Commercial Laws,* published by the National Association of Credit Management, would be a "must." This volume should be referred to whenever such factors as state "exemption" laws or guarantees enter into the determination of a credit risk, or when adjustment or bankruptcy of an account becomes an issue. It is a valued guide on many other details of credit practice. If the company is a member of a credit association affiliated with the National Association of Credit Management, the bookshelf will contain the file of *Credit and Financial Management* published by the NACM, and possibly the file of such a magazine as *Credit Executive* published by the local association. A copy of a recent edition of a good textbook on credits and collections will be of aid to junior members of the department who are learning credit and collections work while on the job, without the benefit of an organized course on the subject; it may also be referred to occasionally by the head of the department to refresh his mind on some point. The National Institute of Credit issues a recommended book list for credit managers which is an excellent guide for starting a credit department library. The Credit Research Foundation publishes a reference library set-up for credit training programs.

The various magazines and government reports which the credit manager should read, so as to know the trends of business conditions in the lines to which his customers belong and the regions in which they are located, probably will not find a resting place in the credit department library. Other department heads must also study this information. These publications will come to the credit manager's desk in the routine of a regular reading sequence, before or after other department heads have had their opportunity to work over these materials.

### CREDIT OFFICE LAYOUT

Planning the layout of a credit department presents few problems that are not covered by the principles of general office layout. In arranging the location of desks, file cases, and other items of credit department equipment, the following principles are applicable:

1. Space should be economized, but not to a point where office efficiency would be impaired.

2. Provision should be made in space allotment, and arrangement of equipment, for subsequent expansion if that appears likely in the reasonably near future.

3. Adequate light, natural or artificial, should be available in all work areas.

4. The customer folder file should be located close to the credit analysts who use it, to minimize movement of materials. If a separate credit and collection correspondence file is maintained, it should be so placed that it is convenient to both the analysts and the collection men.

Formerly it was deemed necessary to locate a company's credit department in close proximity to, if not actually combined with, the receivables division of its accounting department, unless a duplicate customer ledger system was maintained. Advances in the technology of intra-office communication have ended this necessity. Mechanical carriers, film strip reproduction of ledger cards, and closed-circuit TV systems now make it possible for credits and receivables divisions to be located in distant parts of a floor, on different floors, in separate buildings, even in different cities.

## CREDIT DEPARTMENT FORMS

A credit department needs only a few special forms. Several of these have already been discussed in earlier chapters and need only be mentioned here. Many credit departments prefer to send their own financial statement forms to customers rather than depend upon whatever form the customer may chance to use. These statement forms based on some standard model may be printed specially for the credit department, or they may be purchased from the National Association of Credit Management. Statement comparison forms may be printed according to the credit manager's design, or a very satisfactory statement comparison sheet may be mimeographed within the office. The department's customer summary cards may likewise be either printed to the credit manager's order or mimeographed in the office.

One important credit department form, not heretofore mentioned, is the Credit Terms Notice. When a credit manager or his assistant approves a new account for regular terms within a certain credit limit, or subsequently raises or lowers that limit, or sets special terms, or otherwise establishes the policy to be followed with an account, his decision should be recorded in a number of places and several people in the credit department and other departments should be informed of it. One record of the decision, to be placed in the account's general credit folder, should be transmitted to the clerk who handles the credit folder file. Notation of the new terms, limit, or arrangements should be made on the account's summary card, and the clerk who has responsibility for maintaining the summary card file should be notified. So, also, the accounting department, which may follow the policy of noting the terms and credit limit for each account on the customer ledger cards. If cooperation between the sales and credit departments of a concern is to mean anything, the sales department should also know about the decision. This information is conveyed by the Credit Terms Notice form.

An example of a Credit Terms Notice form that would meet all the

---

CREDIT TERMS NOTICE

Date....................

To  __ CREDIT FOLDER FILE
    __ CREDIT CARD FILE
    __ SALES DEPARTMENT
    __ ACCOUNTING DEPARTMENT
    __ ...............................

From CREDIT DEPARTMENT

Account No. .....................

Name  ...................................................

Address  ...............................................

     ......................................................

__ 1. Regular terms.

__ 2. C.O.D., standard sizes, only.

__ 3. Cash in advance.

__ 4. Special terms  ....................................

     ......................................................

__ 5. Set credit limit at $............

__ 6. *Raise* credit limit from $............ to $............

__ 7. *Lower* credit limit from $............ to $............

__ 8. If ........................... account in the amount of

$............ not paid on or before ........................,

put on C.O.D. basis.

__ 9. Do not accept post-dated checks.

__10.  ................................................

     ......................................................

     ......................................................

                         Signed....................

---

ILLUSTRATION 20-4.   Example of Credit Terms Notice Form

needs of an ordinary credit office is shown in Illustration 20-4. The credit manager or assistant need only check off requisite instructions and enter the pertinent figures or other items of information. Such forms would be used in pads. By slipping the required number of carbon papers between the top sheets of the pad, one writing would produce as many copies of the instruction as were needed; the individuals or departments to which they were to be sent would be checked off after the sheets were pulled from the pad.

Another common credit office form is the Customer Ledger Card Requisition Slip. This is filled out with the account name and number whenever the credit department requires a customer ledger card from the accounting department. The receivables clerk clips the slip to a blank ledger card and inserts this in place of the card sent to the credit department. Thus the customer ledger file always contains a record of cards temporarily held by the credit department.

### Customer authorization cards

Certain concerns (such as building supply companies and chain auto service stations that serve, among others, trucking companies which prefer to make monthly settlements) face the problem that their customers, or their customers' employees, often drive up to the warehouse or service station and desire immediate delivery of the products they come to buy. One solution would be to provide all the warehouses or service stations belonging to the concern with full sets of credit summary cards on all of its credit customers. A more practicable solution, and one that has been generally adopted to meet this situation, is to provide the credit customers with individual "authorization" cards, signed by the credit manager and with the identifying signature of the customer. The customer has merely to present his authorization card at the warehouse or service station to obtain his purchase on the company's regular terms. To cover the circumstance that a customer's credit status may change so that he is no longer a good risk, it is generally provided that each set of authorization cards is good only for the current month or quarter; renewal cards are issued to all customers who have been prompt in paying their obligations.

### SUPPLEMENTARY READINGS

See page 422 of this volume.

### REVIEW

1. Discuss the functions and responsibilities of the head of a large credit department.

2. How may the credit and collection work of a large credit department be divided among the junior credit personnel?

3. Discuss the qualifications of a junior credit man or woman.

4. Discuss the qualifications of a credit manager.

5. Discuss the contents of credit office manuals, and their contribution to credit office personnel management.

6. Discuss possibilities of arranging a customer ledger file so that it may be conveniently used by the credit department.

7. Explain the credit department's account folder file.

8. Explain the credit department's summary card file.

9. Explain the use of tickler files by a credit department.

10. What should be the contents of a credit department library?

11. What considerations should be borne in mind in planning credit department layout?

12. What are the two office forms most likely to be used by a credit department? Describe them.

13. What credit information on an account may be incorporated in punch-card ledgers? How is such information made available to a credit manager?

## PROBLEM

1. You are credit manager for a rapidly growing perfume manufacturer which sells through wholesalers and direct to large department stores. Heretofore, you have handled all the credit and collection work of the company with the assistance of only a secretary. The number of the company's accounts has reached a point where the top management agrees that you need a junior credit man or woman. For the personnel department, prepare a job analysis for the position and a statement of the qualifications of the person to be hired.

2. Outline a training program for the person hired.

# CHAPTER 21

# The Credit Department: Operation and Control

A credit manager does not operate independently. He is part of a business unit that buys, sells, perhaps manufactures, and engages in all the other functions incident to its activity. He must fit into the administrative organization, and his credit and collection work should be so conducted that it contributes in all possible ways to the ultimate objective of earning maximum profits for the business. He is in constant relationship with its customers—the very men and companies whose purchases are the foundation of his company's profits. His dealings with these customers must be made to contribute in every way possible to winning and maintaining their good will. In both his analysis and collection work he has a difficult course to chart—he must avoid both the Scylla of excessive leniency which would result in an unwarranted bad debt loss, and the Charybdis of excessive strictness which would lose his company profitable customers. Chance or good judgment may start a credit manager on the properly balanced course, but only by the application of the statistical control techniques described at the close of this chapter can he have consistent assurance that he is keeping to that course through the changing currents of market shifts and business fluctuations.

## INTERNAL RELATIONSHIPS OF
## A CREDIT DEPARTMENT

Small companies rarely have separate credit departments. Even in some large concerns, credits and collections are the responsibility of a division of some other department. Under such circumstances the issue arises—within which major department should a subordinate credit division be placed?

When there is enough credit work in a business to warrant the hiring of a credit manager who will devote himself exclusively to such activity, a new set of internal management problems appears. These involve the relationship of the credit department to the other departments of the concern, and the procedures of cooperation that should be established.

Large organizations with branch sales offices may find it advisable to establish branch credit divisions to work with the subordinate sales units. If this occurs, the relations between the branch credit offices and the central office present still another managerial problem.

### The subordinate credit division

When the credit work of a business is not sufficient to require the employment of an individual who is a specialist in the field and devotes his time exclusively to that operation, it must obviously be made the co-responsibility of someone in the business who is charged with other operations as well. The most common arrangement in small businesses is to have credit checking and collections performed by the sales manager, or by the treasurer or comptroller, or by the bookkeeper or accountant. One or more clerks may be assigned to the routine aspects of the credit and collection work thus handled by some other department head, but determination of the general credit and collection policy and the decisions that must be made on individual accounts are the responsibility of the sales manager or other executive charged with the credit function.

Good argument can be offered for having the credit work of a small business performed by the sales manager. Through his sales force, he has a source of information and contact with the company's customers that can be utilized effectively for credit purposes. He is sales-minded, and will certainly make the credit operation contribute all that it possibly can to sales promotion. The danger that he may be too sales-minded and approve sales to inferior credit risks for the sake of added sales volume is, in practice, reduced by the fact that a qualified sales manager would not risk his job by selling to poor accounts.

The treasurer or comptroller of a small corporation is frequently given credit and collection responsibilities. Through his intimate acquaintance with the finances of his company, he is in a good position to determine its credit policy.

Assigning the credit and collection operations to the bookkeeper of a small business is also a quite common arrangement. The bookkeeper has control of the customer ledger, and can readily adapt it to serve as a credit and collection tool. His meticulous, conservative attitude of mind may sometimes be more consonant with sound credit analysis than the driving optimism of a sales manager. Generally, however, a bookkeeper is not well qualified for rendering credit judgment.

### The separate credit department

A business that started as a small enterprise, with the credit function assigned to some other department head, may grow to a point where its credit and collection work demands the attention of a full-time credit manager, and he is accordingly hired. No change in departmental organization is made, however, and the credit manager becomes a subordinate of the sales manager, or of the head of the accounting department, or of the treasurer or comptroller, as the case may be.

To allow such an arrangement to persist is generally a mistake. The business now has a credit manager presumably capable of assuming all its credit and collection work, yet without the ultimate responsibility for it. If subordinated to a sales manager or the head of the accounting department, he may have his sound judgments frequently overruled by a superior who is less competent in credit matters, to the ultimate detriment of the company's profit. Furthermore, to a sales manager, or accountant, or treasurer, the credit and collection work of the company must always appear a matter distinctly secondary to his major function. He turns an unwilling or deaf ear to the credit manager's requests for more clerical help, better files, automatic equipment, or a larger appropriation for agency reports, and the credit work naturally suffers.

As soon as the credit and collection work of a business has attained sufficient volume to necessitate the hiring of a credit manager, a separate credit department should be established, even if it consists only of this credit manager operating with clerical assistance. This gives him the final responsibility, which should be his, upon credit and collection decisions. He should be free, as a co-equal executive, to work out with the sales manager the necessary cooperation between the two departments. If the head of the accounting department refuses to adapt the form or location of the customer ledger to credit use, the credit manager should have authority to bring the issue to the attention of the marketing manager or top management. At budget committee hearings he should have authority, as a department head, to voice his claims for additional personnel, equipment, or supplies directly. He may have a place on his concern's marketing and finance committees.[1]

The credit and collection work of a business that has grown beyond "small-scale" size can not be developed to maximum efficiency unless it has been given independent departmental status.

## The credit department and other departments

A credit department can accomplish its work effectively only through cooperation with other departments. Its closest and most continuous inter-relations are with the sales and accounting departments. Not infrequently, however, it must coordinate policies and procedures with its company's finance, law, personnel, advertising, and public relations departments. Interdepartmental cooperation involving the credit department should not be limited, as was formerly too often the case, to a mutual grudging tolerance. It can, and should take, and to an increasing extent is taking, the positive form of concordant teamwork.

The least that a credit department owes to the sales department is immediate notice of the refusal of credit terms to a new account, or the withdrawal of credit terms from an old account, with a brief statement of the reason. Such notice should be given by the credit manager to the sales manager. The latter can then pass it on to the particular salesmen concerned, so that they may be spared the embarrassment of calling upon a customer only to discover from him, in none too friendly words, that the company is refusing him credit terms. Sometimes it is helpful for salesmen to know the credit limits set for their accounts. If there is collection difficulty with a customer, and the sales department is notified, a salesman dealing with the customer face to face may, in some cases, be able to clear up the difficulty better than the credit manager can by correspondence.

Mere notice to the sales department of credit refusals or collection difficulties is, however, only a beginning to the possible cooperation that a credit department can offer to a sales department. Some credit departments check the credit status of sales *prospects* before salesmen's calls may be made upon them.[2] Many credit managers have undertaken intensive education of their sales departments on their companies' credit policies, so that the salesmen may be credit-minded in their sales efforts—seek new prospects among better-class risks rather than poor ones where a choice is possible, collect and transmit appropriate credit information to the credit department, understand and not be resentful when credit terms are refused on an order from a customer who is a poor risk, and co-

---

[1] "Is Credit Distribution a Treasury Function?" *Credit and Financial Management,* June 1955, p. 8.

[2] S. Gartner, "Pre-Selling—Credit's Boon to Sales Can Keep Cart Behind the Horse and Swindler Off the Books," *Credit and Financial Management,* April 1960, p. 16.

operate with the credit department in speeding up collections. Such credit instruction may be given to the salesmen periodically at sales meetings when the credit manager, upon invitation of the sales manager, addresses them on the credit aspects of their work. Or the credit manager may prepare a credit manual for the salesmen of the company, in which he explains the company's credit and collection policies and indicates how the salesmen can contribute to their smooth application. The credit manager may also arrange with the bookkeeping department periodically to "age" each salesman's accounts according to the extent of their delinquency in payment. These "aging" statements can be transmitted to the salesmen via the sales manager, thus giving the salesmen an actual check upon the credit aspects of their work, and possibly giving the sales manager an additional measure for rating his salesmen.

There are not so many possible points of friction between the credit and accounting departments as there are between the credit and sales departments. The most common source of irritation between credit and accounting departments is the form and location of the customer ledger. The wishes of a credit department in this matter already have been indicated. Whether a credit manager gains his objectives in these matters depends on his exercise of "office diplomacy."

### Central and branch office organization

Large business organizations that have branch sales offices located in various cities are faced with the issue whether to centralize their credit and collection work at the principal office of the enterprise, or to establish branches of the credit department to correspond with those of the sales department. There are advantages and disadvantages to both arrangements, depending on the special circumstances of the concern's business and administrative organization.

The great advantage of a decentralized organization of the credit department, with each branch credit office associated with a branch sales office, is the close cooperative relationship that can be maintained between each branch credit manager and his associated branch sales manager. The very physical proximity of their offices, and the correspondence of their interests in an identical set of customers, is likely to foster such cooperation. If a branch sales manager has to send his orders for confirmation to a central credit office in some other city, where the analysis is made by a junior credit man who does not know him, there is no real contact and understanding between the departments. The time element enters as a further drawback; it may take days until the branch sales manager receives an order confirmation.

But a branch credit office organization has offsetting disadvantages. It is more difficult for the central credit manager to supervise and control the analysis and collection work of a group of branch credit managers than of a group of junior credit men working directly under his eye. Each branch credit manager tends to develop his own individual policies towards his accounts, and the central manager may find it a complicated task to enforce uniformity of procedure and policy. Presumably the central credit manager is more experienced in credit and collection work than the branch managers, so that his decision, or at least his advice, should be obtained on particularly difficult cases. But the semi-independence of the branch managers may make it difficult to establish a routine whereby doubtful cases will be regularly referred to the central office. Finally, to make the supervision of the central office effective, some duplication of records may be necessary. Considerable additional "paper work," in the form of periodic reports, summaries of credit decisions, and correspondence between the branch and central offices, cannot be avoided.

Where circumstances make it advisable to establish one or more branch credit offices, the central credit manager must formulate a workable administrative routine that will coordinate the work of the branch and central offices. If the customer ledger is kept at the central office, the central credit manager should arrange for duplicate invoices and duplicate receipt memos to be sent to the branch offices, so that they can maintain duplicate ledgers; or he may arrange for photographic or other reproductions of the customer ledger to be sent periodically to the branch offices. He will probably insist on having the ultimate decision on the credit limits and other aspects of particularly large or borderline accounts of the branch offices. If the original customer ledger is kept at the branch office, the central credit manager must have duplicate ledger material on these particular accounts made available to him. A common arrangement is for the branch offices to refer accounts whose delinquency exceeds a prescribed time to the central credit manager, together with information needed for his decisions. Finally, the central credit manager has to maintain constant check upon the efficiency of the credit analysis and collection work done in the branch offices. He accomplishes this by personal contact and by studying period "control" statements, of types discussed later in this chapter, prepared by the branch credit managers.[3]

---

[3] Interesting examples of the varying accents on centralization vs. decentralization in the relations between central and branch credit offices are presented by large concerns such as Du Pont and Lever Brothers. At Du Pont the central credit office in Wilmington, Del. establishes the "credit control lines" (credit limits) for all accounts; the regional offices may impose further restrictions, but if the issue is one of exceeding limits they must refer orders to Wilmington. At Lever Brothers there is more decentralization in credit management. The general credit manager in New York sets over-all policies, but the regional offices have authority within the scope of these policies. The general credit manager maintains duplicate files on marginal accounts only. (Credit Research Foundation, *Punched Card Accounting and the Credit Department,* New York, 1957, p. 21.)

## CUSTOMER RELATIONSHIPS OF
## A CREDIT DEPARTMENT

A credit department, quite as much as a sales department, should so perform its functions that it builds up the respect and good will of the customers for the company. Short of approving orders to accounts that are not proper credit risks and indulgently foregoing payment from a delinquent customer who is able to pay, a credit department should seize every opportunity, and develop opportunities where they do not otherwise exist, to promote customer good will and win friends.

### Correspondence

Every letter that a credit office sends out should endeavor to build up the customer's good will as well as perform whatever may be its primary purpose. When a first order is received from a new customer, and shipping of that order must be delayed until a credit inquiry is completed, a letter should be sent to him welcoming him enthusiastically to the company's growing clientele, informing him of the delay, explaining the credit inquiry in terms that impute esteem rather than discredit to him, and perhaps suggesting cash or C.O.D. terms for this first order so that it may be shipped immediately before the inquiry is completed. The following is an example of such a *welcome* letter:

Dear Mr. _____:

We have just received your order for 10,000 ABC cartons to Mr. Jones, our sales representative. It is a pleasure to welcome you cordially to the rapidly growing number of ABC customers.

Mr. Jones has asked us to ship your order on a "RUSH" basis. We would like to do so, for we want you to have the satisfaction of using ABC cartons at the earliest possible moment.

We and all other reputable members of the cardboard carton industry follow the practice of making a credit inquiry about new customers to confirm their good credit standing. This inquiry will take about a week to complete.

To avoid a delay on your first order, will you authorize us to ship it immediately on a C.O.D. basis? If you will send us a wire collect to that effect immediately upon receipt of this letter, your order will be on its way to you before the close of business tomorrow. If we do not receive a wire from you, we will ship your order on regular terms immediately upon the receipt of confirmatory credit information about you.

Will you help us complete our inquiry in the shortest possible time by filling out the enclosed financial statement form and mailing it back to us at your early convenience?

Very truly yours,

Should the credit inquiry on a new customer indicate that he is not a satisfactory credit risk, or should an old customer deteriorate from an acceptable status to an unacceptable one, a well-phrased letter informing him that he cannot be accorded regular credit terms may, despite this refusal, salvage him for C.O.D. selling or other special terms. The annual request for a financial statement can be built around the complimentary idea of "confirming" the customer's good credit standing. As we saw in Chapter 16, collection letters to customers who are, despite their delinquency, good present credit risks or potentially good risks at some future time can be so phrased that they preserve the customers' self-respect and maintain his friendly appreciation of the seller in spite of the pressure for payment.

Many credit managers overlook the promotional possibilities of "appreciation" letters to good customers who are never delinquent and to whom, consequently, the credit office has little occasion to write. They are the very cream of any company's clientele, yet little or nothing is ordinarily done to foster their good will. The following *appreciation* letter, sent by a credit manager to an account who had consistently discounted, should elicit warm, heartfelt response and undoubtedly do much to bind a top-grade customer to his company:

Dear Mr. _____:

It is one of the ironies of credit work that our files accumulate correspondence to and from customers who are slow in their payments, while there is never reason to send a letter to or receive one from our best and most appreciated customers, men like yourself who buy more and more of our merchandise with each succeeding year and who regularly discount their payments.

This thought struck me forcibly as I was reading over your latest financial statement. I remembered the modest beginning of your store five years ago. I reflected on the sheer brilliance with which you have built yourself up so that now you are one of the leading, if not already the foremost, _____ retailer in _____.

I am writing this letter simply to tell you, Mr. _____, that our company deeply appreciates the cooperation and friendship you have always given us, and deems it a privilege to serve you.

Cordially yours,

Analysis of a customer's financial statement sometimes indicates an element of weakness, possibly not realized by the customer, which he could readily correct if he were made aware of it. A credit manager may help his own company as well as the customer by pointing out the weakness and suggesting the remedy, since its correction will make the customer a safer credit risk. The right way of giving such advice may win the customer's appreciation. The wrong way may arouse his resentment.

An *advice letter* should preserve the customer's pride by praising his accomplishments or by presuming that he has already given thought to the indicated weakness. It ought to recognize that the customer knows more about his particular business than the supplier or any outsider, but that the credit manager has knowledge and experience about the line of business in general that may be helpful. It should avoid equally a patronizing tone, or a wheedling, self-deprecating apology for offering intelligent, helpful suggestions. Finally, the advice letter has to indicate the advantage to the customer of the improvements suggested, and the supplier's interest in the customer's advantage. The following is an example of a well-planned advice letter:

Dear Mr. _____:

I want to thank you for taking time out to send me a financial statement and write me a detailed letter in the midst of the pressing duties that are incident to the chairmanship of such a committee as you mention.

I know it is gratifying to you that you held your own during this past year, and even made a small profit. With business on the upswing, that will undoubtedly be substantially larger this year.

There is one thing that occurred to me in studying your statement, as it no doubt has to you, too. While your capital is entirely adequate for your business, much of it is tied up in an inventory which, in my opinion, is too heavy, even in view of a probable increase in sales. If your stock could be brought down to a point where you could show a turnover of about 3½ to 4 times, this would solve the problem of retiring your indebtedness more promptly.

Please do not think I am trying to tell you how to run your business. I don't know the first thing about merchandising, but I do have an opportunity to study and compare hundreds of statements that come in here from all types of businesses. Once in a while a suggestion of this kind coming from the outside is helpful, and it is in that spirit I have mentioned what occurred to me.

What is your opinion?

Very truly yours,[4]

### Personal visits by credit manager to customers

The nature of credit and collection work tends to produce a depersonalized relationship between a credit manager and his company's customers. To many credit managers their accounts become, after a time, not individual businessmen struggling in their personal ways with the business problems forever besetting them, but merely impersonal subjects of mercantile agency reports and financial statement analysis or meaningless names signed to letters explaining non-payment of past-due items. To the customers the credit manager of a supplier is often only a signature affixed to a form collection letter.

Promotional credit work—credit work that contributes positively to building up and maintaining customer good will instead of merely negatively eliminating poor credit risks and collecting on delinquent accounts—demands that the credit manager become recognized by the customers as a friendly personality. Good correspondence technique may go far towards achieving this objective. Periodic field trips, whereby the

---

[4] H. Sommers, "Psychology," *Credit and Financial Management,* February 1943, p. 7.

credit manager or a member of his staff meets his accounts face to face and they become acquainted with each other as individuals, are a more effective means to this end. As previously indicated, such field trips are an established routine for many credit departments. They provide opportunity for the credit manager or his representative to get information from a customer or a potential customer,[5] make arrangements for payment by a delinquent account, and give advice and encouragement where needed. Such first-hand approach to a buyer is particularly valuable in borderline cases that cannot be judged easily on the basis of correspondence and reports.

**The credit manager as customer counselor**

An experienced credit manager, upon studying financial statements, salesmen's reports, and the correspondence file on a down-grade account, can often spot the developing or continuing cause of business failure. His knowledge of business management and his broad experience with the customer's field may further enable him to determine a possible remedy. If he is sufficiently wise in his handling of human relations to be able to indicate the trouble and suggest its cure in such a manner that his advice is not resented but is appreciated and followed, he improves his chances of getting paid on the past purchases of the account, he retains a sales outlet, and he cements the good will of the account.

Sometimes such suggestions on improvement of the customer's business may be made in a diplomatically worded letter. Sometimes, if the salesman handling the account is intelligent and experienced, the credit manager can discuss the situation with him and prime him to do the talking to the customer. The credit manager may also perform this customer rehabilitation service on his field trips. Finally, in large enterprises, the credit department may have on its staff a "customers' trouble shooter," or there may be a special "customer rehabilitation department" to which cases spotted by the credit department can be referred. It should always be borne in mind, however, that a credit department should offer advice to customers only if some special position of the supplier or some special relationship with a customer justifies it; otherwise, this "interference" may be strongly resented.

## STATISTICAL CONTROLS OF CREDIT AND COLLECTION MANAGEMENT

A credit manager may believe that he is consistently sound in his determination of acceptable and unacceptable credit risks,

---

[5] See Chap. 7.

and that in his collection policy he pursues a policy that is properly balanced between courteous consideration and firmness. Between that belief and the fact, however, there may be considerable discrepancy. For his own guidance, a credit manager should *know*, not merely believe, that his credit and collection policies are sound. He should be able to present concrete evidence of this when his departmental policies are under review by the management of his company. The means of showing how his policies are operating are certain statistical control procedures.

### Ratio of cash and C.O.D. sales to total sales

In most lines of business other than retail, cash or C.O.D. sales are rare and made only to customers who are poor credit risks. A customer refused regular credit terms by a supplier who maintains a high standard of acceptable risks will ordinarily endeavor to obtain credit accommodation from other suppliers with less strict standards. Therefore, if a customer accepts proffered C.O.D. terms, it is a fair indication that his credit standing is so low that he has been refused credit generally throughout the line, and that he is now merely choosing among C.O.D. suppliers. It might appear, consequently that a credit manager could congratulate himself on a higher ratio of cash and C.O.D. sales to total sales than is normal for his company's field, as reflecting such superior diplomacy in refusing regular terms to submarginal customers that they prefer his company to the others that have also refused regular terms. This could well be the correct interpretation. But there is also the possibility that the credit manager may be over-strict in his judgment of acceptable risks for regular terms, and that while some of the rejects may be retained on a C.O.D. basis, some may be lost to competitors.

Calculation of this ratio should be upon an annual basis, as any monthly variations would be attributable primarily to chance factors rather than to considerations of credit policy.

### Rejection ratio

Dividing the number (or dollar total) of refused orders by the total number (or amount) of orders for a period provides another yardstick for measuring credit department effectiveness. This ratio reflects the liberality or severity of the department's customer judgments. A high rejection percentage might also indicate inability of the credit department to cope with one of its most important responsibilities: accepting marginal customers and nursing them through to profitability.

### Bad debt ratio

Most sellers who experienced no bad debt losses over long periods of time would stand convicted of applying unsound credit or collection policy. Either they would be setting their standard of acceptable credit risks so high that they were turning away profitable risk categories of prospects, or would be applying so strict a collection policy that many good but slow-pay customers were driven away.[6] For each company there is some optimum ratio of bad debts to credit sales, determined by such factors as its gross profit margin, the relation of its actual production to its production capacity, and the trend of business conditions. An approach to establishing a company's optimum bad debt ratio may be made by a risk rating analysis of sales of the type described below, or by comparison with the long-term bad debt ratios of other suppliers in the same line of business known to have good credit and collection departments.[7]

Calculation of the actual bad debt ratio for a year just past, and comparison of it with the optimum ratio, provides some guide as to whether a healthy credit and collection policy is being followed, but there is a big margin of error in this comparison. Some accounts that have become insolvent may be written off as bad debts within a brief period after they have become delinquent. Others may be carried as merely delinquent for many months before they are eventually written off. Consequently, a substantial portion of the bad debts recorded for a given calendar or fiscal year may have resulted from credit decisions or collection procedures of the preceding year. Yet they are compared with credit sales of the year just past, and conclusions drawn from the ratio are applied to the credit and collection policies of this recent year. Moreover, a substantial change in sales volume between two years may introduce still another misleading variation into the bad debt ratio. A high volume of earlier-year sales may produce a correspondingly high volume of bad debt losses which are compared with the lower volume of the following-year sales, thus producing a high bad debt ratio which has no relation to the actual situation.

To avoid these misleading distortions of a bad debt ratio based on the actual credit sales and writing off of debts during a calendar or fiscal year, two adustments in the bad debt figure should be made:

1. All accounts past due for some specified period—six months, or eight

---

[6] This does not apply to companies operating at top capacity and not wishing to expand, or whose production and sales are limited by scarce supplies. In such circumstances, sellers can choose their customers, and there is nothing wrong with a bad debt ratio of zero.

[7] A word of caution must be given on using the bad debt ratios of other sellers to determine an optimum ratio for one's own company. The bad debt ratio of any other concern for a single year would be of little value as a guide because of the "lag" factor discussed in the next paragraph. Furthermore, if the other operates on a higher or lower profit margin, its optimum bad debt ratio should, accordingly, be larger or smaller than one's own; if the difference in profit margins is known, an adjustment can be made for it. There may, moreover, still be other differentiating factors, such as the production capacity situation.

months, or ten months—should, for purposes of calculating the bad debt ratio, be counted as bad debts. This procedure limits the lag that is involved in relating bad debts to the sales which produced them.

2. All bad debts should be attributed back to the year of the sales which produced them. This procedure eliminates the other lag distortions noted above. As a consequence, however, the bad debt ratio for any calendar or fiscal year cannot be calculated until after the lapse of the regular credit period plus the arbitrary delinquency period established as suggested in (1) above—from seven to twelve months after the close of the year.

With these two adjustments made, a bad debt ratio lower than the optimum one for the company will indicate either that:

(a) the credit department's standard of acceptable risks during the year to which the bad debts were related was too high, and profitable categories of risks were probably rejected; or

(b) the credit department's collection policy during the latter part of that year and the early part of the following year was too strict, and that good but slow-pay customers may have been lost.

A bad debt ratio higher than the optimum one would indicate the opposite alternatives—either that the credit department had established too low a standard of acceptable risks or that its collection policy was too lax. Variation either way from the optimum bad debt ratio is warning that the credit department was not functioning at full efficiency during the prior year, but the ratio of itself does not indicate whether credit policy or collection policy was at fault.

Trend analysis of a company's bad debt ratio over a year or two will not, by itself, indicate whether its credit or collection policies are becoming stricter or more lax. General business cycle fluctuations, and particular regional and trade developments, as they affect the solvency of the company's customers, are likely to influence the bad debt ratio more profoundly than changes in its credit and collection policy. Such trend analysis, however, does provide some indication whether a credit department had successfully maintained flexible credit and collection policies that were duly adjusted to changes in the outlook for their customer's line of business. A credit department could rightly take pride in a series of bad debt ratios that stayed close to the optimum ratio for the company; it would show excellent forecasting and credit and collection policies effectively geared to anticipated changes in the conditions of the customers' businesses.

### Credit rating analysis

Some companies have experimented with periodic tabulations of their accounts receivable classified by their Dun & Bradstreet ratings. Such tabulations show where the credit department is currently setting its margin of acceptable credit risks, and indicate to some extent the sales volume attributable to the marginal class of risks accepted. This may be a valuable guide when issues involving the balance of sales volume and credit risks are under consideration. Tabulations of this sort based on credit sales instead of accounts receivable would be a more accurate indicator of credit policy and its relation to sales volume, but would be more costly to prepare.

## Collection ratios

The usefulness of the bad debt ratio as an indicator of the soundness of a company's credit and collection policies is mitigated, as noted above, by the lag of several months before the ratio can be determined. A more immediate, though less accurate, indication is provided by the ratio of collections to credit sales, which may be calculated annually, quarterly, or even monthly.

If the total of a company's collections for the year is divided by the total of its credit sales, infallibility in credit judgment and perfection in collection technique—i.e., a consistent record of payment by every customer on or before his due dates—would produce a ratio close to 100 per cent. The reason for the "perfect" percentage being not exactly 100 per cent is that, because of the lag between sales and collections thereon as a result of the terms of sale, sales made during the last months of one year may result in collections during the early months of the next year, and the sales of two successive years may not run parallel. Thus, assume that a supplier giving 60-day terms of sale made exactly $10,000 sales each month during one year, $10,000 sales each month during the first ten months of the next year, and $11,000 sales during each of the last two months of the second year. If its collections were "perfect" in the second year, they would amount to $120,000, since exactly $10,000 would be collected each month. This figure for collections would be divided by $122,000 of sales, since sales in each of the last two months of the year were $11,000 instead of $10,000. This would give a "perfection" ratio of 98.4 per cent. If sales in each of the last two months of the second year had been $9,000, the "perfection" ratio would have been 100.5 per cent.

"Perfect" collections, however, like a "perfect" record of no bad debts, in most cases, would be an indication of bad credit and collection policy. Sound credit policy involves extending credit to risk categories that produce some bad debt loss, and sound collection policy involves a leniency towards slow-paying customers that sometimes results in losses which harsh policy might have prevented. An optimum annual ratio of collections to credit sales should fall short of 100 per cent by the amount of the optimum bad debt ratio for the company, plus or minus any adjustment for lag factors.

Should the actual collection ratio for a concern for any year be below its optimum ratio, the credit department has notice, as in the case of an excessive bad debt ratio, that its standard of acceptable credit risks may be too low, or that its collection policy may be too lenient, or both. There is another possible explanation of a low collection ratio, however, that does not exist in the case of a high bad debt ratio—the company's collection policy may have become more lenient during the year, with the result that some collections that would otherwise have been made in the year do not get recorded until the following year. This last possibility is not necessarily an unfavorable one; the earlier collection policy may have been too strict, and by easing it the credit department is approaching a sounder collection technique. Of course, if the previous policy had been sound or too lenient, a further softening would definitely be unfavorable. A collection ratio higher than the optimum ratio would indicate either too high a standard of credit acceptability, or too harsh a collection technique, or a combination of these policies.

Collection ratios may be calculated quarterly, or even monthly, thus providing a credit manager with a current, but loose, indicator of the results of his credit and collection policies. No consistent optimum ratio can be used as a standard of comparison of these quarterly or monthly ratios, because of the distortions produced by seasonal variation of sales and the lag resulting from terms of sale. In the hypothetical example analyzed in Illustration 21-1, the "perfect" monthly collection ratio varied between 25 per cent and 600 per cent. Current monthly or quarterly collection ratios may be compared with those of other companies in

ILLUSTRATION 21-1.  "Perfect" Monthly Collection Ratios for a Hypothetical Concern with 60-Day Terms and Seasonal Variation of Sales

| Month | Sales | Collections | Collections/ Sales Ratio |
|---|---|---|---|
| January | $10,000 | $ 5,000 | 50  % |
| February | 20,000 | 5,000 | 25 |
| March | 30,000 | 10,000 | 33⅓ |
| April | 20,000 | 20,000 | 100 |
| May | 5,000 | 30,000 | 600 |
| June | 5,000 | 20,000 | 400 |
| July | 5,000 | 5,000 | 100 |
| August | 5,000 | 5,000 | 100 |
| September | 5,000 | 5,000 | 100 |
| October | 5,000 | 5,000 | 100 |
| November | 5,000 | 5,000 | 100 |
| December | 5,000 | 5,000 | 100 |

the same line of business with similar credit terms and a similar pattern of seasonal sales variation provided that the necessary data are available. Such comparison will not determine whether a credit department's policies are sound, but it will indicate whether they are in line with the credit and collection policies current in the line of business. Or a company may compare its current quarterly or monthly ratios with those for the corresponding quarter or month of earlier years. If its terms of sale and the seasonal pattern of its sales have remained the same, such comparison will show whether its credit or collection policies are changing and in what direction.

### Delinquency ratios

Instead of collections or bad debts, the volume of past-due accounts may be compared with credit sales for a specified period—a year, a quarter, or a month—and some norm may be established, by the company's own experience or by the comparative experience of other companies in the same line of business, that will indicate sound credit and collection policies. A lag factor is involved in this comparison also, so that there will be annual and seasonal deviations from the optimum norm that will not reflect credit and collection factors, but variations in the volume of sales. This lag factor, however, is less marked for delinquency ratios than for collection or bad debt ratios, since the delinquency of a past-due account occurs sooner after the sale than its collection or its becoming a bad debt. Therefore the lag factor is less of a distortion in delinquency ratios than in collection and bad debt ratios.

Allowing for the lag factor, a delinquency ratio that exceeded the optimum figure would indicate either too liberal credit extension, a too lenient collection procedure, a collection policy that was becoming more lenient, or a combination of these. Contrariwise, a low delinquency ratio would indicate too strict credit methods, and/or too strict collection procedures, and/or a collection policy that was becoming stricter.

### Aging of accounts

Accounts are "aged" when the amounts due on each are set up in accordance with the periods they have been outstanding. Illustration 21-2 shows a typical form used for aging accounts. Assuming that the company whose aged account schedule appears in this illustration sells on 60-day terms, the entries in column (3) represent its current accounts, and the entries in columns (4) through (7) classify its delinquent accounts according to the degree of their delinquency. Columns (8) and (9) further classify the amounts reported in columns (4) through (7) as

TRADE ACCOUNTS RECEIVABLE AGED

December 31, 1961

| Account (1) | Total Balance (2) | Under 60 Days (3) | 60–90 Days (4) | 90–120 Days (5) | 120–180 Days (6) | Over 180 Days (7) | Doubtful (8) | Uncollectible (9) |
|---|---|---|---|---|---|---|---|---|
| Alapa Mills | 1,420 | 1,300 | 110 | 10 | | | | |
| Arthur Co. | 68 | 68 | | | | | | |
| Ball Co. | 147 | 110 | 37 | | | | | |
| Bell Mills | 34 | | | | 34 | | | |
| Bitter Creek | 101 | 65 | 36 | | | | | |
| Bolls Corp. | 28 | | | | | 28 | | |
| Zenith Mills | 995 | 800 | 195 | | | | | |
| Total Amount | 100,000 | 70,000 | 21,000 | 5,000 | 2,800 | 1,200 | | |
| Total Number | 1,000 | 910 | 460 | 85 | 45 | 10 | | |

ILLUSTRATION 21-2.  Aged Accounts Sheet

"doubtful" and "uncollectible," as a guide to determining bad debt reserves.[8]

Account aging is a common accounting practice, usually undertaken at the time of the annual audit. The results are used for the purpose of informing the management of the general condition of the customers' accounts, and for determining bad debt reserve. If no further use is made of an aged account schedule, the credit department and the over-all management are missing a valuable opportunity to check upon the credit department's work.

If a company has a large number of customers whose accounts are more or less comparable in amount, analysis of its aged accounts can be made on the basis of the amounts involved. Where, however, there are some accounts of much greater amount than the general run, and particularly if some of these large accounts appear in the delinquent columns, the analysis should be made on the basis of the number of accounts, as the relative weight of the large accounts might distort the picture presented.

A company pursuing sound credit and collection policies will have a few delinquent accounts that will eventually develop into bad debts, and a larger number of delinquencies that represent good but slow-paying accounts that are currently past due but will eventually pay their obliga-

---

[8] In calculating the delinquency of an account in *percentages* from month to month, it is advisable to relate the outstanding debt to the original shipment. If $1,000,000 were sold on 60-day terms due on February 10, and $50,000 remained unpaid on March 1, 5 per cent would be entered in the "60-90 days" column of Illustration 21-2. If a month later $20,000 were still open, 2 per cent would be noted in the "90-120 days" column.

tions. Theoretically, there should be an optimum distribution of accounts among the several age categories for any seller, but there is no way this optimum distribution can be calculated in advance, as can be done in the case of bad debt and collection ratios. But comparison by any one concern of its age distribution of accounts with those of other concerns in its line will indicate whether its credit and collection policies are stricter or more lenient than those of the others, and this information may provide a valuable guide to credit department policy. In this connection, some trade associations and credit groups perform a worthy service for their members by collecting and tabulating the annual aged account schedules of their members, and then distributing the results, in comparative percentages, to these members. Trend analysis of the distribution of aged accounts—comparison of the current distribution with those of prior years—will indicate whether a company's credit or collection policies have been changed over the period of the comparison.

Many credit managers have the accounting departments of their concerns prepare monthly aged account statements for them. The percentage distributions of these monthly schedules are, for many companies, comparable month by month—not merely with the corresponding month of preceding years as in the case of monthly collection ratios. In such cases a credit department does not have to wait for the passing of a year before it can ascertain the results of a policy change that may have been designed or incidental. The results manifest themselves, with scarcely any time lag, as shifts of the percentage distribution of accounts between the high and low delinquency columns. When the customers of a company are themselves engaged in a seasonal line, some or even many of them may show a seasonal variation in the promptness of their payments. They may tend to become somewhat delinquent before and during the early part of their seasonal selling period, and clear such delinquencies in the latter part of the season. The change in the percentage distributions of the seller's monthly aged account schedules will show this. Such seasonal variations would have to be taken into account if the credit manager of the concern were trying to check his credit and collection policies by comparison of his monthly aged account schedules.

## Credit department budgets

If a company operates upon a budget, its credit manager must periodically prepare a forecast of the operations and expenses of his department. Apart from its budgetary significance, this obligation to pre-plan in considerable detail the work of a credit department may enhance its efficiency. Too often a credit manager is so pressed by routine duties that he neglects long-range planning. Budgetary deadlines force him to deal annually or semianually with this important function. Furthermore, in analyzing the department's current costs as a basis for budgetary forecasts, the credit manager has an opportunity to measure departmental accomplishments and to weigh alternative procedures.

## SUPPLEMENTARY READINGS

Bermont, L. E., "Data Processing Unlimited," *Credit and Financial Management,* November 1960, p. 8.

————, "Electronics' Jet Age Automates the Office," *Credit and Financial Management,* November 1959, p. 8.

California Workshop of Credit Management, *Customer Counselling,* Credit Research Foundation, New York, 1959.

Credit Research Foundation, *A Study on Credit Management Reporting,* New York, 1953.

————, *Analysis and Evaluation of Credit Management Functions,* New York, 1953.

————, *A Study on Measurement of Credit Department Effectiveness,* New York, 1954.

————, *Credit Management Handbook,* New York, 1958.

————, *Training for Credit Management,* New York, 1954.

"Credits Ties to Sales," *Credit and Financial Management,* July 1957, p. 8.

Curtis, E. T., *Credit Department Organization and Operation,* American Management Association, New York, 1958.

"Data Processing for Small Companies—Service Bureaus Effecting Economies by Use of Punched Paper Tape," *Credit and Financial Management,* November 1960, p. 14.

Dun & Bradstreet, Inc., *How to Control Accounts Receivable for Greater Profits—The Function, Control and Effective Collection of Receivables,* New York, 1959.

"Educating the Customer Helps Build His Credit Position," *Credit and Financial Management,* August 1960, p. 20.

"Four Steps to Profit by Sales-Credit Team," *Credit and Financial Management,* February 1957, p. 8.

Marks, L., *Credit Orientation and Training for Salesmen,* Credit Research Foundation, New York, 1958.

"Microfilm Handling of Receivables Gives Better Control, Speeds Data Processing," *Credit and Financial Management,* May 1956, p. 18.

Moran, E. B., *The Credit Side of Selling, A Manual for Salesmen,* Dartnell Corp., Chicago, 1951.

National Association of Credit Management, *Business Building Through Credit Management,* New York, n.d.

————, *Triple Function of Today's Credit Management,* New York, n.d.

New York Credit and Financial Management Association, *Credit Letters That Increase Sales,* New York, 1952.

————, *Electronic Accounting as it Affects the Credit Department,* New York, 1961.

————, *What Your Salesman Should Know about Credit and Collections*, New York, 1953.

Phelps, C. W., *Credit and Collection Controls for Small Marketers*, Small Business Administration Bulletin No. 33, Washington, D.C., 1958.

Stauffacher, C. B., "Whatever its Godfather, Credit Department is Judged Essential to Overall Management," *Credit and Financial Management*, April 1958, p. 15.

Wood, J. L., *Better Sales Through Credit*, Vantage Press, New York, 1954.

## REVIEW

1. What are the pros and cons of assigning responsibility for credits and collections in a small company to the sales manager? To the bookkeeper? To the treasurer or comptroller?

2. Why should the credit work of a company large enough to have a full-time credit manager be a separate departmental function?

3. What are some of the important issues on which there must be cooperation between the credit and sales departments of a business? Between the credit and accounting departments?

4. Is credit work more efficiently handled if branch office sales managers must have their orders approved by a central credit department, or if branch credit managers are assigned to these branch offices?

5. Discuss the problems of coordinating the work of a branch credit office and its central credit department.

6. Discuss the possibilities of introducing a promotional element into the letters sent by a credit manager to his accounts.

7. Should a credit manager offer a weak customer advice on the latter's business?

8. What would be the significance of (a) a higher proportion of cash and C.O.D. sales for a particular business than is common for the line; (b) a higher-than-normal rejection ratio?

9. What would be the significance of an unusually low bad debt ratio for a particular company? What qualifications must be applied to the use of bad debt ratios as a control factor on a company's credit and collection policy?

10. What would be the significance of an unusually low collection ratio for a particular concern? What qualifications must be applied to the use of collection ratios as a control factor on a concern's credit and collection policy?

11. What would be the significance of an unusually low delinquency ratio? What qualifications must be applied to the use of delinquency ratios as a control factor on a company's credit and collection policy?

12. Explain the use of accounts aging in connection with credit and collection policy control.

## PROBLEM

You are the partner who handles the credits and collections of a wholesale drug house that sells on 2/10 net 60 terms. You check all new accounts in the D&B *Reference Book*. If an account is rated "limited" or "fair," or if it is rated "good" or "high" and the order exceeds an amount related to its letter rating, you draw a report. Otherwise you approve immediately first orders from "good" and "high" accounts.

1. Prepare a "welcome" form letter to be sent to customers whose first orders you have immediately approved.
2. Prepare a "welcome" form letter to be sent to customers approval of whose first orders is being held up for the day or two necessary to get a D&B report.

**PART V**

# SPECIAL APPLICATIONS
# OF BUSINESS CREDIT
# AND COLLECTION MANAGEMENT

# CHAPTER 22

# Industrial Instalment Credit

Sales upon instalment terms are commonly thought of as peculiar to retailing. Before the War Between the States, however, agricultural machinery was sold to farmers on instalment terms involving annual payments. Today a substantial proportion of hotel, restaurant, barber, and beauty shop equipment, machinery, construction equipment, motor trucks, and many other items of business and industrial equipment are sold this way. Manufacturers and distributors of equipment can make many sales on instalment terms that could never be consummated if the purchasers had to pay immediately. For buyers with limited resources, instalment purchase provides an opportunity to obtain equipment they could not acquire if it had to be paid for immediately.[1]

## INDUSTRIAL INSTALMENT TERMS AND INSTRUMENTS

The three elements of mercantile instalment terms are: (1) the down payment, (2) the period over which payment is

---

[1] An alternative method of obtaining equipment without the necessity of immediate payment is leasing it. This procedure is also increasing. Although some prior investigation is usually made by the lessor, the procedure itself is not inherently a credit one. Hence it is not studied in this volume, except for the special "lease-purchase" form.

spread, and (3) the security taken in the form of a conditional sales contract or a chattel mortgage on the equipment sold. The instalment obligation is always evidenced by some form of signed instrument, which may be prepared as an independent document or may be embodied in the sales contract.

### Down payment

Neither custom nor Federal Reserve regulation have established any uniform or minimum down payment proportion for instalment equipment sales. The down payment proportion may be as low as 10 per cent, as high as 50 per cent. High down payments are demanded from purchasers who appear to be poor credit risks, while good credit risks may make strikingly low initial payments. Repossession value of the equipment is also a factor in determining the proportion of down payment.

Many of these sales involve "trade in" of old equipment. In such cases the "trade in" allowance is often considered the full down payment, and the entire balance is covered by the instalment terms.

### Payment period

A businessman usually arranges for instalment purchase of an equipment item costing several hundred or several thousand dollars because he has no capital funds immediately available. He expects to cover the payments out of the profits of the business, to which the new equipment will contribute. Ordinarily he cannot devote all his profits for any given period to this purpose. Therefore he generally seeks extended periods of payment, so that each instalment will be small and leave a substantial remainder of unencumbered profit.

Equipment sellers commonly set one-fourth of the estimated productive life of the equipment as the maximum payment term they will allow. Another procedure for establishing a maximum term is to set, as minimum payments, one-third of the savings or additional earnings expected to result from use of the equipment. This monthly amount, divided into the total initial unpaid balance, sets the term of payment.

Instalment periods of less than a year are ordinarily arranged on business equipment sales only if the value is under $1,000. Twelve-month and eighteen-month terms are common. Two-year and three-year terms may be allowed on heavy industrial equipment. Four-year and five-year terms are not uncommon in the sale of farm machinery.

Monthly payments are generally arranged on sales of business equipment. Payments on farm equipment may be made annually, at crop payment times.

## Interest and special charges

When equipment is sold on an instalment plan, the seller incurs special costs that would not arise with cash or open account sales. There is the cost of the credit investigation, which sometimes is more extended and expensive than in the case of an open-account sale. There is the cost of the long credit extended to the purchaser—an actual cost if the seller discounts the purchaser's note with a bank or finance company, an indirect cost if the seller finances its credit extensions with its own funds and thus operates with a larger capital than would be necessary for cash or short-term sales. There is the risk of loss which must be dealt with as a cost. Under some contracts whereby insurance on the sold equipment is carried by the seller, the insurance premium is an additional cost item.

Instalment sellers usually cover their costs by adding them to the net price of the equipment sold. They generally impose a lump sum "carrying" or "finance" charge to reimburse the cost of the credit inquiry and to cover in some arbitrary fashion the risk of bad debt loss. If the seller carries the insurance on the sold item, the premium is included in this charge. It may also incorporate interest calculated in advance at a rate of 4 to 6 per cent or even higher on the instalment price or, more usually, on the unpaid balance.

Some instalment sellers prefer to have the interest calculated and paid separately with the monthly instalments. If the interest is calculated on each instalment as paid, counting from the contract date, it increases with each payment. If it is calculated month by month on the unpaid balance, it decreases accordingly.

## Conditional sale and chattel mortgage

An important consideration in making instalment equipment sales is the protection the law establishes for the seller. He can recover the sold equipment if the purchaser fails to make payment in full under the terms of the contract. These recovery procedures exist under the law of conditional sales and that of chattel mortgages.

Eight states, including New York and New Jersey, have adopted a Uniform Conditional Sales Act. Another six, among them Pennsylvania, have enacted in recent years the Uniform Commercial Code (see footnote, p. 319 of this volume) which has conditional sales provisions that parallel those of the Uniform Act. Most of the other states provide for validation of various classes of conditional sales through one or another procedure.

A conditional sale is defined by the Uniform Conditional Sales Act as "any contract for the sale of goods under which possession is delivered to the buyer and the property in the goods is to vest in the buyer at a subsequent time upon the payment of part or all of the price." Title to goods subject to a conditional sale thus remains with the seller until payment is completed. If the buyer defaults in his payments, the seller as owner of the property can repossess it, usually without further legal action provided he can do so without causing a breach of the peace. If the buyer resists such repossession, the seller can recover by such common law actions as replevin or detinue or by specified statutory actions. In some states the seller is required to resell repossessed property after a period during which the buyer may redeem it by making payment. Any excess of the resale proceeds over the unpaid balance due the seller has to be paid to the buyer. If a purchaser under a conditional sales contract becomes insolvent, the property covered by the conditional sale does not become part of the assets subject to the liquidation proceeding. It is directly recoverable by the seller, provided he has properly recorded the contract.

An example of a formal conditional sales contract, of a type recommended by the National Association of Credit Management for industrial instalment sales, is shown in Illustration 22-1. Many lawyers and credit managers feel that the terminology of contracts of this sort is antiquated, obsolete, and complex, and hence needlessly confusing and discouraging to purchasers. They hold that the same legal result can be accomplished by a clause in an ordinary sales contract or in the buyer's promissory note that the buyer agrees that the title to the property sold, and to all repairs, replacements of and accession to said property, shall remain in the seller until the purchase price is fully paid.

To make his right of recovery valid as against third parties, such as other creditors or subsequent mortgagees of the buyer, a seller under a conditional sales contract must either file or record the contract, or a copy or memorandum of it, within a designated number of days after the contract is signed. Under the Uniform Conditional Sales Act, the period within which such filing or recording must be made is ten days. The place of filing is usually the office of the recorder or clerk of the county in which the purchaser has his principal place of business or in which the property is located.

In most states a chattel mortgage gives an instalment seller of equipment the same right and procedures of recovery as a conditional sale contract, but under a different legal theory. If a sale is covered by a chattel mortgage on the sold property, title in the property passes to the buyer at the time of sale but is immediately transferred back to the seller by the mortgage and remains with him until the mortgage is cleared. With title thus restored to the seller, he can generally effect recovery of the property under the same procedures as permitted under conditional sales contracts. In some states, however, a chattel mortgage does not transfer

# CONDITIONAL SALES CONTRACT

This agreement, made this . . . . . . . . . . . . . day of . . . . . . . . . . . . .
19 . . . . . ., between . . . . . . . . . . . . of the city of . . . . . . . . . . . . . ,
party of the first part and . . . . . . . . . of the city of . . . . . . . . . ., party
of the second part:

Witnesseth, The said party of the first part has this day delivered to
the said second party the following property, to wit: (*Here insert description*)

upon the terms and conditions hereinafter agreed.

The said second party agrees to receive said property and to pay
said first party therefor the sum of . . . . . . . . . . . . . . . . . . dollars, in
instalments, as follows: the sum of . . . . . . . . . . . . . . . . . . dollars on
the . . . . . . . . . . . . day of each and every month hereafter until the
whole sum of . . . . . . . . . . . . . . . . dollars is fully paid.

It is expressly understood and agreed that the absolute legal title
to all of said property is to remain in said first party until the sum
of . . . . . . . . . . . . . . dollars is paid in full and the said second party
shall have no title to said property until said sum of . . . . . . . . . . . . .
dollars is fully paid.

It is further agreed that in the event of the failure of said second
party to pay any of said instalments when the same shall become due,
then the said first party may enter upon the premises and search for
said property on the premises and in the house and buildings occupied by said second party, and take possession of and remove said property therefrom, with or without any legal process, and that for his acts
in so doing the first party shall be subjected to no proceedings, civil
or criminal, and in such case it is also expressly agreed that the said
first party may retain all the instalments previously paid, as and for
compensation for the use of said property by said second party.

It is further agreed that when said sum of . . . . . . . . . . . . . . . dollars
shall have been fully paid in the manner aforesaid, the absolute legal
title to all of said property shall then, and not until then, vest in the
said second party.

No verbal contract or agreement contrary to any of the terms and
conditions of the foregoing contract has been made. This contract is
executed in duplicate, and each party has one.

In Witness Whereof, the parties hereto have hereunto set their hands
the day and year first above written.

. . . . . . . . . . . . . . . . . . . . . . . . . . . . . . . . .

. . . . . . . . . . . . . . . . . . . . . . . . . . . . . . . . .

ILLUSTRATION 22-1. Conditional Sales Contract Form Recommended by National
Association of Credit Management (from *Credit Manual of
Commercial Laws 1961*, pp. 704-705)

# CHATTEL MORTGAGE

KNOW ALL MEN BY THESE PRESENTS, That ............... of
the town of ................, in the county of ................ and
state of ...................., in consideration of the sum of ...........
dollars to ................. paid by ................. of the county
of ................. and state of ................, the receipt whereof
is hereby acknowledged, does hereby grant, sell, convey and confirm, unto the
said .............. and to .............. heirs and assigns, the following
goods and chattels, to wit: (*Describe property here*). . . .

TO HAVE AND TO HOLD ALL and singular the said goods and chattels,
unto the said mortgagee herein, and his heirs, executors, administrators and
assigns, to his and their sole use, forever. And the mortgagor herein, for himself
and his heirs, executors and administrators, does hereby covenant to and with
the said mortgagee, his heirs, executors, administrators and assigns, that said
mortgagor is lawfully possessed of the said goods and chattels, as of his own
property, and that the same are *free from all encumbrances,* and that he will,
and his executors and administrators shall, warrant and defend the same to
................ the said mortgagee, his heirs, executors, administrators and
assigns, against the lawful claims and demands of all persons.

PROVIDED, NEVERTHELESS, That if said mortgagor ..........., his
executors or administrators, shall well and truly pay unto the said mortgagee
.............., his executors, administrators, or assigns .... (*Describe notes
or debt secured*) ........................................ then this
mortgage is to be void, otherwise to remain in full force and effect.

AND, PROVIDED, ALSO, That it shall be lawful for the said mortgagor,
his executors, administrators and assigns, to retain possession of the said goods
and chattels and at his own expense to keep and use the same, until he or his
executors, administrators or assigns, shall make default in the payment of the
said sum of money above specified, either in principal or interest, at the time
or times, and the manner hereinbefore stated. And the said mortgagor hereby
covenants and agrees that in case default shall be made in payment of the
note . . . . aforesaid, or of any part thereof, or the interest thereon, on the
day or days respectively on which the same shall become due and payable; or
if the mortgagee, his executors, administrators, or assigns, shall feel himself
insecure or unsafe, or shall fear diminution, removal or waste of said property;
or if the mortgagor shall sell or assign or attempt to sell or assign, the said
goods and chattels, or any interest therein; or if any writ, or any distress warrant, shall be levied on said goods and chattels, or any part thereof; then, and
in any or either of the aforesaid cases, all of said note . . . . and sum of money,
both principal and interest, shall at the option of the said mortgagee, his
executors, administrators or assigns, without notice of said option to anyone,
become at once due and payable, and the said mortgagee, his executors, administrators or assigns, or any of them, shall thereupon have the right to take immediate possession of said property, and for that purpose may pursue the same
wherever it may be found, and may enter any of the premises of the mortgagor,
with or without force or process of law, wherever the said goods and chattels
may be, or be supposed to be, and search for the same, and if found, to take
possession of, and remove, and sell, and dispose of the said property or any
part thereof, at public auction, to the highest bidder, after giving ..........
days' notice of the time, place and terms of sale, together with a description of
the property to be sold, by notices posted up in three public places in the
vicinity of such sale, or at private sale, with or without notice, for cash or on

ILLUSTRATION 22-2. Chattel Mortgage Form Recommended by National Association
of Credit Management (from *Credit Manual of Commercial
Laws,* 1961, pp. 708-709)

credit, as the said mortgagee, his heirs, executors, administrators or assigns, agents or attorneys, or any of them, may elect; and, out of the money arising from such sale, to retain all costs and charges for pursuing, searching for, taking, removing, keeping, storing, advertising, and selling such goods and chattels, and all prior liens thereon, together with the amount due and unpaid upon said note . . . ., rendering the surplus, if any remain, unto said mortgagor . . . . or his legal representatives.

In Witness Whereof, I have hereunto set my hand and affixed my seal this . . . . . . . . day of . . . . . . . . . . . . . . , 19 . . . . .

In the presence of:

. . . . . . . . . . . . . . . . . . . . . . . . . . . . .

. . . . . . . . . . . . . . . . . . . . . . . L.S.

. . . . . . . . . . . . . . . . . . . . . . .

ILLUSTRATION 22-2. *(Concluded)*

title back to the seller, but merely gives him a lien upon it. Before he can recover the property he must foreclose under the lien.

A chattel mortgage, an example of which is shown in Illustration 22-2, is a more formal document than a conditional sales contract. Its effect cannot be encompassed by the introduction of a clause into an ordinary sales contract or into a buyer's promissory note. Because of this formalism, a chattel mortgage may seem to some purchasers to be a more enveloping document than a conditional sales contract. It may thus act as a deterrent factor on the consummation of instalment sales. To give protection against third parties, the seller must file or record a chattel mortgage in the same way as a conditional sales contract.

For instalment sales purposes a chattel mortgage apparently possesses no advantage over a conditional sales contract. It may even embody some psychological disadvantage. There is still sharp dispute among the credit managers of equipment companies as to the respective merits of conditional sales contracts and chattel mortgages. The trend of opinion seems to be in favor of the former, for the reasons indicated.

The conditional sales laws and chattel mortgage laws of the several states vary in many important particulars. No credit manager should depend on his general textbook knowledge of the law in these fields. In every case, the law of the particular state involved should be carefully studied, preferably from some law service on conditional sales and chattel mortgages, such as that published by Prentice-Hall, Inc. The summary of these laws published in the National Association of Credit Management's *Credit Manual of Commercial Laws* is a useful guide but is not intended as a manual covering the important, intricate details. Preparation of the documents for conditional sales contracts or chattel mortgages adapted to the laws of the various states wherein the company operates should be assigned to attorneys in these states.

## The buyer's promise to pay

The buyer's obligation on an instalment purchase of equipment is always evidenced by a signed instrument—a clause of the sales contract, or a promissory note or a series of such notes.

Should the buyer be requested to sign a series of notes, each for a specific instalment payment and dated for the time of such payment? Such procedure would provide the seller with a set of collection instruments which could be sent to the buyer's bank for collection. Default upon any payment in the series could then occur only if the buyer had insufficient funds in his bank account, or if he notified his bank to stop payment on the note. But the cumbersome procedure of having to sign 12, or 18 or more promissory notes might influence the buyer against the purchase. It would certainly be poor selling technique.

Most instalment sellers of equipment prefer to have the customer sign a single obligation which lists both the over-all amount and the specific payments to be made. An example of a promissory note embodying such an obligation is shown in Illustration 22-3. Collection of the individual instalments is then made upon the basis of notices sent to the customer in advance of the payment date, or by giving the customer a coupon book covering the series of his payments to be made.[2] Another effective col-

ILLUSTRATION 22-3. Instalment Payment Promissory Note

lection technique is the use of drafts drawn by the seller and sent to the buyer's bank; an example of such a draft is shown in Illustration 22-4. Such a draft is not automatically payable out of a buyer's bank account,

---

[2] An example of a retail instalment coupon book is shown in Illustration 29-1. With a few slight variations, it would serve as an example of an equipment instalment coupon book.

| TO COLLECTING BANK: | |
|---|---|
| This instrument represents a payment due on our customer's time payment account. | |

$.......................................... Cleveland, Ohio.........................................
PLUS INTEREST                                         (To be inserted at home office)

On.............................................pay to the order of
(To be inserted at home office)
THE UNION BANK OF COMMERCE (6-15), Cleveland, Ohio

through.....................................................................................................................................the
(Please insert name, branch and city of customer's bank)

**Please do not protest.**

sum of.......................................................................................................................dollars
with interest at 6% from the date of this instrument. Value received and charge the same to
the account of:

**Notify our bank of disposition by mail.**

.................................................................          THE LINCOLN ELECTRIC COMPANY
(Name of Customer)                                    12818 Coit Road
                                                      Cleveland 1, Ohio
.................................................................
(Street)

CL307 5M 11-45

.................................................................          By.................................................................
(City and State)                                           (Authorized Signature)

ILLUSTRATION 22-4. Draft Drawn under Instalment Promissory Note

as is a promissory note bearing the buyer's signature. This difficulty may be overcome, however, by a "letter of authorization," prepared by the seller, submitted to the buyer for his signature and sent by the buyer to his bank. It authorizes the bank to honor the series of drafts under the promissory note as they are presented. No difficulty is reported in collecting on such drafts.

Instalment notes should always contain an "acceleration clause." It provides that if any payment is defaulted, the entire unpaid balance immediately becomes due. Without such a clause, a buyer could be in default on past instalments while he would not be in default on payments whose dates had not yet arrived. This situation would clearly hamper any action by the seller to recover his equipment or its price for the duration of the entire instalment term. An acceleration clause remedies this situation by, in effect, making default upon any payment a default of the full unpaid balance. However, a seller who does not wish to press or embarrass a buyer who is in default upon one or two payments, but who may be expected to carry through his full schedule of payments with a slight lag, can waive the operation of the acceleration clause with respect to one or several defaulted payments, without sacrificing his right to apply it to future defaults. An acceleration clause may be seen in the instalment sale promissory note shown in Illustration 22-3.

### "Lease-purchase" of equipment

An interesting hybrid between instalment sale and leasing of equipment is the "lease-purchase" plan. It is used in the marketing of many kinds of equipment, from machinery and trucks to office appliances. Under this arrangement the instalment purchaser does not buy his equipment as of the date of the contract, but rents it. The monthly rental agreed upon is the instalment price of the item (including "carrying charges") divided by the number of months included in the instalment term. Upon satisfactory payment of all rental charges through the instalment period, the lessee may (and usually does) exercise an option to have the lease converted to a purchase, with the rental payments previously made accepted as the purchase price. If the lessee defaults upon his rental payments, the lease provides that he must return the property and the lessor is given full authority to recover it.

Unless other provision is made, the first rental payment under a lease-purchase agreement—equivalent to the down payment of a regular instalment sale—is the fractional part of the total price of the equipment determined by the number of months of the contract term. Under an 18-month contract, this would amount to only 5.55 per cent of the price. As an instalment down payment this would be too low for any lessee-buyer who was not the highest type of credit risk. The difficulty can be overcome by the requirement of a "security deposit," which may be applied toward the purchase price if and when the customer exercises his option; the "lease" period is shortened by the number of months' rent represented by the "security deposit."

Decisions in the federal courts and in most state courts have held that a lease-purchase arrangement is, in the eyes of the law, a conditional sales contract and subject to the laws governing such contracts. In most practical and legal respects the two procedures of acquiring equipment operate identically. Why, then, should the lease-purchase agreement have developed as a substitute for the conditional sale contract? The answer is that many purchasers of equipment prefer to "expense" its cost over the year or two during which the "rental" payments are made rather than treat it as a capital item to be recovered through protracted depreciation. Accounting convention permits "rental" payments to be treated on companies' books as current cost items, whereas instalment payments under a conditional sales contract can not be so entered.[3] Exercise of the purchase option upon payment of the final "rental" does not change the original treatment of the payments as current costs. The lessor company commonly treats the transaction as a sale, with the equipment price plus finance charges less the first monthly payment entered as a receivable.

## REFINANCING INDUSTRIAL INSTALMENT SALES

Most distributors and some manufacturers who sell business and industrial equipment on instalment terms have these sales

---

[3] Lease-purchase payments may not be treated as deductible expense for federal income tax purposes, however (Internal Revenue Service, Rulings 55-541 and 55-542, *Bulletin 35*, August 29, 1955).

refinanced. They either discount their customers' notes with, or assign such notes to, finance companies or commercial banks.

The down payment required and the maximum term of payment allowed in such refinancing is generally established in advance by the finance company or bank. The financing institution makes an independent credit investigation of the customer, and arrives at its own credit decision. If it finds the customer acceptable, he is usually notified that his instalment purchase is being refinanced by the institution in question, and that his note should be made out to, and his instalments paid to, the financing institution instead of to the seller.

Most instalment equipment financing is done upon a "recourse" basis— if the customer fails in his payments to the financing institution, the seller must assume the liability. A common arrangement in such cases is to require the seller to take up a customer's note if three monthly payments are missed. As further protection, financing institutions often advance the seller something less than the face amount of their customers' notes. The proportion advanced may be 90 per cent, or 80 per cent, or 75 per cent, or even as low as 66⅔ per cent. Lease-purchase contracts may be similarly refinanced.

## SOURCES OF CREDIT INFORMATION

The credit manager of an instalment seller of business equipment uses all the regular sources of mercantile credit information— mercantile agency rating books and reports, NACM interchange reports, queries to references and banks, salesmen's reports, financial statement analysis. In addition, he will often obtain a special inquiry report on a possible customer from one of the agencies that specialize in such reports. The hundreds or even thousands of dollars that may be risked by his company on a single equipment sale warrant the extra cost of such individual inquiry reports when the mercantile agency report and other ordinary information on a customer—particularly a new company that is acquiring equipment to start a business—prove to be inadequate as a basis for forming a credit decision.

## THE CREDIT DECISION

It might seem, at first thought, as though an instalment sale of equipment under a conditional sales contract or a chattel mortgage could not result in any bad debt loss for the seller. Should the buyer default at any stage of his payment schedule, the seller can repossess the equipment. Because of deterioration, its repossessed value will be less than its original value. But the down payment, and the instalment payments made prior to the default are likely to cover, if not exceed, the difference.

Why, under such circumstances, should a seller bother to make any credit inquiry at all? Why not sell to any buyer who is prepared to make a down payment of 25 or 30 per cent of the instalment price? There are four arguments why the right of repossession should not lower standards of instalment credit judgment:

1. Indifference to the credit status of instalment purchasers of business equipment would probably involve a seller in substantial losses despite the power of repossession. It would be an open invitation to credit racketeers to purchase valuable equipment upon down payments that represented only a fraction of its cost, then disappear and dispose of the equipment through underworld channels.

2. A large proportion of the bad-risk customers would default on their payments. The seller could avoid direct loss by repossessing the equipment, but his reputation and future sales possibilities would be unfavorably affected. Prospective customers, sound credit risks as well as poor ones, would avoid a seller reputed to make extensive resort to repossession.

3. Excessive repossessions would overload the seller with used equipment. It could probably be resold at a profit over its repossession value. Many of these used-item sales, however, would be in place of new-equipment sales at higher profit margins.

4. An irresponsible attitude of an equipment seller towards credit risks would make it difficult for him to refinance his customer instalment notes. Banks as well as finance companies require thorough credit investigations.

Instalment sales of equipment should be, and generally are, based on just as careful analysis of credit factors ascertained from information on a customer as are ordinary mercantile credit sales. A customer who would be unacceptable as a mercantile credit risk would generally be unacceptable as a risk for instalment purchase of equipment. In many cases, indeed, a customer who might be considered acceptable by a mercantile seller for a small credit limit—say $50 or $75—might be deemed unacceptable by an instalment seller of equipment since the amount involved would be several hundred or thousand dollars. A larger proportion of business enterprises with low credit ratings than of high-credit ones buy equipment on instalment terms, but this is only because high-credit companies are generally able to purchase their equipment on cash terms and do not have to apply for instalment credit.

There is one important case, however, where a risk deemed unacceptable for mercantile credit might be given instalment credit on the purchase of equipment. A man just starting a small business with a limited capital is often denied credit by suppliers of merchandise until he has proved himself by several months' operations, or at best he may be allowed only small arbitrary credit limits. If equipment sellers were to adopt the same policy, the business might never be started since the man's available capital might not cover cash purchase of the necessary equipment. Because of the large unit values involved in equipment sales, and the substantial unit profit on such sales if they are duly paid, it is worth while for an equipment seller to obtain a special inquiry report on such a purchaser. If this shows that the man starting a business has character and background that promise a reasonable chance of success, an equipment seller will usually extend instalment terms. Such dependence on the character factor alone is not rash indiscretion. The special inquiry report, after all, has provided the equipment seller with a fuller picture of the customer's character than a mercantile seller can obtain from the ordinary agency report. And, at the worst, the equipment seller always has the ultimate protection of repossession.

## COLLECTION

In mercantile collection procedure, the responsibility for making prompt payment rests with the customer. At most, the seller's credit department may, as a reminder, send him a duplicate statement or duplicate invoice shortly before the due date. In instalment equipment sale procedure, on the contrary, collection initiative commonly rests with the seller. He must mail each current promissory note, or each notice or draft under an over-all promissory note, to the customer's bank in time for it to arrive on or before the due date.

An indispensable collection control instrument in the credit office of an instalment equipment seller, then, is a tickler file. If a series of promissory notes are signed by the buyer, these are immediately placed in the file in such manner that, over the entire period of the instalment terms, each one in turn comes out on the day when it must be mailed to the buyer's bank so as to arrive on or just before the due date. If the buyer signs an over-all promissory note, the notices or drafts under it are prepared immediately afterwards, and they are placed in the tickler file in the same manner as a series of individual notes.

### Correspondence upon default

Default upon an instalment notice, note, or draft is treated quite differently from delinquency upon an open-account obligation. Default upon an instrument is more decisive and more serious than neglect to pay an account obligation on time. There can be no preliminary courteous assumption that a notice, note, or draft was overlooked. The only possible reasons for its not being paid is that the purchaser had no funds in his bank account or that he specifically stopped payment on the instrument. There can be no graduated series of collection appeals, possibly extending over several months, for a specific past-due amount. A default on one instalment payment will probably be followed by another in a month's time, and then by another, with the total amount in default increasing with each succeeding month. Such default is likely to be cumulative, with the possibility of collection decreasing rapidly the longer the default continues.

The first collection step usually taken when an equipment instalment note or draft is returned unsatisfied is to notify the customer that the default has occurred, and that the note or draft will be returned to the bank in a few days' time for recollection. No recriminations or reproaches are made. No apology is made for the prompt return of the note or draft for recollection. If the default resulted from a momentary financial embarrassment of the customer, the few days' delay before the note or draft is received again by the bank gives the purchaser opportunity to build up his account to meet the note or draft on its return. The impersonality of the letter allows the matter to be passed off without loss of face to the customer. If more than a temporary embarrassment is involved, the purchaser has time to write, telephone, or telegraph the seller an explanation of his difficulty and request that the note or draft should not be resubmitted to his bank.

If no reply to this initial letter is received from the customer, and if the note or draft is returned unsatisfied a second time, another letter is sent, courteously requesting an explanation of the default, and pointing to the acceleration clause in the sales contract or promissory note. No threat of repossession is ordinarily made in this second letter, but the implication is clearly there.

Should this letter also remain unanswered, a third letter will not merely warn of repossession, but will set a date when repossession will be undertaken if no reply has been received.

Silence in response to collection letters sent by an instalment equipment seller is less frequent than to ordinary mercantile collection letters. The customer knows that the seller has the weapon of repossession in reserve. He must come to an agreement with the seller, and that quickly, or he will lose his equipment. Hence the very first letter ordinarily brings a reply giving either an excuse or a good reason for the default, and requesting an extension or some other form of leniency. In only a small proportion of cases are the second and third letters in the series needed. Almost without exception the third brings some sort of response.

### Use of collectors

A personal call by a member of the credit department staff is considered by many equipment credit managers to be the most effective method of clearing up a default on an instalment equipment purchase.

Talking man-to-man with the customer, the credit department representative is often able to obtain a check for the amount in default—which the customer may have intended to devote to some personal or other business purpose. If it is absolutely impossible for the purchaser to make his payment, the visiting credit man is in a strategic position to probe into the causes of the default, and to discover whether the customer will be able to meet future notes or drafts under the instalment contract. Such information is of prime importance to the credit manager in determining how to treat the account.

Accordingly the credit office of a small equipment seller usually has one member of its force who, in addition to other duties, serves as visiting collector for delinquent accounts within a reasonable radius of the home office. The credit departments of large equipment sellers often include one or more full-time collectors.

### Extensions and compromises

As stated earlier in this chapter, no instalment seller of business equipment wishes to acquire the reputation of ready resort to repossession. Therefore, whenever it is manifest that a purchaser cannot meet the payment obligations originally established by the purchase contract and his promissory note, he will be allowed an extension on one or two instalments, or the balance of his payment schedule will be rearranged to permit him to make smaller monthly payments over a longer period of time, or some other adjustment will be worked out. Some equipment sellers even follow a tacit policy of foregoing repossession and writing off as bad debts the unpaid balances on defaulted accounts whenever prior payments cover the cost of the equipment and other cost factors in the transaction, and repossession of the equipment would deprive the customer of the means of his livelihood.

When an extension is granted on one or two defaulted payments which come early in the series, they are rarely deferred as lump sums for some specified period of time. The customer, after all, has a further series of payments coming due month after month. To extend time on a defaulted payment as a lump sum would mean that in some future month the customer would have to try to meet a double instalment payment. If circumstances previously caused him to default on a single payment, it is unlikely that soon thereafter he will be able to make a double payment. Therefore when a deferment is granted, the amount in default is usually divided and spread over a number of months to come. While it might be impossible for the customer to meet a double payment in any one month, he may be able to stretch his resources sufficiently to cover a one-and-one-fifth or a one-and-one-quarter payment in each of several successive months. If the default occurs in one of the last of a series of instalment payments, the extension may take the form of adding it as one more payment to be made after the series as originally planned has been completed.

It is customary to charge interest on late instalment payments and extended payments.

## SUPPLEMENTARY READINGS

Cagle, C. H., "Security Pledged on Business Loans at Member Banks," *Federal Reserve Bulletin*, September 1959, p. 1114.

"Capital Goods on the Cuff; Industry Installment Pay Plan," *Sales Management*, October 1, 1950, p. 29.

Celia, A. P., *Financing Industrial Equipment Leases*, Credit Research Foundation, New York, 1959.

Federal Reserve System, "Credit from Large to Small Business," in *Financing Small Business*, (Report to the Committees on Banking and Currency and the Select Committees on Small Business, Washington, D.C., 1958), Part II, vol. 2, p. 482.

Saulnier, R. J., and N. H. Jacoby, *Financing Equipment for Commercial and Industrial Enterprise*, National Bureau of Economic Research, Studies in Business Financing, New York, 1944.

## REVIEW

1. What is the customary industrial instalment down payment?
2. How is the payment period of an industrial instalment contract usually determined?
3. What costs are commonly added to the cash price of equipment when it is sold on instalment terms?
4. Explain a "conditional sale."
5. Explain a "chattel mortgage."
6. Explain how payment procedure under an industrial instalment sale may be arranged.
7. Explain "lease purchase" of equipment.
8. Does financing of equipment instalment sales by a bank or finance company make any difference in terms or procedures?
9. What sources of credit information are used by equipment instalment sellers?
10. Why should careful credit judgment be exercised in industrial instalment selling, even though the seller has the protection of repossession?
11. Why is a tickler file essential to effective collection of industrial instalment obligations?
12. Explain the sequence of collection steps taken if a customer defaults upon equipment instalment payment.
13. Discuss the use of collectors by equipment manufacturers who sell on instalment terms.
14. Discuss the attitude of equipment company credit managers toward granting adjustments to delinquent customers.

# CHAPTER 23

# Mercantile Loan Practices of Banks, Factors, and Finance Companies

Heretofore we have studied the credit and collection practices of business enterprises that *sell goods or services* on credit terms to other business enterprises. Now we turn to the credit operations of certain classes of financial institutions—commercial banks, factors, and finance companies—that make *mercantile* credit available to manufacturers, wholesalers, retailers, and service enterprises through short-term loans [1] and through financing accounts receivable.

The credit information utilized by business concerns selling on credit terms and by financial institutions extending mercantile credit is generally similar, though there are significant differences in the relative dependence placed on the various sources. Similar considerations also influence mercantile credit decisions of business concerns and financial institutions. The problems and procedures of bank loan departments and of factors and finance companies constitute, therefore, a specialized development of ordinary domestic credit and collection management.

---

[1] A bank *mercantile* or *commercial* loan is a short-term one to an enterprise to enable it to carry seasonal inventories of materials, goods or receivables, or to meet exceptional working capital demands. It is to be distinguished from an intermediate-term *working capital* loan, and from a *financial* loan sought by the borrower for investment or speculative purposes.

## TERMS AND INSTRUMENTS OF
## BANK MERCANTILE LOANS

We must survey certain features of bank mercantile loans as a background for understanding bank loan management.

### Secured loans

A substantial proportion of bank mercantile loans are unsecured. They are made exclusively on the basis of the credit standing of the borrowing concern. The balance are made on the basis of collateral security or strength of guarantee. Acceptable forms of collateral security are: (1) stocks and bonds, (2) commodity paper—public warehouse receipts covering commodities stored by the borrower, (3) customer paper—promissory notes and trade acceptances received by the borrowing concern from its customers,[2] (4) savings accounts and the cash surrender value of life insurance policies on principals of the borrowing concern, and (5) accommodation endorsements.[3]

Secured loans are made by banks under three circumstances: (1) when the credit standing of the applicant does not warrant granting an unsecured loan; (2) when an applicant who would rate an unsecured loan prefers to borrow upon security in order to take advantage of the lower interest rate; (3) when the purpose of the loan is to carry a warehoused commodity inventory whose sale will provide the funds to repay the loan, thus making it "self-liquidating."

When a bank considers making a secured mercantile loan, its loan officers must study both the character of the collateral and the credit standing of the applicant. The better the collateral the poorer can be the credit status of the borrowing concern, and vice versa. A bank loan officer must therefore be expert not merely in judging the financial position of clients, but also in appraising the worth of the collateral security. Upon his judgment of the *quality* of the collateral offered depends the *quantity* needed adequately to secure a requested loan. Rarely, if ever,

---

[2] In rare instances, a bank will "discount" customer paper when the customers in question are top-grade risks. In such cases the bank "buys" the customer paper for its face value less a prepaid interest charge, but the "borrower" remains secondarily liable on the assigned notes or acceptances through his endorsement.

More common by far is the loan arrangement whereby the borrower negotiates a regular time or call loan with an amount of customer paper providing ample collateral for the loan. As customer notes or acceptances included in the collateral mature and are paid, either the loan is correspondingly reduced, or the matured paper must be replaced by additional customer paper or other collateral.

[3] Financing assigned accounts receivable might be considered a form of secured bank loan. It is here treated as a special type of mercantile financing and is studied in a later section of this chapter.

does a bank make a secured loan up to the full market value of the collateral pledged. Some fraction of this value is deemed a *margin* over and above the amount of the loan to cover possible decline in the value of traded securities or collateral representing traded commodities, and possible default on customer paper. The necessary margin may vary from a small percentage of the loan to several times its amount, according to the quality of the collateral and the relative credit standing of the borrower.

### Restrictive covenants

A bank may safeguard a mercantile loan, in place of or in addition to requiring security, by incorporating restrictive covenants in the loan agreement. A borrowing concern may, for example, be required to maintain a specified working capital balance during the duration of the loan. Or dividend declarations, or payment of certain elements of officers' salaries, or withdrawals from a partnership may require the bank's permission until the loan is cleared.

### Period of bank mercantile loans

Bank mercantile loans may be classified, according to the period for which they are extended, into two categories: (1) specific-term or "time" loans, and (2) demand or call loans.

*Time* loans are usually made for 30, 60, 90, or 120 days. Very large loans, on which the interest charge is so substantial that every day counts, may be negotiated for some other specific number of days. In case a period longer than 120 days is warranted, a loan is commonly granted for 120 days with the understanding that it will be renewed for another term upon maturity; this renewal may even be repeated. A bank cannot call a time loan before maturity unless special circumstances warrant it, such as the decline of the value of the collateral for a secured loan below a specified figure. The borrower may repay in advance of the due date. Technically this should give him no advantage, since on time loans the interest charge for the full term is customarily prepaid; under such circumstances, however, a bank may allow some rebate on interest previously "discounted."

A *demand* or *call* mercantile loan has no specific term. The bank may demand repayment at any time, and the borrower also has the right to repay whenever he wants. Such loans are usually negotiated by manufacturers or wholesalers with warehoused stocks of commodities, who cannot foretell with any degree of accuracy for how long they will retain these stocks and hence need the borrowed funds. They borrow and repay repeatedly at intervals, depending on their own schedules of payments and receipts.

## Lines of credit

The needs of many business enterprises for bank credit follow seasonal patterns. Purchases of an agricultural raw material may be concentrated in the few months of a crop season while its processing and sale, or its resale, are spread fairly evenly through the year. Or a raw material may be bought and processed rather uniformly throughout the year while the sale of the finished commodity, in response to seasonal demand, is concentrated in a couple of months. Some wholesalers and retailers are also subject to seasonal discrepancies between payments and receipts. Bank loans are a normal recourse for bridging the gaps. But instead of negotiating one loan after another as seasonal needs expand, a business man usually arranges with his bank for a "line of credit," that is, an advance determination of the maximum cumulated total of loans that he will be allowed to incur during the season. Thereafter, during the period of the line, he can borrow any amount within this limit by simply telephoning his wish to the bank. Interest is charged only on the balance outstanding. The line can usually be renewed when it expires. The bank may reduce or even cancel a line of credit at its discretion, though it usually feels morally obligated to adhere to its agreement. If a borrower wants an irrevocable *commitment* from the bank, he has to negotiate such an arrangement at a slightly higher cost.

There are two tacit understandings between bank and borrower with regard to lines of credit. One is the *compensating balance* requirement under which the borrower maintains a minimum account balance equal to some percentage—generally 10, 15, or 20 per cent—of the line. The other is *annual clearance*—complete payment of all debt balance under a line at least once a year. This gives periodic assurance that the line is fulfilling its proper, seasonal purpose and has not become frozen into an investment in the borrower's business. Both requirements are subject to flexible interpretation.

## Instruments of bank credit

The instrument upon which bank loans are generally made is the promissory note, described in Chapter 3 of this volume. If for a demand or call loan, the note is made payable "on demand" and the rate of interest is stated. If for a time loan, the note is made payable "............ days after date" and no interest rate is generally stated, since the interest charge is usually deducted in advance as discount. The note is made to the *order* of the bank, and thereby established as a negotiable instrument, with consequent protection and advantages to the bank as payee. The bank may, for example, rediscount such a note with its federal reserve bank.

If accommodation endorsers are required as security for the loan, the back of the note will contain lines for their names and addresses. In the case of such a third-party guaranty for a line of credit rather than for a

$____________ ____________________ 19___

________________________after date, for value received, the undersigned promise(s) to pay to

THE CHASE MANHATTAN BANK (hereinafter called the Bank), or order, at its Head Office, in the City of New York, in lawful money of the United States,

________________________________________Dollars,

with interest at the rate of__________per cent. per annum, having deposited with the Bank as security for the payment of this note and of all other Liabilities of the undersigned as hereinafter defined, the following property, viz:____________________

The term "Liabilities" as herein used shall include any and all indebtedness, notes, bonds, debentures, obligations and liabilities of any kind of the undersigned to the Bank and also to others to the extent of their participations granted to or interests therein created or acquired for them by the Bank, now or hereafter existing, arising directly between the undersigned and the Bank or acquired outright, conditionally or as collateral security from another by the Bank, whether absolute or contingent, joint or several, or joint and several, secured or unsecured, due or not due, direct or indirect, including, without limiting the generality of the foregoing, liabilities to the Bank of the undersigned as a member of any partnership, syndicate, association or other group, arising by operation of law, contractual or tortious, liquidated or unliquidated, at law, in equity, in admiralty or otherwise, and whether heretofore or hereafter incurred or given by the undersigned as principal, surety, endorser, guarantor or otherwise. The term "Security" as herein used shall include the balance of every deposit account, now or at any time hereafter existing, of the undersigned with the Bank or any other claim of the undersigned against the Bank, all money, negotiable instruments, commercial paper, notes, bonds, stocks, credits, choses in action, claims, demands, or any interest in any thereof, and any other property, rights and interests, of the undersigned, or any evidence thereof, which have been or at any time shall be delivered to or otherwise come into the possession or custody or under the control of the Bank or any of its agents, associates or correspondents, for any purpose, whether or not accepted for the purpose or purposes for which they are delivered or intended. The Bank shall be deemed to have possession, control or custody of any of the Security actually in transit to or set apart for it or any of its agents, associates, correspondents or others acting in its behalf.

As security for the payment of this note and/or of any and all the Liabilities, the undersigned hereby pledge(s) to the Bank all such Security capable of pledge and bargain(s), sell(s), assign(s) and transfer(s) to the Bank, and/or give(s) it a general lien upon, and/or right of set-off of, all right, title and interest of the undersigned in and to any thereof incapable of pledge or inadequately pledged, such pledge and/or sale, assignment, transfer and/or lien and/or right of set-off being made or created for the protection and security of the Bank and/or any other or others (but in such proportions as the Bank may determine if held for the benefit of more than one, such determination of the Bank to be conclusive) having participations or interests in the Liabilities as aforesaid, and in trust in the proportions aforesaid for the benefit of such other or others to the extent of the said participations or interests of any other or others therein.

To the extent and in the manner permitted by law, the right is expressly granted to the Bank, at its option, to transfer or cause to be transferred to, or registered in the name of, itself or its nominee or nominees, any and all stocks, bonds, and other securities and property included in the Security, and whether or not so transferred or registered, to receive the income and dividends thereon, including stock dividends and rights to subscribe, and to hold the same as a part of the Security and/or apply it on the principal of and/or interest on any of the Liabilities, at its discretion to exchange all or any of the Security for other property upon the reorganization, recapitalization or other readjustment of any corporation and in connection with any such reorganization, recapitalization or readjustment to deposit all or any of the Security with any committee or depositary upon such terms and conditions as it may determine, after such transfer or registration to vote or cause its nominee or nominees to vote all or any of such stocks, bonds and securities, and to exercise or cause its nominee or nominees to exercise all or any powers with respect to any stocks, bonds or other securities or property forming a part of the Security, with the same force and effect as an absolute owner thereof, all without notice and without liability except to account for property actually received by it.

The Bank, at its discretion may, whether or not any of the Liabilities be due, in its name and/or in the name of anyone for whom it has acted or shall act as agent in connection with any such Liability, or in the name of the undersigned, demand, sue for, collect and/or receive any money, securities or other property at any time due, payable or receivable on account of or in exchange for, or make any compromise or settlement deemed desirable with respect to, any Security, but shall be under no obligation so to do. If the Security shall consist of or include negotiable instruments and/or other choses in action and/or promises or agreements of any character to pay money, they may be sold in the manner hereinafter provided with respect to the sale of any of the Security; or the Bank may extend the time of payment of any such obligation, arrange for payment of any thereof in instalments, or otherwise modify the terms thereof as to any other party liable thereon, without thereby incurring responsibility to, or discharging or otherwise affecting any liability of, the undersigned thereon or in connection therewith. The Bank upon default (in payment, furnishing security or otherwise) hereunder or in connection with any of the Liabilities (whether such default be that of the undersigned or of any other party obligated thereon or in respect thereto in whole or in part), may sell or cause to be sold in the Borough of Manhattan, New York City, or elsewhere, in one or more sales or parcels, at such price or prices as the Bank may deem best, and either for cash or on credit, or for future delivery, without assumption of any credit risk, all or any of the Security, at any broker's board or at public or private sale, without demand of performance or notice of intention to sell or of time or place of sale, and the Bank and/or anyone in whose behalf it has acted or shall act as hereinbefore provided, or anyone else, may be the purchaser of any or all property, rights and/or interests so sold and thereafter hold the same absolutely, free from any claim or right of whatsoever kind, including any equity of redemption, of the undersigned, any such demand, notice or right and equity being hereby expressly waived and released. The undersigned will bear and pay all expenses (including expense for legal services of every kind) of, or incidental to, the enforcement of any of the provisions hereof or of any of the Liabilities, or any actual or attempted sale, or any exchange, enforcement, collection, compromise or settlement of any of the Security, and/or receipt of the proceeds thereof, and for the care of the Security and defending or asserting the rights and claims of the Bank in respect thereof, by litigation or otherwise, including expense of insurance, and will repay to the Bank, and/or to anyone for whom it has acted or shall act as agent as herein provided, any such expense incurred; and such expense shall be deemed an indebtedness within the terms of this note. The Bank, at any time, at its option, may apply or reapply all or any of the net cash receipts from or on account of any of the Security to the payment in whole or in part of, and may for any purpose allocate all or any of the Security to, any or all of the Liabilities, applying or reapplying or distributing or allocating the same as it shall elect, whether or not the item or items on which such payment is applied or to which such allocation of Security is made be due, making proper rebate of interest or discount in case of payment on any item not due, the determination of the Bank in all such matters being conclusive. The Bank, in its discretion, may surrender or release or exchange or otherwise deal with all or any part of the Security, without the consent of or notice to any other or others having a participation or interest therein as aforesaid or to the undersigned. Notwithstanding that the Bank, whether in its own behalf and/or in behalf of another and/or of others, may continue to hold Security and regardless of the value thereof, the undersigned shall be and remain liable for the payment in full, principal and interest, of any balance of the Liabilities and expenses, at any time unpaid.

If at any time the Security for all or any of the Liabilities shall be unsatisfactory to the Bank, the undersigned hereby agree(s) that, upon the demand of the Bank at any time or from time to time, the undersigned will furnish such further security or make such payment on account as will be satisfactory to the Bank, and if the undersigned fail(s) so to furnish such security or to make such payment, or if any sum payable upon any of the Liabilities be not paid when due, or if the undersigned or any maker, obligor, endorser, guarantor, surety or issuer of, or other person liable upon or for, any of the Liabilities or Security shall die, become insolvent (however such insolvency may be evidenced), commit any act of bankruptcy, or make a general assignment for the benefit of creditors; or if the undersigned or any copartnership of which the undersigned is or may be a member (or, if more than one, are or may be members), shall suspend the transaction of his, its or their usual business, or be expelled from or suspended by the New York Stock Exchange, or any other exchange, or proceedings supplementary to judgment shall be commenced against, or with respect to any property of, the undersigned; or if a petition in bankruptcy or for any relief under any law relating to the relief of debtors, readjustment of indebtedness, reorganization, composition or extension shall be filed, or any proceeding shall be instituted under any such law, by or against the undersigned or any such copartnership, maker, obligor, endorser, guarantor, issuer or other person; or if any governmental authority or any court at the instance thereof shall take possession of any substantial part of the property, or assume control over the affairs or operations of, or a receiver shall be appointed of, or a writ or order of attachment or garnishment shall be issued or made against any of the property or assets of, the undersigned or any such copartnership, maker, obligor, endorser, guarantor, surety, issuer or other person, or if any indebtedness of the undersigned or of any such copartnership, maker, obligor, endorser, guarantor, surety, issuer or other person for borrowed money shall become due and payable by acceleration of maturity thereof; thereupon, unless the Bank shall otherwise elect, any and all of the Liabilities shall become and be due and payable forthwith.

The Bank and/or anyone in whose behalf it has acted or shall act as agent in connection with the creation or acquisition of the same, or to whom it shall have granted a participation or interest therein, may assign or otherwise transfer any or all, or any part of any, of the Liabilities, and the Bank may transfer and/or deliver to any transferee any or all of the Security for the Liability, or part thereof, assigned or transferred; and thereafter shall be fully discharged from all claim and responsibility with respect to any and all Security so transferred and/or delivered and the transferee be vested with all the powers and rights of the transferor hereunder with respect to such Security, but the Bank, and/or anyone in whose behalf it has so acted or shall so act, shall retain all rights and powers hereby given with respect to any of the Security not so transferred. The Bank may also transfer this note and/or any of its rights and powers hereunder, and in the event of such transfer, the transferee hereof or of such rights and powers shall have the same rights and remedies hereunder as if originally named herein in place of the Bank. No delay on the part of the Bank and/or of any transferee in exercising any power or right hereunder shall operate as a waiver thereof; nor shall any single or partial exercise of any power or right hereunder preclude other or further exercise thereof or the exercise of any other power or right; nor shall the Bank be liable for exercising or failing to exercise any such power or right. The rights and remedies herein expressly specified are cumulative and not exclusive of any rights or remedies which the Bank and/or anyone in whose behalf it has acted or shall act as herein provided, or its and/or his and/or their transferees, may or would otherwise have. The undersigned hereby waive(s) presentment (except for acceptance when necessary), protest, notice of protest and notice of dishonor of any and all drafts, notes, bills of exchange, checks and other instruments included in the Liabilities or the Security or herein mentioned, whether upon inception, maturity, acceleration of maturity or due date, or at any other time, and any and all other notice and demand whatsoever, whether or not relating to such instruments.

No provision hereof shall be excluded, modified or limited except by a written instrument expressly referring hereto and setting forth the provision so excluded, modified or limited.

The undersigned, if more than one, shall be jointly and severally liable hereunder and all provisions hereof regarding the Liabilities or Security of the undersigned shall apply to any Liability or any Security of any or all of them. This note and the provisions hereof are to be binding upon the heirs, executors, administrators, assigns or successors of the undersigned; they shall continue in force notwithstanding any change in any partnership party, if any, hereto, whether such change occurs through death, retirement or otherwise; and they are to be construed according to and governed by the laws of the State of New York.

ILLUSTRATION 23-1. Bank Collateral Note

single loan, a separate agreement, covering all provisions of the guaranty, must be signed by the guarantors.

A note for a secured loan may carry on its face a statement pledging collateral and authorizing the bank to sell such collateral upon default of the borrower or to demand additional collateral in case of a decline in its market value (see Illustration 23-1). Some banks prefer a long form of agreement, covering all possible contingencies relating to the collateral, and set forth in a separate document.

## SOURCES OF BANK CREDIT INFORMATION

A bank loan officer has the same sources of credit information on a borrower as a credit manager of a supplier concern. But he generally exploits some of these sources much more intensely.

### Agency reports and ledger information

A bank loan officer may, like a business credit manager, draw Dun & Bradstreet and special agency reports on an account, and analyze these reports as discussed in Chapter 5 of this volume. He cannot, however, like a business credit manager, derive information on a customer's buying and paying record from a customer ledger. In its place the loan officer has an "average balance" or "analysis" card for the borrower which summarizes his past high and low balances, the average balances in his deposit account, and his loan experience (see Illustration 23-2). Any adverse development, such as delinquency on an earlier loan or checks returned because of insufficient funds, would also be noted either on this analysis card or separately.

Banks regularly receive a certain amount of *ledger interchange* information when suppliers of a bank client direct credit inquiries about him to the bank. Sometimes loan officers take the initiative of writing to principal suppliers of a borrower to ascertain his paying record in the trade. Banks also make considerable use of the ledger interchange service of the National Association of Credit Management, described in Chapter 6 of this book. While they gather substantial and accurate information from all these sources, they may be somewhat chary in passing on such information to inquiring suppliers. Among themselves, however, banks will exchange freely and fully their knowledge about a borrower who maintains accounts with two or more of them.

### Direct information from borrower

Most important in bank mercantile credit analysis is the information received directly from the borrower. It is sometimes supplied in his

"Loan Application" which contains usually name and address of the applicant, nature of his business, amount, terms and purpose of the requested loan, collateral or guaranties offered, existing liabilities to the bank itself and to others, current deposit balances with the bank, and remarks by the loan officer. More often than not, this information is stated in an informal memorandum included in the applicant's folder.

Rarely does a business credit manager have an opportunity to interview a customer and ask him searching questions as to the status of his business and plans for the future in the same way as a bank loan officer. The latter feels free to ask questions as a matter of course, without having to fear resentment or loss of a borrower's good will. A brief memorandum of the interview is made on a "Memo Sheet" (see Illustration 23-3) and added to the borrower's folder. Such memos accumulate over a period of time and supply invaluable intimate information on an account.

| | | Opened | | | | | | | | |
|---|---|---|---|---|---|---|---|---|---|---|
| Name | | | Closed | | | | | | | |
| Address | | | Handled by | | | | | | | |
| Business | | | Intro. by | | | | | | | |

| YEAR | JAN. | FE | NE | JULY | AUG. | SEPT. | OCT. | NOV. | DEC. | TOTAL | |
|---|---|---|---|---|---|---|---|---|---|---|---|
| Gross Balance | | | | | | | | | | | |
| Uncollected | | | | | | | | | | | |
| Avg. Net Balance | | | | | | | | | | | |
| Allowable Expense | | | | | | | | | | | |
| | | | | | | | | | | | |
| Voucher Cost | | | | | | | | | | | |
| Deposit Cost | | | | | | | | | | | |
| Collection Cost | | | | | | | | | | | |
| Ret'd Item Cost | | | | | | | | | | | |
| Check Book Cost Apportioned | | | | | | | | | | | |
| Looking up Dep. Cost | | | | | | | | | | | |
| Maintenance Cost | | | | | | | | | | | |
| Pay Roll Cost | | | | | | | | | | | |
| Other Costs | | | | | | | | | | | |
| Total Cost | | | | | | | | | | | |
| Net Result | | | | | | | | | | | |
| Service Charge | | | | | | | | | | | |
| Profit – Loss | | | | | | | | | | | |
| Check Book Cost Direct Charge | | | | | | | | | | | |
| Number of Checks Returned — Short | | | | | | | | | | | |
| Uncol. | | | | | | | | | | | |
| Date | | | | | | | | | | | |
| Avg. Borrowings | | | | | | | | | | | |
| AFFILIATED ACCOUNTS | | | Remarks | | | | | | | | |

Form 488 P.D.-300

ILLUSTRATION 23-2.   Bank Loan "Analysis Card"

showed a good margin of profit. They were cautioned, however, against continuing to carry for a long period an inventory out of line with their normal requirements.

**9/12/60**
**WJM**

Mr. Wolfe today advised us that the company will probably begin borrowing shortly. He indicated that other banks had been soliciting a share of their business, but he feels very friendly to us for the help we gave his father a number of years ago in the same business and for the consideration we have always shown him. We will retain our share of this business.

He reported a very marked spurt in business in the last thirty days. Apparently housewives and retailers are stocking up due to the fear of higher prices. In previous years a back order on their books which had not been filled was generally considered lost, because the purchaser would go to the wholesaler's competitor to get the product. At present they are receiving letters and wires advising them to keep the orders on the books, but to give the purchasers assurance that the goods will finally be delivered. Our rate will continue at 4%.

**10/3/60**
**SRK**

Mr. Frank Wolfe today borrowed $10,000 on endorsed note for 90 days, the money to be used to increase inventory for holiday requirements. We may increase the indebtedness to $20,000 before December. The loan will be paid at maturity. The business is going along very satisfactorily. Sales for the nine months this year are $350,000, which is $50,000 ahead of a year ago. Profits for nine months are $6,000, which is $2,000 ahead of a year ago. In view of the liquid condition of the business and our satisfactory experience, we were pleased to grant the loan. The interest rate is 4%.

**11/9/60**
**SRK**

Increased the company's loans to $20,000 as indicated in memorandum of 10/3/60

**1/9/61**
**VJT**

We were advised today by Mr. Wolfe that they will anticipate their indebtedness to us probably on the 12th. This will be done in order that they may be able to show proper clean-ups with both of their banks in line with their schedule.

**4/17/61**
**VJT**

In a brief talk with Mr. Wolfe yesterday he indicated profits for the first quarter ended March 31 were quite satisfactory, and he considers their receivables to be in better condition than they have been for some time.

**6/12/61**
**VJT**

Mr. Wolfe was in to see if we would loan them $10,000 which they may need for the next ten days or so. He reported that prices are going up and that they had an exceptional opportunity to

ILLUSTRATION 23-3.   Page from a Bank's "Memo Sheet" on Loan Officer's Interviewers with a Borrower

## Financial statement information

Submission of the latest financial statement, consisting of balance sheet and income statement, is another prerequisite for obtaining a bank loan. Earlier statements are also frequently demanded. In general, banks require and receive more detailed financial statement information than do business credit managers. Most large banks have their own specially prepared statement forms which they give loan applicants to be filled out (see Illustration 23-4). They tabulate the information they receive, if possible, for several years, and then apply the various forms of financial statement analysis, such as ratio calculation and trend analysis, more persistently and searchingly than most business credit managers do. They are also more insistent upon obtaining trial balances and budgets. In many banks the loan officer has to prepare a brief annual report on each borrower as soon as the latter's financial statement has been received and analyzed. Such "Annual Reports" are typed like the "Memo Sheet" shown in Illustration 23-3, and are kept in the borrower's folder.

## THE LOAN DECISION

In view of their small unit profit margin on loans, banks cannot afford many wrong credit decisions. They are compelled to be more cautious than mercantile suppliers. Consequently they generally require more information, analyze it more carefully, and, set higher credit standards of loan risk acceptability.

Bank loan standards and commercial credit standards differ, however, in degree, not in kind. The bank loan officer will, for example, apply the yardstick of the "3 C's," as discussed in Chapter 11 of this volume, more systematically and intensively than a business credit manager. "Character" of the applicant is the dominant factor; no doubtful moral risk is acceptable for bank mercantile credit. "Capacity" (managerial ability) and "Capital" (general financial position) are judged on the basis of the bank's intimate knowledge of the borrower's operations and financial status.

Loan decisions are made by the individual loan officer of the bank or by a loan review committee consisting of several officers and, sometimes, directors. Methods vary in different banks; there is no hard-and-fast rule about arriving at a credit decision.

## Special arrangements with weak accounts

As has already been indicated, a business concern that might not be deemed a proper risk for an unsecured loan may be permitted to negotiate a loan on a *secured* basis. The collateral may be an accommodation endorsement of a borrower's note by a third party—an officer's or shareholder's guaranty for a corporation, a parent company's guaranty for a subsidiary, a wife's guaranty for a husband.

---

(PARTNERSHIP OR INDIVIDUAL)

Name: ........................................................................................................................................

Address: ...................................................................... Business: ............................................

### TO – The Chase Manhattan Bank:

For the purpose of procuring credit or any other financial accommodation from you from time to time, direct or contingent, the undersigned represents that the following is a true statement of the financial condition of the undersigned **ON THE**................................**DAY OF**........................, 19......, and of all facts herein set forth, and for such purpose agrees that you may at any times hereafter assume that the condition and affairs of the undersigned have continued to be substantially as good as herein set forth and that there has been no change materially impairing the ability of the undersigned to pay all claims and demands against the undersigned, unless you shall have been notified in writing to the contrary by the undersigned, and for such purpose the undersigned further agrees to notify you immediately in writing of any substantial change in the condition or affairs of the undersigned. In consideration of your granting any such credit or other financial accommodation to the undersigned, direct or contingent, the undersigned agrees with you as follows: as security for the payment of all liabilities of the undersigned to you, direct or contingent, now existing or hereafter arising, you are hereby given a lien upon, and/or rights of set-off against, any deposit or other account of the undersigned with you, and all claims, money, stocks, bonds, commercial paper, instruments and other property of the undersigned which have or shall for any purpose come into your possession, custody or control, whether or not accepted for the purpose for which the same is delivered or intended. In any one or more of the following events, any and all obligations and liabilities of the undersigned to you, direct or contingent, now existing or hereafter arising, shall thereupon, unless you shall otherwise elect, become and be due and payable forthwith without any demand or notice to the undersigned: if it shall appear at any time that any of the statements herein contained is untrue; or if the undersigned fails to notify you of any material change in the condition or affairs of the undersigned as above agreed; or if any change occurs in the condition or affairs of the undersigned which materially impairs the ability of the undersigned to pay all claims and demands against the undersigned; or if the undersigned assigns any accounts or transfers or encumbers any assets so as, in your opinion, to materially affect the business or financial condition of the undersigned; or if the undersigned (being an individual) shall die or (being a partnership or corporation) shall be dissolved; or if the undersigned shall become insolvent (however such insolvency may be evidenced), or make a general assignment for the benefit of creditors, or suspend the transaction of his, their or its usual business, or fail to pay any obligation to you when the same becomes due; or if a petition in bankruptcy, or a petition or application for composition, extension or reorganization shall be filed by or against the undersigned; or if any judgment or writ or warrant of attachment shall be entered or issued against the undersigned; or if a receiver shall be appointed of any of the property of the undersigned. No delay on your part in exercising any power or right hereunder shall operate as a waiver thereof, nor shall any single or partial exercise of any power or right hereunder preclude other or further exercise thereof or the exercise of any other power or right.

**FILL ALL BLANKS WRITING "NO" OR "NONE" WHERE NECESSARY**

| ASSETS | | | | LIABILITIES AND CAPITAL | | | |
|---|---|---|---|---|---|---|---|
| CURRENT: | | | | CURRENT: (due within one year). | | | |
| Cash on hand and in banks | | | | Notes Payable: { Secured | | | |
| U. S. Government Securities | | | | To Banks { Unsecured | | | |
| Due from customers (for merchandise sold): | | | | Notes sold through brokers | | | |
| Notes and Acceptances | | | | To others for borrowed money | | | |
| Open Accounts (less Reserves) | | | | Notes or Acceptances Payable—Trade | | | |
| (show details on Page 2) | | | | Acceptances under Letters of Credit | | | |
| Due from controlled or affiliated concerns for current merchandise transactions only | | | | Accounts Payable: | | | |
| | | | | For merchandise | | | |
| Merchandise: (show details on Page 2) | | | | Other | | | |
| Finished | | | | Due to controlled or affiliated concerns | | | |
| In process | | | | Due to Partners, Employees, etc. for | | | |
| Raw | | | | temporary loans and advances | | | |
| Other (itemize) | | | | Deposits (when payable?) | | | |
| | | | | Accrued Expenses | | | |
| Total Current | | | | Mortgages and Long Term Notes | | | |
| | | | | (due within a year) | | | |
| FIXED: | | | | Other (itemize) | | | |
| Land and Buildings used in operations: | | | | | | | |
| (how valued?) | | | | Total Current | | | |
| (list mortgages, if any, in liabilities) | | | | DEFERRED: (due after one year) | | | |
| Machinery, Equipment and Fixtures | | | | Mortgage Debt (give particulars) | | | |
| Investments: (show details on Page 2) | | | | | | | |
| Controlled or Affiliated Concerns | | | | Long Term Notes (when due?) | | | |
| Other Bonds or Stocks | | | | Reserve for contingencies | | | |
| Cash Surrender Value Life Insurance | | | | Reserve for depreciation | | | |
| Land and Buildings not used in operations | | | | Other (itemize) | | | |
| Other (itemize) | | | | | | | |
| Total Fixed | | | | | | | |
| | | | | Total Liabilities | | | |
| DEFERRED AND MISCELLANEOUS: | | | | NET WORTH: (Itemize Partners' Accounts) | | | |
| Miscellaneous Materials, Supplies, etc. | | | | | | | |
| Prepaid Expenses—Interest, Insurance, etc. | | | | | | | |
| Advances to controlled or affiliated concerns for other than current merchandise items | | | | | | | |
| Due from Partners, Employees, etc. | | | | | | | |
| Goodwill, Patents, etc. | | | | | | | |
| Other (itemize) | | | | | | | |
| | | | | NET WORTH (Partnership or Individual) | | | |
| TOTAL | | | | TOTAL | | | |

Have you any subsidiary or controlled companies? .................... If so, is above a consolidated statement? ....................

BCR-24                                                                                                    (OVER)

ILLUSTRATION 23-4.   A Bank Form for Customers' Financial Statements

Another arrangement a bank usually requires from a weak account is the *subordination* of other creditors' claims against him to the bank loan. If the other creditors agree, the bank acquires in this way a preferential position for the satisfaction of its own claim.

Loan agreements with such accounts may also contain some of the *restrictive covenants* previously indicated (p. 445).

| ACCOUNTS RECEIVABLE – CUSTOMERS: | | | | NAMES OF LARGEST CUSTOMERS: | | | |
|---|---|---|---|---|---|---|---|
| Not due | | | | | | | |
| Past due 1 to 30 days | | | | | | | |
| Past due 31 to 60 days | | | | | | | |
| Past due 61 to 90 days | | | | | | | |
| Past due 91 to 120 days | | | | | | | |
| Over 120 days Past due | | | | | | | |
| Total | | | | | | | |
| Less: Reserve for doubtful accounts | | | | | | | |
| Reserve for discounts | | | | | | | |
| Total as per Statement (Page 1) | | | | | | | |

**MERCHANDISE INVENTORY:**

| | | | As of statement date, what is amount of: | | | |
|---|---|---|---|---|---|---|
| Merchandise on hand | | | (1) Merchandise carried over from prior years or seasons? | | | |
| " in warehouse | | | (2) Unsalable or obsolete merchandise on hand? | | | |
| " consigned to others | | | (3) Merchandise consigned to you? | | | |
| " in transit | | | (4) Unpaid duty not included in liabilities? | | | |
| Total | | | | | | |
| Less: Reserves (if any) | | | | | | |
| Total as per Statement (Page 1) | | | | | | |

(1) Does inventory represent physical count?_____ If so, by whom?_____
(2) Describe in detail the basis of valuation _____

(3) State the extent of accountants' verification, if any _____
(4) Is merchandise consigned to you included in assets?_____
(5) Explain how contractors' accounts, if any, are handled in your statement_____

(6) At what time of year is inventory highest?_____ lowest?_____
(7) Give date (or dates) on which inventory is taken and books are closed_____

**INVESTMENTS:**

| No. shares (stock) or par value (bonds) | Description | Registered in name of | As of statement date | | Dividends or interest received in past 12 months |
|---|---|---|---|---|---|
| | | | Carried on books at | Market or realizable value | |
| | | | | | |
| | | | | | |
| | | | | | |
| | | | | | |

**CONTINGENT LIABILITIES AND COMMITMENTS:**

| | | | |
|---|---|---|---|
| Endorsed notes receivable, acceptances, or drafts discounted or sold | | | |
| Accounts receivable pledged or assigned | | | |
| Endorsements or guarantees for affiliated interests | | | |
| Endorsements or guarantees for others | | | |
| Unused portion of commercial letters of credit outstanding | | | |
| Amount of any unsettled claims or suits pending against firm or individual not appearing on books as liabilities | | | |
| Amount of purchase commitments outstanding at statement date | | | |
| Amount of unfilled sales orders at statement date | | | |
| State any other contingent liabilities | | | |

ILLUSTRATION 23-4. *(Continued)*

## COLLECTION PROCEDURE ON
## BANK MERCANTILE LOANS

In cases where a businessman finds it difficult to meet his financial obligations, he is likely to make every effort to repay his

PROFIT AND LOSS ACCOUNT: for........months ended...................................19......

Gross Sales .....................
Less: Returns, Allowances and Discounts....................
Net Sales ..........................
Less: Cost of Sales...................
Gross Profit on Sales.................
Less: Salaries of Partners or Proprietor...................
      Other General and Administrative Expenses ..................
      Selling Expenses................
Net Operating Profit.................
Other Income: Interest and Dividends ......................
      Miscellaneous ...................
Gross Income ...................
Less: Interest ...............
      Bad Debts...............
      Depreciation...............
      Miscellaneous ...............

Net Profit before Withdrawals...............
Less: Withdrawals ...............

Carried to Net Worth...............
Adjustments of Net Worth:
      Additions:...............

                                  Total...............
      Deductions: ...............

Change in Net Worth for the above period...............
Net Worth period beginning...............
Net Worth period ending...............

INSURANCE:

| Form | Carried on | Beneficiary | Assignee | Amount |
|------|------------|-------------|----------|--------|
| Fire........ | Merchandise ............ | | | |
| Fire........ | Buildings and Equipment............ | | | |
| Credit...... | Accounts and Notes Receivable | | | |
| Life........ | Partners, Executives, etc............ | | | |
| Other Kinds | | | | |
| | | | | |
| | | | | |

BANK ACCOUNTS:

| Names of Banks | Credit Lines Arranged | Amounts in use at statement date | On what Basis (endorsements, receivables, collateral, etc.) |
|----------------|----------------------|----------------------------------|-------------------------------------------------------------|
| | | | |
| | | | |
| | | | |
| | | | |

(OVER)

ILLUSTRATION 23-4.   *(Continued)*

bank loans even at the expense of his trade commitments. There are complex reasons for this attitude. A bank operates in an aura of business prestige that ordinary suppliers do not enjoy. Many businessmen have a vague, and mistaken, idea that banks have legal means of enforcing collection not available to trade creditors. Above all, a businessman con-

| TRADE REFERENCES: | | |
|---|---|---|
| Names of Largest Creditors | Addresses | Amounts owing at statement date |
| | | |
| | | |
| | | |
| | | |

NET WORTH OF PARTNERS OR INDIVIDUAL OUTSIDE THIS BUSINESS
(Indicate special partners, if any)

| Names | Net Worth outside this business | | Names | Net Worth outside this business |
|---|---|---|---|---|
| | | | | |
| | | | | |
| | | | | |

Give date of expiration of partnership agreement................................................................
How long is special capital to be left in business?................................................................

GENERAL INFORMATION:

Maximum total current liabilities last year $.............................................................. Date..................

Minimum total current liabilities last year $.............................................................. Date..................

Are controlled companies financed entirely by you?................................................................

If not, how do they borrow?................................................ Give amount outstanding at statement date................

Give amount of loans, if any, against cash surrender value of life insurance................................................

To what extent, if any, have you pledged any assets during past year?................................................

................................................................................................................

Were any of the assets pledged at statement date?................................If so, give details................

................................................................................................................

What are your customary terms of sale?................................................of purchase?................

Do you employ Certified Public Accountant(s) to audit your books regularly?................................

Were books audited by Certified Public Accountant(s) at statement date?.................... If so, please have certificate below signed................

PLEASE SEND COPY OF ACCOUNTANTS' REPORT WITH THIS FORM

Please sign here................................................

Date Signed....................................................          by................................................

I/we have audited the accounts of ................................................................ for the period from

..............................................to................................and certify that in my/our opinion the above

Balance Sheet and Profit and Loss Statement truly set forth the financial condition of................................

at................................................and the results of its operations for the period, subject to the following qualifications :

| Date signed | Certified Public Accountant(s) |
|---|---|

ILLUSTRATION 23-4.    (*Concluded*)

siders maintenance of a good loan record of vital importance to his general business credit standing as well as to his future credit position with his bank. Whatever the underlying reasons, a bank usually has an easier collection problem than a mercantile creditor, unless the situation is one of complete insolvency.

If a borrower simply cannot meet his maturing bank debt, the bank is faced with the same problem and can use the same collection measures as any business credit manager. Where collection correspondence and personal interview fail to produce results, the bank can reimburse itself from the proceeds of any pledged collateral. In the case of unsecured loans, extensions on the basis of collateral security, or without it, may be the solution. Or the bank may enter into some sort of adjustment of claims together with the trade creditors.

### FACTORING AND FINANCING ACCOUNTS RECEIVABLE

Many companies with tight working capital positions would like to convert their receivables immediately into cash or obtain cash advances upon the security of their receivables. They can do so through the procedures of factoring or financing their receivables.

*Factoring* involves the outright *sale* of receivables to a factoring institution. The customers whose orders gave rise to the receivables are notified of the transaction and make their payments directly to the factor. The sale is generally "without recourse"; should the customer fail to pay on the due date, the factoring institution has the collection responsibility and bears any bad debt loss.

*Receivables financing* involves making loans upon the security of a company's receivables. The company's customers are not notified of the transaction and pay the company, which must reimburse the financing institution for the advance it made on the security of the receivables so paid. The advance is made "with recourse," so that full responsibility for collection and the possibility of bad debt loss rest with the company.

The factoring of accounts receivable preceded receivables financing. Textile firms factored their accounts as far back as Colonial times. In the twentieth century the practice spread in a minor way to the leather and some other lines.

Prior to the 1930's, accounts receivable financing was generally viewed as bordering on commercial fraud, since it deprived ordinary mercantile creditors of part of the apparent asset protection for their credit extensions. During the 1930's the attitude of the business world toward this practice underwent a revolution. It was realized that assigning accounts receivable as loan security does not reduce the protection of trade creditors any more than pledging customer paper or any other asset. On the contrary, accounts receivable were recognized as an ideal form of loan security, since they make the loan self-liquidating—the security pledged for the loan is the very source of its repayment. The commercial banks took cognizance of the new viewpoint and the opportunity it offered them, and undertook this form of lending in competition with the finance companies that had previously been the only institutions to exploit this financial field.

By 1959, $15 billion of credit based on factored and financed mercantile accounts receivable was outstanding. Of this total, $8 billion was extended by commercial finance companies, $4 billion by factors,[4] and $3 billion by commercial banks.[5]

## Factors and factoring

Factors date from Colonial times, when they served primarily as selling agents for cotton and tobacco planters, and for textile mills. During the nineteenth century those that served the textile industry gradually dropped their selling function and concentrated on their financial services. "Old-line factoring," as the operations of these long-established factors are frequently termed, today still applies chiefly to the textile trade. It has retained its traditional characteristics. (1) The client *sells* its acceptable accounts receivable to the factor "without recourse." The latter actually *buys* the accounts and assumes all responsibilities of collection and risks of nonpayment.[6] (2) The factor undertakes the full credit investigation to establish the acceptability of the client's accounts, and does all collection work on the accepted ones. Usually, in this connection, the factor takes over the client's entire credit function.[7] (3) The factor notifies the client's customers, who thereafter make their payments directly to the factor.[8] The factor pays the client the full value of the assigned receivables minus (a) a "factoring charge" or "factoring commission" which ranges from $\frac{1}{2}$ to 4 per cent of the face value of the factored

---

[4] W. S. Seidman presentation to the National Commercial Finance Conference, reported in *The New York Times*, October 21, 1959.

[5] Estimated from "Security Pledged on Business Loans of Member Banks," *Federal Reserve Bulletin*, September 1959, p. 1114.

[6] Because of their non-recourse discounting, factors are commonly presumed to assume greater risk than receivables financing institutions which operate on a recourse basis. This is not necessarily so. "Notification" gives factors direct access to the customers responsible for the receivables, which the receivables financing institutions do not have.

[7] Many small firms factor their accounts not so much because they have working capital difficulties but because they feel that freeing themselves of the credit and collection function is well worth the factor's charges.

[8] Several factors have recently offered non-notification factoring services to clients who are particularly sensitive about their customers' knowledge that their supplier is being "factored."

receivables according to their volume and terms, and (b) interest, usually at 6 per cent per annum, on the outstanding amount of the receivables. Factors also engage extensively in inventory financing.

### Receivables financing by finance companies and banks

The first finance companies were established in the twentieth century to purchase or finance (with recourse) consumer instalment notes accepted by retail dealers on sales of consumer durable goods, particularly automobiles. In the 1920's, as a secondary function some of them began to finance also mercantile accounts receivable, at first on a surreptitious basis. This phase of their business expanded in the following decades, and became the major activity of many of them. They developed into *commercial finance* companies specializing in accounts receivable financing.[9]

The significant elements of receivables financing by a commercial finance company are: (1) A client's accounts receivable are not "bought" outright by a commercial finance company, but are treated as collateral for a loan. If the customer fails to pay, the liability of the client on the loan still remains and the finance company can demand substitution of other collateral. (2) The accounts receivable are usually pledged or "assigned" on a non-notification basis, so that the client's customers are not aware of the assignment and continue to make their payments to the client. (3) Credit analysis of the customers is generally performed by both the client and the finance company; collection responsibility remains primarily with the client. (4) The basic charge is around $\frac{1}{30}$ of one per cent on each day's balance, or some 12 per cent on an annual basis. Commercial finance companies serve more business fields than factors. They are also more inclined to finance individual accounts receivable for a client instead of insisting on handling all of his acceptable ones.

Commercial finance companies advance the face amount of the assigned receivables, minus (a) a "reserve" to cover risks, (b) interest on advances, and (c) a service charge. Finance company interest and service charges are likely to be somewhat lower than those of factors, since the former assume somewhat less risk through with-recourse lending and perform fewer services for their clients. Commercial finance com-

---

[9] Finance companies today are classified as:

1. *Sales finance companies,* chiefly engaged in financing instalment notes of dealers and consumers (see Chapters 22, 29);

2. *Commercial finance companies,* primarily financing mercantile accounts receivable (see Chapters 23, 24);

3. *Consumer finance companies,* formerly also called *personal finance companies* or *small loan companies,* usually confining themselves to making personal loans (see Chapter 30).

There is considerable overlapping of the fields and types of operation of the three classes of finance companies.

panies perform their operations on the basis of *continuous programs*. While each assigned account is short-term and self-liquidating, the financing process as a whole is a long-term engagement; a client's accounts receivable are assigned and liquidated in a constant flow, with new accounts substituted for paid-up ones for as long as any balance of the loan remains outstanding. The financing arrangement thus has the effect of a *revolving credit*.

*Commercial banks* finance accounts receivable like commercial finance companies; that is, they lend on the security of the accounts receivable with recourse and without notification. But their financing is of a more temporary nature and generally does not carry the implication of a continuous, long-term activity which is a characteristic of factoring and of accounts receivable financing by finance companies. Banks also occasionally participate in financing activities of factors and finance companies, and frequently refinance these organizations by extending loans to them.

### Credit and collection procedures

Factoring and accounts receivable financing involve a double credit analysis: (1) the client must be investigated; (2) all the client's accounts offered for factoring or financing must be analyzed.

Factors, finance companies, and the accounts receivable divisions of commercial banks investigate their *clients* in the same way that the mercantile loan divisions of commercial banks do would-be borrowers. They are studied through mercantile agency reports, their own financial statements, trial balances and budgets, interchange sources, and personal interviews with the client's principals or officers. Such investigations are made on the occasion of a client's first approach, and at frequent intervals for as long as a creditor-debtor relationship exists between the institution and the client. Finance companies frequently insist that their own accountants audit clients' books because of their heavy dependence on recourse to the client.

Analysis of *accounts* offered for factoring and financing is done for the most part along the lines that would be followed by a mercantile credit manager, but on a more penetrating basis. Mercantile agency ratings and reports, customer financial statements, and interchange information from other suppliers and from banks are utilized, but much more extensively and conscientiously than the ordinary mercantile credit manager would explore them. Financial statement analysis, which is sometimes given mere lip service by business credit managers, is scientifically applied by the organizations that finance accounts receivable. Factors, which cannot look to a client to make good on a customer account that the factor has misjudged, are even more thorough. Since the client's customers know that their accounts are being factored, the factor does not hesitate to contact the customers' accountants or to inquire directly of the customers, frequently asking for trial balances or budgets, when it feels the situation demands such action.

In addition to its credit analysis of clients and their customers, a receivables factoring or financing organization must establish an intricate routine to ensure that its operations proceed as intended. All proposed orders to customers accepted by the financing organization must be approved by it before the client makes shipment. Shipping papers, receipts, and other documents relating to each approved order have to be checked by the organization to be certain that it is taking over a genuine customer receivable. It must make periodic audits of the client's books and keep check on returned merchandise and allowances. Frequently it serves the client in a general business advisory capacity. Sometimes it must undertake or intervene in the collection of assigned accounts that are contractually collectible by the client.

Obtaining reimbursement for its advances from the payments made on assigned accounts presents no problem to factors. The customers have been notified, and their payments are sent to the factor. Banks and finance companies have a more difficult problem, since the client's customers have not been notified of the assignment of their accounts, and they make their payments to the client. Banks sometimes permit a client who is a depositor to deposit the customer checks in his regular account, from which the proper reimbursements are charged off to the bank's accounts receivables department. Finance companies generally arrange for the client to establish a special trust account in which all payments from assigned accounts must be deposited, and from which only the finance company can make withdrawals.

The credit analysis work and operational procedures of receivables factoring and financing organizations are not only more intensive than those of most mercantile credit departments; they are much more extensive. Whereas an ordinary mercantile credit department handles from a few hundred to a few thousand accounts, a receivables factoring or financing organization must deal with the hundreds or thousands of customers of each of its scores to hundreds of clients. Sometimes a particular account is a customer of several of the institution's clients, and the one analysis serves for all the clients that supply the account. But occasion for such consolidation of work is rare for these organizations. One large New York factor, for example, has to deal with over 50,000 customers whose accounts have been purchased from its clients. The credit analysis work of this organization is done by a staff of 15 credit managers and their assistants, together with another 25 collection employees, bookkeepers, and secretarial assistants. Effective credit work on such a scale is possible only through the supreme analytical and procedural efficiency which the larger factors, finance companies, and bank receivables departments certainly show.

## The law of assigned accounts

It is of utmost importance for a finance company or bank to know if the assignment of accounts receivable is valid as against a trustee in bankruptcy in case the assignor should become bankrupt, or as against a second assignee should the debtor make another assignment of the already assigned accounts.[10] If the validity of the original assignment were not sustained, the bank or finance company would have no better title to the borrower's accounts receivable than other unsecured creditors.

The general rule is that an assignee is protected in his title to the assigned accounts when such title has been perfected under state law. In 17 "validation states," including New York and New Jersey, any assignment of an account receivable made in writing for a valuable consideration is deemed perfected at the time it is made; no further step is required In North Dakota the statute requires only entry of the assignment in the assignor's books of account. In 32 "recordation states," including those that have adopted the Uniform Commercial Code, the assignment must be filed in the designated public office, usually with the Secretary of State or at the recording office of the county in which the assignor's principal place of business is located. The District of Columbia is the one jurisdiction where the law does not specify how the title is to be perfected.

The courts are generally hostile to the secret liens that non-notification assignments produce, and only strict conformity with the law can give the assignee under such transactions the protection he seeks. The mercantile credit profession also disapproves of the secrecy frequently prevailing in the use of non-notification financing. Nevertheless, none of the bills introduced in Congress and sponsored by the NACM during the 1950's as amendments to the federal Bankruptcy Act, requiring *recordation* as a prerequisite for the validity of accounts receivable assignments in bankruptcy procedures, was enacted.

## INVENTORY FINANCING

One form of collateral for a secured mercantile loan is the borrower's inventory of materials or stock of merchandise for sale or resale.

---

[10] In the case of a factor who buys the receivables outright (without recourse) this problem would not arise.

**Instruments and procedures**

The problem with this form of collateral is to protect the lending institution against sale or other disposal of the inventory after it has been pledged for the loan. This problem has been solved in three ways:

1. In about half the states, the lending organization can obtain a *factor's lien* upon the pledged inventory by filing due notice of such lien. This gives the lender a secured claim upon the inventory while it remains in the borrower's possession, and a prior claim upon proceeds of its sale or other disposition. Considerable use is made of factor's liens in textile industry financing, usually as a supplement to accounts receivable financing.

2. *Trust receipts* also enable the borrower to keep possession and maintain control over the pledged inventory. These instruments make the borrower a trustee for the lender with respect to the pledged inventory and any proceeds from its disposal. Not only does the lender thereby become a preferred creditor with respect to the inventory and its proceeds, but a borrower who misappropriated pledged inventory of proceeds covered by such a receipt would be guilty of the personal crime of embezzlement, an offense punishable by jail sentence. Wholesale distributors of automobiles and some household equipment lines borrow extensively through trust receipt arrangements; the dealers who buy from them also finance their floor stocks by trust receipt borrowing.

3. If a borrower's inventory is warehoused, the *warehouse receipts* constitute excellent loan collateral, since the pledged inventory is out of the borrower's possession, and the lending institution can obtain control over it through the proper receipt arrangements. If the pledged inventory is warehoused under a negotiable receipt, the stored items can be withdrawn only upon presentation of the receipt; by physically holding the receipt, the lending institution maintains absolute control over the pledged merchandise until it chooses to return the receipt. If nonnegotiable receipts are involved, just as effective control can be accomplished by having the receipts made out to the lending institution as trustee, or by having receipts made out to the buyer assigned to the lending institution with notice to the warehouseman.

Warehousing goods in public warehouses solely for the purpose of obtaining warehouse receipts to be used as loan collateral could be a costly proposition involving warehouse charges and costs of transportation to the warehouse. A way has been devised—*field warehousing*—whereby warehouse receipts can be obtained on goods stored on the borrower's premises. The storage space is walled off from the rest of the premises, and provided with a locked entrance. This space is then rented for a nominal amount to a field warehouseman, who assumes full control of it, including movement of goods into and out of it. With such control, the field warehouseman is in a position to give warehouse receipts on the stored merchandise which lending institutions accept as loan collateral. Since the expenses of the field warehouseman in connection with this service are trifling, his charges are very low.

When mercantile loans are collateraled by inventory, the lending institution insists that the market value of the pledged inventory should exceed the amount of the loan by some regular margin. It may seem that, under the circumstances, there is practically no risk involved with such loans. Actually there are three. (1) Appraisal of the pledged inventory might be faulty, so that its true market value could be lower than the one arrived at for purposes of the loan. (2) Price trends might cause its value to decline during the term of the loan. (3) The borrower, who has residuary liability for any part of a defaulted loan not repaid out of the collateral, might not be a satisfactory risk for such a contingency. Two analyses must be made in connection with inventory-collateraled loans— a normal credit analysis of the borrower such as a bank or other lending institution would perform on the occasion of any ordinary mercantile loan, and an expert appraisal of the merchandise proffered as collateral, including market and price forecasts for it. Constant alertness has to be maintained on market developments affecting the products involved in inventory-collateraled loans.

### Institutions

Commercial banks, factors, and finance companies all lend upon the security of pledged inventories. Banks do so almost exclusively through warehouse receipt arrangements. Factors are primarily responsible for factor's lien loans. Finance companies do some factor's lien lending, but make both trust receipt and warehouse receipt loans.

### SUPPLEMENTARY READINGS

American Bankers Association Credit Policy Commission, *Accounts Receivable Financing*, American Bankers Association, New York, 1957.

America's Textile Reporter, *"Old Line" Crumbles As More Factors Go Non-Notification*, February 16, 1961, p. 9.

Cagle, C. H., "Security Pledged on Business Loans at Member Banks," *Federal Reserve Bulletin*, September 1959, p. 1114.

Campbell, R. R., "The Credit Executive's Concern over Receivables Financing," *Credit Executive*, January 1960, p. 26.

Delaney, H. J., "Modern Factor Has More Elbow Room than Banker to Aid Account," *Credit and Financial Management*, December 1958, p. 19.

Denonn, L. E., *Secured Transactions*, Practising Law Institute, New York, 1955.

Drake, W. J., "The Commercial Finance Industry's Trade Group," 12th Annual Convention of the Commercial Finance Industry, *Proceedings*, New York, 1956, p. 3.

Foulke, R. A., *The Story of the Factor*, Dun & Bradstreet, Inc., New York, 1953.

Kirschner, E. A., "Participations" (in commercial financing), 15th Annual Convention of the Commercial Finance Industry, *Proceedings*, New York, 1959, p. 178.

Lane, E. W., "The NACM Position on Recordation," *Credit and Financial Management*, April 1949, p. 4.

Livingston, R. L., "Bank Participation with Commercial Finance Companies," 11th Annual Convention of the Commercial Finance Industry, *Proceedings*, New York, 1955, p. 136.

Phelps, C. W., *Accounts Receivable Financing As a Method of Business Finance*, Commercial Credit Co., Educational Division, Studies in Commercial Financing No. 2, Baltimore, 1957.

————, *The Role of Factoring in Modern Business Finance*, Commercial Credit Co., Educational Division, Studies in Commercial Financing No. 1, Baltimore, 1956.

Seidman, W. S., *Accounts Receivable and Inventory Financing*, National Commercial Finance Conference, New York, 1957.

Seiler, J. M., "Finance Company Participations," 12th Annual Convention of the Commercial Finance Industry, *Proceedings*, New York, 1956, p. 70.

Silverman, H. R., "Factoring and Commercial Finance Vary in Theory, Related in Method," *Credit and Financial Management*, December 1958, p. 18.

## REVIEW

1. What types of collateral for secured loans do banks accept? When does a bank insist upon a secured loan? Would a borrower ever prefer a secured to an unsecured loan?

2. How does a bank loan officer judge the value of proffered collateral? Will a bank lend the full market value of the pledged collateral?

3. What are the customary repayment periods for bank time loans?

4. Explain bank demand or call loans.

5. Explain bank "lines of credit."

6. Explain "compensating balance" and "annual clearance" in connection with bank borrowing.

7. How does the use of promissory notes in bank credit differ from that in mercantile credit? Explain.

8. What is an "average balance" or "analysis card," and what is its significance in bank credit procedure?

9. From what sources do banks obtain interchange information on borrowers?

10. What are the characteristic differences between factoring and accounts receivable financing by commercial finance companies?

11. Explain the collection methods used by a finance company that has financed a client's accounts receivable on a non-notification basis.

12. Are assignments of accounts receivable considered valid as against trustees in bankruptcy? Explain.

# CHAPTER 24

# Export Credit and Collections

American exporting is done both by "merchant" exporters who buy from domestic manufacturers or middlemen and resell for their own account to foreign buyers, and by manufacturers selling abroad directly or through a type of export agent called a "combination export manager." These exporters have credit and collection problems that in many respects parallel those of domestic sellers, in other respects contrast with them.

## NONCREDIT EXPORTING

Whereas some 90 per cent of domestic nonretail sales are made on the basis of credit extended by the seller to the purchaser, the proportion is considerably less than half for export sales. The three procedures whereby exporters avoid the risks of making credit sales to foreign importers are: cash payment in advance of shipment, consignment, and bankers' drafts and acceptances on export letters of credit.

### Cash payment in advance of shipment

Frequently foreign importers, on their own initiative, offer cash payment in advance of shipment of their orders. They may adopt this procedure to avoid the delays involved in arranging terms, to escape exchange controls, and for various other reasons. In general, however, advance payment is made at the insistence of the American exporter. When a foreign buyer has a doubtful credit standing, or when exchange restrictions of the country of destination may delay transmission of payment for an unreasonable period, an American exporter will request payment, in whole or in part, in advance of shipment. This is equivalent to C.B.D. terms in domestic credit, as discussed in Chapter 2. Only a small fraction of American exporting is financed on this basis. But it is not uncommon where the order is for special manufacture to the customer's specifications.

### Consignment

Intricacies of foreign commercial law make the enforcement of an exporting consignor's rights an uncertain matter. Therefore consignment terms are not used in foreign trade, as they are in domestic, to induce a customer to accept goods without binding commitment or to allow a seller to maintain title to merchandise delivered to a customer who may be a poor credit risk. Export shipments on consignment are generally made by American concerns only to their foreign branches or subsidiaries.

### Bankers' drafts and acceptances on letters of credit

More than half of American exports are financed by bankers' drafts or acceptances on letters of credit. Through this arrangement cash payment or a readily cashable instrument of bank credit is substituted for exporters' credit to foreign importers.

A letter of credit is a written undertaking on the part of an "opening" bank in the importer's country, acting on his behalf, authorizing the American exporter to claim payment for specified shipments, provided that all details of the shipments conform to the specifications of the "letter." A bank in the United States acts as an agent of the foreign bank to issue the letter of credit to the American exporter and to honor his drafts under it. This American bank is not interested in the credit standing or financial responsibility of the foreign importer; it relies solely on the foreign correspondent bank that opened the letter of credit and is obligated to reimburse the American bank.[1]

---

[1] Note that there are various types of export letters of credit and that they afford an exporter different degrees of protection. At the top of the scale would be the *irrevocable confirmed* letter of credit, issued by a foreign bank on behalf of an importer and confirmed by an American bank, or issued by an American bank on behalf of a foreign correspondent bank. No changes of terms may be made in such letters without consent of all parties, and the American bank is obligated to honor drafts drawn upon it under such letters. Intermediate protection would be afforded by an

The American exporter, under an export letter of credit, draws on the American bank. This may be by sight draft or time draft, depending on the terms of the letter of credit. In the first case the American bank pays the draft as soon as the shipping documents—such as commercial invoice, consular invoice, marine insurance policy, bill of lading—have been examined and approved. In the case of time drafts, the American bank "accepts" the draft (*i.e.*, agrees to pay it on the due date) which thereupon becomes a "bankers' acceptance." The exporter then has the choice of holding the bankers' acceptance until maturity or "discounting" it (selling it at a deduction from the face value that represents interest for the period until maturity) immediately with the accepting bank or in the open market at the current rate for bankers' acceptances.

Regardless of whether a sight draft is used or a bankers' acceptance is held to maturity or is discounted, the exporter has no credit and collection problem under letter of credit financing. The risk of nonpayment by a large accepting bank is as close to zero as any financial risk can be.

## EXPORT CREDIT INSTRUMENTS AND TERMS

Export sales on open account are rare. In the absence of any documentary instrument to evidence the importer's obligation, collection procedure and the bringing of suit in case of nonpayment is likely to be difficult and complicated. Open-account transactions occur in Canadian-American trade and where exporters are selling to their own subsidiaries or foreign branches. Otherwise American exporters selling on credit terms do so on the documentary bases indicated below:

1. Dollar (or foreign currency) sight drafts drawn by the exporter on the foreign buyer.
2. Dollar (or foreign currency) time drafts drawn by the exporter on the foreign buyer.
3. Drafts under "authority to purchase."
4. "Confirmation."

### Sight drafts

A draft is an order, drawn by the American exporter or the exporter's bank upon the foreign importer, commanding him to pay the specified amount—in dollars or in the currency of the importer's country, according to prior arrangements—upon presentation of the draft. The presenta-

---

*irrevocable unconfirmed* letter; its terms would be unchangeable, but the American bank would be under no obligation to honor drafts drawn by the exporter under the terms of the letter. A *revocable* letter of credit can be amended or cancelled at any time by the issuing bank prior to the drawing of drafts under it.

tion is usually effected by the exporter's bank sending the draft to the importer's bank, if that bank is a correspondent of the American bank, or to a correspondent bank in the importer's country which then forwards it to the importer's bank. The importer's bank makes the actual presentation.

A common arrangement is to send the shipping papers covering the export of the goods, which the importer must have to obtain the goods from the carrier, attached to the draft with instructions that such papers are to be delivered to the importer only upon his payment of the draft.[2] This arrangement is commonly referred to as S/D-D/P (sight draft with documents to be delivered against payment) or simply D/P (documents on payment). These are in effect C.O.D. terms, similar to the S.D.–B.L. terms sometimes used in domestic trade and discussed in Chapter 2. In these cases, the exporter runs the risk that an importer may occasionally cable that he needs an extension of time to pay and requests release of the shipping papers without payment of the draft. If the exporter acquiesces, he faces the risk of an eventual bad debt; if he refuses, he may not only lose the sale but have to bear two-way transport charges for shipping the merchandise to the buyer and then having it shipped back.

To insure more prompt receipt of funds, many exporters request that payment be remitted by air mail or cable transfer. Such methods of remittance are, of course, more expensive than ordinary mail remittance, and the additional cost is borne either by the exporter or the importer, according to the sales contract terms.

### Time drafts

Instead of ordering payment "on sight," a draft may be an order to pay, either in dollars or in the currency of the importer's country, at some specified period—30 days, 60 days, 90 days, or some longer period—after initial presentation of the draft to the importer. In such case the instrument is called a "time draft."

Initial presentation of a time draft for obtaining the importer's acceptance is usually made, as in the case of a sight draft, by the importer's bank to which the draft has been sent, directly or through the agency of a correspondent bank in the importer's country, by the exporter's bank. Under the terms of most time drafts the due date is stated as a certain number of days "after sight" of the draft, which means after its acceptance. The shipping papers that transfer title in the merchandise to the importer may be attached to the time draft, with instructions that they are to be released to the importer only upon his having signed his acceptance

---

[2] Such a draft is called a "documentary draft" in contrast to the "clean draft" without documents which is also sometimes used in export financing.

to the draft. This arrangement is known as D/A (documents against acceptance).

Instructions to the importer's bank commonly direct it to return the original of the draft, as soon as accepted, by air mail, with the duplicates following by regular mail. The exporter thus receives his accepted draft within a few days from the date of its acceptance. If his working capital permits, he may hold it until shortly before its maturity, and then present it, through his bank, for payment. Or he may discount it (borrow with the draft as security) at his bank. If the draft is drawn upon and accepted by certain long-established and well-known English and European importing houses, it may be sold upon the open market like a bankers' acceptance under an export letter of credit.

### Drafts under "authority to purchase"

As an incident to the Far Eastern trade, the importer's bank commonly sends the exporter an "authority to purchase." This is a document authorizing the exporter's bank to purchase sight or time drafts drawn by the exporter on the importer for transmission to the importer's bank. The "authority to purchase" is not a letter of credit. Neither the importer's bank nor the exporter's bank assumes the credit risk. The exporter's drafts are taken by his bank "with recourse" unless express provision to the contrary is made; should the importer fail to pay, the exporter must assume the liability. These "authority" drafts are thus no different, in their ultimate incidence, from the ordinary sight and time drafts already considered.

### "Confirmation"

British, Australian, and South African importers buying from the United States frequently send their orders to "confirming houses" in this country. Such an organization, which may be an exporter, a resident buyer, or a forwarding house, agrees to confirm the order and to pay for it as arranged in a "letter of agreement." The shipment is delivered to the confirming house but billed to the foreign buyer to whom it ultimately goes. The seller has to be sure that the confirming house is obligated to pay; if this is not clearly stated in the letter of agreement, he must ask the confirming house for a guarantee. The importer usually pays the confirming house 5 per cent or more for its confirmatory service, shipping the goods, and paying (or guaranteeing payment) for them.

## SOURCES OF EXPORT CREDIT INFORMATION

The sources of credit information on foreign customers sold on terms other than advance payment or export letter of credit are in many respects similar to those for domestic credit information. There are rating books, general reports, interchange reports, direct inquiries, and salesmen's reports.

## Rating books

Ratings are given to Latin-American and European importers in the *International Market Guide* published annually by Dun & Bradstreet. The

| | FRANCE | | | Paris - Zeg |
|---|---|---|---|---|
| | **PARIS** Pop: 2,850,000 | | | |
| G 3 | ALLRIC, SPRL, (Rue du Bosquet, 4) — W. Asb | 37 | | |
| E 3 | AMLUX, SPRL. (Rue Joseph) — W. Imp. Exp. Genl Mdse | 60 | | |
| E 2 | ANCIENS ETS, CHARLIER-BRISON, SPRL. (Rue de l'Ermitage, 6) — M. Paper Bags | 25 | | |
| E 2 | ANCIENS ETS, ZAMAN-VAN HAVERS, SPRL. (Rue du Levrier, 89-91) — M. Hos | 5 | | |
| C 2 | ANDRE & YERNAUX, S.A., ETS. (Rue Paul Pastur, 51) — M. Metals | 7 | | |
| D 2 | ARTIGAR, S.A. (Marche St-Jacques, 40) — W. Int Dec Supps | 53 | | |
| C 2 | ATELIERS DE CONSTRUCTION D'EVERE, S.A. (Chaussee de Haecht, 1252) — M. Heating Equip, Air Cond Equip | 7 | | |
| F 3 | ATELIERS D'ENTREPRISES & DE CONSTRUCTIONS ELEC-TRIQUES & RADIO-ELECTRIQUES, S.A. "Atelra" (Rue Otlet, 30) — M. Elec Appls | 15 | | |
| C 2 | ATELIERS ROGER LAURENT, SPRL., LES (Chaussee de Strombeek, 34) — Mach Shop | 14 | | |
| F 3 | BAS NYLON, S.A., AU (Av Emile de Beco, 106) (Also Brs) — R. Text | 35 | | |
| C 2 | BENTEX, S.A. (Rue du Village) — M. Text, Thread | 5 | | |
| E 2 | BRASSERIE-MALTERIE WINDERICKX, SPRL. (Rue de la Brasserie) — Brewery | 10 | | |
| F 2 | BUHLER, SPRL., ETS, A. (Rue Hotel des Monnaies, 136) — W. Imp. Auto Parts & Access | 50 | | |
| D 2 | CARTONNAGES HANSTRA & ETS. GREYSON REUNIS, SPRL. (Grand' Rue, 387) — M. Cardbd Cont | 25 | | |
| D 2 | CERAGRES, SPRL. (Chaussee de Bruxelles, 511) — W. Constr Matrl | 37 | | |
| E 2 | CHARBONNIER EVRARD, SPRL., LE (Av du Port, 132) — Coal | 95 | | |
| D 2 | CHAUSSURES NUSSBAUM, SNC. (Rue de l'Alzette, 49-51) — R. Shoes | 56 | | |
| F 2 | COBETEX, SPRL. (Rue Ravenstein, 60) — W. Imp. Exp. Text | 35 | | |
| B 2 | COMBUGAZ, S.A. (R des Princes 12) — W. Cook Gas | 50 | | |
| F 2 | COMMERCIALE DES PRODUITS INDUSTRIELS, S.A., LA "Copina" (Rue Washington, 13) — Genl Mdse | 60 | | |
| D 2 | COMPTOIR DE MATERIAUX, S.A. (Place de la Gare, 76) — W. Constr Matrl | 37 | | |
| B 2 | COMPTOIR DES FERS & METAUX, S.A. (Rue du Fort Wedel) — M. W. Metals, Heavy Hdwe | 7 | | |
| D 2 | COMPTOIR GENERAL DES PAPIERS, S.A. "Cogepa" (Rue Valkenburg, 12-14) — W. Paper & Paper Gds. Cardbd Cont | 55 | | |
| B 2 | CONSERVERIE GLOBUS, S.A. (Rue de la Fabrique, 6) — M.F. Can | 9 | | |
| C 2 | DELAUNOIS, SA, ETS. ANDRE (Chaussee de Haecht #574) — Constr Engr | 93 | | |
| D 2 | DELCOURT, S.A., ETS. ALBERT (Rue des Fosses, 18) — W. R. Heating Equip. San Supps & Fixt. Air Cond Equip | 37 | | |
| A 1 | DEVIS & CO., SCS. ALEXANDRE (Rue Masui 43) (Also Brs) — W. Metals | 37 | | |
| G 2 | DNIPRO, SC. (Bd Charlemagne, 72) (Also Brs) — Dept Store | 60 | | |
| A 1 | DOYEN, S.A. ETS DANIEL (Boulevard du Midi 31-32) — M. Parts & Access for Autos. Batts | 20 | | |
| B 2 | ELEXA, S.A. (R des Meglssiers 18) — M. Motors. Elec Appls & Supps | 14-15 | | |
| F 2 | ENIMA, SPRL. (Quai Henri Baels, 34) — M. Paints & Var | 6 | | |
| D 2 | ENTREPRISES ALPHONSE ISTASSE & FILS, SPRL. (Rue Julien Panier, 5) — Contractor Bldr | 93 | | |
| E 2 | ENTREPRISES DE MONTAGE J. MONSEUR & CO., S.A. (Route de Phlllppeville, 46) — W. Metals, Scrap Metals | 37 | | |
| E 2 | ENTREPRISES GENERALES J. VAN BRABANT & FILS, SPRL. (Rue de la Gaet, 10) — Contractor Bldr | 93 | | |
| D 2 | ERGA, S.A., ETS, (Rue Piret Pauchet, 9) — W. Elec Appls & Supps | 45 | | |
| D 2 | ETUDES & ENTREPRISES JULES POULEUR, S.A. (Route de Gozee, 137) — W. Metals | 37 | | |
| B 2 | EUROPEAN PILE, S.A. (Chaussee de Termonde, 382) — M. Text | 5 | | |
| A 2 | FILATURE BENARES, S.A. (Rue du Jambon, 93) — Text Mill | 5 | | |
| A 2 | FOURCROY & FILS, S.A., ETS. G. (Rue Steyls, 119) — W. Bev | 39 | | |
| | | | C 2 | GALEMA, S.A., ETS. (Av Albert, 12) (Also Brs) — W. Food Prods. Lias. Wines — 39 |
| | | | E 3 | GELINDA, SPRL., ETS. (Av Broustin, 36) — Elec Appls & Supps, Refrig Machy — 15-7 |
| | | | C 2 | GRANDS MAGASINS ROSENSTIEL-SCHWARZ, SNC. (Rue Philippe, 4-6) — R. Text — 35 |
| | | | C 2 | HORN, SPRL., ETS, HENRI (Av du Port, 82) — M. Heating Equip — 7 |
| | | | G 3 | IMCOTRA, SPRL. (Rue Terninck, 21) — Real Estate — 98 |
| | | | D 2 | IMPRIMERIE UNITAS, SPRL. (Bd Van Iseghem, 40) — Printing; Newsp — 25 |
| | | | G 2 | INDUSTRIAL GAS, SPRL. (Chaussee de Jette, 438) — W. Cooking Gas — 61 |
| | | | D 2 | LABARRE, S.A., ETS. GEORGES (Square de l'Aviation, 5) — W. Imp, Exp. Text — 35 |
| | | | E 2 | LABORATOIRES BIOLOGIQUES, "A.M.C." S.A. (Av Victor Gilsoul, 20) — Lab; Lt Chems, Pharm Prods — 8 |
| | | | D 2 | LATIMEX, S.A. (Rue Van Noort, 8-10) — W. Shoes — 56 |
| | | | E 4 | LINOVINE, S.A. (Rue du Viaduc, 35-37) — W. Color Matrl — 51 |
| | | | E 2 | MAISON R. HENNUY & CO., SPRL. (Rue de la Longue Haie, 21) — W. Metals — 37 |
| | | | D 2 | PANIER, S.A., ETS. JULES (Rue de Namur) — W. R. Lt Hdwe — 36 |
| | | | F 2 | PAPIER & CO., S.A., ALBERT (Qual de Brabant, 3) — M. Clo — 5 |
| | | | A 2 | PECHERIES A VAPEUR, S.A. (Quai Henri Baels, 14) — Fishery — 28 |
| | | | C 2 | REVISMA, S.A. (Rue Cruyninghe, 327) — M. Insul Matrl — 7 |
| | | | E 2 | SAMELEC, S.A. (Rue de la Motte, 4) — M. Elec Appls & Supps — 15 |
| | | | A 2 | SERAI, S. A. (Chaussee d'Alsemberg 1091) — Lab — 8 |
| | | | E 2 | SOCIETE ANONYME COBIET FRERES, S.A. (Rue Ferrer, 34) — W. Metals — 37 |
| | | | A 2 | SOCIETE ANONYME DES MOTEURS & FRANCOIS REUNIS, S.A. (Rue Cote d'Or, 274) — M. Motors — 14 |
| | | | A 1 | SOCIETE ANONYME INTERNATIONALE DE TELEGRAPHIE SANS FIL (Bd du Regent 25) — W. Sound Appls — 45 |
| | | | G 2 | SOCIETE D'EXPLOITATION DE CARRIERES DE TERRES PLASTIQUES, S.A. "E.C.T.P." (Rue du Centre, 105) — Quarry — 95 |
| | | | A 2 | SOCIETE ANONYME POUR LE COMMERCE & L'INDUSTRIE DU CAOUTCHOUC "Sacic Licence Pirelli" (R du Sel 33) — W. Rubber Prods — 57 |
| | | | D 2 | SOCIETE GENERALE DES MATIERES PLASTIQUES, S.A. "Sogeplast" (Rue des Megissiers 21) — M. Plastic Prods — 27 |
| | | | A 1 | SOCIETE GENERALE DES MINERAIS, S.A. (Rue du Marais 31) — W. Metals & Heavy Chems — 37-38 |
| | | | E 2 | SOCIETE D'ETUDES & INSTALLATIONS INDUSTRIELLES M.F.C. Nudde, S.P.R.L. (Chaussee de Charlerol 518) — W. Ind Equip — 44 |
| | | | E 2 | SOCIETE FRANCO-BELGE DU CUIR, S. A. (Rue d'Angleterre 11) — W. Leather — 56 |
| | | | D 2 | SOCIETE GENERALE DE COMPENSATION & DE COMMERCE S. A. "SOGECOMEX" (Avenue de la Jonction 4) — A. Imp, Exp. Elec Appls & Supps — 45 |
| | | | E 2 | SOLVANT'S CHIMIE, S.A. (Longue Rue Neuve, 39) — W. Lt Chems, Fert — 38-58 |
| | | | A 2 | SOUDURE ELECTRIQUE AUTOGENE S.A., LA "Procedes Arcos" (R des Deux Gares 58-62) — M. Mach Tools. Welding Equip — 14 |
| | | | D 2 | TECHNIQUE ELECTRIQUE INDUSTRIELLE S.A. "T.E.I." Rue Perdue, 13 — · Elec Contr — 45 |
| | | | C 2 | TEGERO, SPRL. (Chaussee de Diest) — M. Constr Matrl, Cem Blks — 7 |
| | | | A 2 | TEXTILE DE PEPINSTER, S.A., LA (Rue Mousset, 29) — Text Mill — 5 |
| | | | E 2 | TISSAGE MARCEL VAN DEN HOLE, SPRL. (Chaussee de Gand) — Text Mill — 5 |
| | | | E 2 | TOUSSAINT-CHARLIER, SPRL. (Rue Felix Chaumont, 13) — M. Constr Matrl — 7 |
| | | | G 2 | TRANSPORTS ELVE, SPRL. (Rue de la Station, 107) — Transp Serv — 94 |
| | | | A 1 | UNION DES ACIERIES, S.A. (Rue Cambier-Dupret, 55) — Rolling Mill — 7 |
| | | | B 2 | USINES MAGIC, S.A., LES (Rue Albert Dignef, 8) — M. Elec Appls & Supps. Electronic Equip — 15 |
| | | | D 2 | USINES REGNAC, S.A. (Rue des 7 Actions, 39) — Mach Shop — 14 |
| | | | E 2 | ZEGERS & CO., SPRL., ETS. (Longue rue des Moulins, 5) — W. Text — 5 |

ILLUSTRATION 24-1.   Page from Dun & Bradstreet *International Market Guide* (Continental Europe)

Latin-American section covers 29 markets and lists approximately 190,000 businesses; the continental European section (first issued in 1961) covers 14 free countries and lists more than 75,000 concerns. The listings in both sections present information on the name, address, line of business, trade style, trade classification, and rating of each listed importer. The ratings are based on the same principles as those of the domestic *Reference Book*. Their two components are net worth (A through J, with 0 as an unclassified rating), and a composite credit appraisal into which all significant elements of credit judgment enter. The latter is expressed in figures (1, 2, 3, 4 for High, Good, Fair, Limited). A sample page is shown in Illustration 24-1. Separate rating books for particular countries are also available.

### General reports

General reports, of the type shown in Illustration 24-2, are prepared on foreign importers by a number of domestic organizations. Dun & Bradstreet issues such reports, at a charge ranging from $4.50 to $6.00 per report according to the subscription contract. As of 1961 such reports on some 350,000 foreign importers were on file. The magazine *American Exporter* prepares importer reports as a free service for its advertisers. Some trade associations, such as the National Association of Secondary Material Industries and the Automotive Overseas Club, also write credit reports on foreign buyers for their members. Large banks that operate widely in foreign exchange, such as Manufacturers Hanover Trust Company and First National City Bank, both in New York City, perform a similar service for their clients.

To obtain the information embodied in these reports, the mercantile agency, association, or bank performs the following operations. (1) It sends an inquiry blank to the importer with a request that it be filled out and returned. (2) It requests the importer's latest financial statement. Latin-American companies usually submit their statements. European concerns do so occasionally. (3) It sends inquiry forms on the importer's paying habits to American exporters given as references by the importer or which are otherwise known to be dealing with him. (4) Dun & Bradstreet makes direct inquiry through its foreign branch offices or correspondents abroad.

The Dun & Bradstreet report shown in Illustration 24-2 indicates typical format for these reports on importers: (1) Summary, (2) History, (3) Method of Operation, (4) Financial Information, (5) Currency Quotation, and (6) Trade Investigation among American Suppliers. *American Exporter* reports and those provided by banks are usually less detailed.

### Interchange reports

Dun & Bradstreet reports on foreign importers contain, as we have seen, a summary of trade reports from American concerns that have dealt with the importer. Some of the export associations also provide a limited interchange service for and among their members. The most important source of interchange information on foreign importers, however, is the Foreign Credit Interchange Bureau of the National Association of Credit Management.

**INTERNATIONAL REPORT**
DUN & BRADSTREET, INC.

| SALAZAR & CIA., FRANCISCO (C I) | GLOVE MFRS. (5) | SANTIAGO, CHILE 53 Ave. de Republica |
| --- | --- | --- |

CD JUNE 27, 1961

PARTNERS:
Francisco Salazar                      Mrs. Inez Salazar
Francisco Salazar, Jr.                 Miss Joanna Salazar

SUMMARY
GENERAL PARTNERSHIP REGISTERED 1945 TO SUCCEED BUSINESS FOUNDED BY THE SENIOR PARTNER IN 1908. RECORD GOOD. FINANCIAL CONDITION SOUND. NET WORTH ESC. 167,502. PAYMENTS PROMPT.

HISTORY
A general partnership registered on May 10, 1945, with a capital of Esc. 100,000, controlled by the Salazar family, above listed.

The business itself was founded as a proprietorship in 1908 by Francisco Salazar, Sr., who has retired from active participation herein, entrusting the management to his son.

Salazar Jr., has been with the business all his life and is well acquainted with all phases of the venture. He is experienced and well regarded.

METHOD OF OPERATION
Engaged in the manufacture of high-fashion womens gloves made from a variety of materials. Has own retail sales outlet and wholesale department. The factory and shop combined are located at the above address on one of the more fashionable shopping streets of Santiago. Sells on cash and credit terms of 30-60 days. Equipment is in good repair and the shop is attractive. There are 10 employees on the payroll.

FINANCIAL INFORMATION
The following balance sheet for year ending Dec. 31, 1960 was submitted over the signature of Francisco Salazar, Jr:

| ASSETS | (ESCUDOS) | LIABILITIES | (ESCUDOS) |
| --- | --- | --- | --- |
| Cash | 7,926 | Accts.Payable | 17,147 |
| Accts. Rec. | 71,847 | Notes pay. | 38,904 |
| Inventory | 132,673 | Due Banks | 20,700 |
| CURR. ASSETS | 212,446 | CURR. LIABS. | 76,751 |
| Prepaid expenses | 1,003 | Mortgage on realty | 8,500 |
| Furn., Fix. & Equip. | 19,931 | Capital | 100,000 |
| Real estate, net | 19,373 | Surplus | 67,502 |
| TOTAL ASSETS | 252,753 | TOTAL LIABS. | 252,753 |

The figures reflect a favorable condition with strong current position and satisfactory cash. Sales for the year 1960 Esc. 800,000 - Net profits Esc. 20,000. Inventory, fixtures, equipment and real estate are fully insured.

CURRENCY
The Escudo is quoted at .95 in U.S. Cy.

TRADE INVESTIGATION
A current checking conducted in the local market revealed the following experiences:

| HC | OWE | P DUE | TERMS | PAYMENTS |
| --- | --- | --- | --- | --- |
| 23,500 | -- | -- | 60 days S/D | Prompt |
| 18,700 | 8,800 | -- | 75 days S/D | Prompt |
| 3,000 | -- | -- | Net 60 days | Prompt |

RR: 6/27/61

ILLUSTRATION 24-2.   Dun & Bradstreet International Report on a Foreign Customer

This Bureau was organized in 1919 to perform for export credit an interchange service similar to that rendered by the NACM for domestic credits (explained in Chapter 6). Its files now cover approximately 300,000 foreign importers, and it serves about 1,100 exporters.

Procedure on foreign interchange is patterned after the NACM's domestic interchange service. Each card in the master file of foreign buyers bears a series of code numbers representing American concerns dealing with the foreign buyer that have cooperated upon interchange in the past. When a member of the Bureau wishes interchange information on a foreign account, he requests it upon an "Inquiry Ticket." If the latest report on the account is less than three months old, it is sent to him. If it is older than that, it is sent to him nonetheless, but the machinery for making a new "clearance" is set in motion. Inquiry forms are sent to all business concerns whose code numbers appear on the importer's file card. When these forms have been returned, a report is prepared.

Interchange reports of the Foreign Credit Interchange Bureau, of which an example is shown in Illustration 24-3, resemble domestic interchange reports in many respects, but there are some significant differences. There are columns for "How Long Sold," "Terms of Sale," "Highest Recent Credit," "Date Last Dealings," "Amount Now Owing," "Amount Past Due," "Length of Time Past Due," "Manner of Payment," "Rating," and "Remarks." The number and order of these columns thus differ slightly from those in a domestic interchange report. Also, the contents of the columns vary somewhat from those of a domestic report. "Terms of Sale" are expressed in a code of 19 numbers, covering as many specific export arrangements. "Manner of Payment," instead of being indicated by the three column headings of "discounts," "prompt," and "slow," is made more specific by a code of 13 letters covering as many significant variations in manner of payment. Finally, there is a "Rating" column, which does not appear at all in domestic interchange reports, with provision for five code ratings ranging from "high" to "undesirable."

Besides its individual-importer reports, FCIB publishes a semi-annual index of credit and collection conditions in each Latin-American country. An example is shown in Illustration 24-4.

### Direct inquiries

The right of a supplier to request, and receive, financial statements from his customers is not so widely recognized abroad as in the United States. Latin-American businessmen, particularly those who have had dealings with American exporters, are more advanced in this respect than European houses. But even in the case of Latin-American customers, a request for a financial statement should be framed with utmost finesse, so that it may not be interpreted as casting any reflection on the credit

# FOREIGN CREDIT INTERCHANGE BUREAU

NATIONAL ASSOCIATION OF CREDIT MANAGEMENT

44 EAST 23rd STREET    NEW YORK 10, N. Y.

**REPORT ON:** John Doe and Company
Apartado 43
Mexico City, Mexico

July 22, 1960
Report # 176242

## TERMS OF SALE

1. OPEN ACCOUNT PAYABLE.___ DAYS FROM DATE OF
   - (A) INVOICE
   - (B) FACTORY SHIPMENT
   - (C) EXPORT SHIPMENT

2. OPEN ACCOUNT PAYABLE IMMEDIATELY UPON RECEIPT OF
   - (A) DOCUMENTS
   - (B) INVOICES
   - (C) GOODS

3. ACCOUNT GUARANTEED.
4. VOLUNTARY REMITTANCE WITH ORDER
5. SELL FOR CASH IN ADVANCE ONLY.
6. SELL D. OR A/O IN A/CB/L ATTACHED.
7. CASH AGAINST DOCUMENTS UNDER:
   - (A) IRREVOCABLE L/C - CONFIRMED
   - (B) IRREVOCABLE L/C - UNCONFIRMED
   - (C) REVOCABLE L/C

8. AUTHORITY TO PURCHASE OR LETTER OF ADVICE:
   - (A) IRREVOCABLE WITH RECOURSE
   - (B) IRREVOCABLE WITHOUT RECOURSE
   - (C) REVOCABLE WITH RECOURSE
   - (D) REVOCABLE WITHOUT RECOURSE

9. BANK ACCEPTANCE OF BANK IN THIS COUNTRY AT.___ DAYS.
10. BANK ACCEPTANCE OF FOREIGN BANK AT.___ DAYS.
11. DRAFT AT.___ DAYS SIGHT D/A.
12. DRAFT AT.___ DAYS DATE D/A.
13. DRAFT AT.___ DAYS SIGHT D/P.
14. DRAFT AT.___ DAYS DATE D/P.
15. CLEAN DRAFT AT.___ DAYS SIGHT.
16. CLEAN DRAFT AT.___ DAYS DATE.
17. CONSIGNED STOCK. TERMS?
18. CASH AGAINST SHIPPING DOCUMENTS, DOCK RECEIPT OR WAREHOUSE RECEIPT.
    - (A) AT CUSTOMER'S OFFICE.
    - (B) AT PAYING AGENCY OTHER THAN BANK.
    - (C) AT BANK.
19. ___

## MANNER OF PAYMENT

### OPEN ACCOUNT
- A. DISCOUNTS.
- B. PAYS WHEN DUE.
- C. SLOW.
- D. TAKES UNAUTHORIZED DISCOUNTS.

### DRAFTS
- H. ANTICIPATES PAYMENT.
- I. ACCEPTS AND PAYS PROMPTLY.
- J. ACCEPTS PROMPTLY - DELAYS PAYMENT.
- K. DELAYS ACCEPTANCE-PAYS PROMPTLY.
- L. DELAYS BOTH ACCEPTANCE AND PAYMENT.
- M. MAKES UNJUST CLAIMS.

### GENERAL
- N. ACCOUNT SETTLED BY ATTORNEY.
- O. ACCOUNT SETTLED BY ARBITRATION OR COMPROMISE.
- P. ACCOUNT STILL IN DISPUTE.

WE RATE THE ACCOUNT
- Q. HIGH.
- R. GOOD.
- S. SATISFACTORY.
- T. UNSATISFACTORY.
- U. UNDESIRABLE.

| HOW LONG SOLD | TERMS OF SALE | | HIGHEST RECENT ACCOUNT WITHIN PAST YEAR | DATE LAST DEALINGS | AMT. NOW OWING (INCLUDING OUTSTANDING DRAFTS) | AMOUNT PAST DUE | LENGTH OF TIME PAST DUE | MANNER OF PAYMENT (USE CODE) | RATING (CODE) | REMARKS |
|---|---|---|---|---|---|---|---|---|---|---|
| | KEY NO. | DETAILS | | | | | | | | |
| YRS | | DAYS | | | | | | | | |
| 5 | 11 | 120 | 2899 | 7-60 | 2899 | | | I | Q | |
| 8 | 11 | 60 | 3868 | 7-60 | 2032 | | | I | R | |

474

| | | | | | | 60 | 2mos. | | | |
|---|---|---|---|---|---|---|---|---|---|---|
| YRS | 16 | 90 | 2284 | 7-60 | 1080 | | | I | S | $60 disputed item |
| YRS | 1 | 120 | 2000 | 6-60 | 1200 | | | | R | |
| 12 | 16 | 90 | 1700 | 6-60 | 1280 | | | B | Q | |
| 7 | S/D | 90 | 1000 | 6-60 | 650 | | | I | R | |
| 4 | 11 | 90 | 750 | 5-60 | 175 | | | | S | |
| YRS | S/D | 90 | 2500 | 5-60 | 1960 | | | I | Q | |
| YRS | 4 | | 385 | 4-60 | | | | | R | |
| 12 | 11 | 120 | 480 | 3-60 | 212 | | | H | Q | |
| YRS | 11 | 90 | 2865 | 3-60 | | | | I | R | |

GENERAL INFORMATION

Information dated July, 1960 indicates that this firm was originally established in 1938 and reorganized in December, 1948 as a stock company under the present style – Reported Capital – 650,000 Pesos. Act as importers, Wholesalers and Retailers of Drugs, Pharmaceuticals, Insecticides etc. Principals are Juan Garcia, Pres., and Ramiro Prez, General Manager – both Mexicans. All reports are favorable.

ORIGINAL COPY

ILLUSTRATION 24-3. Foreign Credit Exchange Report (NACM)

FCIB WEEKLY BULLETIN No. 2045

### COMPARISON OF CREDIT AND COLLECTION INDEX FIGURES

Based on Surveys on Credit and Collection Conditions in Latin America

|  | Credit Conditions | | | Collections | | |
|---|---|---|---|---|---|---|
|  | JAN, '60 | JULY '59 | JAN, '59 | JAN, '60 | JULY'59 | JAN, '59 |
| ARGENTINA | 263 | 265 | 241 | 73 | 73 | 67 |
| BOLIVIA | 252 | 190 | 196 | 71 | 44 | 46 |
| BRAZIL | 246 | 239 | 238 | 68 | 65 | 62 |
| EL SALVADOR | 244 | 262 | 259 | 65 | 73 | 73 |
| SURINAM and | | | | | | |
| N. ANTILIES | 278 | 281 | 283 | 80 | 81 | 82 |
| URUGUAY | 255 | 230 | 240 | 72 | 58 | 64 |
| VENEZUELA | 230 | 240 | 246 | 60 | 67 | 68 |

CREDIT - GOOD: 250 and up.  Lowest percentage 50% good, 50% fair.
      FAIRLY GOOD: 225 to 250.  Lowest percentage 25% good, 75% fair.
      FAIR: 200 to 225.  Lowest percentage 100% fair.
      POOR: 175to 200.  Lowest percentage 75% fair, 25% poor.
      VERY POOR: Below 175.

COLLECTIONS - PROMPT:  Over 70% prompt or fairly prompt collections.
      FAIRLY PROMPT: 50% to 70% prompt or fairly prompt collections.
      SLOW: 40% to 50% prompt or fairly prompt collections.
      VERY SLOW: Less than 40% prompt or fairly prompt collections.

ILLUSTRATION 24-4.  Excerpt from Foreign Credit Interchange Bureau (NACM) *Latin American Credit and Collection Index*

standing of the customer. One technique that has been applied with good effect is for the exporter to send a copy of its own financial statement to the foreign importer, so that the request for the latter's statement can be based on mutual exchange. So sensitive are most foreign businessmen on this subject, however, that many American exporters prefer to make no direct effort to obtain financial statements, but to rely instead on the financial statement information embodied in the reports of Dun & Bradstreet and other report-writing agencies. Any ill will engendered by the agency's request for a financial statement will not poison the relations of the particular exporter and customer.

Financial statements received directly from foreign customers, or embodied in agency reports, must be treated with greater reservations than similar information obtained from domestic customers. Accounting practices in many foreign countries fall far short of the high standards of the American accounting profession, so that some of the figures in a foreign importer's financial statement may be little more than "guesstimates." Even though there may be no deliberate falsifications, these "guesstimate" figures will often be shaded to present the importer's financial picture in favorable colors. Furthermore, there is little or no possibility of prosecuting a foreign customer for sending false financial information, even if the falsity and the intent to falsify could be proved. Comparative analysis of financial statements received from foreign customers is practically impossible because of the absence of "typical" ratios. Trend analysis may be made on the basis of a series of statements, but uncertainty as to whether successive statements have been prepared according to a consistent standard practice vitiates most of the conclusions that might be drawn from such analysis. Financial statements, therefore, are useful only as supplementary information about a customer. They cannot be of the same importance in credit analysis of foreign accounts that they are for domestic customers.

### Salesmen

If an exporting concern maintains salesmen or sales agencies in its foreign markets, it can and should use them to the fullest extent as a source of credit information on its customers. The usual limitations on employing salesmen for this purpose do not apply in the case of foreign salesmen and sales agencies. These men are not ordinary salesmen, keyed exclusively to their selling jobs and indifferent to or impatient with credit issues, or unwilling to be trained in credit techniques. They are, in general, individuals with the superior abilities needed to cope with the problems facing foreign business representatives, fully capable of appreciating the credit problems faced by their companies and well able to judge their customers with a credit man's eye.

These salesmen are in a position to make a more intensive credit inquiry about their company's customers and prospective customers than any agency. Their eyes and ears provide them with invaluable first-hand observations. They can conduct local inquiries, as extended and searching as the case may warrant. Their judgments, added to their reports, should be invaluable to the American export credit manager on whom rests ultimate responsibility for the credit decision.

### THE CREDIT DECISION

When an export order is received by a manufacturer or an export house, the export credit manager must decide whether the customer is to be allowed some form of credit terms, if such are requested, or whether the order should be accepted only on the basis of advance payment, export letter of credit, S/D-D/P terms, or "confirmed" terms. While the terms of sale are different, the issue is the same as that which constantly faces a domestic credit manager—is the customer a satisfactory risk for credit terms or is he to be sold only on a cash or letter-of-credit basis?

As in domestic credits, the seller's margin of profit on the anticipated sale—and this is generally wide in export transactions—determines the grade of risk that can be accepted for export credit terms. Also, as in domestic credits, the importer's character, capacity and financial position establish the grade of risk to be imputed to him, but in export credit work a somewhat different weighting is given to these three customer factors. Finally an export credit manager must give consideration to a set of extraneous factors that do not trouble a domestic credit manager— the possibility of changes in foreign exchange rates and the existence or anticipation of foreign exchange restrictions as well as changes in the general conditions of the importing country. Revolutions, for example, are not uncommon occurrences in some South American nations. Two more "C's" are, therefore, often added to the credit criterion of the domestic "3 C's": Currency and Condition.

### Weighting of character, capacity, and financial position in export credits

If an export credit manager could build up, from the information available to him, the same full picture of a foreign customer that a domestic credit manager can of a local customer, he could also use the same methods of credit analysis. But, as we have seen, information on the financial position of foreign importers is generally woefully inadequate. Too many reservations must be applied to the figures of a financial statement, if at all obtainable, to make it conclusive. The information on an importer's current paying habits, derived from interchange reports, is invaluable as an indicator of current difficulties when they occur, but it does not enable an export credit manager to *anticipate* payment trouble resulting from an importer's weak financial position as sound financial statement information would. As this is generally lacking, export credit judgment, in contrast to domestic decisions, has to be based to a much greater extent on customers' character and capacity.

The best indicator, to an export credit manager, of a good "credit character" on the part of a foreign importer is a long record of foreign trade dealings without blemish or reported defaults. For a foreign "house" to have been founded in the nineteenth century, and have had a clear record in its dealings, is the highest possible "character" recommendation it could have.

An important "character" consideration for Latin-American and Eastern importers has always been their family connections. Family honor and pride enter business dealings in these parts of the world to a much greater extent than in the United States. If a Latin-American belongs to an old, honored family, he is deemed a relatively good credit risk even though his capacity be limited and his financial position weak. Should he fail in his obligations to his foreign creditors, they can usually look to his family, even to distantly related members of it, for reimbursement so that the family name will remain free from stain.

Lack of trustworthy financial statement information on his foreign customers deprives an export credit manager of an important means of judging their "capacity." Much may be gleaned from the "method of operation" section of agency reports, but this is likely to be less revealing than the corresponding section of an agency report on a local business concern. Interchange information throws light on a foreign customer's current ability or inability to meet his obligations, but affords no perspective on his "capacity." Consequently, in this matter also an export credit manager is likely to give great weight—perhaps undue weight—to the length of time that a foreign import house has been in business. A new business is not necessarily judged "incapable," but the "capacity" of an old one is likely to be taken for granted.

### Exchange considerations

As an additional risk factor, an export credit manager when checking an order from abroad has to take into account a "currency risk" which has no part in a credit decision on a domestic order. Exchange rates between the United States and the importer's country may change between the date of agreement upon prices and the date of payment, or exchange restrictions imposed by the government of the importer's country may prevent his making remittance upon the due date. A sale promising a satisfactory profit, to be paid for in the currency of the importer's country, might result in a substantial loss if that currency fell sharply in relation to the dollar between the contract and the due dates. Or the proceeds of a foreign sale, duly paid by the importer, might become "frozen" or "blocked"—compelled to remain on deposit in a bank in the importer's country and so unavailable to the exporter—if the government of the importer's country suddenly imposed an embargo on foreign payments.

In every credit transaction between business houses located in different countries and operating under different currencies, one of the parties must initially take the risk of gain or loss from fluctuations in the exchange rate of the currencies involved. The party initially assuming this risk is the one that agrees to receive or make later payment in the currency of the other party's country. Thus, if an American exporter agreed to accept payment from an English importer in pounds, the former would suffer a speculative loss if the pound rose on the exchanges against the dollar between the contract and payment dates, but he would enjoy a speculative gain if the dollar rose against the pound. Contrariwise, if the contract called for payment in dollars, the English importer would enjoy a gain if the pound rose against the dollar, and would suffer a loss if the dollar rose against the pound.

The risk of exchange variation can be shifted by the party that initially assumes it by "hedging" through forward exchange contracts. An American exporter who had drawn a 90-day draft for £1,000 on an English importer to cover a shipment could immediately, through one of several New York banks that engage in such transactions, arrange to sell £1,000, delivery to be made 90 days later, at the current quotation for 90-day "forward" pounds (which would differ from the "spot" rate for pounds primarily by the amount of an interest charge and certain transaction allowances). Delivery on this transaction would be satisfied, whatever might be the intervening changes in the exchange rate between the pound and the dollar, by the matured 90-day draft. Contrariwise, an English importer who accepted a 90-day draft for $3,500 drawn upon him for a shipment could protect himself through a forward purchase of dollars at an English bank.

Obviously, if all American export sale contracts called for payment in dollars, American exporting manufacturers and export houses would run no risk from variation of the exchanges. But in many cases the importers insist on making payment in their own currencies, on the ground that facilities for hedging are not available in their cities or are more expensive than they would be to the exporter. To make the sale, or to maintain the good will of the customer, the exporter must agree to accept payment in the currency of the importer's country. This exposes him to the risk of foreign exchange fluctuation. Conservative prudence dictates that he should hedge the transaction. But this hedging involves costs that must either be added to the sales price or reduce the exporter's profit. Accordingly, if the dollar seems likely in the near future to maintain or improve its exchange position relative to the currency of the importer's country, many exporters take the chance of leaving a foreign-currency sale "unhedged." The responsibility for such a decision does not rest exclusively on the export credit manager, but he is generally looked upon as the concern's expert on foreign exchange matters and his advice is asked for and usually heeded.

There is no comparable way of safeguarding against the blocking of foreign payments by the government of an importer's country. It happened with unhappy frequency in the 1930's, and entailed much financial embarrassment and in some cases disaster to American exporters. During World War II it became almost universal. More favorable development of international financial payment balances has to some extent eliminated this stumbling block to international trade. But for some time to come, export credit managers will still have to take the possibility of such payment "blocks" into consideration when weighing the advisability of granting credit terms to foreign customers.

An export credit manager, then, must not only know credit analysis, but he must also be a careful student of international financial developments as they affect the countries where his firm's customers are located. He has several sources of information on such developments. *Foreign Commerce Weekly,* published by the Department of Commerce, and the *Federal Reserve Bulletin* contain data on foreign financial developments which, if analyzed properly, may foreshadow exchange movements and indicate the possibility of foreign payment blockings. The monthly "bulletins" or "letters" of certain New York City banks, like First National City Bank, which are active in foreign exchange dealings, often carry valuable interpretative pointers on international financial developments. Export credit managers whose companies are members of the Foreign Credit Interchange Bureau of the National Association of Credit Management have exceptionally valuable sources of information not only on international financial developments but also on how payments are currently being made by importers of various countries. These sources are the Bureau's *Weekly Bulletin,* its *Minutes of the Monthly Round Table Conference on Foreign Finance, Credit, Collection and Exchange Problems,* and its *Semiannual Survey of Credit and Collection Conditions Throughout South America.*

## COLLECTION OF EXPORT ACCOUNTS

Because of the previously indicated weaknesses in credit information on foreign accounts, and because of the many difficulties of conducting collection proceedings by remote control should the necessity arise, standards of credit acceptability on foreign accounts are generally much higher than for domestic accounts. Therefore a much smaller proportion of foreign than of domestic accounts becomes delinquent. The common use of documentary evidences of liability, such as the accepted draft, with only a small proportion of export sales made on open account, probably also contributes to this lower degree of delinquency. But occasional defaults occur, and the export credit manager, like the domestic credit manager, has a collection problem.

### Correspondence

When a foreign customer fails to make remittance on an open account, or his draft is returned unpaid, an export credit manager's initial recourse is to cable and letter writing. The principles of domestic collection letter writing, discussed earlier in this volume, apply also to export collection letters, but with some important qualifications and modifications. If the amount involved in a dishonored draft is substantial, an immediate cable is desirable. A cable not only cuts down the time lag in correspondence between countries, but it also impresses the defaulting importer with the alertness of the exporter's collection department. An initial letter referring to the cable should be sent on the same date. There can be no fictional assumption that nonpayment of the draft was an "oversight" on the importer's part. This first letter in such a case notes the return of the draft, regrets and expresses surprise at the occurrence, and requests an early remittance.

The strongest of all appeals in follow-up collection letters to foreign customers is "pride." The honor of an established "house" means much to a foreign importer—more than it does to most American business concerns. Tactfully made, this appeal alone suffices in most cases where collection is at all possible. An appeal to the customer's self-interest may be made by pointing out that the default, if continued, will have to be reported to a credit agency or an interchange service. So, too, final warning can be given that the account will be turned over to an attorney of the importer's country for collection, even though no such action is intended.

Foreign businessmen expect a more personal touch in correspondence, more courtesy in letter style, and a more delicate treatment of their sensitivity than do American businessmen. Collection letters addressed to them therefore demand a finer exercise of the epistolary art. Few export credit managers prepare files of form collection letters. Each letter, written originally in or translated into the importer's language, is individually tailored to the circumstances of the particular recipient.

If an export credit manager's own collection letters have failed to produce results, he has one further correspondence recourse. Dun & Bradstreet offers the services of its International Mercantile Claims Department, which start with letters to the debtor and follow through, when necessary, to "personal collection" by the Department's branch offices. A similar service is provided by the Foreign Credit Interchange Bureau of the NACM through its network of agents and attorneys in every major city of the free world. Its charges are 20 per cent on the first $750, 15 per cent on the next $750, and 13 per cent on the amount over $1,500.

### Salesmen

If the exporter maintains salesmen or a sales agency in the country of a delinquent customer, collection of the account may be turned over to them after correspondence from the home office has failed to obtain a remittance. It is part of the function of foreign salesmen and sales agencies to handle collections on delinquent accounts as well as obtain credit information for the home office.

### Suit

Collection by suit in the courts of the defaulting importer's country, conducted by an attorney of that country, is rarely satisfactory. American export creditors discover to their dismay that the laws of some other countries give them very little redress, even in clear cases, against nationals of those countries. Where recovery can be had, the costs of the suit, the attorney's charges, and various costs of conducting a suit by remote control may absorb the greater part of the recovered amount. Many exporters prefer to write off as a bad debt any obligation of a foreign customer that cannot be recovered through correspondence. If decision is made to bring suit against a foreign customer, it can be handled by Dun & Bradstreet's International Mercantile Claims Department which has contact with attorneys in all free-world countries, or the Trade Adjustment Service of the U.S. Bureau of Foreign and Domestic Commerce may be asked for assistance.

## EXPORT CREDIT INSURANCE
## AND GUARANTEES

The insurance of export credits was started in 1921 by American Manufacturers Foreign Credit Service Exchange, with credit rating and other services performed by American Foreign Credit Underwriters. During the next ten years some $250 million of American export credits were insured by the Exchange, with $50 million to $60 million of applications rejected as unsatisfactory risks. Because of the greater uncertainty of credit analysis in the export field than in domestic credits, manufacturers and export houses insured their foreign accounts to a greater extent than did domestic sellers.

The American Manufacturers Foreign Credit Insurance Exchange suspended underwriting and was liquidated in December 1932 as a result of the abnormal export credit situation resulting from England's abandonment of the gold standard. It was succeeded, on a more restricted basis, by the Export Credit Indemnity Exchange, also served by American Foreign Credit Underwriters. This export credit insurance by the Export Credit Indemnity Exchange continued until the United States entered World War II. Then, because of the decline in commercial exporting and the deterioration in the character of foreign credit risks, this insurance service was also suspended. After the war, with the revival of exports, new attempts were made to have some form of insurance or guarantee provided for American exporters.[3]

The Export-Import Bank of Washington (Eximbank), engaged primarily in helping finance American exports, has for some time extended

---

[3] Export credit insurance is available in other countries, for example, in Canada, South Africa, England, and the major continental European exporting nations.

guarantees against political and commercial risks [4] for *medium-term* export credits.[5] Prior to 1960, however, neither political nor comprehensive guarantees were available for the *short-term* financing which constitutes the bulk of export credit. Eximbank assumed such guarantees only incidentally when it engaged in direct financing of exporters and bought their notes without recourse. In 1960, Eximbank started its *political* guarantee coverage of short-term export credits; short-term *commercial* risk insurance was left to insurance companies. The latter cooperated with Eximbank by offering exporters a "package plan" which was actually a comprehensive policy combining Eximbank's political risks guarantee with the insurance companies' commercial risk insurance. In 1961 Eximbank extended its guarantee coverage also to short-term commercial risks.[6]

## SUPPLEMENTARY READINGS

Bank for International Settlements (B.I.S.), *Export Credit Insurance and Export Credit at the End of 1960*, Basle, 1961.

Guaranty Trust Company of New York, *A Review of Export and Import Procedure*, rev. ed., 1957.

Jackson, O. A., "What's in Export-Import Credit," *Credit and Financial Management*, May 1952, p. 14.

Reimann, G., and E. F. Wigglesworth, *International Guide to Foreign Commercial Financing*, 2 vol., International Reports, Inc., New York, 1961.

Sánchez, J. R., *Foreign Credits and Collections*, Prentice-Hall, Inc., Englewood Cliffs, N.J., 1947.

Shaterian, W. S., *Export-Import Banking*, rev. ed., 1956. The Ronald Press, New York, 1956.

Ward, W., "Foreign Credit Insurance—Is It a Myth?" *Credit and Financial Management*, September 1945, p. 10.

————, and Harfield, H., *Bank Credit and Acceptances*, 4th ed., The Ronald Press, New York, 1959.

---

[4] "Political risk" is defined as including: (1) inconvertibility or nontransferability of foreign currencies; (2) imposition of laws and regulations beyond control of exporter and buyer which prevent delivery of goods; (3) cancellation of import license; (4) war, hostilities, rebellion, and civil commotion; and (5) expropriation of exported items by foreign authorities. "Commercial" or "credit risk" is defined as insolvency of the buyer, failure to pay within a stated period from due date, etc. Eximbank provides its guarantees in two forms: a "political" guarantee covering only political risks, and a "comprehensive" guarantee covering both political and commercial risks.

[5] "Medium term" credits are those for from 180 days to 5 years (7 years in the case of jet aircraft).

[6] Two private companies, Continental Casualty Company and Federal Insurance Company, offered this form of export risk insurance at that time. Since 1962, FCIA (Foreign Credit Insurance Association) composed of 72 insurance companies sells combined policies against political and commercial risks. The latter is shared equally by Eximbank and FCIA, the former is carried by Eximbank alone.

## REVIEW

1. Discuss the following terms for export sale: (a) cash deposit in advance of shipment, (b) export letter of credit, (c) sight draft, (d) time draft, (e) "authority to purchase," (f) open account, (g) "confirming house."
2. Discuss the "rating books" available on customers in foreign countries.
3. What sort of information on a foreign buyer may be obtained from an agency report on such buyer?
4. Discuss the reports of the Foreign Credit Interchange Bureau of the National Association of Credit Management.
5. Discuss the possibility of obtaining financial statements from foreign customers. What is the value of such statements when available?
6. Are foreign salesmen a good source of credit information on their customers?
7. What customer factors are more important, and which less important, in judging the credit status of a foreign customer in comparison with such judgment on a domestic customer?
8. Discuss the "currency risk" that enters export credit decisions, and what protection may be obtained against such risk.
9. How does collection correspondence directed to a foreign customer differ from that directed to a domestic customer?
10. What are the possibilities of collection suits brought against defaulting foreign customers?
11. How can an American exporter obtain protection on his credit risks?

## PROBLEM

Alphega Electronics, through its Export Division, sells electronic equipment component parts, made to specific order, to manufacturers in many foreign countries. It maintains five sales engineers in Europe, two in Canada, and two in Latin America. The credit period on its export sales is usually 120 to 180 days. Alphega maintains an account with the Chase Manhattan Bank.

1. From what sources can its export credit manager obtain credit information on new and established accounts?
2. What terms or payment arrangements would be made in the following cases: (a) a first order from an Italian concern on which credit information is scanty? (b) repeat orders from a Brazilian firm which appears, from available information, to be doing well and expanding, but seems to be undercapitalized and is reported to be occasionally slow in its domestic payments? (c) orders from Britannic Industries, Ltd., the century-old "Rock of Gibraltar" of the English machine-tool industry?
3. Is there any way Alphega Electronics can protect itself, in its Latin-American sales, against: (a) "blocking" of export payments by the governments of the importing countries? (b) insolvency of the importing concerns?

# CHAPTER 25

# Credit Insurance

As was indicated in Chapter 11, sound credit policy dictates that credit terms should also be extended to categories of credit risks certain to produce some loss. That such "normal" bad debt losses will occur regularly can be readily anticipated. Their amount may be predetermined with considerable degree of accuracy. Provision can be made for their inclusion in accounting and budgetary procedure by treating them as a special type of operating expense or by absorbing them through a bad debt reserve. It would be contrary to all principles of insurance to insure against such normal bad debt losses.

There are, however, several causes of "abnormal" bad debt loss, which cannot be anticipated as to occurrence or amount by any individual seller. The four most important of these possibilities are:

1. Loss resulting from insolvency of one or more large customers whose accounts constitute a disproportionate fraction of the selling company's total receivables.

2. Loss resulting from insolvency of a substantial proportion of a company's customers, all engaged in a particular line of business which is affected by some unusual event—for example, a technological development, a protracted strike, a raw material shortage.

3. Loss resulting from insolvency of a substantial proportion of a com-

pany's customers located in an area affected by some unusual regional event—for example, a flood, a crop failure, a protracted strike in an industry which economically dominates the region.

4. Loss resulting from customer insolvencies in excess of the "normal" as a result of a general business depression.

Such abnormal bad debt losses cannot be anticipated by an individual seller, nor can provision be made for absorbing such losses without severe financial dislocation. But while the individual seller is powerless to make provision against these abnormal bad debt losses, they can be "averaged out" for large aggregates of sellers with customers in all lines of business and located in all parts of the country, operating over full cyclical periods. This "averaging out" of abnormal bad debt loss risks can be and is accomplished by credit insurance.

## DEVELOPMENT OF CREDIT INSURANCE

In 1885 and 1886 the legislatures of New York, New Jersey, and Louisiana authorized the incorporation of companies to write credit insurance. A U. S. Credit System Company was organized under the New Jersey statute in 1889, failed in 1899. The London Guarantee and Accident Co., Ltd. established a credit insurance department in this country in 1892. A year later the American Credit Indemnity Company of New York, an outgrowth of the American Credit Indemnity Company of Louisiana, was organized and commenced business. These two credit insurance companies—the London company and the American Credit Indemnity Company of New York—have continued in business on an expanding scale to the present day, and write all the present American credit insurance. Five other credit insurance companies entered the field, but all subsequently either failed or were absorbed by the London or the American companies.

A major difficulty faced during the first quarter century of credit insurance was the failure to reduce credit losses from business failures to an actuarial basis. This shortcoming was partially met in 1919 by the publication of the first manual of credit insurance rates and coverages. A revision of this manual was made in 1923 to meet New York requirements; other revisions in 1959 and 1960, which introduced major modifications, serve as basis for present-day credit insurance underwriting.

Credit insurance has never been a major insurance field. Even with a doubling during the postwar years, total premium payments in 1959 were only $9 million. Loss payments in this year were $1.7 million.[1]

---

[1] The major source for credit insurance figures are the *Reports* of the Alfred M. Best Co., Inc.

## ELEMENTS OF A
## CREDIT INSURANCE POLICY

The issues involved in credit insurance, for which specific provision must be made in a credit insurance policy, are:

1. Nature of the credit transaction covered by the policy.
2. Number and extent of seller's accounts covered by the insurance.
3. Period of the policy.
4. Provision for collection of past-due accounts which may give rise to liability under the policy.
5. Claim and adjustment procedure.

All credit insurance policies make uniform provision as to the nature of the credit loss covered. With respect to the other issues, a seller is offered considerable choice. The insurance companies have prepared a wide variety of standard policies and special riders (or endorsements) to cater to the particular needs and wishes of individual sellers.

### Nature of credit loss insured against

Credit insurance covers bad debt losses resulting from the insolvency or delinquency of customers. According to current policy forms (see Illustration 25-1), such insolvency is deemed to occur when:

1. a debtor absconds;
2. a sole debtor dies;
3. a sole debtor is adjudged insane;
4. a receiver is appointed for a debtor;
5. the stock in trade of a debtor is sold under the Bulk Sales Act;
6. a writ of attachment or execution is levied on a debtor's stock in trade and said stock is sold thereunder, or the writ is returned unsatisfied;
7. a debtor makes a general offer of compromise to his creditors for less than his indebtedness;
8. possession is taken under a chattel mortgage given by a debtor on his stock in trade;
9. a debtor's assets are assigned to or taken over by a creditors' committee for the sole purpose of liquidation;
10. possession is taken of a debtor's assets under an assignment or deed of trust executed by a debtor for the benefit of his creditors;
11. a voluntary or involuntary proceeding is instituted to adjudge a debtor bankrupt;
12. a proceeding for an arrangement of the debtor's liabilities is instituted in a Court of Bankruptcy.

Delinquency of an account is established for insurance purposes when the insured seller, under a mandatory or optional policy provision, files such account with the insurance company for collection according to the policy terms.

## Types of policies

There are two types of credit insurance policies:

1. *Regular policies* cover only accounts with "preferred" mercantile agency ratings.[2]

2. *Combination policies* cover both "preferred" ratings and accounts with "inferior" or "blank" ratings and accounts not listed by mercantile agencies. Such policies account for over 90 per cent of all credit insurance written in recent years.

*Single accounts* may be insured, instead of all accounts or all "preferred" accounts, but the insurance companies discourage this procedure. They generally urge that a substantial proportion of a company's accounts be covered. If this is not done, they are inclined to raise the primary loss deduction (see below) to such an extent that the policy is likely to become unattractive to the prospective insured.

## Period of policy

The usual term of credit insurance is one year. Occasionally longer-term policies are drawn. With regard to the loss period they cover, there are two basic policy forms:

1. *Back coverage* policies reimburse for losses occurring during the policy period on shipments made within the policy period. By a back sales rider, such policies can be extended to cover losses during the policy period on sales made before the policy date. Filing of accounts for collection is not mandatory under back coverage policies.

2. *Forward coverage* policies reimburse for losses sustained on sales made during the policy period, even though such losses occur after the policy period. Such a policy remains effective for transactions covered by it for a period equal to the terms of sale on these transactions plus three months but not more than seven months from the expiration date of the policy. Filing of accounts for collection is not mandatory at a specific time under forward coverage policies, but there is an additional coinsurance deductible for claims filed more than three months past due date.

## Collection provisions

If a delinquent insured account is turned over to the insurance company within a reasonable period after it becomes past due, the company may be able to take more aggressive and effective collection action than

---

[2] In the case of Dun & Bradstreet ratings, the "preferred" categories are "high" and "good."

A FORM
160 EDITION

# AMERICAN
# CREDIT INDEMNITY
# COMPANY
## OF NEW YORK

ESTABLISHED 1893

EXECUTIVE OFFICE                                BALTIMORE 2, MD.

(HEREINAFTER CALLED THE COMPANY)

1       IN CONSIDERATION of the warranties and representations made
2   in the application for this Policy of Credit Insurance, and of the payment
3   of the premium as hereinafter provided, and subject to the other conditions
4   hereinafter set forth and to the provisions of the Policy Declaration which
5   are hereby made a part of this Policy, hereby guarantees the Insured named
6   in the Policy Declaration against loss due to insolvency, as hereinafter
7   defined, of debtors, provided such insolvency occurs within the Insolvency
8   Period. Such loss shall consist of the unpaid invoice price of bona fide
9   sales of the Insured, shipped during the Shipment Period and actually
10  delivered in the usual course of business to individuals, firms, copartnerships
11  or corporations located in the United States of America and Canada, and
12  shall have been covered, filed and proved as hereinafter provided. From the
13  aggregate amount of net covered losses, ascertained as hereinafter pro-
14  vided, there shall be deducted a Primary Loss, established by the Primary Loss Per-
15  centage of total gross sales so made during the Shipment Period, less all allow-
16  ances actually made on said sales during the Shipment Period, and less the
17  invoice price of any of said sales returned and accepted by the Insured dur-
18  ing the Shipment Period. Such Primary Loss, however, shall in no event be
19  less than the Minimum Primary Loss. The remainder, not exceeding the Policy
20  Amount, less any amount owing to the Company, shall be the amount payable
21  to the Insured by the Company.
22      This Policy shall not cover any loss occurring prior to the payment
23  of the premium, although the Policy may have been delivered; nor any
24  loss that is not a valid and legally sustainable indebtedness or has not been
25  allowed against the debtor or the debtor's estate.

ILLUSTRATION 25-1.   Credit Insurance Policy

the seller, make a collection that the seller would not obtain, and thus avoid liability on the account.

Some credit managers feel that a policy provision compelling or permitting them to refer delinquent accounts to the insurance company gives them a pronounced advantage in their own collection procedure. They can warn their delinquent accounts of the impending collection action, while proclaiming that their contract with the insurance company allows them no discretion in the matter and regretting that their hand is thus

# CONDITIONS

## 1—GOVERNING RATING AND COVERAGE

26 The governing rating is defined and agreed
27 to be the rating of a debtor at date of shipment
28 by the Governing Mercantile Agency, herein-
29 after called Agency.
30 The latest published rating book of the
31 Agency shall be used to determine a debtor's
32 governing rating for coverage on shipments
33 made from the first day of the month named by
34 that book through the last day of the month
35 preceding the month named by the next subse-
36 quent book, but if the Agency shall have
37 changed a rating by written report, compiled
38 during the currency of the latest published book
39 or within 4 months prior to the date thereof,
40 that report, of which the Insured shall have
41 received a copy from the Agency, or written
42 notice thereof from the Company, shall be used
43 to determine the debtor's governing rating for
44 coverage on shipments made after receipt by
45 the Insured of that written report from the
46 Agency, or written notice thereof from the
47 Company. If the Agency issues supplements
48 to the rating book, then, every issued supple-
49 ment shall be treated the same as a written re-
50 port received by the Insured from the Agency, so
51 that a change in rating in any such supple-
52 ment shall govern the same as a change in
53 rating by written report received by the Insured.
54 Every issued supplement shall be construed to
55 have been received by the Insured within 5 days
56 from the issuance date shown in the supplement.
57 Coverage on any loss under this Policy
58 shall be limited to that portion of the indebted-
59 ness of a debtor to the Insured which consists
60 of the unpaid invoice price of shipments made
61 within the Shipment Period, in the name of
62 the Insured or under any name authorized by
63 endorsement; provided, the debtor to whom
64 the goods were shipped and delivered shall
65 have had, at the date of shipment, a governing
66 rating for which coverage is specified in the
67 Table of Ratings and Coverage, as set forth in
68 the Policy Declaration. Coverage shall be
69 limited also to that portion of the indebtedness

70 on which Notification of Claim has been filed
71 as required in Condition 4.
72 The gross amount covered on the total
73 indebtedness of any one debtor shall neither
74 exceed the total amount owing to the Insured
75 by that debtor at date of insolvency, nor exceed
76 the amount set opposite the governing rating
77 of the debtor in the Table of Ratings and
78 Coverage.
79 The amount of coverage applicable to a
80 debtor by rating under Columns 1 and 2 of the
81 Table of Ratings and Coverage at the be-
82 ginning date of the Shipment Period as set forth
83 in the Policy Declaration, or thereafter, shall
84 not be reduced by reason of shipments subse-
85 quently made the debtor while assigned a
86 rating as high or higher as to Capital accom-
87 panied by as high or higher Credit Rating as
88 tabulated in the Table of Ratings and Cover-
89 age; that is, if at the date of shipment under
90 such improved rating, the prior rating affords
91 a higher amount of coverage, then the prior
92 rating shall govern instead of the improved
93 rating. However, should the foregoing pro-
94 visions of this Paragraph not be applicable,
95 then, if the indebtedness of a debtor at the date
96 of insolvency be for shipments made under
97 different governing ratings, the gross amount
98 covered on the total of such indebtedness shall
99 not exceed the largest amount set opposite any
100 one of that debtor's governing ratings in the
101 Table of Ratings and Coverage. Should a
102 change of rating reduce the limit of coverage
103 applicable to a debtor, shipments made there-
104 after shall not be covered unless and until the
105 covered prior indebtedness be less than the
106 amount set opposite the latest rating, in which
107 event the gross amount covered on the total of
108 such indebtedness shall not exceed the amount
109 set opposite said latest rating.
110 A shipment to a debtor whose name, at
111 date of shipment, does not appear in the latest
112 published book, shall be governed by the
113 rating in the latest report of the Agency on

ILLUSTRATION 25-1 *(Continued)*

forced. Slow collections are hastened by this threat-appeal, according to some credit managers, without any sacrifice of customer good will.

Other credit managers do not want to be limited to some specified period, say three months, during which they may pursue their own collection procedures with delinquent customers. An insurance company, in its collection procedure, employs the forthright, aggressive tactics of a collection agency. These tactics may obtain payment from a good but slow-pay customer, but lose his good will in spite of the credit manager's

114 the debtor compiled within 4 months prior to
115 the shipment, and if no such report shall have
116 been compiled within 4 months prior to the
117 shipment, then by the rating in the first report
118 of the Agency on the debtor compiled within 4
119 months after the shipment.

120      Merchandise placed with a debtor on con-
121 signment for the debtor's own use or for resale
122 shall be covered to the extent used or resold,
123 and the date of withdrawal for use or resale
124 shall be construed as the date of shipment within
125 the meaning of this Policy.

126      Every prepayment made by the Insured
127 for freight on any shipment covered by this
128 Policy, and for which the debtor is legally
129 liable, shall, for all the purposes of this Policy,
130 be treated as part of the invoice price payable
131 by the debtor to the Insured for the merchandise,
132 and shall accordingly be so treated both in the
133 calculation of the gross sales of the Insured and
134 of the gross losses of the Insured. When the
135 freight charges are not prepaid by the Insured,
136 the basis of sale of merchandise under this
137 Policy shall be computed at the invoice price
138 of merchandise F.O.B. at shipping point, and
139 freight charges shall not be considered as any
140 part of such transaction.

141      A debtor's name as listed in the agreed
142 books of the Agency, or the name under which
143 a report is issued on a debtor by the Agency,
144 shall for the purposes of this Policy be construed
145 as the legal name of the debtor. If a debtor
146 should use a Division, Style or Trade name in
147 the conduct of his business, shipments made
148 to the debtor under such other names shall be
149 construed as having been made to the debtor
150 under the debtor's legal name. Shipments made
151 to a Branch location of a debtor shall be con-
152 strued as having been made to the debtor at the

153 location maintained as headquarters of the
154 debtor.

155      If, at the date of shipment to a debtor, the
156 Insured should hold an absolute guaranty of a
157 third party, in writing, securing payment of
158 the indebtedness, and such guaranty be valid
159 and legally binding at all times, then, as to a
160 loss on such debtor, the coverage applicable
161 to the guarantor at the date of shipment, if
162 higher than the coverage applicable to the
163 debtor, may, at the option of the Insured, be
164 used to govern coverage on the loss, but not
165 to exceed the amount guaranteed if that amount
166 be less than the amount of coverage applicable
167 to the guarantor. If more than one debtor's
168 account due the Insured shall have been secured
169 by written guaranty of the same guarantor,
170 and the Insured elects to have a loss on more
171 than one debtor governed by the coverage
172 applicable to the guarantor, as aforesaid, or
173 if the Insured also sustains a loss on sales, ship-
174 ments and deliveries made directly to the
175 guarantor, the limit of coverage applicable to
176 such combined obligation of the guarantor
177 shall not exceed the limit of coverage that would
178 have been applicable had the loss on such
179 combined obligation resulted entirely from
180 sales, shipments and deliveries made directly
181 to the guarantor.

182      If the Insured, without the consent of the
183 Company in writing, shall make any agreement
184 with respect to the account of a debtor which
185 would, at the date of filing with the Company
186 or subsequent thereto, prevent or delay any
187 action thereon, or which would interfere with
188 the exercise of the Company's judgment on
189 any proposal made by the debtor to his creditors,
190 coverage on such account under this Policy shall
191 terminate and cease.

## 2—OPTIONAL FILING OF PAST DUE ACCOUNTS

192      The Insured, during the Insolvency Period
193 of this Policy, shall be permitted to file with
194 the Company for collection an account against
195 a debtor not insolvent as defined in Condition
196 3 at the time the account was so filed, and
197 so much of such account that was due and
198 payable at the date of filing, but not more
199 than 3 months past due under the original
200 terms of sale, shall be treated in any Claim

201 Settlement under this Policy as though the
202 debtor had become insolvent. The date of
203 filing of the account by the Insured shall be
204 the date postmarked or the date otherwise
205 delivered to the Company. Every such account so
206 filed shall include all indebtedness then due and
207 payable and shall be accompanied with a Notifica-
208 tion of Claim as described in Condition 4.

ILLUSTRATION 25-1   *(Continued)*

explanation that referring the account to the company is not a matter of choice but of contractual necessity. In general, however, the insurance companies must preserve customer good will for their clients, or these clients will not continue using the insurance companies' collection service. Hence insurance company collection procedure applies "iron fist in velvet glove" techniques.

To meet these divergent views of credit managers, credit insurance policies offer a choice of collection provisions. Forward coverage policies

### 3—INSOLVENCY DEFINED

209 Insolvency for the purposes of this Policy
210 shall be determined to have occurred only when:
211     (1) a debtor shall have absconded;
212     (2) a sole debtor shall have died;
213     (3) a sole debtor shall have been adjudged
214     insane;
215     (4) a receiver shall have been appointed
216     for a debtor;
217     (5) legal notice shall be given by the pro-
218     posed purchaser of the stock in trade
219     of a debtor under the Bulk Sales Act;
220     (6) a writ of attachment or execution shall
221     have been levied on a debtor's stock in
222     trade and said stock sold thereunder,
223     or the writ returned unsatisfied.
224     (7) a debtor shall have made a general offer
225     of compromise to his creditors for less
226     than his indebtedness;
227     (8) possession shall have been taken under
228     a chattel mortgage given by a debtor
229     on his stock in trade;
230     (9) a debtor's assets shall have been as-
231     signed to or taken over by a committee
232     for the sole purpose of liquidation;
233     (10) possession shall have been taken of a
234     debtor's assets under an assignment or
235     deed of trust executed by the debtor
236     for the benefit of his creditors;
237     (11) a voluntary or involuntary proceeding
238     shall have been instituted to adjudge a
239     debtor bankrupt, or
240     (12) a proceeding for an arrangement of
241     the debts of a debtor shall have been
242     instituted in a Court of Bankruptcy.

### 4—NOTIFICATION AND FILING OF CLAIMS

243 When a debtor, within the Insolvency
244 Period of this Policy, becomes insolvent as
245 defined in Condition 3, the Insured, within
246 10 days after acquiring knowledge thereof
247 and during the Insolvency Period, shall file
248 Notification of Claim with the Company on
249 a form furnished by the Company and place
250 the entire account with the Company for
251 attention and collection. If knowledge of a
252 debtor's insolvency as defined in Condition 3
253 be received too late to file the claim with the
254 Company during the Insolvency Period, then a
255 grace period of 20 days shall be permitted for the
256 filing of such claim.
257 Every Notification of Claim filed shall be
258 accompanied with an itemized statement in
259 triplicate, showing fully the dates of shipment,
260 terms of sale, and the condition of the account,
261 together with all notes and other papers evi-
262 dencing the same, and all guarantees, securities,
263 or other documents relating thereto; and the In-
264 sured shall, upon request, promptly furnish all
265 proofs, or any information and assistance necessary
266 for the proper handling of any account in any
267 proceeding.
268 All Notifications of Claim must be received
269 by the Company within the time above speci-
270 fied, in the office designated in the Policy Declara-
271 tion, and shall be handled upon the terms and
272 subject to all the conditions of this Policy. The
273 date of receipt of the Notification of Claim shall
274 be the date postmarked or otherwise delivered
275 to the Company.
276 The filing of any Notification of Claim by
277 the Insured under this Policy shall constitute
278 authority for the Company to place the account
279 represented thereby for collection with any at-
280 torney selected by the Company.
281 Any claim withdrawn by the Insured may
282 not be refiled under this or any other Policy issued
283 by the Company.
284 The receipt, retention or handling by the
285 Company of any claim filed by the Insured shall
286 not constitute a waiver of any of the terms or con-
287 ditions of this Policy, nor shall it be an acceptance
288 of such claim as covered by this or any other Policy.

ILLUSTRATION 25-1 *(Continued)*

provide a final date by which delinquent insured accounts must be filed if full recovery is to be allowed in claim settlement. Back coverage policies make the filing of past-due accounts optional. A rarely-used variant of the back coverage policy provides for no collection by the insurance company; the insured must assume all collection responsibilities, and where insolvency procedures are involved, must prove and press his claims.

In handling covered accounts placed with it for collection, the insurance company gives free service on all collections made within 10 days

## 5—COLLECTION OF ACCOUNTS AND SCHEDULE OF CHARGES

289     The Company assumes responsibility for all 290 money collected by its employees and by attorneys 291 of its selection, and will promptly account for 292 collections due the Insured, subject to the following 293 conditions:

### Free Service:

294

295 No Charge shall be made on any collection
296 effected within 10 days after demand has been
297 made by the Company; neither shall any
298 Charge be made on any collection effected on
299 any undisputed or unlitigated account insofar
300 as covered, provided the debtor, at date of
301 filing, is insolvent as defined in Condition 3.

302 If any balance remain unpaid at the expira-
303 tion of the 10 Day Free Service period, the
304 account shall remain with the Company for
305 handling. On every collection effected other-
306 wise than as hereinbefore limited and defined,
307 the following Charges shall be paid by the
308 Insured:

### On Collections Effected Without Forwarding Service:

309

310 15% on the first $750.00
311 10% on the excess of $750.00

312 Minimum charge $15.00, except on collections
313 under $30.00, charge to be 50%.

### Forwarding Service:

314

315 **Attorney Minimum Commissions:**

316 15% on the first $750.00 collected
317 10% on collections in excess of $750.00
318 $15.00 on collections of $100.00 or less,
319 except on collections of $45.00 or less, charge
320 to be 33⅓%. In localities where charges
321 are established by law, or by Bar Associations,
322 or where the above rates are not recognized
323 and higher rates are demanded, such rates
324 shall govern.

325 **Company Service Charges:**

326 In addition to the Commission charges of
327 attorneys, the Company will charge the fol-
328 lowing rates:
329 5% on the first $1,500.00 collected
330 3% on amounts collected in excess of
331 $1,500.00
332 $5.00 on collections of $100.00 or less, ex-
333 cept on collections of $30.00 or less, 16⅔%.

334     The invoice price of merchandise returned
335 or any amount paid direct to the Insured, on
336 any account filed with the Company, or the bal-
337 ance of an account withdrawn by the Insured,
338 shall be subject to the above Charges in effect at
339 date of notice to the Company.
340     If an account be disputed, in whole or in
341 part, or if the Company consider it necessary, for
342 the purpose of enforcing collection from the
343 debtor, guarantor, surety or endorser, or to par-
344 ticipate in any proceeding involving the estate of
345 the debtor, guarantor, surety or endorser, the In-
346 sured shall authorize suit or other proceeding and
347 shall pay expenses required in connection there-
348 with, promptly advancing court costs and legal

349 fees when requested; failure to do so shall be
350 construed as a withdrawal of the account by the
351 Insured.
352     When litigation or any proceding shall have
353 been authorized by the Insured, the amount
354 charged by the attorney as a non-contingent legal
355 fee shall be paid by the Insured; in addition thereto,
356 the Insured shall pay the stipulated Charge on col-
357 lections effected, but such stipulated Charge shall
358 be limited to the amount that the non-contingent
359 legal fee is less than 50% of the amount collected.
360     The Company shall have authority, in the
361 handling of an account under this Policy, to en-
362 dorse notes, checks or drafts on behalf and in
363 the name of the Insured, and to deposit them,

ILLUSTRATION 25-1   *(Continued)*

after date of filing. Otherwise its collection charges are, if no attorney services are required:

50% on collections under $30,
15% on the first $750 collection, and
10% on any excess over $750.

If an attorney must be employed, the insurance company charges an override on his legal fee.

364 or the proceeds of collection thereof, in the ac-
365 count or to the credit of the Company, in any
366 of its depository banks.
367         The remittance to the Insured, with or with-
368 out charge, of any amount collected on any account
369 filed, and acceptance thereof by the Insured, shall
370 not be construed as a determination of coverage,
371 nor as a waiver either by the Company or the
372 Insured of any of the terms or conditions of this
373 Policy.

## 6—FINAL STATEMENT OF CLAIM

374         When a claim for loss be made under this
375 Policy, the Insured shall complete a Final State-
376 ment of Claim form, which will be furnished by
377 the Company upon request. The completed form
378 must be received by the Company at its Executive
379 Office, Baltimore 2, Maryland, within one month
380 after the expiration of the Insolvency Period.

## 7—CLAIM SETTLEMENT

381         Settlement shall be made within 2 months
382 after receipt by the Company of a Final State-
383 ment of Claim, and the amount then ascertained
384 to be due the Insured shall be paid.
385         To ascertain the net loss in any settlement,
386 there shall be deducted from each gross loss cov-
387 ered, filed and proved hereunder:
388         (1) all amounts collected from the debtor
389              or obtained from any other source;
390         (2) the invoice price of merchandise re-
391              turned, reclaimed or replevined, when
392              such merchandise is in the undisputed
393              possession of the Insured;
394         (3) any discount to which the debtor
395              would be entitled at time of settlement;
396         (4) any legally sustainable set-off that the
397              debtor may have against the Insured;
398              and
399         (5) any amount mutually agreed upon as
400              thereafter obtainable.
401         If no mutually satisfactory agreement can
402 be reached as to the amount thereafter obtain-
403 able on any loss, the Company will allow the
404 unpaid portion of such loss, so far as covered.
405 If at the date of insolvency of a debtor the entire
406 indebtedness of the debtor to the Insured be in
407 excess of the gross amount covered by this Policy,
408 then the above deductions shall be made pro
409 rata, in the ratio which the gross amount covered
410 bears to the whole of the indebtedness. Having
411 made the foregoing deductions from each gross
412 loss covered, filed and proved under this Policy,
413 the result shall be the net loss.
414         From the aggregate amount of net losses
415 there shall be deducted the amount of Primary
416 Loss; the remainder, not exceeding the amount of
417 this Policy, less any amount owing to the Com-
418 pany, shall be the amount payable to the Insured.
419         If any covered claim of the Insured against
420 a debtor be disputed, in whole or in part, the
421 same shall not be allowed in any settlement under
422 this Policy until such disputed claim shall have
423 been finally determined to be a valid and legally
424 sustainable indebtedness against the debtor or the
425 debtor's estate, at which time that claim, so far
426 as covered under this Policy, shall be settled and
427 the amount due the Insured shall be paid.
428         The Insured shall assign to the Company, on
429 forms furnished and in the manner prescribed
430 by the Company, all claims allowed in settlement,
431 together with all securities and guarantees re-
432 lating thereto, execpt those claims upon which
433 the amount thereafter obtainable shall have been
434 mutually agreed upon, and shall warrant the legal
435 validity of the indebtedness for the amount of
436 such claims, and shall upon demand reimburse the
437 Company for any amount paid by the Company to
438 the Insured on any indebtedness which may not
439 be allowed against the debtor or the debtor's
440 estate, together with the expense of any action
441 thereon. Any claim assigned to the Company
442 which shall not have been covered in full by this
443 Policy shall be handled by the Company for the
444 joint benefit of the Insured and the Company as
445 their interests appear.

ILLUSTRATION 25-1   (Continued)

## LIMITATIONS OF COVERAGE

As stated earlier, a credit insurance policy does not purport to reimburse a seller for all bad debt losses which he suffers on his accounts. Three further limitations are placed upon the coverage provided:

1. Stipulated coverage, limited by a specified maximum, is set for each individual account;

### 8—DISPOSAL OF ASSIGNED CLAIMS

446 On claims assigned to it in Claim Settlement, the Company will promptly remit to the Insured, after deduction of all charges and expenses, their pro rata interest, if any, in the amount realized on any Claim.

451 In the event the Company considers it necessary for the purpose of enforcing collection from the debtor, guarantor, surety or endorser, or to participate in any proceeding involving the estate of the debtor, guarantor, surety or endorser, the Company and the Insured shall share the expenses required in connection therewith as their interests appear.

459 Any interest of the Insured in any security acquired by the Company in relation to any claim assigned to it will be evidenced, whenever possible, by a separate instrument and delivered to the Insured. If not so evidenced and any amount be realized in connection with such security, remittance will be made, less all charges and expenses, to the Insured in proportion to its interest in the proceeds.

468 If, after the deductions and remittances, the remaining net amounts realized by the Company should, in the aggregate, exceed the total amount paid to the Insured in Claim Settlement, the Company will remit to the Insured the excess and all net amounts thereafter realized, less any amount owing to the Company. The Company will then, upon the written request of the Insured, reassign all claims assigned to the Company in such Claim Settlement.

### 9—COLLATERAL BENEFITS

478 This Policy shall not be assignable but, upon written request of the Insured, the Company may provide that any loss, ascertained to be payable as provided in Condition 7, shall be paid to a Bank, Trust Company or other payee designated by, and for the account of, the Insured.

### 10—TERMINATION

484 If, during the Shipment Period, the Insured, or any included entity guaranteed by this Policy, should become insolvent as defined in any of the subdivisions of Condition 3, or should cease to continue the business described in the Policy Declaration, as heretofore carried on, or should go into liquidation, or being a partnership should be dissolved, then this Policy shall thereupon terminate as to coverage on shipments made thereafter. Temporary interruption by fire, flood, tornado or by strike, or by the death, withdrawal or admission of a member of a partnership composed of more than two members, shall not so terminate this Policy.

### 11—WAR RISK EXCLUSION

498 Coverage under this Policy shall not apply to any claim, if the direct cause of the past due status of the account under Condition 2, or of the insolvency under Condition 3, be due to an enemy attack by a Foreign Government or Sovereign Power or any action taken by the United States of America, Canada, or other Ally in resisting such attack.

### 12—GENERAL PROVISIONS

506 The premium for this Policy shall be paid by check to the order of American Credit Indemnity Company of New York and shall accompany the application. The Company may at its option accept premium notes or premium agreements. If premium notes or premium agreements so ac-

ILLUSTRATION 25-1    *(Continued)*

2. Most policies include a coinsurance provision;

3. Most policies provide a "primary loss" deduction.

## Maximum limitations on individual account coverage

In determining the maximum coverages allowable on the individual accounts insured under general coverage policies, these accounts are classified according to the capital-and-risk ratings given them by the mercan-

512 cepted be paid at or before maturity, the premium
513 for this Policy shall be construed as having been
514 paid as of the date of such instruments. If any note
515 or agreement be in default, then at the option of
516 the Company, to be exercised within 60 days
517 after any such default, by written notice to the
518 Insured by any Officer or Assistant Officer, this
519 Policy may be cancelled from its inception, with
520 full refund of any portion of the premium paid.
521 Should the Company not exercise its privilege of
522 cancellation as herein provided, the Policy shall
523 remain in effect, but no coverage shall attach
524 to any loss occurring prior to the payment of any
525 premium instrument in default.
526      The Company will acknowledge the receipt
527 of all Notifications of Claim and the Final State-
528 ment of Claim, but neither the acknowledgment
529 nor the retention thereof by the Company, nor
530 its failure to acknowledge receipt thereof, shall
531 be an admission of liability or a waiver by the
532 Company of any of the terms or conditions of
533 this Policy.
534      The warranties and representations made in
535 the application for this Policy of Credit Insur-
536 ance are the basis for this Policy and a part thereof
537 and are conclusively presumed to be material to
538 the risk assumed by the Company under this
539 Policy. False warranty, misrepresentation, con-
540 cealment or fraud in obtaining this Policy, or
541 in any Notification of Claim or Final Statement
542 of Claim filed under this Policy, or in the proof
543 or settlement of any claim for loss under this
544 Policy, shall void this Policy from its beginning
545 and the premium paid shall be forfeited to the
546 Company. The Insured shall permit the Company
547 at any reasonable time to examine and take ex-
548 tracts from the books, securities and papers of the
549 Insured bearing upon any matter involved in any
550 Notification of Claim or Final Statement of Claim
551 filed under this Policy, or in any Claim Settle-
552 ment under this Policy, or in any warranty or
553 representation made in the application for this
554 Policy, or in any claim made either by the Insured
555 or by the Company under this Policy, and in that
556 connection the Insured shall give such assistance
557 and information as the Company shall require,
558 but no such examination, investigation or proceed-
559 ing shall be an admission of liability or waiver
560 of any of the terms or conditions of this Policy. If,
561 by the law of the State named in the Policy
562 Declaration as the address of the Insured, war-

563 ranties are prohibited or not recognized in the
564 application for a Policy, then in conformity there-
565 with, statements of the Insured in the application
566 for this Policy shall be accepted as representations.
567      The rendering of any estimate or statement,
568 or the making of any settlement, shall not bar
569 the examination herein provided for, nor the
570 Company's right to unpaid Charges, nor the
571 Company's right to a refund of any amount
572 overpaid the Insured by the Company, nor bar the
573 right of the Insured to a refund of any amount
574 overpaid the Company.
575      This Policy shall be a valid and binding
576 obligation of the Company only if both it and
577 the Policy Declaration issued in connection there-
578 with be authenticated, as indicated thereon, by
579 the manual signature of an Officer or Assistant
580 Officer of the Company. It shall consist of this
581 printed form of Policy, any endorsements
582 thereto presently or hereafter issued by the Com-
583 pany, and the Policy Declaration. No notice to or
584 knowledge of any Agent or other person shall
585 effect a waiver of any provision thereof. No
586 Agent shall be authorized to make any alteration
587 therein or addition thereto, either verbally or in
588 writing, or to waive any such provision, and no
589 addition, alteration or waiver shall be valid unless
590 expressed in writing over the signature or fac-
591 simile signature of the President of the Company.
592      No suit or action on this Policy shall be
593 brought or be sustainable until after the full com-
594 pliance by the Insured with its terms and condi-
595 tions, nor unless commenced within 12 months
596 after its termination. If the said limitation of
597 time for the commencement of suit be prohibited
598 by any specific statutory provision in relation
599 thereto, in force in the State named in the Policy
600 Declaration as the address of the Insured, the said
601 limitation is hereby amended to conform to the
602 minimum period of limitation permitted by said
603 statutory provision.
604      Any provision of this Policy which, on its
605 effective date, is in conflict with the statutes of
606 the State named in the Policy Declaration as the
607 address of the Insured, is hereby amended to con-
608 form to the minimum requirements of such
609 statutes.
610      All terms and conditions of this Policy shall
611 be conditions precedent to any claim by the
612 Insured.

ILLUSTRATION 25-1 *(Continued)*

tile agency whose ratings are used by the insured. A maximum individual account coverage is specified in the policy for each such capital-and-risk classification. As indicated in Illustration 25-2, these maximum loss allowances range from $500 for a K 3 or J 3½ customer (D&B rating system) to $150,000 for an Aa A1 customer. At the request of the insured, the insurance company may approve higher stipulated limitations for individual accounts. In such cases an endorsement (rider) has to be added to the policy with the names and addresses of all the customers so

### 13—POLICY ACCEPTANCE

613    This Policy and the Policy Declaration as       615    Insured, shall be considered to have been issued
614    issued by the Company, upon acceptance by the    616    on terms mutually agreed upon.

---

IN WITNESS WHEREOF the AMERICAN                    has caused this Policy to be signed by the signature
CREDIT INDEMNITY COMPANY OF NEW YORK              or facsimile signature of its President at Balti-
                                                  more, Maryland.


                                                                        *President*

AUTHENTICATED:


.........................................................
                                *Assistant Secretary*

ILLUSTRATION 25-1    *(Concluded)*

covered; for accounts with "preferred" mercantile ratings this rider is called "Increased Coverage Endorsement," for others it is called "Extraordinary Coverage Endorsement" (see p. 504).

ILLUSTRATION 25-2.    Maximum Account Coverage Under a "Regular Rating" Credit Insurance Policy, as of 1960
(on the basis of Dun & Bradstreet ratings)

| Capital Rating | | | First Credit Rating | | Second Credit Rating | | Third Credit Rating | |
|---|---|---|---|---|---|---|---|---|
| | | | Risk Rating | Limitation | Risk Rating | Limitation | Risk Rating | Limitation |
| Aa | over | $1,000,000 | A1 | $150,000 | 1 | $25,000 | 1½ | $10,000 |
| A+ | over | 750,000 | A1 | 50,000 | 1 | 25,000 | 1½ | 10,000 |
| A | $500,000 to | 750,000 | A1 | 50,000 | 1 | 25,000 | 1½ | 10,000 |
| B+ | 300,000 to | 500,000 | 1 | 50,000 | 1½ | 25,000 | 2 | 10,000 |
| B | 200,000 to | 300,000 | 1 | 50,000 | 1½ | 25,000 | 2 | 10,000 |
| C+ | 125,000 to | 200,000 | 1 | 50,000 | 1½ | 25,000 | 2 | 10,000 |
| C | 75,000 to | 125,000 | 1½ | 30,000 | 2 | 15,000 | 2½ | 7,500 |
| D+ | 50,000 to | 75,000 | 1½ | 25,000 | 2 | 12,500 | 2½ | 6,250 |
| D | 35,000 to | 50,000 | 1½ | 20,000 | 2 | 10,000 | 2½ | 5,000 |
| E | 20,000 to | 35,000 | 2 | 10,000 | 2½ | 5,000 | 3 | 2,500 |
| F | 10,000 to | 20,000 | 2½ | 5,000 | 3 | 3,000 | 3½ | 1,500 |
| G | 5,000 to | 10,000 | 3 | 2,500 | 3½ | 1,500 | | |
| H | 3,000 to | 5,000 | 3 | 1,500 | 3½ | 750 | | |
| J | 2,000 to | 3,000 | 3 | 1,000 | 3½ | 500 | | |
| K | 1,000 to | 2,000 | 3 | 500 | | | | |
| Blank | | | 1 | 50,000 | 2 | 15,000 | 3 | 1,500 |

### Stipulated individual account coverage

An insured seller must stipulate a maximum individual account coverage for each of the capital-and-risk classes in which he has accounts. This stipulated coverage must never exceed the policy maximum, previously discussed.

In calculating stipulated individual account coverage, an insured tabulates his accounts according to the same capital-and-risk rating classification used to establish his policy maximum coverages. Then he enters, on a calculation sheet supplied by the insurance company, the highest balance which each customer is likely to incur during the policy year, as shown in Illustration 25-3.

ILLUSTRATION 25-3.  Illustrative Determination of Stipulated Individual Account Credit Insurance Coverages for Certain Ratings
(Dun & Bradstreet ratings)

| Aa A1 | A+ A1 | A A1 | B+ 1 | B 1 | C+ 1 | C 1½ | D+ 1½ |
|---|---|---|---|---|---|---|---|

*Individual maximum account coverage permitted by policy*

| Aa A1 | A+ A1 | A A1 | B+ 1 | B 1 | C+ 1 | C 1½ | D+ 1½ |
|---|---|---|---|---|---|---|---|
| $150,000 | $50,000 | $50,000 | $50,000 | $50,000 | $30,000 | $25,000 | $20,000 |

*Maximum balance each customer expected to incur*

| Aa A1 | A+ A1 | A A1 | B+ 1 | B 1 | C+ 1 | C 1½ | D+ 1½ |
|---|---|---|---|---|---|---|---|
| $    500 | $80,000 | $500 | $1,000 | | $15,000 | $2,000 | $1,000 |
| 800 | | | | | 1,000 | 1,500 | 1,000 |
| 5,000 | | | | | 1,000 | 3,500 | 1,000 |
| 500 | | | | | 500 | 300 | 600 |
| 25,000 | | | | | | 2,000 | |
| 15,000 | | | | | | | |
| 60,000 | | | | | | | |
| 1,000 | | | | | | | |

*Stipulated individual account coverage for each risk class*

| Aa A1 | A+ A1 | A A1 | B+ 1 | B 1 | C+ 1 | C 1½ | D+ 1½ |
|---|---|---|---|---|---|---|---|
| $60,000 | $50,000 | $10,000 | $10,000 | | $15,000 | $3,500 | $1,500 |

The seller deals separately with each group of customers tabulated in each capital-and-risk classification. In each classification he studies the largest balance listed there, since whatever coverage he decides upon for the largest account in a classification will apply to all the smaller ones. Does he want this account fully covered? Usually he does, for a lower figure, while effecting a small premium saving, would involve a penny-wise, pound-foolish sacrifice of coverage. He may decide to set his capital-and-risk class coverage higher than the largest balance he has entered in it, on the possibility that he may, during the policy period, obtain still larger customers in this capital-and-risk classification. Such added coverage for any particular capital-and-risk classification will increase the face coverage of the policy and, for reasons explained later in this chapter, such expanded face coverage may be desirable. In Illustration 25-3, higher class coverage than is currently needed for accounts in the class has been stipulated for Classes A A1, B+ 1, and D+ 1½.

A stipulated account coverage for a capital-and-risk class is binding on all accounts in that class. Any new accounts obtained after the policy is drawn are covered by the stipulated amounts for their classes. It is always possible, where situations develop that were unforeseen at the time the policy was put into effect, to amend it so as to increase or decrease stipulated coverages for the accounts in particular classes. Under a special "available coverage" policy, an insured can set a stipulated individual coverage for each customer class under his policy, pay an annual basic premium for this stipulated coverage, and arrange for supplemental coverage for future changes in customers' balances. The policy holder pays for this "excess" coverage, up to the amount he has actually used, at the end of each month. Thus, in the case of Illustration 25-3, an insured might stipulate a general $3,500 coverage for his C 1½ accounts, but provide for additional coverage up to $5,000 in any month for which such extra coverage was required.

### Coinsurance provision

Under some policies—those with first, second, and third credit ratings (see Illustration 25-2)—a deduction of 10 per cent is made against the allowed amount on any loss, in determining both the coverage on any individual account and the adjustment paid on any loss sustained. For policies involving lower-rated accounts, the deduction is 20 per cent; for policies with nonrated accounts it is 25 per cent. The insured must "coinsure" or bear this proportion of bad debt loss himself.

There are two reasons for this coinsurance provision. (1) The insured is thereby given an incentive to more careful credit extension. (2) Part of many bad debt losses is loss of profit on sales, and it is not desirable that credit insurance embrace profit insurance.

In the past, credit insurance companies occasionally waived the coinsurance provision on consideration of a higher premium. New types of policies without coinsurance have recently come into use, and their popularity is increasing despite their higher premium rates.

### "Primary loss" deduction

As stated previously, it should be no part of credit insurance to cover the normal bad debt losses that can, and should, be anticipated as a result of the application of sound credit policy and collection technique. General coverage policies take this into consideration by providing that a "primary loss allowance" should be deducted from the net covered amount after deduction of the coinsurance. This primary loss may be calculated in either of two ways: on the basis of a table prepared by the insurance companies, or upon the basis of the insured's previous experience.

The insurance company's primary loss table is based upon three factors. One is the field of business within which the insured is engaged. The second is the insured's annual volume of sales. The third is the extent of coverage provided by the policy. On this basis insurance companies use one set of tables for firms whose shipments go for the most part to manufacturers and wholesalers, and another slightly higher set of primary loss tables for firms selling primarily to retailers.

Experience has taught the insurance companies that in general the larger a selling firm, the more efficient is its credit department, with consequent reduction of avoidable credit losses. Accordingly, the insurance companies have established various annual sales categories with different proportions of primary loss deduction. Thus, for a seller with $100,000 sales, the proportion of primary loss deduction to sales under a "combined rating" policy is 0.85 per cent; if his annual sales are $1 million, it is 0.285 per cent; if they are $10 million, it is 0.098 per cent.

A seller who wishes to reduce his coverage and thus lower his premium may increase his primary loss deduction in accordance with one of several formulas established by the insurance companies.[3] On the other hand, the primary loss deduction may be reduced, and coverage thus increased, if the average actual bad debt loss of the seller during the three years preceding the insurance contract is lower than the manual loss. Thus, if a company's average actual loss was between 60 and 70 per cent of its manual primary loss deduction, the deduction would be reduced by 10 per cent. If its average actual loss was under 50 per cent of the primary loss deduction, the deduction would be reduced by 30 per cent. Furthermore, by a slight increase of the premium, a policyholder can obtain waiver of the primary loss deduction with respect to certain first and second credit rating accounts with a net worth over $35,000.

---

[3] Since many companies think of credit insurance primarily as a shock absorber, they are less interested in recovering small losses. They prefer a higher primary loss deduction in consideration of a reduced premium.

### Face coverage of policy

The face coverage of a general coverage credit insurance policy—*i.e.*, the maximum amount that the insurance company is obligated to pay under a policy—is not determined, as might be thought, by totaling the individual account coverages and subtracting coinsurance and primary loss deduction. Instead, it is calculated by multiplying the basic premium on the policy by 25.

As will be indicated later, the basic premium on a general coverage policy is determined separately for each account risk class by multiplying the stipulated coverage for accounts in that class by a premium rate for the class. The resulting basic premiums for the separate classes are then added together to obtain the total basic premium. This total basic premium determines the face coverage of the policy.

It could happen that all of a seller's accounts were concentrated in a few risk classes, with the result that he stipulated no account coverages for the other risk classes. His total basic premium, accordingly, would be low, since it would be the total of only a few risk class premiums. The face coverage of the policy, as a consequence, would also be low—too low, perhaps, to give the seller the full protection he needs and wants. To take an extreme hypothetical example, suppose a seller had a hundred customers, all of whom happened to have Dun & Bradstreet C 2 ratings, and that he stipulated a $10,000 account coverage for the class under a "regular rating" policy. His basic premium would be $200, giving him a face coverage on his policy of $5,000. No matter how many of his accounts failed to pay him, nor how great his total bad debt loss, he could recover only $5,000.[4]

Whenever a seller discovers, on the basis of an initial calculation, that the face coverage of a policy would be inadequate for his needs, he can increase such coverage by paying more premium than would be established by his stipulated class coverages.

## CLAIM AND ADJUSTMENT PROCEDURE

Credit insurance policies require that the insured file notice of claim with the company within 10 days of receiving knowledge of the insolvency of an account. Filing of a past-due account with the insurance company for collection, under the collection provisions of a policy, also constitutes a notification of claim (see Illustration 25-1).

A final statement of claim for losses covered by a policy must be made within 30 days of the expiration of the policy.

---

[4] Actually, face coverage on a credit insurance policy must be at least equal to the highest coverage on any single rating.

Adjustment and payment of claims by the insurance company is made within 60 days of the filing of the final statement (unless an Interim Adjustment Endorsement or Rider is provided).

### Adjustment calculation

Adjustment of loss claims under a "general coverage" policy is made on the basis of:

1. the actual proved loss sustained on each account (up to the amount of the stipulated coverage), or the covered loss (if the actual loss exceeds the stipulated account coverage);
2. less any recoveries received by the insured prior to the date of adjustment;
3. less coinsurance on each account;
4. less the over-all primary loss deduction.

A "recovery" on any loss account is any amount less than the full liability on a bad debt received by the insured from any source. It may be an amount collected by or for the insured subsequent to filing notice of claim. It may be an amount obtained by the insured in the course of bankruptcy, receivership, or creditors' adjustment proceedings. Or it may be the value of any goods returned to the insured or replevined by him. If full actual loss on an account is allowed, the full amount of any recovery must be deducted. If the covered loss is less than the full amount of the loss, only a pro rata share of the recovery is deducted.

Illustration 25-4 shows the calculation of a credit insurance adjustment under a "regular rating" policy on four bad debt losses sustained by an insured seller. Note that while the gross loss of the seller was $13,800, the net allowance is only $10,485, and the primary loss deduction reduces the

ILLUSTRATION 25-4.   Illustrative Credit Insurance Adjustment Computation

| Customer's D & B Rating | Stipulated Loss Coverage | Actual Loss | Allowed Gross Loss | Actual Salvage | Salvage Deduction | Net Loss Allowed | Coinsurance | Net Allowance |
|---|---|---|---|---|---|---|---|---|
| D+ 1½ | $12,000 | $ 8,300 | $8,300 | $300 | $300 | $8,000 | $800 | $ 7,200 |
| G   3½ | 1,500 | 3,000 | 1,500 | 100 | 50 | 1,450 | 145 | 1,305 |
| K   3½ | — | 300 | — | — | — | — | — | — |
| F   3 | 3,000 | 2,200 | 2,200 | — | — | 2,200 | 220 | 1,980 |
| Total | | $13,800 | | | | | | $10,485 |

Less: primary loss deduction ............................. 4,000

Adjustment loss payment ............................. $ 6,485

adjustment on this to $6,485. Although a $3,000 loss was sustained on the second account, the gross loss allowance on it is $1,500—the individual account maximum for a G 3½ rating. Since allowed loss on this account is only 50 per cent of the actual loss, only $50 of the actual $100 salvage is charged as a salvage deduction. The third loss is not allowed at all, since it was sustained on a nonacceptable account not covered by the "regular rating" policy.

At the time of the loss payment the policyholder assigns to the company for salvage purposes all the accounts entering into the adjustment. The assignment, however, is only to the extent of the company's interest. For example, the D+ 1½ account, which was covered in full, would be assigned to the company for 90 per cent—the 10 per cent coinsurance interest is retained by the policyholder, and he would share on a pro rata basis in all salvage later obtained. The G 3½ account, which was covered for only 50 per cent, would be assigned to the company on a 45 per cent basis—the difference being the coinsurance applying to the covered portion of the account as it relates to the $3,000 loss. No assignment would be taken on a K 3½ account because it was not covered by the policy.

The insuring company has no interest in any further salvage after recovering on a net basis an amount equal to the loss payment. Thereafter, all salvage belongs to the policyholder.

## ENDORSEMENTS

Various endorsements (or riders) to cover extraordinary coverage, policy term, and claim settlement situations, or amending coinsurance or primary loss, or revising coverage, may be attached to the standard general coverage policy forms. Among these are:

*L or "Limited Coverage" Endorsement,* to cover accounts whose ratings do not qualify for coverage under the Table of Ratings and Coverage in Condition 1;

*Specially Purchased and/or Processed Merchandise Endorsement,* to cover customer insolvency occurring between acceptance of a special order and its delivery;

*Back Sales Endorsement,* making a new policy apply to shipments under the previous policy;

*Construed Coverage Endorsement,* making the date of acceptance of an order instead of the date of shipment govern the credit rating of the account;

*Increased Coverage Endorsement,* for accounts with "preferred ratings," to provide coverage higher than the regular maximum allowed on stipulated accounts;

*Extraordinary Coverage Endorsement,* for other accounts, to provide the above coverage;

*Sales Exclusion Endorsement,* excluding certain accounts from coverage, so as to reduce the primary loss deduction;

*Interim Claim Settlement "B" Endorsement,* providing for adjustment and payment of claim before the end of the policy period;

*Bank Endorsement,* providing for loss payment under the policy to be made directly to a bank or other lending institution to whom the accounts have been assigned.

## PREMIUM RATES

The basic factor in determining premium charges for general coverage policies is the stipulated individual account coverage on accounts of customers in the various rating classes. For example, the basic premium rate for the individual account coverage stipulated for Aa A1 accounts is $3 for $1,000; the $50,000 coverage stipulated for this class of risks in Illustration 25-3 would thus involve a premium payment of $150. The rate on stipulated coverage for C 2 accounts is $20 per $1,000; that for E 2½ accounts is $30 per $1,000. The total basic premium on a general coverage policy is the sum of the basic premiums calculated on the stipulated account coverages for all the risk classes covered by the policy, plus a charge for sales volume.

This basic premium is a minimum. It may be, and commonly is, increased by the charge for special endorsements, and by adjustments for increase of face coverage.

No studies have been published on the costs of different kinds of credit insurance in relation to insured sales, but generally premiums on most policies constitute a cost factor of less than 0.1 per cent of sales.

## GENERAL CONSIDERATIONS ON ADVISABILITY OF CREDIT INSURANCE

There is still considerable confusion in the minds of many credit men as to what the advantages and disadvantages of credit insurance are, and whether such insurance is warranted in the case of any individual seller. Much of this confusion is due to lack of knowledge on the part of many credit managers as to just what credit insurance is and how it operates. To some extent it is due to misunderstanding of the value of credit insurance as related to the interests of an individual seller.

Before weighing the advantages and disadvantages of credit insurance in general, it should be clearly understood that a general coverage policy with its lower premium does not cover any and all bad debt losses that a seller may sustain as a result of sales made during the policy period. Because of the primary loss deduction, only *excessive* losses from the insured accounts are covered. However, all accounts can now be covered in a general coverage policy.

A seller is not relieved of bad debt losses by taking out credit insurance. Under a general coverage policy, years may go by during which no claim payments are received from the insurance company or during which such payments are less than the premiums paid to the company. Considering all insured sellers as a group, their premium payments over the long term must exceed the adjustment payments made to them, the difference being represented by the operating costs of the insurance companies and accumulation of reserves by them.

This is as it should be. Credit insurance is not intended to cover ordinary bad debt losses. It is intended as protection against the exceptional bad debt loss that might otherwise be crippling.

### Supplementary advantages

Besides the primary advantage of credit insurance, noted above, there are possible supplementary advantages.

An insured seller may submit each delinquent account to the insurance company within a prescribed period—usually three months. With aggressive collection action taken by the company at such an early date, the chances of collecting the account are greatly increased. If the seller's credit department anticipates such submission of the account to the insurance company by a diplomatic letter to the customer explaining its contract with the insurance company and that it has no choice but to submit the account if payment is not forthcoming, such a letter will in most cases obtain the payment and thus obviate turning the account over to the company. No loss of customer good will should result from such a letter, any more than from any other courteous but strong collection appeal. Should this demand letter produce no results, so that the account must be filed with the insurance company, the customer is probably in such a weak financial position that he can no longer be considered a good account; hence any loss of his good will resulting from the insurance company's aggressive collection action is little real loss to the seller. Thus credit insurance under a policy with a compulsory or optional collection provision tends to improve the seller's collection efficiency, with the many advantages naturally flowing from increased turnover of working capital.

Another supplementary advantage is the review of his accounts and their risk distribution which a seller must make when determining his stipulated account coverages. As indicated in Illustration 25-3, to make this determination a seller must group all of his accounts by their risk classes. This classification may indicate to him an unbalanced distribution of his accounts according to relative risk factors. Moreover, comparison of the figures for anticipated maximum balances in each risk category may spot accounts that deserve more intensive selling; it may likewise spot accounts that are being allowed to maintain balances which are excessive in view of their risk ratings.

Finally, credit insurance facilitates financing of accounts receivable with a bank or finance company. With the danger of *excessive* loss for a borrower's accounts eliminated, the lending institution can afford to be more generous in its judgment of the discount acceptability of such accounts. Apart from the special purpose of accounts receivable financing, a supplier who carries credit insurance on some of his accounts is generally considered a better loan risk by a bank.

## Disadvantages

Premium payments on a credit insurance policy are an additional business cost. As such they either operate to increase the prices of the seller's goods, or they reduce his profits. However, this is true of all insurance costs. If the protection afforded against unexpected crippling bad debt losses is deemed worth this cost, then it can no more be considered a special disadvantage of credit insurance than can the premiums paid for fire insurance, or liability insurance, or any other form of business insurance.

Another disadvantage of credit insurance is the tendency it may induce in some credit departments to rely upon the insurance policy in its credit decisions instead of upon its own considered judgments. The mercantile credit agency ratings upon which credit insurance is so largely based are a valuable guide to the credit risk status of customers, but only a guide. They are not a substitute for detailed inquiry and careful analysis. Yet, if an account can be covered by insurance up to the maximum for its risk class, a credit manager may be tempted to reduce his labor by arbitrarily using such coverage as the account's credit limit. He then blindly approves all orders within the credit limit, and just as blindly refuses to check orders in excess of the limit. Such blind approval of all orders within the covered amount tends to increase the volume of bad debts sustained by the seller and so prevents him from obtaining a lower normal loss deduction on his experience rating. Also, by increasing the adjustments that must be made by the insurance companies, it results in higher premium rates than would otherwise be necessary. Categorical refusal to check orders above policy maximum may often result in the turning down of good business and possibly in the eventual loss of good customers.

In fairness to the institution of credit insurance, it should be noted that fire insurance, liability insurance or any other form of business insurance can have the effect of causing the insured enterprise to relax precautions which it would otherwise take against the risk involved. Insurance companies in any field, while insuring against a risk, exert themselves to reduce the risk on which they give coverage. Fire insurance companies, far from inviting their policy holders to ignore precautions against fire, take the lead in fire prevention activities. Liability insurance companies promote safety campaigns. Similarly, the credit insurance companies endeavor to impress upon their policyholders that their policies are no substitute for careful credit analysis and effective collection procedures. American Credit Indemnity Company of New York offers a guide to improved credit checking techniques and closer handling of collection procedures.


## CONCLUSION

The considerations that warrant other forms of business insurance likewise warrant credit insurance in the case of any company that has one or more accounts much larger than its average, or whose customers are largely grouped in a particular region, or most of whose customers belong to a line of business susceptible to special unfavorable developments. In contrast, a large enterprise, with a wide and scattered list of customers, none of whom account for a disproportionate part of its receivables, would be justified in feeling that it faced little or no possibility of unexpected crippling bad debt losses from the three causes previously noted above, and hence did not need credit insurance on this account.

For such a company there would still remain the issue of whether it should insure against the higher-than-ordinary bad debt losses that must be expected in a period of general business recession or in a recession peculiar to its line. Such recessions occur periodically, but it is not possible to anticipate their exact timing. If the company's financial position is such that it is amply prepared to weather any business collapse through which the credit insurance companies themselves would survive, the higher level of its bad debt losses during the recession would be but one of several classes of loss it would have to absorb, and probably not the most serious. The cumulation of premiums it would have to pay during the years other than those in which sharp recession occurred would exceed any readjustments it received for the recession years, since the premium rates would be determined by other risk factors besides that of recession. Under such circumstances, a company that did not fear unexpected crippling credit losses because of other factors would find no gain in taking out credit insurance merely against recession losses. However, should a large company that otherwise did not need credit insurance find itself temporarily in such a straitened financial position that the extra bad debt losses which a recession would produce might make the difference between solvency and insolvency, then the cost of such insurance should not deter it from obtaining this protection for the crucial period.

## SUPPLEMENTARY READINGS

Churella, Y. A., *An Evaluation of Credit Insurance and its Effects on Business Management,* American Credit Indemnity Co. of N.Y., Baltimore, 1958.

Cowan, G. T. C., "Reinsurance—What It Is and What It Does," *Credit and Financial Management,* October 1959, p. 24.

Karrer, H., *Elements of Credit Insurance—An International Survey,* Pitman, London, 1957.

Levi, A., *Credit Insurance—a Valuable Tool of the Credit Department,* American Credit Indemnity Co. of N.Y., Baltimore, 1960.

McCauley, Y. L., *Credit Insurance—Its History and Functions,* American Credit Indemnity Co. of N.Y., Baltimore, rev. ed., 1959.

Phelps, C. W., *Commercial Credit Insurance as a Management Tool,* Studies in Commercial Financing, No. 3, Educational Division, Commercial Credit Company, Baltimore, 1961.

Trapp, Y. T., *Credit Insurance—A Factor in Bank Lending,* American Credit Indemnity Co. of N.Y., Baltimore, 1954.

## REVIEW

1. What are the types of "abnormal" bad debt loss properly covered by credit insurance?

2. For credit insurance purposes, under what circumstances are customers deemed "insolvent"?

3. Explain the difference between "regular" and "combination" credit insurance policies.

4. What determines the term of a credit insurance policy?

5. What provisions are made, under various types of credit insurance policies, for collection of past-due accounts?

6. Explain stipulated individual account coverage under credit insurance.

7. Explain the "coinsurance" provision of a credit insurance policy.

8. Explain the "primary loss" deduction provisions of a credit insurance policy.

9. How is the face coverage of a credit insurance policy determined?

10. How is a claim settlement payment under a credit insurance policy determined?

11. What is meant by a credit insurance policy endorsement or rider? What are the most common endorsements or riders?

12. How is the premium on a credit insurance policy determined?

13. What are the principal arguments for and against credit insurance?

14. How does credit insurance assist a policyholder in obtaining bank credit?

## PROBLEM

Company A and Company B both insured their accounts last year. Company A had a "regular" back coverage policy, with stipulated individual account coverages of $5,000 for accounts with over $125,000 net worth and $1,000 for others, for the risk classes in which it was interested. Company B had a combination forward coverage policy with the same stipulated account coverages as Company A. The period of both policies was the calendar year. How much can be included in primary loss for each company in each of the following cases?

1. $2,000 sale on net 60 terms in November of last year to a company rated C + 1. The company filed petition in bankruptcy in January of this year.

2. $500 sale in April of last year on net 30 terms to a company rated D 2. A receiver was appointed for the company in November.

3. $1,000 sale in June of last year on net 30 terms to a company rated D 1½. As of end of year, the company had refused to pay without price adjustment on grounds that the delivery was not in accord with specifications.

4. $500 sale in June of last year on net 30 terms to a company rated E 2. The claim was filed with the insurance company in November. The customer had not paid by the end of the year.

5. Shipments during the year to twelve "high" risk customers who became insolvent, all balances within the stipulated individual risk coverages, totaling $38,000, plus shipments during the year to fifteen "good" and "fair" risk customers who became insolvent, all balances within the stipulated individual risk coverages, totaling $12,000. What adjustments to primary loss would be made to determine recovery?

**PART VI**

# CONSUMER CREDIT

# CHAPTER 26

# Consumer Credit— General

Consumer credit takes two forms: retail credit and personal loan credit.

Retail credit is extended by stores and financial institutions, as charge account credit and instalment credit, upon the occasion of retail purchases.

Personal loan credit is extended by various types of financial institutions. Its purpose may be indirectly to finance borrowers' intended retail purchases, but it can have other objectives totally unrelated to retail buying. To the extent that it provides borrowers with funds with which to pay cash for retail purchases, it substitutes for retail credit. Where it is for other purposes, it supplements retail credit.

Prior to World War II, over one-third of retail sales were financed by retail credit—over 20 per cent by charge accounts and from 11 to 13 per cent by instalment credit, as shown in Illustration 26-1. During the war and immediate postwar years shortages of consumer durable goods and government restriction on instalment buying forced the proportion down to 22 per cent. Most of this shrinkage was in instalment sales.

Charge account sales have not quite reacquired their pre-war relative status. As indicated in Illustration 26-1, whereas they represented 23 per cent of retail sales in 1939, they fell short of 20 per cent in 1948 and were

ILLUSTRATION 26-1.   Retail Sales and Reported Retail Credit Sales, 1929, 1939, 1948, and 1958

| Year | Retail Sales (billions) | PROPORTION OF RETAIL CREDIT SALES | | |
|---|---|---|---|---|
| | | Total | Charge Account | Instalment |
| 1929 | $ 48 | 34.3% | 21.3% | 13.0% |
| 1939 | 42 | 34.2 | 22.8 | 11.4 |
| 1948 | 131 | 25.3 | 19.7 | 5.6 |
| 1958 | 200 | 24.0 | 19.0 | 5.0 |

Source: 1929, 1939, and 1948 figures from *U.S. Census of Business 1948*, Vol. II, "Retail Trade—General Statistics," Part 2, and "Merchandise Line Sales Statistics," Washington, D.C., 1952. p. 28. 1958 figures from U.S. Bureau of the Census, *Retail Trade Annual Report 1958*, Washington, D.C., 1959. p. 9.

down to 19 per cent in 1958. Whereas retail sales tripled between 1939 and 1948, and quintupled by 1958, charge account credit outstanding fell short of doubling between 1939 and 1948 and had increased by only 270 per cent by 1958, according to the figures presented in Illustration 26-2. The reasons for this post-war decline in relative importance of charge account credit are explored later in this chapter.

According to the Federal Reserve figures on consumer credit outstanding shown in Illustration 26-2, instalment credit had not recovered its prewar status, relative to retail sales, by 1948, but surged far ahead during the succeeding decade. According to the Census figures of Illustration 26-1, however, the proportion of sales on instalment terms was only 5 per cent in 1958 against 11 per cent in 1939. One explanation of this discrepancy, according to the Bureau of the Census, is that in spite of explicit instructions most automobile dealers in 1948 and 1958 reported as cash sales those instalment sales which they immediately refinanced through financial institutions—and the greater part of their instalment sales is refinanced. Only 24 per cent of automobile sales in 1958 were reported as instalment sales,[1] though indications are that the actual proportion was much higher.[2] Under the circumstances, the Federal Reserve figures showing instalment credit outstanding in 1958 as nearly nine times the 1939 figure, while retail sales increased only fivefold, more truly reflect actual developments in retail instalment selling.

The increase in the proportion of instalment sales during the 1940's and 1950's to some extent offset the decrease in the proportion of charge account sales. It is therefore a reasonable estimate that total retail credit sales (charge account and instalment combined) may be less than the

---

[1] U.S. Bureau of the Census, *Retail Trade Annual Report 1958*, p. 9.

[2] About 60 per cent of all automobile purchases are made on instalment terms (R. I. Robinson and others, *Financial Institutions*, 3rd ed., Richard D. Irwin, Inc., Homewood, Ill., 1960, p. 562).

ILLUSTRATION 26-2.   Consumer Credit Outstanding, End of Year, 1939-1960
(Amounts in billions)

| Year | Total | Charge Accounts | Service Credit | INSTALMENT CREDIT | | | Personal Loans |
|---|---|---|---|---|---|---|---|
| | | | | Total | Automobiles | Other Consumer Goods | |
| 1939 | $ 7.2 | $1.4 | $ .5 | $ 3.1 | $ 1.5 | $ 1.6 | $ 2.2 |
| 1940 | 8.3 | 1.5 | .6 | 3.9 | 2.1 | 1.8 | 2.1 |
| 1941 | 9.2 | 1.6 | .6 | 4.4 | 2.5 | 1.9 | 2.5 |
| 1942 | 6.0 | 1.4 | .7 | 1.9 | .7 | 1.2 | 1.9 |
| 1943 | 4.9 | 1.4 | .7 | 1.2 | .4 | .8 | 1.6 |
| 1944 | 5.1 | 1.5 | .8 | 1.2 | .4 | .8 | 1.6 |
| 1945 | 5.7 | 1.6 | .8 | 1.3 | .5 | .8 | 1.9 |
| 1946 | 8.4 | 2.1 | 1.0 | 2.3 | 1.0 | 1.3 | 3.0 |
| 1947 | 11.6 | 2.4 | 1.2 | 4.1 | 1.9 | 2.1 | 4.0 |
| 1948 | 14.4 | 2.7 | 1.3 | 5.9 | 3.1 | 2.8 | 4.5 |
| 1949 | 17.1 | 2.7 | 1.4 | 8.2 | 4.7 | 3.5 | 4.9 |
| 1950 | 20.8 | 3.0 | 1.5 | 10.7 | 6.3 | 4.3 | 5.6 |
| 1951 | 21.5 | 3.1 | 1.6 | 10.5 | 6.2 | 4.3 | 6.3 |
| 1952 | 25.7 | 3.3 | 1.6 | 13.4 | 8.1 | 5.3 | 7.3 |
| 1953 [a] | 31.4 | 4.3 | 1.9 | 16.6 | 9.8 | 6.8 | 8.6 |
| 1954 | 32.5 | 4.5 | 2.0 | 16.6 | 9.8 | 6.8 | 9.4 |
| 1955 | 38.9 | 4.8 | 2.1 | 21.1 | 13.5 | 7.6 | 10.9 |
| 1956 | 42.5 | 5.0 | 2.4 | 23.0 | 14.5 | 8.6 | 12.1 |
| 1957 | 45.3 | 5.1 | 2.6 | 24.2 | 15.4 | 8.8 | 13.4 |
| 1958 [b] | 45.6 | 5.1 | 2.8 | 23.2 | 14.2 | 8.9 | 14.6 |
| 1959 | 52.1 | 5.1 | 3.0 | 27.0 | 16.5 | 10.5 | 17.0 |
| 1960 | 56.1 | 5.2 | 3.3 | 29.1 | 17.9 | 11.2 | 18.5 |

[a] From 1953 on, "credit card" credits of such organizations as American Express Co., Diners Club, and oil companies are included under "Charge Accounts."

[b] From 1958 on, commercial bank "credit card" credits are included partly under "Personal Loans," partly under "Instalment Credit—Other Consumer Goods"; department store option-term-account credits are included partly under "Charge Accounts," partly under "Instalment Sales—Other Consumer Goods," depending on how the account holders exercised these options; commercial bank and store revolving consumer credits are included under "Instalment Sales—Other Consumer Goods."

Source: *Federal Reserve Bulletin*, April 1953, pp. 346-347 and 398-399; May 1960, p. 542; February 1961, p. 206.

one-third prewar proportion but certainly constitute more than one-quarter.

Whether or not there was a decline in the proportion of *retail credit sales* during the 1940's and 1950's, there was a substantial expansion in *credit financing of retail purchasing.* Personal loan credit expanded by more than $16 billion during this twenty-year period. In view of rising real family disposable incomes during these two decades, particularly in the lower income ranges, most if not all of this increase in personal loan credit may be attributed to financing "big ticket" consumer buying rather than distress borrowing. Consumers discovered that they could save on finance charges by borrowing from commercial banks, industrial banks, and consumer finance companies and paying cash for automobiles and household equipment instead of buying them "on time." Such personal loans are in effect substitutes for retail instalment credit, so that a considerable proportion of "big ticket" cash sales should, from economic and marketing standpoints, be counted in with retail instalment sales. If this is done, the proportion of *credit-financed retail sales* becomes well over two-fifths.

Is consumer credit a stable element or an expanding one in the consumer economy? Because of the indicated defects in the reporting of automobile instalment sales, and the growing substitution of personal loan credit for retail instalment credit, it has been possible to establish only the crudest of trend indications through use of the proportion of credit sales or credit-financed sales. Another approach to this problem is to compare trends in total consumer credit outstanding, total retail sales, and disposable personal income. This is done in Illustration 26-3, where 1939-1959 figures for these three series are plotted on a logarithmic chart. This shows that, with the exception of the war years when consumer credit was restrained, all three series move in the same direction. However, no conclusions can be drawn from this chart as to cause-and-effect relationships.

## DEVELOPMENT OF CONSUMER CREDIT

Records of retail selling on credit, and of personal loans which in direct or indirect ways help to finance consumption, are available from earliest historical times. In our survey, however, we are interested only in the development of consumer credit in the United States, and more particularly in its large-scale institutionalization in five basic forms: (1) charge account and service credit, (2) travel and dining credit, (3) store instalment credit, (4) "community" credit, and (5) personal loan credit.

### Charge account and service credit

*Charge accounts* (accounts established by the stores through which the credit purchases are made) began in the United States with the first Colonial country general stores. The farmers of that period had little cash with which to pay for the necessities they bought. Country store-keepers extended them credit until the next crop season. When the crops were harvested, such part as was not kept by the farmers for their own consumption was commonly purchased by the local store-keepers, and most of the purchase price was usually applied to clearing the farmers' debt. The store-keepers thus acted as middlemen in the distribution of the farm

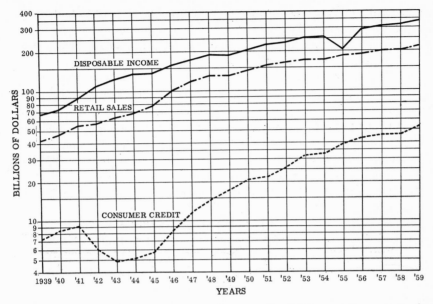

ILLUSTRATION 26-3. Disposable Personal Income, Retail Sales and Consumer Credit, 1939-1959

products. This pattern of rural retail credit lasted well into the nineteenth century.

Urban charge account credit developed along two lines. Neighborhood food stores carried individual customers through times of need, on humanitarian rather than business considerations. Clothing and specialty stores gladly established accounts for customers of known social standing. No true credit inquiry was made in this latter case; the credit was extended primarily on repute.

Institutionalized charge account credit began with the appearance of urban department stores. These stores recognized the promotional opportunity in opening accounts to a wider circle of customers than the social elite of the community. They recognized also the danger of bad debt losses if some check were not made upon applications for charge accounts. Applicants not well known to the store management, at least by reputation, were requested to fill out brief information forms. Thereby the store obtained the names and addesses of an applicant's employer, landlord, and possibly bank. Letters of inquiry were written to these parties, and the credit decision was made on the basis of the replies.

Charge account credit remained on a shaky foundation and involved substantial bad debt losses until the development of retail credit bureaus during the first decade of the twentieth century. As soon as the comprehensive information on credit customers provided by these bureaus became available, more expert credit analysis made it possible both to increase the volume of charge account credit supplied to customers and to reduce the percentage of bad debt loss. By the close of the 1930's some 23 per cent of retail sales volume was made on a charge basis.

Charge account sales increased in absolute amount during the 1950's but, as indicated earlier, their proportion to total retail sales declined. This occurred in the face of a concerted successful drive by department, apparel, and home furnishings stores to "sell" the opening of new charge accounts as a promotional device for attracting and holding new patronage. Such stores increased their charge-account sales, but the effect of this on the overall picture of charge-account retailing was more than offset during the decade by the expansion of cash-basis retailing through supermarkets and discount houses.

*Service credit* is extended to individuals by utilities, hospitals, doctors and dentists, hotels, and other professional and institutional sellers of consumer services. During the past quarter century it has been expanding rapidly. Recently there has been some substitution of "travel and dining" credit for regular service credit in the hotel field.

### Travel and dining credit

During the 1930's several gasoline distributor companies established "credit card" systems which enabled motorists to "charge" their gasoline and oil purchases at the service stations affiliated with the distributor. Payment was made on monthly statements submitted by the distributor. The service stations were reimbursed, with a service charge deducted, by the distributor.

The 1950's saw a widespread application of this "credit card" system to travel expenses. The Diners' Club was created for this express purpose in 1950. American Express Company announced its credit card plan in 1959. Hotels, restaurants, other travel facilities, and some stores agreed to honor the credit cards issued by these organizations. As in the case of the gasoline credit card plans, the credit card holder paid the credit organization on a monthly basis, and it reimbursed the hotels, restaurants, and other businesses that had provided the charged services. One hotel chain, the Hilton, established its own credit card system.[3]

Travel-card spending in 1960 totaled some half billion dollars.

### Store instalment credit

The earliest reported use of instalment selling procedures in the United States was by a New York furniture house during the first decade of the

---

[3] It was on a Hilton credit card that a 19-year-old Brooklyn boy in 1959 went on a $10,000 travel and spending spree before he was apprehended.

nineteenth century. Instalment terms played an important part in the marketing of Singer sewing machines during the 1850's. Piano and other musical instruments, and stoves and ranges, were sold on time payment arrangements during the closing decades of the nineteenth century.

Retail instalment selling received a tremendous impetus during the 1920's as a result of the expansion of the automobile and radio markets, and because of the development of finance companies which financed the receivables of retail instalment dealers.[4] Besides automobiles and radios, jewelry and durable household equipment items such as furniture, refrigerators, stoves, and vacuum cleaners were also sold extensively on instalment plans during the 1920's. During the 1930's instalment financing spread to various "soft goods" fields, particularly men's clothing. Department stores, which had for some time been selling expensive durable items such as furniture on "budget" plans, now offered instalment coupon books that enabled customers to make all sorts of purchases in the store up to a prescribed amount, which was paid off over a series of months.

During the 1950's many department and home furnishings stores instituted revolving instalment or "continuous budget" credit accounts; a customer could purchase at any time up to a pre-established credit limit, constantly paying off any outstanding balance at a pre-agreed rate. By the late 1950's these revolving accounts were responsible for one-third of the total of department store instalment credit.[5]

From 1943-1945, war shortages of consumer durable goods and government credit restrictions cut down instalment buying to a level where the debt balance outstanding remained at only slightly over $1 billion. During the second half of the 1940's, and throughout the 1950's, the American public gave itself over to a splurge of instalment buying that carried the debt balance outstanding at the close of 1960 to over $29 billion. Nearly $18 billion of this total was the result of automobile purchases.

This extraordinary expansion of consumer instalment credit is attributable in some part to its increasing availability as automobile dealers, finance companies, and stores developed and promoted various "budget plans" to encourage consumers to buy "on time." The major cause was probably the culmination in the postwar period of a sociological change in the mores of American personal finance. The older virtues of frugality and "living within one's income" sank into social disrepute; "living ahead" by discounting future income became the normal standard of living for

---

[4] See Chapter 23.
[5] "Expansion in Instalment Credit," *Federal Reserve Bulletin*, April 1959, p. 350.

large elements of the population.[6] Credit plans for teen-agers, to accustom them to "living," were not uncommon by 1961.[7]

"Optional" accounts are a recent department store cross between charge and instalment accounts. The customer buys "big ticket" items on charge account arrangements but has the option, upon receipt of the statement, of converting payment arrangements to a time basis.

### "Community" credit

Until the middle 1950's, charge account and instalment credit was always associated with the store in which the credit-financed purchase was made. The store might refinance its instalment accounts with finance companies. This might be done on a notification, nonrecourse basis, so that all risk of the debt, and all collection responsibility, was transferred from the store to the refinancing institution. Still, the initiative in establishing the instalment credit remained with the store and usually related to specific purchase transactions.

During the 1950's and early 1960's, a growing number of banks established "community" or "central" consumer credit plans. The best known of these is the Chase-Manhattan Bank of New York charge plan ("CMCP"). Under such plans a bank investigates each applicant and then extends him a revolving fund credit which can be used at his option as either a charge account or an instalment credit line. Upon showing the credit card provided by the bank, the card-holder can make purchases "on charge" at any store or service establishment in the community which has become a "member" of the bank's credit plan. The store is reimbursed by the bank, less a service charge ranging from 3½ to 10 per cent, the average being 6 per cent. The indebtedness thus accumulated by the card-holder is repaid to the bank upon a monthly statement or an instalment plan; in the latter case a finance charge is added.

The advantages of these "community" credit plans to a consumer are that he can make charge or instalment purchases in many different stores, yet be concerned with only one financing contract, and that he has only one consolidated payment to make on all his purchases. The stores and service establishments that become "members" of one of these "community" credit plans are relieved of all credit analysis work on sales made to holders of the bank's "plan" cards, and notice that they are "plan" members may bring additional customers who are "plan" card-

---

[6] For interesting analyses of this sociological shift of values, see David Riesman, *The Lonely Crowd* (Yale University Press, New Haven, Conn., 1950), and W. H. Whyte, Jr., *The Organization Man* (Doubleday & Company, Inc., New York, 1957).

[7] K. Corinth, "Credit and the Teen-Age Market, 1959-1960," *Credit Management Year Book* (National Retail Merchants Association, New York, 1960), p. 58; "More Teen-Agers Saying 'Charge It'," *New York Times*, October 8, 1961.

holders into the store. The bank, of course, obtains a profitable form of credit extension.

## Personal loan credit

Through the 1930's, nearly all personal borrowing was of the "distress" type. People borrowed only when they were, temporarily at least, in financial distress. For a long time the only "distress" lenders were pawnbrokers and "loan sharks." Statutory limitations on interest rates were ignored, and the interest rates charged were generally exorbitant, sometimes amounting to several hundred per cent a year.

In 1907, the Russell Sage Foundation of New York started an investigation of "loan shark" practices. As a result of a nine-year study of the problem, the Foundation recommended the drafting of legislation to permit incorporation of companies authorized to make personal loans up to $300 at interest charges not in excess of 3½ per cent a month. The recommendation was received with wide favor. Thirty-eight states subsequently passed special "small loan company" statutes. Most of these laws now have loan amount ceilings far above the original $300.

Maximum interest rates are set on a sliding scale starting with 3½ per cent per month or less for small loan amounts, with lower rates for larger amounts. Hundreds of *consumer finance companies* (or "small loan companies" as they were formerly called), some of them operating through numerous branches, have been organized under these statutes. Their loan volume has increased steadily; their credit outstanding at the end of 1960 was $3.6 billion (see Illustration 26-4).

While the Russell Sage Foundation study was under way, but before the Foundation had proposed its small loan law, and before any consumer finance companies had been set up under such laws, the first of the "Morris Plan" or *industrial banks* was organized in Norfolk, Virginia, in 1910. The original basis of their loans was the securing of two co-makers on each borrower's note. They were not subject to the $300 limit of the small loan companies. Nearly 500 industrial banks have been organized. They pioneered in making loans available, and by 1952 their loan volume amounted to over $1 billion. Since then they have turned increasingly to other credit fields, and their contribution to consumer finance has declined.

A *credit union* is a mutual depositor-borrower association usually set up by the employees of some large organization such as a municipal government, the post office system, a railroad, or a major business corporation, or by the members of a fraternal organization or farm credit association. The first credit union was established in Manchester, New Hampshire, in 1909, one year before the first industrial bank was organized in Virginia. Most of the states have passed legislation governing

ILLUSTRATION 26-4.  Personal Loan Credit Outstanding, End of Year, 1946-1960, by Classes of Lending Institutions

(Amounts in millions)

| Year | Total | Single Payment Cash Loans [1] | Repair and Modernization Instalment Loans [2] | INSTALMENT CASH LOANS | | | | |
|------|-------|-------|-------|-------|-------|-------|-------|-------|
| | | | | Commercial Banks [3] | Sales Finance Companies | Consumer Finance Companies [5] | Credit Unions [5] | Other Financial Institutions [4][5] |
| 1946 | $ 3,023 | $1,122 | $ 405 | $ 546 | $ 92 | | $ 858 | |
| 1947 | 3,984 | 1,356 | 718 | 747 | 126 | | 1,037 | |
| 1948 | 4,517 | 1,445 | 848 | 839 | 166 | | 1,219 | |
| 1949 | 4,863 | 1,532 | 900 | 913 | 142 | | 1,376 | |
| 1950 | 5,632 | 1,821 | 997 | 1,037 | 162 | | 1,615 | |
| 1951 | 6,259 | 1,934 | 968 | 1,122 | 276 | | 1,959 | |
| 1952 | 7,336 | 2,120 | 1,105 | 1,374 | 341 | | 2,396 | |
| 1953 | 8,578 | 2,187 | 1,610 | 1,521 | 377 | | 2,883 | |
| 1954 | 9,416 | 2,408 | 1,616 | 1,676 | 402 | | 3,314 | |
| 1955 | 10,854 | 3,002 | 1,689 | 1,916 | 465 | $2,152 | $1,627 | |
| 1956 | 12,111 | 3,253 | 1,895 | 2,118 | 567 | 2,500 | 1,000 | $ 778 |
| 1957 | 13,356 | 3,364 | 2,089 | 2,351 | 670 | 2,835 | 1,240 | 807 |
| 1958 | 14,566 | 3,646 | 2,350 | 2,612 | 750 | 2,928 | 1,460 | 820 |
| 1959 | 16,825 | 4,176 | 2,704 | 3,119 | 899 | 3,211 | 1,807 | 909 |
| 1960 | 18,511 | 4,311 | 3,008 | 3,505 | 1,001 | 3,571 | 2,105 | 1,010 |

[1] Commercial banks currently account for over 80 per cent of single payment loans.

[2] Commercial banks currently account for over 70 per cent of repair and modernization loans.

[3] Includes a small proportion of loans by industrial banks.

[4] Industrial loan companies, mutual savings banks, savings and loan associations, employee loan funds, and remedial, fraternal, and church loan groups.

[5] Figures from 1946 through 1954 are for consumer finance companies, credit unions, and other financial institutions combined. The 1955 figure is for credit unions and other financial institutions combined.

Sources: Board of Governors of the Federal Reserve System, the National Consumer Finance Association, and Rudolf Modley's Reports, Inc. (Kent, Conn.).

the creation and operation of credit unions; a Federal Credit Union Act was passed in 1934. At the close of 1960 there were nearly 20,500 federal- and state-chartered credit unions with over 12 million members; their personal loans outstanding totalled over $2 billion.

*Sales finance companies,* mainly designed to refinance store instalment credit, and with the core of their activities in this field (see Chapter 29), have also expanded into the personal loan field. By the end of 1960 they had outstanding over $1 billion in personal loans, primarily cash loans, but also to a small extent repair and modernization loans on residential housing.

Making personal loans, usually for specific terms and upon security, has always been an activity of *commercial banks.* They were originally handled, however, like regular business loans, and ordinary wage- or salary-earners could rarely qualify for them. Prior to 1926 only nine banks were known to have personal loan departments. The success of the personal loan companies and industrial banks during the 1920's turned the attention of the commercial banks to this profitable credit field. First National City Bank (New York) in 1928, and Bank of America (San Francisco) in 1929, opened personal loan departments. Some banks sustained substantial losses on their personal loans during the 1929-1932 depression, and this gave a set-back to the movement. The Modernization Loan program of the Federal Housing Administration, initiated in 1934, under which banks were insured against losses up to 20 per cent of personal loans made for financing alterations, repairs, and improvement of property, gave a new impetus to the creation of bank personal loan departments. By the close of the 1940's commercial banks were extending a larger volume of personal instalment loans than either small loan companies or industrial banks; counting in their single-payment personal loans, they were responsible for a greater volume of personal loan credit than all other agencies combined.

## Consumer credit management

Early charge account credit was extended on the basis of store managers' personal knowledge of their customers and on the general community reputation of the customers. Early instalment credit was based almost exclusively on the security given to the seller by a conditional sales contract or chattel mortgage, which enabled him to repossess the goods sold in case of nonpayment. Analysis of the credit risk of retail purchasers was sadly superficial or nonexistent.

A prerequisite to effective evaluation of retail customers as credit risks was dependable sources of information about them. There was no need, as in the case of mercantile credit, for organizations capable of reporting on a national scale. An overwhelming proportion of the patrons of a store, or the borrowers from a consumer credit organization, are located within the retail market area of its community. A *local* credit bureau can satisfy nearly all consumer credit reporting requirements. The special cases of families moving from one retail market area to another, and the special credit report needs of hotels and a few other classes of consumer institutions that draw extra-local patronage, can be met by interchange of information among local bureaus. Consumer credit reporting consequently developed through a large number of independent local retail credit bureaus, instead of a small number of national mercantile agencies.[8]

The first retail credit bureaus were privately owned and operated for profit. Most of the bureaus established in small communities continued to be private enterprises. The large bureaus in metropolitan centers were either started as mutual organizations, or were transformed from private to mutual ownership.

In 1906, a group of privately owned retail credit bureaus organized a National Association of Mercantile Agencies to coordinate their activities. Six years later a second national organization, the National Retail Credit Association, was organized by a group of retail credit managers and managers of retail credit bureaus. These two organizations maintained their separate entities for nine years, were merged in 1921 under the name of the National Retail Credit Association.

The National Retail Credit Association endeavored for a number of years to represent the interests of both credit grantors and credit bureaus. Eventually it was realized that while these two groups have a common interest in establishing and maintaining retail credit on a sound basis, the attention of the credit bureaus is centered on the techniques of collecting and disseminating credit information and making collections from delinquent customers, while the credit grantors are primarily interested in the promotional aspects of retail credit and in authorization and billing techniques. In 1937 a fission was effected, and the Associated Credit Bureaus of America, Inc. was organized as a national association to aid the retail credit bureaus in the technical aspects of their work.

The National Retail Credit Association holds annual conventions for retail credit managers, maintains a research department on retail credit matters, publishes a monthly magazine *Credit World,* prepares forms to be used by store credit departments and advertisements on promptness in credit payment to be published by local credit bureaus, and speaks for the retail credit managers of the country when issues affecting retail credit are before Congress or federal agencies. The Associated Credit

---

[8] The Retail Credit Company, with its offices in Atlanta, Ga., is an exception. It prepares "character credit reports" on a national basis. These are used primarily by insurance companies and for personnel inquiries, but are also available to retail credit managers.

Bureaus of America, Inc. fosters the creation of credit bureaus in interested communities, maintains an interchange system whereby any local member bureau can obtain reports on persons covered by other local bureaus, and promotes uniform methods of compiling and issuing credit reports.

Another organization that has greatly contributed to promotional as well as educational aspects of retail credit is the Credit Management Division of the National Retail Merchants Association. It publishes annually a *Credit Management Year Book* and monthly a journal, *Credit Currents,* in addition to various studies on retail credit.

## PROTECTION OF BORROWERS AND INSTALMENT BUYERS

It has long been recognized that the general public needs protection not only from sharp practices of unethical elements of the business world but also from its own stupidity and wilfulness. One area where both types of protection have been necessary is consumer credit. The protection has taken two forms: prescribed "ceilings" on personal loan interest rates, and prevention of misleading statements of personal loan and instalment purchase terms.

Every state has a "usury" law, limiting the interest that may be charged upon a debt. The so-called "legal rate," which applies to debts on which the interest rate has not been specified by contract, varies from 4 per cent in North Dakota to 7 per cent in four states; the most common rate is 6 per cent. Most states permit a higher rate to be specified by contract. In four states no limit is set for such rates on maximum contractual obligations in excess of $300; in other states maximum "contract rates" range from 6 per cent (New York) to 30 per cent (Rhode Island). Violation of these statutes is penalized in some states by the forfeiture of the excessive interest, in others by forfeiture of all interest, in others by a forfeiture of double or triple the amount of excessive interest. In a few states the charging of usurious interest constitutes a crime, punishable by fine and imprisonment.

In one important consideration these usury laws for a long time failed of their objective. The administrative expense of handling small loans, and the bad debt losses associated with them—particularly small "distress" loans—are so high that the interest charges allowed, even the contractual rates, did not permit the development of legitimate small loan businesses. As a consequence "loan sharks," who took their chance at flouting the laws and charged fantastically exorbitant rates, were the only resource of "distress" borrowers. Accordingly, exceptions had to be made to the general usury law limitations on interest rates. Pawnbrokers were early authorized to charge rates in excess of the statutory maxima. Beginning in 1916, as stated earlier, 38 states have authorized the creation of consumer finance companies permitted to make small loans at *monthly* rates that in most states go up to three per cent and in one case (Alaska) to four per cent. Industrial banks and commercial banks have also been released from the limitations of the usury laws with respect to their personal loans.

Further protection has been given to the instalment buyer and borrowing public by preventing the interest and service charges on instalment purchases and personal loans from being stated in a misleading manner. Several states have passed legislation licensing and regulating consumer finance companies and instalment sellers; such regulation generally precludes any misrepresentations of rates or charges. Some 30 states have also enacted "full disclosure" laws that require a borrower or instalment buyer to be specifically informed about *all* charges involved in a loan or instalment purchase.

## SUPPLEMENTARY READINGS

Black, H., *Buy Now, Pay Later,* William Morrow & Co., Inc., New York, 1961.

Blankertz, D. F., "Instalment Credit in the Affluent Society," *Quarterly Review of Economics and Business,* February 1961, p. 30.

Chiang, A. C., "Installment Credit Control: a Theoretical Analysis," *Journal of Political Economy,* August 1959, p. 363.

Claget, T. F., "Laws Affecting Credit Granting and Collections," *Credit World,* July 1960, p. 19.

Cole, R. H., *Revolving Credit,* University of Illinois, Urbana, 1957.

Dauten, C. A., "Recent Institutional Developments in the Field of Consumer Credit," *The Journal of Finance,* May 1960, p. 206.

Farrar, R. T., "Hilton's Carte Blanche," *Credit Management Year Book 1959/1960,* p. 87.

Garcia, J. J., "American Express Credit Card," *Credit Management Year Book 1959/1960,* p. 86.

Hoffman, W. F., "Bank Charge Account Plan," *Credit Management Year Book 1959/1960,* p. 78.

Huegy, H. W., and R. S. Hancock, *Consumer Credit, Analysis and Decision,* Stipes Publishing Co., Champaign, Ill., 1954.

Mors, W. A., "Recent Trends in State Regulation of Instalment Credit," *The Journal of Finance,* May 1960, p. 191.

Neifeld, M. R., *Neifeld's Manual on Consumer Credit,* Mack Publishing Co., Easton, Pa., 1961.

————, *Trends in Consumer Finance,* Mack Publishing Co., Easton, Pa., 1954.

Phelps, C. W., *The Role of the Sales Finance Company in the American Economy,* Commercial Credit Co., Baltimore, 1952.

Rossant, M. T., "The Credit Card Industry—Prospective Problems," National Consumer Credit Conference for 1959, *Proceedings*, p. 115.

Stedehouder, J. P., "Central Charge Service," *Credit Management Year Book 1959/1960*, p. 80.

Stockton, W., "Laws Affecting Credit Card Abuses," *Credit World*, January 1960, p. 12.

White, A. F., "A Growing Need for Legislation Against Credit Card Abuse," *Credit World*, June 1960, p. 3.

## REVIEW

1. How recent a development are retail store charge accounts?
2. What factors account for the rapid expansion of retail instalment credit during the 1920's, 1930's, and after World War II?
3. What organizations other than department stores and specialty stores give charge accounts and related forms of retail credit?
4. What new types of consumer sales credit, other than store charge accounts and instalment accounts, have developed since 1950? What are their characteristics?
5. What types of financial institutions make personal loans? For how long has each of these types of financial institutions engaged in personal finance activities?
6. What are retail credit bureaus? What services do they perform for retail credit managers?
7. What protection do personal borrowers and instalment buyers have against excessive rates or charges?

# CHAPTER 27

# Sources and Significance of Consumer Credit Information

If an applicant for a charge account, instalment purchase, or personal loan owns an unincorporated business, his status as a retail credit risk is identical with his mercantile credit standing. His gross business income must meet both his personal obligations and his business liabilities; the probabilities of his continued personal and business solvency are determined by the same considerations. The principles of mercantile credit risk analysis, discussed in Chapter 11 of this volume, are guides to whether he intends and is able to fulfill all his obligations. Sources of information are the same whether he is being considered as a consumer credit risk or as a mercantile credit risk.

The principles of mercantile credit risk analysis do not apply, however, to a *wage earner* or *salary earner* who asks for a charge or instalment account or for a personal loan. He must, of course, be a good "character" risk, in the sense of having no record of criminal activity or fraudulent dealings, and giving evidence of responsibility and stability. But "business capacity," and "capital" in the sense of a good financial position, are not considerations in consumer credit. The nature and stability of the applicant's employment, his income from wages and other sources, and certain elements of his personal wealth, are important factors.

The facts which a retail credit manager seeks about a wage or salary earner are obviously quite different from those a mercantile credit manager needs on a business customer. So, too, are his sources of information. Much of this information comes directly from the applicant through the filling out of an application blank. Reports prepared by retail credit bureaus, strikingly different in content and presentation from mercantile agency reports on business enterprises, confirm and complement this information.

## THE RETAIL CREDIT APPLICATION FORM

When a prospective customer requests a charge account, or wishes to buy on an instalment basis, or when a personal loan is requested, the first step is the filling out of a "credit application." The questions on this form are put to the applicant by the store's interviewer, who records the answers. The completed form may or may not be signed by the applicant, according to the policy of the store. Instalment sellers and personal loan organizations prepare their own credit application forms. So do the stores selling on charge account, though a considerable number of them purchase pads of standardized credit application forms which have been designed by the National Retail Credit Association. Banks and other organizations operating non-store charge account plans use their own forms.

### Store charge account application form

A standard charge account application form like the one prepared by the National Retail Credit Association (see Illustration 27-1), probes deeply into the circumstances that determine the credit status of the applicant. The items of information covered by this form are:

*Names* and *ages* of the applicant and of his wife or her husband. A retail credit man is interested in the age of only the income-earning member of a family. Consequently if a husband applies to open a charge account, no request is made for the age of his wife. If a housewife makes application, she is asked for her husband's age, but not her own. An employed woman applicant is not asked her specific age, but the credit interviewer judges her approximate age from her appearance, and enters it upon the application form.

*Number of children* in the applicant's family, and whether any of them are employed.

*Present address, preceding address,* and *term of residence* at each.

Whether the *residence* is *owned* or *rented.* If the latter, whether it is a house, an unfurnished apartment, or a furnished apartment, and the amount of the rent.

Present and preceding *occupation* of the income-earning member of the family, names and addresses of the present and preceding employers, and term of employment in each case.

Approximate total *family income.*

*Real estate, bank accounts,* and *life insurance* owned.

ILLUSTRATION 27-1. Store Charge Account Application Form Prepared by National Retail Credit Association

*Trade references*—the names of other stores where the applicant has charge accounts or has bought on the instalment plan. If the applicant has not had store credit before, any past creditor—a hospital, a doctor, a loan organization—is listed as a trade reference.

*Personal references,* and the name and address of the applicant's *nearest relative* (other than husband or wife).

Many credit managers, particularly those of department stores and specialty shops selling to a clientele of high social standing, feel that applicants for charge accounts in their stores—most of whom, after all, seek such accounts as a shopping convenience and not because they need credit extensions—would resent such probing into their personal affairs. Accordingly they use their discretion as to the questions put to the applicant, or they prepare brief account application forms which call only for information that will permit identification of the applicant. Credit decisions in such stores are based, not on any information given in the applications, but on the reports on the applicants obtained from the local retail credit bureau, or even on personal impression and a check in the *Social Register.*

### Instalment application form [1]

A credit application form devised by an instalment house embodies all the queries contained in the ordinary charge account application form, and in addition provides space for tabulating other outstanding debt. Information may be requested on the current outstanding debt balances and on the weekly or monthly rate of repayment. This knowledge is essential for determination of whether the applicant is an acceptable credit risk, and also to establish a practical schedule of payments.

### Retail credit application procedure

A retail credit application to a store is frequently filled out by a credit interviewer, not by the applicant. But many stores, particularly large establishments, use a "silent interview" procedure in which the applicant fills out the form at a designated desk, then hands it to the interviewer who reads it and may ask further questions.

In small stores a credit application interview may be conducted by the credit manager or by a member of the staff in charge of credit work as well as other functions. Large stores have specialized interviewers.

An applicant for credit commonly has a sense of reserve about opening an account or requesting a loan. He or she prefers not to be under the

---

[1] Application forms of consumer finance companies, which differ in some important details from those used by charge account and instalment sellers, are discussed in Chapter 30.

eyes of the world during the application interview. Therefore provision should be made for a private or semiprivate office in which the interview may be conducted.

There is a skilled technique of eliciting the information required for a retail credit application.[2] A series of direct, point-blank questions might irritate the sensibilities of many applicants. Therefore a number of the queries are phrased indirectly, or are accompanied by a semi-apologetic explanation. For example, instead of asking an applicant how long she has resided at her present address, she is generally asked, "Is this a new address?" In answering, the applicant will generally state how long she has lived at her present address. Again, when asking about the husband's employment, a diplomatic procedure is to say, "As a matter of record, Mrs. . . . . . . . ., we should like to have the business connection and business address of Mr. . . . . . . . ."

During such a conversation, the interviewer should be forming a series of mental judgments upon the applicant which may be very valuable in determining the risk. He may note these upon blank parts of the form in some code system used by the credit department. Such code notations are meaningless to the applicant when she takes the application form in hand to sign it but influence the credit judgment of the store.

Application procedure for a "community" or "travel" credit account is more impersonal. The filled-in application form is mailed to the bank or other financing institution. In border-line cases, or where the application form is incomplete, the applicant may be requested to appear for a personal interview. Otherwise acceptance as well as submission of the application is made by mail.

## RETAIL CREDIT BUREAU REPORTS

Consumer credit reporting is handled by some 2,300 local credit bureaus. They collect the data presented in their reports and supply these reports to stores and institutions that subscribe to their services. They also provide a "notification" service—any seller or lender who has drawn a report on a customer is automatically notified if, at any subsequent date, derogatory information on that customer is received by the bureau. Most of the bureaus issue weekly, biweekly, or monthly bulletins which warn of credit frauds and other developments which might cause credit losses to the subscribers. They also maintain collection services and trace "skips." Many of them undertake promotional campaigns to encourage credit buying and promptness of credit payment on behalf of their members.

---

[2] N. A. Brisco and R. M. Severa, *Retail Credit* (Prentice-Hall, Inc., Englewood Cliffs, N.J., 1942), pp. 71 ff.

Mail order houses, and distributors of consumer goods that operate through widely scattered branch outlets, would find it inconvenient if not impractical to maintain membership in all the local credit bureaus of all the communities in which their customers are located. For their convenience, Credit Bureau Reports (formerly the National Consumer Credit Reporting Corporation) has been established. Through this organization a distributor can obtain, under a single contract, any report issued by any local credit bureau which is a member of the Associated Credit Bureaus of America.

### Derivation of retail credit bureau information

A retail credit bureau derives the information which it incorporates in its reports on credit applicants from the following sources:

1. the applications made by customers at member stores, which provide information on the customer's identity, address, business connections, bank and credit or personal references;
2. telephone or personal contact with the customer's landlord, neighbors, neighborhood dealers, employer, and bank;
3. credit experience of stores, loan companies, and other credit granting institutions given as reference by the customer, or which have previously inquired on the account;
4. litigation records, including suits, judgments, bankruptcies;
5. other public records, such as births, deaths, marriages, mortgage records, liens filed;
6. items clipped from newspapers and periodicals.

A request for a credit bureau report on a customer is made either upon an "inquiry ticket" of the type shown in Illustration 27-2, or by sending a copy of the customer's original application to the credit bureau. Stores which have telephone, teletypewriter, or telescriber facilities may give their inquiries to the bureau through these devices. The inquiry ticket serves as a basis for initiating the investigation. If no up-to-date report is available, an investigation is initiated.

By telephone or personal interview, the customer's or borrower's employer, landlord, bank, and all other parties who have had business dealings with him are contacted. The employer is asked to verify the applicant's statement as to position held and salary received. The landlord is queried as to the customer's character and reputation, the length of residence, size of apartment, rental paid, and promptness with which the obligation is met. The bank gives in round numbers the account balance maintained by the customer or borrower and states whether there is any record of loans or returned checks. Any parties who have previously dealt

F1

| PLEASE MAKE ALL INQUIRIES IN DUPLICATE | C R E D I T  B U R E A U OF GREATER NEW YORK. INC. | FURNISH FULL NAMES AND ADDRESSES |

853 BROADWAY, NEW YORK 3, N. Y.

Reports - SPring 7-3900
Executive - SPring 7-9500

| PULLER | IN | S | C | NC. | OUT |
| | | J | Q | | |

MEMBER'S NAME                                        ATTENTION OF

BLANKE & CO., INC.          H. I. Jaye

| CODE NUMBER | YOUR ACCT. NO. | DATE |
| 9902 | | 9/1/61 |

| LAST NAME | FIRST NAME | MIDDLE NAME | HUSBAND'S NAME |
| PUBLIC | JOHN | Q. | Mary A. WIFE'S NAME |

PRESENT ADDRESS                                        CITY

7500 Parkway, Forest Hills, L.I.

FORMER ADDRESS                                        CITY

729 West 57th Street, N.Y.C.

| AGE | NEW ACCOUNT | REVISION | SOLICITED | DELINQUENT | INACTIVE |

OCCUPATION (HUSBAND)          TITLE          DEPARTMENT

Sales Representative

NAME OF BUSINESS          ADDRESS OF BUSINESS          CITY

Never-Rip Shirt Corp., 8000 Broadway, N.Y.C.

OCCUPATION (WIFE)          TITLE          DEPARTMENT

NAME OF BUSINESS          ADDRESS OF BUSINESS          CITY

BANK OF REFERENCE          BRANCH OR ADDRESS          SPECIAL CHECKING ☐

Chase Manhattan          Main          REG.—CHECKING ☒

STORE OR BUSINESS REFERENCES          ADDRESSES          CITY

**SPECIAL INSTRUCTIONS**

**CHECK TYPE OF SERVICE DESIRED—SEE PRICE LIST**

| LOCAL TRADE | S | OUT-OF-TOWN TRADE | SPECIAL | RUSH |
| CLEARANCE ☐ | S S | CLEARANCE ☐ | REPORT ☒ | SPECIAL ☐ |
| IN-FILE | INSTALLMENT | SPECIAL HANDLING | RESIDENCE ☐ | PRIVATE |
| TRADE ☐ | CLEARANCE ☐ | ☐ REPORT | BUSINESS CHECK ☐ | INVESTIGATION ☐ |

☐ IF NO TRADE IN FILE, CHANGE TO SPECIAL REPORT

FILL IN ON THIS LINE NAME OF OTHER TYPE REPORT DESIRED

ILLUSTRATION 27-2.   Retail Credit Bureau Inquiry Ticket

with the customer on credit terms are asked about the credit terms given, highest credit extended, current balance, any past-due amount, and the manner of payment.

Records of all suits against local residents are entered in a credit bureau's files—in the case of the Credit Bureau of Greater New York this means daily recording of about 2,000 suits brought in New York City's municipal courts and in courts of the suburban counties adjacent to New York City. Items from local papers, which affect the credit, character, or financial standing of any individual living or working in the community, are clipped and filed.

## Files and cards

Some credit bureaus maintain a folder for every individual who has become, or is likely to become, a borrower or a credit customer of any store in the community. Into this folder go the inquiry tickets submitted by stores seeking reports on the individual, memoranda of replies to inquiries directed to his employer, bank, and creditors, any investigators' reports, and all clippings upon him.

Most credit bureaus maintain a file of "master record" cards, which occupies less space than a folder file. Each card summarizes the latest available information on a customer or borrower and his paying habits, including the code numbers of inquirers and the most recent "trade clearance" obtained from the stores where he maintains charge or instalment accounts. By referring to the master record card on an individual, a credit bureau can give an immediate report, by letter, telephone, or telescriber, upon his current credit status.

## Reports

Retail credit bureaus offer several different kinds of reports, varying in price, to meet the needs of inquiring members.

A few bureaus publish annual *rating books* on residents of their communities. Experience with these retail credit rating books has not always been satisfactory. The cost of compiling and publishing them is high. Some bureau members, moreover, tend to base their credit judgments arbitrarily on these ratings, with the result that they follow a superficial credit policy and the bureau misses an opportunity to sell the reports which provide a substantial element of its income. Many credit bureaus which once published rating books have consequently discontinued them.

The *special report* is the most comprehensive type of report published by retail credit bureaus. Written in abbreviated style, it covers the age, marital status, and number of dependents of a customer. A description is given of the customer's or borrower's residence, with information on its ownership and rental status, and on the surrounding neighborhood. A section is devoted to his employment, including his length of service, position held, salary received, opinion of the employer, and the financial rating of the employer's business. If the customer has a bank account, a statement is given of how long the account has been carried, the approximate average balance maintained, whether or not he has borrowed

PUBLIC,    JOHN Q.    (MARY A.)                      REC'D: 9/4/61              WRITTEN: 9/5/61

SURNAME            GIVEN NAMES         WIFE OR HUSBAND      OCCUPATION  SALES REPRESENTATIVE
7500 Parkway, Forest Hills, L.I.                     FIRM NAME   Never-Rip Shirt Corp.
RESIDENCE                         CITY     STATE            ADDRESS     8000 Broadway, N.Y.C.
FORMER   } 729 West 57th Street, N.Y.C.
RESIDENCES                                                  OCCUPATION

                                                           FIRM NAME

                                                           ADDRESS

---

**IDENTITY:**
Mr. Public is married, approximately 45 years of age, two dependent children of school
age - 10 and 14 years old.

**RESIDENTIAL HISTORY:**
He and his family are residents at 7500 Parkway, a good class elevator apartment house
in favorable surroundings.  Have been tenants here since 1954 and are leasing apartment
3-A, 4 rooms, at a rental of $120. monthly.  Live under good circumstances, and the
building management reports them to be prompt pay and satisfactory tenants.  They formerly lived for 6 years at 729 W. 57th Street, New York City, under similar conditions.

**BUSINESS AND RESOURCES:**
Mr. Public is in the employ of the Never-Rip Shirt Corp., 8000 Broadway, New York City.
This is a large well established concern, manufacturers of men's shirts.  Firm has a
mercantile rating of $500,000/750,000.  Mr. Jones, Secretary of the firm, advises Mr.
Public has been with them since 1952 as a sales representative.  He covers both local
and out-of-town territory.  Works on salary and commission basis and his earnings are
reported to be about $9500. annually.  Highly regarded by his employers.

**BANK:** Local bank reports joint account since 6/56.  Medium 3-figure balances, non-
borrowing, satisfactory.  Came well introduced; impressions favorable.

**LITIGATION:** CLEAR

**TRADE INFORMATION**

| DATE CLEARED | MEMBER | SELLING SINCE | HIGH CREDIT | PAYS | REMARKS |
|---|---|---|---|---|---|
| 8/29/61 | 7 | old | $24. | 30-60 | owes $19. for August |
|  | 8 | 1944 | 17. | 30 |  |
| 8/5/61 | 2 | inq. |  |  |  |
| 4/3/61 | 3 . | 1937 |  |  | inactive |
|  | 104 | 1941 | 24. | 30-90 |  |
|  | 204 | 1934 | 13. | 30 |  |
| 12/16/60 | 330 | old | 55. | 30 |  |
| 11/29/60 | 146 | 1938 | 57. | 30 |  |
|  | 418 | old |  |  | inactive |

FOR: #9902
BY: J-1 (FF)

| | CREDIT BUREAU OF GREATER NEW YORK, Inc. | |
|---|---|---|
| SPECIAL | 853 BROADWAY, NEW YORK 3, N. Y. | TELEPHONES: |
| REPORT | The above information is communicated to the inquirer subject to the condition that it be held in strict confidence and not revealed to the subject of inquiry or anyone else; that it was obtained from sources deemed reliable, the accuracy of which is however in no way guaranteed. | SERVICE:  SPring 7-3900 EXECUTIVE: SPring 7-9500 |

52

ILLUSTRATION 27-3.   Retail Credit Bureau Special Report

from the bank, and if so on what basis the loans were extended and how
they were repaid. Reports from personal and business references are included. Suits and judgments against the customer are noted, and the gist
of any news clipping bearing upon his character or credit standing is
given. Finally the latest "trade clearance"—the summary report of his
obligations to stores and other creditors, and his record of payment—is
included. An example of a special report is given in Illustration 27-3.

Among the other and less comprehensive types of reports offered by
retail credit bureaus are the following:

*Residence check,* covering a verification of the age, marital status, number in family, living conditions, and residence ownership or rental paid by a customer or borrower.

*Employment check,* covering a verification of the customer's or borrower's position, length of employment, salary, and other information about his occupation.

*Property report,* covering details of ownership of any parcel of real estate, such as owner of record, date title was taken, assessed valuation, mortgages, payments of taxes, foreclosure proceedings, and so forth.

*Local trade clearance*—a summary of the current file record, or the results of a special interchange clearance, of a customer's paying record with all stores extending credit to him. An example of a trade clearance is shown in Illustration 27-4.

---

PUBLIC, JOHN Q. (MARY A.)      REC'D 9/4/61   WRITTEN 9/5/61   FOR: 9902

NAME
7500 Parkway, Forest Hills, L.I.     OCCUPATION    SALES REPRESENTATIVE

RESIDENCE

FORMER
RESIDENCES } 729 West 57th St., N.Y.C.    FIRM NAME    Never-Rip Shirt Corp.

ADDRESS    8000 Broadway, New York City

| DATE CLEARED | MEMBER | SELLING SINCE | HIGH CREDIT | PAYS | REMARKS |
|---|---|---|---|---|---|
| 8/29/61 | 7 | old | $24. | 30-60 | owes $19. for August |
|  | 8 | 1944 | 17. | 30 |  |
| 8/5/61 | 2 | inq. |  |  |  |
| 4/3/61 | 3 | 1937 |  |  | inactive |
|  | 104 | 1941 | 24. | 30-90 |  |
|  | 204 | 1934 | 13. | 30 |  |
| 12/16/60 | 330 | old | 55. | 30 |  |
| 11/29/60 | 146 | 1938 | 57. | 30 |  |
|  | 418 | old |  |  | inactive |

TRADE CLEARANCE REPORT      T-6

CREDIT REPORTS    **CREDIT BUREAU OF GREATER NEW YORK, Inc.**    EXECUTIVE OFFICES
SPring 7-3900     853 BROADWAY, NEW YORK 3, N. Y.     SPring 7-9500

---

ILLUSTRATION 27-4.   Retail Credit Bureau Trade Clearance

## Credit bureau report procedure

The credit department of a charge account store, or of an instalment seller, or of a personal loan institution, may obtain any of the above reports on a customer by mailing an "inquiry ticket," of the kind shown in Illustration 27-2, to the credit bureau. The report is usually sent by return mail.

Many credit bureaus have developed, under the title of *selective screening service* or *progressive reporting,* new time- and cost-saving reporting procedures. Here the member does not ask for a specific type of report but leaves it to the cedit bureau to decide what information is required to check fully on the customer as a credit risk. The bureau in turn puts "screeners" to work on the customer's file. They determine whether the information contained in it is sufficient or has to be supplemented from other sources.

In cases where charge or instalment account applicants wish to take merchandise with them on the same day on which the application is made, the store may communicate with the credit bureau by telephone or teletypewriter while the customer waits in the credit office, and obtain a summary report of the customer's credit record which will enable the credit department to make a quick decision. Within a few minutes, the customer may be authorized to make the purchases, or if the information is unfavorable, this privilege may be withheld until complete information is received and a final decision arrived at as to the desirability of accepting the account.

Summary reports received by telephone, teletype, or telescriber are often sufficient basis for a final credit decision. In some cases they are followed up by request for a special report or some other comprehensive report suitable to the circumstances.

## OTHER SOURCES OF CONSUMER CREDIT INFORMATION

A store that is not a member of its local retail credit bureau must make its own inquiries and verifications of the information given in the customer's application. By letter or telephone the credit department checks with the employer, the landlord, and the customer's bank as to the accuracy of the statements on the application. Other stores given as references are requested to give interchange information on the credit they have extended to the customer and on paying habits.

Some large stores, service enterprises, "community" credit institutions, and personal loan institutions that are credit bureau members nonetheless make their own inquiries about applicants who, on the basis of their applications, appear to be gilt-edge risks—applicants, for example, who have stable, well-paying positions and own their own homes clear of mortgage. The cost of making such direct inquiries is less than the price of a bureau report. Against this saving must be set the possibility, however, that there may be some hidden weakness in the applicant's credit status which would be revealed by a report but which is not disclosed by mere verification of the information given in the application. Banks with "community" credit plans usually have their own credit information systems, but they also use retail credit bureau information services.

## EVALUATION OF CONSUMER
## CREDIT INFORMATION

Information derived from an application and from a credit bureau report cannot, of itself, establish whether a customer is a satisfactory or an unacceptable credit risk. Inferences from some of the facts given, rather than the facts themselves, indicate the probabilities of payment or nonpayment. Careful analysis of the information given, and correlation of various facts and inferences, must underlie any retail credit decision.

### Significance of specific items

If the credit applicant is a man or a single woman with independent means, credit judgment is based upon the facts given and inferences derived about him or her. In the case of a married woman supported by her husband, it is the husband's circumstances that determine the credit risk. Where both husband and wife are employed, their combined circumstances must be taken into account.

The *age* of a person subject to credit consideration has some bearing upon the risk. Should the income earner be a minor, he or she is, for obvious legal reasons, not generally an acceptable risk without the guaranty of a parent or some other adult. From majority age to 30 years, a person is deemed to grow more stable and responsible, and hence to improve as a retail credit risk. From the age of 50 on, the chances of death,[3] serious illness, and loss of occupation are presumed to increase, so that retail credit status tends to deteriorate.

Attention is given to the *number of children* and other dependents in the family. An income-earner with several children may be regarded as a more stable and responsible individual than a childless person; but to bring up three or a greater number of children is also viewed as a substantial burden which frequently makes it difficult to maintain financial equilibrium. If children are older and contribute to the family income, their evaluation as credit risk factors, of course, changes.

---

[3] Creditor's risk deriving from the possibility of the debtor's death is obviated by *credit life insurance*, taken on the debtor's life, with the creditor as beneficiary, to cover the balance of a personal loan or instalment purchase debt outstanding at the time of the debtor's demise. An increasing proportion of personal loans and retail instalment accounts are coming to be so protected. Nearly $27 billion of credit life insurance (about five-sixths of it applicable to consumer credit) was reported outstanding in 1959 (Institute of Life Insurance, *1960 Life Insurance Fact Book*, New York, 1960, p. 30). Thus more than half of the total of consumer credit outstanding is insurance-covered. Credit health and accident insurance has also recently become available; less than $100 million was outstanding in 1960.

Important inferences may be drawn from the *residence* of the applicant. An owned home is deemed an indication of stability of character. Moreover, unless its value is completely covered by a mortgage, there is an equity which can be reached by judgment liens in case of the debtor's default. If the applicant lives in rented premises, the nature of these premises has a bearing on the credit risk. An applicant renting an unfurnished apartment is deemed a poorer risk than one renting a house, but better than one renting a furnished apartment; the tenant of a furnished apartment can "skip" at a moment's notice with no problem of disposing of furniture. The rental paid for an apartment is also significant, since it may be an indication of an extravagant manner of living, and in any case is an important determinant of the margin of the applicant's income left over to cover payment of credit obligations.

*Length of residence* at the current address and at the preceding address, in the case of applicants who rent premises, is taken as an indication of stability of character.

Information about the *occupation* of the income-earning member of a family is vital to determination of credit risk. Certain occupational groups are deemed less acceptable than others. People with independent occupations, including professional ones, or who own small businesses, tend to be poorer risks. If the applicant, or her husband, is an employee, the position held and the nature of the employer's business are important considerations. Seasonal employment, of course, provides hardly any basis for retail credit extension. An employee of a business that is barely maintaining solvency does not have much job security, and hence he too may be deemed a poor credit risk. In contrast, a civil service employee, or a railroad worker with seniority tenure, is deemed to have the highest type of job security and other things being equal, is regarded as an exceptionally good risk. The position or occupational rank held by a wage or salary earner is taken both as an indicator of relative job security and as a reflection of ability and stability of character.

Knowledge of the *approximate family income,* including income from other sources than wages or salaries, is obviously important in determining the credit risk involved and setting a credit limit. Approximately 15 per cent of an instalment purchaser's annual income is sometimes taken as basis for an instalment debt limit. Up to two weeks' salary is used as a basis for a 30-day charge account, if purchases exceed the store's "floor release" limit and are referred for decision to the credit office.

An applicant's *wealth* as represented by real estate, investments, and bank accounts, and the carrying of life insurance, has important bearing on the credit risk involved. It is deemed to reflect a stable and responsible character. Furthermore, such capital items constitute an element of collateral security, since credit obligations may be paid out of them in case current income should unexpectedly be cut off or reduced.

The amount of *current outstanding obligations*—bank loans, unpaid charge accounts, instalment debt balances, mortgage repayment and life insurance premium payment obligations—is an important credit determinant. If an instalment sale is under consideration, the terms on which the customer must repay his prior obligations may be a major factor in arranging the terms for the new obligation.

*Trade reports* on how an applicant or customer is paying his other accounts are highly valuable in arriving at a credit judgment, provided they are properly interpreted. An occasional record of delinquent payment does not necessarily throw a shadow across a man's consumer credit status. It may be the result of oversight, which happens frequently to even the most careful businessmen when they, or their wives, are handling their personal accounts. It may occur because the customer is dissatisfied with some purchase and is withholding payment while seeking an adjustment from the store. It may be the consequence of any one of a number of other causes which have no bearing on the customer's general credit status. Even consistent lateness in the payment of charge accounts does not mark a person as a poor retail credit risk. Some of the best customers of expensive stores are utterly casual about paying their accounts; some actually look upon their accepted delinquency in payment as a recognition of a superior social standing. If a well-to-do customer's income is ample to cover all purchases being made, consistent delinquency in payment marks him only as a delicate collection problem, not as a poor credit risk. But if consistent delinquency in the payment of charge accounts can be traced to a customer's "living beyond his means," it is to be viewed as a damaging factor in determining his credit status.

A change from general reasonably prompt payment to delinquency on all accounts may be the first warning to a retail credit manager that a customer's credit position has severely deteriorated. If a worker has lost his position, if a businessman is approaching insolvency, the indication will ordinarily appear in the retail trade report upon him long before the specific fact is reported to or uncovered by the retail credit bureau. Hence the first action a retail credit manager takes when he discovers that a previously satisfactory customer is falling two or three months in arrears on his account is to obtain a trade clearance, so that he may find out whether the customer's delinquency is general or confined only to his store. However, even a sudden general delinquency in payments should not be made the occasion for immediately closing a customer's account to further credit purchasing, without allowing him to explain the situation. Illness may have temporarily prevented him from earning his usual income. Some unusual heavy payment—a hospital bill, clearing the balance on a mortgage or some other prior debt, the costs of a funeral or wedding in the family, any one or a combination of countless other possibilities—may have absorbed several months' margin of income over ordinary expenditures which would otherwise have been available for payment of current accounts. After having been forced to fall three, four, five months or even longer behind on all bills, the customer may start clearing some of his accumulated obligations and gradually work himself back to a current position. To discontinue credit to such a customer immediately upon discovery of the general delinquency without giving him an opportunity to explain the reasons for it might cost a store the patronage of a worth-while customer.

Many retail credit application forms provide, as we have seen, for notation of *personal references* and the name of the applicant's *nearest relative* (other than husband or wife). Such names are requested more for moral effect than as sources of valuable information. Every individual can usually find some one or two people willing to write well of him in answer to a credit inquiry, so that the comments of these references will always be favorable. The name and address of a near relative, however, is a useful clue for locating a customer who subsequently "skips" leaving an account unpaid.

### Credit information rating systems

The informational items that determine an individual's retail credit standing are much less complex than those which determine the mercantile credit standing of a business. There are almost infinite possibilities of success and failure for enterprises in any line of business, whereas anticipated stability of income for individuals in a given type of employment is fairly uniform. Stability of character of the group of persons who determine the managerial policy of a corporation can only be guessed at by scattered hints in their individual business biographies and in the history of the corporation. In contrast, the employment and residence records of a retail customer or personal loan applicant provide a surprisingly close and reliable index to his or her personality from a credit risk viewpoint.

Consequently, it has been found possible to give quantitative values to various items of retail credit information, so as to permit over-all quantitative retail credit *rating*. Experience with such rating or scoring systems is beyond the experimental stage but no standard ratings suitable for general use in the retail credit field, or even for use by particular categories of retail credit grantors, have yet been developed. They are, therefore, infrequently applied. As a matter of policy, most credit bureaus rate only "good" credit risks and refer doubtful or inferior ones back to the inquiring credit manager together with available information so that he can make his own decision.

## SUPPLEMENTARY READINGS

Associated Credit Bureaus of America, Inc., *Credit Reporting Fundamentals*, St. Louis, Mo., 1951.

"Effective Use of the Credit Bureau," *Credit Management Year Book, 1959/ 1960*, New York, 1960, p. 167.

Garth, J., "12 Million Reports A Year," *American Business*, April 1952, p. 8.

Meyers, A. C., Jr., "Analysis of Current Economic Trends," *Credit Management Year Book, 1959/1960*, New York 1960, p. 113.

Retail Credit Company, *Retail Credit Company—Description-Principles-Practices*, Atlanta, Ga., n.d.

Small Business Administration, Management and Technical Publications, Annuals, Washington, D.C., 1960; particularly, "Credit and Collection Controls for Small Marketers" (Small Marketers Aids No. 5), and "Building Sound Credit Policy for Small Stores" (SMA No. 6); "Operating Costs and Ratios-Retail" (Small Business Bulletin No. 8); and "Ratio Analysis for Small Business" (Small Business Management Series booklet), Catalogue No. 1.12:20.

## REVIEW

1. What information about an applicant for a charge account may be entered upon his application blank? Would more or less information be requested of an instalment credit applicant?

2. Discuss the technique of interviewing charge account applicants.

3. Describe the contents of a retail credit bureau special report.

4. What other types of reports, besides the special report, do retail credit bureaus supply?

5. Discuss the interpretations, from a credit analysis viewpoint, placed upon the various items of information obtained about an applicant for retail credit or a personal loan.

6. How can life insurance be used to minimize consumer credit risks?

## PROBLEM

Make a two-column tabulation of the credit information on Mr. and Mrs. John Q. Public from the credit bureau report on p. 536, putting all favorable items in one column and the unfavorable ones in the other. Indicate why each item is either favorable or unfavorable and evaluate the desirability of this account for the department store whose credit manager you are.

# CHAPTER 28

# Charge Account
# Management

Charge account management differs from mercantile credit management and from instalment credit and personal loan management, to be discussed in the next two chapters, in one important respect. Many, often most, of the patrons of a store or service establishment want charge accounts, not because they are unable to pay cash, but as *a shopping convenience.* They could pay immediately for their purchases, but when a woman goes "shopping," she rarely knows in advance how much or how little she may actually buy. If she did not have charge accounts in the shops she visits, she would be put to the inconvenience and worry of carrying substantial amounts of currency upon her person. With charge accounts available to her, she can start her shopping tour with no more than carfare and lunch money and buy according to what she sees in the stores. The same consideration of convenience rather than financial necessity dictates the opening of most charge accounts with local grocery stores, tailor shops, hardware stores, and auto service stations.

Most charge account customers, accordingly, are "gilt-edge" risks from a credit viewpoint. But some seek the accommodation because they definitely need credit. A salary earner paid monthly may well be short of cash during the last two weeks of each month. The recipient of a weekly wage or salary, living with no financial margin, may need the time permitted under charge account practice to accumulate the price of even a moderate purchase of home furnishings or an item of clothing. Even a well-to-do person who is living up to his means or beyond, may desire to make an immediate purchase without having the necessary cash and look to the time allowance of a charge account for opportunity to save up the amount involved.

Charge account credit and collection procedure, then, has to be geared to two objectives. It must smooth the way for shopping and cause no embarrassments to the "convenience" buyer. But it must also detect the seeker of credit accommodation, determine whether he is an acceptable credit risk, and apply an effective collection procedure to him should he become delinquent.

## CHARGE ACCOUNT TERMS

Charge account terms are standardized by custom at "10 prox." which means that payment on all purchases made during a month is due either by the tenth of the following month or, under cycle billing (to be discussed later in this chapter), ten days after the billing date. When stores offer "option terms," that is, when they permit the customer either to pay off his charge account within the usual period or to shift to a deferred payment plan, they generally allow an extra ten days for the customer's decision, so that payment is not due until twenty days after billing.

## OPENING NEW ACCOUNTS AND THE CREDIT DECISION

The steps taken by a store in opening a charge account for a customer are: (1) accepting the application, (2) investigating the risk, (3) analyzing the credit information received and making a decision, and (4) notifying the customer. With the account opened, a follow-up procedure must be established, so that if the credit status of the customer should deteriorate, the account can be suspended or closed.

### Processing the application

Applications for charge accounts originate either upon the initiative of the customer, or by invitation from the store or other credit-granting establishment. Merchants have long recognized the value of the patronage supplied by charge account customers. The practice of soliciting accounts is therefore widespread, particularly among stores which are about to open branches in suburban communities or locations in which they have not previously operated. Charge account solicitation may take various forms. Tag lines can be used in regular newspaper advertising, calling the attention of customers to the charge account facilities offered by the store. Radio and television broadcasts may include promotional messages. A direct mail approach can be applied. Door-to-door canvasses are feasible in desirable neighborhoods. Sales clerks in the store may take credit applications directly from customers after selling them on the idea. "Silent interviewer" desks with application forms may be spotted in convenient locations in the store, with an invitation to the customer to fill out an application and deposit it in a receptacle. These techniques are used concurrently or alternately, depending on the nature of the retailing operation and how successful they prove.

It is generally recognized that the best way of obtaining complete credit information from an applicant is to have a trained interviewer take the application and enter into direct conversation with the customer. This method, however, is not always practicable. In many stores, if an application indicates that a customer already has other charge accounts, she is asked no further questions, since full information will be available through the credit bureau. This method works well with the exclusive stores that cater to a better class patronage. It cannot be applied haphazardly to the operation of the so-called "mass" stores.

Charge account applications of local customers are usually processed within a period of three to five days; out-of-town applications take more time. Many stores, however, make their initial credit decision within 24 hours. They use short cuts of communication with the credit bureau, such as the telephone, teletypewriter, or telescriber to obtain the customer's credit record. Frequently, also, customers wish to make "take home" purchases the same day they apply for an account; in such cases the store may release a limited amount of credit so that the initial purchases may be delivered promptly, without waiting for the definitive credit decision. Or, the initial purchases may be held up until the decision is made and then only freed for delivery. In such cases the customer may be permitted to place "charge-send" orders that very day, but "charge-take" authorizations must be postponed until the usual credit inquiry has been completed.

### The credit decision

Most charge account applicants in department stores and specialty shops are excellent risks who desire shopping convenience, not credit facilities. The credit decision in such cases is a simple one.

But some applications are made by people who will be almost certain to defraud the store if they are given accounts, or who may yield to the temptation to commit a fraud if the circumstances permit. Such cases must be spotted and accounts refused to them.

Reports on some applicants indicate that, while they have comfortable incomes, they are extravagant in their expenditures, are behind in payment on their other accounts, and possibly commit themselves to obligations beyond their capacity. Such cases confront the credit manager with a delicate problem of judgment. There is no arbitrary standard of acceptability, based on measurable data, that can be established for his guidance. He must weigh each such case as it comes before him in the balance of his personal judgment and experience.

If it is evident that an applicant seeks a charge account because she really needs credit accommodation, the credit manager must decide whether the family finances would permit prompt clearing of monthly charge account balances. If his judgment is in the affirmative, an account can be opened, but subject to a strict account limit.

Not infrequently there is disagreement between the information given by the applicant on the application form and that received from the credit bureau. The applicant may have magnified her husband's occupation, overstated the family income slightly, or neglected to mention outstanding debts. Such discrepancies are not taken as an indication of dishonesty, but as a manifestation of an all-too-human tendency of people to present themselves as a little better than they are. Procedure in such cases is to hold up any charge-send orders that may have been placed, and request the applicant to call at the credit office for further discussion of the account. At this second interview the credit manager gently raises the question of the discrepancies, in such a way as to avoid giving offense or causing the customer to "lose face." More often than not, on the basis of the resulting explanations, the credit manager is able to approve the account and inform the customer that the ordered goods will be shipped promptly.

### Account and floor release limits

Many customers are deemed acceptable risks for any amount they may choose to buy and charge at a store. But it would be most unwise thus to extend unlimited charge account credit to people with small or moderate incomes, or to customers known to be extravagant in their buying and delinquent in their payments. Accordingly most stores establish a series of *account limits* to be assigned to customers for whom limits are deemed advisable. The principal factors that determine such a limit are the income of the customer's family group, the number in the family group, and existence of financial obligations which would lower the margin otherwise available for clearing charge account obligations. Some weight may also be given to the interviewer's impression of the applicant's appearance, to the applicant's statement of the amount of buying she expects to do in the near future, and to the high balances reported by other stores in the credit bureau's trade report on the applicant. As an example of the relation between income and the account limit, a city department store might well assign a $200 limit to a family group with a $5,000 income and one child, while a $75-a-week garage employee with three children might be given a $50 account limit.

An *account limit* is not a hard and fast maximum on a customer's credit purchasing, but a "stop, look, listen" sign. Each limit set is entered on the customer's ledger card. When, by reason of extra heavy purchases in any month, or because a prior month's bill has not been paid and purchases are continued in the current month, the charge balance on the ledger card reaches or exceeds the limit, the ledger clerk "refers" the account to the credit manager. The latter calls for the customer's information file and reviews the case. Perhaps he obtains a new trade report on the customer from the credit bureau. On the basis of his review he may decide to let the limit stand and stop further purchasing on the account until the balance is reduced. Or he may decide that the customer's circumstances have so changed that the old limit is too low, and he sets a higher one. If the account is to be temporarily suspended, the authorization department is notified, and the account entry there is tabbed. Next time the customer charges an order to the account, the authorization department will see the tab, and the sales department will be notified to request the customer to drop in at the credit office for a conversation with the manager. The conversation will be conducted in a friendly, informal manner. On the basis of the customer's explanations, the credit manager may approve the purchases which the customer is making, or he may regretfully insist that the account must be temporarily closed until the balance is reduced.

To simplify credit authorization routine, some stores set *floor release limits* for charge account customers, ranging from $10 to $50, the size depending on the type of store and patronage. A clerk in any department can give an identified charge-account customer a charge-take order within the floor release limit without referring it to the authorization department. A customer's total charge-take purchases from different departments under her floor release limit might, of course, exceed her account limit. Stores that use floor release limits feel that an occasional occurrence of this sort is a small price to pay for the resulting simplification of authorization procedure.

### Notification

As soon as the investigation on a charge account application has been completed, and the application accepted, a letter is sent to the customer over the signature of the credit manager, or even over that of the manager of the store, informing her that the account has been opened and is at her disposal. This letter offers a favorable opportunity for a promotional effort, which should not be wasted. The following is an example of a notification letter with good promotional effect:

Dear Mrs. _____:

It is my pleasure to inform you that the X Store has opened a charge account in your name.

To three generations of New Yorkers the X Store has stood for the highest in quality, the most economical in prices, and the foremost in serv-ice. Our quality, our economical prices, our services, are at the command of you and your family, Mrs. _____.

Come in soon and just say—"Charge it."

Cordially yours,

If an application for a charge account must be rejected, the notification letter should state the refusal in the most soothing terms possible, seeking meanwhile to retain the applicant as a cash customer. The following is offered as an example of a rejection letter:

Dear Mrs. _____:

Thank you for your recent application for a charge account at the X Store. It is truly appreciated and has been given careful consideration.

As is customary on all applications, we have endeavored to obtain in-formation on yours that would serve as a basis for credit. The complete report, based on information supplied us by the Credit Bureau of Greater New York, does not meet the definite requirements we are compelled to follow. For the present, therefore, we shall be unable to comply with your wish.

Anticipating that we shall be able to establish an account for you in the near future, may we invite you meanwhile to take fullest advantage of the superior quality, the economical prices and the many special services that X Store offers its current-paying customers.

Cordially yours,[1]

## Follow-up

A credit decision on a charge account application is not a final matter. Customers' circumstances often change in such a way as to alter their credit status. An increase in a customer's earning power may warrant the raising of his account limit. Deterioration in his financial position may dictate the lowering of an account limit, or even the suspension of his ac-count.

The first indication of a change in a customer's credit status is com-monly provided by his ledger card. Increased purchasing that over-runs the account limit may point to an increase in income that warrants a higher limit. Delinquency in payments may reflect an adverse change in

---

[1] Many examples of effective notification and rejection letters appear in the monthly "Credit Department Communications" pages in *Credit World.*

family circumstances. Early warning of unfavorable developments is often obtained from the weekly bulletin or special warning notices issued by the credit bureau.

Before any action is taken, upon indication of some change in a customer's credit status, a credit manager should review all his available information on the account. Time is saved on this review if the information has been consolidated in a single file instead of having been scattered through several. Modern retail credit office procedure has been simplified through the use of the *credit history card* file. A credit history "card" is prepared for each charge account customer. Data from the application may be entered on the face of this card, or the actual application may be attached to it. The established account or floor release limits are also noted on the face. The reverse of the card is ruled for summary records of credit bureau trade clearances on the customer and of collection follow-ups when and if the account becomes delinquent. The credit history card may have a pocket for credit bureau reports and notices.

At the first hint of deterioration in a customer's credit status, a credit manager should ask for a trade clearance from the credit bureau, to determine whether the adverse indications he has noted are peculiar to the customer's account in his store or are general. If the tendency is general, the account should be suspended pending a general check upon the customer by the credit bureau, and possibly a personal interview with the customer by the credit manager.

## IDENTIFICATION

Identification of customers having charge accounts would not be necessary if all charged orders were "charge-sends." The period of time between taking a charge-send order and the placing of the goods in the delivery truck is usually ample to permit the authorization department to check the order to see if it is a valid charge. But if a customer wishes to take a charged order with her, some prompt system of identification is necessary.

The sales people of a small store or specialty shop may know all of its charge account customers by sight, and recognize them instantly upon their entrance. Such personal recognition is impossible in a large department store which has thousands of charge account customers and scores or hundreds of sales people, or with "community" and "travel" credit plans where the organization that establishes the account is not the one that sells the merchandise or provides the service. Some mechanical method of identification of charge account customers is needed.

Most department stores and credit plan organizations give each charge account customer a small card upon which is written or stamped the customer's name and address, the account number, and sometimes a code number or letter to indicate the floor or order limit. An improved variant of the card system is the "Charga-Plate"—a thin metal or plastic plate on which the name, address, account number, and order limit code of the customer are stamped in raised letters. The plate not only serves as identification, but it can also be inserted by the sales person in a holder (see Illustration 28-1) and used to stamp the sales check, thus ensuring its absolute accuracy.

ILLUSTRATION 28-1.   Charga-Plate and Stamper

In many cities, stores have formed community Charga-Plate groups, using one common plate as identification in all the stores that belong to the group. The Charga-Plate may be notched by those stores with which the customer has accounts, or it may be used unnotched, depending on which system is considered most desirable in the community concerned. The advantages of such a group plate are obvious. The customer need carry only one means of identification in all stores of the group. The expense of preparing plates and reissuing them in case of changes of address is cut to a minimum. Loss of a plate and its use by an unauthorized person presents a problem though such a misuse may be spotted where the customer is asked to sign the sales check and the signature does not conform to that on the plate.

Unfortunately, customers do not always remember to have their identification cards or Charge-Plates with them when they go shopping. To insist that a customer without her store identification wait while the sales slip for every purchase is sent to the authorization department and a return report received would probably arouse resentment. Consequently, most stores permit customers who say they have charge accounts to take small purchases—under five or ten dollars—upon showing a driver's license, or social security card, or some other official or semiofficial means of identification. The assumption is that, should the customer not have a charge account, he or she can be traced by the address shown on the identification. Of course, false identifications could be and are produced, so that department stores suffer some losses through this self-identification privilege. Because of the speed with which such a fraud can be spotted by the authorization department, only few purchases of this kind could be made in a store before a warning went out to apprehend the buyer. The fraud could not be duplicated in a series of stores, since the local credit bureau would be immediately notified by telephone or telescriber, and a warning would be broadcast to all other stores where the fraud might be repeated. The stores are willing to bear these small losses, for the sake of maintaining the good will of valid charge account customers whose forgetfulness or impulse leads them to shop without their credit cards or Charga-Plates.

If a charge-take order exceeds a store's ten to twenty-five dollar "floor limit," self-identification is not permitted. Should the customer not be recognized by the sales clerk or floor manager, the sales slip must be referred to the authorization department for signature identification. The customer is told apologetically that the wrapping will take a few minutes, and is invited to continue her shopping in other departments while the wrapping is being done. By the time she returns for the parcel, the authorization routine has been completed.

Identification under "community" and "travel" credit plans presents no special problems. The numbered account card issued by the sponsoring organization provides complete and exclusive identification. With it acceptance is absolute; without it, there is no substitute. The store or provider of service assumes no risk in extending credit to a card-holder within the limits indicated by the card; the sponsor bears all risks of fraudulent misuse of its cards.[2]

### AUTHORIZATION

"Authorization" is the approval of credit on purchases made by a customer once the account has been established and a credit limit assigned to it. The basic purposes of authorization are: (1) to provide speedy service to customers who wish to charge their purchases and either take them home or have them sent, and (2) to maintain control

---

[2] The sponsors of these credit "plans" send periodic "stop lists"—and occasionally "flash" ones—to the stores and service organizations cooperating with them. The lists note the numbers and holders of credit cards that have been lost, stolen, or otherwise cancelled but not yet surrendered. If through oversight credit is extended on one of these accounts, the store or service organization, not the sponsor, bears the loss.

against overextension of credit to customers who are not deemed good risks beyond the limit set on the account. Management of authorizations is, therefore, a daily function and one of the most important operations in the credit department. Authorizations frequently run into the thousands and sometimes tens of thousands daily while new applications for charge accounts rarely average more than a handful in a small store and one or two hundred daily in a large establishment.

### Methods of authorization

Charge account customers at stores will do either of two things: they will *take* the merchandise purchased with them, or request that it be *sent*. On charge-take transactions, authorization must be immediate, for the customer waits for the package. If the amount is below the floor release limit, the sales clerk simply wraps the purchase and hands it to the customer. If it is over the floor-release limit, the clerk must communicate with the authorization unit and obtain a specific authorization before releasing the purchase. This can be done by dispatching the sales check to the authorization unit by pneumatic tube, or by using a telephone system. Some stores have elaborate internal dialing systems whereby the sales clerk can reach the alphabetical authorization file which contains the customer's name.

Under the old systems of authorization, it was customary to keep a separate *authorization index*, with the names, addresses, and account limits of customers. All authorization work was performed from such an index, frequently in a "tube room" into which the pneumatic tubes from all over the store ran. This system was cumbersome and often ineffective, for the index did not show the accumulated balance owed by the customer, and no record was made of the purchases as they were authorized. Later a *sliding indicator* was developed which could be used to show the approximate cumulative amount of the purchases authorized. However, keeping the indicator up to date was costly. It also tended to duplicate the efforts of the bookkeeping department. The modern practice is to authorize *directly from the customer's ledger* which reflects the immediate status of the account.

Many stores applying cycle billing methods maintain alphabetical divisions in their combined bookkeeping and authorizing departments. Divisional clerks perform several functions within their own alphabetical section—authorizing, sales check sorting and filing, and preliminary collection dunning. This permits each clerk to attain a high degree of specialization within her own division, and also makes her task more flexible and more interesting.

Authorization of charge-send transactions does not have to be a split-second procedure. It is performed throughout the day, and into the night hours after the selling departments of a store have closed. In some stores all charge-sends are referred to the authorization unit before the packages are released for delivery. In others, all orders up to $50 or $100 are automatically released, with provision for subsequent "drawback" from the delivery platforms if the authorization unit discovers that the credit is not warranted. Under so-called "negative authorization" systems, automatic release of orders under the specified figure does not apply for customers on a "stop list" of closed or suspended accounts.

### Treatment of overlimits

If for any reason there is doubt as to the advisability of releasing a purchase because the account is delinquent, or because the outstanding balance plus the new orders would go over the established account limit, the authorizer refers the sales check to an "overlimit clerk," or directly to one of the assistant credit managers. The latter either approves the credit, rejects it flatly, or communicates with the customer before arriving at a decision. The same procedure is followed if an account is found to be overlimit because of charge-take sales made under a floor release limit.

Customers who persistently make purchases on overlimit or delinquent accounts are usually treated aggressively, sometimes over the telephone, often by personal visit of a credit department representative where no telephone connection can be made. If the activity continues, such an account may be suspended.

### STATEMENT PROCEDURE

Manual methods of charge-account bookkeeping, still used in many small stores, involve a daily routine of separately posting sales-check charges, payment credits, and other charges and credits to a customer ledger and to a statement sheet. At the close of each month, charges and credits are totaled and the balance for each account determined on both ledger and statement sheet. Certain machine bookkeeping systems—the so-called "dual" systems—likewise require separate posting to ledger and statement sheet. They differ from the manual method, however, among other details, in that a cumulated balance can be calculated and posted for each day's entries to each account. With the so-called "unit" systems of machine bookkeeping, entries and balance calculations are posted simultaneously to both ledger card and statement sheet.

For "unit" machine bookkeeping, statement sheets, already stamped by addressograph with each customer's name, address and account number, are interleaved with the ledger cards in their file. Such a file is usually of the visible-index type. The posting of a day's vouchers begins with the sorting of these vouchers according to the classification used in the ledger file—alphabetical, numerical, geographic, or other. The ledger card with attached statement sheet is then drawn for each voucher, or set of vouchers for the same customer, and the card and sheet are inserted in the bookkeeping machine. The preceding balance is picked up, the new postings are made on both statement and ledger card, and the machine calculates and prints the new balance. Ledger card and statement sheet are then returned to the file.

At the close of the month the statement sheets need only be drawn from the file and mailed to the customers. The last balance shown on the sheet is the amount to be paid. In some systems the ledger cards have pockets to hold copies of the sales checks, and these copies are sent to the customer with the statement. A new set of statement sheets is interleaved in the ledger file for the next month.

It is desirable to have a copy of each statement sheet in case reference must be made to it or a duplicate sent to the customer. With some machine bookkeeping systems, duplicate statements are posted by a carbon paper procedure. Many stores have found it more efficient to obtain duplicates of each month's set of completed statements by some microfilm process.

Electronic accounting is beginning to make some contribution to charge account bookkeeping. A large store or service enterprise that has acquired electronic data-processing equipment for other management purposes can frequently establish a charge account ledger and authorization system to be handled through the new equipment. Where this is done, substantial operating economies, a general speeding-up of authorization and statement procedures, and improved accuracy in these procedures may result.

### Cycle billing

The need for a radical change in methods of keeping customers' accounts in retail stores was accentuated by the personnel shortages immediately prior to and during World War II. A system of "cycle" billing of charge-account customers was developed which is now in use in many, if not most, large stores and service organizations. Customer accounts are divided into similar-sized alphabetical or numerical groups. Statements for customers within each group are mailed on successive days of the month—not all at the end of the month as under the old practice. The billing date for each group is the same, or varies not more than a day or two, from month to month. If there are 20 groups (or "cycles," or "controls," as they are sometimes called), there are 20 billing dates during the month. Thus the preparation and mailing of statements is spread fairly evenly through the month. The due date for the customers in each group is ten days after the billing date for the group.

Under the earlier form of cycle billing, still widely used, each ledger card had a pocket in which the customer's duplicate sales checks and payment memos were filed during his monthly cycle period. At the billing date the account was billed by taking a pre-addressed statement form, inserting it into a statement posting machine with the ledger card, filling in any opening balance and the amounts of the debit and credit items for the cycle period, and calculating the new balance. This was printed simultaneously on the statement and the ledger card. The statement was mailed to the customer with the accompanying sales checks and payment memos. Newer electronic bookkeeping methods permit charges and payments to be posted to the ledger and statement as they occur.

Cycle billing has a number of advantages. (1) It amounts to a staggered procedure of mailing customer statements, avoiding a cumulation of work at the end of each month. (2) Payments are received in a more even flow throughout the month, thereby easing the cashier's work. (3) Bookkeeping is facilitated by the spreading of billing dates and also by the practice of cumulated statement entry. (4) Collection procedures are levelled out.

The major disadvantage of cycle billing is that customers who receive statements from a number of stores and service enterprises are more likely to overlook some if they are scattered through a month than if they all arrive during the first week of the month. Cycle billing may increase casual delinquencies.


## COLLECTION PROCEDURE

Charge account collection, like mercantile collection, involves not merely getting the payments owed to the store but also keeping the customers' good will. This dual problem as applied to delinquent charge account customers is even more delicate than in mercantile collection, since people are often more sensitive in their personal financial relations than their business relations, and since many gilt-edge charge account customers frequently become delinquent, and seriously so, purely because of carelessness or indifference in the management of their personal finances.


### Statement reminder

Should a charge account customer with a good credit standing merely fail to pay by the due date—usually ten days after statement date—absolutely nothing is done about it for the first month. The next statement merely starts with the balance carried over from the preceding statement; at most a National Retail Credit Association collection sticker may be attached to this statement as the gentlest of reminders that there is a past-due item on the statement.

Most stores take no action during a second month of delinquency in the case of customers tabbed as good risks. The third statement merely picks up the delinquent balance from the preceding one, plus any new balance incurred during the second month. A gentle reminder in the form of a printed notice may be enclosed calling attention to the past-due amount.

### Interest charge

Prior to the 1950's, imposing an interest penalty on delinquent charge accounts was unheard of. Now it is a spreading practice, particularly on the part of "community" and "travel" credit plans. The grace period allowed is usually 90 days from due date.

### Suspension of account

Most stores suspend ordinary charge accounts after two months of delinquency. Customers whose credit status is uncertain may have their accounts closed, due warning having been given on the tenth or fifteenth day of the second month of delinquency. If derogatory information about a customer has been received from the credit bureau, the account may be suspended during the first month of delinquency, or at any time during a current month before the outstanding amount actually becomes due.

In the case of "community" and "travel" credit plans, suspension of an account has to be something more than merely notifying the delinquent customer and posting his name on a store "stop list." He has a credit card which is presumptive evidence to stores and other member organizations of the credit plan that he is still entitled to full credit. If he voluntarily surrenders the card, well and good. Otherwise all the member organizations must be notified and put on guard. Some states have made it a punishable offense to retain or use an invalidated credit card.

### Collection follow-up

Apart from regular monthly statements, which are sent to a delinquent charge account customer throughout the period of the collection procedure, the follow-up consists chiefly of letters and telephone calls.

The timing of the collection letters is leisurely in the case of a customer believed to be a good credit risk. Some stores do not send their first letter until the middle of the third month of delinquency. Others, because of the type of their patronage, take more aggressive action and begin collection procedure 45 days after rendering the initial bill. Three, four, or five more letters in the series will alternate with statements during the following months; dunning inserts may accompany the statements. A telephone call is usually made to the customer in the fourth or fifth month of delinquency.

Should a delinquent customer be a consistent slow-payer, or be considered a doubtful credit risk, the timing of the collection follow-up is much more rapid. The first collection letter is sent out earlier; in the case of a doubtful credit risk, it may be sent as early as the 15th or 20th of the first month of delinquency. The letters follow at shorter intervals—20 days, or even 15 days, apart. Resort may be had to the phone quite early in the collection procedure; in the case of a doubtful risk, the first phone call would probably be made shortly after the tenth of the second month of delinquency. Attempts at telephone collection would not be limited to one call, as in the case of good risks, but the customer would be subjected to a second phone dun, and a third, and a fourth. At the end of a third month of delinquency, or certainly during the fourth month, a delinquent poor account would be referred to a collection agency.

### Collection correspondence

Most retail collection letters are of the "reminder" variety, and properly so. People well able to pay their personal bills promptly fail, to an amazing extent, to do so through oversight and carelessness. A customer receives a statement from a store, puts it aside with intent to make out a check at a more convenient time, and then forgets about it. This can happen for several months in succession. The only collection approach to such a customer is to remind him of his oversight, again and again.

A store's first reminder notice should be impersonal, thereby implying that the customer's delinquency is not deemed a reflection upon his ability or willingness to pay, but is recognized as the result of a common and nonreprehensible oversight. Many stores use printed cards, sometimes not even bearing the customer's name and address, for this first reminder. Others use printed notices combined with self-mailing envelopes in which the customers can place their remittances (see Illustration 28-2). If a letter is sent, it is multigraphed and so prepared that it is unmistakably a form letter.

The second and even the third reminder letters to good customers should also be impersonal. Formal brevity may be replaced, however, by a somewhat lighter touch. The following second reminder letter has been used with excellent results by the Chicago store which originated it and by several others that have copied it:

Dear Mr. _____:

The Mexicans say "Mañana—I'll do it tomorrow."

There's a little bit of that in all of us when it comes to taking care of statements. We know. We get a lot of them ourselves.

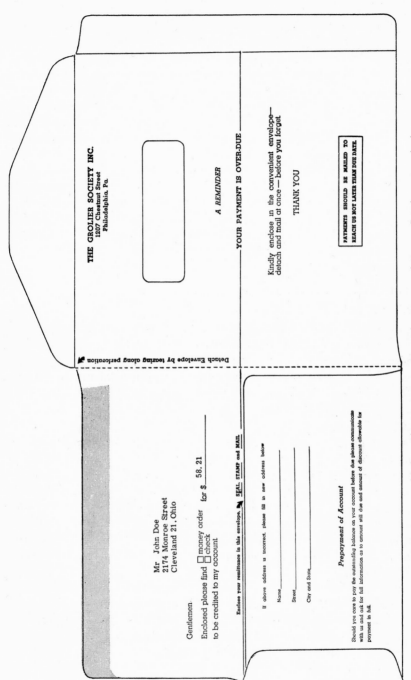

ILLUSTRATION 28-2.   Charge Account Reminder Letter with Return Envelope Attached

559

And once you put them aside for a day or so, it's easy to forget. This is only to remind you that the amount of our _____ statement is $ _____.

Yours very truly,

In general, the payment appeals that can be addressed to delinquent retail customers are weaker than those which are effective with mercantile buyers who are usually anxious to maintain their credit standing in the trade. Personal pride in a record of prompt payment is a mild incentive for the retail customer, although mention of possible loss of standing with the credit bureau because of extreme delinquency is frequently an effective collection lever in advanced dunning. The appeal to a sense of fair play, moderately successful when addressed to men, draws little response from women. Weak though these intermediate appeals are, they represent all a retail collection man has to work with, and he must make the most of them. The following is an example of effective combination of the appeals to pride and fair play:

Dear Mrs. _____:

As a charge customer of the X Department Store you are one of a select group. You were selected because we were confident of your desire to pay your accounts promptly when due.

We believe you have patronized us because you had confidence in us and in our willingness to be fair to our customers.

It is our sincere desire to maintain this mutual feeling of confidence and we are sure you want it maintained.

Won't you help us by getting in touch with us within the next day or two or by sending your check to bring your account up to date?

Yours very truly,

One or two final warning letters are always sent to a customer before his account is placed with an agency for collection. To retain the customer's good will for what it may still be worth, these warning letters often embody a note of apology or regret. But their tone must be firm, for the customer must be made to realize that his delinquency has reached a serious stage. Some stores, to make a greater impression on the delinquent customer, send the last of the final warning letters on the letterhead of the president or manager of the store, and it is apparently signed by him. The following example of such a warning letter could be sent by the collection manager, or might be adapted for signature by the president or manager:

Dear Mrs. _____:

We regret to inform you that our auditors have requested that your account of $ _____ be placed with our agency for collection.

We earnestly suggest that you arrange for payment of the account to avoid the embarrassment an action of this kind may create.

This reference will be deferred for seven days in the belief that you will cooperate with us and will forward your check in settlement.

Very truly yours,

Dear Mr.  ................

Usually there are two sides to a story.

| THIS IS OUR SIDE | THIS IS YOUR SIDE |
|---|---|
| Credit is a mutual arrangement. We have tried to perform our part of the agreement by carrying the best merchandise obtainable to sell at the lowest possible price. | |
| It has also been our endeavor to keep our service up to a high standard. | |
| Are we unfair in expecting our customers to cooperate with us by paying their accounts each month, according to our terms? Your account is past due for the months shown below. If you can send a check in full, fine: just attach it to your half of the letter- no explanation necessary. If not, send part now and tell us on the other side of this "half way" letter when you will send the rest. If you just can't possibly send a cent now, tell us your side of the story on your side of the letter. It helps a lot to know just when we may expect the money that is due. | |
| Will you meet us half-way? | |
| Cordially yours, | |
| SEARS, ROEBUCK & CO. | |

"Stunt" collection letters, which often produce unfavorable reactions in mercantile collection procedure, apparently are more effective with retail customers. Among the most successful are those with humorous illustrations printed on the letterhead to which the letter refers in developing a "reminder" message. Such "stunt reminders" are often based on current holiday dates. Sears Roebuck claims effective results from the "stunt" letter shown above.

Banks that sponsor "community" credit plans and "travel" credit sponsors are generally firmer, in tone as well as timing, in their collection correspondence than stores. They can afford to be, since they do not risk store good will should the feelings of a hypersensitive past-due debtor be injured. Moreover, recipients of dunning correspondence from a bank or other credit-plan sponsor apparently accept a stern tone in letters from such institutions as normal and proper under the circumstances, and not a matter for resentment.

There is some dispute among retail credit managers, as among mercantile credit managers, on the relative merits of form collection letters versus individually dictated letters. The arguments for form letters in retail collection, however, are much stronger than in mercantile collection. A larger proportion of retail charge accounts than of mercantile accounts become delinquent. The amounts involved in charge account delinquencies are generally much smaller than in the case of mercantile delinquencies. With hundreds, even thousands, of accounts unpaid each month, the collection departments of large department stores and credit-plan sponsors cannot, as a practical matter, devote individual attention to a particular account unless a letter from the customer has raised some exceptional consideration. Furthermore, the impersonal quality desirable in "reminder" letters, which constitute by far the greater part of retail collection letters, would be lost in dictated letters.

Accordingly all but a trifling minority of charge account collection letters are form letters. "Reminder" notices and many "reminder" letters are printed, with space provided for *writing* in the past-due amount. No attempt is made to camouflage them as personally dictated letters; on the contrary, every effort is made to emphasize their impersonal quality.

In preparing a supply of printed or multigraphed charge account collection letters, it is not enough to prepare a series of letters for each class of customer to be dealt with—for the good customer who has overlooked one or more statements, for the good but consistently slow-paying customer, and for the doubtful risk. Several series should be prepared for each class of customer, so that repetition will not occur if several collection follow-ups have to be applied to any customer in the course of a year. Many special form letters must be prepared such as one to propose in a suitable case the conversion of a past-due balance to an instalment debt, or one to cover the situation of a customer who has made a part payment on a past-due account. Some large department stores have as many as a hundred different form letters in stock, so that the circumstances when their collection departments must dictate special letters are exceedingly few.

### Personal calls by collectors

Most large stores have one or more members of their collection department who are experienced in making personal visits to delinquent customers. These collectors' calls are unquestionably effective. Retailers agree that if payment on a delinquent account is at all obtainable, it can be obtained by a collector even when all other approaches to the customer have failed.

However, no matter how diplomatic a collector is in his conversation with a delinquent customer, she is likely to resent the visit. Furthermore, personal visits on delinquents by collectors is an expensive procedure. Therefore stores that have collectors customarily send them to delinquent customers only when all possibilities of dunning by letter and by phone have been exhausted.

### Collection by attorney or agency [3]

As in the case of mercantile buyers, some delinquent accounts that have proved unresponsive to the efforts of a store's collection department can be induced to pay by an attorney or a collection bureau. They employ a harsher approach to the delinquent than collection departments are accustomed to take. In the case of attorneys, there is the implication that noncompliance with the order to pay will be followed by suit—whether or not that is the intention of the store that has placed the account in the attorney's hands. Collection agencies have at their command the sending of collectors to make personal visits to the delinquent customers, a procedure which is not available to small or even medium-sized stores.

Most of the collection agencies used by stores and other organizations with unpaid charge accounts are operated by or in conjunction with local retail credit bureaus. These, and a number of responsible private agencies, are supervised by the Collection Service Division of the Associated Credit Bureaus. The advantage of having collection action undertaken by the collection department of the local credit bureau is that all the credit files of the bureau are at its disposal and aid it in determining the best method of making collection. In the first appeal to the delinquent, the department's connection with the bureau is referred to, and he is advised to maintain a good credit record with the bureau since his credit standing throughout the community is determined by this bureau record. This appeal in itself generally brings payment from any delinquent whose finances permit him to pay the account.

### Compromise

Personal reverses may place a charge account customer in a position where he simply cannot meet all his personal debts. He may present this situation to a store collection manager after a series of dunning letters or phone calls. Or it may come to light when one or more creditors have placed their accounts with the collection department of the local credit bureau. Under such circumstances a compromise may be the only practicable solution of the situation.

---

[3] Banks sponsoring "community" credit plans usually collect through their legal departments rather than through agencies or outside attorneys.

Compromises on retail credit obligations are rare, but occasionally they are warranted. If they occur they are generally worked out by a credit bureau collection department. The bureau may arrange the conversion of the customer's outstanding debts into instalment obligations, to be paid off on some pre-arranged plan. Sometimes, with the agreement of the creditors, it is arranged that the customer shall make his weekly or monthly payments to the bureau, which in turn distributes them pro rata to the creditors. Possibly a personal loan from a consumer finance company, to be repaid in instalments, may be arranged as a means of clearing a group of delinquent charge accounts. If circumstances warrant, the debts may all be scaled down, with provision for instalment repayment of the balance.

For an informal compromise agreement of this sort to be binding on all of a customer's creditors, it must be agreed to by all the creditors. Should some of them endeavor to hold out for full settlement of their claims, they can be compelled to conform to a compromise agreeable to the majority by a wage-earner's bankruptcy proceeding under Chapter XIII of the Federal Bankruptcy Act. This is available to any wage or salary earner, regardless of income. It is a voluntary proceeding initiated by a petition of the debtor. A plan, providing for the applying of any assets of the debtor to liquidation of his debt and for submission of some part of his future wages or salary for payment on the debt, is presented. It may and often does provide for some scaling down of the debt. If this plan is accepted by a majority in number and amount of the creditors, it will, under certain conditions, be confirmed by the court and become binding upon all creditors.

### Suit

Suits for collection upon charge accounts are relatively rare. In the first place, the type of customer deemed an acceptable charge account risk is generally amenable to collection procedure provided he can possibly meet his obligation. In the second place, a considerable proportion of charge account customers who actually become insolvent are judgment-proof—they have no property subject to judgment lien and no wage or salary in excess of the statutory exemption that could be garnisheed. Finally, reputable stores do not want to incur the odium that attaches to a reputation for pressing suit against customers caught in the web of misfortune.

Most collection suits are brought against delinquent charge account customers to meet two situations. The first is the case of the customer who cannot meet his debt out of current funds or even out of future income, but who owns real estate. A judgment against such a customer cannot be paid when obtained, but properly filed it constitutes a lien against the real property and must be satisfied at some future time to clear title to the property.

The second situation is that of the employee currently unable to meet his obligations, who could satisfy them on some instalment basis out of his future wage or salary, but refuses to bind himself or conform to such an arrangement. Upon judgment obtained against him, his salary can be garnisheed—the employer is compelled to withhold and pay to the judgment creditor a specified proportion of the employee's wage or salary until the debt is cleared. Garnishment procedure as it applies to wages and salaries [4] is limited in various ways by the laws of the several states, but where these limitations permit its application it is a valuable legal collection procedure.

## PROMOTION

Department store credit managers consider their promotional function at least as important as their credit and collection functions, and in some cases more so. Among their more important promotional efforts are the following:

1. Solicitation of charge accounts from suitable credit risks among the store's cash customers.
2. Door-to-door or mail solicitation of charge accounts among newcomers or established residents in suitable communities.
3. Cordially welcoming each new charge account customer.
4. Cooperating with the advertising department in the enclosure of advertising notices with the monthly statements.
5. Following up inactive accounts to restore them to the active list.
6. So phrasing reminder letters to slow accounts that they are also promotional.
7. Sending occasional good will letters to prompt-paying customers to flatter their self-esteem and win friendship for the store.

## SUPPLEMENTARY READINGS

Ashby, D., "Effect of Option Accounts on Consumer Buying Habits," *Credit Management Year Book 1959/1960*, National Retail Merchants Association, New York, p. 52.

Bollman, D. W., "Planning and Scheduling Promotion of Charge Accounts for Branch Stores," *Credit Management Year Book 1959/1960*, p. 22.

Boxberger, J. J., "Mechanized Files for Credit Bureaus," *Credit World*, January 1960, p. 8.

---

[4] For a general discussion of the law of garnishment, see Ch. 17.

Breth, R. D., "How Much is a Charge Account Worth?" *Credit World*, April 1960, p. 3.

Jedlicka, C. J., "Revolving Credit and Charge Account Financing," *Credit World*, July 1960, p. 11, and August 1960, p. 7.

Landis, H., "Charge Account Authorization Limits—Are They Scientific?" *Credit Currents*, September 1960, p. 1.

Samuel, T. C., "Evaluation of Cycle Billing Procedures," *Credit Management Year Book 1959/1960*, p. 80.

## REVIEW

1. What are the customary charge account terms of sale?

2. How should the charge account application of a customer who wants to make "charge-take" purchases be handled?

3. Is a record of consistent delinquent payment of itself a sound reason for turning down a charge account application?

4. Explain "account," "order," "floor-release," and "negative authorization" limits on charge accounts.

5. How may notification to a customer that her application for a charge account has been accepted or rejected be made promotionally effective?

6. What information is entered upon a customer's credit history card? When is this card used?

7. Why is a charge account customer identification procedure necessary in department stores? Discuss some common ways of identification.

8. What is the purpose of (a) an "authorization file," (b) a "negative authorization list"? How would they be prepared? Explain charge-send authorization and charge-take authorization under each of these systems.

9. How does the timing of charge account collection procedure compare with that of mercantile collection procedure?

10. How long is a charge account allowed to be delinquent before it is suspended?

11. What appeals can be embodied in charge account collection letters?

12. Are form letters desirable in charge account collection correspondence?

13. Under what circumstances should collectors be sent by a store's credit department to delinquent charge account customers?

14. What collection techniques can be applied by attorneys and collection bureaus to delinquent charge account customers that are not available to store credit departments?

15. Under what circumstances would it be proper to compromise the obligation of a delinquent charge account customer?

16. Explain wage-earners' bankruptcy proceedings.

17. When is a collection suit against a delinquent charge account customer advisable?

18. What are some of the ways in which a retail store credit manager can make his work promotional?

## PROBLEM

You are credit manager of the Zeta Department Store in Forest Hills, N.Y., which has both charge accounts and "budget" (instalment) accounts. A Mrs. Mary Public wishes to open a charge account. You draw the credit bureau report shown on p. 536. There is no conflict between any of the information in this report and Mrs. Public's statements in her application sheet.

1. On the basis of this information, would you open an account for Mrs. Public? Why?

2. If you did open an account for Mrs. Public, would you set account and floor limits? If so, how much? Why?

3. Assume that you opened an account for Mrs. Public. For a year she made scattered purchases. The largest amount outstanding during the year was $63. All payments were prompt. On May 26 last she bought some furnishings items totaling $151. She did not pay on her June 14 "cycle" statement, nor on her July statement which contained a reminder notice. It is now July 24, and you send her your regular "form" first collection letter. Write this "form" letter.

4. Assume that you receive no answer to your July 24 letter. Outline your collection procedure from this point on, assuming that you get no favorable result from any preceding step, and that no one answers your calls in two attempts at telephoning.

5. A final letter to Mr. Public warning of suit brings a reply that in early July Mrs. Public had a serious operation, is still convalescent, that he has been too harassed to do anything about your previous communications, and that with the expenses and debts from Mrs. Public's illness he doesn't know when he will be able to pay the Zeta bill. Write your reply. What plans will you make about the Public account?

# CHAPTER 29

# Retail Instalment
# Credit Management

In one respect only is retail instalment credit management identical to charge account credit management. Sources of credit information are the same. Otherwise the differences between the two fields are more marked than their likenesses. Whereas most applicants for charge accounts seek only a shopping convenience, most applicants for retail instalment credit definitely want, and usually need, credit.[1] There is no standardization of retail instalment terms as there is of charge account terms, and determination of terms that will both meet the customer's wish or need and still be sound in view of the credit risk involved is one of the major problems of retail instalment credit management. Special instruments record the instalment buyer's obligation. Discounting of customers' notes with finance companies or banks is an accepted element of instalment credit financing. The decision on instalment purchase transactions is commonly more difficult than on charge account applications, because of the greater risk implied. Collection procedure has to be

---

[1] The advent of option-term accounts during the 1950's (whereby a charge-account customer may decide, after receiving his statement, whether to pay it in one sum or upon a "time" basis) may blur the dividing line between these two forms of retail credit. In practice, the option-term customer is more a "charge account type" than an "instalment type."

much more alert and vigorous on instalments than on charge accounts. The issue of repossession, which does not exist for charge accounts is often an important one in retail instalment credit management. Administrative costs for instalment credit are considerably higher than those for charge account credit.

## FIELDS OF RETAIL INSTALMENT CREDIT

About half of the retail instalment credit outstanding during the 1950's was accounted for by automobile sales. Another quarter to a third represented credit extensions of department stores, furniture stores, and sellers of household appliances. A substantial portion of the instalment credit extended by department stores covered sales of furniture, household equipment, and other durable items. In all, sales of durable consumer goods were responsible for 75 to 80 per cent of the total of retail instalment credit.

### Instalment sale of "soft" goods and services

When the first essays were made at selling men's and women's clothing on "three-payment" (monthly), "ten-payment" (weekly), and other instalment "plans" we do not know. By the late 1920's there were numerous instances of successful instalment merchandising of "soft" goods. During the 1930's the sale of clothing and other "soft" goods on instalment terms became common. Not only did it become an advertised feature of many clothing stores, but under the guise of "budget plans" it was widely adopted by department stores and mail order houses. This type of instalment buying was restricted during the 1940's, but it recovered after the war.

Some instalment payment of heavy medical bills has always existed. A new broad area of service instalment credit came into being during the 1950's when "time" payment plans for cruise and vacation travel were arranged.

### Department store instalment sale procedures

"Budget plans"—that is, instalment payment terms—for furniture and household appliance sales were widely adopted by department stores during the 1920's. Department stores were at first very reluctant to extend the instalment principle to apparel sales, since they felt that in doing this they would attract a cheaper class of customers and thereby drive away their more exclusive clientele. Their fears proved groundless. They gained or retained low-income customers who would otherwise have patronized the clothing and specialty stores offering instalment terms, and apparently lost none of their exclusive clientele.

So satisfactory was the department stores' experience with instalment selling of "soft" goods that in the late 1930's a number of stores developed coupon-book and letter-of-credit techniques to permit store-wide application of instalment selling. Under the coupon-book plan, a customer purchases, upon arrangement for instalment payment, a booklet like the one shown in Illustration 29-1. It contains "merchandise coupons." These may be all of one denomination, say 50 cents, or they may be in pages of various denominations such as 10 cents, 25 cents, 50 cents and one dollar. Books of various total values—$10, $25, $50, and $100—are provided to meet the varying needs and credit capacities of customers. The coupons from one of these books may be used to pay for purchases made in any of the departments of the store. Where the amount of a purchase does not coincide with the denominations of the coupons, the difference is paid in cash.

The letter-of-credit plan accomplishes the same objective. Instead of a coupon book the customer is given a "letter-of-credit" for a specified amount, to be repaid on instalment terms. The border of this certificate is a sequence of amounts, rising by 25-cent intervals, up to the face value of the "letter." As the customer makes her purchases in the different departments of the store, the clerks punch the cumulative amounts of the purchases. From all reports this application of the instalment principle to "store-wide" purchasing has been successful.

The "revolving credit" or "permanent budget" account is a more recent and growing development in instalment selling among department stores and specialty shops. It permits customers to establish accounts with set credit limits, such as $60 or $90 or $120 or more, and fixed monthly payments of $10, or $15, or more. The customer is permitted to purchase up to the credit limit at any time, as long as the monthly payments are met promptly. This type of account is used in the same way as a regular charge account, except that the authorization policy is more cautious. There is also a service charge, usually $1\frac{1}{2}$ per cent per month, imposed on the outstanding balance, to cover the costs of managing the revolving account. Some stores provide flexible schedules of monthly payments on these accounts, allowing longer terms, often up to 15 or 18 months, on sizable purchases. The revolving credit account is designed primarily for purchases of "soft" goods, but may also be used, at the customer's option, for buying durable merchandise.

### RETAIL INSTALMENT TERMS

There is little uniformity in retail instalment terms. Instalment sellers usually suggest that customers make as heavy a down payment and arrange as short a maturity as they find convenient. Thereby

## GIMBEL BROTHERS, INC., PHILADELPHIA
### CREDIT BOND --- COUPON BOOK

AUTHORIZED FOR
GIMBEL BROTHERS, INC.
BY CASHIER.

When issued this Credit Bond contains coupons good for **$50.00** in trade (and each coupon herein is good for the amount in trade represented on its face) for merchandise purchased at Gimbel Brothers, Philadelphia, subject to terms and conditions printed on the back cover hereof. Coupons not good if detached.

*Accepted:*
*Purchaser's Signature*_____

*Purchaser's Address*_____

ILLUSTRATION 29-1. Department Store Instalment Coupon Book

an instalment seller minimizes his credit risk. Most customers endeavor to make the lowest down payment and obtain the longest maturity that the seller will agree to, thereby minimizing their current burden. As a consequence of these divergent pressures and also in view of the strong competition among sellers, there is wide variation in the terms actually granted in any line of instalment selling. Apparently there is also a long-term trend toward more liberal terms.

### Minimum down payment

When instalment sellers looked primarily to repossession for their security, the generalization was frequently made that a down payment should at least equal the depreciation in value of the sold item between its original sales price and the "used" price at which it would have to be resold after repossession.

This principle was valid so long as instalment selling was limited to durable items and the customer's credit status was not taken into account. It was not applicable to instalment sale of "soft" goods that would have practically no resale value on repossession or to instalment-paid services. Such sales could be made on instalment terms only to acceptable credit risks. If a customer is established in this category, the "protection" factor in the down payment loses most of its significance.[2] Accordingly, instalment sellers of "soft" goods and services developed the principle that a down payment should not be less than a unit instalment payment. This example was followed by instalment sellers of durable goods, as they too came to base their sales on credit judgments rather than on the security of repossession.[3]

### Maturity of instalment debt

Instalment sellers prefer to have a customer's debt repaid in the largest instalments that a customer can manage in view of his income and current expenses. The information they obtain upon their customers often enables them to determine with considerable accuracy the margin of a customer's income over expenses and other obligations which is available for instalment debt repayment, and they try to persuade the customer to devote all of that margin to the instalment obligation. In such case, the

---

[2] To promote their instalment sales, some companies send paid-up customers "Privileged Customer Certificates," which entitle these customers to make their next instalment purchases without any down payment. Other companies—the two largest mail order houses—have recently started to generally eliminate down payments (*Wall Street Journal*, April 19, 1961).

[3] In certain fields like automobile selling, where trade-in of an old car is usual and serves as part payment on the new purchase, the trade-in has come to be accepted as the customary down payment, or at least as part of it.

unit payment agreed upon may establish a relatively short maturity for the total debt.

In many cases, however, the customer's margin of income that can be devoted to payments on the instalment debt is very thin. Then the seller must decide the minimum unit payment that he will accept—or, from another viewpoint, the maximum maturity he will agree to. In the "soft" goods fields a clear-cut rule has developed. The term of the debt should not exceed the usable life of the purchased item, so that the purchaser always has an equity in the item on which he is making payments. If a customer still owed for a suit of clothes after it was worn out, it would be a difficult proposition in many cases to induce him to continue payments on it. This principle is not applicable in many of the durable goods fields, since the life of many durable items sold on instalment terms may be quite a number of years. Accordingly certain maximum instalment maturities have been established by custom. For most consumer durables it is 18 months. Automobiles may be sold on terms up to three years.

It happens quite frequently that a customer, all of whose available income margin for some time to come is earmarked for payments on prior instalment buying, seeks to make additional purchases of this type. If the customer is an acceptable risk even though payments on the new purchase will have to be postponed until after the old debt is cleared, and he buys from the seller to whom he is already obligated, the latter will generally approve the sale, consolidate the two debts, and arrange a new payment schedule for the combined debt. If the seller from whom the new purchase is sought is some other than the one to whom the old debt is owed, a payment schedule may be established which does not begin until the outstanding debt has been cleared.

### Frequency of payments

Instalment payment dates may be arranged weekly, semimonthly, or monthly. The determining consideration in dealing with wage earners used to be the periodicity of the customer's pay-days. The credit manager endeavored to have the due dates for the instalment debt follow immediately upon the customer's pay-days, whether they were weekly or monthly. To an increasing extent large stores that carry their instalment accounts, and small stores and automobile agencies that refinance theirs, arrange monthly payments for all sales so that they will conform to the requirements of modern large-scale instalment bookkeeping procedures.

### Charges

Instalment selling involves the seller in five special costs. They are: (1) the cost of the credit inquiry, (2) the bookkeeping cost of maintaining a ledger account for each customer, (3) the collection costs involved in following up slow-paying customers, (4) the financing cost (if the seller discounts the customer's note with a finance company, or borrows from a bank to carry his receivables, he must pay interest for the borrowed funds; if he finances his receivables with his own capital, he foregoes the profit that could be derived from other use of the capital), (5) the bad debt loss which must be expected on some of the accounts.

The seller must obtain reimbursement for these special costs in one way or another, or his instalment business will be a profitless or losing proposition. One technique of reimbursement is to set the store's general schedule of prices higher than those that could be offered if the business were conducted on a cash basis. The special costs of the instalment business are thus charged to the cash as well as the instalment customers. This procedure allows the store to advertise that it arranges instalment terms without any instalment charges. It has the disadvantage that its prices, which must be charged to cash and instalment customers alike, are higher than those of competing cash stores and also of competing credit stores that sell on a charge account or option-term basis.

Occasionally prices are set sufficiently high so that instalment selling costs are covered by the instalment sales alone. Cash customers are then allowed a discount. This arrangement is generally considered worse, from a merchandising viewpoint, than the preceding one. The quoted price schedule must be set even higher than under the preceding arrangement, since the instalment selling costs must be covered entirely by the instalment sales. The allowance of a discount to cash customers, and the feature of no carrying charges for instalment buyers, do not overcome the disadvantage of the high price schedule that must be initially quoted.

The most common arrangement for covering instalment selling costs is to quote the cash price and superimpose on it one or more "carrying charges." Sometimes these include a fixed "credit inquiry charge" unrelated to the amount of the sale or the unpaid balance. Sometimes an "inquiry charge" is graduated in such a way that its ratio to small amounts is higher than to large amounts. Whether or not an "inquiry charge" is made, a "credit service charge" is customarily imposed. Sometimes this "service charge" is calculated on the total unpaid balance after the down payment is made; more rarely it is calculated in relation to each instalment payment. The most common charge rate is 10 per cent per annum for the payment period. "Carrying charges," however determined, are ordinarily precalculated and added to the balance remaining unpaid after the down payment; the resulting total is divided evenly among the number of payments to be made.[4]

---

[4] The opportunities open to sellers of misleading instalment purchasers as to the true character and burden of "carrying charges" are obvious. Some 30 states have "full disclosure" laws requiring instalment sellers to specify the detail of their "carrying charges."

Because of the inclusion of fixed or regressive "inquiry charges" in the carrying charge, and because the "interest charge" is commonly calculated on the total unpaid balance after the down payment, the cost of instalment buying to consumers is not uniform, even for a particular store. The cost tends to be greater for small purchases than for large ones, and for short payment periods than for long ones. The true cost, calculated on an annual basis as interest upon balances outstanding, may range from under 10 per cent for large purchases paid over a maximum period to over 25 per cent for small purchases paid over a three- or four-month period

## INSTRUMENTS OF RETAIL INSTALMENT CREDIT

The customer's promissory note or agreement to pay in instalments is the basic instrument of retail instalment credit. In most instances, the security of the seller-creditor is further buttressed by a conditional sales contract or chattel mortgage. Still more security may be obtained by a wage assignment or a third-party guaranty.

### The customer's promissory note

The obligation of a customer under a retail instalment sale is generally evidenced by a promissory note. Such a note differs from an ordinary mercantile promissory note only in that, instead of providing for a specific payment date, it establishes a series of payments that must be made under the instalment obligation. It is fairly common practice to embody the promissory note, together with the conditional sales contract or chattel mortgage, as part of the customer's application form.

### Conditional sales and chattel mortgages

Where the subject of a retail instalment sale is durable goods, the retailer may require the execution of a conditional sales contract or a chattel mortgage as security for payment of the purchase price. There is some tendency to forego such provision of "security title." Department stores and specialty shops have found that the convenience afforded customers in simply charging merchandise to their time payment accounts without pausing to sign new contracts each time they make an instalment purchase is a valuable sales stimulant, and the good will so engendered may outweigh the value of the security title, even though a certain risk is involved. In the automobile field and in the sale of many types of bulk appliances, however, security title is still regarded as desirable, particularly in view of the refinancing of such instalment accounts with banks and other financial institutions.

F 2125B

### RETAIL INSTALMENT CONTRACT
#### (Conditional Sales Contract)

........................................................
DATE

1. In consideration of your extending credit, when and if approved, I/we the buyer or buyers agree to purchase the goods and/or services described below at the prices and at the terms set forth. I/we agree that title to this merchandise shall remain in Gimbels until it is fully paid for.

| Description of Mdse, and/or services | | | | | | |
|---|---|---|---|---|---|---|
| | | | 1. Cash Sale price | | | |
| | | | 2., Less: Down Payment Trade in Allowance | | | |
| | | | 3. Principal Balance | | | |
| | | | 4. Credit Service Charge | | | |
| Sales tax (If any) | | | 5. Time Balance (Sum of items 3 & 4) | | | |
| Federal excise tax (If any) | | | 6. Time sole price (Sum of items 1 & 4) | | | |

| First Payment | Due on | Monthly Payments | |
|---|---|---|---|
| | | Number | amount |
| $ | | | $ |

2. If I/we should default in the payment of any sum payable under this contract or in the performance of any of the other terms and provisions hereof, any and all amounts then remaining unpaid hereunder, shall at the option of the seller become due and payable forthwith. Should the amount due and payable be referred to an attorney for collection, I/we shall pay, in addition to that amount a further amount equal to twenty percent (20%) thereof.

3. Acceptance of payments in lesser amounts or after they are due shall not be a waiver of any of your rights under this contract.

4. The credit service charges you may charge, receive, and collect on the principal balance of the contract from the date thereof to and including the date when the final instalment is payable, cannot exceed the following rates:
   (a) On so much of the principal balance as does not exceed five hundred dollars, ten dollars per one hundred dollars per annum;
   (b) If the principal balance exceeds five hundred dollars, eight dollars per one hundred dollars per annum on the excess over five hundred dollars; or
   (c) If the credit service charge so computed is less than twelve dollars, twelve dollars, but if the due date of the last instalment of the contract or obligation is eight months or less after its date, ten dollars.

5. This agreement shall not be effective until approved by the Credit Office of Gimbel Brothers I/We agree to notify Gimbel Brothers promptly and in writing of any change of address.

I hereby acknowledge receipt of an executed copy of this **RETAIL INSTALMENT CONTRACT.**

Seller:
**GIMBELS**
1275 Broadway, N. Y., N. Y.

.........................................................
Buyer's Signature

.........................................................
Buyer's Address

By:

NOTICE TO THE BUYER: 1. DO NOT SIGN THIS AGREEMENT BEFORE YOU READ IT OR IF IT CONTAINS ANY BLANK SPACE. 2. YOU ARE ENTITLED TO A COMPLETELY FILLED IN COPY OF THIS AGREEMENT. 3. UNDER THE LAW, YOU HAVE THE RIGHT TO PAY OFF IN ADVANCE THE FULL AMOUNT DUE AND UNDER CERTAIN CONDITIONS TO OBTAIN A PARTIAL REFUND OF THE CREDIT SERVICE CHARGE.

ILLUSTRATION 29-2. Retail Instalment Conditional Sales Contract

Under a conditional sales contract, title remains in the seller until the purchase price is paid in full; upon default in payment, the seller may assert his right by repossession. In the case of a chattel mortgage, title initially passes to the purchaser; upon default, the seller regains title through foreclosure of the mortgage and then may repossess under the regained title. The net effect of the two types of security title is practically the same, and in some states the procedures under both forms of contract have been merged into one known as "action to foreclose a lien on a chattel."

## Wage assignment

When soft goods or department store purchase coupon books are sold on instalment terms, there is commonly no provision for repossession. In such cases the seller often seeks protection by a wage assignment agreement. Wage assignment is commonly combined with a repossession arrangement in the case of durable goods sales, to give the seller double protection.

By a wage assignment an instalment buyer assigns his wages and other earnings from a specified employer or employers to the seller until payments on the instalment contract [5] have been completed (see Illustration 29-3). If these payments are defaulted, the seller can, by simple legal procedure, garnishee (obtain legal attachment upon) the purchaser's wages and have them paid directly to himself until the debt is cleared. Some states permit the full amount of the purchaser's wages to be garnisheed under such assignments, but in most states a limitation—usually 10 per cent—is placed on the proportion that may be paid to the creditor.

---

### ASSIGNMENT OF WAGES DUE AND TO BECOME DUE

KNOW ALL MEN BY THESE PRESENTS, that I, _____, of _____, in the county of _____, in consideration of _____ to the value of $ _____, delivered to me by the X Store, the receipt of which I do hereby acknowledge, do hereby assign and transfer to the said X Store all claims and demands which I now have, and all which at any time between the date hereof and the _____ day of _____ next I may and shall have against _____ of _____, for all sums of money due, and for all sums of money and demands which, at any time between the date hereof and the said _____ day of _____ next, may and shall become due to me for services as a _____; to have and to hold the same to the said X Store and its assigns, forever. And I, the said _____, do hereby constitute and appoint the said X Store to be my attorney irrevocable in the premises, to do and perform all acts, matters, and things touching the premises in like manner to all intents and purposes as I would if personally present.

In witness, etc.

_____L. S.

---

ILLUSTRATION 29-3.  Wage Assignment Applicable to an Instalment Sales Contract (adapted from National Association of Credit Management, *Credit Manual of Commercial Laws*, 1961, p. 701)

### Third-party guarantee

If an instalment purchaser's credit status is poor, so poor that a wage assignment would not afford the seller sufficient protection, or if wage

---

[5] New York and some other states permit assignment of wages as security for loans but not for instalment purchases.

assignments for such transactions are not permissible—and this is the case under some state laws as already indicated—the seller may insist on a third-party guarantee as condition of the sale. Such guarantees may cover only a particular sale, or they may be "open" or continuing so as to cover also extensions and "add-ons." A guarantor may be asked to sign a special agreement or his obligation may be established by making him a co-signer or endorser of the customer's promissory note. Co-signers are often preferred because they are primarily liable for the payment. Upon default, the seller may demand payment immediately from the co-signer as well as from the signer, where both have signed the original obligation. In the case of a separate third-party agreement, the seller must first attempt to collect from the buyer before requiring payment from the guarantor.

"Continuing guarantees" are limited in some states by law to a certain number of years. In New York, for example, such a guarantee is good for only two years from the date of its signing by the guarantor, and any subsequent transaction would not bind the guarantor. The purpose of such limitations is to prevent sellers from demanding payment from guarantors on continuing guarantees signed several years ago for transactions they never contemplated assuming responsibility for at the time the agreement was originally signed.

## PROCEDURE ON APPLICATIONS

The processing of instalment purchase applications and the decisions made upon them resemble closely those of charge account credit procedure. Because of differences in the nature of the two types of credit already noted, however, certain dissimilarities in procedure have developed.

An applicant for a charge account in any store ordinarily need make such application only once; the account remains open indefinitely unless suspended for extreme delinquency or some other exceptional circumstance. An instalment customer, on the contrary, must make a new application on the occasion of every new instalment purchase.

The first time that a customer seeks to buy on instalment in a store, he must fill out an application form of the type discussed in Chapter 27. Ordinary sales clerks are not customarily entrusted with the function of assisting a customer in preparing it. This requires specialized training or experience, and even the smallest instalment store commonly designates some individual of its staff to act as its "finance man" and handle all applications. A large store will have a credit man, or a credit department, to take care of this procedure.

A customer who has already made one instalment purchase in a store is not called upon to fill out application forms on the occasions of his subsequent instalment purchases. His original application, amended to cover any changed circumstances, serves for these later purchases. A single application is all that is needed for the "revolving credit" or "continuous budget" arrangements described in Chapter 26.

## Further inquiry

In many cases where a charge account is opened obviously as a shopping convenience, the store's credit department does not put itself to the expense of ordering a complete report from the local credit bureau, but assures itself upon what seems to be a clearly acceptable credit risk by merely obtaining a trade clearance report in order to be sure that no derogatory information is on record. Where instalment applications are concerned, such superficial checking is inadvisable. The mere fact that instalment terms have been requested generally indicates that the customer needs credit, and his credit standing must therefore be carefully examined.

Almost without exception a full report will be obtained from the credit bureau. In addition, many instalment stores that sell to the poorer sections of a community employ their own investigators who visit the applicant's landlord and the local shops that he patronizes.

## Factors in the credit decision

Credit analysis on instalment purchase applications is generally more careful and more searching than upon charge account applications. Primary weight is given to the nature of the applicant's occupation and its permanence. If the applicant has made previous instalment purchases in the store in question or in other stores, equal or greater consideration is given to his record of past payments. The relation of the terms of the proposed payment to the customer's income is taken into account. Allowance is also made for the payments he may be under obligation to make to other creditors. In cases where an applicant's present credit status is satisfactory, but his employment does not have long-term security, the credit decision may turn upon the applicant's willingness to accept terms that will result in speedy liquidation of the instalment obligation.

## PAYMENT PROCEDURES

Payments on an instalment sale may be arranged to be made by personal visits of the customer to the store, by mail, or to collectors. Each method has its advantages and disadvantages. According to its merchandising policy and the circumstances of its customers, an instalment store may find one or another, or a combination, of these payment procedures the most advantageous.

### Payment to collectors

To send collectors out to receive payments from instalment customers and pay them a commission on their collections, is expensive. The cost involved means that merchandise sold on instalment terms must be priced much higher than would otherwise be necessary. But if the customers of a store are of a financially irresponsible type, who would not themselves take the initiative to pay their instalment obligations, collectors must be used. Few stores now use outside collectors, except on delinquent accounts. However, many house-to-house instalment sellers do their own collecting by personal visit which, at the same time, gives them access to their customers for further sales.

### Payment in the store

If a customer has no checking account—and checking accounts are not too common among instalment buyers—the suggestion that he should come to the store weekly or monthly and make cash payments is a natural one. But customers with checking accounts, too, are persuaded, whenever possible, to pay at the store instead of mailing checks. Any suggestion of mailing postal money orders is gently discouraged.

Many instalment stores prefer that their customers pay in cash at the store. With the customer actually in the store for the purpose of making his payment, he can often be persuaded to make a new purchase.

Store-paying customers are provided with payment books of the type shown in Illustration 29-4.

### Payment by mail

When payment is to be made by mail, the customer may be provided with a payment book, which he encloses with each payment and which must be mailed back to him after record of the payment has been entered.

A common arrangement is to provide the customer with a booklet of detachable payment coupons. Each coupon provides space for the customer's name, address, account number, and the amount of the payment. A coupon is sent to the store with each payment. The customer's receipt is the cancelled check or the money order stub which she retains.

A variation of the coupon book method, used by some stores, is a folder of detachable payment envelopes. The inside of the flap of each envelope is printed to serve as a payment coupon. The inside of the folder is printed so that it can serve the customer as a record of his payments. Promotional sentences may appear on the payment envelopes.

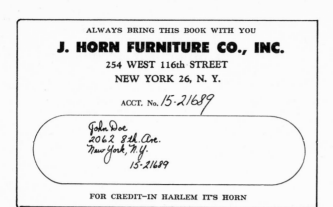

ALWAYS BRING THIS BOOK WITH YOU

# J. HORN FURNITURE CO., INC.

### 254 WEST 116th STREET
### NEW YORK 26, N. Y.

ACCT. No. *15-21689*

*John Doe*
*2062 8th. Ave.*
*New York, N.Y.*
*15-21689*

FOR CREDIT—IN HARLEM IT'S HORN

---

## J. HORN FURNITURE CO., INC.

THE MERCHANDISE delivered to you on this account is covered by a chattel mortgage which you signed at the time of purchase. It is illegal to remove this merchandise, put it in storage, or sell it without the written consent of J. Horn Furniture Co., Inc.

YOUR BALANCE as it appears in this book at any date, is a memo for your convenience, and is subject to corrections, as a result of possible errors or omissions which may be disclosed upon comparison with the original ledger record at our office.

**PLEASE NOTIFY US**
**WHEN YOU MOVE**

---

| FIRST PAYMENT DUE: *10/15/60* | | PAYMENT AS AGREED: $*10⁰⁰* EVERY *M0* | | | |
|---|---|---|---|---|---|
| **DATE** | **TRACER** | **CHARGE** | **CREDIT** | **BALANCE** | **TRANS.** |
| SEP 15 60 | 1396 | 200.00 | | | H |
| 1 SEP 15 60 | 1397 | | 20.00 | 180.00 | AT |
| 2 OCT 17 60 | 1400 | | 10.00 | 170.00 | AR |
| 3 NOV 17 60 | 1404 | | 10.00 | 160.00 | AR |
| 4 | | | | | |
| 5 | | | | | |
| 6 | | | | | |
| 7 | | | | | |
| 8 | | | | | |
| 9 | | | | | |
| 10 | | | | | |
| 11 | | | | | |
| 12 | | | | | |

ALLOW $*15⁰⁰* IF PAID BEFORE *3 mos.*

YOUR ACCOUNT IS ALWAYS OPEN!

ILLUSTRATION 29-4.  Pages from Instalment Payment Book

## COLLECTION OF DELINQUENT ACCOUNTS

Instalment collection procedure is more sharply timed and more aggressive than charge account collection procedure. It must be, for delinquency in an instalment payment is usually not the result of oversight on the part of a customer well able to meet his obligation but of sheer inability to make the payment or willful disregard of his obligation. If two successive payments on an instalment obligation are missed, the credit manager must proceed rapidly to strong measures, or he will probably have a bad debt on his hands.

### The customer ledger

The starting point for retail instalment collection procedure is the customer ledger. From this ledger the credit department receives its notice that a customer has missed one of his instalment payments on its due date.

Formerly instalment houses made it a practice to have a clerk check through the customer ledger weekly and note the accounts that were delinquent. Now most instalment stores use "visible index" ledger card files of the type shown in Illustrations 13-1 and 13-2. Each ledger card is held, by means of slots, on a file "pocket" that is hinged to a panel. Each pocket has at its top or bottom, according to whether the panels stand in a holder or are pulled out like drawers from a cabinet, a folded transparent slip which contains the account's name, a scale of the weeks of the year, and a transparent colored slide. When a payment on an instalment account is received, it is posted to the ledger card, and the slide is pushed along to cover the week or month for which the payment is made.[6] If all accounts were paid up to date on any week or month, the slides would stand at the same position on all the pockets, and would make a straight band of color down the panel. If any accounts are delinquent, they show up at a glance, because their slides stand in from the general line of the prompt accounts.

With one of these visible file systems, there is no need of a weekly check through all the ledger cards to ascertain which customers are paid-up and which are delinquent. A swift glance down the visible index panels enables a clerk to note the past-due accounts, and it takes but a moment to remove the ledger cards of these accounts from their pockets so that collection action can be taken upon them.

---

[6] Under an alternative system, the slide is pushed ahead to the week or month when the next payment is due. This system is preferable when the store sells on both weekly and monthly payment terms, and both sets of accounts are covered by a single ledger system.

Cycle billing, with monthly statements prepared in alphabetical sequence from copies of credit and debit items filed in pocket ledger cards, may be more difficult to apply to instalment credits than to charge account systems (see Chapter 28), but is being widely adopted by large establishments. It may tend to increase "oversight" delinquencies somewhat. Effective systems of "flagging" late accounts, however, can overcome this tendency.

### The reminder notice

The first reminder notice on a missed instalment payment may be sent out two or three days after the due date in the case of accounts that are paid weekly, and five days after the due date in the case of monthly accounts, provided the older manual bookkeeping methods are used. With the tendency of retailers to favor monthly payments to lessen the work-load caused by weekly bookkeeping, the tendency to incorporate the preliminary dunning procedures into the monthly bookkeeping and statement mailing operations is increasing. The adoption of a particular procedure will depend on the need of each individual store.

Regardless of the timing of notices, the message which the first and succeeding reminders should contain, is an important and sometimes highly controversial point. Some credit managers advocate the use of a formal printed notice or card bearing a legend such as this:

> PAYMENT OF $ _____ ON YOUR ACCOUNT WITH US DOES
> NOT APPEAR TO HAVE REACHED US BY THE DUE DATE. IF IT
> HAS BEEN SENT, PLEASE ACCEPT OUR THANKS. IF NOT, WILL
> YOU PLEASE SEND IT PROMPTLY?
> THANK YOU.

The stark formality of such a notice, its proponents feel, saves it from the possibility of being interpreted as a personal reflection on the particular customer.

Other instalment credit managers prefer the reminder to be in the form of a personal letter. They believe that the sting of apparent individual attention can be removed by combining the reminder with a promotional appeal, as in the following letter intended for delinquent customers of an instalment furnishings store who come to the store to make their payments:

Dear Mr. Doe:

   We have not received payment of $ _____ on your account, due _____. Please clear this payment this week.

   While you are in the store, be sure to look at the wonderful silverware bargains we are featuring this week. This is the opportunity of a lifetime to get that new table set you and Mrs. Doe have wanted for so long.

Cordially yours,

## Collection correspondence follow-up

A series of instalment collection letters should be so planned that it leads up to a warning that the acceleration clause will be applied and the full balance of the debt be deemed due, then that collection action on such balance will be taken, finally that the seller's right to repossession will be exercised. Where weekly payments are involved, a third letter (counting the original reminder as the first one), warning the customer that the full balance of the debt will be deemed due upon continued nonpayment, is commonly sent ten days after the original due date and three days after payment has been missed on a second instalment. An "attorney" collection letter calling for payment of the full balance with warning of repossession is mailed at the end of two weeks. A "notice of repossession" is sent on or shortly after the 20th day of delinquency.

Where monthly instalment payments are involved, the timing of the collection correspondence is slower. The letters generally go out at ten-day intervals, after the original reminder notice. Thus the warning that the entire balance will be deemed due is ordinarily not sent until five days after the customer has missed a second payment. The "attorney" letter, warning of repossession and suit, is not mailed until the third month, after a third payment has been missed.

In general, instalment collection letters are more formal and more forceful than charge account collection letters. Many stores have their instalment collection letters printed or multigraphed, and the customer's name and address does not even appear on the letter. Not only is this a time-saving and cost-saving device, but the bare impersonality of the letters may well make a more striking impression upon the type of customer who fails to make instalment payments. The following is one of a series of instalment collection letters used by Gimbels, New York:

Dear Customer:

We recently called your attention to the fact that the terms on your Easy Payment account called for payments at the rate of $ _____ per month payable within ten days after receipt of your monthly statement.

To date, the payments promised have not been received. We are anxious to help you retain your good credit standing and urge, therefore, that you bring your account up to date without further delay.

A self-addressed envelope is attached for your convenience in so doing. Thank you.

Very truly yours,
G i m b e l s
Credit Sales Office

P.S. If payment has already been made, please disregard this notice.

A final notice, printed in red, has sometimes been used with effect to impress seriously delinquent customers with the imminence of legal action and the costs of such action to the customer. Such notices are banned by law in many states, however, as coercive.

### Telephone follow-up

A telephone call cannot be ignored like a collection letter. It pins the customer down to an explanation of why he has not made his past-due payment, and usually to a promise and specific arrangement for correcting the delinquency. All efficient instalment credit departments therefore look upon the telephone as one of their most efficient collection instruments. But a customer who has been forced to make embarrassing explanations over a telephone, and unwillingly agrees to a method of payment which will probably inconvenience him, is likely to resent the pressure thus put upon him and transfer his custom to some other store. Therefore, the telephone is not ordinarily used in the opening stages of an instalment collection procedure but only when the credit department decides that the customer would not be an acceptable risk for further purchases. Such a conclusion is likely if there is no immediate reply to the letter warning that the full balance of the debt will become immediately payable if the due instalment is not paid. From this point on, however, telephone calls are alternated with letters, or two or more calls may be made between successive letters.

### Collectors and collection agencies

As was noted above, some instalment stores selling to poorer and financially irresponsible elements of the community may depend entirely on collectors for obtaining weekly payments from their customers. Otherwise collectors and collection agencies are resorted to only when correspondence, telephoning, and the strongest warnings of impending repossession do not produce payment. Where all other methods of persuasion have failed, however, the personal visit of a collector sometimes results in the customer scraping together the money to make at least a part payment.

Large instalment stores usually have one or more members of the credit department staff who act as collectors. Smaller stores use the services of collection agencies. While there are many private agencies that undertake this service, most stores use the collection departments associated with their local credit bureaus. Their collectors are experienced in the special problems of retail collections, including tracing "skips," that is, debtors who have moved from their known addresses.[7] The prestige

---

[7] Some credit bureaus have special divisions for this purpose.

of the credit bureau they represent is of great assistance in making collections. The bureaus themselves, and their collectors, are all bonded to protect the stores that employ them.

## REPOSSESSION

The conditional sales contract or the chattel mortgage, which a customer signs when he purchases durable goods on an instalment plan, entitles the seller to repossess the goods if payments are not made in strict accordance with the sales contract. But instalment sellers are loath to exercise this right. The legal procedure of repossession involves numerous expenses and fees, and various costs are associated with the reconditioning, storing, and resale of the goods that have been repossessed; more often than not, instalment sellers sustain net losses on their repossessions. Furthermore, if a store gains the reputation of quick and frequent resort to repossession, customers become wary of dealing with it. Hence instalment stores usually forego exercise of this right of repossession until every other possibility of obtaining payment has been exhausted. Rather than repossess, they will agree to liberal readjustment of the payment terms, and often compromise the remaining balance of an obligation. Many stores, in cases where the unpaid balance amounts to less than 25 per cent of the original price, will threaten to repossess in an effort to obtain payment, but will waive repossession if such payment cannot be made by the customer and write it off as a bad debt.

If repossession cannot be avoided, the store tries to arrange a "friendly" surrender of the goods. In many cases customers whose financial circumstances have so changed that they cannot meet the obligations of an instalment contract return the merchandise without protest. Sometimes a permissible legal deceit may be practiced to obtain peaceable repossession. A truck and crew are sent to the customer's house. The truckman presents a "notice of demand for goods or payment" which looks official but has no legal status. The customer, unaware that force may not be employed under the circumstances and that he could simply refuse the "demand," surrenders the merchandise.

Should a customer categorically refuse to surrender merchandise covered by a conditional sale or chattel mortgage, the seller must then proceed according to the due process of law.[8] The detail of repossession law is intricate, and differs from state to state. The matter should be placed in the hands of a competent attorney.

---

[8] In England a delinquent instalment debtor can be jailed. The United States is less enlightened.

## DEALER REFINANCING

Over seven-eighths of retail instalment credit is re-financed.[9] Most instalment retailers, including practically all automobile dealers, sell their instalment accounts to banks and sales finance companies. These institutions buy them partly on a "full recourse" basis (the merchant remaining liable for bad debt losses), partly on a "non-recourse" basis (the financial institution taking over the full risk), and partly on a combined-risk or "limited recourse" basis (the dealer and the financing institution sharing any credit losses on an agreed basis).

Commercial banks and sales finance companies divide this dealer re-financing business, with the former slightly predominating.[10] Three sales finance companies are national in scope. A few more operate in several states. There are several thousand local ones. Most sales finance companies are independent units. A few are "captive," that is, owned by large manufacturers or by large retailers such as general mail order houses.

The primary activity of these companies is purchasing or discounting dealers' retail instalment contracts. Many of them lend on the security of auto dealers' floor stocks. Some also finance commercial accounts receivable (see Chapter 23) and make personal loans (see Chapter 30). Retail automobile instalment financing, however, constitutes two-thirds or more of their activity.

When a store's or dealer's instalment sales are refinanced, the customer may be so notified at the time of the sale. In this case his notes are made out to the sales finance company or bank which does the refinancing. Subsequent payments are usually made directly to the refinancing institution. In some cases the store or dealer acts as its collecting agent. This is an advantage to the institution; it shifts the administrative burden of handling collections to the seller. But the seller, too, may derive advantages. If the customer makes his payments in person, his repeated visits to the store provide it with further opportunities to make sales to him. Even if he pays by mail, "envelope stuffers" may be enclosed with the store's notices of payment due, affording it an extra direct-mail promotion.

Non-notification refinancing is also quite common. In such case the customer does not know that his notes have been discounted. He makes his payments to the store, which acts as trustee for the refinancing institution with respect to these payments.

---

[9] Dauten, C. A., "Recent Institutional Developments in the Field of Consumer Credit," *The Journal of Finance*, May 1960, p. 207.

[10] Board of Governors of the Federal Reserve System, "Consumer Credit Statistics," published currently in the *Federal Reserve Bulletin*.

Under all circumstances—with and without notification, with and without recourse—instalment refinancing institutions are keenly concerned with the credit status of the customers whose notes they discount, and also with the downpayment and maturity terms of the refinanced sales contracts. Even under "full recourse" refinancing, where the seller remains liable for any failure of the customer to make his payments, the refinancing institution must assure itself that each customer is a sound credit risk. Bankruptcy of a refinanced seller would render any "full recourse" provisions valueless. With "limited recourse" or "non-recourse" arrangements, refinancing institutions have a still more immediate interest in an instalment purchaser's reliability. They usually, therefore, make careful credit analyses of instalment sellers' customers, sometimes a more careful analysis than that made by the sellers themselves. They may also set minimum downpayment and payment-term requirements which the sellers must apply if they want their contracts refinanced. Where sales finance companies lend against a "portfolio" of retail contracts instead of against individual contracts, they cannot pursue credit risk analysis of each component of a "portfolio," but they may still stipulate and thereby to some extent standardize the instalment sales terms of the seller.

All bank activities, including their refinancing of retail instalment sales, are under statutory control. Sales finance companies are not so fully regulated, but there is a growing tendency for instalment sales legislation to extend to refinancing, including licensing of companies engaged in this business and regulation of various aspects of their operations.[11]

## SUPPLEMENTARY READINGS

Baker, C. B., "Long-Term Sources of Capital for Consumer Financing," National Consumer Credit Conference for 1958, *Proceedings*, p. 64.

Barnes, E. H., *Barnes on Credit and Collection* (Prentice-Hall, Inc., Englewood Cliffs, N.J., 1961).

Brisco, N. A. and R. M. Severa, *Retail Credit* (Prentice-Hall, Inc., Englewood Cliffs, N.J., 1942).

Burland, E. L., "Revolving Credit Plans in Retailing," National Consumer Credit Conference for 1959, *Proceedings*, p. 77.

Cheyney, W. J., "New Perspectives in Consumer Financial Management," National Consumer Credit Conference for 1959, *Proceedings*, p. 19.

Hayes, J. A., "Write-Off Policy," *Credit Management Year Book 1959/1960*, p. 101.

---

[11] National Association of Credit Management, *Credit Manual of Commercial Laws, 1961*, New York, p. xxxvii.

Hogan, W. E., "A Survey of State Retail Instalment Sales Legislation," *Cornell Law Quarterly*, Fall 1958, p. 38.

Landis, G. H., "Old Line Instalments vs. Continuous Instalment Accounts for Durables," *Credit Management Year Book 1959/1960*, p. 241.

Paradiso, L. J., and M. A. Smith, "Consumer Purchasing and Income Patterns," *Survey of Current Business*, March 1959, p. 18.

Phelps, C. W., *Important Steps in Retail Credit Operations* (1959), *Retail Credit Fundamentals* (1956), *Retail Credit Management* (1955), National Retail Credit Association, St. Louis, Mo.

————, *Using Instalment Credit*, Commercial Credit Co., Baltimore, Md., 1955.

Sasser, W., "Bad Debts and Authorizing Costs," *Credit Management Year Book 1959/1960*, p. 95.

Silbert, T. H., "Short-Term Sources of Capital for Consumer Financing," National Consumer Credit Conference for 1958, *Proceedings*, p. 59.

Tannrath, A. M., *How to Locate Skips and Collect*, publ. by the author, Chicago, Ill., 1961.

Trotta, A. L., "1958 Credit Department Operating Results," *Credit Management Year Book 1959/1960*, p. 205.

Weber, P. M., "Instalment Credit Terms Before and During Regulation," *Federal Reserve Bulletin*, July 1951, p. 800.

Woll, M., and F. C. Lewis, "Preparation for Automation," *Credit Management Year Book 1959/1960*, p. 256.

## REVIEW

1. What are the principal fields of retail instalment selling?
2. Explain the department store "coupon book," "letter of credit," and revolving credit system of instalment merchandising.
3. How should the minimum down payment permitted on an instalment sale be determined?
4. What considerations determine the period over which instalment payments are spread?
5. How is the "instalment charge," "financing charge," or "service charge" on an instalment purchase calculated?
6. What sort of promissory note is customarily signed by an instalment purchaser?
7. Why do retail instalment sellers often prefer the security of a chattel mortgage to that of a conditional sale?
8. Explain the use of wage assignments in connection with instalment purchase contracts.
9. Explain the use of third-party co-signatures, endorsements, and guarantees in connection with instalment purchase contracts.
10. In what ways may retail instalment sellers be refinanced by finance companies and banks?
11. Compare the credit inquiry made upon instalment customers with that made upon charge account applicants.

12. What are the most important factors in determining the credit status of an applicant for instalment credit?

13. Is it practicable to use collectors to obtain regular instalment payments?

14. Assuming the customer is agreeable to making his instalment payments either by mail or at the store, which arrangement is preferable? Why?

15. Contrast instalment collection correspondence with charge account collection correspondence.

16. What part do telephone calls play in instalment collection procedure?

17. Under what circumstances should an instalment seller's right of repossession under a conditional sale or chattel mortgage be exercised?

## PROBLEM

1. You are credit officer of the Alpha Finance Company. Mr. John Public is buying a new automobile. With his trade-in counted as down payment, he will have a balance of $2,000 to pay. The proposed arrangement is twelve monthly instalments. The dealer plans to refinance the instalment credit on a nonrecourse basis with Alpha Finance Company. Will you approve the transaction on the basis of the credit bureau report on Mr. Public shown on p. 536? Explain.

2. Mr. Public has made seven payments to Alpha Finance Company, but has failed to make his eighth. You have received no reply to your reminder notice or first letter. Write the next "form" letter that would be used in this case.

# CHAPTER 30

# Personal Loan Credit

Personal loan credit—*loans made* to individuals as distinguished from *credit extended* to them incident to purchases made by them—constitutes a substantial element of consumer credit. The $18.5 billion of personal loans outstanding at the close of 1960 represented 33 per cent of the total consumer credit outstanding at that date. Whereas charge account credit outstanding doubled during the 1950's, and instalment credit tripled, the increase in personal loan credit was nearly four-fold.[1]

In its economic aspects, personal loan credit is closely related to the forms of consumer credit already studied. Credit analysis for personal loan credit is similar to that for charge account and instalment credit. In many respects, however, there are marked contrasts between personal loan credit and the other two forms of consumer credit. Different borrowing motivations are sometimes involved. Certain types of financial institutions not heretofore encountered are involved in personal credit extension. Its terms and instruments deserve special study. The loan decisions may involve different factors, or different weighting of factors. Personal loan collection procedure, while resembling in many respects instalment collection methods, has distinctive features.

---

[1] See Illustration 26-2.

## DEMAND FOR PERSONAL LOAN CREDIT

Personal loans are negotiated for four reasons: (1) meeting "distress" needs—obtaining funds for urgently required clothing or fuel which could not otherwise be bought, or for medical services which would otherwise be unobtainable, or for meeting mortgage or interest obligations whose nonpayment would result in foreclosure; (2) consolidating and refinancing pre-existing debt; (3) obtaining funds for cash purchase of consumer goods and services as an alternative to instalment buying; and (4) obtaining funds for business or investment use.

### Refinancing and other personal reasons

A major proportion of personal loans are made for the purpose of refinancing pre-existing debt. This is a type of business the personal loan institutions have been encouraging. An instalment purchaser sometimes finds that he has loaded himself with an over-heavy or inconvenient sequence of instalment payments. The stores, in order to keep their own capital liquid, prefer not to readjust and lengthen his payment schedules but recommend him to a consumer finance company or personal loan department of a bank. The personal loan so negotiated is used to clear the troublesome instalment debt.

In many cases the purchaser of an automobile, of furniture, or of expensive household equipment discovers that the charges on a personal loan will be less than the finance charges on an instalment purchase. He borrows the purchase price from a personal loan institution, and pays cash. Automobile purchase loans, particularly those based on used cars, account for a substantial proportion of current loans by consumer finance companies and credit unions. Personal loans to finance travel, house repair, education,[2] adjusting contracts, paying insurance premiums, and moving may be included here.

Some sellers of "big ticket" merchandise or services take the initiative of arranging with financial institutions to make personal loans to their customers so that the latter can pay on a cash instead of an instalment basis. In such cases, instead of signing a conditional sales contract, the customer gives a personal loan note to the lending institution, possibly with a chattel mortgage on the purchased goods as security. On such loans, the lending institution usually has "recourse" to the seller—the

---

[2] Some consumer finance companies and sales finance companies make intermediate-term loans (one to four years) for education purposes through wholly-owned subsidiaries, for example, Household Finance Corporation's "Education Funds, Inc." and "The Tuition Plan, Inc." of C.I.T. Financial Corporation. Other personal loan institutions handle such credits as an element of their regular personal loan business.

seller must reimburse the financing organization for any unpaid balance upon default.

"Distress" loans, which accounted for as much as 25 per cent of personal loan credit in the 1930's, now constitute a much smaller proportion of the total.[3]

### Business loans

Farmers and proprietors of small businesses occasionally find personal instalment loans a convenient method of obtaining funds for the purchase of equipment. Sometimes such loans are made to enable a small business man to take advantage of cash discounts.

A large volume of single-payment loans are granted by banks to individuals, usually on a secured basis. Since in these cases the borrowers are able to submit collateral security of greater value than the face amount of their loans, the loans can hardly be considered motivated by "distress" considerations. The larger part of these single-payment loans is probably for business and investment purposes. The balance is negotiated to enable the borrowers to make cash payments for expensive purchases, so that they can save the cost of instalment terms, but avoid inconvenient liquidation of capital assets which would provide the wherewithal for cash payment.

## PERSONAL LOAN INSTITUTIONS

Personal loans are made by seven classes of lenders: (1) most of the 13,500 commercial banks, (2) an unknown number of pawnbrokers and other nonregulated lenders, (3) some 3,500 consumer finance companies, (4) an unknown number of industrial banks, (5) an unknown number of industrial loan companies, (6) some 20,500 credit unions, and (7) some sales finance companies.[4]

### Commercial banks

The National Banking Act and most state banking laws never placed any restriction on personal lending by the banks chartered under their authority. In the few cases where state banking laws originally prevented such lending, amendments have removed the bars. Although thus free

---

[3] No comprehensive figures are available on the distribution of personal loans outstanding by purpose of loan, but the above conclusions are sustained by figures in M. R. Neifeld, *Personal Finance Comes of Age* (Harper & Bros., New York, 1939), pp. 129, 137, and *Trends in Consumer Finance* (Mack Publishing Co., Easton, Pa., 1954), pp. 105-107.

[4] In addition, savings and loan associations and mutual savings banks make a small volume of "passbook" loans. Both classes of institutions also extend repair and modernization loans.

to make personal loans, most commercial banks showed little interest in this field of credit until the late 1920's. Once their interest was aroused, however, the commercial banks moved rapidly and massively into the field. With over $18½ billion of personal loans currently outstanding, they account for about half of the amount.

The common range of commercial bank personal loans is between $100 and $1,500. Thus commercial banks are in direct competition with the specialized small-loan institutions.[5]

Commercial banks make quite a large volume of unsecured personal loans, chiefly instalment loans, to persons with good credit standing. The greater part of their personal loans, however, are secured. Some are collateraled by co-makers; others by stocks and bonds, life insurance policies, or savings bank pass books. Those personal loans that are negotiated to enable borrowers to make cash purchases of automobiles and other consumer durable items are secured by chattel mortgage on the purchased equipment. Commercial banks make few "distress" loans collateraled by wage assignments, third-party guarantees, or chattel mortgages on household furniture.

Commercial banks, like the other institutions extending personal credit, are generally bound by the "contract" rates of the usury laws of the states in which they operate. But they usually discount the interest charge on the entire amount of the loan and deduct it in advance, so that the effective rate on their loans may actually be more than double the nominal rate. They also frequently charge moderate inquiry fees, and add the premium charge for term life insurance on the borrower to cover the unpaid balance of the loan.

Maturities of bank personal loans average 12 months. The terms for loans to finance purchases of automobiles and other expensive durable goods may run from 24 to 36 months and over.

Commercial banks have recently inaugurated two specialized ways of extending personal loans: on the basis of *check-credit plans* and through *in-plant banking services.* Under a check-credit plan, such as the "Citibank Ready-Credit" of the First National City Bank of New York, a bank permits a customer to use personalized special checks to make any payment he wishes, within a prearranged limit; repayment of the outstanding debit balance, plus interest, is made monthly in amounts that would extinguish the debt, if no more were incurred, in a year or some shorter period. This arrangement amounts to a personal "line of credit," comparable to that used in most bank mercantile loans (see Chapter 22), but involving instalment repayment. It differs from the "community" credit plans described in Chapter 26 under which a customer can buy on

---

[5] Yet, as will be indicated subsequently, they also provide many of these institutions with a substantial proportion of their working capital by lending to them or refinancing them by purchasing some of their customer paper.

credit only in stores and service establishments that are members of such a plan; "check-credit" checks, are in effect ordinary checks drawn on a checking account established by a loan instead of a deposit, and are acceptable wherever ordinary checks would be. Under "in-plant banking" service,[6] a bank arranges with a business organization to provide various services for its employees, among them the extension of personal loans. This is a convenient way for an employee to get such services and for the bank to expand them. It substantially reduces a bank's costs and risks in opening personal loan facilities; the borrower, for example, is always reachable "on the spot"; his repayments, if he so chooses, may be made through payroll deductions. With "in-plant banking," the commercial banks are entering a field of personal loan operations which was to some extent taken care of by the employer-companies themselves, but by and large dominated heretofore by the credit unions.

## Pawnbrokers and other nonregulated lenders

Pawnbrokers are sometimes considered purchasers of personal property rather than lenders. Whatever may be the original intention of the borrowers, many pawned items are never redeemed. When they are, however, pawnbrokers can be said to be performing a personal loan function.

There are two classes of pawnbrokers. The majority make advances on cheap jewelry and miscellaneous personal property. These advances range from 50 cents to $10, and average in some cases as low as $2 or $3. The second class lends on the security of precious stones and precious metals, in amounts ranging from one dollar to several thousand dollars; the average is from $10 to $50.

Both classes of pawnbrokers employ the same method of operation. A borrower brings some item of value to be pledged for the "loan." No credit inquiry is made. The pawnbroker looks only to the value of the pledge. He appraises it and advances 60 to 70 per cent of its auction value. The customer is given a loan ticket on which is entered the amount of the advance, a description of the property pledged, and other pertinent information. The pledge may be redeemed at any time within a year by payment of the advance and the pawnbroker's charges. If the pledge is not redeemed, the pawnbroker is supposed to sell it at auction and remit any excess of the auction price over the advance to the borrower. Where an auction procedure is actually conducted, the pawnbroker himself is usually the only bidder for his pledges. Rarely, if ever, is there any balance to be remitted.

---

[6] In 1960 the Bank of America operated "in-plant" service in 3000 companies (*Wall Street Journal,* March 10, 1960). The First National City Bank of New York has started a similar "in-plant" program under the name "Ready-Banking Service."

Pawnbrokers are sometimes regulated by municipal ordinances and occasionally by state law. They are subject to the general or special usury laws of their states. Enforcement of these usury laws is spasmodic, however, and the charges of many pawnbrokers are probably a few per cent above the legal limit. But in general pawnbrokers' charges are not so excessive as to be a social abuse. Handling costs for their advances are generally high because of the small amounts of the loans. A pawnbroker's profits are not derived primarily from the charges on the advances that are repaid, but from resale of the pledges that are not redeemed. Therefore, when pawnbrokers do charge more than the legal rates under the usury laws, their overcharge is generally modest; in most cases the ratio of their charges to the principal of the loan is less than the ratio of the charges legally permitted to personal finance companies.

So-called "loan sharks" do not, like pawnbrokers, lend upon pledges of personal property, but upon assignments of wages. In defiance of the usury laws, their rates range up to 240 and 300 per cent (on an annual basis) upon the unpaid balance of the loan. The "sharks" are not interested in collecting the principal of a loan but in obtaining their exorbitant charges; they prefer that a victim involve himself ever more deeply as to the principal of his obligation, up to whatever figure his circumstances can sustain, so that they can continue to collect their charges for a correspondingly longer period. Their collections are enforced by the threat to act on the wage assignment and to cause the debtor to lose his employment. In many cases they threaten and even use physical violence. Their victims could at any time seek legal protection, but ignorance and sometimes fear prevent this. Drives by public bodies and civic agencies can suppress "loan shark" activities temporarily, but only for the period while the drive is in force. The only long-term cure for this evil is a revision of the usury law of a state to provide for organization of consumer finance and other controlled small-loan organizations. Where advances can be obtained from such controlled sources, and the borrowing public has been educated to use the facilities of these institutions, their competition generally ends the menace of the "loan shark."

### Consumer finance companies

The legal basis of a consumer finance company is a state law authorizing the existence of such organizations, permitting them to charge a specified rate in excess of the maximum under the state's usury law, and subjecting their activities to certain limitations and controls. Thirty-eight states have such laws based on the Uniform Small Loan Act. A few other states have small-loan laws not based on this act.

The Uniform Small Loan Act, first published in 1916, has undergone several revisions. Some states have amended their small-loan laws to accommodate the new provisions of the Uniform Act. Others have allowed their statutes to remain based on its earlier forms. Consequently there is considerable divergence in the details of the state small-loan laws. They are in substantial agreement in their main provisions, however, of which the following are the most significant:

1. Loans are limited to a maximum ranging from $300 to $5,000; for most the stipulated maximum is between $300 and $800.

2. A maximum monthly interest charge is established. The highest is 3½ per cent on the unpaid balance. Most states provide for "combination rates"—for example, in New York the charge is 2½ per cent on the first $100, 2 per cent on the part of the loan between $100 and $300, ¾ per cent on the amount exceeding $300. No extra fee can ordinarily be charged, and interest cannot be deducted in advance or compounded.

3. A state license is required for each loan office. Applicants must have some liquid sum—usually $25,000—per office. No other business may be conducted in connection with the loan business without consent of the licensing authority.

4. Lenders must file annual reports and permit examination at least once a year.

5. Misleading advertising is forbidden. A borrower must receive a clear written statement of the terms of his contract, receipts for payments made, and the canceled note and any pledged security upon final payment.

6. A lender may not accept a power of attorney or confession of judgment from a borrower. Loans require the written consent of both husband and wife when made on the security of a wage assignment or chattel mortgage on household furniture.

A small loan business under these statutes may be conducted by an individual, a partnership, or a corporation. Most of the 3,500 consumer finance companies currently operating are incorporated. Chain organization of these companies has developed on a major scale, and two chains, the Beneficial Finance Company and the Household Finance Corporation, dominate the personal finance field.

The loan funds of consumer finance companies are derived initially from their invested capital and surplus. Some of the larger ones have raised substantial amounts of additional operating capital by bond issues. Small companies, as well as the large ones, borrow on short-term bases from commercial banks.

Consumer finance company loans are made upon the basis of instalment repayment, with terms ranging from three months to two years, depending upon the amount of the loan and the credit of the borrower. The smaller the loan, the shorter is the period usually allowed for repayment;

some companies establish a maximum repayment term—ten months, for example—for loans under $50. Longer terms are commonly permitted on secured loans than on unsecured ones.

Between 25 and 30 per cent of finance company loans are unsecured, being based exclusively on the credit status of the borrower as determined by the finance companies' analysis.[7] The most common collateral taken for secured consumer finance company loans is a chattel mortgage on the house furnishings or automobile of the borrower. In a small proportion of cases, loans are secured by third-party guaranty, through the use of endorsed or co-maker notes. Loans secured by wage assignments are an insignificant proportion of consumer finance company loans in most states.[8]

### Industrial ("Morris Plan") banks

The original idea of the industrial or "Morris Plan" bank was that it would make personal loans from $50 to $5,000 on the borrower's note secured by two endorsers or co-makers of satisfactory credit standing. Repayment of the loan would be made in 12 or fewer monthly instalments, usually through purchase of noninterest "investment certificates" of the company. At the maturity of the note, the accumulated "investment certificates" thus purchased would be surrendered to the company in payment of the note. A "credit investigation fee" amounting to 1 or 2 per cent of the loan would be charged, together with the maximum interest rate permitted under the state's usury law. Since no interest was paid on the "investment certificates" purchased monthly, the true interest rate was in effect double the face rate. Thus a 2 per cent "credit investigation fee" plus an 8 per cent interest rate would amount, in effect, to an 18 per cent charge for the loan.

In most states industrial banks can be organized under the regular state banking laws. In seven states special statutes authorizing their creation and operation were enacted. These special statutes originally set restrictions, not too severe, on the type and size of loans they could make and the interest rates and fees they could charge. In recent years many of these restrictions have been removed so that even in the special-statute states industrial banks can engage in general commercial banking.

The first industrial bank was established in Norfolk, Virginia, in 1910. Through the next three decades industrial banks engaged primarily in the small-loan business for which they were originally intended. During the 1940's and 1950's they expanded generally into commercial banking

---

[7] To a growing extent borrowers are required to take out term life insurance for the amount and term of the loan.

[8] Because of unfavorable public reaction to the enforcement of such assignments, the two large personal finance company chains have voluntarily discontinued the practice of taking wage assignments.

and now are classified, for statistical purposes, with commercial banks.[9]

Personal loans currently account for about one half of the loan operations of industrial banks—a higher proportion than for regular commercial banks. The character of industrial bank personal loans has changed significantly in recent years. Co-maker loans, which they pioneered, and loans on third-party guarantees are now rarely made. Most of their present personal loans are automobile purchase loans secured by chattel mortgages and F.H.A. insured improvement loans on houses. The balance is largely unsecured instalment loans.

## Industrial loan companies

Industrial loan companies, organized under special laws in 18 states and under the general banking laws in the others, differ from industrial banks in three respects: (1) they cannot be called "banks," (2) they cannot accept deposits, and (3) they are not elegible for federal deposit insurance or membership in the Federal Reserve System. Like the industrial banks, in recent years the industrial loan companies have evolved away from their original distinctive and rather narrow type of operation, and have become practically indistinguishable from consumer finance companies, with which they are now statistically grouped.

## Credit unions

Credit unions are cooperative saving and personal loan organizations, operated on a nonprofit basis, whose members have some common bond of interest.

All but six states have statutes covering organization and operation of credit unions. They may also be organized under a federal law enacted in 1934. Half of the present credit unions were chartered under state laws, half under the federal statute.[10]

The distinctive feature of a credit union is its organization by and for a group with some common interest. The members may all be employees of a particular company or government unit, or members of a particular labor union, or of a fraternal association, or of a religious association, or of a farm cooperative. Without this extraneous binding interest among the membership, credit unions languish and fail. Federal efforts to develop neighborhood credit unions have generally been unsuccessful. Credit unions have grown substantially in number and activities in recent years. They have extended their operations from making personal loans to refinancing retail instalment sales.

---

[9] Board of Governors of the Federal Reserve System, *Consumer Instalment Credit,* Part I, Vol. 1, Washington, D.C., 1957, p. 37.

[10] Credit Union National Association, *Credit Union Yearbook 1960,* Washington, D.C., 1960, p. 33.

The operating premises of a credit union are generally supplied by the employer or the membership group. The officers, with the possible exception of a paid manager, usually contribute their services without compensation. Investigating loan applicants is rendered easy and inexpensive in view of the group relationship of members. Thus both overhead costs and operating expenses of a credit union are relatively low.

Operating capital of a credit union is derived from two sources. The members purchase limited-dividend shares; 6 per cent is the usual legal dividend limit, but 3½ to 4½ per cent is the average actual payment. Members with excess funds deposit them with the union as in a savings account; interest paid on these accounts is generally higher than the rate currently paid on savings bank accounts. The accumulated funds are lent to members who wish to borrow; rarely if ever are loans made to non-members. The average credit union loan today is around $600. In some states and under federal statute, maximum amounts are stipulated for unsecured loans; large loans must be secured by co-makers or by collateral. State statutory provisions commonly set maximum interest charges of one per cent per month on the unpaid balance, or six per cent per annum on the loan amount if the interest is deducted in advance. Federally-chartered unions are limited to basing their interest charge on the unpaid balance. Most credit unions protect themselves and their borrowers by requiring loan balances to be covered by term life insurance.

### Sales finance companies

Some sales finance companies have expanded into the personal loan business. In this case their procedures are generally similar to those of commercial banks. Sales finance companies, however, operate their personal loan divisions under various statutes: some under small loan company laws, some under industrial bank statutes, and others under the loan requirements of the state usury laws. Accordingly size of loan, interest rates, and repayment and security arrangements differ among sales finance companies.

A high proportion of sales finance company personal loans are negotiated for the purchase of automobiles; they are usually secured by chattel mortgage. Some loans are extended for home repair and modernization; these are usually FHA-insured. Otherwise sales finance company personal loans are largely unsecured.

Personal loans by sales finance companies are all repaid on a monthly basis; there are no single-payment loans. Maturities generally run up to two years; loans for purchase of automobiles and marine equipment may have 30-month terms. The companies favor having their loans covered by term life insurance, but this protection is not always applied.

## INSTRUMENTS OF PERSONAL LOAN CREDIT

All personal loans are based on promissory notes—single-payment or instalment—signed by the borrower and sometimes by an endorser or co-maker.

Many personal loan institutions have developed a form of promissory note which can be used equally for an unsecured loan, for a co-maker loan, or for a third-party guaranteed loan. An example is shown in Illustration 30-1. For an unsecured loan, such a note needs only the signature of the borrower on the front. If a co-maker loan is in question, the co-makers' names and addresses follow that of the borrower on the front of the note. If the security is to take the form of a third-party endorsement, the guaranty is printed and space is provided for the endorsement on the reverse of the note. Observe that this note, like all instalment notes, contains an "acceleration" clause which provides that the entire unpaid balance of the note shall become due if any payment under it is defaulted.

A chattel mortgage may be made part of an instalment note, or it may be a separate instrument, as shown in Illustration 22-2.

## SOURCES OF PERSONAL LOAN CREDIT INFORMATION

Personal credit institutions utilize three sources of information on the credit status of their loan applicants—the application forms which the applicants must fill out, investigators, and retail credit bureau reports.

### Application

The application form submitted to a would-be borrower from a consumer finance company, industrial bank, or the personal loan department of a commercial bank, is similar to that submitted to applicants for charge account or instalment credit in a department or specialty store (see Illustration 27-1). It calls for information on the applicant's age, marital status, and number of dependents, on his length of residence at his present and preceding addresses, on his present and preceding employment and employer, on his income, and whether he has a bank account and life insurance. But the inquiry into the circumstances of an applicant for a personal loan must be more searching than that on an applicant for charge account or instalment credit, so the application form provided for the former contains additional inquiries (see Illustration 30-2). The applicant is queried as to the purpose of the loan. He is required to give

NOTE

**LENDER**

The Lender's name and address above and the items set forth in the box directly below are expressly made a part of this Note.

| First Instalment Due Date | Borrowers' Name and Address | | Wife |
|---|---|---|---|
| Loan Number | | | |
| Instalments Number – Amount $ | | | |
| Final Instalment Due Date | ☐ Chattel NATURE SECURITY (as checked) | | ☐ Wage Assignment |
| | ☐ Mortgage ☐ Accommodation Maker | | |
| Date of Loan | | Actual Amount of Loan $ | |

**For Value Received**, the undersigned jointly and severally promise to pay to said Lender, at its said office, the Actual Amount of Loan shown hereon, together with interest at the rate of 2½% per month on that part of the unpaid principal balance of said loan not exceeding $300, and ½ of 1% per month on any remainder of such unpaid principal balance, in successive monthly instalments, the Number and Amount of which are shown hereon, the first of said instalments being due on the First Instalment Due Date shown hereon and each subsequent instalment on the same day of each succeeding month thereafter, the final instalment being due and owing on the Final Instalment Due Date shown hereon. Each instalment shall be in the Amount of instalment shown hereon, except that the final instalment shall be equal to the unpaid principal plus interest accrued and unpaid at the time said final instalment is paid. The Nature of Security for this note is as shown hereon. If this note is not paid at maturity, the unpaid principal balance shall bear interest thereafter at said rate. A default in the payment of the full amount of any instalment of the principal or interest hereof, at the option of the holder hereof and without notice or demand, shall render the entire unpaid balance of the principal hereof and accrued interest thereon at once due and payable. Payment in advance may be made in any amount at any time. All payments hereon shall be applied first to interest to date of payment and remainder to principal. All parties hereto severally waive demand and presentment for payment, notice of non-payment, notice of protest and protest of this note and agree that their liability hereunder shall not be affected by any extension of the time of payment of all or any part of the amount owing hereon at any time or times, and further waive all rights of exemption under the laws of this or any other state.

Said Actual Amount of Loan is the actual amount of money lent and paid to the undersigned.

The undersigned acknowledge receipt of a Statement in English as required by Section 17:10-15 of the Revised Statutes of New Jersey.

IN WITNESS WHEREOF, the undersigned have hereunto set their hands and seals on the Date of Loan above written.

Witness:................................................ ...................................................................(SEAL.)

Witness:................................................ ...................................................................(SEAL.)

Witness:................................................ ...................................................................(SEAL.)

ILLUSTRATION 30-1.  Personal Loan Note Form (Consumer Finance Company)

**LENDER**

The Lender's name and address above and the items set forth in the box directly below are expressly made a part of the Statement of Loan on the reverse side hereof.

| First Instalment Due Date | Borrowers' Name and Address | | Wife |
|---|---|---|---|
| Loan Number | | | |
| Instalments Number – Amount $ | | | |
| Final Instalment Due Date | NATURE SECURITY (as checked) ☐ Chattel Mortgage ☐ Accommodation Maker ☐ Wage Assignment | | |
| Date of Loan | | | |
| | | Actual Amount of Loan $ | |

| Date | Total Payment | Interest | Principal | Unpaid Balance | Rec'd By |
|---|---|---|---|---|---|
| | | | | | |
| | | | | | |
| | | | | | |
| | | | | | |
| | | | | | |
| | | | | | |
| | | | | | |
| | | | | | |
| | | | | | |
| | | | | | |
| | | | | | |
| | | | | | |
| | | | | | |
| | | | | | |
| | | | | | |
| | | | | | |
| | | | | | |
| | | | | | |

## IMPORTANT INFORMATION

This is your receipt book. Please bring it with you every time you visit our office.

Your payments are due at our office each month as indicated hereon. Payments may be sent by mail. Please do not send currency through the mail. Make all Checks, Post Office or Express Money Orders payable to the company shown hereon.

If you need more money, see us whether you owe us at the time or not.

**NOTIFY US PROMPTLY OF ANY CHANGE OF ADDRESS**

ILLUSTRATION 30-1 *(Concluded)*

\* \* \*

This loan, if granted, will be protected by insurance on the borrower's life until maturity (whether expressed or accelerated) for the unpaid balance up to $10,000 less the outstanding balance of any other similarly insured loan(s), provided the borrower has not reached his 70th birthday. In certain cases the cost of such insurance is paid by the borrower.

## APPLICATION FOR CREDIT

### TO THE CHASE MANHATTAN BANK
INSTALMENT CREDIT DIVISION
NEW YORK 15, N. Y.

DATE_____

I hereby apply for personal credit of $_____repayable in _____ monthly payments beginning

☐ one month from date of loan,
☐ on the following date

Purpose_____

MR.
MRS.
MISS
FULL NAME_____                AGE_____

☐ MARRIED
☐ SINGLE    NO. OF DEPENDENTS_____

SEND MAIL TO

HOME ADDRESS_____

NUMBER-STREET            CITY OR TOWN         ZONE      STATE       YEARS THERE_____

☐ HOME ADDRESS

APARTMENT NO._____ TELEPHONE NO._____ PLACE OF BIRTH_____

☐ BUSINESS ADDRESS

LAST PREVIOUS ADDRESS_____                YEARS THERE_____

NEAREST RELATIVE
WITH WHOM NOT LIVING_____

NAME                              ADDRESS                    RELATIONSHIP_____

### EMPLOYMENT OR BUSINESS

NAME OF COMPANY_____

STREET ADDRESS_____

CITY_____ ZONE_____ STATE_____

PHONE NO._____ EXT. NO._____YEARS THERE_____

BADGE OR EMPLOYEE NO._____ DEPARTMENT_____

ANNUAL SALARY $_____ POSITION_____

KIND OF BUSINESS_____

OTHER INCOME $_____ SOURCE_____

PREVIOUS EMPLOYER
IF WITHIN LAST 2 YEARS_____

ADDRESS_____YEARS THERE_____

NAME OF WIFE OR HUSBAND_____

IF EMPLOYED, WHERE?_____

### LIFE INSURANCE

AMOUNT $_____ CASH SURRENDER VALUE $_____

PLACED WITH _____

### BANK REFERENCES

PERSONAL CHECKING _____
                          BANK              BRANCH

BUSINESS CHECKING _____
                          BANK              BRANCH

SPECIAL CHECKING _____
                          BANK              BRANCH

SAVINGS _____
                          BANK              BRANCH

### REAL ESTATE

LOCATION _____

IN NAME OF_____ VALUE $_____

1ST MORTGAGE $_____ 2ND MORTGAGE $_____

HELD BY _____

### MISCELLANEOUS

DO YOU OWN AN AUTOMOBILE?_____ MAKE_____ YEAR_____

HAVE YOU EVER HAD AN ACCOUNT IN THIS DEPARTMENT?_____

ARE YOU A MEMBER OF CHASE MANHATTAN CHARGE PLAN?_____

HAVE YOU ANY JUDGMENTS OR LEGAL PROCEEDINGS AGAINST YOU?_____
IF SO, PLEASE EXPLAIN BY LETTER.

### LIST ALL LOANS OR DEBTS NOW OUTSTANDING. IF NONE, PLEASE STATE "NONE".

| NAME OF BANK, COMPANY OR INDIVIDUAL | ADDRESS | ACCOUNT NO. | ORIGINAL AMOUNT | BALANCE UNPAID | AMOUNT DUE EACH MONTH |
|---|---|---|---|---|---|
| | | | | | |
| | | | | | |
| | | | | | |
| | | | | | |

I hand you herewith a Note. I understand that if this loan is made, it will be discounted at a rate not exceeding six dollars per annum per one hundred dollars of the amount of the loan.

I authorize you to obtain any information you may require relative to this application from my employer, if any, and from any other sources to which you may apply, each such source being hereby authorized by me to provide you with such information. I agree that if any situation arises before this loan is made which materially changes any of the representations made by me in this application, I will promptly notify you thereof.

If this loan is made, I further authorize you: (A) to deduct, at your option, any moneys owing by me to you, (B) to remit the proceeds or balance of the proceeds to me by ordinary mail at my sole risk, (C) to return the note, as and when paid in full, by ordinary mail at my sole risk to any of the signers thereof. If this loan is not made return the note to me by ordinary mail at my sole risk; but in any event you may retain this application for your records.

I represent, warrant, and confirm that all the statements made by me in this application are correct and have been made by me for the purpose of inducing you to make this loan and knowing that you will rely thereupon; without in any way limiting the foregoing and for the same purpose, I reaffirm and represent and warrant that I have no outstanding obligations to any bank, loan company, corporation or any individual, and that no suits, judgments or legal claims of any kind whatsoever are now pending against me, except as stated by me in this application.

No._____                SIGNATURE OF APPLICANT_____

I.C.D. 27

ILLUSTRATION 30-2.    Personal Loan Application Form (Commercial Bank)

an estimate of his living expenses, the cash surrender value of any life insurance policy he holds, the purchase and assessed values of any real estate he owns, and the details of any mortgages on such property and of any unpaid assessments against it. He has to state the details of any instalment or other personal loan obligations outstanding against him. He is queried as to whether he has ever gone through bankruptcy, or had legal proceedings brought against him, or is contingently liable as an endorser or guarantor for others.

If a co-maker loan is in question, the co-maker is asked to fill out an application form similar to that of the borrower, but less detailed.

### Investigators

Consumer finance companies formerly checked upon their loan applicants by investigators' visits to the applicants' homes. This personal-call method is giving way to telephone check-ups. To the extent that visits are still used—and this may be essential if a chattel mortgage on home furnishings is offered by a borrower and the lending organization wishes to appraise the collateral—they also provide an opportunity for the investigator to see the applicant's home surroundings. An investigator's judgment on this detail may be a factor in the loan decision.

### Credit bureau reports

Many of the details on a personal loan application can be verified by telephone or letter inquiry. But such verification would not establish whether full statement had been made of outstanding liabilities, or whether the applicant was a good or a poor moral risk. These important details can be ascertained only by drawing a report from the local retail credit bureau, as discussed in Chapter 27. Such reports are usually drawn by personal loan agencies on all applicants except those who offer a collateral security that gives the lending institution full protection. Commercial banks use them particularly if they operate "community" credit plans as previously described and have to check on a large number of applicants.

Note that in the case of co-maker and guaranteed loans, credit bureau reports are usually drawn on the co-makers and guarantors, as well as on the borrowers.

## THE CREDIT DECISION

On a loan secured by stocks or bonds, or the cash surrender value of a life insurance policy, or a savings-bank deposit book, a personal loan institution can afford to be liberal, even superficial, in its credit analysis, assuming that the validity of the collateral has been verified. The chance that the lending institution will sustain any net loss on the loan is practically nil.

Where the security for a personal loan is a chattel mortgage on the borrower's household furniture, as in the case of many consumer finance company loans, or on purchased items, as in the case of purchase loans made by industrial and commercial banks, the lending institution does not have automatic protection against loss. In the first place, the repossession value of a borrower's household furniture may be merely nominal; the chattel mortgage on it is often taken more for moral effect than as true security. In the second place, a record of numerous repossessions would be just as disastrous to the business of a lending institution as to that of an instalment seller. Foreclosure under a chattel mortgage is a collection weapon of last resort.

Loans upon the security of chattel mortgage, then, are in most instances viewed as in almost the same category as unsecured loans—the probability of repayment of the loan depends essentially upon the credit status of the borrower. In judging this credit risk, a personal loan agency must apply stricter standards than charge-account or instalment sellers. The latter in many cases make substantial gross profits upon the sales promoted by the credit terms, and this extra gross profit may warrant the risk of a substantial bad debt loss. A personal loan institution derives no such compensation. Any bad debt losses it sustains must be covered by the margin, often very narrow, between its loan charges and its operating and finance costs. The ordinary personal loan institution would court failure if it had to absorb the proportion of bad debt loss that reflects sound credit management for the ordinary instalment seller. Thus it may well happen that an individual who would be an acceptable risk to any instalment seller is unacceptable to a personal loan institution when he seeks to borrow the cash price of an item that he might buy on instalment terms.

In the case of co-maker loans, the loan officer must make a decision not merely upon the credit status of the borrower, but upon that of each co-maker as well. If any one of the co-makers is a clearly acceptable credit risk in his own right by the lending institution's standards, there is an obviously clear case for approving the loan. But it is quite possible for a co-maker loan to be acceptable when neither the borrower nor any of the co-makers, considered individually, would be a fully acceptable risk for an unsecured loan. If there were one chance in ten that a borrower and one co-maker, taken individually, would fail to pay an obligation, the chance of their collective failure would be one in a hundred, provided there were no common influence conducive to failure operating upon both of them. If there were a borrower and two co-makers, each with an individual one-in-ten probability of failure, the collective probability would be one in a thousand. The co-maker loan principle, by substituting collective for individual responsibility, thus permits loans to be made safely to principals of distinctly inferior credit status.

Some personal loan agencies, placing reliance on this collective security, may have been lax in the credit standards they applied to loan principals. The more responsible institutions, however, realize that such laxity results in the co-makers being frequently compelled to assume the obligations of

This loan (FHA improvement loans and secured loans excepted), if granted, will be protected by insurance on the borrower's life until maturity (whether expressed or accelerated) for the unpaid balance up to $10,000.00 less the outstanding balance of any other similarly insured loan(s), provided the borrower has not reached his 70th birthday.

## STATEMENT OF CO-MAKER

TO THE CHASE MANHATTAN BANK
INSTALMENT CREDIT DIVISION, NEW YORK, N. Y.

DATE_____

I have read the application of_____ for a loan of $_____ and consent to act as co-maker. You are entitled to rely on the truth of my answers given below and on my liability on the note as co-maker which I now acknowledge signing.

MR.
MRS.
FULL NAME MISS_____ AGE_____ ☐ MARRIED ☐ SINGLE   NO. OF DEPENDENTS_____

SEND MAIL TO

HOME ADDRESS_____ YEARS THERE_____
NUMBER - STREET          CITY OR TOWN      ZONE   STATE

☐ HOME ADDRSS
☐ BUSINESS ADDRSS

APARTMENT NO._____ TELEPHONE NO._____ PLACE OF BIRTH_____

LAST PREVIOUS ADDRESS_____ YEARS THERE_____

### EMPLOYMENT OR BUSINESS

NAME OF COMPANY_____

STREET ADDRESS_____

CITY_____ ZONE_____ STATE_____

PHONE NO._____ EXT. NO._____ YEARS THERE_____

BADGE OR EMPLOYEE NO._____ DEPARTMENT_____

ANNUAL SALARY $_____ POSITION_____

KIND OF BUSINESS_____

OTHER INCOME $_____ SOURCE_____

### BANK REFERENCES

PERSONAL CHECKING_____
BANK          BRANCH

BUSINESS CHECKING_____
BANK          BRANCH

SPECIAL CHECKING_____
BANK          BRANCH

SAVINGS_____
BANK          BRANCH

### MISCELLANEOUS

STATE RELATIONSHIP OF APPLICANT TO YOU_____

HAVE YOU EVER BEEN A BORROWER IN THIS DIVISION?_____

HAVE YOU EVER BEEN A CO-MAKER IN THIS DIVISION?_____

HAVE YOU ANY JUDGMENTS OR LEGAL PROCEEDINGS AGAINST YOU?_____

IF SO, PLEASE EXPLAIN BY LETTER.

### REAL ESTATE

LOCATION_____

IN NAME OF_____ VALUE $_____

AMOUNT OF MORTGAGE $_____

SIGN HERE➤ _____
SIGNATURE OF CO-MAKER

RESERVED FOR USE OF BANK

| ACCOUNT NUMBER | ORIG. AMOUNT | BAL. | | ACCOUNT NUMBER | ORIG. AMOUNT | BAL. | |
|---|---|---|---|---|---|---|---|
| B | | | | C | | | |
| B | | | | C | | | |
| B | | | | C | | | FILED_____ |

No.

ICO.196  8-57

ILLUSTRATION 30-3.   Co-Maker Statement Form

the principals, with the consequence that people, even close relatives of would-be borrowers, refuse to be co-makers on personal loans. Any wide spread of this feeling would, obviously, strip the foundation from an important fraction of the personal loan business. Therefore responsible personal loan agencies to an increasing extent refuse to substitute the collective security of the borrower and co-makers for the individual borrower's credit responsibility. At most they allow the added security of the co-makers to liberalize only slightly their judgment of the credit accept-ability of the loan applicant.

## COLLECTION

Personal loan collection procedure closely resembles instalment collection procedure.

Many borrowers plan to make their payments by personal visit to the lending agency. They are given pass books which contain a statement of the loan and its terms, with provision for entry of payments and computa-tion of the remaining balance. In other cases, particularly in connection with large institutions extending personal loans, a borrower finds it more convenient to make payment by check or money order, and he arranges to mail his payments and pass book to the lending institution. Sometimes he is given a booklet of payment coupons and envelopes similar to those used by some instalment sellers, as shown in Illustration 29-4.

Borrowers on personal loans are generally more prompt in their pay-ments than instalment purchasers. Delinquency on consumer finance com-pany loans ranges between 10 and 15 per cent; it is less than one per cent on commercial bank personal loans. When delinquency occurs,[11] however, it must be dealt with promptly. Hence all personal loan institutions utilize some sort of visible index system for their ledgers, so that delinquencies can be noted within a day or two of their development. The tone of their collection reminders and letters, like those used by instalment sellers, is firm. In the case of co-maker loans, the co-makers as well as the borrower are notified of the latter's delinquency, so that the influence of the co-makers can be enlisted to hold the borrower to prompt payments. The telephone is employed at an early stage concurrently with correspondence. Investigators may make personal calls. Collection follow-up is so timed that the threat of legal action is reached shortly after two monthly or three weekly payments have been missed.

Bad debt losses on most classes of personal loans run rather low—gen-erally about one-fourth of one per cent. For consumer finance companies the ratio is over one per cent.

---

[11] Consumer finance companies take the end of the month as the "cut-off" date for delinquency. This means that any account that should have paid during the month is "one month delinquent," whether it is past-due one day or 31 days. In the same way "two-month delinquency" may represent a past-due range from 32 to 61 days. This method tends to overstate the delinquency rates of consumer finance companies com-pared with other lending institutions, which base their calculations on the actual due date.

## Adjustments

A personal loan institution seeks repayment of its loan, not enforcement of whatever penalties the loan contract and the law allow it for nonpayment. Therefore, whenever a borrower finds himself unable to repay a personal loan according to the terms of the original transaction, the lending institution's first approach to the problem is an attempt to work out a new schedule of payments that the borrower will be able to meet. Sometimes this is accomplished by amending the terms of the original loan contract. More commonly a new contract is arranged to cover the unpaid balance of a loan in default. Quite frequently the borrower is given additional money in the form of a new loan, if his difficulty is attributable to the fact that the original loan was insufficient for his needs or a new emergency has arisen.

## Procedure on security

If a borrower cannot complete payments upon a personal loan under any adjustment acceptable to the lending institution, the latter must reimburse itself as far as it can from the security pledged for the loan. It need not wait until the full term of an instalment loan has expired to take such action, since the acceleration clause in the promissory note signed by the borrower provides that the entire unpaid balance becomes due if the borrower defaults on any instalment. The lending institution may have waived enforcement of this acceleration provision while it sought to discover if an adjustment was possible, but the clause remains fully effective until the lending institution resorts to its application.

Stocks or bonds, savings bank pass books, and the cash surrender value of life insurance policies pledged as collateral for personal loans can be immediately liquidated by the lending institution under the terms of the "collateral" note signed by the borrower. The lending institution reimburses itself to the amount of the unpaid balance of the loan and the interest thereon, and transmits the balance of the collateral or any balance from its liquidation to the borrower.

When a borrower has given a chattel mortgage on household furnishings or other personal property as security for a personal loan, and finds himself unable to meet his obligation, he usually hands over his security without forcing the lending agency to take legal action against him. Three-quarters of the security "repossessed" by consumer finance companies is thus obtained by "voluntary surrender." Failing such compliance, the lending institutions must foreclose under the mortgage in accordance with the laws of the state of the debtor's residence. Repossessions and foreclosures ordinarily cover only part of the unpaid balances which caused them.

Collection experience on co-maker loans is surprisingly good. Loyalty of the borrower to his co-makers, and pressure by the co-makers on the borrower, are obviously powerful influences in holding borrowers to their obligations. In the small proportion of cases where default does occur, the lending institution notifies the co-makers of their liability for the unpaid balance still outstanding. While each of several co-makers is fully liable for the unpaid balance of a co-maker loan, a lending institution usually endeavors to negotiate a division of payment between or among them. It generally has no objection to a co-maker's acknowledgment of his obligation as a debt to the lending institution instead of making immediate cash payment, provided he is an acceptable credit risk or can give acceptable security. His debt becomes a personal loan of the institution to him, with regular charges to be paid—an additional item of business for the lending institution.

### SUPPLEMENTARY READINGS

Cohen, J. B. and Hanson, A. W., *Personal Finance—Principles and Case Problems*, Richard D. Irwin, Homewood, Ill., rev. ed., 1958.

Cottle, S., "The Earnings Performance of the Consumer Finance Industry," *The Journal of Finance*, September 1960, p. 387.

Credit Union National Association, *Credit Union Yearbook 1960*, Madison, Wis., 1960.

————, *The Federal Credit Union: Policy and Practice*, Harper & Bros., New York, 1956.

Diefenbacher, F., "Citibank Ready-Credit," *Credit World*, January 1960, p. 18.

Donaldson, E. F., *Personal Finance*, The Ronald Press, 2nd ed. New York, 1956.

Hackney, C. V., "Developments in Instalment Cash Lending," National Consumer Credit Conference 1959, *Proceedings*, University of Florida, Gainesville, Fla., 1959.

Neifeld, M. R., *Guide to Instalment Computations*, Mack Publishing Company, Easton, Pa., 1951.

————, *Neifeld's Manual on Consumer Credit*, Mack Publishing Company, Easton, Pa., 1961.

————, *Trends in Consumer Finance*, Mack Publishing Company, Easton, Pa., 1954.

Phelps, C. W., "Consumer Finance Company Charges," *The Journal of Marketing*, April 1952, p. 397, and July 1952, p. 22.

Robbins, W. D., *Consumer Instalment Loans*, Ohio State University, Columbus, Ohio, 1955.

Rossant, M. J., "The Credit Card Industry—Prospects and Problems," National Consumer Credit Conference 1959, *Proceedings*, University of Florida, Gainesville, Fla., 1959, p. 115.

## REVIEW

1. To whom, and for what purposes, are the loans of personal loan institutions made?
2. Discuss the personal loan operations of commercial banks. What is "in-plant banking" and what are its advantages?
3. Discuss pawnbrokers as sources of personal loan funds.
4. Why are "loan sharks" still operating in some states?
5. Discuss consumer finance companies and their operations.
6. Discuss the personal loan operations of industrial banks and industrial loan companies.
7. Discuss credit unions and their operations.
8. Discuss the personal loan operations of sales finance companies.
9. Describe the types of promissory notes used in connection with instalment personal loans.
10. Contrast charge account, instalment purchase, and personal loan application forms.
11. Are personal visits by an investigator a usual means of obtaining information on a personal loan applicant?
12. Do personal loan institutions make much use of retail credit bureau reports?
13. Are personal loan institutions stricter or more liberal in their credit risk judgments than instalment sellers? Why? How may the fact of co-makers on a personal loan influence the credit risk involved?
14. Compare personal loan payment and collection procedure with retail instalment payment and collection procedure.
15. Do personal loan institutions ever agree to adjustments on payment terms with delinquent borrowers? Explain.
16. How may personal loan institutions realize on the various forms of loan security they take when a borrower defaults?

# CHAPTER 31

# Economics of Consumer and Mercantile Credit

Consumer credit has long been recognized as a contributory factor to economic fluctuations; only in recent years has attention been devoted to its role in long-term shaping of the national economy.[1] Less study has been made of the economic effects of mercantile credit.[2] Our concluding chapter will survey current knowledge and judgment on these two subjects.

---

[1] Some of the earlier studies and some of the more recent ones: E. R. A. Seligman, *The Economics of Instalment Selling* (Harper & Brothers, New York, 1927); R. Nugent, *Consumer Credit and Economic Stability* (Russell Sage Foundation, New York, 1939); National Bureau of Economic Research, *Studies in Consumer Instalment Financing*, 10 vols., New York 1940/1944; Board of Governors of the Federal Reserve System, *Consumer Instalment Credit*, 6 vols., Washington, D.C., 1957/1958 (hereafter referred to as "Federal Reserve Consumer Credit Study 1957/1958"); articles in the *Journal of Finance:* L. L. Werboff, "The Effects of Instalment Term Variation," September 1959, p. 379; W. P. Mors, "Consumer Finance—Recent Trends in State Regulation of Instalment Credit," May 1960, p. 191; C. A. Dauten, "Consumer Finance —Recent Institutional Developments in the Field of Consumer Credit," May 1960, p. 206; S. Cottle, "The Earnings Performance of the Consumer Finance Industry," September 1960, p. 387; J. T. Croteau, "Sources of Consumer Credit—Instalment Debt Among Institutional Creditors," December 1960, p. 531; R. M. Neifeld, *Neifeld's Manual on Consumer Credit*, Section III "Economic Aspects of Consumer Credit" (Mack Publishing Co., Easton, Pa., 1961).

[2] Until 1956, some exploration on this subject was made only by the authors of this book (see earlier editions of *Credit and Collection Management*, Chaps. 1 and 26). Recent and more penetrating studies are: Federal Reserve Bank of Kansas City,

## ECONOMICS OF CONSUMER CREDIT

Charge account credit and consumer instalment credit [3] differ in both long-term and short-term effects upon the national economy.

### Economic effects of charge account credit

As was indicated in Chapter 28, charge account credit is largely requested and provided as a shopping convenience, rather than as a true credit extension to individuals unable to pay cash. Both the woman who uses a charge account in a department store and the householder who arranges with a fuel oil supplier to bill him monthly for home oil deliveries usually have ample cash on hand, or balances in checking or savings accounts, to pay for their purchases. But how much more convenient it is to buy in store after store with only taxi and restaurant fare in a handbag, or to make out a single check for all oil deliveries during a winter month!

Because charge accounts make retail buying more convenient, more "painless," they unquestionably spur such buying and add somewhat to its overall volume. In a modest way they stimulate propensity to spend and subdue propensity to save. Any expansion of charge accounts thus tends to add an increment to retail buying which, magnified by the "multiplier" effect, makes a built-in contribution to national income. The steady expansion of charge account credit has thus been a modest factor in our long-term economic growth.

---

"Trade Credit, A Factor in the Rationing of Capital," *Monthly Review*, June 1957, p. 3, and "Forces Behind the Growth of Trade Credit," *Monthly Review*, October 1959, p. 3; H. Reinhardt, "Economics of Mercantile Credit—A Study in Methodology," *The Review of Economics and Statistics*, November 1957, p. 468, reprinted in *Credit Executive*, March 1958, p. 3, adapted into German, "Zur Volkswirtschaftlichen Bedeutung des Warenkredits in den Vereinigten Staaten," *Oesterreichisches Bank Archiv*, Vienna, January 1959, p. 13; Federal Reserve System, "Credit from Large to Small Business" (Report to the Committees on Banking and Currency and the Select Committees on Small Business), Washington, D.C., 1958, Part II, vol. 2, p. 482; the *Radcliffe Report* (Committee on the Working of the Monetary System), section "Trade Credit," London, 1959, p. 103; B. Tew and R. F. Henderson, *Studies in Company Finance* (Cambridge University Press, Cambridge, 1959), Chap. 7; A. H. Meltzer, "Mercantile Credit, Monetary Policy, and Size of Firm," *The Review of Economics and Statistics*, November 1960, p. 429; Board of Governors of the Federal Reserve System, "Small Business Financing: Corporate Manufacturers," *Federal Reserve Bulletin*, January 1961, p. 2; Commission on Money and Credit, *Money and Credit, Their Influence on Jobs, Prices and Growth* (Prentice-Hall, Inc., Englewood Cliffs, N.J., 1961), section "Business Credit," p. 75; M. H. Seiden, *Trade Credit—Quantitative and Qualitative Analysis*, National Bureau of Economic Research, New York, to be published in 1962.

[3] The term "consumer instalment credit" in this chapter includes both retail instalment credit extended by retailers and service organizations and personal loans made by banks and finance companies to individuals to enable them to purchase "big ticket" merchandise and services with provision for instalment repayment.

Charge accounts also have some monetary effect, although slight. Charging purchases causes part of an individual's cash on hand and on deposit, which would otherwise have been used for immediate payment of the purchase, to remain idle for a few days or weeks. Thus utilization of charge account credit tends to lower the velocity of monetary circulation. If the stores and institutions that extend charge account credit financed such extensions entirely out of invested capital, there would be no offset to the depressant effect of the slowed-down circulation of consumers' cash holdings. But most stores and other institutions that offer charge account credit do finance some part of their receivables through borrowing from banks or finance companies. Where finance companies are involved, they obtain much of their operating capital from commercial bank loans. Directly or indirectly, then, charge accounts are responsible for calling into existence an added element of bank credit. This addition to monetary stock offsets the inertness of the personal accounts affected by the charge account buying.

In summary, charge accounts operate as a continuing mild stimulant to consumer buying by sharpening somewhat the propensity to spend. Increases in the outstanding volume of charge account credit produce readjustments of monetary stock and velocity that tend to sustain this stimulation.

### Derivation of consumer instalment credit

The first approach to analyzing either the long-term or short-term economic effects of consumer instalment credit is to establish the proportions in which it is derived from invested capital and from bank credit. Federal Reserve series on consumer credit outstanding permit this calculation to be made from 1939 on. Illustration 31-1 shows the calculations for December 31, 1960.

Credit outstanding on retail instalment sales as of this date was $29.1 billions. The automobile dealers, stores, and service organizations that made these sales had financed approximately four-fifths of their customer receivables through sales finance companies and banks, and held only $5.8 billion themselves.[4]

Sales finance companies derive their operating funds approximately one-third from their own invested capital (equity funds and long-term debt) and two-thirds from bank borrowing.[5] Applying these proportions

---

[4] Probably considerably less than half of this $5.8 billion should be deemed derived from the retailers' own invested capital. The greater part should be attributed to mercantile credit which these retailers received from their suppliers. This mercantile credit, as we shall see later in this chapter, was derived part from the invested capital of the businesses involved, part from bank credit which they received directly or indirectly.

[5] *Federal Reserve Consumer Instalment Credit Study*, Part I, Vol. 2, pp. 6-7.

ILLUSTRATION 31-1.   Derivation of Consumer Instalment Credit Outstanding December 31, 1960
(Amounts in billions)

| Holders of Consumer Instalment Obligations | Amounts Extended [a] | Derivation of Retailers' Credit Extensions | Derivation of Sales Finance Companies' Credit Extensions | Derivation of Consumer Finance Institutions' Credit Extensions | Ultimate Derivations |
|---|---|---|---|---|---|
| Retailers | $29.1 | $ 5.8 | | | $ 5.8 |
| Sales Finance Companies | | 11.1 | $3.7 | | 3.7 |
| Consumer Finance Institutions | 10.0 | | | $5.0 | 5.0 |
| Commercial Banks | 4.2 | 12.2 | 7.4 | 5.0 | 28.8 |
| Total | $43.3 | | | | $43.3 |

[a] *Federal Reserve Bulletin*, April 1961, p. 456.

to the $11.1 billion of retailers' instalment receivables financed by the sales finance companies gives $3.7 billion derived from the invested capital of these companies, $12.2 from the commercial banks.

Credit unions, consumer finance companies, and other consumer loan institutions had $10.0 billion outstanding on personal loans to finance consumer purchases. Some $5.0 billion of this total was derived from their own invested capital and savings deposits, some $5.0 billion from bank borrowings.[6]

Commercial banks made some $4.2 billion of personal loans to consumers to finance "big ticket" purchases. In addition, as we have seen, they financed $12.2 billion of retailers' instalment credit and refinanced $12.4 billion of the consumer instalment credit provided by sales finance companies and consumer finance institutions. In all they provided nearly $29.0 billion of the $43.3 billion—some two-thirds—of consumer instalment credit outstanding at the close of 1960.

This two-thirds proportion for commercial bank derivation of consumer instalment credit is not a constant. In periods when consumer instalment credit is expanding more rapidly than it was at the close of 1960 the proportion could be higher; in periods when it was leveling off or shrinking the proportion could be lower. As a safe working hypothesis, we can say that in the present American economy between three-fifths and three-quarters of consumer instalment credit consists of, or is derived from, bank credit.

This element of bank credit constitutes an addition to the monetary supply of the country. It is a "revolving fund," brought into existence by forward-shifted consumer purchasing, retired by consumer repayments, recreated by additional forward-shifted buying. For the most part it is a passive factor in the economy, expanding or contracting according to whether new forward-shifted consumer buying exceeds or falls short of repayment of prior-incurred debt. It could become an active factor controlling the volume of forward-shifted buying if, through bank or public action, utilization of bank credit for this purpose was limited or discouraged, or if prior limitations or damping were discontinued.

### Long-term effects of consumer instalment credit

Basic to an understanding of the long-term effects of consumer instal-

---

[6] On the basis of S. Cottle's study, *op. cit.* p. 388, which centers on the "Big 5" of the consumer finance industry, it is assumed that about 60 per cent of the credit extension provided by the large consumer finance companies—and they account, taking the 10 largest, for over one-half of all loan extensions by consumer finance companies—is derived from bank credit. The proportion may be somewhat lower for the smaller consumer finance companies, and is certainly lower for credit unions and other consumer loan institutions that finance their credit extensions to a substantial degree from their savings deposits. Accordingly, a 50 per cent proportion for bank-credit-financed instalment loans for all consumer instalment loan institutions is a conservative estimate.

ment credit is the realization that in general *it does not produce sales that otherwise would not have occurred;* it merely makes possible *a temporal forward-shifting of sales volume* that would have appeared at a later date. *Expansion* of consumer instalment credit outstanding during any period does enable an increment to be added to the sales volume *for that period* by the forward-shifting process. But during any period when consumer instalment credit outstanding remains constant, as it did during 1958, reflecting no net forward-shifting of consumer purchases, sales fall back to whatever their level would have been had the institution of consumer instalment credit never come into existence. And in any period when there is a decline in consumer credit outstanding, sales fall below whatever their level would have been in a cash economy because consumer income which otherwise would have been available for cash purchases during that period becomes subject to the "compulsory" saving of instalment debt repayment. Consumer instalment credit produces no *built-in* long-term increment of consumer buying; what it provides is a series of discrete periodic increments which may or may not continue through a long term.

Three qualifications must be made to the above generalization:

1. Throughout the postwar period, except in 1958, consumer instalment credit outstanding has expanded. The annual increases have ranged from $2.3 to $5.8 billion. In every year except 1958, therefore, what would otherwise have been the level of consumer cash spending has been increased by an increment of forward-shifted buying. There is no reason to believe that this trend will not continue. This continuing series of increments is not a permanent built-in element of consumer buying. It could disappear if ever the outstanding volume of consumer instalment credit became stabilized at any level. But since any such stabilization appears to be an unlikely eventuality, we can reasonably look upon this increment of consumer buying, with its "multiplier" effect, as a present continuing element in our economy.

2. Availability of consumer instalment credit unquestionably produces some stimulation of consumers' propensity to spend. This expansive pressure on the economy is an inherent factor of consumer instalment credit, which would operate just as much if the total of credit outstanding were stabilized or declining as when it is increasing.

3. As we have seen, consumer instalment credit is derived in major proportion from bank credit. Stabilization of consumer instalment credit outstanding at any level would not cause the volume of bank credit it has called into existence to disappear. This bank credit would remain an element of our monetary stock, with its built-in pressure to sustain operations, or prices, or both.

Our conclusion must be that, while consumer instalment credit does not exercise anywhere near as expansive an effect on the economy as has been argued by some writers who interpret the outstanding volume of such credit as an annual increment to consumer purchasing, it has had some, possibly considerable, long-term expansive influence.

Apart from this "growth" effect, the development of consumer instalment credit has produced a significant long-term modification of the pattern of consumer spending. Availability of instalment and consumer-loan credit favors purchase of "big ticket" merchandise such as automobiles and other consumer durables, and "big ticket" services such as travel tours. With all allowance for consumer budget flexibility made possible by the forward-shifting of credit-financed purchases, in the long run the greater emphasis on "big ticket" spending leaves a smaller fraction of consumer incomes available for "small ticket" spending. For many "time purchase" families there is a definite check to spending on the extraneous trivia of living. In some cases, the squeeze extends even to the semi-necessities of family life; many a family head has a tight lunch-money allowance and raveled shirt cuffs because of the pressure of finance-company payments for the TV set and the family car. The country's production pattern has been significantly influenced by this modification in the pattern of consumer spending.

### Short-term effects of consumer instalment credit

We have seen that an increase of credit-financed forward-shifted consumer purchasing can add billions to the national income for a specific period, and a decline could temporarily reduce national income by billions. Furthermore, the accompanying expansion or contraction of outstanding consumer instalment credit would be accomplished by changes in bank credit volume rather than in invested capital. Obviously developments in forward-shifted consumer purchasing and the credit structure that supports it can be significant factors in business fluctuations. These expansions and contractions of credit-financed forward-shifted purchasing and related bank credit do not have an isolated influence. Their effects on national income combine with the effects of changes in capital plant creation, inventory accumulation, residential construction, public finance, and other factors.

The significant question is: If credit-financed forward-shifted purchasing is allowed to develop uncontrolled, do its expansions and contractions in general operate as a stabilizing influence on business fluctuations, countering contractions and expansions of other factors, or do they operate as a destabilizing influence tending to exaggerate business upswings and downswings?

Evidential data currently available on this important issue are too thin for firm conclusions and point to conflicting tendencies. Present tentative findings are as follows:

1. Consumer "attitudes" and "intentions," which exercise a strong influence on forward-shifted buying, do not parallel expansion and contraction of other fluctuation-producing factors, and at various crucial phases of economic fluctuations tend to counter them. To the extent that these "attitudes" and "intentions" shape forward-shifted consumer buying and the volume of bank credit derivative from it, these operate as a *stabilizing* influence on the economy.[7]

2. Some of the newly developed procedures in consumer credit aim at a better balance of credit extension and amortization. Increasing availability and utilization of revolving and optional terms accounts and bank "community credit" plans work in this direction. This is a *stabilizing* influence.

3. As soon as a recessive trend becomes obvious, retail credit managers and bank personal loan officers become more selective in judging the creditworthiness of applicants for instalment and personal loan credit. Even before unemployment reaches substantial proportions, this tends to cut forward-shifted consumer buying, with *destabilizing* effect.

4. A recession that produces substantial long-continued unemployment cuts off a consumer group which otherwise would make some forward-shifted purchases, while leaving them still with the obligation of paying off prior-incurred debt. While repayment terms may be extended,[8] thus slowing the reduction of consumer credit outstanding, the check to forward-shifted buying is absolute. This aggravates the existing recessive trend, thereby continuing the *destabilizing* influence noted in the preceding paragraph.

5. When a store or other selling organization expands its instalment credits and refinances them in any manner other than their outright sale without recourse, it adds an item of receivables to its assets balanced by an equal payables item added to its liabilities. If its current ratio was previously better than 1:1, such addition of equal amounts to current assets and current liabilities lowers its current ratio; its balance sheet position becomes less liquid and more sensitive to adverse short-term developments. And such adverse developments come with a recession, both because its sales fall off with the check to forward-shifted consumer buying and because it must face an increase in delinquencies on its instalment accounts and even outright bad debt loss. Increase of instalment buying has thus rendered broad segments of our retailing system more vulnerable in the face of protracted recessions. This may be considered an indirect *destabilizing* effect of expansion of instalment credit.

---

[7] G. Katona, *The Powerful Consumer* (McGraw-Hill Book Company, Inc., New York, 1960), p. 242.

[8] Banks and finance companies are less flexible in this respect than instalment sellers. Thus the recent shift from instalment credit to personal-loan credit (see Ch. 26) has reduced this ameliorative element.

### Control

Regardless of whether uncontrolled credit-financed forward-shifted consumer buying acts on balance as a stabilizing or a destabilizing factor in our economy, the possibilities of favorably influencing business fluctuations through controlling this buying should be explored. We cannot here rely on individual policies developed by credit managers or retail top management, for their decisions must deal primarily with the soundness of the credit extension made and the effects of these extensions on sales and bad debt risks. Credit controls related to the broad economic impact of instalment sales must be the responsibility of the national monetary authorities. There are two approaches to such control. (1) Since so much of this buying is made possible, directly or indirectly, through bank credit, can general bank credit controls favorably influence this buying? (2) Can specific controls be applied to instalment selling and personal loans to finance "big ticket" buying?

General bank credit controls take three forms: (a) central bank discount rate control, (b) central bank open market operations, and (c) commercial bank reserve requirement changes.

The theory of discount rate control is that the commercial banks, compelled to pay higher rates when they borrow from the central bank, pass on the added cost by charging higher interest rates to their borrowers, including sales finance companies, consumer finance companies, and individuals seeking personal loans to finance forward-shifted purchases. The consumer finance companies would pass their higher interest cost on to their individual borrowers, and the sales finance companies would pass on theirs to the stores and dealers whose instalment accounts they refinance. These, in turn, would increase their finance charges to instalment purchasers. Presumably this higher cost of "time purchases" would discourage some marginal cases of instalment buying or personal borrowing, and so reduce the total volume of forward-shifted buying. Conversely, according to the theory, a lowering of the central bank discount rate should result in lower borrowing and finance-charge rates for "time purchase" credit, and stimulate such purchases.

Even if changes in central bank discount rates consistently produced changes in bank loan rates, which is not the case, this would be a bungling approach to controlling forward-shifted consumer buying. Consumer demand for credit to finance such buying is more inelastic than any other class of borrowing except consumer "necessity" loans. The fact that consumers are willing to pay finance charges that range from 12 to over 30 per cent on an annual basis for the privilege of time payment should indicate that a difference of one or two per cent a year would have no appreciable effect on the volume of instalment or consumer-loan credit and hence on forward-shifted purchasing. The effects of changes in the discount rate on commercial and investment borrowing would be titanic before the slightest impression was made on consumer credit.

The second form of general bank credit control by the central banking authority, open market operations, involves inducing commercial banks to buy or sell federal debt securities by adjusting the central bank's offer or bid prices. Such purchases by the commercial banks reduce their reserves and hence their lending capacity. Contrariwise, sales raise bank reserves and loan potential. As their lending capacity contracts or expands, the banks tighten or loosen their credit requirements and lines, including those relating to personal loans and loans to sales and consumer finance companies. In this case the extreme inelasticity of consumer demand for "time" credit has no bearing on the matter. The decision of how a contractive "open market" pressure will be passed on to the various classes of bank credit rests with the commercial banks. There is some indication that they may apply the screws more vigorously to refinancing sales finance companies and, possibly, consumer loans than to business or investment loans. Thus, open-market control of general bank credit, at least in its contractive phases, may be transmitted in intensified form to some elements of consumer credit and through it to forward-shifted consumer purchasing.

The third form of general bank credit control through changing bank reserve requirements is also a method of modifying the commercial banks' lending potential, but a less flexible one than open market operations. Its effects on consumer instalment credit would be similar to those of open market operations and, in some instances, more intensive due to the inherent rigidity of this measure.

Specific regulation of credit-financed forward-shifted consumer purchasing has been effected three times—from 1941 to 1947, from 1948 to 1949, and from 1950 to 1952—by "Regulation W." Under this regulation, the Board of Governors of the Federal Reserve System established the maximum periods to be allowed for repayment of consumer instalment debts and minimum down payments on instalment purchases. Promulgation of Regulation W requires Congressional authorization. The authorizations for the 1941 and 1950 controls were based on war emergency legislation. The 1948 promulgation rested on a peace-time act whose constitutionality was untested.

The 1941 and 1950 utilizations of Regulation W were parts of broader "crash" programs intended primarily to dampen the diversionary effect of "nonessential" consumer demand on scarce material and personnel resources. The objective of reducing the rampant inflationary pressures at these times, while recognized and appreciated, was secondary. In 1948 the purpose of the control measure was primarily anti-inflationary. It is generally accepted that Regulation W was effective in both objectives.

There have been a number of recent proposals that authorization for

Regulation W be re-enacted on a "standby" basis, so that it can be utilized at any time by the Board of Governors of the Federal Reserve System as an element of its control on economic fluctuations. Quite naturally the proposal is bitterly opposed by producers of goods sold largely "on time" and by the finance companies. No sound arguments have been advanced against the effectiveness of Regulation W if wisely applied. The main attack has been upon this control as an additional element of government interference with a "free economy." There is also some question as to whether there is constitutional foundation for peace-time authorization of this Regulation.

## ECONOMICS OF MERCANTILE CREDIT

As was indicated in Chapter 1, nearly 90 per cent of nonretail sales are made on credit terms. Yet the only figures available on mercantile credit are those on manufacturers' and wholesalers' credit sales occasionally calculated for the Censuses of Manufactures and Business. Accordingly no quantitative approach, such as was presented on consumer credit, is possible in analyzing the economics of mercantile credit.

### The "network" concept of mercantile credit

Mercantile credit is sometimes described as passing through the business economy as a "flow," or a series of straight-line "flows," starting with producers of raw materials and moving on through manufacturers and wholesalers to retailers. A better analogy might be that of a "network" of channels or flows. Each point in the network in which converging flows meet and from which new flows diverge is a business unit. The network starts at the top with many complicated closed circuits representing credit extensions among producers of industrial materials and supplies. It works down unbroken through the levels of consumer goods manufacturers and wholesalers. The flows diverging downward from most points involve greater quantities, either because of greater number of outgoing flows or greater volume of individual flows than those converging into it, since most businesses grant more credit than they receive. At the bottom is a fringe of "open" flows representing mercantile credit extensions to retailers who may pass on consumer credit but never mercantile credit.

### Derivation of mercantile credit

We have noted that most business units extend more mercantile credit than they receive—that the flows diverging from each point in the credit network are generally more numerous, or of greater volume, or both, than the flows converging upon it. This tendency reflects two obvious characteristics of business operation. First, the movement of manufactured consumer goods and some industrial goods is one of dispersion. Practically all consumer-goods manufacturers and middlemen have more customers than suppliers. Although this is not so consistently true in industrial marketing, it probably holds for a good majority of the enterprises in this field. Second, for all businesses the gross sales which determine their credit extensions must exceed the cost of goods or materials and supplies purchased. These two factors provide the basis for the credit they receive. Thus new elements of mercantile credit keep entering the network at most of its points. Their major derivation is threefold: (1) the invested capital of the business units, (2) commercial bank credit, and (3) factors and finance companies.

Practically every business (other than some retail units) must expect to sell on credit terms. Of course it will receive credit from its suppliers but, on balance, as indicated above, it must anticipate that its receivables will exceed its payables. Some units, as indicated below, can cover part of this difference by borrowing from banks or refinancing with factors and sales finance companies. But, all businesses must have a net worth sufficient, among all the other claims upon it, to meet part or all of the continuing excess of receivables over payables.

All through the mercantile credit network are business units, small as well as large, that are acceptable, on either a secured or unsecured basis, as bank credit risks. Those with seasonal swings in their production or marketing operations negotiate bank loans to carry them through the peak periods. Not all of these loans are applied to carry the expanded volume of receivables in the borrowing concerns' peak marketing periods (these bank loans finance, to an even greater extent, wage payments, inventory accumulations, and other costs); but some part of the loan proceeds may be deemed translated into the concerns' peak period credit extensions.

As was indicated in Chapter 23, the practice of refinancing mercantile accounts receivable through factors and finance companies is increasing. These financial institutions in effect provide their clients with the credit that the latter extend to their customers. The factors and finance companies, in turn, derive the funds they advance in some part from their invested capital, in substantial part from bank borrowing. Through this channel a second element of bank credit is thus fed into the mercantile credit network.

### Bank credit as a substitute for mercantile credit

So far we have seen bank credit flowing into the mercantile credit network and providing some part of its substance. But to some extent bank credit also serves as a substitute for mercantile credit, thereby reducing the over-all flow through the network. This occurs when business purchasers who are acceptable bank credit risks negotiate bank loans to enable them to take advantage of cash discounts. When a customer borrows from a bank and discounts his payables, the amount of mercantile credit his suppliers extend to him is reduced. The credit flows to these customers from their suppliers are thinner than they otherwise would be.

These cash-discounting businesses of course extend the same amounts of mercantile credit to their customers that they would if their purchases were financed by mercantile credit instead of bank credit. The lower stretches of the mercantile credit network are unaffected by this substitution of bank for mercantile credit at higher levels. But the reduction in the volume of the mercantile credit flow at the higher levels is unquestionable.

### Monetary effects of mercantile credit

To the extent that mercantile credit is derived from invested capital it has no monetary effect. It is simply a financial mechanism whereby such capital is applied, not to the business operations of the concern with the capital, but to its customers' operations.

When a company's mercantile credit extensions are made possible in any part through its bank borrowing, it is its own credit extensions that create the need for the bank loan, rather than the bank loan that provokes its extensions of trade credit. So mercantile credit can be deemed to call into existence the bank credit from which it is derived, wherever such derivation occurs. Likewise, when a customer borrows from a bank to take advantage of cash discounts offered by suppliers, the causative factor in the substitution is a mercantile credit consideration.

We cannot measure the amount or proportion of bank credit brought into existence by mercantile credit in these two ways. Whatever its amount or proportion, this bank credit exercises the same monetary effects in our economy as any other elements of bank credit. As the proximate cause of this element of bank credit, mercantile credit can be viewed as contributing, at one remove, to the monetary stock of the nation.

### Contributions of mercantile credit to long-term economic growth

That the existence of mercantile credit is generally beneficial to business, and thereby sustains it at a higher level than would otherwise be possible, goes without saying. It would long since have disappeared from the business scene, or at least have been sharply limited, had its balance of effect been detrimental. Its three major contributions to business and economic growth are:

1. Business men with ability but with insufficient investment capital to

conduct a business on as large a scale as would otherwise be possible can operate with resources in part provided by their suppliers. In many cases such business men would not be valid risks for bank credit, but are proper subjects for mercantile credit with its broader risk margin. The extension of mercantile credit to such customers enables them to operate businesses at greater profit to themselves and at greater value to their communities, and enlarges the sales possibilities of their suppliers.

2. Seasonal enterprises that are not valid bank credit risks but measure up to mercantile credit standards can operate with a net worth sufficient for their off-season operations and base some or all of their in-season expansion on mercantile credit. If such credit were not available, they would either have to operate with large amounts of inactive investment capital during off-season months, or they would find their operations restricted when the time for seasonal expansion arrived. The first alternative would constitute inefficient use of the nation's store of investment capital. The second would limit the service and profit of seasonal enterprises on the one hand and their suppliers' sales possibilities on the other.

5. Through the interflow of bank and mercantile credit analyzed above, the growth effects of bank credit upon the business system are extended to cases where bank credit could not be directly accorded. A strong seller with a liberal line of bank credit, or one who refinances his receivables through his bank or a factor or finance company, translates bank credit into mercantile credit which enables some of these customers, who would not be eligible bank credit risks, to pass on this "derived" mercantile credit to their customers in turn. Thus mercantile credit serves as an instrumentality for more extended percolation of bank credit through the business structure.

One long-term disadvantage of mercantile credit should be noted. The units of a business structure interpenetrated by mercantile credit are more vulnerable when caught by adverse individual chance or general business downswings than if they operated on a cash basis. Part of the assets of credit-extending concerns consists of accounts receivable which can become "frozen" or lost as bad debts through their customers' inability to pay. The accounts payable of credit-receiving concerns, so long as they remain unpaid, are a liability whose amount remains fixed while asset elements may be shrinking. Neither of these risks would exist in a cash-operating business structure.

Mercantile credit can be abused, moreover, introducing additional elements of weakness into the business system. Many a buyer, in a position to develop a sound business on a modest scale consonant with his limited capital, has been led astray by his ability to obtain more mercantile credit than was warranted by his financial condition. Such a buyer, overexpanding his business on his suppliers' funds, renders himself vulnerable to all the slight breezes of the business atmosphere that hardly affect more stable enterprises. His mushroom concern fails, with ruin for himself and loss to his creditors, when a sounder, less over-generous credit policy toward him might have produced a lasting business. A seller who endeavors to force his sales volume by "selling credit"—*i.e.*, being unwarrantedly liberal in his credit policy—soon finds his work-ing capital frozen in overdue receivables and his earnings eaten up by excessive bad debt losses.

These two long-term disadvantages of mercantile credit are trifling beside its benefits. On balance it serves as a useful business catalyst, producing continuously an economically valuable series of business trans-actions that otherwise could not occur without itself being consumed in the process.

### Mercantile credit and business fluctuations—demand considerations

Superficially it might seem that demand for mercantile credit should bear a strict mathematical relation to business purchasing demand. There is a basic relation between the two, of course, but there are two modifying factors.

As a business recession progresses, many companies that have pre-viously been acceptable risks for bank credit for the purpose of taking cash discounts lose their acceptability. Instead of discounting, they now shift to paying at the end of the net period. In effect, in a recession, elements of bank credit that had previously substituted for mercantile credit are withdrawn. The shift from cash discounting to net payment means that suppliers' receivables remain outstanding for a longer period, thereby introducing a growing pressure on their mercantile credit exten-sions.

Also, many prompt-paying customers become delinquent, and previous late payers become still slower in meeting their trade obligations, thus adding to the pressure on suppliers' credit extensions.

With business recovery these credit demand developments are naturally reversed.

### Mercantile credit and business fluctuations—supply factors

During the early stages of a recession the working capital position of most suppliers is tightened. The effort to achieve more liquidity gives them strong inducement to cut down not only on their inventories *but also on their receivables*. Their credit managers find themselves under pres-sure to step up collections, even to shorten credit terms.

In such a period, moreover, the credit risk standing of many customers deteriorates. Accounts that had previously been acceptable slip into the nonacceptable category. The case for refusing to approve further orders from them would seem to become categorical.

A psychological factor also enters. Credit managers are no more immune than any other managerial category to recession-engendered pessimism. In judging the credit risk status of their accounts, they are inclined to lean ever more toward conservative rather than liberal interpretations of their accounts' prospects.

These three considerations would seem to point to the conclusion that the development of a recession tends to instigate an acute contraction of the supply of mercantile credit, which in turn further destabilizes the economy. But two strong offsetting factors also come into play as recessions develop.

As sales start turning down, sales managers become panicky and, among other desperate measures, bring pressure on the credit managers of their firms to be more lenient in approving marginal orders. Sometimes top management backs this attempt. Frequently it cannot be resisted and against their better judgment credit managers have to maintain questionably high credit limits and accept orders from accounts that have become doubtful.

Furthermore, as a recession progresses, many suppliers find that a growing proportion of their receivables become "frozen." They are forced more or less to "carry" some moderately-weakened customers, not only allowing present balances to run long past due, but continuing to sell to them, sometimes on extended terms. They might gladly force collections on other less desirable delinquent accounts, but know that the only result of drastic collection action would be to drive the accounts into bankruptcy with no hope of recovering any significant fraction of the amounts due. Further sales may not be made to these accounts, but the credit previously extended to them remains outstanding, in many cases eventually to be written off as bad debts.

Do the contractive pressures on mercantile credit supply during the development and progress of a recession predominate, so that on balance it becomes one more destabilizing factor in the picture? Or are the two expansive factors ascendant, so that some net stabilizing effect results? Quantitative evidence of the respective strengths of the contradictory tendencies is lacking and probably always will be.

During business upswings mercantile credit, in its supply aspects, plays a more passive role. The liquidation of the past-due balances of customers that survived the downswing constitutes a reduction of mercantile credit outstanding, but it is an elimination of a previously "frozen" element that had been inactive in stimulating business, and it is usually accomplished without straitjacketing the customers' expanding operations. As recovery progresses and moves into "boom," suppliers are able and willing to extend whatever credit their customers need, but this attitude is in response to the customers' demand and is not a conditioning influence on that demand.

Experienced credit managers perform an important function in these developments. In "boom" times, particularly inflationary ones, their inherent caution may serve as a salutary brake on mercantile credit expansion. By holding to prior-established credit limits and by taking a conservative attitude toward orders that reflect speculative or over-enthusiastic buying, they put a rein on credit supply that serves as a "built-in" check on inflationary progress. In the same economic-minded vein, credit executives are in a position, by maintaining credit extension in a period of business recession, to provide much of the necessary implements to stem the tide.

## Control

Possibilities of external control of mercantile credit, and thereby business purchasing, are slight.

In recession times the factors that tend to contract the supply of mercantile credit are, as we have seen, the worsening of the credit risk standing of customers and the psychological bias of credit managers. Neither of these is amenable to external manipulation.

Can there be any external means of checking the granting of mercantile credit at a time when pressures of business buying might contribute to inflationary developments?

Any specific regulation of mercantile credit, such as Regulation W applied to consumer credit, would appear to be out of the question. The complexity of mercantile credit terms cannot be reduced to two elements —down payment and period of repayment—with uniform limitations established for a few broad categories, as in the case of consumer credit.

Since, as we have seen, mercantile credit derives to some extent from bank credit, there might appear to be some possibility of controlling mercantile credit through general bank credit regulation. But the points of such derivation are too scattered through the network of mercantile credit flows, and the application of bank credit at such points is too mixed with other business uses, to permit specific *directed* control of mercantile credit through bank credit regulation. At most we can only observe that any contraction of bank credit accomplished through present control tools among its other consequences probably exercises some constrictive effect upon the supply of mercantile credit and thereby may to some extent discourage some business purchasing.

# Index

Page numbers for major treatment of a topic are printed in *italic* type. Page numbers for incidental references to a topic are printed in roman type.

**635**